Surely, those who believe,
those who are Jewish,
the Christians,
the converts;
anyone who
(1) believes in God, and
(2) believes in the Hereafter, and
(3) leads a righteous life,
will receive their recompense
from their Lord;
they have nothing to fear,
nor will they grieve.
[2:62, 5:69]

QURAN

THE
FINAL
TESTAMENT
[Authorized English Version]

Translated from the Original
by
Rashad Khalifa, Ph.D.

(Revised Edition)

Proclaiming
One Unified Religion
for All the People

All religions of the world—Judaism, Christianity, Islam, Hinduism, Buddhism, and others—have been severely corrupted through innovations, traditions, and the idolization of humans such as the prophets and the saints.

God's plan, as stated in the Old Testament (Malachi 3:1), the New Testament (Luke 17:22-36 & Matthew 24:27), and this Final Testament (3:81), calls for the sending of God's Messenger of the Covenant after all the scriptures have been delivered. The main function of God's Messenger of the Covenant is to purify the scriptures and unify them into one universal message to this world from the Creator and Sustainer of this world.

This major scriptural prophecy has now been fulfilled. God's Messenger of the Covenant has arrived, supported by overwhelming tangible proof (see Appendix Two). The purification and unification process has begun. God's plan is supported by God's invisible forces, and the enormous dimensions of this divine plan is manifest in the recent exposure of false religionists, and the removal of such anti-freedom barriers as the Berlin Wall, the Iron Curtain, and the bamboo curtain.

Henceforth, there is only one religion acceptable to God—Submission. Anyone who submits to God and devotes the worship to God ALONE is a "Submitter." Thus, one may be a Jewish Submitter, a Christian Submitter, a Buddhist Submitter, a Hindu Submitter, or a Muslim Submitter.

The only religion acceptable to God is Submission.　　*[3:19]*

Anyone who seeks other than Submission as his religion,
it will not be accepted from him and, in the Hereafter,
he will be with the losers.　　*[3:85]*

(Rashad Khalifa, November, 1989)

A prophet like me will the Lord, your God, raise up for you from among your kinsmen; to him you shall listen.   *(Moses in Deuteronomy 18:15)*

I will raise up for them a prophet like you from among their kinsmen, and will put My words into his mouth; he shall tell them all that I command him. If any man will not listen to My words which he speaks in My name, I Myself will make him answer for it.   *(Deuteronomy 18:18-19)*

I will ask the Father, and He will give you another Paraclete — to be with you always: THE SPIRIT OF TRUTH.   *(Jesus in John 14:16-17)*

When THE SPIRIT OF TRUTH comes to you, he will guide you to all truth, and will announce to you the things to come.   *(Jesus in John 16:13)*

God's Messenger of the Covenant
Lo, I am sending My messenger to prepare the way before Me; and suddenly there will come to the temple the Lord whom you seek, and the messenger of the covenant whom you desire.
Yes, he is coming, says the Lord of hosts. But who will endure the day of his coming? And who can stand when he appears?
For he is like the refiner's fire... he will sit purifying....   *(Malachi 3:1-3)*

When God ALONE is mentioned, the hearts of those who do not believe in the Hereafter shrink with aversion. But when others are mentioned besides Him, they rejoice.   **[39:45]**

On the 27th night of Ramadan, 13 B.H. (Before Hijra) (610A.D.), the prophet Muhammad (the soul—the real person—not the body) was summoned to the highest possible point, millions of light years from the planet Earth, and this Quran was placed into his heart (2:185, 17:1, 44:3, 53:1-18, 97:1).

Subsequently, the Quran was released into Muhammad's memory, with Gabriel's mediation, over a period of 23 years, 610 to 632 A.D. (17:106). At the moment of release, Muhammad scrupulously wrote it down with his own hand (Appendix 28). What Muhammad left was the complete Quran, written in the chronological sequence of revelation, with detailed instructions for putting the revelations into the sequence decreed by God.

During the re-arrangement process, the scribes who idolized the Prophet added two verses at the end of Sura 9, the last sura revealed in Medina. This blasphemous act resulted in a 50-year war between Ali Ibn Abi Taaleb and his supporters on one side and the distorters of the Quran on the other side. The war ended when Hussein ibn Ali and his family were martyred in Karbala.

It was the Umayyad ruler Marwan Ibn Al-Hakam (died in 684 AD) who destroyed the original Quran that was written by Muhammad's hand, "fearing the eruption of new disputes."

God's Messenger of the Covenant has presented overwhelming evidence that 9:128-129 do not belong in the Quran (Appendix 24). With the removal of these false verses, the Quran has finally been restored. Our generation is the first ever to receive the Quran in its purified and finalized form (see Appendices 1 and 28).

CONTENTS

Sura No.	Name		No. of Verses	Page

PREFACE

On January 31, 1990, sometime before dawn, Dr. Rashad Khalifa, God's Messenger of the Covenant, was martyred by one or more disbelievers who broke into the masjid earlier that night and waited for him to come in. It was a well known fact that Dr. Khalifa would come every day in the early hours to carry on his work on this translation.

By God's grace, he had completed his review of the majority of this translation, having finished through Sura 49 the evening before. He had given detailed instructions to the people who were involved in the proof reading about specific changes he had already made and the changes he planned to make. Except for these changes specified by him, and obvious grammatical or printing errors, the text has been left untouched.

New material has been added to two of the Appendices—15 and 17. In the last few months before Dr. Khalifa died, the awesome mathematical miracle confirming the 5 Contact Prayers was discovered by brothers of Masjid Tucson. Dr. Khalifa had detailed these miracles in the January, 1990, issue of the *Submitters Perspective*, the monthly newsletter of United Submitters International, of which he was the editor. They are herein reproduced in Appendix 15 under the section on the Contact Prayers.

In the February, 1990, issue of *Submitters Perspective*, also written and printed before he died, Dr. Khalifa confirmed through Quran the fact that the righteous do not really die—they go directly to Paradise. That article is reproduced in Appendix 17 on Death.

Thus, the appendices have been updated using his own material. Minor corrections to some of the mathematical tables in Appendices 1, 2, 24 and 29 were also required; and two tables were found to be incorrect and therefore deleted.

In the months since Dr. Khalifa's martyrdom we have had reassurances that the channel which he opened for the discoveries of the numerical parameters embedded in the Quran is not closed. These discoveries continue to flow, and will continue to be published in other works.

Dr. Rashad Khalifa, God's Messenger of the Covenant, has departed, just like all the other messengers before him, but the purified message is alive and will continue to sustain this world until the very end. It is Quran.

You will surely die, just like they will die. (39:30)

God: there is no god except He; the Living, the Eternal. (3:2-3)

Universal Unity
Ramadan, 1412 (March, 1992)

INTRODUCTION

In the name of God, Most Gracious, Most Merciful

This is God's final message to humanity. All of God's prophets have come to this world, and all the scriptures have been delivered. The time has come to purify and consolidate all the messages delivered by God's prophets into one message, and to proclaim that henceforth, there is only one religion acceptable to God, "Submission" (3:19, 85). "Submission" is the religion whereby we recognize God's absolute authority, and reach an unshakeable conviction that God ALONE possesses all power; no other entity possesses any power that is independent of Him. The natural result of such a realization is to devote our lives and our worship absolutely to God ALONE. This is the First Commandment in all the scriptures, including the Old Testament, the New Testament, and this Final Testament.

Hear, O Israel! The Lord our God is One God!
Therefore you shall adore the Lord your God
with all your heart,
with all your soul,
with all your mind,
and with all your strength.   *[Deuteronomy 6:4-5, Luke 12:29-30, Quran 3:18]*

Let us meditate on God, His glorious attributes,
who is the basis of everything in this universe as its Creator,
who is fit to be worshiped as Omnipresent, Omnipotent, Omniscient
and self existent conscious being,
who removes all ignorance and impurities from the mind
and purifies and sharpens our intellect.   *[Gayatri Mantra, Yajur Veda]*

While every religion has been corrupted by innovations, traditions, and false, idolatrous doctrines, there may be "Submitters" within every religion. There may be Submitters who are Christian, Jewish, Muslim, Hindu, Buddhist, or anything else. These Submitters, collectively, constitute the only religion acceptable to God. As emphasized by the theme on the front page of this book, all Submitters who are devoted to God ALONE, and do not set up any idols beside God, are redeemed into God's eternal kingdom (2:62). A criterion of the true submitters is that they will find nothing objectionable in the Quran.

With the advent of this Testament, God's message to the world is now complete. We have now received the long awaited answers to our most urgent questions—who we are, the purpose of our lives, how we came into this world, where do we go from here, which religion is the right one, was it evolution or creation, etc.

Some may wonder: "Why did God wait all this time to perfect and consolidate His message? What about all the people since Adam who did not receive the complete scripture?" Bearing in mind that the Quran answers this question in 20:52, it is a matter of simple statistics that the world's population from the beginning until now did not exceed 7,000,000,000. From now to the end of the world, 2280 A.D. (Appendix 25), it is estimated that the total world population will exceed 75,000,000,000. Thus, the vast majority of people are destined to receive God's purified and consolidated message (see diagram).

> *World population from now (1990) to the end of the world (2280).*
> *[The black section represents the world population since Adam]*

Before Genesis

It all began billions of years ago when one of God's high-ranking creatures, Satan, developed a supercilious idea that he could run a dominion as an independent god besides God. This challenge to God's absolute authority was not only blasphemous, it was also erroneous. Satan was ignorant of the fact that God alone possesses the ability to be a god, and that there is much more to godhood than he realized. It was the ego—arrogance augmented by ignorance—that led Satan to believe that he could take care of a dominion, as a god, and run it without disease, misery, war, accidents, and chaos. The vast majority of God's creatures disagreed with Satan. Yet, the minute egotistic minority that agreed with him to various extents were in the billions. Thus, a profound dispute erupted within the Heavenly Community (38:69). The rebels' unjustifiable challenge to God's absolute authority was met and resolved in the most efficient manner. After giving the rebels sufficient chances to denounce their crime and submit to Him, God decided to exile the hard core rebels on a space ship called Earth, and give them yet another chance to redeem themselves.

If you claim that you can fly a plane, the best way to test your claim is to give you a plane and ask you to fly it. This is precisely what God decided to do in response to Satan's claim that he could be a god; God appointed him a temporary god on the tiny speck Earth (2:30, 36:60). As for those who agreed with Satan, they were given a chance to kill their egos and submit to God's absolute authority. While the vast majority of the guilty creatures took advantage of this opportunity, a minuscule minority consisting of about 150 billion creatures failed to take advantage of this offer (33:72).

The dispute in the Heavenly Community led to the classification of God's creatures into different categories:

(1) The Angels

Creatures who never questioned God's absolute authority were classified as angels; they knew that God *alone* possesses the ability and qualifications to be a god. The vast majority of God's creatures—countless numbers—belong in this category. The number of the angels is so enormous, even the angels do not know how many of them there are; only God knows their number (74:31).

(2) The Animals

Although the angels suggested that the rebels and their leader should be exiled from God's kingdom (2:30), the Most Merciful willed to give the rebels a chance to denounce their crime, repent, and submit to His absolute authority (33:72). As represented in the diagram above, the vast majority of the rebels took advantage of God's gracious offer to re-enter His kingdom. They agreed to kill their egos, come to this world to perform a submissive role, as an expiation for their blasphemy. In return for their submissive role in this world, these creatures are redeemed back to God's eternal kingdom (6:38). The horse, the dog, the tree, the sun, the moon, the stars, as well as deformed and retarded children are among the intelligent creatures who denounced their crime and repented:

Do you not realize that   *to God prostrates everything*   *in the heavens and the earth;*   *the sun, the moon, the stars,*   *the mountains, the trees, the animals,*   *as well as many people?*   *Many people, however, are destined for retribution.*   *(22:18)*

The stars and the trees prostrate.   *(55:6)*

The horse has no ego. The horse's owner can be rich or poor, tall or short, fat or thin, young or old, and the horse will serve them all. The dog has no ego; it will wag its tail to its owner, no matter how rich or poor the owner might be. The sun rises and sets every day at precisely the times prescribed by God. The moon follows its synchronized orbit around the earth, without the slightest deviation. The human body—a temporary garment—belongs to the Earth; as such, it is a submitter. The heart, lungs, kidneys, and other organs, perform their functions without our control.

xv

(3) The Humans

The hard-core rebels—humans and jinns—refused to denounce their crime, and opted for witnessing a demonstration of Satan's claim. These egotistic creatures who failed to submit to God's absolute authority, even when offered a chance to do so, were divided in half. The half that were less convinced of Satan's point of view became classified as humans. Although they harbored doubts about Satan's claim, they failed to make a firm stand regarding God's absolute authority. It is the ego that prevented these creatures from appreciating God's omnipotence, it is the ego that prevented them from submitting when such an opportunity was offered to them (33:72), and it is the ego that stands between most of us and redemption to God's kingdom (25:43). This is why "Kill your ego" is one of the first commandments in the Quran (2:54).

(4) The Jinns

The other half of the guilty creatures, those who leaned closer to Satan's point of view and exhibited the biggest egos, became classified as jinns. It was God's plan to assign one jinn to every human being from birth to death. The jinn companion represents Satan and constantly promotes his point of view (50:23, 27). Both the jinns and the humans are given a precious chance in this world to re-educate themselves, denounce their egoism, and redeem themselves by submitting to God's absolute authority. Whenever a human being is born, a jinn is born and is assigned to the new human. We learn from the Quran that the jinns are Satan's descendants (7:27, 18:50). When a jinn being is born and assigned to a human being, the jinn remains a constant companion of the human until the human dies. The jinn is then freed, and lives on for a few centuries. Both humans and jinns are required to worship God alone (51:56).

God Does Not Want Robots

The dispute in the Heavenly Community as stated in 38:69 and described above proves that God's creatures possess the freedom of choice; they have minds of their own. The rebellion of a minuscule minority among God's creatures has served to emphasize the wonderful fact that God's creatures serve Him because they appreciate His infinite magnificence. Without the rebellion, we would have never known that freedom is God's gift to His creatures.

Most Gracious, Most Merciful

Even in our worldly dimension, any enterprise expects its employees to be loyal and devoted to the welfare of the enterprise. If an employee is not totally dedicated to the enterprise, or is shown to have divided loyalties, he is immediately dismissed. Since the humans and the jinns sided with Satan, then turned down God's offer to reconsider their rebellious acts, the angels expected Satan and his allies to be banished from God's kingdom (2:30). It was immense mercy from God that He granted us this additional chance to denounce our crime and redeem ourselves.

To carry out this extremely merciful plan of redemption, God "created death" (67:1-2). The divine plan called for bringing the rebels into another existence, where they have no recollection of the heavenly feud. Under the circumstances of this life, the humans and the jinns receive both God's messages and Satan's messages, then freely choose either side. Based on their freewill decision, they are either redeemed to God's kingdom, or become permanently exiled with Satan.

Satan's Temporary Dominion

To emphasize the utter insignificance of Satan's projected dominion, God created a billion galaxies, a billion trillion stars, within a vast universe that spans billions of light years. If we travel towards the sun (93,000,000 miles) at the speed of light, we will reach it in eight minutes. If we keep going, we will reach the border of our Milky Way Galaxy after 50-70,000 years at the speed of light. To reach the nearest galaxy, it will take us 2,000,000 years at the speed of light, and there are at least 2,000,000,000 galaxies in "our universe." With the most powerful telescopes, the earth is utterly invisible from the edge of our own galaxy, let alone from the edge of our universe. As if our universe were not vast enough, God created six more, even larger universes surrounding our universe (2:29, 67:3). God then informed Satan that a tiny mote within the smallest and innermost universe, the planet Earth, shall be his dominion. God's plan called for placing the humans and jinns in a universe that cannot stand His physical presence (7:143). Thus, Satan rules his minute kingdom far from the physical presence of God, though with God's full knowledge and control. It should also be noted that the number of rebels who repented was so vast, that the planet earth could not possibly accommodate all of them. As it is, the animals vastly outnumber the humans on this planet. It would take an unmanagable earth to accommodate all the repentant rebels. Hence the placement of uncountable decillions of creatures in outer space.

Adam and Eve

The body of the first human being was shaped on earth by God's angels, in accordance with God's instructions (7:11). God then assigned the first person, Adam, to that body. When God informed the angels that they will be serving the humans throughout the test period—guarding them, driving the winds, distributing the rain and provisions, etc.—Satan was the only one who refused to "fall prostrate" (2:34, 15:31, 38:74). Adam's mate was cloned, with feminine features, from Adam, and God assigned the second human being to her body. While the empty (soulless) bodies of Adam and Eve remained here on earth, their souls, the real persons, resided in Heaven. Adam and Eve remained in Heaven for as long as they upheld God's commandments. Once they listened to Satan instead, they reflected a flawed human nature in all of us, and they immediately belonged to Satan's dominion down on Earth—"their bodies became visible to them" (7:20, 20:121). The rest is history.

Satan: Father of All the Jinns

Putting the jinns and the humans to the test stipulated that Satan shall reproduce whenever a human being is born. As mentioned above, every time a human being is born, a jinn being is born to serve as a constant companion of the human person. Every human being is subjected to the incessant persuasions of Satan's representative who lives in the same body from birth to death. Satan's representative tries to convince the human companion of Satan's point of view: that God alone is not enough. On the Day of Judgment, the jinn companion serves as a witness against the human counterpart (43:38; 50:23,27). Many jinn companions are converted to God's point of view by the human companions.

God did not leave the human being without preparation. To help the humans in their final chance to reconsider their blasphemy, every person is born with instinctive knowledge that God ALONE, and no one else, is our Lord and Master (7:172-173). The jinns were not given this instinctive knowledge, but they are given a much longer life span and greater abilities to study God's signs throughout the innermost universe. Since they represent Satan's point of view, their instinctive nature leans strongly in favor of polytheism. In addition to our built-in instinct to worship God alone, God sent messengers to help us redeem ourselves. With all these elements in view, we can appreciate the fact that the only unforgivable offense (if maintained until death) is idol worship: believing that anyone besides God possesses any power.

Forty Years Grace Period

The human being is given forty years to study, look around, reflect, and examine all points of view before making this most important decision—to uphold Satan's point of view, or God's absolute authority. Anyone who dies before the age of forty is chosen by God for redemption due to circumstances known only to God. Anyone who dies before the age of 40 goes to Heaven (46:15, Appendix 32). God's immense mercy is evident from the fact that even those who believe in the Quran find it difficult to accept such a compassionate divine law.

God's messengers delivered the good news of our God-given chance to redeem ourselves, and they were supported by formidable signs. When Moses went to Pharaoh, he was supported by such miracles as the turning of his staff into a serpent. Jesus created live birds from clay by God's leave, healed the leprous and the blind by God's leave, and revived the dead by God's leave. The prophet Muhammad, God's messenger who delivered this Final Testament, did not exhibit such miracles (10:20). The Quran itself was the miracle supporting Muhammad's mission (29:50-51). It was divine wisdom that separated the Miracle of the Quran from Muhammad by 14 centuries. Now that we understand the momentous dimensions of the Quran's mathematical miracle (Appendix 1), we realize that millions of people would have worshiped Muhammad as God incarnate if this Miracle were revealed through him.

Proof of Authenticity:
Physical, Tangible, Irrefutable.

With the advent of the computer age, we discover that the Quran's mathematical code is "One of the great miracles" as stated in 74:30-35. While the miracles given to previous messengers were limited in time and place, the Quran's miracle is perpetual. Only a few people witnessed the miracles of Moses and Jesus, but the Quran's miracle can be witnessed by anyone at any time. Furthermore, the Quran's miracle documents and proves all the previous miracles (5:48).

As detailed in Appendix 1, the Quran's mathematical miracle is based on the number "19." To share this awesome miracle with the reader, the word "**GOD**" is printed throughout the English text in bold capital letters and the cumulative number of occurrences is shown at the lower left corner of every page. The total occurrence of this most important word is shown at the end of the Quran to be 2698. This total is a multiple of 19. Additionally, when we add the numbers assigned to every verse where the word "God" occurs, the total comes to 118123, also a multiple of 19 (19x6217). The cumulative sum of verse numbers where the word "God" occurs is shown on the lower right corner of every page. These simple physical facts are easily verifiable by the reader, and they suffice to prove the super-human nature of the Quran's mathematical composition.

Total Count of the Word "God"   *Total Sum of Verse Numbers*
(Shown at the lower left corner of every page)   *(Shown at the lower right corner)*

2698 (19x142)   *118123 (19x6217)*

Proof of Authenticity to be Verified by the Reader

In addition to the Quran's extraordinary mathematical composition, we find a large number of Quranic facts which are proven or theorized by modern science. Here are a few examples of such advance scientific information:
1. The earth is egg-shaped (39:5, 79:30).
2. The earth is not standing still; it moves constantly (27:88).
3. The sun is a source of light, while the moon reflects it (10:5, 25:61, 71:16).
4. The proportion of oxygen diminishes as we climb towards the sky (6:125).
5. The "Big Bang Theory" is confirmed (21:30).
6. The "Expansion of the Universe Theory" is confirmed (51:47).
7. The universe started out as a gaseous mass (41:11).
8. Evolution is a fact; within a given species, evolution is a divinely guided process (21:30, 24:45, 32:7-9, 18:37, 15:28-29, 7:11, 71:13-14, Appendix 31).
9. The man's seminal fluid decides the baby's gender (53:45-46).

No Nonsense

Equally miraculous is the absence of any nonsense in the Quran. This is particularly significant in view of the dominance of ignorance and superstition at the time of revelation of the Quran. For example, the most respected exegesis among the traditional Muslims is that of Ibn Kathir. In this famous reference, written centuries after the Prophet, we read that the earth is carried on 40,000 horns of a giant bull, who stands on top of a giant whale (see Ibn Kathir's interpretation of Verse 68:1).

As recently as 1975, and in the same location where the Quran was revealed, the president of the Islamic University of Medina, Saudi Arabia, Sheikh Abdul Aziz Ben Baz, declared that the earth is flat and standing still (see insert)!!

من مطبوعات الجامعة الاسلامية
بالمدينة المنورة ١٣٩٥ هـ

الأدلة النقلية والحسّيّة

على جَرَيان الشَّمس وسُكون الأَرض

عبد العَزيز بن بَاز

ولو كانت الأرض تدور كما
يزعمون لكانت البلدان ، والجبال ، والأشجار ، والأنهار ، والبحار
لا قرار لها ، ولشاهد الناس البلدان المغربية في المشرق ، والمشرقية في المغرب ؛
ولتغيرت القبلة على الناس حتى لا يقرّ لها قرار

Translation from Ben Baz' book, Page 23: "If the earth is rotating as they claim, the countries, the mountains, the trees, the rivers, and the oceans will have no bottom and the people will see the eastern countries move to the west and the western countires move to the east."

Perfect Happiness: Now and Forever

One of the most elusive objectives of every human being is "Happiness." The Quran reveals the secret of attaining perfect happiness in this life and forever. We learn from the Quran that happiness is an exclusive quality of the soul. Thus, a body that attains all the material successes it longs for—money, power, fame, etc.—often belongs to an unhappy person. Happiness depends totally on the degree of growth and development attained by the soul, the real person. The Quran provides a detailed map towards perfect happiness for both body and soul, both in this world and in the eternal Hereafter (Appendix 15).

In numerous verses throughout this proven Testament, God personally guarantees the believers' happiness, now and forever:

Absolutely, God's allies will have nothing to fear,
nor will they grieve.
They are those who believe
and lead a righteous life.
For them happiness in this life, and in the Hereafter.
Such is God's inviolable law.
This is the true triumph.   *[10:62-64]*

All Believers Constitute the One Acceptable Religion

As expected from the Creator's final message, one of the prominent themes in the Quran is the call for unity among all believers, and the repeated prohibition of making any distinction among God's messengers. If the object of worship is one and the same, there will be absolute unity among all believers. It is the human factor, i.e., devotion and prejudice to such powerless humans as Jesus, Muhammad, and the saints that causes division, hatred, and bitter wars among the misguided believers. A guided believer is devoted to God ALONE, and rejoices in seeing any other believer who is devoted to God ALONE, regardless of the name such a believer calls his or her religion.

> *Surely, those who believe,*
> *those who are Jewish,*
> *the Christians,*
> *and the converts;*
> *anyone who*
> *(1) believes in God,*
> *(2) believes in the Last Day, and*
> *(3) leads a righteous life,*
> *will receive their recompense from their Lord;*
> *they have nothing to fear, nor will they grieve.*   *[2:62, 5:69]*

God's Messenger of the Covenant

As detailed in Appendix 2, the publication of this book marks the advent of a new era – the era where God's messages, delivered by all His prophets, are consolidated into one. God's one and only religion, "Submission," shall dominate all other religions (9:33, 48:28, and 61:9). Today's corrupted religions, including Judaism, Christianity, Hinduism, Buddhism, and Islam, will simply die out, and "Submission" will prevail. This is not the wishful thinking of a human being or a collection of humans; this is God's inviolable law (3:19, 9:33, 41:53, 48:28, 61:9, 110:1).

Rashad Khalifa
Tucson
Ramadan 26,1409*

* The final draft of the first printing was completed on the Night of Destiny 1409. If we add the day, month, and year of this date, we get 1444, or 19x19x4. [Ramadan 26,1409: 9 + 26 + 1409 = 1444.]

Sura 1: The Key (Al- Fãtehah)

1. In the name of **GOD**, Most Gracious, Most Merciful.*

2. Praise be to **GOD**, Lord of the universe.

3. Most Gracious, Most Merciful.

4. Master of the Day of Judgment.

5. You alone we worship. You alone we ask for help.

6. Guide us in the right path;

7. the path of those whom You blessed; not of those who have deserved wrath, nor of the strayers.

1:1 The first verse in the Quran represents the foundation upon which a superhuman 19-based mathematical miracle is built. This important statement consists of 19 Arabic letters, and every word in it occurs in the whole Quran in multiples of 19 (see Appendices 1 & 29 for the details).

1:1-7 Sura 1 is God's gift to us to establish contact with Him through the daily Contact Prayers. This fact is supported by an earth-shattering, simple-to-understand-but-impossible-to-imitate mathematical composition that challenges the greatest mathematicians on earth, and stumps them; it is far beyond human capabilities:

(1) The sura number, followed by the numbers of verses, next to each other, give 1 1 2 3 4 5 6 7. This number is a multiple of 19.

(2) If we substitute the number of letters per verse in place of verse numbers, we get 1 19 17 12 11 19 18 43. This number is also a multiple of 19.

(3) If we insert the total gematrical value of every verse, we get 1 19 786 17 581 12 618 11 241 19 836 18 1072 43 6009. This number is a multiple of 19.

(4) The number shown above includes all parameters of Sura 1, and consists of 38 digits (19x2).

(5) It is noteworthy that this 38-digit number is still divisible by 19 when we write its components backwards, from right to left, as practiced by the Arabs. Thus, 6009 43 1072 18 836 19 241 11 618 12 581 17 786 19 1 is also a multiple of 19.

(6) The mathematical representations mentioned above participate in numerous extraordinary mathematical phenomena to confirm all details of the five daily Contact Prayers (Appendix 15).

Verse #	No of Letters	Gematrical Value
1	19	786
2	17	581
3	12	618
4	11	241
5	19	836
6	18	1072
7	43	6009
Totals	139	10143

(7) Many more astounding phenomena are given in Appendix One. Thus, the reader is handed, at the outset, tangible proof that this is God's message to the world.

Cumulative frequency of the word GOD=

Cumulative sum of verses where GOD occurs=

Sura 2: The Heifer (Al-Baqarah)

In the name of God,
Most Gracious, Most Merciful

1. A.L.M.*

2. This scripture is infallible; a beacon for the righteous;

Three Categories of People
(1) The Righteous.

3. who believe in the unseen, observe the Contact Prayers (*Salat*),* and from our** provisions to them, they give to charity.

4. And they believe in what was revealed to you, and in what was revealed before you, and with regard to the Hereafter, they are absolutely certain.*

5. These are guided by their Lord; these are the winners.

(2) The Disbelievers

6. As for those who disbelieve, it is the same for them; whether you warn them, or not warn them, they cannot believe.*

7. **GOD** seals their minds and their hearing, and their eyes are veiled. They have incurred severe retribution.

(3) The Hypocrites

8. Then there are those who say, "We believe in **GOD** and the Last Day," while they are not believers.

---

*2:1 These initials remained a divinely guarded secret for 1400 years. Now we recognize them as a major component of the Quran's extraordinary mathematical code (see Appendices 1, 2, 24, and 26). The meaning of A.L.M. is pointed out in Verse 2: "This scripture is infallible." This is incontrovertibly proven by the fact that the frequencies of occurrence of these three initials in this sura are 4502, 3202, and 2195, respectively. The sum of these numbers is 9899, or 19x521. Thus, these most frequent letters of the Arabic language are mathematically placed according to a super-human pattern. These same initials also prefix Suras 3, 29, 30, 31, and 32, and their frequencies of occurrence add up to multiples of 19 in each one of these suras.

*2:3 Since the Contact Prayers are decreed five times a day, they constitute the prime source of nourishment for our souls. Along with all other practices in Submission, the Contact Prayers were originally revealed through Abraham (21:73, 22:78). Although these five daily prayers were practiced before the revelation of the Quran, each Contact Prayer is specifically mentioned in the Quran (24:58, 11:114, 17:78, & 2:238). Appendices 1 & 15 provide physical evidence supporting all the details of the Contact Prayers, including the number of units (Rak'aas) and the numbers of bowings, prostrations, and Tashahhuds in each prayer.

**2:3 When God uses the plural tense, this indicates that other entities, usually the angels, are involved. When God spoke to Moses, the singular form was used (20:12-14). See Appendix 10.

*2:4 Despite severe distortions that afflicted the previous scriptures, God's truth can still be found in them. Both the Old Testament and the New Testament still advocate absolute devotion to God ALONE (Deuteronomy 6:4-5, Mark 12:29-30). All distortions are easily detectable.

*2:6-7 Those who make a decision to reject God are helped in that direction; they are prevented by God from seeing any proof or guidance for as long as they maintain such a decision. The consequences of such a disastrous decision are spelled out in Verse 7.

9. In trying to deceive **GOD** and those who believe, they only deceive themselves without perceiving.

10. In their minds there is a disease. Consequently, **GOD** augments their disease. They have incurred a painful retribution for their lying.

11. When they are told, "Do not commit evil," they say, "But we are righteous!"

12. In fact, they are evildoers, but they do not perceive.

13. When they are told, "Believe like the people who believed," they say, "Shall we believe like the fools who believed?" In fact, it is they who are fools, but they do not know.

14. When they meet the believers, they say, "We believe," but when alone with their devils, they say, "We are with you; we were only mocking."

15. **GOD** mocks them, and leads them on in their transgressions, blundering.

16. It is they who bought the straying, at the expense of guidance. Such trade never prospers, nor do they receive any guidance.

17. Their example is like those who start a fire, then, as it begins to shed light around them, **GOD** takes away their light, leaving them in darkness, unable to see.

18. Deaf, dumb, and blind; they fail to return.

19. Another example: a rainstorm from the sky in which there is darkness, thunder, and lightning. They put their fingers in their ears, to evade death. **GOD** is fully aware of the disbelievers.

The Light of Faith

20. The lightning almost snatches away their eyesight. When it lights for them, they move forward, and when it turns dark, they stand still. If **GOD** wills, He* can take away their hearing and their eyesight. **GOD** is Omnipotent.

21. O people, worship only your Lord—the One who created you and those before you—that you may be saved.

22. The One who made the earth habitable for you, and the sky a structure. He sends down from the sky water, to produce all kinds of fruits for your sustenance. You shall not set up idols to rival **GOD**, now that you know.

Mathematical Challenge

23. If you have any doubt regarding what we revealed to our servant,* then produce one sura like these, and call upon your own witnesses against **GOD**, if you are truthful.

Allegorical Description of Hell

24. If you cannot do this—and you can never do this—then beware of the Hellfire, whose fuel is people and rocks; it awaits the disbelievers.

---

*2:20 *"He" and "she" do not necessarily imply natural gender in Arabic (Appendix 4).*

*2:23-24 *The Quran's miraculous mathematical code provides numerous proofs as it spells out the name "Rashad Khalifa" as God's servant mentioned here. Some literary giants, including Al-Mutanabby and Taha Hussein, have answered the literary challenge, but they had no awareness of the Quran's mathematical composition. It is the Quran's mathematical code, revealed through God's Messenger of the Covenant, Rashad Khalifa, that is the real challenge—for it can never be imitated. See Appendices 1, 2, 24, & 26 for the detailed proofs.*

Allegorical Description of Paradise

25. Give good news to those who believe and lead a righteous life that they will have gardens with flowing streams. When provided with a provision of fruits therein, they will say, "This is what was provided for us previously." Thus, they are given allegorical descriptions. They will have pure spouses therein, and they abide therein forever.

26. **GOD** does not shy away from citing any kind of allegory,* from the tiny mosquito and greater. As for those who believe, they know that it is the truth from their Lord. As for those who disbelieve, they say, "What did **GOD** mean by such an allegory?" He misleads many thereby, and guides many thereby. But He never misleads thereby except the wicked,

27. who violate **GOD**'s covenant after pledging to uphold it, sever what **GOD** has commanded to be joined, and commit evil. These are the losers.

Two Deaths and Two Lives for the Disbelievers*

28. How can you disbelieve in **GOD** when you were dead and He gave you life, then He puts you to death, then He brings you back to life, then to Him you ultimately return?

29. He is the One who created for you everything on earth, then turned to the sky and perfected seven universes therein,* and He is fully aware of all things.

Satan: A Temporary "god"*

30. Recall that your Lord said to the angels, "I am placing a representative (*a temporary god*) on Earth." They said, "Will You place therein one who will spread evil therein and shed blood, while we sing Your praises, glorify You, and uphold Your absolute authority?" He said, "I know what you do not know."

The Test Begins

31. He taught Adam all the names* then presented them to the angels, saying, "Give me the names of these, if you are right."

2:26 See Appendix 5 for further discussion of Heaven and Hell.

2:28 The righteous do not really die; they go straight to Heaven. When their interim on this earth comes to an end, the angels of death simply invite them to go to the same Paradise where Adam and Eve once lived (2:154, 3:169, 8:24, 22:58, 16:32, 36:20-27, 44:56, 89:27-30). Thus, while the righteous experience only the first death following our original sin, the unrighteous go through two deaths (40:11). At the time of death, the disbelievers know their miserable fate (8:50, 47:27), then they suffer a continuous nightmare that lasts until Hell is created (40:46, 89:23, Appendix 17).

2:29 Our universe with its billion galaxies, spanning distances of billions of light years, is the smallest and innermost of seven universes (Appendix 6). Please look up 41:10-11.

2:30-37 These verses answer such crucial questions as: "Why are we here?" (See Appendix 7).

2:31 These are the names of the animals, the automobile, the submarine, the space satellite, the VCR, and all other objects to be encountered by the human beings on Earth.

---

32. They said, "Be You glorified, we have no knowledge, except that which You have taught us. You are the Omniscient, Most Wise."

33. He said, "O Adam, tell them their names." When he told them their names, He said, "Did I not tell you that I know the secrets of the heavens and the earth? I know what you declare, and what you conceal."

34. When we said to the angels, "Fall prostrate before Adam," they fell prostrate, except Satan; he refused, was too arrogant, and a disbeliever.

35. We said, "O Adam, live with your wife in Paradise, and eat therefrom generously, as you please, but do not approach this tree, lest you sin."

36. But the devil duped them, and caused their eviction therefrom. We said, "Go down as enemies of one another. On Earth shall be your habitation and provision for a-while."

Specific Words*

37. Then, Adam received from his Lord words, whereby He redeemed him. He is the Redeemer, Most Merciful.

38. We said, "Go down therefrom, all of you. When guidance comes to you from Me, those who follow My guidance will have no fear, nor will they grieve.

39. "As for those who disbelieve and reject our revelations, they will be dwellers of Hell, wherein they abide forever."

Divine Commandments
to All Jews:
"You Shall Believe in This Quran."

40. O Children of Israel, remember My favor, which I bestowed upon you, and fulfill your part of the covenant, that I fulfill My part of the covenant, and reverence Me.

41. You shall believe in what I have revealed herein, confirming what you have; do not be the first to reject it. Do not trade away My revelations for a cheap price, and observe Me.

42. Do not confound the truth with falsehood, nor shall you conceal the truth, knowingly.

43. You shall observe the Contact Prayers (*Salat*) and give the obligatory charity (*Zakat*), and bow down with those who bow down.

44. Do you exhort the people to be righteous, while forgetting yourselves, though you read the scripture? Do you not understand?

45. You shall seek help through steadfastness and the Contact Prayers (*Salat*). This is difficult indeed, but not so for the reverent,

46. who believe that they will meet their Lord; that to Him they ultimately return.

47. O Children of Israel, remember My favor which I bestowed upon you, and that I blessed you more than any other people.

48. Beware of the day when no soul can avail another soul, no intercession will be accepted, no ransom can be paid, nor can anyone be helped.

---

*2:37 Similarly, God has given us specific, mathematically coded words, the words of Sura 1, to establish contact with Him (see Footnote 1:1 and Appendix 15).

49. Recall that we saved you from Pharaoh's people who inflicted upon you the worst persecution, slaying your sons and sparing your daughters. That was an exacting test from your Lord.

50. Recall that we parted the sea for you; we saved you and drowned Pharaoh's people before your eyes.

51. Yet, when we summoned Moses for forty nights, you worshiped the calf in his absence, and turned wicked.*

52. Still, we pardoned you thereafter that you may be appreciative.

53. Recall that we gave Moses scripture and the statute book, that you may be guided.

Kill Your Ego*

54. Recall that Moses said to his people, "O my people, you have wronged your souls by worshiping the calf. You must repent to your Creator. You shall kill your egos. This is better for you in the sight of your Creator." He did redeem you. He is the Redeemer, Most Merciful.

Physical Evidence*

55. Recall that you said, "O Moses, we will not believe unless we see **GOD**, physically." Consequently, the lightning struck you, as you looked.

56. We then revived you, after you had died, that you may be appreciative.

57. We shaded you with clouds (*in Sinai*), and sent down to you manna and quails: "Eat from the good things we provided for you." They did not hurt us (*by rebelling*); they only hurt their own souls.

Lack of Confidence in God: They Refuse to Enter Jerusalem

58. Recall that we said, "Enter this town, where you will find as many provisions as you like. Just enter the gate humbly, and treat the people nicely. We will then forgive your sins, and increase the reward for the pious."

59. But the wicked among them carried out commands other than the commands given to them. Consequently, we sent down upon the transgressors condemnation from the sky, due to their wickedness.

More Miracles

60. Recall that Moses sought water for his people. We said, "Strike the rock with your staff." Whereupon, twelve springs gushed out therefrom. The members of each tribe knew their own water. Eat and drink from **GOD**'s provisions, and do not roam the earth corruptingly.

---

*2:51 This incident reflects the humans' idolatrous tendency. Despite the profound miracles, Moses' followers worshiped the calf in his absence, and Moses ended up with only two believers (5:23). As pointed out in the Introduction, the humans are rebels whose egos are their gods.

*2:54 It is the ego that led to Satan's fall. It is the ego that caused our exile to this world, and it is the ego that is keeping most of us from redemption to God's Kingdom.

*2:55 It is noteworthy that the word "GOD" in this verse is the 19th occurrence, and this is the verse where the people demanded "physical evidence." The Quran's mathematical code, based on the number 19, provides such physical evidence. Note also that 2 + 55 = 57=19x3.

Israel Rebels

61. Recall that you said, "O Moses, we can no longer tolerate one kind of food. Call upon your Lord to produce for us such earthly crops as beans, cucumbers, garlic, lentils, and onions." He said, "Do you wish to substitute that which is inferior for that which is good? Go down to Egypt, where you can find what you asked for." They have incurred condemnation, humiliation, and disgrace, and brought upon themselves wrath from **GOD**. This is because they rejected **GOD**'s revelations, and killed the prophets unjustly. This is because they disobeyed and transgressed.

Unity of
All Submitters

62. Surely, those who believe, those who are Jewish, the Christians, and the converts; anyone who
   (1) believes in **GOD**, and
   (2) believes in the Last Day, and
   (3) leads a righteous life, will receive their recompense from their Lord. They have nothing to fear, nor will they grieve.

Covenant with Israel

63. We made a covenant with you, as we raised Mount Sinai above you: "You shall uphold what we have given you strongly, and remember its contents, that you may be saved."

64. But you turned away thereafter, and if it were not for **GOD**'s grace towards you and His mercy, you would have been doomed.

65. You have known about those among you who desecrated the Sabbath. We said to them, "Be you as despicable as apes."

66. We set them up as an example for their generation, as well as subsequent generations, and an enlightenment for the righteous.

The Heifer*

67. Moses said to his people, "**GOD** commands you to sacrifice a heifer." They said, "Are you mocking us?" He said, "**GOD** forbid, that I should behave like the ignorant ones."

68. They said, "Call upon your Lord to show us which one." He said, "He says that she is a heifer that is neither too old, nor too young; of an intermediate age. Now, carry out what you are commanded to do."

69. They said, "Call upon your Lord to show us her color." He said, "He says that she is a yellow heifer, bright colored, pleases the beholders."

70. They said, "Call upon your Lord to show us which one. The heifers look alike to us and, **GOD** willing, we will be guided."

71. He said, "He says that she is a heifer that was never humiliated in plowing the land or watering the crops; free from any blemish." They said, "Now you have brought the truth." They finally sacrificed her, after this lengthy reluctance.

---

*2:67 Although this sura contains important laws and commandments, including the contact prayers, fasting, Hajj pilgrimage, and the laws of marriage, divorce, etc., the name given to the sura is "The Heifer." This reflects the crucial importance of submission to God and immediate, unwavering obedience to our Creator. Such submission proves our belief in God's omnipotence and absolute authority. See also the Bible's Book of Numbers, Chapter 19.

Purpose of the Heifer

72. You had killed a person, then disputed among yourselves. **GOD** was to expose what you tried to conceal.

73. We said, "Strike (*the victim*) with part (*of the heifer*)." That is when **GOD** brought the victim back to life, and showed you His signs, that you may understand.

74. Despite this, your hearts hardened like rocks, or even harder. For there are rocks from which rivers gush out. Others crack and release gentle streams, and other rocks cringe out of reverence for **GOD**. **GOD** is never unaware of anything you do.

Distorting the Word of God

75. Do you expect them to believe as you do, when some of them used to hear the word of **GOD**, then distort it, with full understanding thereof, and deliberately?

*Concealing the
Word of God*

76. And when they meet the believers, they say, "We believe," but when they get together with each other, they say, "Do not inform (*the believers*) of the information given to you by **GOD**, lest you provide them with support for their argument concerning your Lord. Do you not understand?"

77. Do they not know that **GOD** knows everything they conceal, and everything they declare?

78. Among them are gentiles who do not know the scripture, except through hearsay, then assume that they know it.

79. Therefore, woe to those who distort the scripture with their own hands, then say, "This is what **GOD** has revealed," seeking a cheap material gain. Woe to them for such distortion, and woe to them for their illicit gains.

*Eternity of
Heaven and Hell**

80. Some have said, "Hell will not touch us, except for a limited number of days." Say, "Have you taken such a pledge from **GOD**—**GOD** never breaks His pledge—or, are you saying about **GOD** what you do not know?"

81. Indeed, those who earn sins and become surrounded by their evil work will be the dwellers of Hell; they abide in it forever.

82. As for those who believe, and lead a righteous life, they will be the dwellers of Paradise; they abide in it forever.

The Commandments

83. We made a covenant with the Children of Israel: "You shall not worship except **GOD**. You shall honor your parents and regard the relatives, the orphans, and the poor. You shall treat the people amicably. You shall observe the Contact Prayers (*Salat*) and give the obligatory charity (*Zakat*)." But you turned away, except a few of you, and you became averse.

---

*2:80-82 It is an established belief among corrupted Muslims that they will suffer in Hell only in proportion to the number of sins they had committed, then they will get out of Hell and go to Heaven. They also believe that Muhammad will intercede on their behalf, and will take them out of Hell. Such beliefs are contrary to the Quran (Appendix 8).

---

84. We made a covenant with you, that you shall not shed your blood, nor shall you evict each other from your homes. You agreed and bore witness.

85. Yet, here you are killing each other, and evicting some of you from their homes, banding against them sinfully and maliciously. Even when they surrendered, you demanded ransom from them. Evicting them was prohibited for you in the first place. Do you believe in part of the scripture and disbelieve in part? What should be the retribution for those among you who do this, except humiliation in this life, and a far worse retribution on the Day of Resurrection? **GOD** is never unaware of anything you do.

86. It is they who bought this lowly life at the expense of the Hereafter. Consequently, the retribution is never commuted for them, nor can they be helped.

The Prophets of Israel

87. We gave Moses the scripture, and subsequent to him we sent other messengers, and we gave Jesus, son of Mary, profound miracles and supported him with the Holy Spirit. Is it not a fact that every time a messenger went to you with anything you disliked, your ego caused you to be arrogant? Some of them you rejected, and some of them you killed.

Tragic Statement:
"My mind is made up!"

88. Some would say, "Our minds are made up!" Instead, it is a curse from **GOD**, as a consequence of their disbelief, that keeps them from believing, except for a few of them.

The Quran
Consummates All Scriptures

89. When this scripture came to them from **GOD**, and even though it agrees with, and confirms what they have, and even though they used to prophesy its advent when they talked with the disbelievers, when their own prophecy came to pass, they disbelieved therein. **GOD**'s condemnation thus afflicts the disbelievers.

90. Miserable indeed is what they sold their souls for—rejecting these revelations of **GOD** out of sheer resentment that **GOD** should bestow His grace upon whomever He chooses from among His servants. Consequently, they incurred wrath upon wrath. The disbelievers have incurred a humiliating retribution.

91. When they are told, "You shall believe in these revelations of **GOD**," they say, "We believe only in what was sent down to us." Thus, they disbelieve in subsequent revelations, even if it is the truth from their Lord, and even though it confirms what they have! Say, "Why then did you kill **GOD**'s prophets, if you were believers?"

Learning From
Israel's History

92. Moses went to you with profound miracles, yet you worshiped the calf in his absence, and you turned wicked.

93. We made a covenant with you, as we raised Mount Sinai above you, saying, "You shall uphold the commandments we have given you, strongly, and listen." They said, "We hear, but we disobey." Their hearts became filled with adoration for the calf, due to their disbelief. Say, "Miserable indeed is what your faith dictates upon you, if you do have any faith."

94. Say, "If the abode of the Hereafter is reserved for you at **GOD,** to the exclusion of all other people, then you should long for death, if you are truthful."

95. They never long for it, because of what their hands have sent forth. **GOD** is fully aware of the wicked.

96. In fact, you will find them the most covetous of life; even more so than the idol worshipers. The one of them wishes to live a thousand years. But this will not spare him any retribution, no matter how long he lives. **GOD** is seer of everything they do.

Gabriel
Mediates
the Revelation

97. Say, "Anyone who opposes Gabriel should know that he has brought down this (*Quran*) into your heart, in accordance with **GOD**'s will, confirming previous scriptures, and providing guidance and good news for the believers."

98. Anyone who opposes **GOD,** and His angels, and His messengers, and Gabriel and Michael, should know that **GOD** opposes the disbelievers.

99. We have sent down to you such clear revelations, and only the wicked will reject them.

100. Is it not a fact that when they make a covenant and pledge to keep it, some of them always disregard it? In fact, most of them do not believe.

Disregarding God's Scripture

101. Now that a messenger from **GOD** has come to them,* and even though he proves and confirms their own scripture, some followers of the scripture (*Jews, Christians, and Muslims*) disregard **GOD**'s scripture behind their backs, as if they never had any scripture.

Witchcraft Condemned

102. They pursued what the devils taught concerning Solomon's kingdom. Solomon, however, was not a disbeliever, but the devils were disbelievers. They taught the people sorcery, and that which was sent down through the two angels of Babel, Haroot and Maroot. These two did not divulge such knowledge without pointing out: "This is a test. You shall not abuse such knowledge." But the people used it in such evil schemes as the breaking up of marriages. They can never harm anyone against the will of **GOD.** They thus learn what hurts them, not what benefits them, and they know full well that whoever practices witchcraft will have no share in the Hereafter. Miserable indeed is what they sell their souls for, if they only knew.

103. If they believe and lead a righteous life, the reward from **GOD** is far better, if they only knew.

---

*2:101 God's Messenger of the Covenant is prophesied in the Old Testament (Malachi 3:1-3), the New Testament (Luke 17:22-37), and this Final Testament (3:81).

Twisting the Words of Supplication

104. O you who believe, do not say, *"Raa'ena"** (be our shepherd). Instead, you should say, *"Unzurna"* (watch over us), and listen. The disbelievers have incurred a painful retribution.

Jealousy Condemned

105. Neither the disbelievers among the followers of the scripture, nor the idol worshipers, wish to see any blessings come down to you from your Lord. However, **GOD** showers His blessings upon whomever He chooses. **GOD** possesses infinite grace.

The Ultimate Miracle:
The Quran's
*Mathematical Code**

106. When we abrogate any miracle, or cause it to be forgotten, we produce a better miracle, or at least an equal one. Do you not recognize the fact that **GOD** is Omnipotent?

107. Do you not recognize the fact that **GOD** possesses the kingship of the heavens and the earth; that you have none besides **GOD** as your Lord and Master?

108. Do you wish to demand of your messenger what was demanded of Moses in the past? Anyone who chooses disbelief, instead of belief, has truly strayed off the right path.

109. Many followers of the scripture would rather see you revert to disbelief, now that you have believed. This is due to jealousy on their part, after the truth has become evident to them. You shall pardon them, and leave them alone, until **GOD** issues His judgment. **GOD** is Omnipotent.

110. You shall observe the Contact Prayers (*Salat*) and give the obligatory charity (*Zakat*). Any good you send forth on behalf of your souls, you will find it at **GOD**. **GOD** is seer of everything you do.

All Believers Are Redeemed,
Regardless of the Name
of Their Religion

111. Some have said, "No one will enter Paradise except Jews or Christians!" Such is their wishful thinking. Say, "Show us your proof, if you are right."

Submission:
The Only Religion

112. Indeed, those who submit themselves absolutely to **GOD** alone, while leading a righteous life, will receive their recompense from their Lord; they have nothing to fear, nor will they grieve.*

113. The Jews said, "The Christians have no basis," while the Christians said, "The Jews have no basis." Yet, both of them read the scripture. Such are the utterances of those who possess no knowledge. **GOD** will judge them on the Day of Resurrection, regarding their disputes.

---

*2:104 The word "Raa'ena" was abused by some Hebrew-speaking people, and twisted to sound like a dirty word (see also 4:46).

*2:106 The Quran's mathematical miracle is perpetual & greater than previous miracles (34:45, 74:35). Like the Quran itself, it confirms, consummates, and supersedes all previous miracles.

*2:111-112 See 2:62 and 5:69.

You Shall Frequent the Masjid

114. Who are more evil than those who boycott **GOD**'s masjids, where His name is commemorated, and contribute to their desertion? These ought not to enter therein except fearfully. They will suffer in this life humiliation, and will suffer in the Hereafter a terrible retribution.

115. To **GOD** belongs the east and the west; wherever you go there will be the presence of **GOD. GOD** is Omnipresent, Omniscient.

Gross Blasphemy

116. They said, "**GOD** has begotten a son!" Be He glorified; never! To Him belongs everything in the heavens and the earth; all are subservient to Him.

117. The Initiator of the heavens and the earth: to have anything done, He simply says to it, "Be," and it is.

118. Those who possess no knowledge say, "If only **GOD** could speak to us, or some miracle could come to us!" Others before them have uttered similar utterances; their minds are similar. We do manifest the miracles for those who have attained certainty.

119. We have sent you* with the truth as a bearer of good news, as well as a warner. You are not answerable for those who incur Hell.

120. Neither the Jews, nor the Christians, will accept you, unless you follow their religion. Say, "**GOD**'s guidance is the true guidance." If you acquiesce to their wishes, despite the knowledge you have received, you will find no ally or supporter to help you against **GOD**.

121. Those who received the scripture, and know it as it should be known, will believe in this. As for those who disbelieve, they are the losers.

122. O Children of Israel, remember My favor which I bestowed upon you, and that I blessed you more than any other people.

123. Beware of the day when no soul will help another soul, no ransom will be accepted, no intercession will be useful, and no one will be helped.

Abraham

124. Recall that Abraham was put to the test by his Lord, through certain commands, and he fulfilled them. (*God*) said, "I am appointing you an imam for the people." He said, "And also my descendants?" He said, "My covenant does not include the transgressors."

125. We have rendered the shrine (*the Ka'aba*) a focal point for the people, and a safe sanctuary. You may use Abraham's shrine as a prayer house. We commissioned Abraham and Ismail: "You shall purify My house for those who visit, those who live there, and those who bow and prostrate."

126. Abraham prayed: "My Lord, make this a peaceful land, and provide its people with fruits. Provide for those who believe in **GOD** and the Last Day." (*God*) said, "I will also provide for those who disbelieve. I will let them enjoy, temporarily, then commit them to the retribution of Hell, and a miserable destiny."

---

*2:119 It is my obligation to point out that the identity of this messenger is confirmed to be "Rashad Khalifa," God's Messenger of the Covenant. By adding the gematrical value of "Rashad" (505), plus the gematrical value of "Khalifa" (725), plus the verse number (119), we get 1349, a multiple of 19. See 3:81 and Appendix Two.

*Abraham Delivered All the
Practices of Submission (Islam)*

127. As Abraham raised the foundations of the shrine, together with Ismail (*they prayed*): "Our Lord, accept this from us. You are the Hearer, the Omniscient.

128. "Our Lord, make us submitters to You, and from our descendants let there be a community of submitters to You. Teach us the rites of our religion, and redeem us. You are the Redeemer, Most Merciful.

129. "Our Lord, and raise among them a messenger to recite to them Your revelations, teach them the scripture and wisdom, and purify them. You are the Almighty, Most Wise."

130. Who would forsake the religion of Abraham, except one who fools his own soul? We have chosen him in this world, and in the Hereafter he will be with the righteous.

131. When his Lord said to him, "Submit," he said, "I submit to the Lord of the universe."

132. Moreover, Abraham exhorted his children to do the same, and so did Jacob: "O my children, **GOD** has pointed out the religion for you; do not die except as submitters."

133. Had you witnessed Jacob on his death bed; he said to his children, "What will you worship after I die?" They said, "We will worship your god; the god of your fathers Abra-ham, Ismail, and Isaac; the one god. To Him we are submitters."

134. Such is a community from the past. They are responsible for what they earned, and you are responsible for what you earned. You are not answerable for anything they have done.

*Submission (Islam):
Abraham's Religion ***

135. They said, "You have to be Jewish or Christian, to be guided." Say, "We follow the religion of Abraham —monotheism—he never was an idol worshiper."

*No Distinction
Among
God's Messengers*

136. Say, "We believe in **GOD**, and in what was sent down to us, and in what was sent down to Abraham, Ismail, Isaac, Jacob, and the Patriarchs; and in what was given to Moses and Jesus, and all the prophets from their Lord. We make no distinction among any of them. To Him alone we are submitters."

137. If they believe as you do, then they are guided. But if they turn away, then they are in opposition. **GOD** will spare you their opposition; He is the Hearer, the Omniscient.

138. Such is **GOD**'s system, and whose system is better than **GOD**'s? "Him alone we worship."

---

*2:135 The Quran repeatedly informs us that Submission is the religion of Abraham (3:95, 4:125, 6:161, 22:78). Abraham received a practical "scripture," namely, all the duties and practices of Submission [the Contact Prayers (Salat), the obligatory charity (Zakat), the fasting of Ramadan, and the Hajj pilgrimage]. Muhammad was a follower of Abraham's religion, as we see in 16:123; he delivered this Final Testament, the Quran. The third messenger of Submission delivered the religion's proof of authenticity (see 3:81 and Appendices 1, 2, 24, & 26).

139. Say, "Do you argue with us about **GOD**, when He is our Lord and your Lord? We are responsible for our deeds, and you are responsible for your deeds. To Him alone we are devoted."

140. Do you say that Abraham, Ismail, Isaac, Jacob, and the Patriarchs were Jewish or Christian? Say, "Do you know better than **GOD**? Who is more evil than one who conceals a testimony he has learned from **GOD**? **GOD** is never unaware of anything you do."

141. That was a community from the past. They are responsible for what they earned, and you are responsible for what you earned. You are not answerable for anything they did.

Abolition of Bigotry and Prejudice*

142. The fools among the people would say, "Why did they change the direction of their *Qiblah*?"* Say, "To **GOD** belongs the east and the west; He guides whoever wills in a straight path."

143. We thus made you an impartial community, that you may serve as witnesses among the people, and the messenger serves as a witness among you. We changed the direction of your original *Qiblah* only to distinguish those among you who readily follow the messenger from those who would turn back on their heels. It was a difficult test, but not for those who are guided by **GOD**. **GOD** never puts your worship to waste. **GOD** is Compassionate towards the people, Most Merciful.

Qiblah Restored to Mecca

144. We have seen you turning your face about the sky (*searching for the right direction*). We now assign a *Qiblah* that is pleasing to you. Henceforth, you shall turn your face towards the Sacred Masjid. Wherever you may be, all of you shall turn your faces towards it. Those who received the previous scripture know that this is the truth from their Lord. **GOD** is never unaware of anything they do.

145. Even if you show the followers of the scripture every kind of miracle, they will not follow your *Qiblah*. Nor shall you follow their *Qiblah*. They do not even follow each others' *Qiblah*. If you acquiesce to their wishes, after the knowledge that has come to you, you will belong with the transgressors.

Abuse of the Scripture: Selective Emphasis and Concealment

146. Those who received the scripture recognize the truth herein, as they recognize their own children. Yet, some of them conceal the truth, knowingly.

147. This is the truth from your Lord; do not harbor any doubt.

148. Each of you chooses the direction to follow; you shall race towards righteousness. Wherever you may be, **GOD** will summon you all. **GOD** is Omnipotent.

*2:142-145 "Qiblah" is the direction one faces during the Contact Prayers (Salat). When Gabriel conveyed to Muhammad the command to face Jerusalem instead of Mecca, the hypocrites were exposed. The Arabs were strongly prejudiced in favor of the Ka'aba as their "Qiblah." Only the true believers were able to overcome their prejudices; they readily obeyed the messenger.

Qiblah Restored to Mecca

149. Wherever you go, you shall turn your face (*during Salat*) towards the Sacred Masjid.* This is the truth from your Lord. **GOD** is never unaware of anything you all do.

150. Wherever you go, you shall turn your face (*during Salat*) towards the Sacred Masjid; wherever you might be, you shall turn your faces (*during Salat*) towards it. Thus, the people will have no argument against you, except the transgressors among them. Do not fear them, and fear Me instead. I will then perfect My blessings upon you, that you may be guided.

151. (*Blessings*) such as the sending of a messenger from among you to recite our revelations to you, purify you, teach you the scripture and wisdom, and to teach you what you never knew.

152. You shall remember Me, that I may remember you, and be thankful to Me; do not be unappreciative.

153. O you who believe, seek help through steadfastness and the Contact Prayers (*Salat*). **GOD** is with those who steadfastly persevere.

Where Do We Go From Here?

154. Do not say of those who are killed in the cause of **GOD**, "They are dead." They are alive at their Lord, but you do not perceive.*

155. We will surely test you through some fear, hunger, and loss of money, lives, and crops. Give good news to the steadfast.*

156. When an affliction befalls them, they say, "We belong to **GOD**, and to Him we are returning."

157. These have deserved blessings from their Lord and mercy. These are the guided ones.

Hajj
Pilgrimage

158. The knolls of Safa and Marwah are among the rites decreed by **GOD**. Anyone who observes *Hajj* or '*Umrah* commits no error by traversing the distance between them. If one volunteers more righteous works, then **GOD** is Appreciative, Omniscient.

Gross Offense

159. Those who conceal our revelations and guidance, after proclaiming them for the people in the scripture, are condemned by **GOD**; they are condemned by all the condemners.

160. As for those who repent, reform, and proclaim, I redeem them. I am the Redeemer, Most Merciful.

161. Those who disbelieve and die as disbelievers, have incurred the condemnation of **GOD**, the angels, and all the people (*on the Day of Judgment*).

2:149 A glaring proof of the idolatry committed by today's "Muslims" is the designation of Muhammad's tomb as a "Sacred Masjid." The Quran mentions only one "Sacred Masjid."

2:154 The righteous do not really die; they simply leave their bodies here and go to the same Paradise where Adam and Eve once lived. See Appendix 17 for the proof and the details.

2:155 The test is designed to prove that we worship God alone under all circumstances (29:2).

---

162. Eternally they abide therein. The retribution is never commuted for them, nor are they reprieved.

163. Your god is one god; there is no god but He, Most Gracious, Most Merciful.

Overwhelming Signs of God

164. In the creation of the heavens and the earth, the alternation of night and day, the ships that roam the ocean for the benefit of the people, the water that **GOD** sends down from the sky to revive dead land and to spread in it all kinds of creatures, the manipulation of the winds, and the clouds that are placed between the sky and the earth, there are sufficient proofs for people who understand.

*The Idols Disown Their Idolizers**

165. Yet, some people set up idols to rival **GOD**, and love them as if they are **GOD**. Those who believe love **GOD** the most. If only the transgressors could see themselves when they see the retribution! They will realize then that all power belongs to **GOD** alone, and that **GOD**'s retribution is awesome.

166. Those who were followed will disown those who followed them.* They will see the retribution, and all ties among them will be severed.

167. Those who followed will say, "If we can get another chance, we will disown them, as they have disowned us now." **GOD** thus shows them the consequences of their works as nothing but remorse; they will never exit Hell.

Satan Prohibits Lawful Things

168. O people, eat from the earth's products all that is lawful and good, and do not follow the steps of Satan; he is your most ardent enemy.

169. He only commands you to commit evil and vice, and to say about **GOD** what you do not know.

Maintaining the Status Quo: A Human Tragedy

170. When they are told, "Follow what **GOD** has revealed herein," they say, "We follow only what we found our parents doing." What if their parents did not understand, and were not guided?

171. The example of such disbelievers is that of parrots who repeat what they hear of sounds and calls, without understanding. Deaf, dumb, and blind; they cannot understand.

*Only Four Meats Prohibited**

172. O you who believe, eat from the good things we provided for you, and be thankful to **GOD**, if you do worship Him alone.

173. He only prohibits for you the eating of animals that die of themselves (*without human interference*), blood, the meat of pigs, and animals dedicated to other than **GOD**. If one is forced (*to eat these*), without being malicious or deliberate, he incurs no sin. **GOD** is Forgiver, Most Merciful.

---

*2:165-166 Jesus, Mary, Muhammad, Ali, and the saints will disown their idolizers on the Day of Resurrection. See also 16:86, 35:14, 46:6, and the Gospel of Matthew 7:21-23.

*2:172-173 Throughout the Quran, only four meats are prohibited (6:145, 16:115, Appendix 16). Dietary prohibitions beyond these four are tantamount to idol worship (6:121,148,150; 7:32).

Corrupted Religious Leaders Conceal the Quran's Miracle*

174. Those who conceal **GOD**'s revelations in the scripture, in exchange for a cheap material gain, eat but fire into their bellies. **GOD** will not speak to them on the Day of Resurrection, nor will He purify them. They have incurred a painful retribution.

175. It is they who chose the straying instead of guidance, and the retribution instead of forgiveness. Consequently, they will have to endure Hell.

176. This is because **GOD** has revealed this scripture, bearing the truth, and those who dispute the scripture are the most ardent opponents.

Righteousness Defined

177. Righteousness is not turning your faces towards the east or the west. Righteous are those who believe in **GOD**, the Last Day, the angels, the scripture, and the prophets; and they give the money, cheerfully, to the relatives, the orphans, the needy, the traveling alien, the beggars, and to free the slaves; and they observe the Contact Prayers (*Salat*) and give the obligatory charity (*Zakat*); and they keep their word whenever they make a promise; and they steadfastly persevere in the face of persecution, hardship, and war. These are the truthful; these are the righteous.

Discouraging Capital Punishment*

178. O you who believe, equivalence is the law decreed for you when dealing with murder—the free for the free, the slave for the slave, the female for the female. If one is pardoned by the victim's kin, an appreciative response is in order, and an equitable compensation shall be paid. This is an alleviation from your Lord and mercy. Anyone who transgresses beyond this incurs a painful retribution.

179. Equivalence is a life saving law for you, O you who possess intelligence, that you may be righteous.

Write A Will

180. It is decreed that when death approaches, you shall write a will for the benefit of the parents and relatives, equitably. This is a duty upon the righteous.

181. If anyone alters a will he had heard, the sin of altering befalls those responsible for such altering. **GOD** is Hearer, Knower.

182. If one sees gross injustice or bias on the part of a testator, and takes corrective action to restore justice to the will, he commits no sin. **GOD** is Forgiver, Most Merciful.

---

*2:174-176 Despite their recognition of God's mathematical miracle in the Quran, the corrupted religious leaders tried for many years to conceal this awesome miracle. Many of them admitted that they resented the fact that Rashad Khalifa, not them, was blessed with the miracle.

*2:178 The Quran clearly discourages capital punishment. Every kind of excuse is provided to spare lives, including the life of the murderer. The victim's kin may find it better, under certain circumstances, to spare the life of the murderer in exchange for an equitable compensation. Also capital punishment is not applicable if, for example, a woman kills a man, or vice versa.

Fasting Emphasized and Modified*

183. O you who believe, fasting is decreed for you, as it was decreed for those before you, that you may attain salvation.

184. Specific days (*are designated for fasting*); if one is ill or traveling, an equal number of other days may be substituted. Those who can fast, but with great difficulty, may substitute feeding one poor person for each day of breaking the fast. If one volunteers (*more righteous works*), it is better. But fasting is the best for you, if you only knew.

185. Ramadan is the month during which the Quran was revealed, providing guidance for the people, clear teachings, and the statute book. Those of you who witness this month shall fast therein. Those who are ill or traveling may substitute the same number of other days. **GOD** wishes for you convenience, not hardship, that you may fulfill your obligations, and to glorify **GOD** for guiding you, and to express your appreciation.

God Answers the Prayers of "His Servants"

186. When My servants ask you about Me, I am always near. I answer their prayers when they pray to Me. The people shall respond to Me and believe in Me, in order to be guided.

187. Permitted for you is sexual intercourse with your wives during the nights of fasting. They are the keepers of your secrets, and you are the keepers of their secrets. **GOD** knew that you used to betray your souls, and He has redeemed you, and has pardoned you. Henceforth, you may have intercourse with them, seeking what **GOD** has permitted for you. You may eat and drink until the white thread of light becomes distinguishable from the dark thread of night at dawn. Then, you shall fast until sunset. Sexual intercourse is prohibited if you decide to retreat to the masjid (*during the last ten days of Ramadan*). These are **GOD**'s laws; you shall not transgress them. **GOD** thus clarifies His revelations for the people, that they may attain salvation.

Bribery, Corruption Condemned

188. You shall not take each others' money illicitly, nor shall you bribe the officials to deprive others of some of their rights illicitly, while you know.

Do Not Beat Around the Bush

189. They ask you about the phases of the moon! Say, "They provide a timing device for the people, and determine the time of Hajj." It is not righteous to beat around the bush;* righteousness is attained by upholding the commandments and by being straightforward. You shall observe **GOD**, that you may succeed.

---

*2:183-187 Like all duties in Submission, fasting was decreed through Abraham (22:78, Appendices 9 & 15). Prior to revelation of the Quran, sexual intercourse was prohibited throughout the fasting period. This rule is modified in 2:187 to allow intercourse during the nights of Ramadan.

*2:189 The literal Quranic idiom says: "Do not enter the homes through the back doors." The question about the phases of the moon is an example of beating around the bush; there were bad ulterior motives behind this question.

Rules of War*

190. You may fight in the cause of **GOD** against those who attack you, but do not aggress. **GOD** does not love the aggressors.

191. You may kill those who wage war against you, and you may evict them whence they evicted you. Oppression is worse than murder. Do not fight them at the Sacred Masjid, unless they attack you therein. If they attack you, you may kill them. This is the just retribution for those disbelievers.

192. If they refrain, then **GOD** is Forgiver, Most Merciful.

193. You may also fight them to eliminate oppression, and to worship **GOD** freely. If they refrain, you shall not aggress; aggression is permitted only against the aggressors.

194. During the Sacred Months, aggression may be met by an equivalent response. If they attack you, you may retaliate by inflicting an equitable retribution. You shall observe **GOD** and know that **GOD** is with the righteous.

195. You shall spend in the cause of **GOD**; do not throw yourselves with your own hands into destruction. You shall be charitable; **GOD** loves the charitable.

Hajj and 'Umrah Pilgrimage*

196. You shall observe the complete rites of *Hajj and 'Umrah* for **GOD**. If you are prevented, you shall send an offering, and do not resume cutting your hair until your offering has reached its destination. If you are ill, or suffering a head injury (*and you must cut your hair*), you shall expiate by fasting, or giving to charity, or some other form of worship. During the normal *Hajj,* if you break the state of *Ihraam* (sanctity) between *'Umrah* and *Hajj,* you shall expiate by offering an animal sacrifice. If you cannot afford it, you shall fast three days during *Hajj* and seven when you return home—this completes ten—provided you do not live at the Sacred Masjid. You shall observe **GOD**, and know that **GOD** is strict in enforcing retribution.

The Four Months of Hajj
(Zul-Hijjah, Muharram, Safar, &
Rabi I)

197. *Hajj* shall be observed in the specified months.* Whoever sets out to observe *Hajj* shall refrain from sexual intercourse, misconduct, and arguments throughout *Hajj.* Whatever good you do, **GOD** is fully aware thereof. As you prepare your provisions for the journey, the best provision is righteousness. You shall observe Me, O you who possess intelligence.

---

*2:190 All fighting is regulated by the basic rule in 60:8-9. Fighting is allowed strictly in self-defense, while aggression and oppression are strongly condemned throughout the Quran.

*2:196 See the details of Hajj and 'Umrah in Appendix 15.

*2:197 Hajj can be observed any time during the Sacred Months: Zul-Hijjah, Muharram, Safar, and Rabi I. Local governments restrict Hajj to a few days for their own convenience. See 9:37.

---

198. You commit no error by seeking provisions from your Lord (*through commerce*). When you file from 'Arafaat, you shall commemorate **GOD** at the Sacred Location (*of Muzdalifah*). You shall commemorate Him for guiding you; before this, you had gone astray.

199. You shall file together, with the rest of the people who file, and ask **GOD** for forgiveness. **GOD** is Forgiver, Most Merciful.

200. Once you complete your rites, you shall continue to commemorate **GOD** as you commemorate your own parents, or even better. Some people would say, "Our Lord, give us of this world," while having no share in the Hereafter.

201. Others would say, "Our Lord, grant us righteousness in this world, and righteousness in the Hereafter, and spare us the retribution of Hell."

202. Each of these will receive the share they have earned. **GOD** is most efficient in reckoning.

Mena: Last Rites of Hajj

203. You shall commemorate **GOD** for a number of days (*in Mena*); whoever hastens to do this in two days commits no sin, and whoever stays longer commits no sin, so long as righteousness is maintained. You shall observe **GOD,** and know that before Him you will be gathered.

Appearances May Be Deceiving

204. Among the people, one may impress you with his utterances concerning this life, and may even call upon **GOD** to witness his innermost thoughts, while he is a most ardent opponent.

205. As soon as he leaves, he roams the earth corruptingly, destroying properties and lives. **GOD** does not love corruption.

206. When he is told, "Observe **GOD**," he becomes arrogantly indignant. Consequently, his only destiny is Hell; what a miserable abode.

207. Then there are those who dedicate their lives to serving **GOD**; **GOD** is compassionate towards such worshipers.

208. O you who believe, you shall embrace total submission; do not follow the steps of Satan, for he is your most ardent enemy.

209. If you backslide, after the clear proofs have come to you, then know that **GOD** is Almighty, Most Wise.

210. Are they waiting until **GOD** Himself comes to them in dense clouds, together with the angels? When this happens, the whole matter will be terminated, and to **GOD** everything will be returned.*

*Miracles Bring Greater Responsibility**

211. Ask the Children of Israel how many profound miracles have we shown them! For those who disregard the blessings bestowed upon them by **GOD, GOD** is most strict in retribution.

*2:210 This world is a test; it is our last chance to restore ourselves back into God's kingdom by denouncing idol worship (see the INTRODUCTION). If God and His angels show up, everyone will believe, and the test will no longer be valid.

*2:211 The Quran's mathematical miracle is a great blessing, and brings with it an awesome responsibility (please see 5:115).

Shortsightedness

212. This worldly life is adorned in the eyes of the disbelievers, and they ridicule those who believe. However, the righteous will be far above them on the Day of Resurrection. **GOD** blesses whomever He wills, without limits.

Disastrous Jealousy

213. The people used to be one community when **GOD** sent the prophets as bearers of good news, as well as warners. He sent down with them the scripture, bearing the truth, to judge among the people in their disputes. Ironically, those who received the scripture were the ones who rejected any new scripture, despite clear proofs given to them. This is due to jealousy on their part. **GOD** guides those who believe to the truth that is disputed by all others, in accordance with His will. **GOD** guides whoever wills in a straight path.*

214. Do you expect to enter Paradise without being tested like those before you? They were tested with hardship and adversity, and were shaken up, until the messenger and those who believed with him said, "Where is **GOD**'s victory?" **GOD**'s victory is near.

Recipients of Charity

215. They ask you about giving: say, "The charity you give shall go to the par-

ents, the relatives, the orphans, the poor, and the traveling alien." Any good you do, **GOD** is fully aware thereof.

Believers:
The Ultimate Victors

216. Fighting may be imposed on you, even though you dislike it. But you may dislike something which is good for you, and you may like something which is bad for you. **GOD** knows while you do not know.

Oppression Condemned

217. They ask you about the Sacred Months and fighting therein: say, "Fighting therein is a sacrilege. However, repelling from the path of **GOD** and disbelieving in Him and in the sanctity of the Sacred Masjid, and evicting its people, are greater sacrileges in the sight of **GOD**. Oppression is worse than murder." They will always fight you to revert you from your religion, if they can. Those among you who revert from their religion, and die as disbelievers, have nullified their works in this life and the Hereafter. These are the dwellers of Hell, wherein they abide forever.

218. Those who believe, and those who emigrate and strive in the cause of **GOD**, have deserved **GOD**'s mercy. **GOD** is Forgiver, Most Merciful.

2:213 All worshipers of God ALONE, from all religions, are truly united.

Intoxicants and Gambling Prohibited*

219. They ask you about intoxicants and gambling: say, "In them there is a gross sin, and some benefits for the people. But their sinfulness far outweighs their benefit." They also ask you what to give to charity: say, "The excess." **GOD** thus clarifies the revelations for you, that you may reflect,

220. upon this life and the Hereafter. And they ask you about the orphans: say, "Bringing them up as righteous persons is the best you can do for them. If you mix their property with yours, you shall treat them as family members." **GOD** knows the righteous and the wicked. Had **GOD** willed, He could have imposed harsher rules upon you. **GOD** is Almighty, Most Wise.

Do Not Marry Idol Worshipers

221. Do not marry idolatresses unless they believe; a believing woman is better than an idolatress, even if you like her. Nor shall you give your daughters in marriage to idolatrous men, unless they believe. A believing man is better than an idolater, even if you like him. These invite to Hell, while **GOD** invites to Paradise and forgiveness, as He wills. He clarifies His revelations for the people, that they may take heed.

Menstruation

222. They ask you about menstruation: say, "It is harmful; you shall avoid sexual intercourse with the women during menstruation; do not approach them until they are rid of it. Once they are rid of it, you may have intercourse with them in the manner designed by **GOD**. **GOD** loves the repenters, and He loves those who are clean."

223. Your women are the bearers of your seed. Thus, you may enjoy this privilege however you like, so long as you maintain righteousness. You shall observe **GOD**, and know that you will meet Him. Give good news to the believers.

Do Not Take God's Name in Vain

224. Do not subject **GOD**'s name to your casual swearing, that you may appear righteous, pious, or to attain credibility among the people. **GOD** is Hearer, Knower.

225. **GOD** does not hold you responsible for the mere utterance of oaths; He holds you responsible for your innermost intentions. **GOD** is Forgiver, Clement.

Laws of Divorce

226. Those who intend to divorce their wives shall wait four months (*cooling off*); if they change their minds and reconcile, then **GOD** is Forgiver, Merciful.

227. If they go through with the divorce, then **GOD** is Hearer, Knower.

2:219 The world now recognizes that the economic benefits from manufacturing alcoholic beverages and illicit drugs are not worth the traffic fatalities, brain damage to children of alcoholic mothers, family crises, and other disastrous consequences. Check with "Alcoholics Anonymous" and "Gamblers Anonymous" for more information. See also 5:90-91.

---

228. The divorced women shall wait three menstruations (*before marrying another man*). It is not lawful for them to conceal what **GOD** creates in their wombs, if they believe in **GOD** and the Last Day. (*In case of pregnancy*), the husband's wishes shall supersede the wife's wishes, if he wants to remarry her. The women have rights, as well as obligations, equitably. Thus, the man's wishes prevail (*in case of pregnancy*). **GOD** is Almighty, Most Wise.

229. Divorce may be retracted twice. The divorced woman shall be allowed to live in the same home amicably, or leave it amicably. It is not lawful for the husband to take back anything he had given her. However, the couple may fear that they may transgress **GOD**'s law. If there is fear that they may transgress **GOD**'s law, they commit no error if the wife willingly gives back whatever she chooses. These are **GOD**'s laws; do not transgress them. Those who transgress **GOD**'s laws are the unjust.

230. If he divorces her (*for the third time*), it is unlawful for him to remarry her, unless she marries another man, then he divorces her. The first husband can then remarry her, so long as they observe **GOD**'s laws. These are **GOD**'s laws; He explains them for people who know.

*Do Not Throw
The Divorcees
Out Onto the Streets*

231. If you divorce the women, once they fulfill their interim (*three menstruations*), you shall allow them to live in the same home amicably, or let them leave amicably. Do not force them to stay against their will, as a revenge. Anyone who does this wrongs his own soul. Do not take **GOD**'s revelations in vain. Remember **GOD**'s blessings upon you, and that He sent down to you the scripture and wisdom to enlighten you. You shall observe **GOD**, and know that **GOD** is aware of all things.

232. If you divorce the women, once they fulfill their interim, do not prevent them from remarrying their husbands, if they reconcile amicably. This shall be heeded by those among you who believe in **GOD** and the Last Day. This is purer for you, and more righteous. **GOD** knows, while you do not know.

233. Divorced mothers shall nurse their infants two full years, if the father so wishes. The father shall provide the mother's food and clothing equitably. No one shall be burdened beyond his ability. No mother shall be harmed on account of her infant, nor shall the father be harmed because of his infant. (*If the father dies*), his inheritor shall assume these responsibilities. If the infant's parents mutually agree to part, after due consultation, they commit no error by doing so. You commit no error by hiring nursing mothers, so long as you pay them equitably. You shall observe **GOD**, and know that **GOD** is Seer of everything you do.

*You Shall Observe
The Pre-Marriage Interims*

234. Those who die and leave wives, their widows shall wait four months and ten days (*before they remarry*). Once they fulfill their interim, you commit no error by letting them do whatever righteous matters they wish to do. **GOD** is fully Cognizant of everything you do.

235. You commit no sin by announcing your engagement to the women, or keeping it secret. **GOD** knows that you will think about them. Do not meet them secretly, unless you have something righteous to discuss. Do not consummate the marriage until their interim is fulfilled. You should know that **GOD** knows your innermost thoughts, and observe Him. You should know that **GOD** is Forgiver, Clement.

Breaking the Engagement

236. You commit no error by divorcing the women before touching them, or before setting the dowry for them. In this case, you shall compensate them—the rich as he can afford and the poor as he can afford—an equitable compensation. This is a duty upon the righteous.

237. If you divorce them before touching them, but after you had set the dowry for them, the compensation shall be half the dowry, unless they voluntarily forfeit their rights, or the party responsible for causing the divorce chooses to forfeit the dowry. To forfeit is closer to righteousness. You shall maintain the amicable relations among you. **GOD** is Seer of everything you do.

You Shall Observe the Contact Prayers*

238. You shall consistently observe the Contact Prayers, especially the middle prayer, and devote yourselves totally to **GOD**.

239. Under unusual circumstances, you may pray while walking or riding. Once you are safe, you shall commemorate **GOD** as He taught you what you never knew.

Alimony For Widows and Divorcees

240. Those who die and leave wives, a will shall provide their wives with support for a year, provided they stay within the same household. If they leave, you commit no sin by letting them do whatever they wish, so long as righteousness is maintained. **GOD** is Almighty, Most Wise.

241. The divorcees also shall be provided for, equitably. This is a duty upon the righteous.

242. **GOD** thus explains His revelations for you, that you may understand.

Striving in the Cause of God

243. Have you noted those who fled their homes—though they were in the thousands—fearing death? **GOD** said to them, "Die," then revived them. **GOD** showers His grace upon the people, but most people are unappreciative.

---

*2:238 *All five prayers are found in 2:238, 11:114, 17:78, & 24:58. When the Quran was revealed, the Contact Prayers (Salat) had already been in existence (Appendix 9). The details of all five prayers—what to recite and the number of units (Rak'aas) per prayer, etc.—are mathematically confirmed. For example, writing down the number of units for each of the five prayers, next to each other, we get 24434, 19x1286. Also, if we use [*] to represent Sura 1 (Al-Fãtehah), where [*] = the sura number (1), followed by the number of verses (7), followed by the number of each verse, the number of letters in each verse, and the gematrical value of every letter, writing down 2 [*] [*] 4 [*] [*] [*] [*] 4 [*] [*] [*] [*] 3 [*] [*] [*] 4 [*] [*] [*] [*] produces a multiple of 19 (see 1:1).*

244. You shall fight in the cause of **GOD**, and know that **GOD** is Hearer, Knower.

245. Who would lend **GOD** a loan of righteousness, to have it repaid to them multiplied manifold? **GOD** is the One who provides and withholds, and to Him you will be returned.

Saul*

246. Have you noted the leaders of Israel after Moses? They said to their prophet, "If you appoint a king to lead us, we will fight in the cause of **GOD**." He said, "Is it your intention that, if fighting is decreed for you, you will not fight?" They said, "Why should we not fight in the cause of **GOD**, when we have been deprived of our homes, and our children?" Yet, when fighting was decreed for them, they turned away, except a few. **GOD** is aware of the transgressors.

*Questioning
God's Wisdom*

247. Their prophet said to them, "**GOD** has appointed Taloot (Saul) to be your king." They said, "How can he have kingship over us when we are more worthy of kingship than he; he is not even rich?" He said, "**GOD** has chosen him over you, and has blessed him with an abundance in knowledge and in body." **GOD** grants His kingship to whomever He wills. **GOD** is Bounteous, Omniscient.

Ark of the Covenant

248. Their prophet said to them, "The sign of his kingship is that the Ark of the Covenant will be restored to you, bringing assurances from your Lord, and relics left by the people of Moses and the people of Aaron. It will be carried by the angels. This should be a convincing sign for you, if you are really believers."

David and Goliath

249. When Saul took command of the troops, he said, "**GOD** is putting you to the test by means of a stream. Anyone who drinks from it does not belong with me—only those who do not taste it belong with me—unless it is just a single sip." They drank from it, except a few of them. When he crossed it with those who believed, they said, "Now we lack the strength to face Goliath and his troops." Those who were conscious of meeting **GOD** said, "Many a small army defeated a large army by **GOD**'s leave. **GOD** is with those who steadfastly persevere."

250. When they faced Goliath and his troops, they prayed, "Our Lord, grant us steadfastness, strengthen our foothold, and support us against the disbelieving people."

251. They defeated them by **GOD**'s leave, and David killed Goliath. **GOD** gave him kingship and wisdom, and taught him as He willed. If it were not for **GOD**'s support of some people against others, there would be chaos on earth. But **GOD** showers His grace upon the people.

---

*2:246 *This same history is narrated in the Bible's Book of I Samuel, Ch. 9 and 10.*

252. These are **GOD**'s revelations. We recite them through you,* truthfully, for you are one of the messengers.

Many Messengers / One Message

253. These messengers; we blessed some of them more than others. For example, **GOD** spoke to one, and we raised some of them to higher ranks. And we gave Jesus, son of Mary, profound miracles and supported him with the Holy Spirit. Had **GOD** willed, their followers would not have fought with each other, after the clear proofs had come to them. Instead, they disputed among themselves; some of them believed, and some disbelieved. Had **GOD** willed, they would not have fought. Everything is in accordance with **GOD**'s will.

*No Intercession ***

254. O you who believe, you shall give to charity from the provisions we have given to you, before a day comes where there is no trade, no nepotism, and no intercession. The disbelievers are the unjust.

255. **GOD**: there is no other god besides Him, the Living, the Eternal. Never a moment of unawareness or slumber overtakes Him. To Him belongs everything in the heavens and everything on earth. Who could intercede with Him, except in accordance with His will? He knows their past, and their future. No one attains any knowledge, except as He wills. His dominion encompasses the heavens and the earth, and ruling them never burdens Him. He is the Most High, the Great.

No Compulsion in Religion

256. There shall be no compulsion in religion: the right way is now distinct from the wrong way. Anyone who denounces the devil and believes in **GOD** has grasped the strongest bond; one that never breaks. **GOD** is Hearer, Omniscient.

257. **GOD** is Lord of those who believe; He leads them out of darkness into the light. As for those who disbelieve, their lords are their idols; they lead them out of the light into darkness—these will be the dwellers of Hell; they abide in it forever.

Abraham's Courageous Debate

258. Have you noted the one who argued with Abraham about his Lord, though **GOD** had given him kingship? Abraham said, "My Lord grants life and death." He said, "I grant life and death." Abraham said, "**GOD** brings the sun from the east, can you bring it from the west?" The disbeliever was stumped. **GOD** does not guide the wicked.

2:252 In keeping with the mathematical composition of the Quran, God has willed that the name of the messenger mentioned here shall be spelled out mathematically. The discovery of the Quran's miraculous 19-based code has been divinely reserved for God's Messenger of the Covenant. By adding this verse number (252), plus the gematrical value of "Rashad" (505), plus the gematrical value of "Khalifa" (725) we get 252 + 505 + 725 = 1482, or 19x78. Please see Appendices 2 and 26 for the complete details related to the proven identity of God's Messenger of the Covenant, to whom this verse clearly refers.

2:254 One of Satan's clever tricks is attributing the power of intercession to powerless human idols such as Jesus and Muhammad (Appendix 8).

Lesson About Death *

259. Consider the one who passed by a ghost town and wondered, "How can **GOD** revive this after it had died?" **GOD** then put him to death for a hundred years, then resurrected him. He said, "How long have you stayed here?" He said, "I have been here a day, or part of the day." He said, "No! You have been here a hundred years. Yet, look at your food and drink; they did not spoil. Look at your donkey—we thus render you a lesson for the people. Now, note how we construct the bones, then cover them with flesh." When he realized what had happened, he said, "Now I know that **GOD** is Omnipotent."

Every Believer Needs Assurance

260. Abraham said, "My Lord, show me how You revive the dead." He said, "Do you not believe?" He said, "Yes, but I wish to reassure my heart." He said, "Take four birds, study their marks, place a piece of each bird on top of a hill, then call them to you. They will come to you in a hurry. You should know that **GOD** is Almighty, Most Wise."

The Best Investment

261. The example of those who spend their monies in the cause of **GOD** is that of a grain that produces seven spikes, with a hundred grains in each spike. **GOD** multiplies this manifold for whomever He wills. **GOD** is Bounteous, Knower.

262. Those who spend their money in the cause of **GOD**, then do not follow their charity with insult or harm, will receive their recompense from their Lord; they have nothing to fear, nor will they grieve.

263. Kind words and compassion are better than a charity that is followed by insult. **GOD** is Rich, Clement.

264. O you who believe, do not nullify your charities by inflicting reproach and insult, like one who spends his money to show off, while disbelieving in **GOD** and the Last Day. His example is like a rock covered with a thin layer of soil; as soon as heavy rain falls, it washes off the soil, leaving it a useless rock. They gain nothing from their efforts. **GOD** does not guide disbelieving people.

Charity

265. The example of those who give their money seeking **GOD**'s pleasure, out of sincere conviction, is that of a garden on high fertile soil; when heavy rain falls, it gives twice as much crop. If heavy rain is not available, a drizzle will suffice. **GOD** is Seer of everything you do.

266. Does any of you wish to own a garden of palm trees and grapes, with flowing streams and generous crops, then, just as he grows old, and while his children are still dependent on him, a holocaust strikes and burns up his garden? **GOD** thus clarifies the revelations for you, that you may reflect.

2:259 The lesson we learn here is that the period of death—only the unrighteous die; the righteous go straight to Heaven—passes like one day (see 18:19-25 and Appendix 17).

What to Give

267. O you who believe, you shall give to charity from the good things you earn, and from what we have produced for you from the earth. Do not pick out the bad therein to give away, when you yourselves do not accept it unless your eyes are closed. You should know that **GOD** is Rich, Praiseworthy.

268. The devil promises you poverty and commands you to commit evil, while **GOD** promises you forgiveness from Him and grace. **GOD** is Bounteous, Omniscient.

Wisdom: A Great Treasure

269. He bestows wisdom upon whomever He chooses, and whoever attains wisdom, has attained a great bounty. Only those who possess intelligence will take heed.

Anonymous Charity Better

270. Any charity you give, or a charitable pledge you fulfill, **GOD** is fully aware thereof. As for the wicked, they will have no helpers.

271. If you declare your charities, they are still good. But if you keep them anonymous, and give them to the poor, it is better for you, and remits more of your sins. **GOD** is fully Cognizant of everything you do.

God is the Only One Who Guides

272. You are not responsible for guiding anyone. **GOD** is the only one who guides whoever chooses (*to be guid-*

ed). Any charity you give is for your own good. Any charity you give shall be for the sake of **GOD**. Any charity you give will be repaid to you, without the least injustice.

273. Charity shall go to the poor who are suffering in the cause of **GOD**, and cannot emigrate. The unaware may think that they are rich, due to their dignity. But you can recognize them by certain signs; they never beg from the people persistently. Whatever charity you give, **GOD** is fully aware thereof.

274. Those who give to charity night and day, secretly and publicly, receive their recompense from their Lord; they will have nothing to fear, nor will they grieve.

Usury Prohibited*

275. Those who charge usury are in the same position as those controlled by the devil's influence. This is because they claim that usury is the same as commerce. However, **GOD** permits commerce, and prohibits usury. Thus, whoever heeds this commandment from his Lord, and refrains from usury, he may keep his past earnings, and his judgment rests with **GOD**. As for those who persist in usury, they incur Hell, wherein they abide forever.

276. **GOD** condemns usury, and blesses charities. **GOD** dislikes every disbeliever, guilty.

---

*2:275-278 It is an established economic principle that excessive interest on loans can utterly destroy a whole country. During the last few years we have witnessed the devastation of the economies of many nations where excessive interest is charged. Normal interest—less than 20%—where no one is victimized and everyone is satisfied, is not usury.

Divine Guarantee

277. Those who believe and lead a righteous life, and observe the Contact Prayers (*Salat*), and give the obligatory charity (*Zakat*), they receive their recompense from their Lord; they will have nothing to fear, nor will they grieve.

278. O you who believe, you shall observe **GOD** and refrain from all kinds of usury, if you are believers.

279. If you do not, then expect a war from **GOD** and His messenger. But if you repent, you may keep your capitals, without inflicting injustice, or incurring injustice.

280. If the debtor is unable to pay, wait for a better time. If you give up the loan as a charity, it would be better for you, if you only knew.

281. Beware of the day when you are returned to **GOD**, and every soul is paid for everything it had done, without the least injustice.

Write Down Financial Transactions

282. O you who believe, when you transact a loan for any period, you shall write it down. An impartial scribe shall do the writing. No scribe shall refuse to perform this service, according to **GOD**'s teachings. He shall write, while the debtor dictates the terms. He shall observe **GOD** his Lord and never cheat. If the debtor is mentally incapable, or helpless, or cannot dictate, his guardian shall dictate equitably. Two men shall serve as witnesses; if not two men, then a man and two women whose testimony is acceptable to all.* Thus, if one woman becomes biased, the other will remind her. It is the obligation of the witnesses to testify when called upon to do so. Do not tire of writing the details, no matter how long, including the time of repayment. This is equitable in the sight of **GOD**, assures better witnessing, and eliminates any doubts you may have. Business transactions that you execute on the spot need not be recorded, but have them witnessed. No scribe or witness shall be harmed on account of his services. If you harm them, it would be wickedness on your part. You shall observe **GOD**, and **GOD** will teach you. **GOD** is Omniscient.

283. If you are traveling, and no scribe is available, a bond shall be posted to guarantee repayment. If one is trusted in this manner, he shall return the bond when due, and he shall observe **GOD** his Lord. Do not withhold any testimony by concealing what you had witnessed. Anyone who withholds a testimony is sinful at heart. **GOD** is fully aware of everything you do.

284. To **GOD** belongs everything in the heavens and the earth. Whether you declare your innermost thoughts, or keep them hidden, **GOD** holds you responsible for them. He forgives whomever He wills, and punishes whomever He wills. **GOD** is Omnipotent.

---

*2:282 Financial transactions are the ONLY situations where two women may substitute for one man as witness. This is to guard against the real possibility that one witness may marry the other witness, and thus cause her to be biased. It is a recognized fact that women are more emotionally vulnerable than men.

*You Shall Not Make Any Distinction
Among God's Messengers*

285. The messenger has believed in what was sent down to him from his Lord, and so did the believers. They believe in **GOD**, His angels, His scripture, and His messengers: "We make no distinction among any of His messengers." They say, "We hear, and we obey.* Forgive us, our Lord. To You is the ultimate destiny."

286. **GOD** never burdens a soul beyond its means: to its credit is what it earns, and against it is what it commits. "Our Lord, do not condemn us if we forget or make mistakes. Our Lord, and protect us from blaspheming against You, like those before us have done. Our Lord, protect us from sinning until it becomes too late for us to repent. Pardon us and forgive us. You are our Lord and Master. Grant us victory over the disbelieving people."

◆◆◆◆

Sura 3: The Amramites (Āli-'Imrān)

In the name of God,
Most Gracious, Most Merciful

1. A.L.M.*

2. **GOD**: there is no god except He; the Living, the Eternal.

3. He sent down to you this scripture, truthfully, confirming all previous scriptures, and He sent down the Torah and the Gospel

4. before that, to guide the people, and He sent down the statute book. Those who disbelieve in **GOD**'s revelations incur severe retribution. **GOD** is Almighty, Avenger.

5. Nothing is hidden from **GOD**, on earth, or in the heaven.

6. He is the One who shapes you in the wombs as He wills. There is no other god besides Him; the Almighty, Most Wise.

7. He sent down to you this scripture, containing straightforward verses—which constitute the essence of the scripture—as well as multiple-meaning or allegorical verses. Those who harbor doubts in their hearts will pursue the multiple-meaning verses to create confusion, and to extricate a certain meaning. None knows the true meaning thereof except **GOD** and those well founded in knowledge. They say, "We believe in this—all of it comes from our Lord." Only those who possess intelligence will take heed.

8. "Our Lord, let not our hearts waver, now that You have guided us. Shower us with Your mercy; You are the Grantor.

2:285 One of the major commandments is: "You shall not make any distinction among God's messengers" (2:136, 3:84, 4:150). The believers react by saying, "We hear and we obey," while the idol worshipers argue back to justify their insistence upon mentioning Muhammad's name next to God's, to the exclusion of all other messengers. The corrupted Muslims mention Muhammad in their profession of faith (Shahaadah) and during their Contact Prayers (see 72:18).

3:1 See Footnote 2:1 and Appendix One.

9. "Our Lord, You will surely gather the people on a day that is inevitable. **GOD** never breaks a promise."

10. Those who disbelieve will never be helped by their money, nor by their children, against **GOD**. They will be fuel for Hell.

11. Like Pharaoh's people and those before them, they rejected our revelations and, consequently, **GOD** punished them for their sins. **GOD** is strict in enforcing retribution.

12. Say to those who disbelieve, "You will be defeated, then gathered in Hell; what a miserable abode!"

Believers:
The Ultimate Victors

13. An example has been set for you by the two armies who clashed—one army was fighting in the cause of **GOD**, while the other was disbelieving. They saw with their own eyes that they were twice as many. **GOD** supports with His victory whomever He wills. This should provide an assurance for those who possess vision.

Different Priorities

14. Adorned for the people are the worldly pleasures, such as the women, having children, piles upon piles of gold and silver, trained horses, livestock, and crops. These are the materials of this world. A far better abode is reserved at **GOD**.

15. Say, "Let me inform you of a much better deal: for those who lead a righteous life, reserved at their Lord, are gardens with flowing streams, and pure spouses, and joy in **GOD**'s blessings." **GOD** is Seer of His worshipers.

16. They say, "Our Lord, we have believed, so forgive us our sins, and spare us the agony of the hellfire."

17. They are steadfast, truthful, submitting, charitable, and meditators at dawn.

The Most Important
Commandment*

18. **GOD** bears witness that there is no god except He, and so do the angels and those who possess knowledge. Truthfully and equitably, He is the absolute god; there is no god but He, the Almighty, Most Wise.

Submission:
The Only Religion

19. The only religion approved by **GOD** is "Submission." Ironically, those who have received the scripture are the ones who dispute this fact, despite the knowledge they have received, due to jealousy. For such rejectors of **GOD**'s revelations, **GOD** is most strict in reckoning.

---

*3:18 The proclamation of faith (Shahaadah) that is decreed by God is: "There is no god except God," in Arabic "La Elaaha Ella Allah" (see also 37:35, 47:19). The corrupted Muslims insist upon adding a second "Shahaadah" proclaiming that Muhammad is God's messenger. This is by definition "Shirk" (idolatry) and a flagrant defiance of God and His messenger. Additionally, it violates the major commandments in 2:136, 2:285, 3:84, & 4:150-152 prohibiting any distinction among God's messengers. By proclaiming that "Muhammad is a messenger of God," and failing to make the same proclamation for other messengers such as Abraham, Moses, Jesus, Saleh, and Jonah, a distinction is committed and a major commandment is violated.

20. If they argue with you, then say, "I have simply submitted myself to **GOD**; I and those who follow me." You shall proclaim to those who received the scripture, as well as those who did not, "Would you submit?" If they submit, then they have been guided, but if they turn away, your sole mission is to deliver this message. **GOD** is Seer of all people.

21. Those who have rejected **GOD**'s revelations, and killed the prophets unjustly, and killed those who advocated justice among the people, promise them a painful retribution.

22. Their works have been nullified, both in this life and in the Hereafter, and they will have no helpers.

23. Have you noted those who were given part of the scripture, and how they are invited to uphold this scripture of **GOD**, and apply it to their own lives, then some of them turn away in aversion?

24. This is because they said, "The hellfire will not touch us, except for a few days." They were thus deceived in their religion by their own fabrications.

25. How will it be for them, when we summon them on that inevitable day? Each soul will be paid for whatever it earned, without the least injustice.

Attributes of God

26. Say, "Our god: possessor of all sovereignty. You grant sovereignty to whomever You choose, You remove sovereignty from whomever You choose. You grant dignity to whomever You choose, and commit to humiliation whomever You choose. In Your hand are all provisions. You are Omnipotent.

27. "You merge the night into the day, and merge the day into the night. You produce the living from the dead, and produce the dead from the living, and You provide for whomever You choose, without limits."

Choose Your Friends Carefully

28. The believers never ally themselves with the disbelievers, instead of the believers. Whoever does this is exiled from **GOD**. Exempted are those who are forced to do this to avoid persecution. **GOD** alerts you that you shall reverence Him alone. To **GOD** is the ultimate destiny.

29. Say, "Whether you conceal your innermost thought, or declare it, **GOD** is fully aware thereof." He is fully aware of everything in the heavens and the earth. **GOD** is Omnipotent.

30. The day will come when each soul will find all the good works it had done brought forth. As for the evil works, it will wish that they were far, far removed. **GOD** alerts you that you shall reverence Him alone. **GOD** is Compassionate towards the people.

31. Proclaim: "If you love **GOD**, you should follow me." **GOD** will then love you, and forgive your sins. **GOD** is Forgiver, Most Merciful.

32. Proclaim: "You shall obey **GOD** and the messenger." If they turn away, **GOD** does not love the disbelievers.

The Birth of Mary

33. **GOD** has chosen Adam, Noah, the family of Abraham, and the family of Amram (*as messengers*) to the people.

34. They belong to the same progeny. **GOD** is Hearer, Omniscient.

35. The wife of Amram said, "My Lord, I have dedicated (*the baby*) in my belly to You, totally, so accept from me. You are Hearer, Omniscient."

36. When she gave birth to her, she said, "My Lord, I have given birth to a girl"—**GOD** was fully aware of what she bore—"The male is not the same as the female. I have named her Mary, and I invoke Your protect-tion for her and her descendants from the rejected devil."

37. Her Lord accepted her a gracious acceptance, and brought her up a gracious upbringing, under the guardianship of Zachariah. When-ever Zachariah entered her sanc-tuary he found provisions with her. He would ask, "Mary, where did you get this from?" She would say, "It is from **GOD**. **GOD** provides for whomever He chooses, without limits."

The Birth of John

38. That is when Zachariah implored his Lord: "My Lord, grant me such a good child; You are the Hearer of the prayers."

39. The angels called him when he was praying in the sanctuary: "**GOD** gives you good news of John; a believer in the word of **GOD**, hon-orable, moral, and a righteous pro-phet."

40. He said, "How can I have a boy, when I am so old, and my wife is sterile?" He said, "**GOD** does what-ever He wills."

41. He said, "My Lord, give me a sign." He said, "Your sign is that you will not speak to the people for three days, except through signals. Com-memorate your Lord frequently; and meditate night and day."

Mary and Jesus

42. The angels said, "O Mary, **GOD** has chosen you and purified you. He has chosen you from all the women.

43. "O Mary, you shall submit to your Lord, and prostrate and bow down with those who bow down."

44. This is news from the past that we reveal to you. You were not there when they drew their raffles to select Mary's guardian. You were not present when they argued with one another.

45. The angels said, "O Mary, **GOD** gives you good news: a Word from Him whose name is 'The Messiah, Jesus the son of Mary. He will be prominent in this life and in the Hereafter, and one of those closest to Me.'

46. "He will speak to the people from the crib, as well as an adult; he will be one of the righteous."

47. She said, "My Lord, how can I have a son, when no man has touched me?" He said, "**GOD** thus creates whatever He wills. To have anything done, He simply says to it, 'Be,' and it is.

48. "He will teach him the scripture, wisdom, the Torah, and the Gos-pel."

49. As a messenger to the Children of Israel: "I come to you with a sign from your Lord—I create for you from clay the shape of a bird, then I blow into it, and it becomes a live bird by **GOD**'s leave. I restore vision to the blind, heal the leprous, and I revive the dead by **GOD**'s leave. I can tell you what you eat, and what you store in your homes. This should be a proof for you, if you are believers.

50. "I confirm previous scripture—the Torah—and I revoke certain prohibitions imposed upon you. I come to you with sufficient proof from your Lord. Therefore, you shall observe **GOD**, and obey me.

51. "**GOD** is my Lord and your Lord;* you shall worship Him alone. This is the right path."

52. When Jesus sensed their disbelief, he said, "Who are my supporters towards **GOD**?" The disciples said, "We are **GOD**'s supporters; we believe in **GOD**, and bear witness that we are submitters.

53. "Our Lord, we have believed in what You have sent down, and we have followed the messenger; count us among the witnesses."

The Death of Jesus*

54. They plotted and schemed, but so did **GOD**, and **GOD** is the best schemer.

55. Thus, **GOD** said, "O Jesus, I am terminating your life, raising you to Me, and ridding you of the disbelievers. I will exalt those who follow you above those who disbelieve, till the Day of Resurrection. Then to Me is the ultimate destiny of all of you, then I will judge among you regarding your disputes.

56. "As for those who disbelieve, I will commit them to painful retribution in this world, and in the Hereafter. They will have no helpers."

57. As for those who believe and lead a righteous life, He will fully recompense them. **GOD** does not love the unjust.

58. These are the revelations that we recite to you, providing a message full of wisdom.

Mathematical Confirmation*

59. The example of Jesus, as far as **GOD** is concerned, is the same as that of Adam; He created him from dust, then said to him, "Be," and he was.

60. This is the truth from your Lord; do not harbor any doubts.

3:51 This is precisely what Jesus is quoted to say throughout the New Testament. See for example the Gospel of John 20:17, and the book "Jesus: Myths and Message" by Lisa Spray, Ch. 4 (Universal Unity, Fremont, California, 1992).

3:54-55 We learn that Jesus' soul, the real person, was raised, i.e., Jesus' life on earth was terminated, prior to the arrest, torture, and crucifixion of his empty, soulless, but physiologically living body (See the details in Appendix 22).

3:59 The "equality" of the creation of Jesus and Adam is confirmed mathematically; Jesus and Adam are mentioned in the Quran the same number of times, 25 times each.

Challenging
the Disbelievers

61. If anyone argues with you, despite the knowledge you have received, then say, "Let us summon our children and your children, our women and your women, ourselves and yourselves, then let us invoke **GOD**'s curse upon the liars."

62. Absolutely, this is the narration of the truth. Absolutely, there is no god except **GOD**. Absolutely, **GOD** is the Almighty, Most Wise.

63. If they turn away, then **GOD** is fully aware of the evildoers.

Invitation
to All Believers

64. Say, "O followers of the scripture, let us come to a logical agreement between us and you: that we shall not worship except **GOD**; that we never set up any idols besides Him, nor set up any human beings as lords beside **GOD**." If they turn away, say, "Bear witness that we are submitters."

65. O followers of the scripture, why do you argue about Abraham, when the Torah and the Gospel were not revealed until after him? Do you not understand?

66. You have argued about things you knew; why do you argue about things you do not know? **GOD** knows, while you do not know.

67. Abraham was neither Jewish, nor Christian; he was a monotheist submitter. He never was an idol worshiper.

68. The people most worthy of Abraham are those who followed him, and this prophet, and those who believe. **GOD** is the Lord and Master of the believers.

69. Some followers of the scripture wish to lead you astray, but they only lead themselves astray, without perceiving.

70. O followers of the scripture, why do you reject these revelations of **GOD** though you bear witness (*that this is the truth*)?

71. O followers of the scripture, why do you confound the truth with falsehood, and conceal the truth, knowingly?

72. Some followers of the scripture say, "Believe in what was sent down to the believers in the morning, and reject it in the evening; maybe someday they will revert.

73. "And do not believe except as those who follow your religion." Say, "The true guidance is **GOD**'s guidance." If they claim that they have the same guidance, or argue with you about your Lord, say, "All grace is in **GOD**'s hand; He bestows it upon whomever He wills." **GOD** is Bounteous, Omniscient.

74. He specifies His mercy for whomever He wills; **GOD** possesses unlimited grace.

Be Honest With All People

75. Some followers of the scripture can be trusted with a whole lot, and they will give it back to you. Others among them cannot be trusted with a single dinar; they will not repay you unless you keep after them. That is because they say, "We do not have to be honest when dealing with the gentiles!"* Thus, they attribute lies to **GOD**, knowingly.

76. Indeed, those who fulfill their obligations and lead a righteous life, **GOD** loves the righteous.

77. As for those who trade away **GOD**'s covenant, and their obligations, for a cheap price, they receive no share in the Hereafter. **GOD** will not speak to them, nor look at them, on the Day of Resurrection, nor will He purify them. They have incurred a painful retribution.

78. Among them are those who twist their tongues to imitate the scripture, that you may think it is from the scripture, when it is not from the scripture, and they claim that it is from **GOD**, when it is not from **GOD**. Thus, they utter lies and attribute them to **GOD**, knowingly.

79. Never would a human being whom **GOD** blessed with the scripture and prophethood say to the people, "Idolize me beside **GOD**." Instead, *(he would say),* "Devote yourselves absolutely to your Lord alone," according to the scripture you preach and the teachings you learn.

80. Nor would he command you to idolize the angels and the prophets as lords. Would he exhort you to disbelieve after becoming submitters?

Major Prophecy Fulfilled:
God's Messenger
*of the Covenant**

81. **GOD** took a covenant from the prophets, saying, "I will give you the scripture and wisdom. Afterwards, a messenger will come to confirm all existing scriptures. You shall believe in him and support him." He said, "Do you agree with this, and pledge to fulfill this covenant?" They said, "We agree." He said, "You have thus borne witness, and I bear witness along with you."

---

*3:75 Prior to the discovery of the Quran's mathematical code, some scholars falsely claimed that Muhammad was an illiterate man who could not write such a great book. They distorted the meaning of the word **"Ummy,"** claiming that it meant "illiterate." This verse proves that **"Ummiyyeen"** means "gentiles" (See also 62:2 & Appendix 28).*

3:81 This major prophecy has now been fulfilled. God's Messenger of the Covenant, as prophesied in this verse and in the Bible's Malachi 3:1-21, Luke 17:22-36 & Matthew 24:27, is to purify and unify God's messages which were delivered by God's prophets. Judaism, Christianity, Islam, Hinduism, Buddhism, etc., have been severely corrupted. It is the will of Almighty God to purify them and unify them under the banner of worshiping Him alone. Overwhelming evidence has been provided by God in support of His Messenger of the Covenant, whose name is incontrovertibly specified in the Quran's mathematical code as "Rashad Khalifa." For example, adding the gematrical value of "Rashad" (505), plus the value of "Khalifa" (725), plus the verse number (81) gives 1311, or 19x69 (see Appendix 2 for the detailed evidence).

Rejectors of God's Messenger of the Covenant are Disbelievers

82. Those who reject this (*Quranic prophecy*) are the evil ones.

83. Are they seeking other than **GOD**'s religion, when everything in the heavens and the earth has submitted to Him, willingly and unwillingly, and to Him they will be returned?

Make No Distinction Among God's Messengers

84. Say, "We believe in **GOD**, and in what was sent down to us, and in what was sent down to Abraham, Ismail, Isaac, Jacob, and the Patriarchs, and in what was given to Moses, Jesus, and the prophets from their Lord. We make no distinction among any of them. To Him alone we are submitters."

Only One Religion Approved by God

85. Anyone who accepts other than Submission as his religion, it will not be accepted from him, and in the Hereafter, he will be with the losers.

86. Why should **GOD** guide people who disbelieved after believing, and after witnessing that the messenger is truth, and after solid proofs* have been given to them? **GOD** does not guide the wicked.

87. These have incurred condemnation by **GOD**, and the angels, and all the people.

88. Eternally they abide therein; the retribution is never commuted for them, nor will they be reprieved.

89. Exempted are those who repent thereafter, and reform. **GOD** is Forgiver, Most Merciful.

When Repentance is Unacceptable

90. Those who disbelieve after believing, then plunge deeper into disbelief, their repentance will not be accepted from them; they are the real strayers.

91. Those who disbelieve and die as disbelievers, an earthful of gold will not be accepted from any of them, even if such a ransom were possible. They have incurred painful retribution; they will have no helpers.

92. You cannot attain righteousness until you give to charity from the possessions you love. Whatever you give to charity, **GOD** is fully aware thereof.

Do Not Prohibit What Is Lawful

93. All food used to be lawful for the Children of Israel, until Israel imposed certain prohibitions on themselves before the Torah was sent down. Say, "Bring the Torah and read it, if you are truthful."

94. Those who fabricate false prohibitions after this, and attribute them to **GOD**, are truly wicked.

---

*3:86 Verses 3:82-90 inform us that those who reject God's Messenger of the Covenant are no longer submitters (Muslims), since they no longer believe the Quran. The proofs mentioned in 3:86 refer to the Quran's mathematical code, which was revealed through God's Messenger of the Covenant. Both 3:86 and 3:90 talk about "disbelieving after believing."

95. Say, "**GOD** has proclaimed the truth: You shall follow Abraham's religion—monotheism. He never was an idolater."

96. The most important shrine established for the people is the one in Becca;* a blessed beacon for all the people.

97. In it are clear signs: the station of Abraham. Anyone who enters it shall be granted safe passage. The people owe it to **GOD** that they shall observe Hajj to this shrine, when they can afford it. As for those who disbelieve, **GOD** does not need anyone.

98. Say, "O followers of the scripture, why do you reject these revelations of **GOD**, when **GOD** is witnessing everything you do?"

99. Say, "O followers of the scripture, why do you repel from the path of **GOD** those who wish to believe, and seek to distort it, even though you are witnesses?" **GOD** is never unaware of anything you do.

100. O you who believe, if you obey some of those who received the scripture, they will revert you, after having believed, into disbelievers.

101. How can you disbelieve, when these revelations of **GOD** have been recited to you, and His messenger has come to you? Whoever holds fast to **GOD** will be guided in the right path.

102. O you who believe, you shall observe **GOD** as He should be ob-served, and do not die except as Submitters.

Believers are United

103. You shall hold fast to the rope of **GOD**, all of you, and do not be divided. Recall **GOD**'s blessings upon you—you used to be enemies and He reconciled your hearts. By His grace, you became brethren. You were at the brink of a pit of fire, and He saved you therefrom. **GOD** thus explains His revelations for you, that you may be guided.

104. Let there be a community of you who invite to what is good, advocate righteousness, and forbid evil. These are the winners.

105. Do not be like those who became divided and disputed, despite the clear proofs that were given to them. For these have incurred a terrible retribution.

106. The day will come when some faces will be brightened (*with joy*), while other faces will be darkened (*with misery*). As for those whose faces are darkened, they will be asked, "Did you not disbelieve after believing? Therefore, suffer the retribution for your disbelief."

107. As for those whose faces are brightened, they will rejoice in **GOD**'s mercy; they abide therein forever.

108. These are **GOD**'s revelations; we recite them to you, truthfully. **GOD** does not wish any hardship for the people.

---

*3:96 This is an M-initialed sura, and this peculiar spelling of "Mecca" as "Becca" causes the occurrence of "M" to conform to the Quran's mathematical code. The normal spelling "Mecca" would have increased the frequency of occurrence of "M" (Appendix One).

109. To **GOD** belongs everything in the heavens and everything on earth, and all matters are controlled by **GOD**.

The Best Community

110. You are the best community ever raised among the people: you advocate righteousness and forbid evil, and you believe in **GOD**. If the followers of the scripture believed, it would be better for them. Some of them do believe, but the majority of them are wicked.

111. They can never harm you, beyond insulting you. If they fight you, they will turn around and flee. They can never win.

112. They shall be humiliated whenever you encounter them, unless they uphold **GOD**'s covenant, as well as their peace covenants with you. They have incurred wrath from **GOD**, and, consequently, they are committed to disgrace. This is because they rejected **GOD**'s revelations, and killed the prophets unjustly. This is because they disobeyed and transgressed.

Righteous Jews & Christians

113 They are not all the same; among the followers of the scripture, there are those who are righteous. They recite **GOD**'s revelations through the night, and they fall prostrate.

114. They believe in **GOD** and the Last Day, they advocate righteousness and forbid evil, and they hasten to do righteous works. These are the righteous.

115. Any good they do will not go unrewarded. **GOD** is fully aware of the righteous.

116. Those who disbelieved can never be helped by their money or their children against **GOD**. They have incurred Hell, wherein they abide forever.

117. The example of their accomplishments in this life is like a violent wind that hits the harvest of people who have wronged their souls, and wipes it out. **GOD** never wronged them; it is they who wronged themselves.

Do Not Befriend Hypocrites

118. O you who believe, do not befriend outsiders who never cease to wish you harm; they even wish to see you suffer. Hatred flows out of their mouths and what they hide in their chests is far worse. We thus clarify the revelations for you, if you understand.

119. Here you are loving them, while they do not love you, and you believe in all the scripture. When they meet you they say, "We believe," but as soon as they leave, they bite their fingers out of rage towards you. Say, "Die in your rage." **GOD** is fully aware of the innermost thoughts.

120. When anything good comes your way they hurt, and when something bad happens to you they rejoice. If you steadfastly persevere, and maintain righteousness, their schemes will never hurt you. **GOD** is fully aware of everything they do.

The Battle of Badr

121. Recall that you (*Muhammad*) were among your people when you set out to assign to the believers their positions for battle. **GOD** is Hearer, Omniscient.

122. Two groups among you almost failed, but **GOD** was their Lord. In **GOD** the believers shall trust.

123. **GOD** has granted you victory at Badr, despite your weakness. Therefore, you shall observe **GOD**, to show your appreciation.

God's Angels
Help the Believers

124. You told the believers, "Is it not enough that your Lord supports you with three thousand angels, sent down?"

125. Indeed, if you steadfastly persevere and maintain righteousness, then they attack you suddenly, your Lord will support you with five thousand* angels, well trained.

126. **GOD** thus informs you, in order to give you good news, and to assure your hearts. Victory comes only from **GOD**, the Almighty, Most Wise.

127. He thus annihilates some disbelievers, or neutralizes them; they always end up the losers.

128. It is not up to you; He may redeem them, or He may punish them for their transgressions.

129. To **GOD** belongs everything in the heavens and the earth. He forgives whomever He wills, and punishes whomever He wills. **GOD** is Forgiver, Most Merciful.

Usury Prohibited*

130. O you who believe, you shall not take usury, compounded over and over. Observe **GOD**, that you may succeed.

131. Beware of the hellfire that awaits the disbelievers.

132. You shall obey **GOD** and the messenger, that you may attain mercy.

Attributes of the Righteous

133. You should eagerly race towards forgiveness from your Lord and a Paradise whose width encompasses the heavens and the earth; it awaits the righteous,

134. who give to charity during the good times, as well as the bad times. They are suppressors of anger, and pardoners of the people. **GOD** loves the charitable.

135. If they fall in sin or wrong their souls, they remember **GOD** and ask forgiveness for their sins—and who forgives the sins except **GOD**—and they do not persist in sins, knowingly.

136. Their recompense is forgiveness from their Lord, and gardens with flowing streams; they abide therein forever. What a blessed reward for the workers!

Victory for the Righteous

137. Precedents have been set for you in the past; roam the earth and note the consequences for the unbelievers.

---

*3:124-125 Thirty different numbers are mentioned in the Quran. Their total comes to 162146, 19x8534. This conforms with the Quran's mathematical miracle (See Appendix One).

*3:130 Interest on bank deposits and interest charged on loans are lawful if they are not excessive (5-15%). Banks invest and their profits are passed on to the depositors. Since all parties are happy and no one is victimized, it is perfectly lawful to take interest from the bank (see 2:275).

138. This is a proclamation for the people, and a guidance and enlightenment for the righteous.

139. You shall not waver, nor shall you grieve, for you are the ultimate victors, if you are believers.

140. If you suffer hardship, the enemy also suffers the same hardship. We alternate the days of victory and defeat among the people. **GOD** thus distinguishes the true believers, and blesses some of you with martyrdom. **GOD** dislikes injustice.

141. **GOD** thus toughens those who believe and humiliates the disbelievers.

Our Claims Must Be Tested

142. Do you expect to enter Paradise without **GOD** distinguishing those among you who strive, and without distinguishing those who are steadfast?

143. You used to long for death before you had to face it. Now you have faced it, right before your eyes.

144. Muhammad was no more than a messenger like the messengers before him. Should he die or get killed, would you turn back on your heels? Anyone who turns back on his heels, does not hurt **GOD** in the least. **GOD** rewards those who are appreciative.

Time of Death Predetermined

145. No one dies except by **GOD**'s leave, at a predetermined time. Whoever seeks the vanities of this world, we give him therefrom, and whoever seeks the rewards of the Hereafter, we bless him therein. We reward those who are appreciative.

146. Many a prophet had godly people fight along with him, without ever wavering under pressure in the cause of **GOD**, nor did they hesitate or become discouraged. **GOD** loves the steadfast.

147. Their only utterance was, "Our Lord, forgive us our sins, and our transgressions, strengthen our foothold, and grant us victory over the disbelievers."

148. Consequently, **GOD** granted them the rewards of this world, and the better rewards of the Hereafter. **GOD** loves the good doers.

149. O you who believe, if you obey those who disbelieve, they will turn you back on your heels, then you end up losers.

150. **GOD** alone is your Lord and Master, and He is the best supporter.

God Controls Your Enemies

151. We will throw terror into the hearts of those who disbelieved, since they set up besides **GOD** powerless idols. Their destiny is Hell; what a miserable abode for the transgressors!

The Battle of Uhud

152. **GOD** has fulfilled His promise to you, and you defeated them by His leave. But then you wavered, disputed among yourselves, and disobeyed after He had shown you (*the victory*) you had longed for. But then, some of you became distracted by the spoils of this world, while others were rightly concerned with the Hereafter. He then diverted you from them to test you. He has pardoned you. **GOD** showers the believers with His grace.

153. Recall that you rushed (*after the spoils*), paying no attention to anyone, even when the messenger was calling from behind you. Consequently, He substituted one misery for another, that you may not grieve over anything you had missed, or agonize over any hardship you had suffered. **GOD** is Cognizant of everything you do.

Moment of Death Predetermined

154. After the setback, He sent down upon you peaceful slumber that pacified some of you. Others among you were selfishly concerned about themselves. They harbored thoughts about **GOD** that were not right—the same thoughts they had harbored during the days of ignorance. Thus, they said, "Is anything up to us?" Say, "Everything is up to **GOD**." They concealed inside themselves what they did not reveal to you. They said, "If it was up to us, none of us would have been killed in this battle." Say, "Had you stayed in your homes, those destined to be killed would have crawled into their death beds." **GOD** thus puts you to the test to bring out your true convictions, and to test what is in your hearts. **GOD** is fully aware of the innermost thoughts.

155. Surely, those among you who turned back the day the two armies clashed have been duped by the devil. This reflects some of the (*evil*) works they had committed. **GOD** has pardoned them. **GOD** is Forgiver, Clement.

156. O you who believe, do not be like those who disbelieved and said of their kinsmen who traveled or mobilized for war, "Had they stayed with us, they would not have died or gotten killed." **GOD** renders this a source of grief in their hearts. **GOD** controls life and death. **GOD** is Seer of everything you do.

157. Whether you get killed or die in the cause of **GOD**, the forgiveness from **GOD**, and mercy are far better than anything they hoard.

158. Whether you die or get killed, you will be summoned before **GOD**.

The Messenger's Kindness

159. It was mercy from **GOD** that you became compassionate towards them. Had you been harsh and mean-hearted, they would have abandoned you. Therefore, you shall pardon them and ask forgiveness for them, and consult them. Once you make a decision, carry out your plan, and trust in **GOD**. **GOD** loves those who trust in Him.*

160. If **GOD** supports you, none can defeat you. And if He abandons you, who else can support you? In **GOD** the believers shall trust.

No One Above the Law

161. Even the prophet cannot take more of the spoils of war than he is entitled to. Anyone who takes more than his rightful share will have to account for it on the Day of Resurrection. That is when each soul is paid for whatever it earned, without the least injustice.

---

*3:159 The currency of the U.S.A. is the only currency that carries the phrase: "In God we trust." It is a fact that the American dollar has been the strongest currency in the world, and the standard by which all other currencies are measured.

---

162. Is one who pursues **GOD**'s pleasure the same as one who incurs wrath from **GOD** and his destiny is Hell, the most miserable abode?

163. They certainly occupy different ranks at **GOD**. **GOD** is Seer of everything they do.

164. **GOD** has blessed the believers by raising in their midst a messenger from among them, to recite for them His revelations, and to purify them, and to teach them the scripture and wisdom. Before this, they had gone totally astray.

165. Now that you have suffered a setback, and even though you inflicted twice as much suffering (*upon your enemy*), you said, "Why did this happen to us?" Say, "This is a consequence of your own deeds." **GOD** is Omnipotent.

166. What afflicted you the day the two armies clashed was in accordance with **GOD**'s will, and to distinguish the believers.

167. And to expose the hypocrites who were told, "Come fight in the cause of **GOD**, or contribute." They said, "If we knew how to fight, we would have joined you." They were closer to disbelief then than they were to belief. They uttered with their mouths what was not in their hearts. **GOD** knows what they conceal.

168. They said of their kinsmen, as they stayed behind, "Had they obeyed us, they would not have been killed." Say, "Then prevent your own death, if you are truthful."

*The Righteous Do Not Really Die**

169. Do not think that those who are killed in the cause of **GOD** are dead; they are alive at their Lord, enjoying His provisions.

170. They are rejoicing in **GOD**'s grace, and they have good news for their comrades who did not die with them, that they have nothing to fear, nor will they grieve.

171. They have good news of **GOD**'s blessings and grace, and that **GOD** never fails to reward the believers.

172. For those who respond to **GOD** and the messenger, despite the persecution they suffer, and maintain their good works, and lead a righteous life, a great reward.

173. When the people say to them, "People have mobilized against you; you should fear them," this only strengthens their faith, and they say, "**GOD** suffices us; He is the best Protector."

174. They have deserved **GOD**'s blessings and grace. No harm ever touches them, for they have attained **GOD**'s approval. **GOD** possesses infinite grace.

Fear: The Devil's Tool

175. It is the devil's system to instill fear into his subjects. Do not fear them and fear Me instead, if you are believers.

176. Do not be saddened by those who hasten to disbelieve. They never hurt **GOD** in the least. Instead, **GOD** has willed that they will have no share in the Hereafter. They have incurred a terrible retribution.

---

*3:169 We learn from the Quran that the righteous do not really die; they simply leave their worldly bodies and go directly to the same paradise where Adam and Eve once lived (2:154, 8:24, 16:32, 22:58, 44:56, & 36:26-27; see also Appendix 17).

---

177. Those who choose disbelief, instead of belief, do not hurt **GOD** in the least; they have incurred a painful retribution.

178. Let not the disbelievers think that we lead them on for their own good. We only lead them on to confirm their sinfulness. They have incurred a humiliating retribution.

179. **GOD** is not to leave the believers as you are, without distinguishing the bad from the good. Nor does **GOD** inform you of the future, but **GOD** bestows such knowledge upon whomever He chooses from among His messengers.* Therefore, you shall believe in **GOD** and His messengers. If you believe and lead a righteous life, you receive a great recompense.

180. Let not those who withhold and hoard **GOD**'s provisions think that this is good for them; it is bad for them. For they will carry their hoardings around their necks on the Day of Resurrection. **GOD** is the ultimate inheritor of the heavens and the earth. **GOD** is fully Cognizant of everything you do.

Humans Continue to Defy God

181. **GOD** has heard the utterances of those who said, "**GOD** is poor, while we are rich." We will record everything they said, just as we recorded their killing of the prophets unjustly, and we will say, "Suffer the retribution of Hell.

182. "This is the consequence of your own works." **GOD** is never unjust towards the people.

183. It is they who said, "**GOD** has made a covenant with us that we shall not believe in any messenger, unless he produces an offering that gets consumed by fire." Say, "Messengers before me have come to you with clear proofs, including what you just demanded. Why then did you kill them, if you are truthful?"

184. If they reject you, messengers before you have been rejected, even though they brought proofs, the Psalms, and the enlightening scripture.

A Great Triumph

185. Every person tastes death, then you receive your recompense on the Day of Resurrection. Whoever misses Hell, barely, and makes it to Paradise, has attained a great triumph. The life of this world is no more than an illusion.

The Inevitable Test*

186. You will certainly be tested, through your money and your lives, and you will hear from those who received the scripture, and from the idol worshipers, a lot of insult. If you steadfastly persevere and lead a righteous life, this will prove the strength of your faith.

3:179 The end of the world is one example of future events revealed to God's Messenger of the Covenant. See Footnote 72:27.

3:186 After passing the admission tests, the proven worshipers of God ALONE enjoy a perfect life, now and forever. See 29:2-3, 10:62, and 24:55.

187. **GOD** took a covenant from those who received the scripture: "You shall proclaim it to the people, and never conceal it." But they disregarded it behind their backs, and traded it away for a cheap price. What a miserable trade.

188. Those who boast about their works, and wish to be praised for something they have not really done, should not think that they can evade the retribution. They have incurred a painful retribution.

189. To **GOD** belongs the sovereignty of the heavens and the earth. **GOD** is Omnipotent.

Those Who
Possess Intelligence

190. In the creation of the heavens and the earth, and the alternation of night and day, there are signs for those who possess intelligence.

191. They remember **GOD*** while standing, sitting, and on their sides, and they reflect upon the creation of the heavens and the earth: "Our Lord, You did not create all this in vain. Be You glorified. Save us from the retribution of Hell.

192. "Our Lord, whomever You commit to Hell are the ones You have forsaken. Such transgressors have no helpers.

193. "Our Lord, we have heard a caller calling to faith and proclaiming: 'You shall believe in your Lord,' and we have believed. Our Lord, forgive us our transgressions, remit our sins, and let us die as righteous believers.

194. "Our Lord, shower us with the blessings you promised us through Your messengers, and do not forsake us on the Day of Resurrection. You never break a promise."

God
Responds

195. Their Lord responded to them: "I never fail to reward any worker among you for any work you do, be you male or female—you are equal to one another. Thus, those who immigrate, and get evicted from their homes, and are persecuted because of Me, and fight and get killed, I will surely remit their sins and admit them into gardens with flowing streams." Such is the reward from **GOD**. **GOD** possesses the ultimate reward.

196. Do not be impressed by the apparent success of disbelievers.

197. They only enjoy temporarily, then end up in Hell; what a miserable destiny!

198. As for those who observe their Lord, they have deserved gardens with flowing streams; they abide therein forever. Such is the abode given to them by **GOD**. What **GOD** possesses is far better for the righteous.

3:191 Your god is whoever or whatever occupies your mind most of the time. The true believers are those who remember God most of the time. See 23:84-89 and Appendix 27.

Righteous Jews and Christians

199. Surely, some followers of the previous scriptures do believe in **GOD**, and in what was revealed to you, and in what was revealed to them. They reverence **GOD**, and they never trade away **GOD**'s revelations for a cheap price. These will receive their recompense from their Lord. **GOD** is the most efficient in reckoning.

200. O you who believe, you shall be steadfast, you shall persevere, you shall be united, you shall observe **GOD**, that you may succeed.

◆◆◆◆

Sura 4: Women (Al-Nesã')

In the name of God,
Most Gracious, Most Merciful

1. O people, observe your Lord; the One who created you from one being, and created from it its mate, then spread from the two many men and women. You shall regard **GOD**, by whom you swear, and regard the parents. **GOD** is watching over you.*

Regard the Orphans

2. You shall hand over to the orphans their rightful properties. Do not substitute the bad for the good, and do not consume their properties by combining them with yours. This would be a gross injustice.

*Grounds For Polygamy**

3. If you deem it best for the orphans, you may marry their mothers—you may marry two, three, or four. If you fear lest you become unfair, then you shall be content with only one, or with what you already have. Additionally, you are thus more likely to avoid financial hardship.

4. You shall give the women their due dowries, equitably. If they willingly forfeit anything, then you may accept it; it is rightfully yours.

5. Do not give immature orphans the properties that **GOD** has entrusted with you as guardians. You shall provide for them therefrom, and clothe them, and treat them kindly.

6. You shall test the orphans when they reach puberty. As soon as you find them mature enough, give them their property. Do not consume it extravagantly in a hurry, before they grow up. The rich guardian shall not charge any wage, but the poor guardian may charge equitably. When you give them their properties, you shall have witnesses. **GOD** suffices as Reckoner.

Women's Inheritance Rights

7. The men get a share of what the parents and the relatives leave behind. The women too shall get a share of what the parents and relatives leave behind. Whether it is a small or a large inheritance, *(the women must get)* a definite share.

8. During distribution of the inheritances, if relatives, orphans, and needy persons are present, you shall give them therefrom, and treat them kindly.

---

*4:1 This is the second longest sura, and the title indicates that it aims at defending the women's rights. Any interpretation must favor the women's rights, not the other way around.

*4:3 See Appendix 30 for a detailed discussion of polygamy.

---

9. Those who are concerned about their own children, in case they leave them behind, shall observe **GOD** and be equitable.

10. Those who consume the orphans' properties unjustly, eat fire into their bellies, and will suffer in Hell.

If No Will
Is Left*

11. **GOD** decrees a will for the benefit of your children; the male gets twice the share of the female.* If the inheritors are only women, more than two, they get two-thirds of what is bequeathed. If only one daughter is left, she gets one-half. The parents of the deceased get one-sixth of the inheritance each, if the deceased has left any children. If he left no children, and his parents are the only inheritors, the mother gets one-third. If he has siblings, then the mother gets one-sixth. All this, after fulfilling any will* the deceased has left, and after paying off all debts. When it comes to your parents and your children, you do not know which of them is really the best to you and the most beneficial. This is **GOD**'s law. **GOD** is Omniscient, Most Wise.

Inheritance
For the Spouses

12. You get half of what your wives leave behind, if they had no children. If they had children, you get one-fourth of what they leave. All this, after fulfilling any will they had left, and after paying off all debts. They get one-fourth of what you leave behind, if you had no children. If you had children, they get one-eighth of what you bequeath. All this, after fulfilling any will you had left, and after paying off all debts. If the deceased man or woman was a loner, and leaves two siblings, male or female, each of them gets one-sixth of the inheritance. If there are more siblings, then they equally share one-third of the inheritance. All this, after fulfilling any will, and after paying off all debts, so that no one is hurt. This is a will decreed by **GOD**. **GOD** is Omniscient, Clement.

God Communicates
With Us Through
His Messenger

13. These are **GOD**'s laws. Those who obey **GOD** and His messenger, He will admit them into gardens with flowing streams, wherein they abide forever. This is the greatest triumph.

14. As for the one who disobeys **GOD** and His messenger, and transgresses His laws, He will admit him into Hell, wherein he abides forever. He has incurred a shameful retribution.

---

*4:11 Generally, the son is responsible for a family, while the daughter is taken care of by a husband. However, the Quran recommends in 2:180 that a will shall be left to conform with the specific circumstances of the deceased. For example, if the son is rich and the daughter is poor, one may leave a will giving the daughter everything, or twice as much as the son.

Health Quarantine

15. Those who commit adultery among your women, you must have four witnesses against them, from among you. If they do bear witness, then you shall keep such women in their homes until they die, or until **GOD** creates an exit for them.*

16. The couple who commits adultery shall be punished.* If they repent and reform, you shall leave them alone. **GOD** is Redeemer, Most Merciful.

Repentance

17. Repentance is acceptable by **GOD** from those who fall in sin out of ignorance, then repent immediately thereafter. **GOD** redeems them. **GOD** is Omniscient, Most Wise.

18. Not acceptable is the repentance of those who commit sins until death comes to them, then say, "Now I repent." Nor is it acceptable from those who die as disbelievers. For these, we have prepared a painful retribution.

19. O you who believe, it is not lawful for you to inherit what the women leave behind, against their will. You shall not force them to give up anything you had given them, unless they commit a proven adultery. You shall treat them nicely. If you dislike them, you may dislike something wherein **GOD** has placed a lot of good.

Protection for Women

20. If you wish to marry another wife, in place of your present wife, and you had given any of them a great deal, you shall not take back anything you had given her. Would you take it fraudulently, maliciously, and sinfully?

21. How could you take it back, after you have been intimate with each other, and they had taken from you a solemn pledge?

Respect for the Father

22. Do not marry the women who were previously married to your fathers —existing marriages are exempted and shall not be broken—for it is a gross offense, and an abominable act.

Incest Forbidden

23. Prohibited for you (*in marriage*) are your mothers, your daughters, your sisters, the sisters of your fathers, the sisters of your mothers, the daughters of your brother, the daughters of your sister, your nursing mothers, the girls who nursed from the same woman as you, the mothers of your wives, the daughters of your wives with whom you have consummated the marriage— if the marriage has not been consummated, you may marry the daughter. Also prohibited for you are the women who were married to your genetic sons. Also, you shall not be married to two sisters at the same time—but do not break up existing marriages. **GOD** is Forgiver, Most Merciful.

4:15 A woman witnessed by four people in the act of committing adultery on four different occasions, with four different partners, represents a danger to public health. Such a woman is a depository of germs, and a health quarantine protects the society from her. A good example of an exit that saves a quarantined woman is marriage— someone may wish to marry her, and thus protect her and the society.

4:16 Public exposure of the sinners is a major deterrent, as we see in 5:38 and 24:2.

Mutual Attraction And
Dowry Required

24. Also prohibited are the women who are already married, unless they flee their disbelieving husbands who are at war with you.* These are **GOD**'s commandments to you. All other categories are permitted for you in marriage, so long as you pay them their due dowries. You shall maintain your morality, by not committing adultery. Thus, whoever you like among them, you shall pay them the dowry decreed for them. You commit no error by mutually agreeing to any adjustments to the dowry. **GOD** is Omniscient, Most Wise.

25. Those among you who cannot afford to marry free believing women, may marry believing slave women. **GOD** knows best about your belief, and you are equal to one another, as far as belief is concerned. You shall obtain permission from their guardians before you marry them, and pay them their due dowry equitably. They shall maintain moral behavior, by not committing adultery, or having secret lovers. Once they are freed through marriage, if they commit adultery, their punishment shall be half of that for the free women.* Marrying a slave shall be a last resort for those unable to wait. To be patient is better for you. **GOD** is Forgiver, Most Merciful.

26. **GOD** wills to explain things for you, and to guide you through past precedents, and to redeem you. **GOD** is Omniscient, Most Wise.

God's Mercy

27. **GOD** wishes to redeem you, while those who pursue their lusts wish that you deviate a great deviation.

28. **GOD** wishes to lighten your burden, for the human being is created weak.

Murder, Suicide, and
Illicit Gains Prohibited

29. O you who believe, do not consume each others' properties illicitly— only mutually acceptable transactions are permitted. You shall not kill yourselves. **GOD** is Merciful towards you.

30. Anyone who commits these transgressions, maliciously and deliberately, we will condemn him to Hell. This is easy for **GOD** to do.

31. If you refrain from committing the gross sins that are prohibited for you, we will remit your sins, and admit you an honorable admittance.

Men and Women Endowed
With Unique Qualities

32. You shall not covet the qualities bestowed upon each other by **GOD**; the men enjoy certain qualities, and the women enjoy certain qualities. You may implore **GOD** to shower you with His grace. **GOD** is fully aware of all things.

Do Not Object to the
Inheritance Laws Proposed by God

33. For each of you, we have designated shares from the inheritance left by the parents and the relatives. Also those related to you through marriage, you shall give them their due share. **GOD** witnesses all things.

4:24 If believing women flee their disbelieving husbands who are at war with the believers, they do not have to obtain a divorce before remarriage. See 60:10.

4:25 This law proves that the punishment for adultery could not possibly be stoning to death as stated in the laws of corrupted Muslims (see 24:2).

Do Not Beat Your Wife*

34. The men are made responsible for the women,** and **GOD** has endowed them with certain qualities, and made them the bread earners. The righteous women will cheerfully accept this arrangement, since it is **GOD**'s commandment, and honor their husbands during their absence. If you experience rebellion from the women, you shall first talk to them, then (*you may use negative incentives like*) deserting them in bed, then you may (*as a last alternative*) beat them. If they obey you, you are not permitted to transgress against them. **GOD** is Most High, Supreme.

Marriage Arbitration

35. If a couple fears separation, you shall appoint an arbitrator from his family and an arbitrator from her family; if they decide to reconcile, **GOD** will help them get together. **GOD** is Omniscient, Cognizant.

Major Commandments

36. You shall worship **GOD** alone—do not associate anything with Him. You shall regard the parents, the relatives, the orphans, the poor, the related neighbor, the unrelated neighbor, the close associate, the traveling alien, and your servants. **GOD** does not like the arrogant show-offs.

37. The ones who are stingy, exhort the people to be stingy, and conceal what **GOD** has bestowed upon them from His bounties. We have prepared for the disbelievers a shameful retribution.

38. They give money to charity only to show off, while disbelieving in **GOD** and the Last Day. If one's companion is the devil, that is the worst companion.

39. Why do they not believe in **GOD** and the Last Day, and give from **GOD**'s provisions to them? **GOD** is fully aware of them.

Divine Justice

40. **GOD** does not inflict an atom's weight of injustice. On the contrary, He multiplies the reward manifold for the righteous work, and grants from Him a great recompense.

41. Thus, when the day (*of judgment*) comes, we will call upon a witness from each community, and you (*the messenger*) will serve as a witness among these people.

---

*4:34 God prohibits wife-beating by using the best psychological approach. For example, if I don't want you to shop at Market X, I will ask you to shop at Market Y, then at Market Z, then, as a last resort, at Market X. This will effectively stop you from shopping at Market X, without insulting you. Similarly, God provides alternatives to wife-beating; reasoning with her first, then employing certain negative incentives. Remember that the theme of this sura is defending the women's rights and countering the prevalent oppression of women. Any interpretation of the verses of this sura must be in favor of the women. This sura's theme is "protection of women."

**4:34 This expression simply means that God is appointing the husband as "captain of the ship." Marriage is like a ship, and the captain runs it after due consultation with his officers. A believing wife readily accepts God's appointment, without mutiny.

42. On that day, those who disbelieved and disobeyed the messenger will wish that they were level with the ground; not a single utterance will they be able to hide from **GOD**.

What Nullifies Ablution

43. O you who believe, do not observe the Contact Prayers (*Salat*) while intoxicated, so that you know what you are saying. Nor after sexual orgasm without bathing, unless you are on the road, traveling; if you are ill or traveling, or you had urinary or fecal-related excretion (*such as gas*), or contacted the women (*sexually*), and you cannot find water, you shall observe *Tayammum* (*dry ablution*) by touching clean dry soil, then wiping your faces and hands therewith. **GOD** is Pardoner, Forgiver.

44. Have you noted those who received a portion of the scripture, and how they choose to stray, and wish that you stray from the path?

45. **GOD** knows best who your enemies are. **GOD** is the only Lord and Master. **GOD** is the only Supporter.

46. Among those who are Jewish, some distort the words beyond the truth, and they say, "We hear, but we disobey," and "Your words are falling on deaf ears," and "*Raa'ena** (*be our shepherd*)," as they twist their tongues to mock the religion. Had they said, "We hear, and we obey," and "We hear you," and "*Unzurna* (*watch over us*)," it would have been better for them, and more righteous. Instead, they have incurred condemnation from **GOD** due to their disbelief. Consequently, the majority of them cannot believe.

47. O you who received the scripture, you shall believe in what we reveal herein, confirming what you have, before we banish certain faces to exile, or condemn them as we condemned those who desecrated the Sabbath. **GOD**'s command is done.

The Unforgivable Sin

48. **GOD** does not forgive idolatry,* but He forgives lesser offenses for whomever He wills. Anyone who sets up idols beside **GOD**, has forged a horrendous offense.

49. Have you noted those who exalt themselves? Instead, **GOD** is the One who exalts whomever He wills, without the least injustice.

50. Note how they fabricate lies about **GOD**; what a gross offense this is!

51. Have you noted those who received a portion of the scripture, and how they believe in idolatry and false doctrine, then say, "The disbelievers are better guided than the believers?!"

52. It is they who incurred **GOD**'s condemnation, and whomever **GOD** condemns, you will not find any helper for him.

53. Do they own a share of the sovereignty? If they did, they would not give the people as much as a grain.

---

*4:46 The word "Raa'ena" was twisted by some Hebrew speaking people to sound like a dirty word. See 2:104.

*4:48 Idol worship is not forgivable, if maintained until death. One can always repent from any offense, including idolatry, before death comes (see 4:18 & 40:66).

dom; we granted them a great authority.

55. Some of them believed therein, and
some of them repelled therefrom;
Hell is the only just retribution for
these.

Allegorical Description of Hell

56. Surely, those who disbelieve in our
revelations, we will condemn them
to the hellfire. Whenever their skins
are burnt, we will give them new
skins. Thus, they will suffer continuously. **GOD** is Almighty, Most
Wise.

57. As for those who believe and lead a
righteous life, we will admit them
into gardens with flowing streams;
they abide therein forever. They will
have pure spouses therein. We will
admit them into a blissful shade.

Honesty & Justice Advocated

58. **GOD** commands you to give back
anything the people have entrusted
to you. If you judge among the people, you shall judge equitably. The
best enlightenment indeed is what
GOD recommends for you. **GOD** is
Hearer, Seer.

59. O you who believe, you shall obey
GOD, and you shall obey the messenger, and those in charge among
you. If you dispute in any matter,
you shall refer it to **GOD** and the
messenger, if you do believe in **GOD**
and the Last Day. This is better for
you, and provides you with the best
solution.

Believers Or Hypocrites?

60. Have you noted those who claim
that they believe in what was revealed to you, and in what was
revealed before you, then uphold
the unjust laws of their idols? They
were commanded to reject such
laws. Indeed, it is the devil's wish to
lead them far astray.

61. When they are told, "Come to what
GOD has revealed, and to the messenger," you see the hypocrites
shunning you completely.

62. How will it be when a disaster hits
them, as a consequence of their own
works? They will come to you then
and swear by **GOD**: "Our intentions
were good and righteous!"

63. **GOD** is fully aware of their innermost intentions. You shall ignore
them, enlighten them, and give them
good advice that may save their
souls.

*Unquestioning Submission:
Quality of the True Believers*

64. We did not send any messenger except to be obeyed in accordance
with **GOD**'s will. Had they, when
they wronged their souls, come to
you and prayed to **GOD** for forgiveness, and the messenger prayed for
their forgiveness, they would have
found **GOD** Redeemer, Most Merciful.

65. Never indeed, by your Lord; they
are not believers unless they come
to you to judge in their disputes,
then find no hesitation in their
hearts whatsoever in accepting your
judgment. They must submit a total
submission.

God's Tests Are Never Unreasonable

66. Had we decreed for them: "You must offer your lives," or "Give up your homes," they would not have done it, except for a few of them. (*Even if such a command was issued,*) had they done what they were commanded to do, it would have been better for them, and would prove the strength of their faith.

67. And we would have granted them a great recompense.

68. And we would have guided them in the right path.

Equality of Believers

69. Those who obey **GOD** and the messenger belong with those blessed by **GOD**—the prophets, the saints, the martyrs, and the righteous. These are the best company.

70. Such is the blessing from **GOD**; **GOD** is the best Knower.

71. O you who believe, you shall remain alert, and mobilize as individuals, or mobilize all together.

72. Surely, there are those among you who would drag their feet, then, if a setback afflicts you, they would say, "**GOD** has blessed me that I was not martyred with them."

73. But if you attain a blessing from **GOD**, they would say, as if no friendship ever existed between you and them, "I wish I was with them, so I could share in such a great victory."

74. Those who readily fight in the cause of **GOD** are those who forsake this world in favor of the Hereafter. Whoever fights in the cause of **GOD**, then gets killed, or attains victory, we will surely grant him a great recompense.

The Believers are Fearless

75. Why should you not fight in the cause of **GOD** when weak men, women, and children are imploring: "Our Lord, deliver us from this community whose people are oppressive, and be You our Lord and Master."

76. Those who believe are fighting for the cause of **GOD**, while those who disbelieve are fighting for the cause of tyranny. Therefore, you shall fight the devil's allies; the devil's power is nil.

77. Have you noted those who were told, "You do not have to fight; all you need to do is observe the Contact Prayers (*Salat*) and give the obligatory charity (*Zakat*)," then, when fighting was decreed for them, they feared the people as much as they feared **GOD**, or even more? They said, "Our Lord, why did You force this fighting on us? If only You respite us for awhile!" Say, "The materials of this world are nil, while the Hereafter is far better for the righteous, and you never suffer the slightest injustice."

*God is the Doer of Everything**

78. Wherever you are, death will catch up with you, even if you live in formidable castles. When something good happens to them, they say, "This is from **GOD**," and when something bad afflicts them, they blame you. Say, "Everything comes from **GOD**." Why do these people misunderstand almost everything?

Nothing Bad Comes From God

79. Anything good that happens to you is from **GOD**, and anything bad that happens to you is from you. We have sent you as a messenger to the people,* and **GOD** suffices as witness.

80. Whoever obeys the messenger is obeying **GOD**. As for those who turn away, we did not send you as their guardian.

81. They pledge obedience, but as soon as they leave you, some of them harbor intentions contrary to what they say. **GOD** records their innermost intentions. You shall disregard them, and put your trust in **GOD**. **GOD** suffices as an advocate.

Proof of Divine Authorship

82. Why do they not study the Quran carefully? If it were from other than **GOD**, they would have found in it numerous contradictions.*

Beware of the Devil's Rumors

83. When a rumor that affects security comes their way, they spread it. Had they referred it to the messenger, and those in charge among them, those who understand these matters would have informed them. If it were not for **GOD**'s grace towards you, and His mercy, you would have followed the devil, except a few.

84. You shall fight for the cause of **GOD**; you are responsible only for your own soul, and exhort the believers to do the same. **GOD** will neutralize the power of those who disbelieve. **GOD** is much more powerful, and much more effective.

Responsibility

85. Whoever mediates a good deed receives a share of the credit thereof, and whoever mediates an evil work, incurs a share thereof. **GOD** controls all things.

You Shall Be Courteous

86. When greeted with a greeting, you shall respond with a better greeting or at least an equal one. **GOD** reckons all things.

87. **GOD**: there is no god except He. He will surely summon you on the Day of Resurrection—the inevitable day. Whose narration is more truthful than **GOD**'s?

4:78 Bad things are consequences of our own deeds (42:30, 64:11), though God is the doer of everything (8:17). God created the fire to serve us, but you can decide to put your finger in it. We thus hurt ourselves. It is God's law that if you put your finger in the fire, it will hurt.

4:79 Muhammad was not given any proof of prophethood. Hence the expression "God suffices as a witness" (29:51-52). The gematrical value of "Muhammad" is 92, and 92 + 79=171 = 19x9.

4:82 Although the Quran was revealed during the dark ages, you cannot find any nonsense in it; another proof of divine authorship (see the Introduction and Appendix One).

How to Deal
With the Hypocrites

88. Why should you divide yourselves into two groups regarding the hypocrites (*among you*)? **GOD** is the one who condemned them because of their own behavior. Do you want to guide those who are sent astray by **GOD**? Whomever **GOD** sends astray, you can never find a way to guide them.

89. They wish that you disbelieve as they have disbelieved, then you become equal. Do not consider them friends, unless they mobilize along with you in the cause of **GOD**. If they turn against you, you shall fight them, and you may kill them when you encounter them in war. You shall not accept them as friends, or allies.*

90. Exempted are those who join people with whom you have signed a peace treaty, and those who come to you wishing not to fight you, nor fight their relatives. Had **GOD** willed, He could have permitted them to fight against you. Therefore, if they leave you alone, refrain from fighting you, and offer you peace, then **GOD** gives you no excuse to fight them.

91. You will find others who wish to make peace with you, and also with their people. However, as soon as war erupts, they fight against you. Unless these people leave you alone, offer you peace, and stop fighting you, you may fight them when you encounter them. Against these, we give you a clear authorization.

You Shall Not Kill

92. No believer shall kill another believer, unless it is an accident. If one kills a believer by accident, he shall atone by freeing a believing slave, and paying a compensation to the victim's family, unless they forfeit such a compensation as a charity. If the victim belonged to people who are at war with you, though he was a believer, you shall atone by freeing a believing slave. If he belonged to people with whom you have signed a peace treaty, you shall pay the compensation in addition to freeing a believing slave. If you cannot find* a slave to free, you shall atone by fasting two consecutive months, in order to be redeemed by **GOD**. **GOD** is Knower, Most Wise.

An Unforgivable Offense

93. Anyone who kills a believer on purpose, his retribution is Hell, wherein he abides forever, **GOD** is angry with him, and condemns him, and has prepared for him a terrible retribution.

94. O you who believe, if you strike in the cause of **GOD**, you shall be absolutely sure. Do not say to one who offers you peace, "You are not a believer," seeking the spoils of this world. For **GOD** possesses infinite spoils. Remember that you used to be like them, and **GOD** blessed you. Therefore, you shall be absolutely sure (*before you strike*). **GOD** is fully Cognizant of everything you do.

---

*4:89 The basic rule controlling all fighting is stated in 60:8-9.

*4:92 Since slavery does not exist, the offender must atone by fasting two consecutive months.

Higher Ranks for the Strivers

95. Not equal are the sedentary among the believers who are not handicapped, and those who strive in the cause of **GOD** with their money and their lives. **GOD** exalts the strivers with their money and their lives above the sedentary. For both, **GOD** promises salvation, but **GOD** exalts the strivers over the sedentary with a great recompense.

96. The higher ranks come from Him, as well as forgiveness and mercy. **GOD** is Forgiver, Most Merciful.

Apathy Condemned

97. Those whose lives are terminated by the angels, while in a state of wronging their souls, the angels will ask them, "What was the matter with you?" They will say, "We were oppressed on earth." They will say, "Was **GOD**'s earth not spacious enough for you to emigrate therein?" For these, the final abode is Hell, and a miserable destiny.

98. Exempted are the weak men, women, and children who do not possess the strength, nor the means to find a way out.

99. These may be pardoned by **GOD**. **GOD** is Pardoner, Forgiver.

100. Anyone who emigrates in the cause of **GOD** will find on earth great bounties and richness. Anyone who gives up his home, emigrating to **GOD** and His messenger, then death catches up with him, his re-compense is reserved with **GOD**. **GOD** is Forgiver, Most Merciful.

101. When you travel, during war, you commit no error by shortening your Contact Prayers (*Salat*), if you fear that the disbelievers may attack you. Surely, the disbelievers are your ardent enemies.

War
Precautions

102. When you are with them, and lead the Contact Prayer (*Salat*) for them, let some of you stand guard; let them hold their weapons, and let them stand behind you as you prostrate. Then, let the other group that has not prayed take their turn praying with you, while the others stand guard and hold their weapons. Those who disbelieved wish to see you neglect your weapons and your equipment, in order to attack you once and for all. You commit no error, if you are hampered by rain or injury, by putting down your weapons, so long as you remain alert. **GOD** has prepared for the disbelievers a shameful retribution.

The Contact Prayers

103. Once you complete your Contact Prayer (*Salat*), you shall remember **GOD** while standing, sitting, or lying down.* Once the war is over, you shall observe the Contact Prayers (*Salat*); the Contact Prayers (*Salat*) are decreed for the believers at specific times.

---

*4:103 Your god is whoever or whatever occupies your mind most of the day. In order to belong in God's kingdom, and enjoy His grace and protection, the Quran exhorts us to remember God "always" (2:152 & 200, 3:191, 33:41-42). This profound fact explains the numerous verses asserting that "most" of those who believe in God are going to Hell (12:106, 23:84-89, 29:61-63, 31:25, 39:38, 43:87). See Footnote 3:191 and Appendix 27.

---

104. Do not waver in pursuing the enemy. If you suffer, they also suffer. However, you expect from **GOD** what they never expect. **GOD** is Omniscient, Most Wise.

105. We have sent down to you the scripture, truthfully, in order to judge among the people in accordance with what **GOD** has shown you. You shall not side with the betrayers.

106. You shall implore **GOD** for forgiveness. **GOD** is Forgiver, Most Merciful.

Do Not Defend the Transgressors

107. Do not argue on behalf of those who have wronged their own souls; **GOD** does not love any betrayer, guilty.

108. They hide from the people, and do not care to hide from **GOD**, though He is with them as they harbor ideas He dislikes. **GOD** is fully aware of everything they do.

You Do Not Help Them by Being "Nice"

109. Here you are arguing on their behalf in this world; who is going to argue with **GOD** on their behalf on the Day of Resurrection? Who is going to be their advocate?

110. Anyone who commits evil, or wrongs his soul, then implores **GOD** for forgiveness, will find **GOD** Forgiving, Most Merciful.

111. Anyone who earns a sin, earns it to the detriment of his own soul. **GOD** is Omniscient, Most Wise.

112. Anyone who earns a sin, then accuses an innocent person thereof, has committed a blasphemy and a gross offense.

113. If it were not for **GOD**'s grace towards you, and His mercy, some of them would have misled you. They only mislead themselves, and they can never harm you in the least. **GOD** has sent down to you the scripture and wisdom, and He has taught you what you never knew. Indeed, **GOD**'s blessings upon you have been great.

114. There is nothing good about their private conferences, except for those who advocate charity, or righteous works, or making peace among the people. Anyone who does this, in response to **GOD**'s teachings, we will grant him a great recompense.

115. As for him who opposes the messenger, after the guidance has been pointed out to him, and follows other than the believers' way, we will direct him in the direction he has chosen, and commit him to Hell; what a miserable destiny!

The Unforgivable Sin

116. **GOD** does not forgive idol worship (*if maintained until death*),* and He forgives lesser offenses for whomever He wills. Anyone who idolizes any idol beside **GOD** has strayed far astray.

117. They even worship female gods besides Him; as a matter of fact, they only worship a rebellious devil.

118. **GOD** has condemned him, and he said, "I will surely recruit a definite share of Your worshipers.*

4:116 A simple definition of idolatry: Believing that anything beside God can help you.

4:118 The majority of believers in God fall into idolatry (12:106).

---

119. "I will mislead them, I will entice them, I will command them to (*forbid the eating of certain meats by*) marking the ears of livestock, and I will command them to distort the creation of **GOD**." Anyone who accepts the devil as a lord, instead of **GOD**, has incurred a profound loss.

120. He promises them and entices them; what the devil promises is no more than an illusion.

121. These have incurred Hell as their final abode, and can never evade it.

122. As for those who believe and lead a righteous life, we will admit them into gardens with flowing streams, wherein they live forever. Such is the truthful promise of **GOD**. Whose utterances are more truthful than **GOD**'s?

The Law

123. It is not in accordance with your wishes, or the wishes of the people of the scripture: anyone who commits evil pays for it, and will have no helper or supporter against **GOD**.

124. As for those who lead a righteous life, male or female, while believing, they enter Paradise; without the slightest injustice.

Abraham:
Original Messenger of Islam *

125. Who is better guided in his religion than one who submits totally to **GOD**, leads a righteous life, according to the creed of Abraham: monotheism? **GOD** has chosen Abraham as a beloved friend.

126. To **GOD** belongs everything in the heavens and the earth. **GOD** is in full control of all things.

127. They consult you concerning women: say, "**GOD** enlightens you regarding them, as recited for you in the scripture. You shall restore the rights of orphaned girls whom you cheat out of their due dowries when you wish to marry them: you shall not take advantage of them. The rights of orphaned boys must also be protected as well. You shall treat the orphans equitably. Whatever good you do, **GOD** is fully aware thereof."

Divorce Discouraged

128. If a woman senses oppression or desertion from her husband, the couple shall try to reconcile their differences, for conciliation is best for them. Selfishness is a human trait, and if you do good and lead a righteous life, **GOD** is fully Cognizant of everything you do.

Polygamy Discouraged*

129. You can never be equitable in dealing with more than one wife, no matter how hard you try. Therefore, do not be so biased as to leave one of them hanging (*neither enjoying marriage, nor left to marry someone else*). If you correct this situation and maintain righteousness, **GOD** is Forgiver, Most Merciful.

130. If the couple must decide to part, **GOD** will provide for each of them from His bounties. **GOD** is Bounteous, Most Wise.

---

*4:125 All messengers since Adam have preached one and the same religion. Abraham was the original messenger of the creed named "Islam" (22:78, Appendix 26). "Islam" is not a name, but rather a description meaning "Submission."

*4:129 See Appendix 30, entitled "Polygamy."

---

131. To **GOD** belongs everything in the heavens and the earth, and we have enjoined on those who received the scripture before you, and enjoined on you, that you shall reverence **GOD**. If you disbelieve, then to **GOD** belongs everything in the heavens and the earth. **GOD** is in no need, Praiseworthy.

132. To **GOD** belongs everything in the heavens and the earth, and **GOD** is the only Protector.

133. If He wills, He can annihilate you, O people, and substitute others in your place. **GOD** is certainly able to do this.

134. Anyone who seeks the materials of this world should know that **GOD** possesses both the materials of this world and the Hereafter. **GOD** is Hearer, Seer.

You Shall Not
Bear False Witness

135. O you who believe, you shall be absolutely equitable, and observe **GOD**, when you serve as witnesses, even against yourselves, or your parents, or your relatives. Whether the accused is rich or poor, **GOD** takes care of both. Therefore, do not be biased by your personal wishes. If you deviate or disregard (*this commandment*), then **GOD** is fully Cognizant of everything you do.

136. O you who believe, you shall believe in **GOD** and His messenger, and the scripture He has revealed through His messenger, and the scripture He has revealed before that. Anyone who refuses to believe in **GOD**, and His angels, and His scriptures, and His messengers, and the Last Day, has indeed strayed far astray.

137. Surely, those who believe, then disbelieve, then believe, then disbelieve, then plunge deeper into disbelief, **GOD** will not forgive them, nor will He guide them in any way.

138. Inform the hypocrites that they have incurred painful retribution.

139. They are the ones who ally themselves with disbelievers instead of believers. Are they seeking dignity with them? All dignity belongs with **GOD** alone.

140. He has instructed you in the scripture that: if you hear **GOD**'s revelations being mocked and ridiculed, you shall not sit with them, unless they delve into another subject. Otherwise, you will be as guilty as they are. **GOD** will gather the hypocrites and the disbelievers together in Hell.

The Hypocrites

141. They watch you and wait; if you attain victory from **GOD**, they say (*to you*), "Were we not with you?" But if the disbelievers get a turn, they say (*to them*), "Did we not side with you, and protect you from the believers?" **GOD** will judge between you on the Day of Resurrection. **GOD** will never permit the disbelievers to prevail over the believers.

142. The hypocrites think that they are deceiving **GOD**, but He is the One who leads them on. When they get up for the Contact Prayer (*Salat*), they get up lazily. That is because they only show off in front of the people, and rarely do they think of **GOD**.

143. They waver in between, neither belonging to this group, nor that group. Whomever **GOD** sends astray, you will never find a way to guide him.

144. O you who believe, you shall not ally yourselves with the disbelievers, instead of the believers. Do you wish to provide **GOD** with a clear proof against you?

They Think That They Are Believers

145. The hypocrites will be committed to the lowest pit of Hell, and you will find no one to help them.

146. Only those who repent, reform, hold fast to **GOD**, and devote their religion absolutely to **GOD** alone, will be counted with the believers. **GOD** will bless the believers with a great recompense.

147. What will **GOD** gain from punishing you, if you became appreciative and believed? **GOD** is Appreciative, Omniscient.

Do Not Use Bad Language

148. **GOD** does not like the utterance of bad language, unless one is treated with gross injustice. **GOD** is Hearer, Knower.

149. If you work righteousness—either declared or concealed—or pardon a transgression, **GOD** is Pardoner, Omnipotent.

You Shall Not Make Any Distinction Among God's Messengers

150. Those who disbelieve in **GOD** and His messengers, and seek to make distinction among **GOD** and His messengers, and say, "We believe in some and reject some," and wish to follow a path in between;

151. these are the real disbelievers. We have prepared for the disbelievers a shameful retribution.

152. As for those who believe in **GOD** and His messengers, and make no distinction among them, He will grant them their recompense. **GOD** is Forgiver, Most Merciful.

Lessons From Israel

153. The people of the scripture challenge you to bring down to them a book from the sky! They have asked Moses for more than that, saying, "Show us **GOD**, physically." Consequently, the lightning struck them, as a consequence of their audacity. Additionally, they worshiped the calf, after all the miracles they had seen. Yet, we pardoned all this. We supported Moses with profound miracles.

154. And we raised Mount Sinai above them, as we took their covenant. And we said to them, "Enter the gate humbly." And we said to them, "Do not desecrate the Sabbath." Indeed, we took from them a solemn covenant.

155. (*They incurred condemnation*) for violating their covenant, rejecting **GOD**'s revelations, killing the prophets unjustly, and for saying, "Our minds are made up!" In fact, **GOD** is the One who sealed their minds, due to their disbelief, and this is why they fail to believe, except rarely.

156. (*They are condemned*) for disbelieving and uttering about Mary a gross lie.

Crucifying "the Body" of Jesus*

157. And for claiming that they killed the Messiah, Jesus, son of Mary, the messenger of **GOD**. In fact, they never killed him, they never crucified him—they were made to think that they did. All factions who are disputing in this matter are full of doubt concerning this issue. They possess no knowledge; they only conjecture. For certain, they never killed him.*

158. Instead, **GOD** raised him to Him; **GOD** is Almighty, Most Wise.

159. Everyone among the people of the scripture was required to believe in him before his death. On the Day of Resurrection, he will be a witness against them.

160. Due to their transgressions, we prohibited for the Jews good foods that used to be lawful for them; also for consistently repelling from the path of **GOD**.

161. And for practicing usury, which was forbidden, and for consuming the people's money illicitly. We have prepared for the disbelievers among them painful retribution.

162. As for those among them who are well founded in knowledge, and the believers, they believe in what was revealed to you, and in what was revealed before you. They are observers of the Contact Prayers (*Salat*), and givers of the obligatory charity (*Zakat*); they are believers in **GOD** and the Last Day. We grant these a great recompense.

God's Messengers

163. We have inspired you, as we inspired Noah and the prophets after him. And we inspired Abraham, Ismail, Isaac, Jacob, the Patriarchs, Jesus, Job, Jonah, Aaron, and Solomon. And we gave David the Psalms.

164. Messengers we have told you about, and messengers we never told you about. And **GOD** spoke to Moses directly.

165. Messengers to deliver good news, as well as warnings. Thus, the people will have no excuse when they face **GOD**, after all these messengers have come to them. **GOD** is Almighty, Most Wise.

166. But **GOD** bears witness concerning what He has revealed to you; He has revealed it with His knowledge. And the angels bear witness as well, but **GOD** suffices as witness.

167. Surely, those who disbelieve and repel from the way of **GOD** have strayed far astray.

168. Those who disbelieve and transgress, **GOD** will not forgive them, nor will He guide them in any way;

169. except the way to Hell, wherein they abide forever. This is easy for **GOD** to do.

---

*4:157-158 Jesus, the real person, the soul, was raised in the same manner as in the death of any righteous person. Subsequently, his enemies arrested, tortured, and crucified his living, but empty, body. See Appendices 17 & 22, and the book "JESUS: MYTHS AND MESSAGE," by Lisa Spray (Universal Unity, Fremont, California, 1992).

170. O people, the messenger has come to you with the truth from your Lord. Therefore, you shall believe for your own good. If you disbelieve, then to **GOD** belongs everything in the heavens and the earth. **GOD** is Omniscient, Most Wise.

Trinity:
A False Doctrine

171. O people of the scripture, do not transgress the limits of your religion, and do not say about **GOD** except the truth. The Messiah, Jesus, the son of Mary, was a messenger of **GOD**, and His word that He had sent to Mary, and a revelation from Him. Therefore, you shall believe in **GOD** and His messengers. You shall not say, "Trinity." You shall refrain from this for your own good. **GOD** is only one god. Be He glorified; He is much too glorious to have a son. To Him belongs everything in the heavens and everything on earth. **GOD** suffices as Lord and Master.

172. The Messiah would never disdain from being a servant of **GOD**, nor would the closest angels. Those who disdain from worshiping Him, and are too arrogant to submit, He will summon them all before Him.

173. As for those who believe and lead a righteous life, He will fully recompense them, and shower them with His grace. As for those who disdain and turn arrogant, He will commit them to painful retribution. They will find no lord beside **GOD**, nor a savior.

The Quran's Mathematical Code:
Tangible, Irrefutable Proof

174. O people, a proof has come to you from your Lord; we have sent down to you a profound beacon.

175. Those who believe in **GOD**, and hold fast to Him, He will admit them into mercy from Him, and grace, and will guide them to Him in a straight path.

176. They consult you; say, "**GOD** advises you concerning the single person. If one dies and leaves no children, and he had a sister, she gets half the inheritance. If she dies first, he inherits from her, if she left no children. If there were two sisters, they get two-thirds of the inheritance. If the siblings are men and women, the male gets twice the share of the female." **GOD** thus clarifies for you, lest you go astray. **GOD** is fully aware of all things.

◆◆◆

Sura 5: The Feast (Al-Mã'edah)

In the name of God,
Most Gracious, Most Merciful

1. O you who believe, you shall fulfill your covenants. Permitted for you to eat are the livestock, except those specifically prohibited herein. You shall not permit hunting throughout Hajj pilgrimage. **GOD** decrees whatever He wills.

2. O you who believe, do not violate the rites instituted by **GOD**, nor the Sacred Months, nor the animals to be offered, nor the garlands marking them, nor the people who head for the Sacred Shrine (*Ka'bah*) seeking blessings from their Lord and approval. Once you complete the pilgrimage, you may hunt.* Do not be provoked into aggression by your hatred of people who once prevented you from going to the Sacred Masjid. You shall cooperate in matters of righteousness and piety; do not cooperate in matters that are sinful and evil. You shall observe **GOD**. **GOD** is strict in enforcing retribution.

Only Four Meats Prohibited
"Animals that
die of themselves" Defined

3. Prohibited for you are animals that die of themselves, blood, the meat of pigs,* and animals dedicated to other than **GOD**. (*Animals that die of themselves include those*) strangled, struck with an object, fallen from a height, gored, attacked by a wild animal—unless you save your animal before it dies—and animals sacrificed on altars. Also prohibited is dividing the meat through a game of chance; this is an abomination. Today, the disbelievers have given up concerning (*the eradication of*) your religion; do not fear them and fear Me instead. Today, I have completed your religion, perfected My blessing upon you, and I have decreed Submission as the religion for you. If one is forced by famine (*to eat prohibited food*), without being deliberately sinful, then **GOD** is Forgiver, Merciful.

4. They consult you concerning what is lawful for them; say, "Lawful for you are all good things, including what trained dogs and falcons catch for you." You train them according to **GOD**'s teachings. You may eat what they catch for you, and mention **GOD**'s name thereupon. You shall observe **GOD**. **GOD** is most efficient in reckoning.

5. Today, all good food is made lawful for you. The food of the people of the scripture is lawful for you. Also, you may marry the chaste women among the believers, as well as the chaste women among the followers of previous scripture, provided you pay them their due dowries. You shall maintain chastity, not committing adultery, nor taking secret lovers. Anyone who rejects faith, all his work will be in vain, and in the Hereafter he will be with the losers.

---

*5:2 Hunting and the cutting of plants are forbidden during pilgrimage for the conservation of natural resources. With thousands of pilgrims converging on Mecca, if hunting were permitted, the land would quickly be stripped of its natural resources. Animal offerings are made part of the pilgrimage to provide for the converging pilgrims, as well as the local population, and to replenish any depleted supplies. See 2:196.

*5:3 The "meat" of the pig is prohibited, not the "fat." Anything that is not specifically prohibited in the Quran must be considered lawful. See 6:145-146.

Ablution

6. O you who believe, when you observe the Contact Prayers (*Salat*), you shall: *(1)* wash your faces, *(2)* wash your arms to the elbows, *(3)* wipe your heads, and *(4)* wash your feet to the ankles. If you were unclean due to sexual orgasm, you shall bathe. If you are ill, or traveling, or had any digestive excretion (*urinary, fecal, or gas*), or had (*sexual*) contact with the women, and you cannot find water, you shall observe the dry ablution (*Tayammum*) by touching clean dry soil, then rubbing your faces and hands. **GOD** does not wish to make the religion difficult for you; He wishes to cleanse you and to perfect His blessing upon you, that you may be appreciative.

7. Remember **GOD**'s blessing upon you, and His covenant that He covenanted with you: you said, "We hear and we obey." You shall observe **GOD**; **GOD** is fully aware of the innermost thoughts.

You Shall Not Bear False Witness

8. O you who believe, you shall be absolutely equitable, and observe **GOD**, when you serve as witnesses. Do not be provoked by your conflicts with some people into committing injustice. You shall be absolutely equitable, for it is more righteous. You shall observe **GOD**. **GOD** is fully Cognizant of everything you do.

9. **GOD** promises those who believe and lead a righteous life forgiveness and a great recompense.

10. As for those who disbelieve and reject our revelations, they are the dwellers of Hell.

God Defends the Believers

11. O you who believe, remember **GOD**'s blessings upon you; when some people extended their hands to aggress against you, He protected you and withheld their hands. You shall observe **GOD**; in **GOD** the believers shall trust.

Conditions for Staying Within God's Protection *

12. **GOD** had taken a covenant from the Children of Israel, and we raised among them twelve patriarchs. And **GOD** said, "I am with you, so long as you observe the Contact Prayers (*Salat*), give the obligatory charity (*Zakat*), and believe in My messengers and respect them, and continue to lend **GOD** a loan of righteousness. I will then remit your sins, and admit you into gardens with flowing streams. Anyone who disbelieves after this, has indeed strayed off the right path."

Consequences of Violating God's Covenant

13. It was a consequence of their violating the covenant that we condemned them, and we caused their hearts to become hardened. Consequently, they took the words out of context, and disregarded some of the commandments given to them. You will continue to witness betrayal from them, excepting a few of them. You shall pardon them, and disregard them. **GOD** loves those who are benevolent.

---

*5:12 If you fulfill the requirements stated in this verse, God will let you know that He is with you; you will have no doubt about it. Prominent among God's signs are mathematical signs for those who understand the Quran's miracle (Appendix One).

Christians, too, Must Obey God's Messenger

14. Also from those who said, "We are Christian," we took their covenant. But they disregarded some of the commandments given to them. Consequently, we condemned them to animosity and hatred among themselves, until the Day of Resurrection. **GOD** will then inform them of everything they had done.

The Quran: God's Message to the Jews and Christians

15. O people of the scripture, our messenger has come to you to proclaim for you many things you have concealed in the scripture, and to pardon many other transgressions you have committed. A beacon has come to you from **GOD**, and a profound scripture.

16. With it, **GOD** guides those who seek His approval. He guides them to the paths of peace, leads them out of darkness into the light by His leave, and guides them in a straight path.

Gross Blasphemy

17. Pagans indeed are those who say that **GOD** is the Messiah, the son of Mary. Say, "Who could oppose **GOD** if He willed to annihilate the Messiah, son of Mary, and his mother, and everyone on earth?" To **GOD** belongs the sovereignty of the heavens and the earth, and everything between them. He creates whatever He wills. **GOD** is Omnipotent.

God's Messenger to the Jews, Christians and Muslims

18. The Jews and the Christians said, "We are **GOD**'s children and His beloved." Say, "Why then does He punish you for your sins? You are just humans like the other humans He created." He forgives whomever He wills and punishes whomever He wills. To **GOD** belongs the sovereignty of the heavens and the earth, and everything between them, and to Him is the final destiny.

God's Messenger of the Covenant

19. O people of the scripture, our messenger has come to you, to explain things to you, after a period of time without messengers, lest you say, "We did not receive any preacher or warner." A preacher and warner has now come to you. **GOD** is Omnipotent.*

20. Recall that Moses said to his people, "O my people, remember **GOD**'s blessings upon you: He appointed prophets from among you, made you kings, and granted you what He never granted any other people.

God Gives the Holy Land to Israel

21. "O my people, enter the holy land that **GOD** has decreed for you, and do not rebel, lest you become losers."

---

*5:19 This verse reports the fulfillment of the biblical and Quranic prophecy regarding the advent of God's Messenger of the Covenent (Malachi 3:1, Quran 3:81). The name of this messenger is mathematically coded into the Quran as "Rashad Khalifa." This very special verse warrants the presentation of specific evidence. By adding the gematrical value of "Rashad" (505), plus the value of "Khalifa" (725), plus the sura number (5), plus the verse number (19), we obtain a total of 505 + 725 + 5 + 19 = 1254, or 19x66. Nineteen is the Quran's common denominator, which was revealed through Rashad Khalifa. More evidence and specific details are in Appendix Two.

22. They said, "O Moses, there are powerful people in it, and we will not enter it, unless they get out of it. If they get out, we are entering."

23. Two men who were reverent and blessed by **GOD** said, "Just enter the gate. If you just enter it, you will surely prevail. You must trust in **GOD**, if you are believers."

Despite All the Miracles They Saw

24. They said, "O Moses, we will never enter it, so long as they are in it. Therefore, go—you and your Lord —and fight. We are sitting right here."

25. He said, "My Lord, I can only control myself and my brother. So, allow us to part company with the wicked people."

26. He said, "Henceforth, it is forbidden them for forty years, during which they will roam the earth aimlessly. Do not grieve over such wicked people."

The First Murder*

27. Recite for them the true history of Adam's two sons. They made an offering, and it was accepted from one of them, but not from the other. He said, "I will surely kill you." He said, "**GOD** accepts only from the righteous.

28. "If you extend your hand to kill me, I am not extending my hand to kill you. For I reverence **GOD**, Lord of the universe.

29. "I want you, not me, to bear my sin and your sin, then you end up with the dwellers of Hell. Such is the requital for the transgressors."

30. His ego provoked him into killing his brother. He killed him, and ended up with the losers.

31. **GOD** then sent a raven to scratch the soil, to teach him how to bury his brother's corpse. He said, "Woe to me; I failed to be as intelligent as this raven, and bury my brother's corpse." He became ridden with remorse.

Grossness of Murder

32. Because of this, we decreed for the Children of Israel that anyone who murders any person who had not committed murder or horrendous crimes, it shall be as if he murdered all the people. And anyone who spares a life, it shall be as if he spared the lives of all the people. Our messengers went to them with clear proofs and revelations, but most of them, after all this, are still transgressing.

*Capital Punishment:
When is it Justified?*

33. The just retribution for those who fight **GOD** and His messenger, and commit horrendous crimes, is to be killed, or crucified, or to have their hands and feet cut off on alternate sides, or to be banished from the land. This is to humiliate them in this life, then they suffer a far worse retribution in the Hereafter.

---

*5:27-31 The names of the two sons involved in this first murder are not relevant. But they are given in the Bible as Abel and Cain (Genesis 4:2-9).

34. Exempted are those who repent before you overcome them. You should know that **GOD** is Forgiver, Most Merciful.

35. O you who believe, you shall reverence **GOD** and seek the ways and means to Him, and strive in His cause, that you may succeed.

The Cost of Disbelief

36. Certainly, those who disbelieved, if they possessed everything on earth, even twice as much, and offered it as ransom to spare them the retribution on the Day of Resurrection, it would not be accepted from them; they have incurred a painful retribution.

37. They will want to exit Hell, but alas, they can never exit therefrom; their retribution is eternal.

Mathematical Proof
Supports Quranic Justice

38. The thief, male or female, you shall mark their hands* as a punishment for their crime, and to serve as an example from **GOD**. **GOD** is Almighty, Most Wise.

39. If one repents after committing this crime, and reforms, **GOD** redeems him. **GOD** is Forgiver, Most Merciful.

40. Do you not know that **GOD** possesses the sovereignty of the heavens and the earth? He punishes whomever He wills, and forgives whomever He wills. **GOD** is Omnipotent.

41. O you messenger, do not be saddened by those who hasten to disbelieve among those who say, "We believe," with their mouths, while their hearts do not believe. Among the Jews, some listened to lies. They listened to people who never met you, and who distorted the words out of context, then said, "If you are given this, accept it, but if you are given anything different, beware." Whomever **GOD** wills to divert, you can do nothing to help him against **GOD**. **GOD** does not wish to cleanse their hearts. They have incurred humiliation in this world, and in the Hereafter, they will suffer a terrible retribution.

42. They are upholders of lies, and eaters of illicit earnings. If they come to you to judge among them, you may judge among them, or you may disregard them. If you choose to disregard them, they cannot harm you in the least. But if you judge among them, you shall judge equitably. **GOD** loves those who are equitable.

*5:38 The practice of cutting off the thief's hand, as decreed by the false Muslims, is a satanic practice without Quranic basis. Due to the special importance of this example, God has provided mathematical proof in support of marking the hand of the thief, rather than severing it. Verse 12:31 refers to the women who so admired Joseph that they "cut" their hands. Obviously, they did not "cut off" their hands; nobody can. The sum of sura and verse numbers are the same for 5:38 and 12:31, i.e., 43. It is also the will and mercy of God that this mathematical relationship conforms with the Quran's 19-based code. Nineteen verses after 12:31, we see the same word (12:50).

43. Why do they ask you to judge among them, when they have the Torah, containing **GOD**'s law, and they chose to disregard it? They are not believers.

Honoring Previous Scripture

44. We have sent down the Torah,* containing guidance and light. Ruling in accordance with it were the Jewish prophets, as well as the rabbis and the priests, as dictated to them in **GOD**'s scripture, and as witnessed by them. Therefore, do not reverence human beings; you shall reverence Me instead. And do not trade away My revelations for a cheap price. Those who do not rule in accordance with **GOD**'s revelations are the disbelievers.

The Law of Equivalence

45. And we decreed for them in it that: the life for the life, the eye for the eye, the nose for the nose, the ear for the ear, the tooth for the tooth, and an equivalent injury for any injury. If one forfeits what is due to him as a charity, it will atone for his sins. Those who do not rule in accordance with **GOD**'s revelations are the unjust.

The Gospel of Jesus: Guidance and Light

46. Subsequent to them, we sent Jesus, the son of Mary, confirming the previous scripture, the Torah. We gave him the Gospel, containing guidance and light, and confirming the previous scriptures, the Torah, and augmenting its guidance and light, and to enlighten the righteous.

47. The people of the Gospel shall rule in accordance with **GOD**'s revelations therein. Those who do not rule in accordance with **GOD**'s revelations are the wicked.

Quran: The Ultimate Reference

48. Then we revealed to you this scripture, truthfully, confirming previous scriptures, and superseding them. You shall rule among them in accordance with **GOD**'s revelations, and do not follow their wishes if they differ from the truth that came to you. For each of you, we have decreed laws and different rites. Had **GOD** willed, He could have made you one congregation. But He thus puts you to the test through the revelations He has given each of you. You shall compete in righteousness. To **GOD** is your final destiny—all of you—then He will inform you of everything you had disputed.

49. You shall rule among them in accordance with **GOD**'s revelations to you. Do not follow their wishes, and beware lest they divert you from some of **GOD**'s revelations to you. If they turn away, then know that **GOD** wills to punish them for some of their sins. Indeed, many people are wicked.

50. Is it the law of the days of ignorance that they seek to uphold? Whose law is better than **GOD**'s for those who have attained certainty?

5:44 The Torah is a collection of all the scriptures revealed through all the prophets of Israel prior to Jesus Christ, i.e., today's Old Testament. Nowhere in the Quran do we find that the Torah was given to Moses.

Certain Jews and Christians Cannot Be Friends*

51. O you who believe, do not take certain Jews and Christians as allies; these are allies of one another. Those among you who ally themselves with these belong with them. **GOD** does not guide the transgressors.

52. You will see those who harbor doubt in their hearts hasten to join them, saying, "We fear lest we may be defeated." May **GOD** bring victory, or a command from Him, that causes them to regret their secret thoughts.

53. The believers will then say, "Are these the same people who swore by **GOD** solemnly that they were with you?" Their works have been nullified; they are the losers.

54. O you who believe, if you revert from your religion, then **GOD** will substitute in your place people whom He loves and who love Him. They will be kind with the believers, stern with the disbelievers, and will strive in the cause of **GOD** without fear of any blame. Such is **GOD**'s blessing; He bestows it upon whomever He wills. **GOD** is Bounteous, Omniscient.

55. Your real allies are **GOD** and His messenger, and the believers who observe the Contact Prayers (*Salat*), and give the obligatory charity (*Zakat*), and they bow down.

56. Those who ally themselves with **GOD** and His messenger, and those who believed, belong in the party of **GOD**; absolutely, they are the victors.

Which Jews and Christians

57. O you who believe, do not befriend those among the recipients of previous scripture who mock and ridicule your religion, nor shall you befriend the disbelievers. You shall reverence **GOD**, if you are really believers.

Recipients of the Scriptures Transgress

58. When you call to the Contact Prayers (*Salat*), they mock and ridicule it. This is because they are people who do not understand.

59. Say, "O people of the scripture, do you not hate us because we believe in **GOD**, and in what was revealed to us, and in what was revealed before us, and because most of you are not righteous?"

60. Say, "Let me tell you who are worse in the sight of **GOD**: those who are condemned by **GOD** after incurring His wrath until He made them (*as despicable as*) monkeys and pigs, and the idol worshipers. These are far worse, and farther from the right path."

61. When they come to you, they say, "We believe," even though they were full of disbelief when they entered, and they are full of disbelief when they leave. **GOD** is fully aware of everything they conceal.

---

*5:51 Relations with other people are governed by the basic rule in 5:57 & 60:8-9. The Jews and Christians who cannot be friends are specifically mentioned in 5:57; they are the ones who mock and ridicule the believers, or attack them.

62. You see many of them readily committing evil and transgression, and eating from illicit earnings. Miserable indeed is what they do.

63. If only the rabbis and the priests enjoin them from their sinful utterances and illicit earnings! Miserable indeed is what they commit.

Blaspheming Against God

64. The Jews even said, "**GOD**'s hand is tied down!" It is their hands that are tied down. They are condemned for uttering such a blasphemy. Instead, His hands are wide open, spending as He wills. For certain, your Lord's revelations to you will cause many of them to plunge deeper into transgression and disbelief. Consequently, we have committed them to animosity and hatred among themselves until the Day of Resurrection. Whenever they ignite the flames of war, **GOD** puts them out. They roam the earth wickedly, and **GOD** dislikes the evildoers.

Salvation For Jews and Christians

65. If only the people of the scripture believe and lead a righteous life, we will then remit their sins, and admit them into gardens of bliss.

They Must Believe in This Quran

66. If only they would uphold the Torah and the Gospel, and what is sent down to them herein from their Lord, they would be showered with blessings from above them and from beneath their feet. Some of them are righteous, but many of them are evildoers.

The Messenger Must Deliver

67. O you messenger, deliver what is revealed to you from your Lord—until you do, you have not delivered His message—and **GOD** will protect you from the people. **GOD** does not guide the disbelieving people.

68. Say, "O people of the scripture, you have no basis until you uphold the Torah, and the Gospel, and what is sent down to you herein from your Lord." For sure, these revelations from your Lord will cause many of them to plunge deeper into transgression and disbelief. Therefore, do not feel sorry for the disbelieving people.

Minimum Requirements For Salvation

69. Surely, those who believe, those who are Jewish, the converts, and the Christians; any of them who *(1)* believe in **GOD** and *(2)* believe in the Last Day, and *(3)* lead a righteous life, have nothing to fear, nor will they grieve.

70. We have taken a covenant from the Children of Israel, and we sent to them messengers. Whenever a messenger went to them with anything they disliked, some of them they rejected, and some they killed.

71. They thought that they would not be tested, so they turned blind and deaf, then **GOD** redeemed them, but then many of them turned blind and deaf again. **GOD** is Seer of everything they do.

Today's Christianity Not Jesus' Religion *

72. Pagans indeed are those who say that **GOD** is the Messiah, son of Mary. The Messiah himself said, "O Children of Israel, you shall worship **GOD**; my Lord* and your Lord." Anyone who sets up any idol beside **GOD**, **GOD** has forbidden Paradise for him, and his destiny is Hell. The wicked have no helpers.

73. Pagans indeed are those who say that **GOD** is a third of a trinity. There is no god except the one god. Unless they refrain from saying this, those who disbelieve among them will incur a painful retribution.

74. Would they not repent to **GOD**, and ask His forgiveness? **GOD** is Forgiver, Most Merciful.

75. The Messiah, son of Mary, is no more than a messenger like the messengers before him, and his mother was a saint. Both of them used to eat the food. Note how we explain the revelations for them, and note how they still deviate!

76. Say, "Would you worship beside **GOD** powerless idols who can neither harm you, nor benefit you? **GOD** is Hearer, Omniscient."

Choose Your Friends Carefully

77. Say, "O people of the scripture, do not transgress the limits of your religion beyond the truth, and do not follow the opinions of people who have gone astray, and have misled multitudes of people; they are far astray from the right path."

78. Condemned are those who disbelieved among the Children of Israel, by the tongue of David and Jesus, the son of Mary. This is because they disobeyed and transgressed.

Apathy Condemned

79. They did not enjoin one another from committing evil. Miserable indeed is what they did.

80. You would see many of them allying themselves with those who disbelieve. Miserable indeed is what their hands have sent forth on behalf of their souls. **GOD** is angry with them and, consequently, they will abide forever in retribution.

81. Had they believed in **GOD**, and the prophet, and in what was revealed to him herein, they would not have befriended them. But many of them are evil.

A Statement of Fact

82. You will find that the worst enemies of the believers are the Jews and the idol worshipers. And you will find that the closest people in friendship to the believers are those who say, "We are Christian." This is because they have priests and monks among them, and they are not arrogant.

---

*5:72-76 In John 20:17, we see that Jesus taught that he was neither God, nor the son of God. Many theologians have concluded, after careful research, that today's Christianity is not the same Christianity taught by Jesus. Two outstanding books on this subject are "The Myth of God Incarnate" (The Westminster Press, Philadelphia, 1977) and "The Mythmaker" (Harper & Row, New York, 1986). On the front jacket of "The Mythmaker" we read the following statement: "...**Hyam Maccoby presents new arguments to support the view that Paul, not Jesus, was the founder of Christianity.... it was Paul alone who created a new religion through his vision of Jesus as a divine Saviour who died to save humanity.**"

83. When they hear what was revealed to the messenger, you see their eyes flooding with tears as they recognize the truth therein, and they say, "Our Lord, we have believed, so count us among the witnesses.

84. "Why should we not believe in **GOD**, and in the truth that has come to us, and hope that our Lord may admit us with the righteous people?"

85. **GOD** has rewarded them for saying this; He will admit them into gardens with flowing streams. They abide therein forever. Such is the reward for the righteous.

86. As for those who disbelieve and reject our revelations, they are the dwellers of Hell.

Do Not Prohibit Lawful Things

87. O you who believe, do not prohibit good things that are made lawful by **GOD**, and do not aggress; **GOD** dislikes the aggressors.

88. And eat from the good and lawful things that **GOD** has provided for you. You shall reverence **GOD**, in whom you are believers.

Do Not Take God's Name in Vain

89. **GOD** does not hold you responsible for the mere utterance of oaths; He holds you responsible for your actual intentions. If you violate an oath, you shall atone by feeding ten poor people from the same food you offer to your own family, or clothing them, or by freeing a slave. If you cannot afford this, then you shall fast three days. This is the atonement for violating the oaths that you swore to keep. You shall fulfill your oaths. **GOD** thus explains His revelations to you, that you may be appreciative.

Intoxicants and Gambling Prohibited

90. O you who believe, intoxicants, and gambling, and the altars of idols, and the games of chance are abominations of the devil; you shall avoid them, that you may succeed.

91. The devil wants to provoke animosity and hatred among you through intoxicants and gambling, and to distract you from remembering **GOD**, and from observing the Contact Prayers (*Salat*). Will you then refrain?

92. You shall obey **GOD**, and you shall obey the messenger, and beware. If you turn away, then know that the sole duty of our messenger is to deliver the message efficiently.

93. Those who believe and lead a righteous life bear no guilt by eating any food, so long as they observe the commandments, believe and lead a righteous life, then maintain their piety and faith, and continue to observe piety and righteousness. **GOD** loves the righteous.

Game Conservation

94. O you who believe, **GOD** will test you with some game within reach of your hands and your arrows (*during pilgrimage*). **GOD** thus distinguishes those among you who observe Him in their privacy. Those who transgress after this have incurred a painful retribution.

95. O you who believe, do not kill any game during pilgrimage. Anyone who kills any game on purpose, his fine shall be a number of livestock animals that is equivalent to the game animals he killed. The judgment shall be set by two equitable people among you. They shall make sure that the offerings reach the Ka'bah. Otherwise, he may expiate by feeding poor people, or by an equivalent fast to atone for his offense. **GOD** has pardoned past offenses. But if anyone returns to such an offense, **GOD** will avenge it. **GOD** is Almighty, Avenger.

All Creatures of the Sea Lawful to Eat

96. All fish of the sea are made lawful for you to eat. During pilgrimage, this may provide for you during your journey. You shall not hunt throughout the pilgrimage. You shall reverence **GOD**, before whom you will be summoned.

97. **GOD** has appointed the Ka'bah, the Sacred Masjid,* to be a sanctuary for the people, and also the Sacred Months, the offerings (*to the Sacred Masjid*), and the garlands marking them. You should know that **GOD** knows everything in the heavens and the earth, and that **GOD** is Omniscient.

98. Know that **GOD** is strict in enforcing retribution, and that **GOD** is Forgiving, Most Merciful.

99. The sole duty of the messenger is to deliver the message, and **GOD** knows everything you declare and everything you conceal.

100. Proclaim: "The bad and the good are not the same, even if the abundance of the bad may impress you. You shall reverence **GOD**, (*even if you are in the minority*) O you who possess intelligence, that you may succeed."

101. O you who believe, do not ask about matters which, if revealed to you prematurely, would hurt you. If you ask about them in light of the Quran, they will become obvious to you. **GOD** has deliberately overlooked them. **GOD** is Forgiver, Clement.

102. Others before you have asked the same questions, then became disbelievers therein.

103. **GOD** did not prohibit livestock that begets certain combinations of males and females, nor livestock liberated by an oath, nor the one that begets two males in a row, nor the bull that fathers ten. It is the disbelievers who invented such lies about **GOD**. Most of them do not understand.

Do Not Follow Your Parents' Religion Blindly

104. When they are told, "Come to what **GOD** has revealed, and to the messenger," they say, "What we found our parents doing is sufficient for us." What if their parents knew nothing, and were not guided?

---

*5:97 The idol-worshiping Muslims have instituted two "Sacred Masjids" by consecrating the Prophet's tomb. The Quran talks only about one Sacred Masjid.

105. O you who believe, you should worry only about your own necks. If the others go astray, they cannot hurt you, as long as you are guided. To **GOD** is your ultimate destiny, all of you, then He will inform you of everything you had done.

Witnessing A Will

106. O you who believe, witnessing a will when one of you is dying shall be done by two equitable people among you. If you are traveling, then two others may do the witnessing. After observing the Contact Prayer (*Salat*), let the witnesses swear by **GOD**, to alleviate your doubts: "We will not use this to attain personal gains, even if the testator is related to us. Nor will we conceal **GOD**'s testimony. Otherwise, we would be sinners."

107. If the witnesses are found to be guilty of bias, then two others shall be asked to take their places. Choose two persons who were victimized by the first witnesses, and let them swear by **GOD:** "Our testimony is more truthful than theirs; we will not be biased. Otherwise, we will be transgressors."

108. This is more apt to encourage an honest testimony on their part, fearing that their oath may be disregarded like that of the previous witnesses. You shall observe **GOD** and listen. **GOD** does not guide the wicked.

The Dead Messengers
Totally Unaware

109. The day will come when **GOD** will summon the messengers and ask them, "How was the response to you?" They will say, "We have no knowledge. You are the Knower of all secrets."

110. **GOD** will say, "O Jesus, son of Mary, remember My blessings upon you and your mother. I supported you with the Holy Spirit, to enable you to speak to the people from the crib, as well as an adult. I taught you the scripture, wisdom, the Torah, and the Gospel. Recall that you created from clay the shape of a bird by My leave, then blew into it, and it became a live bird by My leave. You healed the blind and the leprous by My leave, and revived the dead by My leave. Recall that I protected you from the Children of Israel who wanted to hurt you, despite the profound miracles you had shown them. The disbelievers among them said, 'This is obviously magic.'

111. "Recall that I inspired the disciples: 'You shall believe in Me and My messenger.' They said, 'We have believed, and bear witness that we are submitters.' "

The Feast

112. Recall that the disciples said, "O Jesus, son of Mary, can your Lord send down to us a feast from the sky?" He said, "You should reverence **GOD**, if you are believers."

113. They said, "We wish to eat from it, and to reassure our hearts, and to know for sure that you have told us the truth. We will serve as witnesses thereof."

Greater Miracles Bring Greater Responsibility*

114. Said Jesus, the son of Mary, "Our god, our Lord, send down to us a feast from the sky. Let it bring plenty for each and every one of us, and a sign from You. Provide for us; You are the best Provider."

115. **GOD** said, "I am sending it down. Anyone among you who disbelieves after this, I will punish him as I never punished anyone else."*

On The Day Of Resurrection

116. **GOD** will say, "O Jesus, son of Mary,* did you say to the people, 'Make me and my mother idols beside **GOD**?'" He will say, "Be You glorified. I could not utter what was not right. Had I said it, You already would have known it. You know my thoughts, and I do not know Your thoughts. You know all the secrets.

117. "I told them only what You commanded me to say, that: 'You shall worship **GOD**, my Lord and your Lord.' I was a witness among them for as long as I lived with them. When You terminated my life on earth, You became the Watcher over them. You witness all things.

118. "If You punish them, they are Your constituents. If You forgive them, You are the Almighty, Most Wise."

119. **GOD** will proclaim, "This is a day when the truthful will be saved by their truthfulness." They have

deserved gardens with flowing streams. They abide therein forever. **GOD** is pleased with them, and they are pleased with Him. This is the greatest triumph.

120. To **GOD** belongs the sovereignty of the heavens and the earth, and everything in them, and He is Omnipotent.

◆◆◆◆

Sura 6: Livestock (Al-An'ām)

In the name of God,
Most Gracious, Most Merciful

1. Praise be to **GOD**, who created the heavens and the earth, and made the darkness and the light. Yet, those who disbelieve in their Lord continue to deviate.

2. He is the One who created you from mud, then predetermined your life span, a life span that is known only to Him. Yet, you continue to doubt.

3. He is the one **GOD** in the heavens and the earth. He knows your secrets and your declarations, and He knows everything you earn.

4. No matter what kind of proof comes to them from their Lord, they turn away from it, in aversion.

5. Since they rejected the truth when it came to them, they have incurred the consequences of their heedlessness.

5:114-115 The Quran's overwhelming miracle (Appendix One) is described in 74:35 as "One of the greatest miracles," and brings with it an uncommonly great responsibility.

5:116 It is noteworthy that the Quran consistently calls Jesus "son of Mary" and the Bible calls him "son of man." God knew that some will blaspheme and call him "son of God"!

6. Have they not seen how many generations before them we have annihilated? We established them on earth more than we did for you, and we showered them with blessings, generously, and we provided them with flowing streams. We then annihilated them because of their sins, and we substituted another generation in their place.

7. Even if we sent down to them a physical book, written on paper, and they touched it with their hands, those who disbelieved would have said, "This is no more than clever magic."

8. They also said, "If only an angel could come down with him!" Had we sent an angel, the whole matter would have been terminated, and they would no longer be respited.

Requirements of the Test

9. Had we sent an angel, we would have sent him in the form of a man, and we would have kept them just as confused as they are confused now.

10. Messengers before you have been ridiculed. It is those who mocked them who suffered the consequences of their ridiculing.

11. Say, "Roam the earth and note the consequences for the rejectors."

12. Say, "To whom belongs everything in the heavens and the earth?" Say, "To **GOD**." He has decreed that mercy is His attribute. He will surely summon you all on the Day of Resurrection, which is inevitable. The ones who lose their souls are those who disbelieve.

13. To Him belongs everything that dwells in the night and the day. He is the Hearer, the Knower.

14. Say, "Shall I accept other than **GOD** as a Lord and Master, when He is the Initiator of the heavens and the earth, and He feeds but is not fed?" Say, "I am commanded to be the most devoted submitter, and, 'Do not be an idol worshiper.' "

15. Say, "I fear, if I disobeyed my Lord, the retribution of an awesome day.

16. "Whoever is spared (*the retribution*), on that day, has attained His mercy. And this is the greatest triumph."

Only God Controls Happiness

17. If **GOD** touches you with adversity, none can relieve it except He. And if He touches you with a blessing, He is Omnipotent.

18. He is Supreme over His creatures. He is the Most Wise, the Cognizant.

Quran, the Whole Quran,
and Nothing But the Quran

19. Say, "Whose testimony is the greatest?" Say, "**GOD**'s. He is the witness between me and you that this Quran* has been inspired to me, to preach it to you and whomever it reaches. Indeed, you bear witness that there are other gods* beside **GOD**." Say, "I do not testify as you do; there is only one god, and I disown your idolatry."

20. Those to whom we have given the scripture recognize this as they recognize their own children. The ones who lose their souls are those who do not believe.

6:19 This verse proclaims the Quran as the only source of religious guidance. Those who uphold additional sources, such as Hadith & Sunna (lies attributed to the Prophet), are defined as idolaters.

21. Who is more evil than one who lies about **GOD**, or rejects His revelations? The transgressors never succeed.

Idol Worshipers Deny Their Idolatry

22. On the day when we summon them all, we will ask the idol worshipers, "Where are the idols you set up?"

23. Their disastrous response will be, "By **GOD** our Lord, we never were idol worshipers."*

24. Note how they lied to themselves, and how the idols they had invented have abandoned them.

25. Some of them listen to you, but we place veils on their hearts to prevent them from understanding, and deafness in their ears. Thus, no matter what kind of proof they see, they cannot believe. Thus, when they come to argue with you, the disbelievers say, "These are tales from the past."

26. They repel others from this (*Quran*), as they themselves stay away from it, and thus, they only destroy themselves without perceiving.

27. If only you could see them when they face the hellfire! They would say then, "Woe to us. Oh, we wish we could go back, and never reject our Lord's revelations, and join the believers."

28. As a matter of fact, (*they only say this because*) their secrets have been exposed. If they go back, they will commit exactly the same crimes.* They are liars.

29. They say (*subconsciously*), "We live only this life; we will not be resurrected."

30. If you could only see them when they stand before their Lord! He would say, "Is this not the truth?" They would say, "Yes, by our Lord." He would say, "You have incurred the retribution by your disbelief."

31. Losers indeed are those who disbelieve in meeting **GOD**, until the Hour comes to them suddenly, then say, "We deeply regret wasting our lives in this world." They will carry loads of their sins on their backs; what a miserable load!

Rearranging Our Priorities

32. The life of this world is no more than illusion and vanity, while the abode of the Hereafter is far better for the righteous. Do you not understand?!

33. We know that you may be saddened by what they say. You should know that it is not you that they reject; it is **GOD**'s revelations that the wicked disregard.

34. Messengers before you have been rejected, and they steadfastly persevered in the face of rejection. They were persecuted until our victory came to them. Such is **GOD**'s system that will never change. The history of My messengers thus sets the precedents for you.

6:23 Now and forever, the idol worshipers vehemently deny that they are idolaters.

6:28 This is because as soon as we enter into our worldly dimension, we become totally unaware of events in the dimension of souls, where God and His angels, and Heaven and Hell, can be seen. Thus, the guilty will not change their behavior, even after seeing that eternal dimension.

35. If their rejection gets to be too much for you, you should know that even if you dug a tunnel through the earth, or climbed a ladder into the sky, and produced a miracle for them (*they still would not believe*). Had **GOD** willed, He could have guided them, unanimously. Therefore, do not behave like the ignorant ones.

36. The only ones to respond are those who listen. **GOD** resurrects the dead; they ultimately return to Him.

37. They said, "If only a certain sign could come down to him from his Lord!" Say, "**GOD** is able to send down a sign, but most of them do not know."

Animals and Birds:
Submitting Creatures*

38. All the creatures on earth, and all the birds that fly with wings, are communities like you. We did not leave anything out of this book.** To their Lord, all these creatures will be summoned.

Overwhelming Miracle
of the Quran

39. Those who reject our proofs are deaf and dumb, in total darkness. Whomever **GOD** wills, He sends astray, and whomever He wills, He leads in a straight path.

40. Say, "What if **GOD**'s retribution came to you, or the Hour came to you: would you implore other than **GOD**, if you are truthful?"

41. The fact is: only Him you implore, and He answers your prayer, if He so wills, and you forget your idols.

42. We have sent (*messengers*) to communities before you, and we put them to the test through adversity and hardship, that they may implore.

43. If only they implored when our test afflicted them! Instead, their hearts were hardened, and the devil adorned their works in their eyes.

The System*

44. When they thus disregard the message given to them, we open for them the gates of everything. Then, just as they rejoice in what was given to them, we punish them suddenly; they become utterly stunned.

45. The wicked are thus annihilated. Praise be to **GOD**, Lord of the universe.

God Alone
Worthy of Worship

46. Say, "What if **GOD** took away your hearing and your eyesight, and sealed your minds; which god, other than **GOD**, can restore these for you?" Note how we explain the revelations, and note how they still deviate!

---

*6:38 Animals were among the creatures who took advantage of God's offer to repent after committing the original sin (see the Introduction).

**6:38 All information relevant to our eternal life of the Hereafter is contained in the Quran. The true believers accept, without hesitation, God's assertion: "We did not leave anything out of this book." The importance of this statement, and similar statements, is reflected in the fact that each of them consists of 19 Arabic letters (Appendix 19).

*6:44 Before the guilty are thrown out the window, they are taken up to a high floor.

47. Say, "What if **GOD**'s retribution came to you suddenly, or after an announcement, is it not the wicked who incur annihilation?"

Role of the Messengers

48. We do not send the messengers except as deliverers of good news, as well as warners. Those who believe and reform have nothing to fear, nor will they grieve.

49. As for those who reject our revelations, they incur the retribution for their wickedness.

50. Say, "I do not say to you that I possess the treasures of **GOD**. Nor do I know the future. Nor do I say to you that I am an angel. I simply follow what is revealed to me." Say, "Is the blind the same as the seer? Do you not reflect?"

51. And preach with this (*Quran*) to those who reverence the summoning before their Lord—they have none beside Him as a Lord and Master, nor an intercessor—that they may attain salvation.

52. And do not dismiss those who implore their Lord day and night, devoting themselves to Him alone. You are not responsible for their reckoning, nor are they responsible for your reckoning. If you dismiss them, you will be a transgressor.

53. We thus test the people by each other, to let them say (*mockingly*), "Are these the people among us who are blessed by **GOD**?" Is **GOD** not aware of the appreciative ones?

54. When those who believe in our revelations come to you, you shall say, "*Salāmun 'Alaykum* (Peace be upon you). Your Lord has decreed that mercy is His attribute. Thus, anyone among you who commits a transgression out of ignorance, and repents thereafter and reforms, then He is Forgiving, Most Merciful."

55. We thus explain the revelations, and point out the ways of the wicked.

56. Say, "I am forbidden from worshiping what you worship besides **GOD**." Say, "I will not follow your opinions. Otherwise, I will go astray, and not be guided."

57. Say, "I have solid proof from my Lord, and you have rejected it. I do not control the retribution you challenge me to bring. Judgment belongs with **GOD** alone. He narrates the truth, and He is the best judge."

58. Say, "If I controlled the retribution you challenge me to bring, the whole matter would have been terminated long ago. **GOD** knows best who the wicked are."

Almighty God

59. With Him are the keys to all secrets; none knows them except He. He knows everything on land and in the sea. Not a leaf falls without His knowledge. Nor is there a grain in the depths of the soil. Nor is there anything wet or dry, that is not recorded in a profound record.

Death and Resurrection:
Every Day*

60. He is the One who puts you to death during the night, and knows even the smallest of your actions during the day. He resurrects you every morning, until your life span is fulfilled, then to Him is your ultimate return. He will then inform you of everything you had done.

61. He is Supreme over His creatures, and He appoints guards to protect you. When the appointed time of death comes to any of you, our messengers put him to death without delay.

62. Then everyone is returned to **GOD**, their rightful Lord and Master. Absolutely, He is the ultimate judge; He is the most accurate reckoner.

63. Say, "Who can save you from the darkness of the land or the sea?" You implore Him loudly and secretly: "If He saves us this time, we will be eternally appreciative."

64. Say, "**GOD** does save you this time, and other times as well, then you still set up idols besides Him."

65. Say, "He is certainly able to pour upon you retribution from above you, or from beneath your feet. Or He can divide you into factions and have you taste each others' tyranny. Note how we explain the revelations, that they may understand."

66. Your people have rejected this, even though it is the truth. Say, "I am not a guardian over you."

67. Every prophecy herein will come to pass, and you will surely find out.

Respect for the Word of God

68. If you see those who mock our revelations, you shall avoid them until they delve into another subject. If the devil causes you to forget, then, as soon as you remember, do not sit with such evil people.

69. The righteous are not responsible for the utterances of those people, but it may help to remind them; perhaps they may be saved.

70. You shall disregard those who take their religion in vain, as if it is a social function, and are totally absorbed in this worldly life. Remind with this (*Quran*), lest a soul may suffer the consequences of its evil earnings. It has none beside **GOD** as a Lord and Master, nor an intercessor. If it could offer any kind of ransom, it would not be accepted. They suffer the consequences of the evil works they earn; they have incurred hellish drinks, and a painful retribution because of their disbelief.

71. Say, "Shall we implore, beside **GOD**, what possesses no power to benefit us or hurt us, and turn back on our heels after **GOD** has guided us? In that case, we would join those possessed by the devils, and rendered utterly confused, while their friends try to save them: 'Stay with us on the right path.' " Say, "**GOD**'s guidance is the right guidance. We are commanded to submit to the Lord of the universe.

---

*6:60 The righteous do not really die; they go straight to the same Paradise where Adam and Eve once lived. The unrighteous die and experience a nightmare that lasts until the Day of Resurrection (see 2:154, 3:169, 8:24, 16:32, 22:58, 36:26-27, 40:46, 44:56, and Appendix 17).

72. "And to observe the Contact Prayers (*Salat*), and to reverence Him—He is the One before whom you will be summoned (*for the reckoning*)."

73. He is the One who created the heavens and the earth, truthfully. Whenever He says, "Be," it is. His word is the absolute truth. All sovereignty belongs to Him the day the horn is blown. Knower of all secrets and declarations, He is the Most Wise, the Cognizant.

Abraham Debates
With Idol Worshipers

74. Recall that Abraham said to his father Āzer, "How could you worship statues as gods? I see that you and your people have gone far astray."

75. We showed Abraham the marvels of the heavens and the earth, and blessed him with certainty:

76. When the night fell, he saw a shining planet. "Maybe this is my Lord," he said. When it disappeared, he said, "I do not like (*gods*) that disappear."

77. When he saw the moon rising, he said, "Maybe this is my Lord!" When it disappeared, he said, "Unless my Lord guides me, I will be with the strayers."

78. When he saw the sun rising, he said, "This must be my Lord. This is the biggest." But when it set, he said, "O my people, I denounce your idolatry.

79. "I have devoted myself absolutely to the One who initiated the heavens and the earth; I will never be an idol worshiper."

80. His people argued with him. He said, "Do you argue with me about **GOD**, after He has guided me? I have no fear of the idols you set up. Nothing can happen to me, unless my Lord wills it. My Lord's knowledge encompasses all things. Would you not take heed?

81. "Why should I fear your idols? It is you who should be afraid, since you worship instead of **GOD** idols that are utterly powerless to help you. Which side is more deserving of security, if you know?"

Perfect Security
for Believers

82. Those who believe, and do not pollute their belief with idol worship, have deserved the perfect security, and they are truly guided.

83. Such was our argument, with which we supported Abraham against his people. We exalt whomever we will to higher ranks. Your Lord is Most Wise, Omniscient.

84. And we granted him Isaac and Jacob, and we guided both of them. Similarly, we guided Noah before that, and from his descendants (*we guided*) David, Solomon, Job, Joseph, Moses, and Aaron. We thus reward the righteous.

85. Also, Zachariah, John, Jesus, and Elias; all were righteous.

86. And Ismail, Elisha, Jonah, and Lot; each of these we distinguished over all the people.

87. From among their ancestors, their descendants, and their siblings, we chose many, and we guided them in a straight path.

88. Such is **GOD**'s guidance, with which He guides whomever He chooses from among His servants. Had any of them fallen into idolatry, their works would have been nullified.

89. Those were the ones to whom we have given the scripture, wisdom, and prophethood. If these people disbelieve, we will substitute others in their place, and the new people will not be disbelievers.

90. These are the ones guided by **GOD**; you shall be guided in their footsteps. Say, "I do not ask you for any wage. This is but a message for all the people."

God's Messages to the World

91. They never valued **GOD** as He should be valued. Thus, they said, "**GOD** does not reveal anything to any human being." Say, "Who then revealed the scripture that Moses brought, with light and guidance for the people?" You put it down on paper to proclaim it, while concealing a lot of it. You were taught what you never knew—you and your parents. Say, "**GOD** (*is the One who revealed it*)" then leave them in their heedlessness, playing.

92. This too is a blessed scripture that we have revealed, confirming the previous scriptures, that you may warn the most important community* and all those around it. Those who believe in the Hereafter will believe in this (*scripture*), and will observe the Contact Prayers (*Salat*).

False Messengers Condemned

93. Who is more evil than one who fabricates lies and attributes them to **GOD**, or says, "I have received divine inspiration," when no such inspiration was given to him, or says, "I can write the same as **GOD**'s revelations"? If only you could see the transgressors at the time of death! The angels extend their hands to them, saying, "Let go of your souls. Today, you have incurred a shameful retribution for saying about **GOD** other than the truth, and for being too arrogant to accept His revelations.

94. "You have come back to us as individuals, just as we created you the first time, and you have left behind what we provided for you. We do not see with you the intercessors that you idolized and claimed that they will help you. All ties among you have been severed; the idols you set up have abandoned you."

Greatness of God

95. **GOD** is the One who causes the grains and the seeds to crack and germinate. He produces the living from the dead, and the dead from the living. Such is **GOD**; how could you deviate!

96. At the crack of dawn, He causes the morning to emerge. He made the night still, and He rendered the sun and the moon to serve as calculation devices. Such is the design of the Almighty, the Omniscient.

---

*6:92 Today's "most important community" is America, where God's message is being restored. When the Quran was revealed, Mecca was the most important community.

---

97. And He is the One who made the stars to guide you during the darkness, on land and on sea. We thus clarify the revelations for people who know.

98. He initiated you from one person, and decided your path, as well as your final destiny. We thus clarify the revelations for people who understand.

99. He is the One who sends down from the sky water, whereby we produce all kinds of plants. We produce from the green material multitudes of complex grains, palm trees with hanging clusters, and gardens of grapes, olives and pomegranate; fruits that are similar, yet dissimilar. Note their fruits as they grow and ripen. These are signs for people who believe.

100. Yet, they set up besides **GOD** idols from among the jinns, though He is the One who created them. They even attribute to Him sons and daughters, without any knowledge. Be He glorified. He is the Most High, far above their claims.

101. The Initiator of the heavens and the earth. How can He have a son, when He never had a mate? He created all things, and He is fully aware of all things.

God

102. Such is **GOD** your Lord, there is no god except He, the Creator of all things. You shall worship Him alone. He is in control of all things.

103. No visions can encompass Him, but He encompasses all visions. He is the Compassionate, the Cognizant.

104. Enlightenments have come to you from your Lord. As for those who can see, they do so for their own good, and those who turn blind, do so to their own detriment. I am not your guardian.

105. We thus explain the revelations, to prove that you have received knowledge, and to clarify them for people who know.

106. Follow what is revealed to you from your Lord, there is no god except He, and disregard the idol worshipers.

107. Had **GOD** willed, they would not have worshiped idols. We did not appoint you as their guardian, nor are you their advocate.

108. Do not curse the idols they set up beside **GOD**, lest they blaspheme and curse **GOD**, out of ignorance. We have adorned the works of every group in their eyes. Ultimately, they return to their Lord, then He informs them of everything they had done.

109. They swore by **GOD**, solemnly, that if a miracle came to them, they would surely believe. Say, "Miracles come only from **GOD**." For all you know, if a miracle did come to them, they would continue to disbelieve.

110. We control their minds and their hearts. Thus, since their decision is to disbelieve, we leave them in their transgressions, blundering.

*A Consequence of
Their Own Decision*

111. Even if we sent down the angels to them; even if the dead spoke to them; even if we summoned every miracle before them; they cannot believe unless **GOD** wills it. Indeed, most of them are ignorant.

*Hadith & Sunna: Fabrications by
the Prophet's Enemies*

112. We have permitted the enemies of every prophet—human and jinn devils—to inspire in each other fancy words, in order to deceive. Had your Lord willed, they would not have done it. You shall disregard them and their fabrications.

Important Criterion

113. This is to let the minds of those who do not believe in the Hereafter listen to such fabrications, and accept them, and thus expose their real convictions.*

Quran: Fully Detailed

114. Shall I seek other than **GOD** as a source of law, when He has revealed to you this book fully detailed?* Those who received the scripture recognize that it has been revealed from your Lord, truthfully. You shall not harbor any doubt.

115. The word of your Lord is complete,* in truth and justice. Nothing shall abrogate His words. He is the Hearer, the Omniscient.

116. If you obey the majority of people on earth, they will divert you from the path of **GOD**. They follow only conjecture; they only guess.

117. Your Lord is fully aware of those who stray off His path, and He is fully aware of those who are guided.

118. You shall eat from that upon which **GOD**'s name has been pronounced, if you truly believe in His revelations.

*Chance to Remember God:
Mention God's Name
Before You Eat*

119. Why should you not eat from that upon which **GOD**'s name has been mentioned? He has detailed for you what is prohibited for you, unless you are forced. Indeed, many people mislead others with their personal opinions, without knowledge. Your Lord is fully aware of the transgressors.

120. You shall avoid obvious sins, as well as the hidden ones. Those who have earned sins will surely pay for their transgressions.

121. Do not eat from that upon which the name of **GOD** has not been mentioned, for it is an abomination. The devils inspire their allies to argue with you; if you obey them, you will be idol worshipers.*

122. Is one who was dead and we granted him life, and provided him with light that enables him to move among the people, equal to one in total darkness from which he can never exit? The works of the disbelievers are thus adorned in their eyes.

6:113 The Quran provides criteria that tell us whether we truly believe in the Hereafter or merely give it lip service. These important criteria are stated here, and in 17:45-46 and 39:45.

6:113-115 Upholding any source beside the Quran reflects disbelief in the Quran (Appendix 18).

6:121 Dietary prohibitions instituted by other than God represent idolatry.

123. We allow the leading criminals of every community to plot and scheme. But they only plot and scheme against their own souls, without perceiving.

Questioning God's Wisdom*

124. When a powerful proof comes to them, they say, "We will not believe, unless we are given what is given to **GOD**'s messengers!" **GOD** knows exactly who is best qualified to deliver His message.* Such criminals will suffer debasement at **GOD**, and terrible retribution as a consequence of their evil scheming.

Quranic Knowledge Far Ahead of Human Progress*

125. Whomever **GOD** wills to guide, He renders his chest wide open to Submission. And whomever He wills to send astray, He renders his chest intolerant and straitened, like one who climbs towards the sky.* **GOD** thus places a curse upon those who refuse to believe.

126. This is the straight path to your Lord. We have explained the revelations for people who take heed.

127. They have deserved the abode of peace at their Lord; He is their Lord and Master, as a reward for their works.

128. The day will come when He summons all of them (*and says*): "O you jinns, you have claimed multitudes of humans." Their human companions will say, "Our Lord, we enjoyed each others' company until we wasted the life span You had set for us." He will say, "Hell is your destiny." They abide therein forever, in accordance with **GOD**'s will. Your Lord is Wise, Omniscient.

129. We thus match the wicked to be companions of each other, as a punishment for their transgressions.

130. O you jinns and humans, did you not receive messengers from among you, who narrated to you My revelations, and warned you about the meeting of this day? They will say, "We bear witness against ourselves." They were totally preoccupied with the worldly life, and they will bear witness against themselves that they were disbelievers.

131. This is to show that your Lord never annihilates any community unjustly, while its people are unaware.

132. Everyone will attain a rank commensurate with their deeds. Your Lord is never unaware of anything they do.

133. Your Lord is the Rich One; possessor of all mercy. If He wills, He can remove you, and substitute whomever He wills in your place, just as He produced you from the progeny of other people.

134. What is promised to you will come to pass, and you can never evade it.

*6:124 Jealousy and ego are human traits that provoke some people to question God's wisdom in selecting His messengers. Corrupted Muslim scholars have uttered this same utterance regarding the revelation of the Quran's mathematical code through God's Messenger of the Covenant.

*6:125 Centuries after the revelation of the Quran, we learned that the proportion of oxygen diminishes as we climb towards the sky, and we gasp for air.

135. Say, "O my people, do your best, and so will I. You will surely find out who the ultimate victors are." Certainly, the wicked will never succeed.

Abusing God's Provisions

136. They even set aside a share of **GOD**'s provisions of crops and livestock, saying, "This share belongs to **GOD**," according to their claims, "and this share belongs to our idols." However, what was set aside for their idols never reached **GOD**, while the share they set aside for **GOD** invariably went to their idols. Miserable indeed is their judgment.

137. Thus were the idol worshipers duped by their idols, to the extent of killing their own children.* In fact, their idols inflict great pain upon them, and confuse their religion for them. Had **GOD** willed, they would not have done it. You shall disregard them and their fabrications.

Religious Innovations Condemned

138. They said, "These are livestock and crops that are prohibited; no one shall eat them except whomever we permit," so they claimed. They also prohibited the riding of certain livestock. Even the livestock they ate, they never pronounced **GOD**'s name as they sacrificed them. Such are innovations attributed to Him.

He will surely requite them for their innovations.

139. They also said, "What is in the bellies of these livestock is reserved exclusively for the males among us, and prohibited for our wives." But if it was a stillbirth, they permitted their wives to share therein. He will certainly requite them for their innovations. He is Most Wise, Omniscient.

140. Losers indeed are those who killed their children foolishly, due to their lack of knowledge, and prohibited what **GOD** has provided for them, and followed innovations attributed to **GOD**. They have gone astray; they are not guided.

*Zakat Must Be Given "On The Day Of Harvest"**

141. He is the One who established gardens, trellised and untrellised, and palm trees, and crops with different tastes, and olives, and pomegranate—fruits that are similar, yet dissimilar. Eat from their fruits, and give the due alms on the day of harvest,* and do not waste anything. He does not love the wasters.

142. Some livestock supply you with transportation, as well as bedding materials. Eat from **GOD**'s provisions to you, and do not follow the steps of Satan; he is your most ardent enemy.

6:137 A perfect example is the internationally infamous incident of the execution of a Saudi Arabian princess in 1978 for alleged adultery. God's law institutes whipping, not execution, as a punishment for adultery (24:1-2), while the idolatrous laws stipulate execution. As pointed out in 42:21, the traditionalists follow a religion that is not authorized by God.

6:141 Zakat charity is so important, the Most Merciful has restricted His mercy to those who give it (7:156). Yet, the corrupted Muslims have lost this most important commandment; they give Zakat only once a year. We see here that Zakat must be given away "on the day we receive income." The proportion that came to us through Abraham is 2.5% of our net income.

*Innovated Dietary Prohibitions
Condemned*

143. Eight kinds of livestock: regarding the two kinds of sheep, and the two kinds of goats, say, "Is it the two males that He prohibited, or the two females, or the contents of the wombs of the two females? Tell me what you know, if you are truthful."

144. Regarding the two kinds of camels, and the two kinds of cattle, say, "Is it the two males that He prohibited, or the two females, or the contents of the wombs of the two females? Were you witnesses when **GOD** decreed such prohibitions for you? Who is more evil than those who invent such lies and attribute them to **GOD**? They thus mislead the people without knowledge. **GOD** does not guide such evil people."

*The Only Dietary Prohibitions**

145. Say, "I do not find in the revelations given to me any food that is prohibited for any eater except: *(1)* carrion, *(2)* running blood, *(3)* the meat* of pigs, for it is contaminated, and *(4)* the meat of animals blasphemously dedicated to other than **GOD**." If one is forced (*to eat these*), without being deliberate or malicious, then your Lord is Forgiver, Most Merciful.

146. For those who are Jewish we prohibited animals with undivided hoofs; and of the cattle and sheep we prohibited the fat, except that which is carried on their backs, or in the viscera, or mixed with bones. That was a retribution for their transgressions, and we are truthful.

147. If they disbelieve you, then say, "Your Lord possesses infinite mercy, but His retribution is unavoidable for the guilty people."

148. The idol worshipers say, "Had **GOD** willed, we would not practice idolatry, nor would our parents, nor would we prohibit anything." Thus did those before them disbelieve, until they incurred our retribution. Say, "Do you have any proven knowledge that you can show us? You follow nothing but conjecture; you only guess."

*The Most Powerful
Argument**

149. Say, "**GOD** possesses the most powerful argument; if He wills He can guide all of you."

150. Say, "Bring your witnesses who would testify that **GOD** has prohibited this or that." If they testify, do not testify with them. Nor shall you follow the opinions of those who reject our revelations, and those who disbelieve in the Hereafter, and those who stray away from their Lord.

---

*6:145-146 Only four kinds of animal products are prohibited: animals that die of themselves, running blood (not trapped within the meat), the meat of pigs, and animals dedicated to other than their Creator. Verse 146 informs us that such prohibitions are very specific; God prohibits either "the meat" or "the fat," or both, if He so wills.

*6:149 The Quran's mathematical code is a tangible and utterly incontrovertible proof that this is God's message to the world. It takes divine intervention to prevent any reader from appreciating this extraordinary phenomenon, then falling prostrate, and accepting this overwhelming miracle (see 17:45-46, 18:57, 56:79, and Appendix One).

The Major Commandments

151. Say, "Come let me tell you what your Lord has really prohibited for you: You shall not set up idols besides Him. You shall honor your parents. You shall not kill your children from fear of poverty—we provide for you and for them. You shall not commit gross sins, obvious or hidden. You shall not kill—**GOD** has made life sacred—except in the course of justice. These are His commandments to you, that you may understand."

Additional Commandments

152. You shall not touch the orphans' money except in the most righteous manner, until they reach maturity. You shall give full weight and full measure when you trade, equitably. We do not burden any soul beyond its means. You shall be absolutely just when you bear witness, even against your relatives. You shall fulfill your covenant with **GOD**. These are His commandments to you, that you may take heed.

153. This is My path—a straight one. You shall follow it, and do not follow any other paths, lest they divert you from His path. These are His commandments to you, that you may be saved.

154. And we gave Moses the scripture, complete with the best commandments, and detailing everything, and a beacon and mercy, that they may believe in meeting their Lord.

155. This too is a blessed scripture that we have revealed; you shall follow it and lead a righteous life, that you may attain mercy.

156. Now you can no longer say, "The scripture was sent down to two groups before us, and we were unaware of their teachings."

Mathematics: The Ultimate Proof*

157. Nor can you say, "If only a scripture could come down to us, we would be better guided than they." A proven scripture has now come to you from your Lord, and a beacon, and a mercy. Now, who is more evil than one who rejects these proofs from **GOD**, and disregards them? We will commit those who disregard our proofs to the worst retribution for their heedlessness.

Requirements of the Test

158. Are they waiting for the angels to come to them, or your Lord, or some physical manifestations of your Lord? The day this happens, no soul will benefit from believing if it did not believe before that, and did not reap the benefits of belief by leading a righteous life.* Say, "Keep on waiting; we too are waiting."

Religious Sects Condemned

159. Those who divide themselves into sects do not belong with you. Their judgment rests with **GOD**, then He will inform them of everything they had done.

6:157 The role of the Quran's mathematical code is evident from the fact that the sum of the verse number (157) plus the gematrical value of "Rashad Khalifa" (1230), through whom the code was revealed, gives 1387, or 19x73.

6:158 After believing, the soul must grow and develop through the worship practices prescribed by God.

---

160. Whoever does a righteous work receives the reward for ten, and the one who commits a sin is requited for only one. No one suffers the slightest injustice.

161. Say, "My Lord has guided me in a straight path—the perfect religion of Abraham, monotheism. He never was an idol worshiper."

162. Say, "My Contact Prayers (*Salat*), my worship practices, my life and my death, are all devoted absolutely to **GOD** alone, the Lord of the universe.

163. "He has no partner. This is what I am commanded to believe, and I am the first to submit."

164. Say, "Shall I seek other than **GOD** as a lord, when He is the Lord of all things? No soul benefits except from its own works, and none bears the burden of another. Ultimately, you return to your Lord, then He informs you regarding all your disputes."

165. He is the One who made you inheritors of the earth, and He raised some of you above others in rank, in order to test you in accordance with what He has given you. Surely, your Lord is efficient in enforcing retribution, and He is Forgiver, Most Merciful.

◆◆◆◆

Sura 7: The Purgatory (Al-A'arāf)

In the name of God,
Most Gracious, Most Merciful

1. A.L.M.S.*

2. This scripture has been revealed to you—you shall not harbor doubt about it in your heart—that you may warn with it, and to provide a reminder for the believers.

3. You shall all follow what is revealed to you from your Lord; do not follow any idols besides Him. Rarely do you take heed.

4. Many a community we annihilated; they incurred our retribution while they were asleep, or wide awake.

5. Their utterance when our retribution came to them was: "Indeed, we have been transgressors."

6. We will certainly question those who received the message, and we will question the messengers.

7. We will inform them authoritatively, for we were never absent.

8. The scales will be set on that day, equitably. Those whose weights are heavy will be the winners.

9. As for those whose weights are light, they will be the ones who lost their souls,* as a consequence of disregarding our revelations, unjustly.

---

*7:1 See Appendix 1 for the role of these initials in the Quran's mathematical miracle.

*7:9 Failing to heed our Creator leads to spiritual starvation and eventual "loss" of the soul.

10. We have established you on earth, and we have provided for you the means of support therein. Rarely are you appreciative.

11. We created you, then we shaped you, then we said to the angels, "Fall prostrate before Adam." They fell prostrate, except Iblees (*Satan*); he was not with the prostrators.

The Test Begins

12. He said, "What prevented you from prostrating when I ordered you?" He said, "I am better than he; You created me from fire, and created him from mud."

13. He said, "Therefore, you must go down, for you are not to be arrogant here. Get out; you are debased."

14. He said, "Grant me a respite, until the Day of Resurrection."

15. He said, "You are granted a respite."

16. He said, "Since You have willed that I go astray,* I will skulk for them on Your straight path.

17. "I will come to them from before them, and from behind them, and from their right, and from their left, and You will find that most of them are unappreciative."

18. He said, "Get out therefrom, despised and defeated. Those among them who follow you, I will fill Hell with you all.

19. "As for you, Adam, dwell with your wife in Paradise, and eat therefrom as you please, but do not approach this one tree, lest you fall in sin."

20. The devil whispered to them, in order to reveal their bodies, which were invisible to them. He said, "Your Lord did not forbid you from this tree, except to prevent you from becoming angels, and from attaining eternal existence."

21. He swore to them, "I am giving you good advice."

22. He thus duped them with lies. As soon as they tasted the tree, their bodies became visible to them, and they tried to cover themselves with the leaves of Paradise. Their Lord called upon them: "Did I not enjoin you from that tree, and warn you that the devil is your most ardent enemy?"

23. They said, "Our Lord, we have wronged our souls, and unless You forgive us and have mercy on us, we will be losers."

24. He said, "Go down as enemies of one another. On earth shall be your habitation and provision for a-while."

25. He said, "On it you will live, on it you will die, and from it you will be brought out."

26. O children of Adam, we have provided you with garments to cover your bodies, as well as for luxury. But the best garment is the garment of righteousness. These are some of **GOD**'s signs, that they may take heed.

---

*7:16 Satan is a proven liar, and so are his constituents (see 2:36, 6:22-23, & 7:20-22).

---

27. O children of Adam, do not let the devil dupe you as he did when he caused the eviction of your parents from Paradise, and the removal of their garments to expose their bodies. He and his tribe see you, while you do not see them. We appoint the devils as companions of those who do not believe.

Examine All Inherited Information

28. They commit a gross sin, then say, "We found our parents doing this, and **GOD** has commanded us to do it." Say, "**GOD** never advocates sin. Are you saying about **GOD** what you do not know?"

29. Say, "My Lord advocates justice, and to stand devoted to Him alone at every place of worship. You shall devote your worship absolutely to Him alone. Just as He initiated you, you will ultimately go back to Him."

Beware: They Believe that They Are Guided

30. Some He guided, while others are committed to straying. They have taken the devils as their masters, instead of **GOD**, yet they believe that they are guided.

Dress Nicely For The Masjid

31. O children of Adam, you shall be clean and dress nicely when you go to the masjid. And eat and drink moderately; Surely, He does not love the gluttons.

Innovated Prohibitions Condemned

32. Say, "Who prohibited the nice things **GOD** has created for His creatures, and the good provi-sions?" Say, "Such provisions are to be enjoyed in this life by those who believe. Moreover, the good provisions will be exclusively theirs on the Day of Resurrection." We thus explain the revelations for people who know.

33. Say, "My Lord prohibits only evil deeds, be they obvious or hidden, and sins, and unjustifiable aggression, and to set up beside **GOD** powerless idols, and to say about **GOD** what you do not know."

34. For each community, there is a predetermined life span. Once their interim comes to an end, they cannot delay it by one hour, nor advance it.

Messengers From Among You

35. O children of Adam, when messengers come to you from among you, and recite My revelations to you, those who take heed and lead a righteous life, will have nothing to fear, nor will they grieve.

36. As for those who reject our revelations, and are too arrogant to uphold them, they have incurred Hell, wherein they abide forever.

37. Who is more evil than those who invent lies about **GOD**, or reject His revelations? These will get their share, in accordance with the scripture, then, when our messengers come to terminate their lives, they will say, "Where are the idols you used to implore beside **GOD**?" They will say, "They have abandoned us." They will bear witness against themselves that they were disbelievers.

Mutual Blaming

38. He will say, "Enter with the previous communities of jinns and humans into Hell." Every time a group enters, they will curse their ancestral group. Once they are all in it, the latest one will say of the previous one, "Our Lord, these are the ones who misled us. Give them double the retribution of Hell." He will say, "Each receives double, but you do not know."

39. The ancestral group will say to the later group, "Since you had an advantage over us, taste the retribution for your own sins."

*Rejecting God's Revelations:
An Unforgivable Offense*

40. Surely, those who reject our revelations and are too arrogant to uphold them, the gates of the sky will never open for them, nor will they enter Paradise until the camel passes through the needle's eye. We thus requite the guilty.

41. They have incurred Hell as an abode; they will have barriers above them. We thus requite the transgressors.

42. As for those who believe and lead a righteous life—we never burden any soul beyond its means—these will be the dwellers of Paradise. They abide in it forever.

By God's Grace

43. We will remove all jealousy from their hearts. Rivers will flow beneath them, and they will say, "**GOD** be praised for guiding us. We could not possibly be guided, if it were not that **GOD** has guided us. The messengers of our Lord did bring the truth." They will be called: "This is your Paradise. You have inherited it, in return for your works."

44. The dwellers of Paradise will call the dwellers of Hell: "We have found our Lord's promise to be the truth, have you found your Lord's promise to be the truth?" They will say, "Yes." An announcer between them will announce: "**GOD**'s condemnation has befallen the transgressors;

45. "who repel from the path of **GOD**, and strive to make it crooked, and, with regard to the Hereafter, they are disbelievers."

46. A barrier separates them, while the Purgatory* is occupied by people who recognize each side by their looks. They will call the dwellers of Paradise: "Peace be upon you." They did not enter (*Paradise*) through wishful thinking.

47. When they turn their eyes towards the dwellers of Hell, they will say, "Our Lord, do not put us with these wicked people."

The Majority Doomed

48. The dwellers of the Purgatory will call on people they recognize by their looks, saying, "Your great numbers did not avail you in any way, nor did your arrogance.

49. "Are those the people you swore that **GOD** will never touch them with mercy?" (*The people in the Purgatory will then be told,*) "Enter Paradise; you have nothing to fear, nor will you grieve."

---

*7:46-49 Initially, there will be 4 places: (1) the High Heaven, (2) the Lower Heaven, (3) the Purgatory, and (4) Hell. The Purgatory will be annexed into the Lower Heaven.

---

50. The dwellers of Hell will call on the dwellers of Paradise: "Let some of your water, or some of **GOD**'s provisions to you flow towards us." They will say, "**GOD** has forbidden them for the disbelievers."

51. Those who do not take their religion seriously, and are totally preoccupied with this worldly life, we forget them on that day, because they forgot that day, and because they spurned our revelations.

Quran:
Fully Detailed

52. We have given them a scripture that is fully detailed, with knowledge, guidance, and mercy for the people who believe.

53. Are they waiting until all (*prophecies*) are fulfilled? The day such fulfillment comes to pass, those who disregarded it in the past will say, "The messengers of our Lord have brought the truth. Are there any intercessors to intercede on our behalf? Would you send us back, so that we change our behavior, and do better works than what we did?" They have lost their souls, and their own innovations have caused their doom.

54. Your Lord is the one **GOD**; who created the heavens and the earth in six days,* then assumed all authority. The night overtakes the day, as it pursues it persistently, and the sun, the moon, and the stars are committed to serve by His command. Absolutely, He controls all creation and all commands. Most

Exalted is **GOD**, Lord of the universe.

55. You shall worship your Lord publicly and privately; He does not love the transgressors.

56. Do not corrupt the earth after it has been set straight, and worship Him out of reverence, and out of hope. Surely, **GOD**'s mercy is attainable by the righteous.

57. He is the One who sends the wind with good omen, as a mercy from His hands. Once they gather heavy clouds, we drive them to dead lands, and send down water therefrom, to produce with it all kinds of fruits. We thus resurrect the dead, that you may take heed.

58. The good land readily produces its plants by the leave of its Lord, while the bad land barely produces anything useful. We thus explain the revelations for people who are appreciative.

Noah

59. We sent Noah to his people, saying, "O my people, worship **GOD**; you have no other god beside Him. I fear for you the retribution of an awesome day."

60. The leaders among his people said, "We see that you are far astray."

61. He said, "O my people, I am not astray; I am a messenger from the Lord of the universe.

62. "I deliver to you the messages of my Lord, and I advise you, and I know from **GOD** what you do not know.

7:54 The six days of creation are allegorical; they serve as a yardstick to let us know the relative complexity of our infinitesimal planet Earth—it was created in "4 days" (see 41:10).

63. "Is it too much of a wonder that a reminder should come to you from your Lord, through a man like you, to warn you, and to lead you to righteousness, that you may attain mercy?"

64. They rejected him. Consequently, we saved him and those with him in the ark, and we drowned those who rejected our revelations; they were blind.

Hûd

65. To 'Ãd we sent their brother Hûd. He said, "O my people, worship **GOD**; you have no other god beside Him. Would you then observe righteousness?"

66. The leaders who disbelieved among his people said, "We see that you are behaving foolishly, and we think that you are a liar."

67. He said, "O my people, there is no foolishness in me; I am a messenger from the Lord of the universe.

68. "I deliver to you my Lord's messages, and I am honestly advising you.

69. "Is it too much of a wonder that a message should come to you from your Lord, through a man like you, to warn you? Recall that He made you inheritors after the people of Noah, and multiplied your number. Remember **GOD**'s blessings, that you may succeed."

Following the Parents Blindly:
A Human Tragedy

70. They said, "Did you come to make us worship **GOD** alone, and abandon what our parents used to wor-

ship? We challenge you to bring the doom you threaten us with, if you are truthful."

71. He said, "You have incurred condemnation and wrath from your Lord. Do you argue with me in defense of innovations you have fabricated—you and your parents—which were never authorized by **GOD**? Therefore, wait and I will wait along with you."

72. We then saved him and those with him, by mercy from us, and we annihilated those who rejected our revelations and refused to be believers.

Sãleh

73. To Thamûd we sent their brother Sãleh. He said, "O my people, worship **GOD**; you have no other god beside Him. Proof has been provided for you from your Lord: here is **GOD**'s camel, to serve as a sign for you. Let her eat from **GOD**'s land, and do not touch her with any harm, lest you incur a painful retribution.

74. "Recall that He made you inheritors after 'Ãd, and established you on earth, building mansions in its valleys, and carving homes from its mountains. You shall remember **GOD**'s blessings, and do not roam the earth corruptingly."

The Message:
Proof of Messengership

75. The arrogant leaders among his people said to the common people who believed, "How do you know that Sãleh is sent by his Lord?" They said, "The message he brought has made us believers."

76. The arrogant ones said, "We disbelieve in what you believe in."

77. Subsequently, they slaughtered the camel, rebelled against their Lord's command, and said, "O Sāleh, bring the doom you threaten us with, if you are really a messenger."

78. Consequently, the quake annihilated them, leaving them dead in their homes.

79. He turned away from them, saying, "O my people, I have delivered my Lord's message to you, and advised you, but you do not like any advisers."

Lot:
Homosexuality Condemned

80. Lot said to his people, "You commit such an abomination; no one in the world has done it before!

81. "You practice sex with the men, instead of the women. Indeed, you are a transgressing people."

82. His people responded by saying, "Evict them from your town. They are people who wish to be pure."

83. Consequently, we saved him and his family, but not his wife; she was with the doomed.

84. We showered them with a certain shower; note the consequences for the guilty.

Shu'aib:
Cheating, Dishonesty Condemned

85. To Midyan we sent their brother Shu'aib. He said, "O my people, worship **GOD**; you have no other god beside Him. Proof has come to you from your Lord. You shall give full weight and full measure when you trade. Do not cheat the people out of their rights. Do not corrupt the earth after it has been set

straight. This is better for you, if you are believers.

86. "Refrain from blocking every path, seeking to repel those who believe from the path of **GOD**, and do not make it crooked. Remember that you used to be few and He multiplied your number. Recall the consequences for the wicked.

87. "Now that some of you have believed in what I was sent with, and some have disbelieved, wait until **GOD** issues His judgment between us; He is the best judge."

88. The arrogant leaders among his people said, "We will evict you, O Shu'aib, together with those who believed with you, from our town, unless you revert to our religion." He said, "Are you going to force us?

89. "We would be blaspheming against **GOD** if we reverted to your religion after **GOD** has saved us from it. How could we revert back to it against the will of **GOD** our Lord? Our Lord's knowledge encompasses all things. We have put our trust in **GOD**. Our Lord, grant us a decisive victory over our people. You are the best supporter."

90. The disbelieving leaders among his people said, "If you follow Shu'aib, you will be losers."

91. The quake annihilated them, leaving them dead in their homes.

92. Those who rejected Shu'aib vanished, as if they never existed. Those who rejected Shu'aib were the losers.

93. He turned away from them, saying, "O my people, I have delivered to you the messages of my Lord, and I have advised you. How can I grieve over disbelieving people."

Blessings in Disguise

94. Whenever we sent a prophet to any community, we afflicted its people with adversity and hardship, that they may implore.

95. Then we substituted peace and prosperity in place of that hardship. But alas, they turned heedless and said, "It was our parents who experienced that hardship before prosperity." Consequently, we punished them suddenly when they least expected.

*Most People Make
the Wrong Choice*

96. Had the people of those communities believed and turned righteous, we would have showered them with blessings from the heaven and the earth. Since they decided to disbelieve, we punished them for what they earned.

97. Did the people of the present communities guarantee that our retribution will not come to them in the night as they sleep?

98. Did the people of today's communities guarantee that our retribution will not come to them in the daytime while they play?

99. Have they taken **GOD**'s plans for granted? None takes **GOD**'s plans for granted except the losers.

100. Does it ever occur to those who inherit the earth after previous generations that, if we will, we can punish them for their sins, and seal their hearts, causing them to turn deaf?

101. We narrate to you the history of those communities: their messengers went to them with clear proofs, but they were not to believe in what they had rejected before. **GOD** thus seals the hearts of the disbelievers.

102. We found that most of them disregard their covenant; we found most of them wicked.*

Moses

103. After (*those messengers,*) we sent Moses with our signs to Pharaoh and his people, but they transgressed. Note the consequences for the wicked.

104. Moses said, "O Pharaoh, I am a messenger from the Lord of the universe.

105. "It is incumbent upon me that I do not say about **GOD** except the truth. I come to you with a sign from your Lord; let the Children of Israel go."

106. He said, "If you have a sign, then produce it, if you are truthful."

107. He threw down his staff, and it turned into a tremendous serpent.

108. He took out his hand, and it was white to the beholders.

109. The leaders among Pharaoh's people said, "This is no more than a clever magician.

110. "He wants to take you out of your land; what do you recommend?"

111. They said, "Respite him and his brother, and send summoners to every city.

---

*7:102 This life is our last chance to redeem ourselves, but most people are proven to be stubbornly rebellious and evil (see the INTRODUCTION).

---

112. "Let them summon every experienced magician."

113. The magicians came to Pharaoh and said, "Do we get paid if we are the winners?"

114. He said, "Yes indeed; you will even become close to me."

115. They said, "O Moses, either you throw, or we are throwing."

116. He said, "You throw." When they threw, they tricked the people's eyes, intimidated them, and produced a great magic.

117. We then inspired Moses: "Throw down your staff," whereupon it swallowed whatever they fabricated.

The Truth Recognized by the Experts

118. Thus, the truth prevailed, and what they did was nullified.

119. They were defeated then and there; they were humiliated.

120. The magicians fell prostrate.

121. They said, "We believe in the Lord of the universe.

122. "The Lord of Moses and Aaron."

123. Pharaoh said, "Did you believe in him without my permission? This must be a conspiracy you schemed in the city, in order to take its people away. You will surely find out.

124. "I will cut your hands and feet on alternate sides, then I will crucify you all."

125. They said, "We will then return to our Lord.

126. "You persecute us simply because we believed in the proofs of our Lord when they came to us."

"Our Lord, grant us steadfastness, and let us die as submitters."

127. The leaders among Pharaoh's people said, "Will you allow Moses and his people to corrupt the earth, and forsake you and your gods?" He said, "We will kill their sons, and spare their daughters. We are much more powerful than they are."

128. Moses said to his people, "Seek **GOD**'s help, and steadfastly persevere. The earth belongs to **GOD**, and He grants it to whomever He chooses from among His servants. The ultimate victory belongs to the righteous."

129. They said, "We were persecuted before you came to us, and after you came to us." He said, "Your Lord will annihilate your enemy and establish you on earth, then He will see how you behave."

The Plagues

130. We then afflicted Pharaoh's people with drought, and shortage of crops, that they may take heed.

131. When good omens came their way, they said, "We have deserved this," but when a hardship afflicted them, they blamed Moses and those with him. In fact, their omens are decided only by **GOD**, but most of them do not know.

132. They said, "No matter what kind of sign you show us, to dupe us with your magic, we will not believe."

The Warnings Go Unheeded

133. Consequently, we sent upon them the flood, the locusts, the lice, the frogs, and the blood—profound signs. But they maintained their arrogance. They were evil people.

134. Whenever a plague afflicted them, they said, "O Moses, implore your Lord—you are close to Him. If you relieve this plague, we will believe with you, and will send the Children of Israel with you."

135. Yet, when we relieved the plague for any length of time, they violated their pledge.

The Inevitable Retribution

136. Consequently, we avenged their actions, and drowned them in the sea. That is because they rejected our signs, and were totally heedless thereof.

137. We let the oppressed people inherit the land, east and west, and we blessed it. The blessed commands of your Lord were thus fulfilled for the Children of Israel, to reward them for their steadfastness, and we annihilated the works of Pharaoh and his people and everything they harvested.

After All the Miracles

138. We delivered the Children of Israel across the sea. When they passed by people who were worshiping statues, they said, "O Moses, make a god for us, like the gods they have." He said, "Indeed, you are ignorant people.

139. "These people are committing a blasphemy, for what they are doing is disastrous for them.

140. "Shall I seek for you other than **GOD** to be your god, when He has blessed you more than anyone else in the world?"

Reminder to the Children of Israel

141. Recall that we delivered you from Pharaoh's people, who inflicted the worst persecution upon you, killing your sons and sparing your daughters. That was an exacting trial for you from your Lord.

*Our World Cannot Stand
the Physical Presence of God*

142. We summoned Moses for thirty* nights, and completed them by adding ten.* Thus, the audience with his Lord lasted forty* nights. Moses said to his brother Aaron, "Stay here with my people, maintain righteousness, and do not follow the ways of the corruptors."

143. When Moses came at our appointed time, and his Lord spoke with him, he said, "My Lord, let me look and see You." He said, "You cannot see Me. Look at that mountain; if it stays in its place, then you can see Me." Then, his Lord manifested Himself to the mountain, and this caused it to crumble. Moses fell unconscious. When he came to, he said, "Be You glorified. I repent to You, and I am the most convinced believer."

144. He said, "O Moses, I have chosen you, out of all the people, with My messages and by speaking to you. Therefore, take what I have given you and be appreciative."

145. We wrote for him on the tablets all kinds of enlightenments and details of everything: "You shall uphold these teachings strongly, and exhort your people to uphold them—these are the best teachings. I will point out for you the fate of the wicked."

---

*7:142 The manner in which these numbers are mentioned is significant As detailed in Appendix 1, all the numbers mentioned in the Quran add up to 162146, 19x8534.

*Divine Intervention Keeps
the Disbelievers in the Dark*

146. I will divert from My revelations those who are arrogant on earth, without justification. Consequently, when they see every kind of proof they will not believe. And when they see the path of guidance they will not adopt it as their path, but when they see the path of straying they will adopt it as their path. This is the consequence of their rejecting our proofs, and being totally heedless thereof.

147. Those who reject our revelations and the meeting of the Hereafter, their works are nullified. Are they requited only for what they committed?

The Golden Calf

148. During his absence, Moses' people made from their jewelry the statue of a calf, complete with the sound of a calf.* Did they not see that it could not speak to them, or guide them in any path? They worshiped it, and thus turned wicked.

149. Finally, when they regretted their action, and realized that they had gone astray, they said, "Unless our Lord redeems us with His mercy, and forgives us, we will be losers."

150. When Moses returned to his people, angry and disappointed, he said, "What a terrible thing you have done in my absence! Could you not wait for the commandments of your Lord?" He threw down the tablets, and took hold of his brother's head, pulling him towards himself. (*Aaron*) said, "Son of my mother, the people took advantage of my weakness, and almost killed me. Let not my enemies rejoice, and do not count me with the transgressing people."

151. (*Moses*) said, "My Lord, forgive me and my brother, and admit us into Your mercy. Of all the merciful ones, You are the Most Merciful."

152. Surely, those who idolized the calf have incurred wrath from their Lord, and humiliation in this life. We thus requite the innovators.

153. As for those who committed sins, then repented thereafter and believed, your Lord—after this—is Forgiver, Most Merciful.

154. When Moses' anger subsided, he picked up the tablets, containing guidance and mercy for those who reverence their Lord.

155. Moses then selected seventy men from among his people, to come to our appointed audience. When the quake shook them, he said, "My Lord, You could have annihilated them in the past, together with me, if You so willed. Would You annihilate us for the deeds of those among us who are foolish? This must be the test that You have instituted for us. With it, You condemn whomever You will, and guide whomever You will. You are our Lord and Master, so forgive us, shower us with Your mercy; You are the best Forgiver.

---

*7:148 How the golden calf acquired the sound of a calf is explained in Footnote 20:96.

---

*Requirements For Attaining God's
Mercy: The Importance of Zakat*

156. "And decree for us righteousness in this world, and in the Hereafter. We have repented to You." He said, "My retribution befalls whomever I will. But My mercy encompasses all things. However, I will specify it for those who *(1)* lead a righteous life, *(2)* give the obligatory charity (*Zakat*),* *(3)* believe in our revelations, and

157. "*(4)* follow the messenger, the gentile prophet (*Muhammad*), whom they find written in their Torah and Gospel.* He exhorts them to be righteous, enjoins them from evil, allows for them all good food, and prohibits that which is bad, and unloads the burdens and the shackles imposed upon them. Those who believe in him, respect him, support him, and follow the light that came with him are the successful ones."

158. Say, "O people, I am **GOD**'s messenger to all of you. To Him belongs the sovereignty of the heavens and the earth. There is no god except He. He controls life and death." Therefore, you shall believe in **GOD** and His messenger, the gentile prophet, who believes in **GOD** and His words. Follow him, that you may be guided.

The Guided Jews

159. Among the followers of Moses there are those who guide in accordance with the truth, and the truth renders them righteous.

Miracles in Sinai

160. We divided them into twelve tribal communities, and we inspired Moses when his people asked him for water: "Strike the rock with your staff," whereupon twelve springs gushed out therefrom. Thus, each community knew its water. And we shaded them with clouds, and sent down to them manna and quails: "Eat from the good things we provided for you." It is not us that they wronged; it is they who wronged their own souls.

Rebellion Despite the Miracles

161. Recall that they were told, "Go into this town to live, and eat therefrom as you please, treat the people amicably, and enter the gate humbly. We will then forgive your transgressions. We will multiply the reward for the righteous."

162. But the evil ones among them substituted other commands for the commands given to them. Consequently, we sent upon them condemnation from the sky, because of their wickedness.

*Observing the Commandments
Brings Prosperity*

163. Remind them of the community by the sea, who desecrated the Sabbath. When they observed the Sabbath, the fish came to them abundantly. And when they violated the Sabbath, the fish did not come. We thus afflicted them, as a consequence of their transgression.

---

*7:156 *The importance of the obligatory charity (Zakat) cannot be over emphasized. As instituted in 6:141, Zakat must be given away upon receiving any income—2.5% of one's net income must be given to the parents, the relatives, the orphans, the poor, and the traveling alien, in this order (see 2:215).*

*7:157 *Muhammad is prophesied in Deuteronomy 18:15-19 and John 14:16-17 & 16:13.*

---

*Mocking and Ridiculing
God's Message*

164. Recall that a group of them said, "Why should you preach to people whom **GOD** will surely annihilate or punish severely?" They answered, "Apologize to your Lord," that they might be saved.

165. When they disregarded what they were reminded of, we saved those who prohibited evil, and afflicted the wrongdoers with a terrible retribution for their wickedness.

166. When they continued to defy the commandments, we said to them, "Be you despicable apes."

167. Additionally, your Lord has decreed that He will raise up against them people who will inflict severe persecution upon them, until the Day of Resurrection. Your Lord is most efficient in enforcing retribution, and He is certainly the Forgiver, Most Merciful.

168. We scattered them among many communities throughout the land. Some of them were righteous, and some were less than righteous. We tested them with prosperity and hardship, that they may return.

169. Subsequent to them, He substituted new generations who inherited the scripture. But they opted for the worldly life instead, saying, "We will be forgiven." But then they continued to opt for the materials of this world. Did they not make a covenant to uphold the scripture, and not to say about **GOD** except the truth? Did they not study the scrip-

ture? Certainly, the abode of the Hereafter is far better for those who maintain righteousness. Do you not understand?

170. Those who uphold the scripture, and observe the Contact Prayers (*Salat*), we never fail to recompense the pious.

171. We raised the mountain above them like an umbrella, and they thought it was going to fall on them: "You shall uphold what we have given you, strongly, and remember the contents thereof, that you may be saved."

*We Are Born With Instinctive
Knowledge About God**

172. Recall that your Lord summoned all the descendants of Adam, and had them bear witness for themselves: "Am I not your Lord?" They all said, "Yes. We bear witness." Thus, you cannot say on the Day of Resurrection, "We were not aware of this."

173. Nor can you say, "It was our parents who practiced idolatry, and we simply followed in their footsteps. Will You punish us because of what others have innovated?"

174. We thus explain the revelations, to enable the people to redeem themselves.*

175. Recite for them the news of one who was given our proofs, but chose to disregard them. Consequently, the devil pursued him, until he became a strayer.

---

*7:172 *Thus, every human being is born with an instinctive knowledge about God.*

*7:174 *This life is our last chance to return to God's Kingdom (See INTRODUCTION).*

---

176. Had we willed, we could have elevated him therewith, but he insisted on sticking to the ground, and pursued his own opinions. Thus, he is like the dog; whether you pet him or scold him, he pants. Such is the example of people who reject our proofs. Narrate these narrations, that they may reflect.

177. Bad indeed is the example of people who reject our proofs; it is only their own souls that they wrong.

178. Whomever **GOD** guides is the truly guided one, and whomever He commits to straying, these are the losers.

*Satan Hypnotizes
His Constituents*

179. We have committed to Hell multitudes of jinns and humans. They have minds with which they do not understand, eyes with which they do not see, and ears with which they do not hear. They are like animals; no, they are far worse—they are totally unaware.

180. To **GOD** belongs the most beautiful names; call upon Him therewith, and disregard those who distort His names. They will be requited for their sins.

181. Among our creations, there are those who guide with the truth, and the truth renders them righteous.

182. As for those who reject our revelations, we lead them on without them ever realizing it.

183. I will even encourage them; My scheming is formidable.

184. Why do they not reflect upon their friend (*the messenger*)? He is not crazy. He is simply a profound warner.

185. Have they not looked at the dominion of the heavens and the earth, and all the things **GOD** has created? Does it ever occur to them that the end of their life may be near? Which *Hadith*, beside this, do they believe in?

186. Whomever **GOD** commits to straying, there is no way for anyone to guide him. He leaves them in their sins, blundering.

187. They ask you about the end of the world (*the Hour*),* and when it will come to pass. Say, "The knowledge thereof is with my Lord. Only He reveals its time.* Heavy it is, in the heavens and the earth. It will not come to you except suddenly."** They ask you as if you are in control thereof. Say, "The knowledge thereof is with **GOD**," but most people do not know.

*Messengers Are Powerless;
They Do Not Know the Future.*

188. Say, "I have no power to benefit myself, or harm myself. Only what **GOD** wills happens to me. If I knew the future, I would have increased my wealth, and no harm would have afflicted me. I am no more than a warner, and a bearer of good news for those who believe."

7:187 The right time to reveal this information was predestined to be 1980 A.D., through God's Messenger of the Covenant (See 15:87, 72:27, and Appendices 2 & 11).

**7:187 The "Hour" comes "suddenly" only to the disbelievers (See Appendix 11).*

Our Children Can be Idols

189. He created you from one person (*Adam*). Subsequently, He gives every man a mate to find tranquility with her. She then carries a light load that she can hardly notice. As the load gets heavier, they implore **GOD** their Lord: "If You give us a good baby, we will be appreciative."

190. But when He gives them a good baby, they turn His gift into an idol that rivals Him. **GOD** be exalted, far above any partnership.

191. Is it not a fact that they are idolizing idols who create nothing, and are themselves created?

192. Idols that can neither help them, nor even help themselves?

193. When you invite them to the guidance, they do not follow you. Thus, it is the same for them whether you invite them, or remain silent.

194. The idols you invoke besides **GOD** are creatures like you. Go ahead and call upon them; let them respond to you, if you are right.

195. Do they have legs on which they walk? Do they have hands with which they defend themselves? Do they have eyes with which they see? Do they have ears with which they hear? Say, "Call upon your idols, and ask them to smite me without delay.

196. "**GOD** is my only Lord and Master; the One who revealed this scripture. He protects the righteous.

197. "As for the idols you set up beside Him, they cannot help you, nor can they help themselves."

198. When you invite them to the guidance, they do not hear. And you see them looking at you, but they do not see.

199. You shall resort to pardon, advocate tolerance, and disregard the ignorant.

200. When the devil whispers to you any whisper, seek refuge in **GOD**; He is Hearer, Omniscient.

201. Those who are righteous, whenever the devil approaches them with an idea, they remember, whereupon they become seers.

202. Their brethren ceaselessly entice them to go astray.

203. If you do not produce a miracle that they demand, they say, "Why not ask for it?" Say, "I simply follow what is revealed to me from my Lord." These are enlightenments from your Lord, and guidance, and mercy for people who believe.

204. When the Quran is recited, you shall listen to it and take heed, that you may attain mercy.

205. You shall remember your Lord within yourself, publicly, privately, and quietly, day and night; do not be unaware.*

206. Those at your Lord are never too proud to worship Him; they glorify Him and fall prostrate before Him.

◆◆◆◆

---

*7:205 Your god is whoever or whatever occupies your mind most of the day. This explains the fact that most of those who believe in God are destined for Hell (See 12:106, 23:84-90, and Appendix 27).

Sura 8: The Spoils of War (Al-Anfãl)

In the name of God,
Most Gracious, Most Merciful

1. They consult you about the spoils of war. Say, "The spoils of war belong to **GOD** and the messenger." You shall observe **GOD**, exhort one another to be righteous, and obey **GOD** and His messenger, if you are believers.

The True Believers

2. The true believers are those whose hearts tremble when **GOD** is mentioned, and when His revelations are recited to them, their faith is strengthened, and they trust in their Lord.

3. They observe the Contact Prayers (*Salat*), and from our provisions to them, they give to charity.

4. Such are the true believers. They attain high ranks at their Lord, as well as forgiveness and a generous provision.

The Weak Believers

5. When your Lord willed that you leave your home, to fulfill a specific plan, some believers became exposed as reluctant believers.

6. They argued with you against the truth, even after everything was explained to them. They acted as if they were being driven to certain death.

7. Recall that **GOD** promised you victory over a certain group, but you still wanted to face the weaker group. It was **GOD**'s plan to establish the truth with His words, and to defeat the disbelievers.

8. For He has decreed that the truth shall prevail, and the falsehood shall vanish, in spite of the evildoers.

God's Invisible Soldiers

9. Thus, when you implored your Lord to come to the rescue, He responded to you: "I am supporting you with one thousand angels in succession."

Victory Guaranteed for the Believers

10. **GOD** gave you this good news to strengthen your hearts. Victory comes only from **GOD**. **GOD** is Almighty, Most Wise.

11. He caused peaceful slumber to overtake you and pacify you, and He sent down water from the sky to clean you therewith. He protected you from the devil's curse, reassured your hearts and strengthened your foothold.

Lessons from History*

12. Recall that your Lord inspired the angels: "I am with you; so support those who believed. I will throw terror into the hearts of those who disbelieved. You may strike them above the necks, and you may strike even every finger."

13. This is what they have justly incurred by fighting **GOD** and His messenger. For those who fight against **GOD** and His messenger, **GOD**'s retribution is severe.

---

*8:12-16 All wars are governed by the basic rule in 60:8-9

---

14. This is to punish the disbelievers; they have incurred the retribution of Hell.

15. O you who believe, if you encounter the disbelievers who have mobilized against you, do not turn back and flee.

16. Anyone who turns back on that day, except to carry out a battle plan, or to join his group, has incurred wrath from **GOD**, and his abode is Hell; what a miserable destiny!

God Is Doing Everything*

17. It was not you who killed them; **GOD** is the One who killed them. It was not you who threw when you threw; **GOD** is the One who threw. But He thus gives the believers a chance to earn a lot of credit. **GOD** is Hearer, Omniscient.

18. Additionally, **GOD** thus nullifies the schemes of the disbelievers.

19. You sought victory (*O disbelievers*), and victory did come; it belonged to the believers. If you refrain (*from aggression*) it would be better for you, but if you return, so will we. Your armies will never help you, no matter how great. For **GOD** is on the side of the believers.

20. O you who believe, obey **GOD** and His messenger, and do not disregard him while you hear.

The Disbelievers Blocked Out

21. Do not be like those who say, "We hear," when they do not hear.

22. The worst creatures in the sight of **GOD** are the deaf and dumb, who do not understand.

23. Had **GOD** known of any good in them, He would have made them hearers. Even if He made them hearers, they still would turn away in aversion.

The Righteous Do Not Really Die*

24. O you who believe, you shall respond to **GOD** and to the messenger when he invites you to what gives you life.* You should know that **GOD** is closer to you than your heart, and that before Him you will be summoned.

25. Beware of a retribution that may not be limited to the evildoers among you.* You should know that **GOD**'s retribution is severe.

God Supports the Believers

26. Remember that you used to be few and oppressed, fearing that the people may snatch you, and He granted you a secure sanctuary, supported you with His victory, and provided you with good provisions, that you may be appreciative.

27. O you who believe, do not betray **GOD** and the messenger, and do not betray those who trust you, now that you know.

---

*8:17 Believing in God necessitates believing in His qualities, one of which is that He is doing everything Without knowing God, there is no belief (23:84-90). Bad things are incurred by us, and executed by Satan, in accordance with God's laws (4:78-79, 42:30).

*8:24 See Appendix 17. When the righteous exit their bodies, they go straight to Heaven.

*8:25 A community that tolerates homosexuality, for example, may be hit by an earthquake.

Money & Children Are Tests

28. You should know that your money and your children are a test, and that **GOD** possesses a great recompense.

29. O you who believe, if you reverence **GOD**, He will enlighten you, remit your sins, and forgive you. **GOD** possesses infinite grace.

God Protects His Messenger*

30. The disbelievers plot and scheme to neutralize you, or kill you, or banish you. However, they plot and scheme, but so does **GOD**. **GOD** is the best schemer.

31. When our revelations are recited to them, they say, "We have heard. If we wanted to, we could have said the same things. These are no more than tales from the past!"

32. They also said, "Our god, if this is really the truth from You, then shower us with rocks from the sky, or pour upon us a painful punishment."

33. However, **GOD** is not to punish them while you are in their midst; **GOD** is not to punish them while they are seeking forgiveness.

34. Have they not deserved **GOD**'s retribution, by repelling others from the Sacred Masjid, even though they are not the custodians thereof? The true custodians thereof are the righteous, but most of them do not know.

The Contact Prayers (Salat)
Existed Before the Quran*

35. Their Contact Prayers (*Salat*) at the shrine (*Ka'bah*) were no more than a mockery and a means of repelling the people (*by crowding them out*). Therefore, suffer the retribution for your disbelief.

Spending Their Money
to Fight God*

36. Those who disbelieve spend their money to repel others from the way of **GOD**. They will spend it, then it will turn into sorrow and remorse for them. Ultimately, they will be defeated, and all disbelievers will be summoned to Hell.

37. **GOD** will sift away the bad from the good, then pile the bad on top of each other, all in one pile, then throw it in Hell. Such are the losers.

---

*8:30 God chose His final prophet, Muhammad, from the strongest tribe of Arabia. It was tribal law and traditions that prevented the disbelievers—by God's leave—from killing Muhammad. Similarly, it was God's will to move His Messenger of the Covenant from the Middle East, where he would have been killed, to the U.S.A. where God's message can flourish and reach every corner of the globe. This is mathematically confirmed: the sura & verse numbers = 8 + 30 = 38 = 19x2.

*8:35 All religious practices in Islam came to us through Abraham; when the Quran was revealed, all rites in "Submission" were already in existence (21:73, 22:78).

*8:36 The idol worshiping leaders of corrupted Islam, Saudi Arabia, have allocated huge sums of money annually to fight God and His miracle. For example, the famous Lebanese publisher Dār Al-'Ilm Lil-Malāyîn (Knowledge for the Millions) published the Arabic version of "The Miracle of the Quran" in March, 1983. The Saudis bought all the copies and destroyed them.

38. Tell those who disbelieved: if they stop, all their past will be forgiven. But if they return, they will incur the same fate as their previous counterparts.

39. You shall fight them to ward off oppression, and to practice your religion devoted to **GOD** alone. If they refrain from aggression, then **GOD** is fully Seer of everything they do.

40. If they turn away, then you should know that **GOD** is your Lord and Master; the best Lord and Master, the best supporter.

41. You should know that if you gain any spoils in war, one-fifth shall go to **GOD** and the messenger, to be given to the relatives, the orphans, the poor, and the traveling alien. You will do this if you believe in **GOD** and in what we revealed to our servant on the day of decision, the day the two armies clashed. **GOD** is Omnipotent.

God Controls Everything and Plans for the Believers

42. Recall that you were on this side of the valley, while they were on the other side. Then their caravan had to move to lower ground. Had you planned it this way, you could not have done it. But **GOD** was to carry out a predetermined matter, whereby those destined to be annihilated were annihilated for an obvious reason, and those destined to be saved were saved for an obvious reason. **GOD** is Hearer, Omniscient.

43. **GOD** made them appear in your dream (*O Muhammad*) fewer in number. Had He made them appear more numerous, you would

have failed, and you would have disputed among yourselves. But **GOD** saved the situation. He is Knower of the innermost thoughts.

44. And when the time came and you faced them, He made them appear fewer in your eyes, and made you appear fewer in their eyes as well. For **GOD** willed to carry out a certain plan. All decisions are made by **GOD**.

45. O you who believe, when you encounter an army, you shall hold fast and commemorate **GOD** frequently, that you may succeed.

46. You shall obey **GOD** and His messenger, and do not dispute among yourselves, lest you fail and scatter your strength. You shall steadfastly persevere. **GOD** is with those who steadfastly persevere.

47. Do not be like those who left their homes grudgingly, only to show off, and in fact discouraged others from following the path of **GOD**. **GOD** is fully aware of everything they do.

The Devil Sees God's Invisible Soldiers

48. The devil had adorned their works in their eyes, and said, "You cannot be defeated by any people today," and "I will be fighting along with you." But as soon as the two armies faced each other, he turned back on his heels and fled, saying, "I disown you. I see what you do not see. I am afraid of **GOD**. **GOD**'s retribution is awesome."

49. The hypocrites and those who harbored doubt in their hearts said, "These people are deceived by their religion." However, if one puts his trust in **GOD**, then **GOD** is Almighty, Most Wise.

50. If you could only see those who disbelieved when the angels put them to death! They will beat them on their faces and their rear ends: "Taste the retribution of Hell.

51. "This is a consequence of what your hands have sent forth. **GOD** is never unjust towards the creatures."

52. This is the same fate as that of Pharaoh's people and those who disbelieved before them. They rejected **GOD**'s revelations, and **GOD** punished them for their sins. **GOD** is powerful, and His retribution is severe.

Retribution:
A Consequence of Sin

53. **GOD** does not change a blessing He has bestowed upon any people unless they themselves decide to change. **GOD** is Hearer, Omniscient.

54. Such was the case with the people of Pharaoh and others before them. They first rejected the signs of their Lord. Consequently, we annihilated them for their sins. We drowned Pharaoh's people; the wicked were consistently punished.

55. The worst creatures in the sight of **GOD** are those who disbelieved; they cannot believe.

56. You reach agreements with them, but they violate their agreements every time; they are not righteous.

57. Therefore, if you encounter them in war, you shall set them up as a deterrent example for those who come after them, that they may take heed.

58. When you are betrayed by a group of people, you shall mobilize against

them in the same manner. **GOD** does not love the betrayers.

59. Let not those who disbelieve think that they can get away with it; they can never escape.

You Shall Be Prepared:
A Divine Commandment

60. You shall prepare for them all the power you can muster, and all the equipment you can mobilize, that you may frighten the enemies of **GOD**, your enemies, as well as others who are not known to you; **GOD** knows them. Whatever you spend in the cause of **GOD** will be repaid to you generously, without the least injustice.

61. If they resort to peace, so shall you, and put your trust in **GOD**. He is the Hearer, the Omniscient.

God Suffices the Believers

62. If they want to deceive you, then **GOD** will suffice you. He will help you with His support, and with the believers.

63. He has reconciled the hearts (*of the believers*). Had you spent all the money on earth, you could not reconcile their hearts. But **GOD** did reconcile them. He is Almighty, Most Wise.

64. O you prophet, sufficient for you is **GOD** and the believers who have followed you.

65. O you prophet, you shall exhort the believers to fight. If there are twenty of you who are steadfast, they can defeat two hundred, and a hundred of you can defeat a thousand of those who disbelieved. That is because they are people who do not understand.

66. Now (*that many new people have joined you*) **GOD** has made it easier for you, for He knows that you are not as strong as you used to be. Henceforth, a hundred steadfast believers can defeat two hundred, and a thousand of you can defeat two thousand by **GOD**'s leave. **GOD** is with those who steadfastly persevere.

67. No prophet shall acquire captives, unless he participates in the fighting. You people are seeking the materials of this world, while **GOD** advocates the Hereafter. **GOD** is Almighty, Most Wise.

68. If it were not for a predetermined decree from **GOD**, you would have suffered, on account of what you took, a terrible retribution.

69. Therefore, eat from the spoils you have earned that which is lawful and good, and observe **GOD**. **GOD** is Forgiver, Most Merciful.

70. O you prophet, tell the prisoners of war in your hands, "If **GOD** knew of anything good in your hearts, He would have given you better than anything you have lost, and would have forgiven you. **GOD** is Forgiver, Most Merciful."

71. And if they want to betray you, they have already betrayed **GOD**. This is why He made them the losers. **GOD** is Omniscient, Most Wise.

72. Surely, those who believed, and emigrated, and strove with their money and their lives in the cause of **GOD**, as well as those who hosted them and gave them refuge, and supported them, they are allies of one another. As for those who believe, but do not emigrate with you, you do not owe them any support, until they do emigrate. However, if they need your help, as brethren in faith, you shall help them, except against people with whom you have signed a peace treaty. **GOD** is Seer of everything you do.

73. Those who disbelieved are allies of one another. Unless you keep these commandments, there will be chaos on earth, and terrible corruption.

74. Those who believed and emigrated, and strove in the cause of **GOD**, as well as those who hosted them and gave them refuge, and supported them, these are the true believers. They have deserved forgiveness and a generous recompense.

75. Those who believed afterwards, and emigrated, and strove with you, they belong with you. Those who are related to each other shall be the first to support each other, in accordance with **GOD**'s commandments. **GOD** is fully aware of all things.

◆◆◆◆

Sura 9: Ultimatum (Barã'ah)

*No Basmalah**

1. An ultimatum is herein issued from **GOD** and His messenger to the idol worshipers who enter into a treaty with you.

2. Therefore, roam the earth freely for four months, and know that you cannot escape from **GOD**, and that **GOD** humiliates the disbelievers.

9:1 The absence of **Basmalah from this sura is not only a profound sign from the Almighty Author of the Quran that this sura has been tampered with, but also represents an awesome miracle in its own right. See the details in Appendices 24 & 29.*

3. A proclamation is herein issued from **GOD** and His messenger to all the people on the great day of pilgrimage, that **GOD** has disowned the idol worshipers, and so did His messenger. Thus, if you repent, it would be better for you. But if you turn away, then know that you can never escape from **GOD**. Promise those who disbelieve a painful retribution.

4. If the idol worshipers sign a peace treaty with you, and do not violate it, nor band together with others against you, you shall fulfill your treaty with them, until the expiration date. **GOD** loves the righteous.

5. Once the Sacred Months are past, (*and they refuse to make peace*) you may kill the idol worshipers when you encounter them, punish them, and resist every move they make. If they repent and observe the Contact Prayers (*Salat*) and give the obligatory charity (*Zakat*), you shall let them go. **GOD** is Forgiver, Most Merciful.

6. If one of the idol worshipers sought safe passage with you, you shall grant him safe passage, so that he can hear the word of **GOD**, then send him back to his place of security. That is because they are people who do not know.

7. How can the idol worshipers demand any pledge from **GOD** and from His messenger? Exempted are those who have signed a peace treaty with you at the Sacred Masjid. If they honor and uphold such a treaty, you shall uphold it as well. **GOD** loves the righteous.

8. How can they (*demand a pledge*) when they never observed any rights of kinship between you and them nor any covenant, if they ever had a chance to prevail. They pacified you with lip service, while their hearts were in opposition, and most of them are wicked.

9. They traded away **GOD**'s revelations for a cheap price. Consequently, they repulsed the people from His path. Miserable indeed is what they did!

10. They never observe any rights of kinship towards any believer, nor do they uphold their covenants; these are the real transgressors.

Repentance: Cleaning the Slate

11. If they repent and observe the Contact Prayers (*Salat*) and give the obligatory charity (*Zakat*), then they are your brethren in religion. We thus explain the revelations for people who know.

12. If they violate their oaths after pledging to keep their covenants, and attack your religion, you may fight the leaders of paganism – you are no longer bound by your covenant with them – that they may refrain.

13. Would you not fight people who violated their treaties, tried to banish the messenger, and they are the ones who started the war in the first place? Are you afraid of them? **GOD** is the One you are supposed to fear, if you are believers.

14. You shall fight them, for **GOD** will punish them at your hands, humiliate them, grant you victory over them, and cool the chests of the believers.

15. He will also remove the rage from the believers' hearts. **GOD** redeems whomever He wills. **GOD** is Omniscient, Most Wise.

The Inevitable Test

16. Did you think that you will be left alone without **GOD** distinguishing those among you who strive, and never ally themselves with **GOD**'s enemies, or the enemies of His messenger, or the enemies of the believers? **GOD** is fully Cognizant of everything you do.

17. The idol worshipers are not to frequent the masjids of **GOD**, while confessing their disbelief. These have nullified their works, and they will abide forever in Hell.

18. The only people to frequent **GOD**'s masjids are those who believe in **GOD** and the Last Day, and observe the Contact Prayers (*Salat*), and give the obligatory charity (*Zakat*), and do not fear except **GOD**. These will surely be among the guided ones.

Question to the Arabs

19. Have you considered the watering of the pilgrims and caring for the Sacred Masjid a substitute for believing in **GOD** and the Last Day, and striving in the cause of **GOD**? They are not equal in the sight of **GOD**. **GOD** does not guide the wicked people.

Good News

20. Those who believe, and emigrate, and strive in the cause of **GOD** with their money and their lives, are far greater in rank in the sight of **GOD**. These are the winners.

21. Their Lord gives them good news: mercy and approval from Him, and gardens where they rejoice in everlasting bliss.

22. Eternally they abide therein. **GOD** possesses a great recompense.

If You Have to Make a Choice

23. O you who believe, do not ally yourselves even with your parents and your siblings, if they prefer disbelieving over believing. Those among you who ally themselves with them are transgressing.

Important Criterion*

24. Proclaim: "If your parents, your children, your siblings, your spouses, your family, the money you have earned, a business you worry about, and the homes you cherish are more beloved to you than **GOD** and His messenger,** and the striving in His cause, then just wait until **GOD** brings His judgment." **GOD** does not guide the wicked people.

---

*9:24 Since the odds are overwhelming against any human being to actually believe and devote the worship to God alone (12:103, 106), it is virtually impossible to see a whole family believe. Thus, most believers have been faced with the choice: "Either me or God and His messenger." This choice is consistently stated by spouses of the believers, or their parents, their children, etc. Consistently, the believers made the right choice. This is a mandatory test for all believers (29:2).

**9:24 The Quranic, mathematical evidence points specifically at God's Messenger of the Covenant. By adding the gematrical value of "Rashad" (505), plus the value of "Khalifa" (725), plus the verse number (24), we get 505 + 725 + 24 = 1254 = 19x66.

25. **GOD** has granted you victory in many situations. But on the day of Hunayn, you became too proud of your great number. Consequently, it did not help you at all, and the spacious earth became so straitened around you, that you turned around and fled.

26. Then **GOD** sent down contentment upon His messenger and upon the believers. And He sent down invisible soldiers; He thus punished those who disbelieved. This is the requital for the disbelievers.

27. Ultimately, **GOD** redeems whomever He wills. **GOD** is Forgiver, Most Merciful.

28. O you who believe, the idol worshipers are polluted; they shall not be permitted to approach the Sacred Masjid after this year. If you fear loss of income, **GOD** will shower you with His provisions, in accordance with His will. **GOD** is Omniscient, Most Wise.

29. You shall fight back against those who do not believe in **GOD**, nor in the Last Day, nor do they prohibit what **GOD** and His messenger have prohibited, nor do they abide by the religion of truth – among those who received the scripture – until they pay the due tax, willingly or unwillingly.

Blasphemies

30. The Jews said, "Ezra is the son of **GOD**," while the Christians said, "Jesus is the son of **GOD**!" These are blasphemies uttered by their mouths. They thus match the blasphemies of those who have disbelieved in the past. **GOD** condemns them. They have surely deviated.

Upholding the Teachings of Religious Leaders Instead of God's Teachings

31. They have set up their religious leaders and scholars as lords,* instead of **GOD**. Others deified the Messiah, son of Mary. They were all commanded to worship only one god. There is no god except He. Be He glorified, high above having any partners.

32. They want to put out **GOD**'s light with their mouths, but **GOD** insists upon perfecting His light, in spite of the disbelievers.

9:31 If you consult the "Muslim scholars" about worshiping God alone, and upholding the word of God alone, as taught in this proven scripture, they will advise you against it. If you consult the Pope about the identity of Jesus, he will advise you to uphold a trinity. If you obey the "Muslim scholars" whose advice is contrary to God's teachings, or if you take the Pope's advice instead of God's, you have set up these religious leaders as gods instead of God.

"Submission" Destined to Prevail*

33. He is the One who sent His messenger* with the guidance and the religion of truth, and will make it dominate all religions, in spite of the idol worshipers.

Beware of Professional Religionists

34. O you who believe, many religious leaders and preachers take the people's money illicitly, and repel from the path of **GOD**. Those who hoard the gold and silver, and do not spend them in the cause of **GOD**, promise them a painful retribution.

35. The day will come when their gold and silver will be heated in the fire of Hell, then used to burn their foreheads, their sides, and their backs: "This is what you hoarded for yourselves, so taste what you have hoarded."

God's System:
Twelve Months Per Year*

36. The count of months, as far as **GOD** is concerned, is twelve.* This has been **GOD**'s law, since the day He created the heavens and the earth. Four of them are sacred. This is the perfect religion; you shall not wrong your souls (*by fighting*) during the Sacred Months. However, you may declare all-out war against the idol worshipers (*even during the Sacred Months*), when they declare all-out war against you, and know that **GOD** is on the side of the righteous.

Altering the Sacred Months *

37. Altering the Sacred Months is a sign of excessive disbelief; it augments the straying of those who have disbelieved. They alternate the Sacred Months and the regular months, while preserving the number of months consecrated by **GOD**. They thus violate what **GOD** has consecrated. Their evil works are adorned in their eyes. **GOD** does not guide the disbelieving people.

38. O you who believe, when you are told, "Mobilize in the cause of **GOD**," why do you become heavily attached to the ground? Have you chosen this worldly life in place of the Hereafter? The materials of this world, compared to the Hereafter, are nil.

---

*9:33 This statement, letter for letter, occurs here and in 61:9. If we write down the gematrical value of "Rashad" (505), followed by the value of "Khalifa" (725), followed by the sura and verse numbers where this statement occurs (9:33 & 61:9), we get 505 725 9 33 61 9, a multiple of 19. This confirms that the messenger here is Rashad Khalifa. Additionally, the number of verses from 9:33 to 61:9 (3902) + 9 + 33 + 61 + 9 + the value of "Rashad Khalifa" (1230) gives 5244, also a multiple of 19. The gematrical value of 9:33 & 61:9, calculated by adding the values of every letter, is 7858. By adding this number, plus the number of letters in the two verses (120), plus the number of verses from 9:33 to 61:9 (3902), plus the value of "Rashad Khalifa" (1230), we get 7858 + 120 + 3902 + 1230 = 13110 = 19x690. See Appendices 1, 2, and 26.

*9:36 The word "month" is mentioned in the Quran 12 times, and "day" 365 times.

*9:37 The Sacred Months according to the corrupted Muslim World are Rajab, Zul-Qe'dah, Zul-Hijjah, and Muharram (7th, 11th, 12th and 1st months of the Islamic Calendar). A careful study of the Quran, however, reveals that they should be Zul-Hijjah, Muharram, Safar, and Rabi I (12th, 1st, 2nd, and 3rd months). See Appendix 15.

39. Unless you mobilize, He will commit you to painful retribution and substitute other people in your place; you can never hurt Him in the least. **GOD** is Omnipotent.

God's Invisible Soldiers

40. If you fail to support him (*the messenger*), **GOD** has already supported him. Thus, when the disbelievers chased him, and he was one of two in the cave, he said to his friend, "Do not worry; **GOD** is with us." **GOD** then sent down contentment and security upon him, and supported him with invisible soldiers. He made the word of the disbelievers lowly. **GOD**'s word reigns supreme. **GOD** is Almighty, Most Wise.

Better Believers Strive
in the Cause of God

41. You shall readily mobilize, light or heavy, and strive with your money and your lives in the cause of **GOD**. This is better for you, if you only knew.

The Sedentary

42. If there were a quick material gain, and a short journey, they would have followed you. But the striving is just too much for them. They will swear by **GOD**: "If we could, we would have mobilized with you." They thus hurt themselves, and **GOD** knows that they are liars.

43. **GOD** has pardoned you: why did you give them permission (*to stay behind*), before you could distinguish those who are truthful from the liars?

44. Those who truly believe in **GOD** and the Last Day do not ask your permission to evade the opportunity to strive with their money and their lives. **GOD** is fully aware of the righteous.

45. The only people who wish to be excused are those who do not really believe in **GOD** and the Last Day. Their hearts are full of doubt, and their doubts cause them to waver.

46. Had they really wanted to mobilize, they would have prepared for it thoroughly. But **GOD** disliked their participation, so He discouraged them; they were told, "Stay behind with those who are staying behind."

47. Had they mobilized with you, they would have created confusion, and would have caused disputes and divisions among you. Some of you were apt to listen to them. **GOD** is fully aware of the transgressors.

48. They sought to spread confusion among you in the past, and confounded matters for you. However, the truth ultimately prevails, and **GOD**'s plan is carried out, in spite of them.

49. Some of them would say, "Give me permission (*to stay behind*); do not impose such a hardship on me." In fact, they have thus incurred a terrible hardship; Hell is surrounding the disbelievers.

50. If something good happens to you, they hurt, and if an affliction befalls you, they say, "We told you so," as they turn away rejoicing.

51. Say, "Nothing happens to us, except what **GOD** has decreed for us. He is our Lord and Master. In **GOD** the believers shall trust."

52. Say, "You can only expect for us one of two good things (*victory or martyrdom*), while we expect for you condemnation from **GOD** and retribution from Him, or at our hands. Therefore, wait, and we will wait along with you."

53. Say, "Spend, willingly or unwillingly. Nothing will be accepted from you, for you are evil people."

The Contact Prayer Existed Before Muhammad*

54. What prevented the acceptance of their spending is that they disbelieved in **GOD** and His messenger, and when they observed the Contact Prayers (*Salat*),* they observed them lazily, and when they gave to charity, they did so grudgingly.

Apparent Worldly Success

55. Do not be impressed by their money, or their children. **GOD** causes these to be sources of retribution for them in this life, and (*when they die*) their souls depart while they are disbelievers.

56. They swear by **GOD** that they belong with you, while they do not belong with you; they are divisive people.

57. If they could find a refuge, or caves, or a hiding place, they would go to it, rushing.

58. Some of them criticize your distribution of the charities; if they are given therefrom, they become satisfied, but if they are not given therefrom, they become objectors.

59. They should be satisfied with what **GOD** and His messenger have given them. They should have said, "**GOD** suffices us. **GOD** will provide for us from His bounties, and so will His messenger. We are seeking only **GOD**."

Distribution System for Charities

60. Charities shall go to the poor, the needy, the workers who collect them, the new converts, to free the slaves, to those burdened by sudden expenses, in the cause of **GOD**, and to the traveling alien. Such is **GOD**'s commandment. **GOD** is Omniscient, Most Wise.

61. Some of them hurt the prophet by saying, "He is all ears!" Say, "It is better for you that he listens to you. He believes in **GOD**, and trusts the believers. He is a mercy for those among you who believe." Those who hurt **GOD**'s messenger have incurred a painful retribution.

62. They swear by **GOD** to you, to please you, when **GOD** and His messenger are more worthy of pleasing, if they are really believers.

Retribution for Opposing God and His Messenger

63. Did they not know that anyone who opposes **GOD** and His messenger has incurred the fire of Hell forever? This is the worst humiliation.

The Hypocrites

64. The hypocrites worry that a sura may be revealed exposing what is inside their hearts. Say, "Go ahead and mock. **GOD** will expose exactly what you are afraid of."

---

*9:54 This is another proof that the Contact Prayers (Salat) existed before the Quran, and were handed down from Abraham (see 21:73). Also, it stumps those who challenge God's assertion that the Quran is complete and fully detailed when they ask, "Where can we find the details of the Contact Prayers in the Quran?" (6:19, 38, 114).

65. If you ask them, they would say, "We were only mocking and kidding." Say, "Do you realize that you are mocking **GOD**, and His revelations, and His messenger?"

66. Do not apologize. You have disbelieved after having believed. If we pardon some of you, we will punish others among you, as a consequence of their wickedness.

67. The hypocrite men and the hypocrite women belong with each other – they advocate evil and prohibit righteousness, and they are stingy. They forgot **GOD**, so He forgot them. The hypocrites are truly wicked.

68. **GOD** promises the hypocrite men and the hypocrite women, as well as the disbelievers, the fire of Hell, wherein they abide forever. It suffices them. **GOD** has condemned them; they have incurred an everlasting retribution.

God's System Does Not Change

69. Some of those before you were stronger than you, and possessed more money and children. They became preoccupied with their material possessions. Similarly, you have become preoccupied with your material possessions, just like those before you have become preoccupied. You have become totally heedless, just as they were heedless. Such are the people who nullify their works, both in this world and in the Hereafter; they are the losers.

The Losers

70. Have they not learned anything from the previous generations; the people of Noah, 'Ãd, Thamûd, the people of Abraham, the dwellers of Midyan, and the evildoers (*of Sod-*

om and Gomorrah)? Their messengers went to them with clear proofs. **GOD** never wronged them; they are the ones who wronged their own souls.

The Winners

71. The believing men and women are allies of one another. They advocate righteousness and forbid evil, they observe the Contact Prayers (*Salat*) and give the obligatory charity (*Zakat*), and they obey **GOD** and His messenger. These will be showered by **GOD**'s mercy. **GOD** is Almighty, Most Wise.

72. **GOD** promises the believing men and the believing women gardens with flowing streams, wherein they abide forever, and magnificent mansions in the gardens of Eden. And **GOD**'s blessings and approval are even greater. This is the greatest triumph.

*You Shall Be Stern
With the Disbelievers*

73. O you prophet, strive against the disbelievers and the hypocrites, and be stern in dealing with them. Their destiny is Hell; what a miserable abode!

74. They swear by **GOD** that they never said it, although they have uttered the word of disbelief; they have disbelieved after becoming submitters. In fact, they gave up what they never had. They have rebelled even though **GOD** and His messenger have showered them with His grace and provisions. If they repent, it would be best for them. But if they turn away, **GOD** will commit them to painful retribution in this life and in the Hereafter. They will find no one on earth to be their lord and master.

75. Some of them even pledged: "If **GOD** showered us with His grace, we would be charitable, and would lead a righteous life."

76. But when He did shower them with His provisions, they became stingy, and turned away in aversion.

77. Consequently, He plagued them with hypocrisy in their hearts, till the day they meet Him. This is because they broke their promises to **GOD**, and because of their lying.

78. Do they not realize that **GOD** knows their secrets, and their conspiracies, and that **GOD** is the Knower of all secrets?

79. Those who criticize the generous believers for giving too much, and ridicule the poor believers for giving too little, **GOD** despises them. They have incurred a painful retribution.

*Satan's Most Effective Bait:
The Myth of Intercession**

80. Whether you ask forgiveness for them, or do not ask forgiveness for them – even if you ask forgiveness for them seventy times – **GOD** will not forgive them. This is because they disbelieve in **GOD** and His messenger. **GOD** does not guide the wicked people.

81. The sedentary rejoiced in their staying behind the messenger of **GOD**, and hated to strive with their money and their lives in the cause of **GOD**. They said, "Let us not mobilize in this heat!" Say, "The fire of Hell is much hotter," if they could only comprehend.

82. Let them laugh a little, and cry a lot. This is the requital for the sins they have earned.

83. If **GOD** returns you to a situation where they ask your permission to mobilize with you, you shall say, "You will never again mobilize with me, nor will you ever fight with me against any enemy. For you have chosen to be with the sedentary in the first place. Therefore, you must stay with the sedentary."

84. You shall not observe the funeral prayer for any of them when he dies, nor shall you stand at his grave. They have disbelieved in **GOD** and His messenger, and died in a state of wickedness.

Worldly Materials Are Nil

85. Do not be impressed by their money or their children; **GOD** causes these to be sources of misery for them in this world, and their souls depart as disbelievers.

86. When a sura is revealed, stating: "Believe in **GOD**, and strive with His messenger," even the strong among them say, "Let us stay behind!"

87. They chose to be with the sedentary. Consequently, their hearts were sealed, and thus, they cannot comprehend.

True Believers are Eager to Strive

88. As for the messenger and those who believed with him, they eagerly strive with their money and their lives. These have deserved all the good things; they are the winners.

---

*9:80 If Muhammad could not intercede on behalf of his own uncles and cousins, what makes strangers who never met him think that he will intercede on their behalf? Abraham could not intercede on behalf of his father, nor could Noah intercede on behalf of his son (11:46 & 60:4).

89. **GOD** has prepared for them gardens with flowing streams, wherein they abide forever. This is the greatest triumph.

90. The Arabs made up excuses, and came to you seeking permission to stay behind. This is indicative of their rejection of **GOD** and His messenger – they stay behind. Indeed, those who disbelieve among them have incurred a painful retribution.

91. Not to be blamed are those who are weak, or ill, or do not find anything to offer, so long as they remain devoted to **GOD** and His messenger. The righteous among them shall not be blamed. **GOD** is Forgiver, Most Merciful.

92. Also excused are those who come to you wishing to be included with you, but you tell them, "I do not have anything to carry you on." They then turn back with tears in their eyes, genuinely saddened that they could not afford to contribute.

93. The blame is on those who ask your permission to stay behind, even though they have no excuse. They have chosen to be with the sedentary. Consequently, **GOD** has sealed their hearts, and thus, they do not attain any knowledge.

Hard Times Serve to Expose the Hypocrites

94. They apologize to you when you return to them (*from battle*). Say, "Do not apologize; we no longer trust you. **GOD** has informed us about you." **GOD** will see your works, and so will the messenger, then you will be returned to the Knower of all secrets and declara-

tions, then He will inform you of everything you had done.

95. They will swear by **GOD** to you, when you return to them, that you may disregard them. Do disregard them. They are polluted, and their destiny is Hell, as a requital for the sins they have earned.

96. They swear to you, that you may pardon them. Even if you pardon them, **GOD** does not pardon such wicked people.

The Arabs

97. The Arabs are the worst in disbelief and hypocrisy, and the most likely to ignore the laws that **GOD** has revealed to His messenger. **GOD** is Omniscient, Most Wise.

98. Some Arabs consider their spending (*in the cause of God*) to be a loss, and even wait in anticipation that a disaster may hit you. It is they who will incur the worst disaster. **GOD** is Hearer, Omniscient.

99. Other Arabs do believe in **GOD** and the Last Day, and consider their spending to be a means towards **GOD**, and a means of supporting the messenger. Indeed, it will bring them nearer; **GOD** will admit them into His mercy. **GOD** is Forgiver, Most Merciful.

100. As for the early vanguards who immigrated (*Muhãjerin*), and the supporters who gave them refuge (*Ansãr*) and those who followed them in righteousness, **GOD** is pleased with them, and they are pleased with Him. He has prepared for them gardens with flowing streams, wherein they abide forever. This is the greatest triumph.

*Retribution Doubled
for the Hypocrites**

101. Among the Arabs around you, there are hypocrites. Also, among the city dwellers, there are those who are accustomed to hypocrisy. You do not know them, but we know them. We will double the retribution for them, then they end up committed to a terrible retribution.

102. There are others who have confessed their sins; they have mixed good deeds with bad deeds. **GOD** will redeem them, for **GOD** is Forgiver, Most Merciful.

103. Take from their money a charity to purify them and sanctify them. And encourage them, for your encouragement reassures them. **GOD** is Hearer, Omniscient.

104. Do they not realize that **GOD** accepts the repentance of His worshipers, and takes the charities, and that **GOD** is the Redeemer, Most Merciful?

105. Say, "Work righteousness; **GOD** will see your work, and so will His messenger and the believers. Ultimately, you will be returned to the Knower of all secrets and declarations, then He will inform you of everything you had done."

106. Others are waiting for **GOD**'s decision; He may punish them, or He may redeem them. **GOD** is Omniscient, Most Wise.

*Masjids that Oppose God
and His Messenger**

107. There are those who abuse the masjid by practicing idol worship, dividing the believers, and providing comfort to those who oppose **GOD** and His messenger. They solemnly swear: "Our intentions are honorable!" **GOD** bears witness that they are liars.

Do Not Pray in Those Masjids

108. You shall never pray in such a masjid. A masjid that is established on the basis of righteousness from the first day is more worthy of your praying therein. In it, there are people who love to be purified. **GOD** loves those who purify themselves.

109. Is one who establishes his building on the basis of reverencing **GOD** and to gain His approval better, or one who establishes his building on the brink of a crumbling cliff, that falls down with him into the fire of Hell? **GOD** does not guide the transgressing people.

110. Such a building that they have established remains a source of doubt in their hearts, until their hearts are stilled. **GOD** is Omniscient, Most Wise.

---

*9:101 The hypocrites sit among the believers, listen to the message and proofs, then spread their poisonous doubts. It is a Quranic law that they receive double the retribution, now and forever.

*9:107 Any masjid where the practices are not devoted absolutely to God ALONE belongs to Satan, not God. For example, mentioning the names of Abraham, Muhammad, and/or Ali in the Azan and/or the Salat prayers violates God's commandments in 2:136, 2:285, 3:84, & 72:18. Unfortunately, this is a common idolatrous practice throughout the corrupted Muslim world.

The Most Profitable Investment

111. **GOD** has bought from the believers their lives and their money in exchange for Paradise. Thus, they fight in the cause of **GOD**, willing to kill and get killed. Such is His truthful pledge in the Torah, the Gospel, and the Quran—and who fulfills His pledge better than **GOD**? You shall rejoice in making such an exchange. This is the greatest triumph.

The Believers

112. They are the repenters, the worshipers, the praisers, the meditators, the bowing and prostrating, the advocators of righteousness and forbidders of evil, and the keepers of **GOD**'s laws. Give good news to such believers.

You Shall Disown God's Enemies: Abraham Disowned His Father

113. Neither the prophet, nor those who believe shall ask forgiveness for the idol worshipers, even if they were their nearest of kin, once they realize that they are destined for Hell.

114. The only reason Abraham asked forgiveness for his father was that he had promised him to do so. But as soon as he realized that he was an enemy of **GOD**, he disowned him. Abraham was extremely kind, clement.

115. **GOD** does not send any people astray, after He had guided them, without first pointing out for them what to expect. **GOD** is fully aware of all things.

116. To **GOD** belongs the sovereignty of the heavens and the earth. He controls life and death. You have none beside **GOD** as a Lord and Master.

117. **GOD** has redeemed the prophet, and the immigrants (*Muhãjireen*) and the supporters who hosted them and gave them refuge (*Ansãr*), who followed him during the difficult times. That is when the hearts of some of them almost wavered. But He has redeemed them, for He is Compassionate towards them, Most Merciful.

Do Not Abandon the Messenger

118. Also (*redeemed were*) the three who stayed behind. The spacious earth became so straitened for them, that they almost gave up all hope for themselves. Finally, they realized that there was no escape from **GOD**, except to Him. He then redeemed them that they may repent. **GOD** is the Redeemer, Most Merciful.

119. O you who believe, you shall reverence **GOD**, and be among the truthful.

120. Neither the dwellers of the city, nor the Arabs around them, shall seek to stay behind the messenger of **GOD** (*when he mobilizes for war*). Nor shall they give priority to their own affairs over supporting him. This is because they do not suffer any thirst, or any effort, or hunger in the cause of **GOD**, or make a single step that enrages the disbelievers, or inflict any hardship upon the enemy, without having it written down for them as a credit. **GOD** never fails to recompense those who work righteousness.

121. Nor do they incur any expense, small or large, nor do they cross any valley, without having the credit written down for them. **GOD** will surely reward them generously for their works.

The Importance of
Religious Education

122. When the believers mobilize, not all of them shall do so. A few from each group shall mobilize by devoting their time to studying the religion. Thus, they can pass the knowledge on to their people when they return, that they may remain religiously informed.

The Disbelievers

123. O you who believe, you shall fight the disbelievers who attack you – let them find you stern – and know that **GOD** is with the righteous.

The Hypocrites

124. When a sura was revealed, some of them would say, "Did this sura strengthen the faith of anyone among you?" Indeed, it did strengthen the faith of those who believed, and they rejoice in any revelation.

125. As for those who harbored doubts in their hearts, it actually added unholiness to their unholiness, and they died as disbelievers.

126. Do they not see that they suffer from exacting trials every year once or twice? Yet, they consistently fail to repent, and fail to take heed?

A Historical Crime Unveiled:
Tampering With the
Word of God*
God Provides Irrefutable Evidence

127. Whenever a sura was revealed, some of them would look at each other as if to say: "Does anyone see you?" Then they left. Thus, **GOD** has diverted their hearts, for they are people who do not comprehend.

◆◆◆◆

Sura 10: Jonah
(Younus)

In the name of God,
Most Gracious, Most Merciful

1. A. L. R.* These (*letters*) are the proofs of this book of wisdom.

2. Is it too much of a wonder for the people that we inspired a man like them? He (*was inspired to say*), "You shall warn the people, and give good news to those who believe that they have attained a position of prominence at their Lord." The disbelievers said, "This is a clever magician!"

---

*9:1 & *9:127 This is the only sura that is not prefixed with the **Basmalah.** This phenomenon has puzzled the students of the Quran for 14 centuries, and many theories were advanced to explain it. Now we realize that the conspicuous absence of the **Basmalah** serves three purposes: (1) It represents an advance divine proclamation that the idol worshipers were destined to tamper with the Quran by adding 2 false verses (9:128-129). (2) It demonstrates one of the functions of God's mathematical code in the Quran, namely, to guard the Quran against any alteration. (3) It provides additional miraculous features of the Quran's code. Due to their extraordinary importance, the details are given in Appendices 24 and 29. One immediate observation is that the number of occurrences of the word "God" at the end of Sura 9 is 1273 (19x67). If the two false verses 128 & 129 are included, this phenomenon – and many more – will vanish.

*10:1 These letters constitute a major portion of the Quran's awesome mathematical code and proof of divine authorship. See Appendix 1 for details.

---

3. Your only Lord is **GOD**; the One who created the heavens and the earth in six days, then assumed all authority. He controls all matters. There is no intercessor, except in accordance with His will. Such is **GOD** your Lord. You shall worship Him. Would you not take heed?

4. To Him is your ultimate return, all of you. This is **GOD**'s truthful promise. He initiates the creation, then repeats it, in order to reward those who believe and lead a righteous life, equitably. As for those who disbelieve, they incur hellish drinks, and a painful retribution for their disbelieving.

5. He is the One who rendered the sun radiant, and the moon a light, and He designed its phases that you may learn to count the years and to calculate. **GOD** did not create all this, except for a specific purpose. He explains the revelations for people who know.

6. Surely, in the alternation of night and day, and what **GOD** created in the heavens and the earth, there are proofs for people who are righteous.

Preoccupation With This World

7. Those who are not expecting to meet us, and are preoccupied with this worldly life and are content with it, and refuse to heed our proofs;

8. these have incurred Hell as their ultimate abode, as a consequence of their own works.

God Guides the Believers

9. As for those who believe and lead a righteous life, their Lord guides them, by virtue of their belief. Rivers will flow beneath them in the gardens of bliss.

10. Their prayer therein is: "Be You glorified, our god," their greeting therein is, "Peace," and their ultimate prayer is: "Praise be to **GOD**, Lord of the universe."

11. If **GOD** hastened the retribution incurred by the people, the way they demand provisions, they would have been annihilated long ago. However, we leave those who do not believe in meeting us in their transgressions, blundering.

12. When adversity touches the human being, he implores us while lying down, or sitting, or standing up. But as soon as we relieve his adversity, he goes on as if he never implored us to relieve any hardship! The works of the transgressors are thus adorned in their eyes.

Lessons from the Past

13. Many a generation we have annihilated before you when they transgressed. Their messengers went to them with clear proofs, but they refused to believe. We thus requite the guilty people.

Now It Is Your Turn

14. Then we made you inheritors of the earth after them, to see how you will do.

*Every Letter Calculated and
Divinely Designed*

15. When our revelations are recited to them, those who do not expect to meet us say, "Bring a Quran* other than this, or change it!" Say, "I cannot possibly change it on my own. I simply follow what is revealed to me. I fear, if I disobey my Lord, the retribution of an awesome day."

16. Say, "Had **GOD** willed, I would not have recited it to you, nor would you have known anything about it. I have lived among you a whole life before this (*and you have known me as a sane, truthful person*). Do you not understand?"

17. Who is more evil than one who fabricates lies about **GOD**, or rejects His revelations. Certainly, the transgressors never succeed.

18. They worship beside **GOD** idols that possess no power to harm them or benefit them, and they say, "These are our intercessors at **GOD**!" Say, "Are you informing **GOD** of something He does not know in the heavens or the earth?" Be He glorified. He is the Most High; far above needing partners.

19. The people used to be one congregation, then they disputed. If it were not for a predetermined word from your Lord, they would have been judged immediately regarding their disputes.

*Miracle of the Quran to be
Unveiled After Muhammad**

20. They say, "How come no miracle came down to him from his Lord?" Say, "The future belongs to **GOD**; so wait, and I am waiting along with you."

Rebellious Humans

21. When we bestow mercy upon the people, after adversity had afflicted them, they immediately scheme against our revelations! Say, "**GOD**'s scheming is far more effective. For our messengers are recording everything you scheme."

22. He is the One who moves you across the land and sea. You get onto the ships, and they sail smoothly in nice breeze. Then, while rejoicing therein, violent wind blows, and the waves surround them from every side. This is when they implore **GOD**, sincerely devoting their prayers to Him alone: "If You only save us this time, we will be eternally appreciative."

23. But as soon as He saves them, they transgress on earth, and oppose the truth. O people, your transgression is only to the detriment of your own souls. You remain preoccupied with this worldly life, then to us is your ultimate return, then we inform you of everything you had done.

10:15 The word "Quran" is mentioned in the Quran 58 times, but since this verse refers to "another Quran," it must be excluded; "This Quran" is mentioned in the Quran 57 times, 19x3.

10:20 In retrospect, we see now that the Quran's miracle, indeed "One of the greatest miracles" (74:30-35), was divinely predestined to be unveiled 14 centuries after Muhammad. In view of the current condition of the traditional Muslims, if Muhammad had been given this miracle, those Muslims, who are already idolizing Muhammad beside God, would have worshiped him as God incarnate. Additionally, this miracle is obviously designed for the computer age, and to be appreciated by mathematically sophisticated generations.

24. The analogy of this worldly life is like this: we send down water from the sky to produce with it all kinds of plants from the earth, and to provide food for the people and the animals. Then, just as the earth is perfectly adorned, and its people think that they are in control thereof, our judgment comes by night or by day,* leaving it completely barren, as if nothing existed the previous day. We thus explain the revelations for people who reflect.

25. **GOD** invites to the abode of peace, and guides whomever He wills in a straight path.

Heaven and Hell are Eternal

26. For the righteous, the reward will be multiplied manifold. Their faces will never experience any deprivation or shame. These are the dwellers of Paradise; they abide therein forever.

27. As for those who earned sins, their requital is equivalent to their sin. Humiliation is their lot, and no one beside **GOD** can protect them. Their faces will seem overwhelmed by masses of dark night. They will be the dwellers of Hell; they abide therein forever.

Idols Disown
Their Worshipers

28. On the day when we summon them all, we will say to those who worshiped idols, "We have summoned you, together with your idols." We will have them confront each other, and their idols will say to them, "We had no idea that you idolized us.

29. "**GOD** suffices as a witness between us and you, that we were completely unaware of your worshiping us."

30. That is when each soul will examine everything it had done. They will be returned to **GOD**, their rightful Lord and Master, and the idols they had fabricated will disown them.

31. Say, "Who provides for you from the heaven and the earth? Who controls all the hearing and the eyesight? Who produces the living from the dead, and the dead from the living? Who is in control of all things?" They would say, "**GOD**." Say, "Why then do you not observe the commandments?"

32. Such is **GOD**, your rightful Lord. What is there after the truth, except falsehood? How could you disregard all this?

33. This is what your Lord's decision does to those who choose to be wicked: they cannot believe.

Reflect on Your Idols

34. Say, "Can any of your idols initiate creation, then repeat it?" Say, "**GOD** initiates the creation, then repeats it."

35. Say, "Does any of your idols guide to the truth?" Say, "**GOD** guides to the truth. Is one who guides to the truth more worthy of being followed, or one who does not guide, and needs guidance for himself? What is wrong with your judgment?"

10:24 God, of course, knows whether His judgment will come during the day, or during the night. But it just happens that the earth will be half day and half night when the end of the world comes. Another "scientific miracle" of the Quran.

36. Most of them follow nothing but conjecture, and conjecture is no substitute for the truth. **GOD** is fully aware of everything they do.

Only God Can Author the Quran

37. This Quran could not possibly be authored by other than **GOD**. It confirms all previous messages, and provides a fully detailed scripture. It is infallible; for it comes from the Lord of the universe.

38. If they say, "He fabricated it," say, "Then produce one sura like these, and invite whomever you wish, other than **GOD**, if you are truthful."

39. Indeed, they have rejected this without studying and examining it, and before understanding it. Thus did those before them disbelieve. Therefore, note the consequences for the transgressors.

40. Some of them believe (*in this scripture*), while others disbelieve in it. Your Lord is fully aware of the evildoers.

41. If they reject you, then say, "I have my works, and you have your works. You are innocent of anything I do, and I am innocent of anything you do."

42. Some of them listen to you, but can you make the deaf hear, even though they cannot understand?

*Humans Freely Choose
Their Paths*

43. Some of them look at you, but can you guide the blind, even though they do not see?

44. **GOD** never wrongs the people; it is the people who wrong their own souls.

45. On the day when He summons all of them, they will feel as if they lasted in this world one hour of the day, during which they met. Losers indeed are those who disbelieved in meeting **GOD**; and chose to be misguided.

46. Whether we show you some (*of the retribution*) we promise them, or terminate your life before that, to us is their ultimate return. **GOD** witnesses everything they do.

47. To each community, a messenger. After their messenger comes, they are judged equitably, without the least injustice.

48. They challenge: "When will this prophecy come to pass, if you are telling the truth?"

The Messenger Possesses No Power

49. Say, "I possess no power to harm myself, or benefit myself; only what **GOD** wills takes place." Each community has a predetermined life span. Once their interim comes to an end, they cannot delay it by one hour, nor advance it.

50. Say, "Whether His retribution comes to you by night or by day, why are the transgressors in such a hurry?

51. "If it does happen, will you believe then? Why should you believe then? You used to challenge it to come?"

52. It will be said to the transgressors, "Taste the eternal retribution. Are you not requited precisely for what you have earned?"

53. They challenge you to prophesy: "Is this really what will happen?" Say, "Yes indeed, by my Lord, this is the truth, and you can never escape."

What Price Faith

54. If any wicked soul possessed everything on earth, it would readily offer it as ransom. They will be ridden with remorse when they see the retribution. They will be judged equitably, without the least injustice.

55. Absolutely, to **GOD** belongs everything in the heavens and the earth. Absolutely, **GOD**'s promise is truth, but most of them do not know.

56. He controls life and death, and to Him you will be returned.

57. O people, enlightenment has come to you herein from your Lord, and healing for anything that troubles your hearts, and guidance, and mercy for the believers.

Joy for the Believers

58. Say, "With **GOD**'s grace and with His mercy they shall rejoice." This is far better than any wealth they can accumulate.

*Human-made
Dietary Prohibitions*

59. Say, "Did you note how **GOD** sends down to you all kinds of provisions, then you render some of them unlawful, and some lawful?" Say, "Did **GOD** give you permission to do this? Or, do you fabricate lies and attribute them to **GOD**?"

60. Does it ever occur to those who fabricate lies about **GOD** that they will have to face Him on the Day of Resurrection? Certainly, **GOD**

showers the people with His grace, but most of them are unappreciative.

Knowing God

61. You do not get into any situation, nor do you recite any Quran, nor do you do anything, without us being witnesses thereof as you do it. Not even an atom's weight is out of your Lord's control, be it in the heavens or the earth. Nor is there anything smaller than an atom, or larger, that is not recorded in a profound record.

Happiness: Now and Forever*

62. Absolutely, **GOD**'s allies have nothing to fear, nor will they grieve.

63. They are those who believe and lead a righteous life.

64. For them, joy and happiness in this world, as well as in the Hereafter. This is **GOD**'s unchangeable law. Such is the greatest triumph.

65. Do not be saddened by their utterances. All power belongs to **GOD**. He is the Hearer, the Omniscient.

66. Absolutely, to **GOD** belongs everyone in the heavens and everyone on earth. Those who set up idols beside **GOD** are really following nothing. They only think that they are following something. They only guess.

67. He is the One who rendered the night for your rest, and rendered the day lighted. These are proofs for people who can hear.

---

*10:62-64 Most people think that they have to wait until the Day of Resurrection before they receive their rewards for righteousness, or the retribution for wickedness. But the Quran repeatedly assures the believers that they are guaranteed perfect happiness here in this world, now and forever. At the end of their interim here, they go directly to Paradise (see Appendix 17).

The Gross Blasphemy

68. They said, "**GOD** has begotten a son!" Be He glorified. He is the Most Rich. To Him belongs everything in the heavens and everything on earth. You have no proof to support such a blasphemy. Are you saying about **GOD** what you do not know?

69. Proclaim: "Those who fabricate lies about **GOD** will never succeed."

70. They get their temporary share in this world, then to us is their ultimate return, then we commit them to severe retribution for their disbelieving.

Noah

71. Recite for them the history of Noah. He said to his people, "O my people, if you find my position and my reminding you of **GOD**'s revelations too much for you, then I put my trust in **GOD**. You should get together with your leaders, agree on a final decision among yourselves, then let me know it without delay.

72. "If you turn away, then I have not asked you for any wage. My wage comes from **GOD**. I have been commanded to be a submitter."

73. They rejected him and, consequently, we saved him and those who joined him in the ark; we made them the inheritors. And we drowned those who rejected our revelations. Note the consequences; they have been warned.

Humans Insist on Their Original Sin

74. Then we sent after him messengers to their people, and they showed them clear proofs. But they were not to believe in what they had rejected in the past. We thus seal the hearts of the transgressors.

Moses and Aaron

75. Then we sent after them Moses and Aaron to Pharaoh and his group, with our proofs. But they turned arrogant; and were transgressing people.

76. When the truth came to them from us, they said, "This is obviously magic!"

77. Moses said, "Is this how you describe the truth when it comes to you? Is this magic? How can any magicians prevail?"

78. They said, "Did you come to divert us from what we found our parents doing, and to attain positions of prominence for yourselves? We will never join you as believers."

The Truth Prevails

79. Pharaoh said, "Bring to me every experienced magician."

80. When the magicians came, Moses said to them, "Throw whatever you are going to throw."

81. When they threw, Moses said, "What you have produced is magic, and **GOD** will make it fail. **GOD** does not support the transgressors' work."

82. **GOD** establishes the truth with His words, despite the criminals.

83. None believed with Moses except a few of his people, while fearing the tyranny of Pharaoh and his elders. Surely, Pharaoh was much too arrogant on earth, and a real tyrant.

84. Moses said, "O my people, if you have really believed in **GOD**, then put your trust in Him, if you are really submitters."

85. They said, "We trust in **GOD.** Our Lord, save us from the persecution of these oppressive people.

86. "Deliver us, with Your mercy, from the disbelieving people."

87. We inspired Moses and his brother. "Maintain your homes in Egypt for the time being, turn your homes into synagogues, and maintain the Contact Prayers (*Salat*). Give good news to the believers."

88. Moses said, "Our Lord, you have given Pharaoh and his elders luxuries and wealth in this world. Our Lord, they only use them to repulse others from Your path. Our Lord, wipe out their wealth, and harden their hearts to prevent them from believing, until they see the painful retribution."

89. He said, "Your prayer has been answered (*O Moses and Aaron*), so be steadfast, and do not follow the ways of those who do not know."

90. We delivered the Children of Israel across the sea. Pharaoh and his troops pursued them, aggressively and sinfully. When drowning became a reality for him, he said, "I believe that there is no god except the One in whom the Children of Israel have believed; I am a submitter."

91. "Too late!* For you have rebelled already, and chose to be a transgressor.

Pharaoh's Body Preserved

92. "Today, we will preserve your body, to set you up as a lesson for future generations."* Unfortunately, many people are totally oblivious to our signs.

93. We have endowed the Children of Israel with a position of honor, and blessed them with good provisions. Yet, they disputed when this knowledge came to them. Your Lord will judge them on the Day of Resurrection regarding everything they disputed.

The Messenger's Doubt

94. If you have any doubt regarding what is revealed to you from your Lord, then ask those who read the previous scripture. Indeed, the truth has come to you from your Lord. Do not be with the doubters.

95. Nor shall you join those who rejected **GOD**'s revelations, lest you be with the losers.

96. Surely, those condemned by a decree from your Lord cannot believe.

97. No matter what kind of proof you show them, (*they cannot believe*), until they see the painful retribution.

Believing Nations Prosper

98. Any community that believes will surely be rewarded for believing. For example, the people of Jonah: when they believed, we relieved the humiliating retribution they had been suffering in this world, and we made them prosperous.

---

*10:91 Believing in God is the first step. Thereafter, one needs to nourish and develop the soul through the practices of worship (see Appendix 15).

*10:92 God endowed the Egyptians with the exclusive knowledge of mummification. Today, Pharaoh's mummified body is on display at the Cairo Museum.

99. Had your Lord willed, all the people on earth would have believed.* Do you want to force the people to become believers?

The Disbelievers Blocked Out*

100. No soul can believe except in accordance with **GOD**'s will. For He places a curse upon those who refuse to understand.

101. Say, "Look at all the signs in the heavens and the earth." All the proofs and all the warnings can never help people who decided to disbelieve.

102. Can they expect other than the fate of their counterparts in the past? Say, "Just wait, and, along with you, I am also waiting."

Guaranteed Victory

103. We ultimately save our messengers and those who believe. It is our immutable law that we save the believers.

104. Say, "O people, if you have any doubt regarding my religion, I do not worship what you worship beside **GOD**. I worship **GOD** alone; the One who will terminate your lives. I am commanded to be a believer."

105. I was commanded: "Keep yourself devoted to the religion of monotheism; you shall not practice idol worship.

106. "You shall not worship beside **GOD** what possesses no power to benefit you or harm you. If you do, you will be a transgressor."

All Power Belongs To God

107. If **GOD** touches you with a hardship, none can relieve it except He. And when He blesses you, no force can prevent His grace. He bestows it upon whomever He chooses from among His servants. He is the Forgiver, Most Merciful.

108. Proclaim: "O people, the truth has come to you herein from your Lord. Whoever is guided is guided for his own good. And whoever goes astray, goes astray to his own detriment. I am not a guardian over you."

109. Follow what is revealed to you, and be patient until **GOD** issues His judgment; He is the best judge.

◆◆◆◆

Sura 11: Hûd (Hûd)

In the name of God,
Most Gracious, Most Merciful

1. A.L.R. This is a scripture whose verses have been perfected, then elucidated.* It comes from a Most Wise, Most Cognizant.

The Quran: Messenger of God

2. Proclaiming: "You shall not worship except **GOD**. I come to you from Him as a warner, as well as a bearer of good news.

---

*10:99-101 The test demands that we denounce idolatry on our own, without divine intervention in our initial decision. God blocks out those who choose to disbelieve.

*11:1 Our generation is fortunate to witness two awesome phenomena in the Quran: (1) an extraordinary mathematical code (Appendix 1), and (2) a literary miracle of incredible dimensions. If humans attempt to write a mathematically structured work, the numerical manipulations will adversely affect the literary quality. The Quran sets the standard for literary excellence.

3. "You shall seek your Lord's forgiveness, then repent to Him. He will then bless you generously for a predetermined period, and bestow His grace upon those who deserve it. If you turn away, then I fear for you the retribution of an awesome day."

4. To **GOD** is your ultimate return, and He is Omnipotent.

5. Indeed, they hide their innermost thoughts, as if to keep Him from knowing them. In fact, as they cover themselves with their clothes, He knows all their secrets and declarations. He knows the innermost thoughts.

Provisions Guaranteed

6. There is not a creature on earth whose provision is not guaranteed by **GOD**. And He knows its course and its final destiny. All are recorded in a profound record.

7. He is the One who created the heavens and the earth in six days—* and His (*earthly*) domain was completely covered with water—** in order to test you, to distinguish those among you who work righteousness. Yet, when you say, "You will be resurrected after death," those who disbelieve would say, "This is clearly witchcraft."

8. And if we delay the retribution they have incurred—for we reserve it for a specific community—they say,

"What is keeping Him?" In fact, once it comes to them, nothing can stop it, and their mocking will come back to haunt them.

9. Whenever we bless the human being with mercy from us, then remove it, he turns despondent, unappreciative.

10. Whenever we bless him, after adversity had afflicted him, he says, "All adversity has gone away from me;" he becomes excited, proud.

11. As for those who steadfastly persevere, and lead a righteous life, they deserve forgiveness and a generous recompense.

God's Revelation is Heavy

12. You may wish to disregard some of that which is revealed to you, and you may be annoyed by it. Also, they may say, "How come no treasure comes down to him, or an angel?" You are only a warner; **GOD** controls all things.

The Quran: Impossible to Imitate

13. If they say, "He fabricated (*the Quran*)," tell them, "Then produce ten suras like these, fabricated, and invite whomever you can, other than **GOD**, if you are truthful."*

14. If they fail to meet your challenge, then know that this is revealed with **GOD**'s knowledge, and that there is no god except He. Will you then submit?

11:7 The six days are simply a yardstick providing us with a lot of information. Thus, we learn that the vast lifeless physical universe was created in two days, while the tiny mote called "Earth" was created in four days (41:10-12). The provision of food, water, and oxygen for the earth's inhabitants had to be precisely calculated and arranged.

**11:7 The earth was initially covered with water. Subsequently, the land mass emerged, and the continents drifted apart.*

11:13 The Quran's mathematical miracle is inimitable (See Appendix 1).

---

15. Those who pursue this worldly life and its material vanities, we will pay them for their works in this life; without the least reduction.

16. It is they who gave up their share in the Hereafter, and, consequently, Hell is their lot. All their works are in vain; everything they have done is nullified.

The Quran's Mathematical Code

17. As for those who are given solid proof* from their Lord, reported by a witness from Him, and before it, the book of Moses has set a precedent and a mercy,** they will surely believe. As for those who disbelieve among the various groups, Hell is awaiting them. Do not harbor any doubt; this is the truth from your Lord, but most people disbelieve.

18. Who are more evil than those who fabricate lies about **GOD**? They will be presented before their Lord, and the witnesses will say, "These are the ones who lied about their Lord. **GOD**'s condemnation has befallen the transgressors."

19. They repel from the way of **GOD** and seek to make it crooked, and they are disbelievers in the Hereafter.

The Disbelievers

20. These will never escape, nor will they find any lords or masters to help them against **GOD**. Retribution will be doubled for them. They

have failed to hear, and they have failed to see.

21. These are the ones who lose their souls, and the idols they had fabricated will disown them.

22. There is no doubt that, in the Hereafter, they will be the worst losers.

The Believers

23. As for those who believe and lead a righteous life, and devote themselves to their Lord, they are the dwellers of Paradise; they abide therein forever.

24. The example of these two groups is like the blind and deaf, compared to the seer and hearer. Are they equal? Would you not take heed?

Noah

25. We sent Noah to his people, saying, "I come to you as a clear warner.

26. "You shall not worship except **GOD**. I fear for you the retribution of a painful day."

27. The leaders who disbelieved among his people said, "We see that you are no more than a human being like us, and we see that the first people to follow you are the worst among us. We see that you do not possess any advantage over us. Indeed, we think you are liars."

28. He said, "O my people, what if I have a solid proof from my Lord? What if He has blessed me out of His mercy, though you cannot see it? Are we going to force you to believe therein?

---

*11:17 The Quran's 19-based mathematical code is a built-in proof of divine authorship. It is noteworthy that the word "Bayyinah" (proof) is mentioned in the Quran 19 times.

**11:17 As it turns out, Moses' book was also mathematically composed, with "19" as the common denominator. See Footnote 46:10 and Appendix 1.

---

29. "O my people, I do not ask you for any money; my wage comes only from **GOD**. I am not dismissing those who believed; they will meet their Lord (*and He alone will judge them*). I see that you are ignorant people.

30. "O my people, who can support me against **GOD**, if I dismiss them? Would you not take heed?

All Power Belongs to God

31. "I do not claim that I possess the treasures of **GOD**, nor do I know the future, nor do I claim to be an angel. Nor do I say to those despised by your eyes that **GOD** will not bestow any blessings upon them. **GOD** knows best what is in their innermost thoughts. (*If I did this,*) I would be a transgressor."

32. They said, "O Noah, you have argued with us, and kept on arguing. We challenge you to bring the doom you threaten us with, if you are truthful."

33. He said, "**GOD** is the One who brings it to you, if He so wills, then you cannot escape.

34. "Even if I advised you, my advice cannot benefit you if it is **GOD**'s will to send you astray. He is your Lord, and to Him you will be returned."

35. If they say, "He made up this story," then say, "If I made it up, then I am responsible for my crime, and I am innocent of any crime you commit."

36. Noah was inspired: "No more of your people are going to believe, beyond those who already believe. Do not be saddened by their actions.

37. "Build the ark under our watchful eyes, and with our inspiration, and do not implore Me on behalf of those who have transgressed; they are destined to drown."

He Who Laughs Last Laughs Best

38. While he was building the ark, whenever some of his people passed by him they laughed at him. He said, "You may be laughing at us, but we are laughing at you, just as you are laughing.

39. "You will surely find out who will suffer a shameful retribution, and incur an everlasting punishment."

40. When our judgment came, and the atmosphere boiled over, we said, "Carry on it a pair of each kind,* together with your family, except those who are condemned. Carry with you those who have believed," and only a few have believed with him.

41. He said, "Come on board. In the name of **GOD** shall be its sailing, and its mooring. My Lord is Forgiver, Most Merciful."

42. As it sailed with them in waves like hills, Noah called his son, who was isolated: "O my son, come ride with us; do not be with the disbelievers."

11:40 & 44 This is God's proven truth: Noah's ark was made of logs, tied together with primitive ropes (54:13). Contrary to common belief the flood was limited to the area around today's Dead Sea, and the animals were only Noah's livestock, not every animal that lived on earth.

43. He said, "I will take refuge on top of a hill, to protect me from the water." He said, "Nothing can protect anyone today from **GOD**'s judgment; only those worthy of His mercy (*will be saved*)." The waves separated them, and he was among those who drowned.

Where Did the Ark Land

44. It was proclaimed: "O earth, swallow your water," and "O sky, cease." The water then subsided; the judgment was fulfilled. The ark finally rested on the hills of Judea.* It was then proclaimed: "The transgressors have perished."

45. Noah implored his Lord: "My Lord, my son is a member of my family, and Your promise is the truth. You are the wisest of the wise."

The Myth of Intercession*

46. He said, "O Noah, he is not of your family. It is unrighteous to ask Me for something you do not know.* I enlighten you, lest you be like the ignorant."

47. He said, "My Lord, I seek refuge in You, lest I implore You again for something I do not know. Unless You forgive me, and have mercy on me, I will be with the losers."

48. It was proclaimed: "O Noah, disembark, with peace and blessings upon you, and upon nations who will descend from your companions. As for the other nations descending from you, we will bless them for awhile, then commit them to painful retribution."

49. This is news from the past that we reveal to you. You had no knowledge about them—neither you, nor your people—before this. Therefore, be patient. The ultimate victory belongs to the righteous.

Hûd:
One and the Same Message

50. To 'Ãd we sent their brother Hûd. He said, "O my people, worship **GOD**; you have no other god besides Him. You are inventing.

51. "O my people, I do not ask you for any wage. My wage comes only from the One who initiated me. Do you not understand?

52. "O my people, seek forgiveness from your Lord, then repent to Him. He will then shower you with provisions from the sky, and augment your strength. Do not turn back into transgressors."

53. They said, "O Hûd, you did not show us any proof, and we are not abandoning our gods on account of what you say. We will never be believers with you.

54. "We believe that some of our gods have afflicted you with a curse." He said, "I bear witness before **GOD**, and you bear witness as well, that I disown the idols you have set up—

55. "beside Him. So, give me your collective decision, without delay.

---

*11:44 See footnote for 11:40.

11:46 Intercession is Satan's most effective bait to entice people into idol worship. However, Abraham could not help his father, nor could Noah help his son, nor could Muhammad help his own relatives (2:254, 9:80 & 114).

56. "I have put my trust in **GOD**, my Lord and your Lord. There is not a creature that He does not control. My Lord is on the right path.

57. "If you turn away, I have delivered to you what I was sent with. My Lord will substitute other people in your place; you cannot harm Him in the least. My Lord is in control of all things."

58. When our judgment came, we saved Hûd and those who believed with him, by mercy from us. We saved them from a terrible retribution.

59. Such was 'Ãd—they disregarded the revelations of their Lord, disobeyed His messengers, and followed the ways of every stubborn tyrant.

60. Consequently, they incurred condemnation in this world, and on the Day of Resurrection. Indeed, 'Ãd rejected their Lord. Indeed, 'Ãd, the people of Hûd, have perished.

Sãleh:
One and the Same Message

61. To Thamoud we sent their brother Sãleh. He said, "O my people, worship **GOD**; you have no other god beside Him. He initiated you from the earth, then settled you in it. You shall seek His forgiveness, then repent to Him. My Lord is always near, responsive."

62. They said, "O Sãleh, you used to be popular among us before this. Are you enjoining us from worshiping what our parents are worshiping? We are full of doubt concerning everything you have told us."

The Disbelievers Always Losers

63. He said, "O my people, what if I have solid proof from my Lord, and mercy from Him? Who would support me against **GOD**, if I disobeyed Him? You can only augment my loss.

64. "O my people, this is **GOD**'s camel to serve as a proof for you. You shall let her eat from **GOD**'s earth, and do not touch her with any harm, lest you incur an immediate retribution."

65. They slaughtered her. He then said, "You have only three days to live. This is a prophecy that is inevitable."

66. When our judgment came, we saved Sãleh and those who believed with him by mercy from us, from the humiliation of that day. Your Lord is the Most Powerful, the Almighty.

67. Those who transgressed were annihilated by the disaster, leaving them in their homes, dead.

68. It was as if they never lived there. Indeed, Thamoud have rejected their Lord. Absolutely, Thamoud have incurred their annihilation.

Abraham and Lot

69. When our messengers went to Abraham with good news, they said, "Peace." He said, "Peace," and soon brought a roasted calf.

70. When he saw that their hands did not touch it, he became suspicious and fearful of them. They said, "Do not be afraid, we are being dispatched to the people of Lot."

71. His wife was standing, and she laughed when we gave her the good news about Isaac, and after Isaac, Jacob.

72. She said, "Woe to me, how could I bear a child at my age, and here is my husband, an old man? This is really strange!"

73. They said, "Do you find it strange for **GOD**? **GOD** has bestowed His mercy and blessings upon you, O inhabitants of the shrine. He is Praiseworthy, Glorious."

74. When Abraham's fear subsided, and the good news was delivered to him, he proceeded to argue with us on behalf of Lot's people.

75. Indeed, Abraham was clement, extremely kind, and obedient.

76. "O Abraham, refrain from this. Your Lord's judgment has been issued; they have incurred unavoidable retribution."

Homosexuality Condemned

77. When our messengers went to Lot, they were mistreated, and he was embarrassed by their presence. He said, "This is a difficult day."

78. His people came rushing; they had grown accustomed to their sinful acts. He said, "O my people, it would be purer for you, if you take my daughters instead. You shall reverence **GOD**; do not embarrass me with my guests. Have you not one reasonable man among you?"

79. They said, "You know well that we have no need for your daughters; you know exactly what we want."

80. He said, "I wish I were strong enough, or had a powerful ally!"

81. (*The angels*) said, "O Lot, we are your Lord's messengers, and these people cannot touch you. You shall leave with your family during the night, and let not anyone of you look back, except your wife; she is condemned along with those who are condemned. Their appointed time is the morning. Is not the morning soon enough?"

Sodom & Gomorrah Destroyed

82. When our judgment came, we turned it upside down, and we showered it with hard, devastating rocks.

83. Such rocks were designated by your Lord to strike the transgressors.

Shu'aib:
One and the Same Message

84. To Midyan we sent their brother Shu'aib. He said, "O my people, worship **GOD**; you have no other god beside Him. Do not cheat when you measure or weigh. I see that you are prosperous, and I fear for you the retribution of an overwhelming day.

85. "O my people, you shall give full measure and full weight, equitably. Do not cheat the people out of their rights, and do not roam the earth corruptingly.

86. "Whatever **GOD** provides for you, no matter how small, is far better for you, if you are really believers. I am not a guardian over you."

87. They said, "O Shu'aib, does your religion dictate upon you that we must abandon our parents' religion, or running our businesses in any manner we choose? Surely, you are known for being clement, wise."

88. He said, "O my people, what if I have solid proof from my Lord; what if He has provided me with a great blessing? It is not my wish to commit what I enjoin you from. I only wish to correct as many wrongs as I can. My guidance depends totally on **GOD**; I have put my trust in Him. To Him I have totally submitted.

89. "And, O my people, do not be provoked by your opposition to me into incurring the same disasters as the people of Noah, or the people of Hûd, or the people of Sāleh; and the people of Lot are not too far from you.

90. "You shall implore your Lord for forgiveness, then repent to Him. My Lord is Most Merciful, Kind."

91. They said, "O Shu'aib, we do not comprehend many of the things you are telling us, and we see that you are powerless among us. If it were not for your tribe, we would have stoned you. You have no value for us."

92. He said, "O my people, does my tribe command a greater respect than **GOD**? Is this why you have been heedless of Him? My Lord is fully aware of everything you do.

93. "O my people, go on doing what you wish, and so will I. You will certainly find out which of us will incur shameful retribution; you will find out who the liar is. Just wait in anticipation, and I will wait in anticipation along with you."

94. When our judgment came, we saved Shu'aib and those who believed with him, by mercy from us. As for the evil ones, they were struck by a disaster that left them dead in their homes.

95. It was as though they never existed. Thus, Midyan perished, just like Thamoud had perished before that.

Moses

96. We sent Moses with our signs and a profound authority.

97. To Pharaoh and his elders. But they followed the command of Pharaoh, and Pharaoh's command was not wise.

98. He will lead his people on the Day of Resurrection, all the way to Hell; what a miserable abode to live in!

99. They have incurred condemnation in this life, as well as on the Day of Resurrection; what a miserable path to follow!

Lessons to be Learned

100. This is news from the past communities that we narrate to you. Some are still standing, and some have vanished.

101. We never wronged them; they wronged their own souls. Their gods, whom they invoked beside **GOD**, could not help them in the least when the judgment of your Lord came. In fact, they only ensured their doom.

102. Such was the retribution enforced by your Lord when the communities transgressed. Indeed, His retribution is painful, devastating.

103. This should be a lesson for those who fear the retribution of the Hereafter. That is a day when all the people will be summoned—a day to be witnessed.

104. We have appointed a specific time for it to take place.

105. The day it comes to pass, no soul will utter a single word, except in accordance with His will. Some will be miserable, and some will be happy.

106. As for the miserable ones, they will be in Hell, wherein they sigh and wail.

107. Eternally they abide therein, for as long as the heavens and the earth endure, in accordance with the will of your Lord. Your Lord is doer of whatever He wills.

108. As for the fortunate ones, they will be in Paradise. Eternally they abide therein, for as long as the heavens and the earth endure, in accordance with the will of your Lord—an everlasting reward.

Following Our Parents Blindly
A Great Human Tragedy

109. Do not have any doubt regarding what these people worship; they worship exactly as they found their parents worshiping. We will requite them their due share fully, without reduction.

110. We have given Moses the scripture, but it was disputed, and if it were not for a predetermined word decreed by your Lord, they would have been judged immediately. They are full of doubt about this, suspicious.

111. Your Lord will surely recompense everyone for their works. He is fully Cognizant of everything they do.

112. Therefore, continue on the path you have been enjoined to follow, together with those who repented with you, and do not transgress. He is Seer of everything you do.

113. Do not lean towards those who have transgressed, lest you incur Hell, and find no allies to help you against **GOD**, then end up losers.

Three of the Five Prayers

114. You shall observe the Contact Prayers (*Salat*) at both ends of the day, and during the night. The righteous works wipe out the evil works. This is a reminder for those who would take heed.

115. You shall steadfastly persevere, for **GOD** never fails to recompense the righteous.

116. If only some of those among the previous generations possessed enough intelligence to forbid evil! Only a few of them deserved to be saved by us. As for the transgressors, they were preoccupied with their material luxuries; they were guilty.

117. Your Lord never annihilates any community unjustly, while its people are righteous.

Why Were We Created

118. Had your Lord willed, all the people would have been one congregation (*of believers*). But they will always dispute (*the truth*).

119. Only those blessed with mercy from your Lord (*will not dispute the truth*). This is why He created them.* The judgment of your Lord has already been issued: "I will fill Hell with jinns and humans, all together."**

120. We narrate to you enough history of the messengers to strengthen your heart. The truth has come to you herein, as well as enlightenments and reminders for the believers.

---

* *11:119 The Most Merciful has created us on this earth to give us yet another chance to denounce our original crime and to be redeemed (see the Introduction and Appendix 7).*

** *11:119 God does not put a single person in Hell; they choose and insist upon going to Hell.*

---

121. Say to those who disbelieve, "Do whatever you can, and so will we.

122. "Then wait; we too will wait."

123. To **GOD** belongs the future of the heavens and the earth, and all matters are controlled by Him. You shall worship Him and trust in Him. Your Lord is never unaware of anything you do.

◆◆◆◆

Sura 12: Joseph (Yousuf)

In the name of God,
Most Gracious, Most Merciful

1. A. L. R. These (*letters*) are proofs of this profound scripture.*

2. We have revealed it an Arabic Quran, that you may understand.*

3. We narrate to you the most accurate history through the revelation of this Quran. Before this, you were totally unaware.

4. Recall that Joseph said to his father, "O my father, I saw eleven planets, and the sun, and the moon; I saw them prostrating before me."

5. He said, "My son, do not tell your brothers about your dream, lest they plot and scheme against you. Surely, the devil is man's worst enemy.

6. "Your Lord has thus blessed you, and has given you good news through your dream. He has perfected His blessings upon you and upon the family of Jacob, as He did for your ancestors Abraham and Isaac before that. Your Lord is Omniscient, Most Wise.

7. In Joseph and his brothers there are lessons for the seekers.

8. They said, "Joseph and his brother are favored by our father, and we are in the majority. Indeed, our father is far astray.

Joseph's Fate
*Already Decided by God**

9. "Let us kill Joseph, or banish him, that you may get some attention from your father. Afterwards, you can be righteous people."*

10. One of them said, "Do not kill Joseph; let us throw him into the abyss of the well. Perhaps some caravan can pick him up, if this is what you decide to do."

11. They said, "Our father, why do you not trust us with Joseph? We will take good care of him.

12. "Send him with us tomorrow to run and play. We will protect him."

13. He said, "I worry lest you go away with him, then the wolf may devour him while you are not watching him."

14. They said, "Indeed, if the wolf devours him, with so many of us around, then we are really losers."

12:1 The Quranic initials constitute a major component of a great miracle (App. 1).

12:2 Why was the Quran revealed in Arabic? See 41:44 and Appendix 4.

12:9 We learn from Joseph's dream that he was destined for a bright future. Thus, while his brothers met to decide his fate, his fate was already decided by God. Everything is done by God (8:17), and is already recorded (57:22).

---

*Believers are Blessed with
God's Assurances*

15. When they went away with him, and unanimously decided to throw him into the abyss of the well, we inspired him: "Some day, you will tell them about all this, while they have no idea."

16. They came back to their father in the evening, weeping.

17. They said, "Our father, we went racing with each other, leaving Joseph with our equipment, and the wolf devoured him. You will never believe us, even if we were telling the truth."

18. They produced his shirt with fake blood on it. He said, "Indeed, you have conspired with each other to commit a certain scheme. All I can do is resort to a quiet patience. May **GOD** help me in the face of your conspiracy."

Joseph is Taken to Egypt

19. A caravan passed by, and soon sent their waterer. He let down his bucket, then said, "How lucky! There is a boy here!" They took him along as merchandise, and **GOD** was fully aware of what they did.

20. They sold him for a cheap price—a few Dirhams—for they did not have any need for him.

21. The one who bought him in Egypt said to his wife, "Take good care of him. Maybe he can help us, or maybe we can adopt him." We thus established Joseph on earth, and we taught him the interpretation of dreams. **GOD**'s command is always done, but most people do not know.

22. When he reached maturity, we endowed him with wisdom and knowledge. We thus reward the righteous.

*God Protects the Believers
From Sin*

23. The lady of the house where he lived tried to seduce him. She closed the doors and said, "I am all yours." He said, "May **GOD** protect me. He is my Lord, who gave me a good home.* The transgressors never succeed."

24. She almost succumbed to him, and he almost succumbed to her, if it were not that he saw a proof from his Lord. We thus diverted evil and sin away from him, for he was one of our devoted servants.

25. The two of them raced towards the door, and, in the process, she tore his garment from the back. They found her husband at the door. She said, "What should be the punishment for one who wanted to molest your wife, except imprisonment or a painful punishment?"

26. He said, "She is the one who tried to seduce me." A witness from her family suggested: "If his garment is torn from the front, then she is telling the truth and he is a liar.

27. "And if his garment is torn from the back, then she lied, and he is telling the truth."

28. When her husband saw that his garment was torn from the back, he said, "This is a woman's scheme. Indeed, your scheming is formidable.

---

* *12:23 Joseph worded this statement in such a way that the governor's wife thought that he was talking about her husband, when in fact he was talking about God.*

---

29. "Joseph, disregard this incident. As for you (*my wife*), you should seek forgiveness for your sin. You have committed an error."

30. Some women in the city gossiped: "The governor's wife is trying to seduce her servant. She is deeply in love with him. We see that she has gone astray."

31. When she heard of their gossip, she invited them, prepared for them a comfortable place, and gave each of them a knife. She then said to him, "Enter their room." When they saw him, they so admired him, that they cut their hands.* They said, "Glory be to **GOD**, this is not a human being; this is an honorable angel."

32. She said, "This is the one you blamed me for falling in love with. I did indeed try to seduce him, and he refused. Unless he does what I command him to do, he will surely go to prison, and will be debased."

33. He said, "My Lord, the prison is better than giving in to them. Unless You divert their scheming from me, I may desire them and behave like the ignorant ones."

34. His Lord answered his prayer and diverted their scheming from him. He is the Hearer, the Omniscient.

35. Later, they saw to it, despite the clear proofs, that they should imprison him for awhile.

36. Two young men were in the prison with him. One of them said, "I saw (*in my dream*) that I was making wine," and the other said, "I saw myself carrying bread on my head, from which the birds were eating. Inform us of the interpretation of these dreams. We see that you are righteous."

37. He said, "If any food is provided to you, I can inform you about it before you receive it. This is some of the knowledge bestowed upon me by my Lord. I have forsaken the religion of people who do not believe in **GOD**, and with regard to the Hereafter, they are really disbelievers.

38. "And I followed instead the religion of my ancestors, Abraham, Isaac, and Jacob. We never set up any idols beside **GOD**. Such is the blessing from **GOD** upon us and upon the people, but most people are unappreciative.

39. "O my prison mates, are several gods better, or **GOD** alone, the One, the Supreme?

40. "You do not worship beside Him except innovations that you have made up, you and your parents. **GOD** has never authorized such idols. All ruling belongs to **GOD**, and He has ruled that you shall not worship except Him. This is the perfect religion, but most people do not know.

41. "O my prison mates, one of you will be the wine butler for his lord, while the other will be crucified—the birds will eat from his head. This settles the matter about which you have inquired."

---

*12:31 *This is the same word used in 5:38 regarding the hand of the thief, and the sum of sura and verse numbers (12 + 31 and 5 + 38) are the same. Therefore, the thief's hand should be marked, not severed as practiced by the corrupted Islam (see Footnote 5:38).*

---

42. He then said to the one to be saved "Remember me at your lord."* Thus, the devil caused him to forget his Lord, and, consequently, he remained in prison a few more years.

The King's Dream

43. The king said, "I saw seven fat cows being devoured by seven skinny cows, and seven green spikes (*of wheat*), and others shriveled. O my elders, advise me regarding my dream, if you know how to interpret the dreams."

44. They said, "Nonsense dreams. When it comes to the interpretation of dreams, we are not knowledgeable."

45. The one who was saved (*from the prison*) said, now that he finally remembered, "I can tell you its interpretation, so send me (*to Joseph*)."

Joseph Interprets the King's Dream

46. "Joseph my friend, inform us about seven fat cows being devoured by seven skinny cows, and seven green spikes, and others shriveled. I wish to go back with some information for the people."

47. He said, "What you cultivate during the next seven years, when the time of harvest comes, leave the grains in their spikes, except for what you eat.

48. "After that, seven years of drought will come, which will consume most of what you stored for them.

49. "After that, a year will come that brings relief for the people, and they will, once again, press juice."

50. The king said, "Bring him to me." When the messenger came to him, he said, "Go back to your lord and ask him to investigate the women who cut their hands. My Lord is fully aware of their schemes."

51. (*The king*) said (*to the women*), "What do you know about the incident when you tried to seduce Joseph?" They said, "**GOD** forbid; we did not know of anything evil committed by him." The wife of the governor said, "Now the truth has prevailed. I am the one who tried to seduce him, and he was the truthful one.

52. "I hope that he will realize that I never betrayed him in his absence, for **GOD** does not bless the schemes of the betrayers.

53. "I do not claim innocence for myself. The self is an advocate of vice, except for those who have attained mercy from my Lord. My Lord is Forgiver, Most Merciful."

Joseph Attains Prominence

54. The king said, "Bring him to me, so I can hire him to work for me." When he talked with him, he said, "Today, you have a prominent position with us."

55. He said, "Make me the treasurer, for I am experienced in this area and knowledgeable."

12:42 When Joseph begged his companion to intercede with the king on his behalf, he exhibited dependence on other than God to be saved from the prison. This does not befit a true believer, and such a serious slip cost Joseph a few years in the prison. We learn from the Quran that only God can relieve any hardship that might befall us. A true believer trusts in God and depends totally on Him alone (1:5, 6:17, 8:17, 10:107).

56. We thus established Joseph on earth, ruling as he wished. We shower our mercy upon whomever we will, and we never fail to recompense the righteous.

57. Additionally, the reward in the Hereafter is even better for those who believe and lead a righteous life.

58. Joseph's brothers came; when they entered, he recognized them, while they did not recognize him.

59. After he provided them with their provisions, he said, "Next time, bring with you your half-brother. Do you not see that I give full measure, and treat you generously?

60. "If you fail to bring him to me, you will get no share from me; you will not even come close."

61. They said, "We will negotiate with his father about him. We will surely do this."

62. He then instructed his assistants: "Put their goods back in their bags. When they find them upon their return to their family, they may come back sooner."

63. When they returned to their father, they said, "Our father, we can no longer get any provisions, unless you send our brother with us. We will take good care of him."

64. He said, "Shall I trust you with him, as I trusted you with his brother before that? **GOD** is the best Protector, and, of all the merciful ones, He is the Most Merciful.

65. When they opened their bags, they found their goods returned to them. They said, "Our father, what more can we ask for? Here are our goods returned to us. We can thus provide for our family, protect our brother, and receive one more camel-load. This is certainly a profitable deal."

66. He said, "I will not send him with you, unless you give me a solemn pledge before **GOD** that you will bring him back, unless you are utterly overwhelmed." When they gave him their solemn pledge, he said, "**GOD** is witnessing everything we say."

67. And he said, "O my sons, do not enter from one door; enter through separate doors. However, I cannot save you from anything that is predetermined by **GOD**. To **GOD** belongs all judgments. I trust in Him, and in Him shall all the trusters put their trust."

Jacob Senses Joseph

68. When they went (*to Joseph*), they entered in accordance with their father's instructions. Although this could not change anything decreed by **GOD**, Jacob had a private reason for asking them to do this. For he possessed certain knowledge that we taught him, but most people do not know.

Back in Egypt

69. When they entered Joseph's place, he brought his brother closer to him and said, "I am your brother; do not be saddened by their actions."

Joseph Keeps His Brother

70. When he provided them with their provisions, he placed the drinking cup in his brother's bag, then an announcer announced: "The owners of this caravan are thieves."

71. They said, as they came towards them, "What did you lose?"

72. They said, "We lost the king's cup. Anyone who returns it will receive an extra camel-load; I personally guarantee this."

73. They said, "By **GOD**, you know full well that we did not come here to commit evil, nor are we thieves."

74. They said, "What is the punishment for the thief, if you are liars?"

75. They said, "The punishment, if it is found in his bag, is that the thief belongs to you. We thus punish the guilty."

76. He then started by inspecting their containers, before getting to his brother's container, and he extracted it out of his brother's container. We thus perfected the scheme for Joseph; he could not have kept his brother if he applied the king's law. But that was the will of **GOD**. We exalt whomever we choose to higher ranks. Above every knowledgeable one, there is one who is even more knowledgeable.

77. They said, "If he stole, so did a brother of his in the past." Joseph concealed his feelings in himself, and did not give them any clue. He said (*to himself*), "You are really bad. **GOD** is fully aware of your accusations."

78. They said, "O you noble one, he has a father who is elderly; would you take one of us in his place? We see that you are a kind man."

79. He said, "**GOD** forbid that we should take other than the one in whose possession we found our goods. Otherwise, we would be unjust."

80. When they despaired of changing his mind, they conferred together. Their eldest said, "Do you realize that your father has taken a solemn pledge from you before **GOD**? In the past you lost Joseph. I am not leaving this place until my father gives me permission, or until **GOD** judges for me; He is the best Judge.

81. "Go back to your father and tell him..."

Back In Palestine

'Our father, your son has committed a theft. We know for sure, because this is what we have witnessed. This was an unexpected occurrence.

82. 'You may ask the community where we were, and the caravan that came back with us. We are telling the truth.' "

83. He said, "Indeed, you have conspired to carry out a certain scheme. Quiet patience is my only recourse. May **GOD** bring them all back to me. He is the Omniscient, Most Wise."

84. He turned away from them, saying, "I am grieving over Joseph." His eyes turned white from grieving so much; he was truly sad.

85. They said, "By **GOD**, you will keep on grieving over Joseph until you become ill, or until you die."

86. He said, "I simply complain to **GOD** about my dilemma and grief, for I know from **GOD** what you do not know.

87. "O my sons, go fetch Joseph and his brother, and never despair of **GOD**'s grace. None despairs of **GOD**'s grace except the disbelieving people."

Israel Goes to Egypt

88. When they entered (*Joseph's*) quarters, they said, "O you noble one, we have suffered a lot of hardship, along with our family, and we have brought inferior goods. But we hope that you will give us full measure and be charitable to us. **GOD** rewards the charitable."

89. He said, "Do you recall what you did to Joseph and his brother when you were ignorant?"

90. They said, "You must be Joseph." He said, "I am Joseph, and here is my brother. **GOD** has blessed us. That is because if one leads a righteous life, and steadfastly perseveres, **GOD** never fails to reward the righteous."

91. They said, "By **GOD**, **GOD** has truly preferred you over us. We were definitely wrong."

92. He said, "There is no blame upon you today. May **GOD** forgive you. Of all the merciful ones, He is the Most Merciful.

93. "Take this shirt of mine; when you throw it on my father's face, his vision will be restored. Bring your whole family and come back to me."*

94. Even before the caravan arrived, their father said, "I can sense the smell of Joseph. Will someone enlighten me?"

95. They said, "By **GOD**, you are still in your old confusion."

96. When the bearer of good news arrived, he threw (*the shirt*) on his face, whereupon his vision was restored. He said, "Did I not tell you that I knew from **GOD** what you did not know?"

97. They said, "Our father, pray for our forgiveness; we were wrong indeed."

98. He said, "I will implore my Lord to forgive you; He is the Forgiver, Most Merciful."

In Egypt

99. When they entered Joseph's quarters, he embraced his parents, saying, "Welcome to Egypt. **GOD** willing, you will be safe here."

100. He raised his parents upon the throne. They fell prostrate before him. He said, "O my father, this is the fulfillment of my old dream. My Lord has made it come true. He has blessed me, delivered me from the prison, and brought you from the desert, after the devil had driven a wedge between me and my brothers. My Lord is Most Kind towards whomever He wills. He is the Knower, the Most Wise."

101. "My Lord, You have given me kingship and taught me the interpretation of dreams. Initiator of the heavens and the earth; You are my Lord and Master in this life and in the Hereafter. Let me die as a submitter, and count me with the righteous."

102. This is news from the past that we reveal to you. You were not present when they made their unanimous decision (*to throw Joseph in the well*), as they conspired together.

12:93 This marks the beginning of the Children of Israel in Egypt Moses led them out of Egypt a few centuries later.

*The Majority of People
Do Not Believe*

103. Most people, no matter what you do, will not believe.

104. You are not asking them for any money; you simply deliver this reminder for all the people.

105. So many proofs in the heavens and the earth are given to them, but they pass by them, heedlessly!

*The Majority of Believers
Destined for Hell*

106. The majority of those who believe in **GOD** do not do so without committing idol worship.

107. Have they guaranteed that an overwhelming retribution from **GOD** will not strike them, or the Hour will not come to them suddenly, when they least expect it?

108. Say, "This is my path: I invite to **GOD**, on the basis of a clear proof, and so do those who follow me. **GOD** be glorified. I am not an idol worshiper."

109. We did not send before you except men whom we inspired, chosen from the people of various communities. Did they not roam the earth and see the consequences for those before them? The abode of the Hereafter is far better for those who lead a righteous life. Would you then understand?

*Victory, Ultimately, Belongs
to the Believers*

110. Just when the messengers despair, and think that they had been rejected, our victory comes to them.

We then save whomever we choose, while our retribution for the guilty people is unavoidable.

The Quran is All We Need

111. In their history, there is a lesson for those who possess intelligence. This is not fabricated *Hadith*; this (*Quran*) confirms all previous scriptures, provides the details of everything, and is a beacon and mercy for those who believe.

Sura 13: Thunder (Al-Ra'ad)

In the name of God,
Most Gracious, Most Merciful

1. A. L. M. R.* These (*letters*) are proofs of this scripture. What is revealed to you from your Lord is the truth, but most people do not believe.

2. **GOD** is the One who raised the heavens without pillars that you can see, then assumed all authority. He committed the sun and the moon, each running (*in its orbit*) for a predetermined period. He controls all things, and explains the revelations, that you may attain certainty about meeting your Lord.

3. He is the One who constructed the earth and placed on it mountains and rivers. And from the different kinds of fruits, He made them into pairs—males and females. The night overtakes the day. These are solid proofs for people who think.

---

*13:1 These initials constitute a major component of the Quran's built-in proof of divine authorship, the miraculous mathematical code. See Appendix 1.

4. On earth, there are adjacent lots that produce orchards of grapes, crops, palm trees—dioecious and non-dioecious. Although they are irrigated with the same water, we prefer some of them over others in eating. These are solid proofs for people who understand.

Belief in the
Hereafter Required
For Salvation

5. If you ever wonder, the real wonder is their saying: "After we turn into dust, do we get recreated anew?" These are the ones who have disbelieved in their Lord. These are the ones who have incurred shackles around their necks. These are the ones who have incurred Hell, wherein they abide forever.

6. They challenge you to bring doom upon them, rather than turning righteous! Sufficient precedents have been set for them in the past. Indeed, your Lord is full of forgiveness towards the people, in spite of their transgressions, and your Lord is also strict in enforcing retribution.

7. Those who disbelieved say, "If only a miracle could come down to him from his Lord (*we will then believe*)." You are simply a warner—every community receives a guiding teacher.

8. **GOD** knows what every female bears, and what every womb releases, or gains. Everything He does is perfectly measured.

9. The Knower of all secrets and declarations; the Supreme, the Most High.

10. It is the same whether you conceal your thoughts, or declare them, or hide in the darkness of the night, or act in the daylight.

11. Shifts (*of angels*) take turns, staying with each one of you—they are in front of you and behind you. They stay with you, and guard you in accordance with **GOD**'s commands. Thus, **GOD** does not change the condition of any people unless they themselves make the decision to change. If **GOD** wills any hardship for any people, no force can stop it. For they have none beside Him as Lord and Master.

12. He is the One who shows you the lightning as a source of fear, as well as hope, and He initiates the loaded clouds.

13. The thunder praises His glory, and so do the angels, out of reverence for Him. He sends the lightning bolts, which strike in accordance with His will. Yet, they argue about **GOD**, though His power is awesome.

14. Imploring Him is the only legitimate supplication, while the idols they implore beside Him, cannot ever respond. Thus, they are like those who stretch their hands to the water, but nothing reaches their mouths. The supplications of the disbelievers are in vain.

All Creation Has Submitted to God

15. To **GOD** prostrates everyone in the heavens and the earth, willingly or unwillingly, and so do their shadows in the mornings and the evenings.*

16. Say, "Who is the Lord of the heavens and the earth?" Say, "**GOD**." Say, "Why then do you set up besides Him masters who do not possess any power to benefit or harm even themselves?" Say, "Is the blind the same as the seer? Is darkness the same as the light?" Have they found idols besides **GOD** who created creations similar to His creations, to the point of not distinguishing the two creations? Say, "**GOD** is the Creator of all things, and He is the One, the Supreme."

The Truth vs Falsehood

17. He sends down water from the sky, causing the valleys to overflow, then the rapids produce abundant foam. Similarly, when they use fire to refine metals for their jewelry or equipment, foam is produced. **GOD** thus cites analogies for the truth and falsehood. As for the foam, it goes to waste, while that which benefits the people stays close to the ground. **GOD** thus cites the analogies.

18. Those who respond to their Lord deserve the good rewards. As for those who failed to respond to Him, if they possessed everything on earth—even twice as much—they would readily give it up as ransom. They have incurred the worst reckoning, and their final abode is Hell; what a miserable destiny.

Believers Versus Disbelievers
(1) The Believers

19. Is one who recognizes that your Lord's revelations to you are the truth equal to one who is blind? Only those who possess intelligence will take heed.

20. They are the ones who fulfill their pledge to **GOD**, and do not violate the covenant.

21. They join what **GOD** has commanded to be joined, reverence their Lord, and fear the dreadful reckoning.

22. They steadfastly persevere in seeking their Lord, observe the Contact Prayers (*Salat*), spend from our provisions to them secretly and publicly, and counter evil with good. These have deserved the best abode.

23. They enter the gardens of Eden, together with the righteous among their parents, their spouses, and their children. The angels will enter to them from every door.

24. "Peace be upon you, because you steadfastly persevered. What a joyous destiny."

(2) The Disbelievers

25. As for those who violate **GOD**'s covenant after pledging to keep it, and sever what **GOD** has commanded to be joined, and commit evil, they have incurred condemnation; they have incurred the worst destiny.

13:15 Even the disbelievers prostrate; they cannot, for example, control their heartbeats, their lungs, or peristalsis. The shadows are predetermined by God's design of the solar and the lunar orbits, and by the peculiar shape of the planet earth which causes the four seasons. The absolute precision of the sun/earth relation is proven by the invention of solar clocks and their shadows.

God Controls All Provisions

26. **GOD** is the One who increases the provision for whomever He wills, or withholds it. They have become pre-occupied with this life, and this life, compared to the Hereafter, is nil.

27. Those who disbelieve would say, "If only a miracle could come down to him from his Lord (*we would believe*)." Say, "**GOD** sends astray whomever He wills, and guides to Him only those who obey."

28. They are the ones whose hearts rejoice in remembering **GOD**. Absolutely, by remembering **GOD**, the hearts rejoice.

29. Those who believe and lead a righteous life have deserved happiness and a joyous destiny.

God's Messenger of the Covenant*

30. We have sent you (*O Rashad*)* to this community, just as we did for other communities in the past. You shall recite to them what we reveal to you, for they have disbelieved in the Most Gracious. Say, "He is my Lord. There is no god except He. I put my trust in Him alone; to Him is my ultimate destiny."

Mathematical Miracle of the Quran

31. Even if a Quran caused mountains to move, or the earth to tear a-sunder, or the dead to speak (*they will not believe*). **GOD** controls all things. Is it not time for the believers to give up and realize that if **GOD** willed, He could have guided all the people? The disbelievers will continue to suffer disasters, as a consequence of their own works, or have disasters strike close to them, until

GOD's promise is fulfilled. **GOD** will never change the predetermined destiny.

All Messengers Must Be Ridiculed

32. Messengers before you have been ridiculed; I permitted the disbelievers to carry on, then I punished them. How terrible was My retribution!

33. Is there any equal to the One who controls every single soul? Yet, they set up idols to rival **GOD**. Say, "Name them. Are you informing Him of something on earth that He does not know? Or, are you fabricating empty statements?" Indeed, the schemes of those who disbelieve have been adorned in their eyes. They are thus diverted from the right path. Whomever **GOD** sends astray can never find a guiding teacher.

34. They have incurred retribution in this life, and the retribution in the Hereafter is far worse. Nothing can protect them against **GOD**.

Heaven Allegorically Described

35. The allegory of Heaven, which is promised for the righteous, is flowing streams, inexhaustible provisions, and cool shade. Such is the destiny for those who observe righteousness, while the destiny for the disbelievers is Hell.

36. Those who received the scripture rejoice in what was revealed to you; some others may reject parts of it Say, "I am simply enjoined to worship **GOD**, and never associate any idols with Him. I invite to Him, and to Him is my ultimate destiny.

---

*13:30 If we add the gematrical value of "Rashad" (505), plus the value of "Khalifa" (725), plus the sura number (13), plus the verse number (30), we get 505 + 725 + 13 + 30 = 1273 = 19x67. God thus specifies the name of His messenger (see Appendix 2 for the details).

Divine Authorization of the
Quran's Mathematical Code*

37. We revealed these laws in Arabic, and if you ever acquiesce to their wishes, after this knowledge has come to you, you will have no ally, nor a protector, against **GOD**.

38. We have sent messengers before you (*O Rashad*), and we made them husbands with wives and children. No messenger can produce a miracle without **GOD**'s authorization, and in accordance with a specific, predetermined time.

39. **GOD** erases whatever He wills, and fixes. With Him is the original Master Record.

40. Whether we show you what we promise them, or terminate your life before that, your sole mission is to deliver (*the message*). It is us who will call them to account.

41. Do they not see that every day on earth, brings them closer to the end, and that **GOD** decides their life span, irrevocably? He is the most efficient Reckoner.

42. Others before them have schemed, but to **GOD** belongs the ultimate scheming. He knows what everyone is doing. The disbelievers will find out who the ultimate winners are.

43. Those who disbelieved will say, "You are not a messenger!" Say, "**GOD** suffices as a witness between me and you, and those who possess knowledge of the scripture."

◆◆◆◆

Sura 14: Abraham (Ibrahîm)

In the name of God,
Most Gracious, Most Merciful

1. A. L. R.* A scripture that we revealed to you, in order to lead the people out of darkness into the light—in accordance with the will of their Lord—to the path of the Almighty, the Praiseworthy.

2. (*The path of*) **GOD**; the One who possesses everything in the heavens and everything on earth. Woe to the disbelievers; they have incurred a terrible retribution.

What is Your Priority?

3. They are the ones who give priority to this life over the Hereafter, repel from the way of **GOD**, and seek to make it crooked; they have gone far astray.

The Messenger's Language

4. We did not send any messenger except (*to preach*) in the tongue of his people, in order to clarify things for them. **GOD** then sends astray whomever He wills, and guides whomever He wills. He is the Almighty, the Most Wise.

Moses

5. Thus, we sent Moses with our miracles, saying, "Lead your people out of darkness into the light, and remind them of the days of **GOD**." These are lessons for every steadfast, appreciative person.

---

*13:37-38 The verse number (38) = 19x2. Placing the values of "Rashad" (505) and "Khalifa" (725) next to 13:37-38, gives 505 725 13 37 38, or 19x26617112302 (Appendix 2).

*14:1 These initials remained a divinely guarded secret until the Quran's mathematical code was discovered in 1974 A.D. See Appendix 1 for the significance of these initials.

The Importance
of Being Appreciative

6. Recall that Moses said to his people, "Remember **GOD**'s blessings upon you. He saved you from Pharaoh's people who inflicted the worst persecution upon you, slaughtering your sons and sparing your daughters. That was an exacting trial from your Lord."

Appreciative vs Unappreciative

7. Your Lord has decreed: "The more you thank Me, the more I give you." But if you turn unappreciative, then My retribution is severe.

8. Moses said, "If you disbelieve, along with all the people on earth, **GOD** is in no need, Praiseworthy."

Egotistic Defiance: A Human Trait

9. Have you not heard about those before you—the people of Noah, 'Ãd, Thamoud, and others who came after them and known only to **GOD**? Their messengers went to them with clear proofs, but they treated them with contempt and said, "We disbelieve in what you are sent with. We are skeptical about your message; full of doubt."

Following Our Parents Blindly:
A Great Human Tragedy

10. Their messengers said, "Do you have doubts about **GOD**; the Initiator of the heavens and the earth? He invites you only to forgive your sins, and to give you another chance to redeem yourselves." They said,

"You are no more than humans like us, who want to repel us from the way our parents used to worship. Show us some profound authority."

11. Their messengers said to them, "We are no more than humans like you, but **GOD** blesses whomever He chooses from among His servants. We could not possibly show you any kind of authorization, except in accordance with **GOD**'s will. In **GOD** the believers shall trust.

12. "Why should we not trust in **GOD**, when He has guided us in our paths? We will steadfastly persevere in the face of your persecution. In **GOD** all the trusters shall trust."

13. Those who disbelieved said to their messengers, "We will banish you from our land, unless you revert to our religion." Their Lord inspired them: "We will inevitably annihilate the transgressors.

14. "And we will let you dwell in their land after them. This is (*the reward*) for those who reverence My majesty, and reverence My promise."

15. They issued a challenge, and consequently, every stubborn tyrant ended up doomed.

16. Awaiting him is Hell, wherein he will drink putrid water.

17. He will gulp it down, though he cannot stand it, as death comes to him from every direction, but he will never die. Awaiting him is a terrible retribution.*

---

*14:17 When we rebelled against God, and agreed with Satan during the great feud (38:69), the angels suggested that we should be banished to Hell (Appendix 7). But the Most Merciful decided to give us another chance to redeem ourselves. He said to the angels, "I know what you do not know" (2:30). God knew that many humans would have protested that they had no idea how bad Hell was. The awesome description of Hell in 14:17 and in 22:19-22, nullifies such a protest. Now we have a pretty good idea how terrible Hell is.

---

18. The allegory of those who disbelieve in their Lord: their works are like ashes in a violent wind, on a stormy day. They gain nothing from whatever they earn; such is the farthest straying.

Worship Only the Omnipotent One

19. Do you not realize that **GOD** has created the heavens and the earth for a specific purpose? If He wills, He can remove you, and substitute a new creation in your place.

20. This is not too difficult for **GOD**.

On the Day of Resurrection

21. When they all stand before **GOD**,* the followers will say to the leaders, "We used to follow you. Can you spare us even a little bit of **GOD**'s retribution?" They will say, "Had **GOD** guided us, we would have guided you. Now it is too late, whether we grieve or resort to patience, there is no exit for us."

Satan Disowns His Followers

22. And the devil will say, after the judgment had been issued, "**GOD** has promised you the truthful promise, and I promised you, but I broke my promise. I had no power over you; I simply invited you, and you accepted my invitation. Therefore, do not blame me, and blame only yourselves. My complaining cannot help you, nor can your complaining help me. I have disbelieved in your idolizing me. The transgressors have incurred a painful retribution."

23. As for those who believe and lead a righteous life, they will be admitted into gardens with flowing streams. They abide therein forever, in accordance with the will of their Lord. Their greeting therein is: "Peace."

Truth vs. Falsehood

24. Do you not see that **GOD** has cited the example of the good word as a good tree whose root is firmly fixed, and its branches are high in the sky?

25. It produces its crop every season, as designed by its Lord. **GOD** thus cites the examples for the people, that they may take heed.

26. And the example of the bad word is that of a bad tree chopped at the soil level; it has no roots to keep it standing.

27. **GOD** strengthens those who believe with the proven word, in this life and in the Hereafter. And **GOD** sends the transgressors astray. Everything is in accordance with **GOD**'s will.

They Remove Their Families From God's Protection

28. Have you noted those who responded to **GOD**'s blessings by disbelieving, and thus brought disaster upon their own families?

29. Hell is their destiny, wherein they burn; what a miserable end!

Idol Worship: The Mother of All Evil

30. They set up rivals to rank with **GOD** and to divert others from His path. Say, "Enjoy for awhile; your final destiny is Hell."

Crucial Commandments

31. Exhort My servants who believed to observe the Contact Prayers (*Salat*), and to give (*to charity*) from our provisions to them, secretly and publicly, before a day comes where there is neither trade, nor nepotism.

14:21 Frequently, the Quran talks about the Hereafter in the past tense. This is because those are future events already witnessed by God, and will surely come to pass.

32. **GOD** is the One who created the heavens and the earth, and He sends down from the sky water to produce all kinds of fruit for your sustenance. He has committed the ships to serve you on the sea in accordance with His command. He has committed the rivers as well to serve you.

33. He has committed the sun and the moon in your service, continuously. He has committed the night and the day to serve you.

34. And He gives you all kinds of things that you implore Him for. If you count **GOD**'s blessings, you can never encompass them. Indeed, the human being is transgressing, unappreciative.

Abraham

35. Recall that Abraham said, "My Lord, make this a peaceful land, and protect me and my children from worshiping idols.

36. "My Lord, they have misled so many people. As for those who follow me, they belong with me. As for those who disobey me, You are Forgiver, Most Merciful.

37. "Our Lord, I have settled part of my family in this plantless valley, at Your Sacred House. Our Lord, they are to observe the Contact Prayers (*Salat*), so let throngs of people converge upon them, and provide for them all kinds of fruits, that they may be appreciative.

38. "Our Lord, You know whatever we conceal and whatever we declare— nothing is hidden from **GOD** on earth, nor in the heavens.

39. "Praise be to **GOD** for granting me, despite my old age, Ismail and Isaac. My Lord answers the prayers.

The Contact Prayers: Gift From God

40. "My Lord, make me one who consistently observes the Contact Prayers (*Salat*), and also my children. Our Lord, please answer my prayers.

41. "My Lord, forgive me and my parents, and the believers, on the day when the reckoning takes place."

42. Do not ever think that **GOD** is unaware of what the transgressors are doing. He only respites them until a day where the eyes stare in horror.

43. As they rush (*out of the graves*), their faces will be looking upward, their eyes will not even blink, and their minds will be horrified.

God Sends His Commands Through His Messengers

44. You shall warn the people of the day when the retribution comes to them. Those who transgressed will say, "Our Lord, give us one more respite. We will then respond to Your call and follow the messengers." Did you not swear in the past that you will last forever?

45. You dwelled in the homes of those before you, who wronged their souls, and you have seen clearly what we did to them. We have set many precedents for you.

46. They schemed their schemes, and **GOD** is fully aware of their schemes. Indeed, their schemes were sufficient to erase mountains.

Guaranteed Victory for God's Messengers

47. Do not think that **GOD** will ever break His promise to His messengers. **GOD** is Almighty, Avenger.

New Heavens and New Earth *

48. The day will come when this earth will be substituted with a new earth, and also the heavens, and everyone will be brought before **GOD**, the One, the Supreme.

49. And you will see the guilty on that day chained in shackles.

50. Their garments will be made of tar, and fire will overwhelm their faces.

51. For **GOD** will pay each soul for whatever it earned; **GOD** is the most efficient reckoner.

52. This is a proclamation for the people, to be warned herewith, and to let them know that He is only one god, and for those who possess intelligence to take heed.

◆◆◆◆

Sura 15: Al-Hijr Valley (Al-Hijr)

In the name of God,
Most Gracious, Most Merciful

1. A.L.R.* These (*letters*) are proofs of this scripture; a profound Quran.

2. Certainly, those who disbelieved will wish they were submitters.

3. Let them eat, enjoy, and remain blinded by wishful thinking; they will find out.

4. We never annihilated any community, except in accordance with a specific, predetermined time.

5. The end of any community can never be advanced, nor delayed.

6. They said, "O you who received this reminder, you are crazy.

7. "Why do you not bring down the angels, if you are truthful?"

8. We do not send down the angels except for specific functions. Otherwise, no one will be respited.

God's Messenger of the Covenant*

9. Absolutely, we have revealed the reminder, and, absolutely, we will preserve it.*

10. We have sent (*messengers*) before you to the communities in the past.

11. Every time a messenger went to them, they ridiculed him.

12. We thus control the minds of the guilty.

13. Consequently, they cannot believe in him. This has been the system since the past generations.

14:48 This prophecy is also found in the Old Testament (Isaiah 65:17 & 66:22) and the New Testament: "What we await are new heavens and a new earth where, according to his promise, the justice of God will reside." (2 Peter 3:13).

*15:1 & *15:9 The divine source and the perfect preservation of the Quran are proven by the Quran's mathematical code (App. 1). God's Messenger of the Covenant was destined to unveil this great miracle. The word "Dhikr" denotes the Quran's code in several verses (15:6, 21:2, 26:5, 38:1, 38:8, 74:31). The value of "Rashad Khalifa" (1230) + 15 + 9= 1254, 19x66.*

14. Even if we opened for them a gate into the sky, through which they climb;

15. they will say, "Our eyes have been deceived. We have been bewitched."

16. We placed galaxies in the sky, and adorned it for the beholders.

17. And we guarded it against every rejected devil.

18. If any of them sneaks around to listen, a mighty projectile will chase him back.

19. As for the earth, we constructed it, and placed on it stabilizers (*mountains*), and we grew on it a perfect balance of everything.

20. We made it habitable for you,* and for creatures you do not provide for.

21. There is nothing that we do not own infinite amounts thereof. But we send it down in precise measure.

22. And we send the winds as pollinators, and cause water to come down from the sky for you to drink. Otherwise, you could not keep it palatable.

23. It is we who control life and death, and we are the ultimate inheritors.

24. And we fully know those among you who advance, and we fully know those who regress.

25. Your Lord will surely summon them. He is Most Wise, Omniscient.

The Human Race

26. We created the human being from aged mud, like the potter's clay.

27. As for the jinns, we created them, before that, from blazing fire.

28. Your Lord said to the angels, "I am creating a human being from aged mud, like the potter's clay.

29. "Once I perfect him, and blow into him from My spirit, you shall fall prostrate before him."

30. The angels fell prostrate; all of them,

31. except Iblis (*Satan*), He refused to be with the prostrators.

32. He said, "O Iblis (*Satan*), why are you not with the prostrators?"

33. He said, "I am not to prostrate before a human being, whom You created from aged mud, like the potter's clay."

34. He said, "Therefore, you must get out; you are banished.

35. "You have incurred My condemnation until the Day of Judgment."

36. He said, "My Lord, respite me until the day they are resurrected."

37. He said, "You are respited.

38. "Until the specified day and time."

39. He said, "My Lord, since You have willed that I go astray, I will surely entice them on earth; I will send them all astray.

---

* 15:20 *When we send astronauts into space, we provide them with precisely measured quantities of food, water, and oxygen. God created the spaceship Earth with billions of astronauts who work and reproduce; He supplied them with a self-supporting system that generates oxygen, fresh water, and a great variety of delicious foods and drinks.*

---

40. "Except those among Your worshipers who are devoted absolutely to You alone."

41. He said, "This is a law that is inviolable.

42. "You have no power over My servants. You only have power over the strayers who follow you.

43. "And Hell awaits them all.

44. "It will have seven gates. Each gate will get a specific share of them."

45. As for the righteous, they will enjoy gardens and springs.

46. Enter therein, peaceful and secure.

47. We remove all jealousy from their hearts. Like one family, they will be on adjacent furnishings.

48. Never will they suffer any fatigue therein; never will they be evicted therefrom.

49. Inform My servants that I am the Forgiver, Most Merciful.

50. And that My retribution is the most painful retribution.

Angels Visit Abraham

51. Inform them about Abraham's guests

52. When they entered his quarters, they said, "Peace." He said, "We are apprehensive about you."

53. They said, "Do not be apprehensive. We have good news for you: an enlightened son."

54. He said, "How can you give me such good news, when I am so old?" Do you still give me this good news?

55. They said, "The good news we give you is true; do not despair."

56. He said, "None despairs of his Lord's mercy, except the strayers."

57. He said, "What is your mission, O messengers?"

58. They said, "We are being dispatched to guilty people.

59. "As for Lot's family, we will save them all.

60. "But not his wife; she is destined to be with the doomed."

Lot

61. The messengers went to Lot's town.

62. He said, "You are unknown people."

63. They said, "We bring to you what they have been doubting.

64. "We bring to you the truth; we are truthful.

65. "You shall take your family during the night. Stay behind them, and make sure that none of you looks back. Go straight as commanded."

66. We delivered to him this command: those people are to be annihilated in the morning.

67. The people of the city came joyfully.

68. He said, "These are my guests; do not embarrass me.

69. "Fear **GOD**, and do not shame me."

70. They said, "Did we not enjoin you from contacting anyone?"

71. He said, "Here are my daughters, if you must."

72. But, alas, they were totally blinded by their lust.

73. Consequently, the disaster struck them in the morning.

74. We turned it upside down, and showered them with devastating rocks.

75. This is a lesson for those who possess intelligence.

76. This will always be the system.

77. This is a sign for the believers.

78. The people of the woods also were transgressors.

79. Consequently, we avenged from them, and both communities are fully documented.

80. The people of Al-Hijr disbelieved the messengers.

81. We gave them our revelations, but they disregarded them.

82. They used to carve secure homes out of the mountains.

83. The disaster hit them in the morning.

84. What they hoarded did not help them.

*End of the World Unveiled**

85. We did not create the heavens and the earth, and everything between them, except for a specific purpose. The end of the world will come, so treat them with benign neglect.

86. Your Lord is the Creator, the Omniscient.

87. We have given you the seven pairs, and the great Quran.

88. Do not be jealous of what we bestowed upon the other (*messengers*), and do not be saddened (*by the disbelievers*), and lower your wing for the believers.

89. And proclaim: "I am the manifest warner."

90. We will deal with the dividers.

91. They accept the Quran only partially.

92. By your Lord, we will question them all,

93. about everything they have done.

94. Therefore, carry out the orders given to you, and disregard the idol worshipers.

95. We will spare you the mockers,

96. who set up another god beside **GOD**. They will surely find out.

97. We know full well that you may be annoyed by their utterances.

98. You shall sing the praises of your Lord, and be with the prostrators.

99. And worship your Lord, in order to attain certainty.*

◆◆◆◆

Sura 16: The Bee (Al-Nahl)

In the Name of God,
Most Gracious, Most Merciful

1. **GOD**'s command has already been issued (*and everything has already been written*), so do not rush it.* Be He glorified; the Most High, far above any idols they set up.

---

*15:85-88 One of the functions of God's Messenger of the Covenant is to deliver the Quranic assertion that the world will end in AD 2280 (20:15, 72:27 & Appendix 25).
*15:99 The practices of worship are our means of attaining certainty (Appendix 15).
*16:1 Everything is already recorded (57:22). See also Appendix 14.

2. He sends down the angels with the revelations, carrying His commands, to whomever He chooses from among His servants: "You shall preach that there is no other god beside Me; You shall reverence Me."

3. He created the heavens and the earth for a specific purpose. He is much too High, far above any idols they set up.

4. He created the human from a tiny drop, then he turns into an ardent opponent.

5. And He created the livestock for you, to provide you with warmth, and many other benefits, as well as food.

6. They also provide you with luxury during your leisure, and when you travel.

God's Blessings

7. And they carry your loads to lands that you could not reach without a great hardship. Surely, your Lord is Compassionate, Most Merciful.

8. And (*He created*) the horses, the mules, and the donkeys for you to ride, and for luxury. Additionally, He creates what you do not know.

9. **GOD** points out the paths, including the wrong ones. If He willed, He could have guided all of you.

10. He sends down from the sky water for your drink, and to grow trees for your benefit.

11. With it, He grows for you crops, olives, date palms, grapes, and all kinds of fruits. This is (*sufficient*) proof for people who think.

12. And He commits, in your service, the night and the day, as well as the sun and the moon. Also, the stars are committed by His command. These are (*sufficient*) proofs for people who understand.

13. And (*He created*) for you on earth things of various colors. This is a (*sufficient*) proof for people who take heed.

14. And He committed the sea to serve you; you eat from it tender meat, and extract jewelry which you wear. And you see the ships roaming it for your commercial benefits, as you seek His bounties, that you may be appreciative.

15. And He placed stabilizers (*mountains*) on earth, lest it tumbles with you, as well as rivers and roads, that you may be guided.

16. And landmarks, as well as the stars; to be used for navigation.

17. Is One who creates like one who does not create? Would you now take heed?

18. If you count **GOD**'s blessings, you cannot possibly encompass them. **GOD** is Forgiver, Most Merciful.

19. And **GOD** knows whatever you conceal and whatever you declare.

The Dead Prophets and Saints

20. As for the idols they set up beside **GOD**, they do not create anything; they themselves were created.

21. They are dead, not alive, and they have no idea how or when they will be resurrected.

22. Your god is one god. As for those who do not believe in the Hereafter, their hearts are denying, and they are arrogant.

23. Absolutely, **GOD** knows everything they conceal and everything they declare. He does not love those who are arrogant.

24. When they are asked, "What do you think of these revelations from your Lord," they say, "Tales from the past."

25. They will be held responsible for their sins on the Day of Resurrection, all of them, in addition to sins of all those whom they misled by their ignorance. What a miserable load!

26. Others like them have schemed in the past, and consequently, **GOD** destroyed their building at the foundation, causing the roof to fall on them. The retribution struck them when they least expected.

27. Then, on the Day of Resurrection, He will disgrace them and ask, "Where are My partners that you had set up beside Me, and had opposed Me for their sake?" Those blessed with knowledge will say, "Today, the shame and misery have befallen the disbelievers."

Death for the Disbelievers

28. The angels put them to death in a state of wronging their souls. That is when they finally submit, and say, "We did not do anything wrong!" Yes indeed. **GOD** is fully aware of everything you have done.

29. Therefore, enter the gates of Hell, wherein you abide forever. What a miserable destiny for the arrogant ones.

The Believers Do Not Really Die*

30. As for the righteous, when they are asked, "What do you think of these revelations from your Lord," they say, "Good." For those who lead a righteous life, happiness, and the abode of the Hereafter is even better. What a blissful abode for the righteous.

31. The gardens of Eden are reserved for them, wherein rivers flow. They have anything they wish therein. **GOD** thus rewards the righteous.

They Go Straight to Paradise

32. The angels terminate their lives in a state of righteousness, saying, "Peace be upon you. Enter Paradise (*now*) as a reward for your works."*

The Disbelievers

33. Are they waiting for the angels to come to them, or until your Lord's judgment comes to pass? Those before them did the same thing. **GOD** is not the One who wronged them; they are the ones who wronged their own souls.

34. They have incurred the consequences of their evil works, and the very things they ridiculed came back to haunt them.

Famous Excuse

35. The idol worshipers say, "Had **GOD** willed, we would not worship any idols besides Him, nor would our parents. Nor would we prohibit anything besides His prohibitions." Those before them have done the same. Can the messengers do anything but deliver the complete message?

---

*16:30-32 *The righteous taste only the first death, which has been already experienced by all of us (see 44:56). At the end of their interim in this world, the angels of death simply invite them to move on to the Paradise where Adam and Eve once lived (2:154, 3:169, 8:24, 22:58, 36:27).*

36. We have sent a messenger to every community, saying, "You shall worship **GOD**, and avoid idolatry." Subsequently, some were guided by **GOD**, while others were committed to straying. Roam the earth and note the consequences for the rejectors.

37. No matter how hard you try to guide them, **GOD** does not guide the ones He had committed to straying. Thus, no one can help them.

Deep In Their Minds

38. They swore solemnly by **GOD**: "**GOD** will not resurrect the dead." Absolutely, such is His inviolable promise, but most people do not know.

39. He will then point out to everyone all the things they had disputed, and will let those who disbelieved know that they were liars.

To Resurrect the Dead

40. To have anything done, we simply say to it, "Be," and it is.

41. Those who emigrated for the sake of **GOD**, because they were persecuted, we will surely make it up to them generously in this life, and the recompense of the Hereafter is even greater, if they only knew.

42. This is because they steadfastly persevere, and in their Lord they trust.

43. We did not send before you except men whom we inspired. Ask those who know the scripture, if you do not know.

44. We provided them with the proofs and the scriptures. And we sent down to you this message, to proclaim for the people everything that is sent down to them, perhaps they will reflect.

45. Did those who scheme evil schemes guarantee that **GOD** will not cause the earth to swallow them, or that the retribution will not come to them when they least expect it?

46. It may strike them while they are asleep; they can never escape.

47. Or it may strike them while they are fearfully expecting it. Your Lord is Compassionate, Most Merciful.

48. Have they not seen all the things created by **GOD**? Their shadows surround them right and left, in total submission to **GOD**, and willingly.

49. To **GOD** prostrates everything in the heavens and everything on earth —every creature—and so do the angels; without the least arrogance.*

50. They reverence their Lord, high above them, and they do what they are commanded to do.

51. **GOD** has proclaimed: "Do not worship two gods; there is only one god. You shall reverence Me alone."

52. To Him belongs everything in the heavens and the earth and therefore, the religion shall be devoted absolutely to Him alone. Would you worship other than **GOD**?

53. Any blessing you enjoy is from **GOD**. Yet, whenever you incur any adversity you immediately complain to Him.

54. Yet, as soon as He relieves your affliction, some of you revert to idol worship.

16:49 The human body, whether it belongs to a believer or a disbeliever, submits to God; the heartbeats, the lungs' movement, and peristalsis illustrate this submission.

---

55. Let them disbelieve in what we have given them. Go ahead and enjoy temporarily; you will surely find out.

56. They designate for the idols they set up out of ignorance, a share of the provisions we bestow upon them. By **GOD**, you will be held accountable for your innovations.

Bigoted Bias Against Baby Girls

57. They even assign daughters to **GOD**, be He glorified, while they prefer for themselves what they like.

58. When one of them gets a baby girl, his face becomes darkened with overwhelming grief.

59. Ashamed, he hides from the people, because of the bad news given to him. He even ponders: should he keep the baby grudgingly, or bury her in the dust. Miserable indeed is their judgment.

60. Those who do not believe in the Hereafter set the worst examples, while to **GOD** belongs the most sublime examples. He is the Almighty, the Most Wise.

The Original Sin

61. If **GOD** punished the people for their transgressions, He would have annihilated every creature on earth. But He respites them for a specific, predetermined time. Once their interim ends, they cannot delay it by one hour, nor advance it.

62. They ascribe to **GOD** what they dislike for themselves, then utter the lie with their own tongues that they are righteous! Without any doubt, they have incurred Hell, for they have rebelled.

63. By **GOD**, we have sent (*messengers*) to communities before you, but the devil adorned their works in their eyes. Consequently, he is now their lord, and they have incurred a painful retribution.

64. We have revealed this scripture to you, to point out for them what they dispute, and to provide guidance and mercy for people who believe.

Additional Proofs
From God

65. **GOD** sends down from the sky water to revive the land after it had died. This should be (*sufficient*) proof for people who hear.

66. And in the livestock there is a lesson for you: we provide you with a drink from their bellies. From the midst of digested food and blood, you get pure milk, delicious for the drinkers.

67. And from the fruits of date palms and grapes you produce intoxicants, as well as good provisions. This should be (*sufficient*) proof for people who understand.

The Bee

68. And your Lord inspired the bee: build homes in mountains and trees, and in (*the hives*) they build for you.

69. Then eat from all the fruits, following the design of your Lord, precisely. From their bellies comes a drink of different colors, wherein there is healing for the people. This should be (*sufficient*) proof for people who reflect.*

16:69 Besides its recognized nutritive value, honey has been scientifically proven as a healing medicine for certain allergies and other ailments.

---

70. **GOD** created you, then He terminates your lives. He lets some of you live to the oldest age, only to find out that there is a limit to the knowledge they can acquire. **GOD** is Omniscient, Omnipotent.

No Partners With God

71. **GOD** has provided for some of you more than others. Those who are given plenty would never give their properties to their subordinates to the extent of making them partners. Would they give up **GOD**'s blessings?*

72. And **GOD** made for you spouses from among yourselves, and produced for you from your spouses children and grandchildren, and provided you with good provisions. Should they believe in falsehood, and turn unappreciative of **GOD**'s blessings?

*Idol Worship:
Not Very Intelligent*

73. Yet, they worship beside **GOD** what possesses no provisions for them in the heavens, nor on earth, nor can provide them with anything.

74. Therefore, do not cite the examples for **GOD**; **GOD** knows while you do not know.

*The Rich Believer is Better
than the Poor Believer*

75. **GOD** cites the example of a slave who is owned, and is totally powerless, compared to one whom we blessed with good provisions, from which he gives to charity secretly and publicly. Are they equal? Praise be to **GOD**, most of them do not know.

76. And **GOD** cites the example of two men: one is dumb, lacks the ability to do anything, is totally dependent on his master—whichever way he directs him, he cannot produce anything good. Is he equal to one who rules with justice, and is guided in the right path?

This Life is Very Short

77. To **GOD** belongs the future of the heavens and the earth. As far as He is concerned, the end of the world (*the Hour*) is a blink of an eye away, or even closer. **GOD** is Omnipotent.

78. **GOD** brought you out of your mothers' bellies knowing nothing, and He gave you the hearing, the eyesight, and the brains, that you may be appreciative.

79. Do they not see the birds committed to fly in the atmosphere of the sky? None holds them up in the air except **GOD**. This should be (*sufficient*) proof for people who believe.

80. And **GOD** provided for you stationary homes where you can live. And He provided for you portable homes made of the hides of livestock, so you can use them when you travel, and when you settle down. And from their wools, furs, and hair, you make furnishings and luxuries for awhile.

81. And **GOD** provided for you shade through things which He created, and provided for you shelters in the mountains, and provided for you garments that protect you from heat, and garments that protect when you fight in wars. He thus perfects His blessings upon you, that you may submit.

16:71 If the humans would not give up their power to that extent, why do they expect God to do this, and create partners for Himself?

82. If they still turn away, then your sole mission is the clear delivery (*of the message*).

The Disbelievers Unappreciative

83. They fully recognize **GOD**'s blessings, then deny them; the majority of them are disbelievers.

On The Day of Resurrection

84. The day will come when we raise from every community a witness, then those who disbelieved will not be permitted (*to speak*), nor will they be excused.

85. Once those who transgressed see the retribution, it will be too late; it will not be commuted for them, nor will they be respited.

The Idols Disown Their Idolizers

86. And when those who committed idol worship see their idols, they will say, "Our Lord, these are the idols we had set up beside You." The idols will then confront them and say, "You are liars."

87. They will totally submit to **GOD** on that day, and the idols they had invented will disown them.

88. Those who disbelieve and repel from the path of **GOD**, we augment their retribution by adding more retribution, due to their transgressions.

89. The day will come when we will raise from every community a witness from among them, and bring you as the witness of these people. We have revealed to you this book to provide explanations for everything, and guidance, and mercy, and good news for the submitters.

90. **GOD** advocates justice, charity, and regarding the relatives. And He forbids evil, vice, and transgression. He enlightens you, that you may take heed.

You Shall Keep Your Word

91. You shall fulfill your covenant with **GOD** when you make such a covenant. You shall not violate the oaths after swearing (*by God*) to carry them out, for you have made **GOD** a guarantor for you. **GOD** knows everything you do.

92. Do not be like the knitter who unravels her strong knitting into piles of flimsy yarn. This is your example if you abuse the oaths to take advantage of one another. Whether one group is larger than the other, **GOD** thus puts you to the test. He will surely show you on the Day of Resurrection everything you had disputed.

93. Had **GOD** willed, He could have made you one congregation. But He sends astray whoever chooses to go astray, and He guides whoever wishes to be guided.* You will surely be asked about everything you have done.

Violating Your Oath:
A Serious Offense

94. Do not abuse the oaths among you, lest you slide back after having a strong foothold, then you incur misery. Such is the consequence of repelling from the path of **GOD** (*by setting a bad example*); you incur a terrible retribution.

95. Do not sell your oaths before **GOD** short. What **GOD** possesses is far better for you, if you only knew.

16:93 God knows the sincere believers among us who deserve to be redeemed. Accordingly, He guides them, while blocking out those who choose to disbelieve.

---

96. What you possess runs out, but what **GOD** possesses lasts forever. We will surely reward those who steadfastly persevere; we will recompense them for their righteous works.

*Guaranteed Happiness
Now and Forever*

97. Anyone who works righteousness, male or female, while believing, we will surely grant them a happy life in this world, and we will surely pay them their full recompense (*on the Day of Judgment*) for their righteous works.

An Important Commandment*

98. When you read the Quran, you shall seek refuge in **GOD** from Satan the rejected.

99. He has no power over those who believe and trust in their Lord.

100. His power is limited to those who choose him as their master; those who choose him as their god.

101. When we substitute one revelation in place of another, and **GOD** is fully aware of what He reveals, they say, "You made this up!" Indeed, most of them do not know.

102. Say, "The Holy Spirit has brought it down from your Lord, truthfully, to assure those who believe, and to provide a beacon and good news for the submitters."

*The Quran Is Not Copied
From The Bible*

103. We are fully aware that they say, "A human being is teaching him!" The tongue of the source they hint at is non-Arabic, and this is a perfect Arabic tongue.

104. Surely, those who do not believe in **GOD**'s revelations, **GOD** does not guide them. They have incurred a painful retribution.

105. The only ones who fabricate false doctrines are those who do not believe in **GOD**'s revelations; they are the real liars.

Lip Service Does Not Count

106. Those who disbelieve in **GOD**, after having acquired faith, and become fully content with disbelief, have incurred wrath from **GOD**. The only ones to be excused are those who are forced to profess disbelief, while their hearts are full of faith.*

*Preoccupation With This Life
Leads to Exile From God*

107. This is because they have given priority to this life over the Hereafter, and **GOD** does not guide such disbelieving people.

108. Those are the ones whom **GOD** has sealed their hearts, and their hearing, and their eyesight. Consequently, they remain unaware.

109. Without a doubt, they will be the losers in the Hereafter.

110. As for those who emigrate because of persecution, then continue to strive and steadfastly persevere, your Lord, because of all this, is Forgiver, Most Merciful.

---

*16:98 Our salvation is attained by knowing God's message to us, the Quran, and Satan will do his utmost to keep us from being redeemed. Hence this commandment.

*16:106 God's wisdom decrees that if someone holds a gun to your head and orders you to declare that you disbelieve in God, you may grant him his wish. What the heart harbors is what counts.

---

111. The day will come when every soul will serve as its own advocate, and every soul will be paid fully for whatever it had done, without the least injustice.

Prohibiting Lawful Food Brings Deprivation

112. **GOD** cites the example of a community that used to be secure and prosperous, with provisions coming to it from everywhere. But then, it turned unappreciative of **GOD**'s blessings. Consequently, **GOD** caused them to taste the hardships of starvation and insecurity. Such is the requital for what they did.

113. A messenger had gone to them from among them, but they rejected him. Consequently, the retribution struck them for their transgression.

114. Therefore, you shall eat from **GOD**'s provisions everything that is lawful and good, and be appreciative of **GOD**'s blessings, if you do worship Him alone.

Only Four Foods Prohibited

115. He only prohibits for you dead animals, blood, the meat of pigs,* and food which is dedicated to other than **GOD**. If one is forced (*to eat these*), without being deliberate or malicious, then **GOD** is Forgiver, Most Merciful.

116. You shall not utter lies with your own tongues stating: "This is lawful, and this is unlawful," to fabricate lies and attribute them to **GOD**. Surely, those who fabricate lies and attribute them to **GOD** will never succeed.

117. They enjoy briefly, then suffer painful retribution.

118. For the Jews, we prohibited what we narrated to you previously.* It was not us who wronged them; they are the ones who wronged their own souls.

119. Yet, as regards those who fall in sin out of ignorance then repent thereafter and reform, your Lord, after this is done, is Forgiver, Most Merciful.

Abraham

120. Abraham was indeed an exemplary vanguard in his submission to **GOD**, a monotheist who never worshiped idols.

121. Because he was appreciative of His Lord's blessings, He chose him and guided him in a straight path.

122. We granted him happiness in this life, and in the Hereafter he will be with the righteous.

Muhammad: A Follower of Abraham*

123. Then we inspired you (*Muhammad*) to follow the religion of Abraham,* the monotheist; he never was an idol worshiper.

16:115 & 118 The most devastating trichinosis parasite, Trichinella spiralis, (also the pork tapeworm Taenia solium) survives in the meat of pigs, not the fat. More than 150,000 people are infected annually in the United States. See 6:145-146, and Appendix 16.

16:123 This informs us that all religious practices, which came to us through Abraham, were intact at the time of Muhammad (see 22:78 and Appendix 9).

The Sabbath Abrogated

124. The Sabbath was decreed only for those who ended up disputing it (*Jews & Christians*). Your Lord is the One who will judge them on the Day of Resurrection regarding their disputes.

How to Spread God's Message

125. You shall invite to the path of your Lord with wisdom and kind enlightenment, and debate with them in the best possible manner. Your Lord knows best who has strayed from His path, and He knows best who are the guided ones.

126. And if you punish, you shall inflict an equivalent punishment. But if you resort to patience (*instead of revenge*), it would be better for the patient ones.

127. You shall resort to patience—and your patience is attainable only with **GOD**'s help. Do not grieve over them, and do not be annoyed by their schemes.

128. **GOD** is with those who lead a righteous life, and those who are charitable.

◆◆◆◆

Sura 17: The Children of Israel (Banî Israel)

In the name of God,
Most Gracious, Most Merciful

1. Most glorified is the One who summoned His servant (*Muhammad*) during the night, from the Sacred Masjid (*of Mecca*) to the farthest place of prostration,* whose surroundings we have blessed, in order to show him some of our signs. He is the Hearer, the Seer.

2. Similarly, we gave Moses the scripture, and rendered it a beacon for the Children of Israel that: "You shall not set up any idol as a Lord and Master beside Me."

3. They are descendants of those whom we carried with Noah; he was an appreciative servant.

4. We addressed the Children of Israel in the scripture: "You will commit gross evil on earth, twice. You are destined to fall into great heights of arrogance.

5. "When the first time comes to pass, we will send against you servants of ours who possess great might, and they will invade your homes. This is a prophecy that must come to pass.

6. "Afterwards, we will give you a turn over them, and will supply you with a lot of wealth and children; we will give you the upper hand.

7. "If you work righteousness, you work righteousness for your own good, but if you commit evil you do so to your own detriment. Thus, when the second time comes to pass, they will defeat you and enter the masjid, just as they did the first time. They will wipe out all the gains you had accomplished."

8. Your Lord showers you with His mercy. But if you revert to transgression, we will counter with retribution. We have designated Gehenna as a final abode for the disbelievers.

---

*17:1 "The Aqsa Masjid" means "the farthest place where there is prostration," many billions of Light Years away. This verse informs us that Muhammad, the soul, was taken to the highest Heaven to be given the Quran (2:185, 44:3, 53:1-18, &. 97:1).

Quran: Our Means to Salvation

9. This Quran guides to the best path, and brings good news to the believers who lead a righteous life, that they have deserved a great recompense.

10. As for those who disbelieve in the Hereafter, we have prepared for them a painful retribution.

11. The human being often prays for something that may hurt him, thinking that he is praying for something good. The human being is impatient.

12. We rendered the night and the day two signs. We made the night dark, and the day lighted, that you may seek provisions from your Lord therein. This also establishes for you a timing system, and the means of calculation. We thus explain everything in detail.

*The Video Tape**

13. We have recorded the fate of every human being; it is tied to his neck. On the Day of Resurrection we will hand him a record that is accessible.

14. Read your own record. Today, you suffice as your own reckoner.

15. Whoever is guided, is guided for his own good, and whoever goes astray does so to his own detriment. No sinner will bear the sins of anyone else. We never punish without first sending a messenger.

16. If we are to annihilate any community, we let the leaders commit vast corruption therein. Once they deserve retribution, we annihilate it completely.

17. Many a generation have we annihilated after Noah. Your Lord is most efficient in dealing with the sins of His servants; He is fully Cognizant, Seer.

Choose Your Priorities Carefully
This Life

18. Anyone who chooses this fleeting life as his priority, we will rush to him what we decide to give him, then we commit him to Gehenna, where he suffers forever, despised and defeated.

The Hereafter

19. As for those who choose the Hereafter as their priority, and work righteousness, while believing, their efforts will be appreciated.

20. For each one of them we provide; we provide those and these from your Lord's bounties. Your Lord's bounties are inexhaustible.

21. Note how we preferred some people above others (*in this life*). The differences in the Hereafter are far greater and far more significant.

Major Commandments

22. You shall not set up any other god beside **GOD**, lest you end up despised and disgraced.

23. Your Lord has decreed that you shall not worship except Him, and your parents shall be honored. As long as one or both of them live, you shall never say to them, "Uff" (*the slightest gesture of annoyance*), nor shall you shout at them; you shall treat them amicably.

---

*17:13 Your life is already recorded, as if on a video tape, from birth to death. This same record will be made accessible to us upon resurrection. See 57:22 & Appendix 14.

24. And lower for them the wings of humility, and kindness, and say, "My Lord, have mercy on them, for they have raised me from infancy."

25. Your Lord is fully aware of your innermost thoughts. If you maintain righteousness, He is Forgiver of those who repent.

26. You shall give the due alms to the relatives, the needy, the poor, and the traveling alien, but do not be excessive, extravagant.

27. The extravagant are brethren of the devils, and the devil is unappreciative of his Lord.

28. Even if you have to turn away from them, as you pursue the mercy of your Lord, you shall treat them in the nicest manner.

Stinginess Condemned

29. You shall not keep your hand stingily tied to your neck, nor shall you foolishly open it up, lest you end up blamed and sorry.

30. For your Lord increases the provision for anyone He chooses, and reduces it. He is fully Cognizant of His creatures, Seer.

Abortion is Murder

31. You shall not kill your children due to fear of poverty. We provide for them, as well as for you. Killing them is a gross offense.

32. You shall not commit adultery; it is a gross sin, and an evil behavior.

33. You shall not kill any person—for **GOD** has made life sacred—except in the course of justice. If one is killed unjustly, then we give his heir authority to enforce justice. Thus, he shall not exceed the limits in avenging the murder, he will be helped.

34. You shall not touch the orphans' money except for their own good, until they reach maturity. You shall fulfill your covenants, for a covenant is a great responsibility.

35. You shall give full measure when you trade, and weigh equitably. This is better and more righteous.

Crucial Advice

36. You shall not accept any information, unless you verify it for yourself. I have given you the hearing, the eyesight, and the brain, and you are responsible for using them.

37. You shall not walk proudly on earth—you cannot bore through the earth, nor can you be as tall as the mountains.

38. All bad behavior is condemned by your Lord.

Quran Is Wisdom

39. This is some of the wisdom inspired to you by your Lord. You shall not set up another god beside **GOD**, lest you end up in Gehenna, blamed and defeated.

40. Has your Lord given you boys, while giving Himself the angels as daughters?! How could you utter such a blasphemy?

41. We have cited in this Quran (*all kinds of examples*), that they may take heed. But it only augments their aversion.

42. Say, "If there were any other gods beside Him, as they claim, they would have tried to overthrow the Possessor of the throne."

43. Be He glorified, He is much too exalted, far above their utterances.

Everything Glorifies God

44. Glorifying Him are the seven universes, the earth, and everyone in them. There is nothing that does not glorify Him, but you do not understand their glorification. He is Clement, Forgiver.

*Disbelievers Cannot
Understand Quran*

45. When you read the Quran, we place between you and those who do not believe in the Hereafter an invisible barrier.

Quran: The ONLY Source

46. We place shields around their minds, to prevent them from understanding it, and deafness in their ears. And when you preach your Lord, using the Quran alone,* they run away in aversion.

47. We are fully aware of what they hear, when they listen to you, and when they conspire secretly—the disbelievers say, "You are following a crazy man."

48. Note how they describe you, and how this causes them to stray off the path.

49. They said, "After we turn into bones and fragments, we get resurrected anew?!"

50. Say, "Even if you turn into rocks or iron.

51. "Even if you turn into any kind of creation that you deem impossible." They will then say, "Who will bring us back?" Say, "The One who created you in the first place." They will then shake their heads and say,

"When will that be?" Say, "It may be closer than you think."

52. The day He summons you, you will respond by praising Him, and you will then realize that you had lasted in this life but a short while.

Treat Each Other Amicably

53. Tell My servants to treat each other in the best possible manner, for the devil will always try to drive a wedge among them. Surely, the devil is man's most ardent enemy.

54. Your Lord knows you best. According to His knowledge, He may shower you with mercy, or He may requite you. We did not send you to be their advocate.

55. Your Lord is the best knower of everyone in the heavens and the earth. In accordance with this knowledge, we preferred some prophets over others. For example, we gave David the Psalms.

56. Say, "Implore whatever idols you have set up beside Him." They have no power to relieve your afflictions, nor can they prevent them.

*The Righteous Idols
Worship God Alone*

57. Even the idols that they implore are seeking the ways and means towards their Lord. They pray for His mercy, and fear His retribution. Surely, the retribution of your Lord is dreadful.

58. There is not a community that we will not annihilate before the Day of Resurrection, or inflict severe retribution upon them. This is already written down in the book.

---

* *17:46 The Arabic word "alone" refers to God in 7:70, 39:45, 40:12 & 84, and 60:4. If you add these numbers, you get 361, 19x19. But if you include 17:46, which refers to the Quran, the product is not a multiple of 19. "Alone," therefore refers to the Quran in 17:46 (Appendix 18).*

Old Kind of Miracles
Made Obsolete

59. What stopped us from sending the miracles is that the previous generations have rejected them. For example, we showed Thamoud the camel, a profound (*miracle*), but they transgressed against it. We sent the miracles only to instill reverence.

60. We informed you that your Lord fully controls the people, and we rendered the vision that we showed you a test for the people, and the tree that is accursed in the Quran.* We showed them solid proofs to instill reverence in them, but this only augmented their defiance.

Satan Dupes the People

61. When we said to the angels, "Fall prostrate before Adam," they fell prostrate, except Satan. He said, "Shall I prostrate to one You created from mud?"

62. He said, "Since You have honored him over me, if You respite me till the Day of Resurrection, I will possess all his descendants, except a few."

63. He said, "Then go; you and those who follow you will end up in Hell as your requital; an equitable requital.

64. "You may entice them with your voice, and mobilize all your forces and all your men against them, and share in their money and children, and promise them. Anything the devil promises is no more than an illusion.

65. "As for My servants, you have no power over them." Your Lord suffices as an advocate.

66. Your Lord is the One who causes the ships to float on the ocean,* that you may seek His bounties. He is Most Merciful towards you.

Bad Weather
Friends

67. If you are afflicted in the middle of the sea, you forget your idols and sincerely implore Him alone. But as soon as He saves you to the shore, you revert. Indeed, the human being is unappreciative.

68. Have you guaranteed that He will not cause the land, on shore, to swallow you? Or, that He will not send upon you a tempest, then you find no protector?

69. Have you guaranteed that He will not return you to the sea another time, then send upon you a storm that drowns you because of your disbelief? Once this happens, we will not give you another chance.

70. We have honored the children of Adam, and provided them with rides on land and in the sea. We provided for them good provisions, and we gave them greater advantages than many of our creatures.

71. The day will come when we summon every people, together with their record. As for those who are given a record of righteousness, they will read their record and will not suffer the least injustice.

---

*17:60 Muhammad's journey to the highest heaven to receive the Quran, as stated in 17:1 and 53:1-18, is a test because the people had to believe Muhammad on faith.

*17:66 We now learn from physics and physical chemistry that water possesses unique qualities that render it perfectly suitable for serving our various needs.

72. As for those who are blind in this life, they will be blind in the Hereafter; even a lot worse.

God Strengthens the Messenger

73. They almost diverted you from the revelations we have given you. They wanted you to fabricate something else, in order to consider you a friend.

74. If it were not that we strengthened you, you almost leaned towards them just a little bit.

75. Had you done that, we would have doubled the retribution for you in this life, and after death, and you would have found no one to help you against us.

76. They almost banished you from the land to get rid of you, so they could revert as soon as you left.

77. This has been consistently the case with all the messengers that we sent before you, and you will find that our system never changes.

The Noon Prayer

78. You shall observe the Contact Prayer (*Salat*) when the sun declines from its highest point at noon, as it moves towards sunset. You shall also observe (*the recitation of*) the Quran at dawn. (*Reciting*) the Quran at dawn is witnessed.

Meditation

79. During the night, you shall meditate for extra credit, that your Lord may raise you to an honorable rank.

80. And say, "My Lord, admit me an honorable admittance, and let me depart an honorable departure, and grant me from You a powerful support."

81. Proclaim, "The truth has prevailed, and falsehood has vanished; falsehood will inevitably vanish."

Healing and Mercy

82. We send down in the Quran healing and mercy for the believers. At the same time, it only increases the wickedness of the transgressors.

83. When we bless the human being, he becomes preoccupied and heedless. But when adversity strikes him, he turns despondent.

84. Say, "Everyone works in accordance with his belief, and your Lord knows best which ones are guided in the right path."

Divine Revelation:
The Source of All Knowledge

85. They ask you about the revelation. Say, "The revelation comes from my Lord. The knowledge given to you is minute."

86. If we will, we can take back what we revealed to you, then you will find no protector against us.

87. This is but mercy from your Lord. His blessings upon you have been great.

Mathematical Composition
of the Quran

88. Say, "If all the humans and all the jinns banded together in order to produce a Quran like this, they could never produce anything like it, no matter how much assistance they lent one another."

89. We have cited for the people in this Quran all kinds of examples, but most people insist upon disbelieving.

God's Messengers Challenged

90. They said, "We will not believe you unless you cause a spring to gush out of the ground.

91. "Or unless you own a garden of date palms and grapes, with rivers running through it.

92. "Or unless you cause masses from the sky, as you claimed, to fall on us. Or unless you bring **GOD** and the angels before our eyes.

93. "Or unless you own a luxurious mansion, or unless you climb into the sky. Even if you do climb, we will not believe unless you bring a book that we can read."* Say, "Glory be to my Lord. Am I any more than a human messenger?"

Messengership: An Essential Test

94. What prevented the people from believing when the guidance came to them, is their saying, "Did **GOD** send a human being as a messenger?"

95. Say, "If the earth were inhabited by angels, we would have sent down to them from the sky an angel messenger."

God Is My Witness

96. Say, "**GOD** suffices as a witness between me and you. He is fully Cognizant of His worshipers, Seer."

97. Whomever **GOD** guides is the truly guided one. And whomever He sends astray, you will never find for them any lords and masters beside Him. We will summon them on the Day of Resurrection forcibly; blind, dumb, and deaf. Their destination is Hell; whenever it cools down, we will increase their fire.

Their Innermost Thoughts

98. Such is their just retribution, since they rejected our revelations. They said, "After we turn into bones and fragments, do we get resurrected into a new creation?"

99. Could they not see that the **GOD** who created the heavens and the earth, is able to create the same creations? He has predetermined for them an irrevocable life span? Yet, the disbelievers insist upon disbelieving.

100. Proclaim, "If you possessed my Lord's treasures of mercy, you would have withheld them, fearing that you might exhaust them. The human being is stingy."

Moses and Pharaoh

101. We supported Moses with nine profound miracles—ask the Children of Israel. When he went to them, Pharaoh said to him, "I think that you, Moses, are bewitched."

102. He said, "You know full well that no one can manifest these except, obviously, the Lord of the heavens and the earth. I think that you, Pharaoh, are doomed."

103. When he pursued them, as he chased them out of the land, we drowned him, together with those who sided with him, all of them.

17:93 God's Messenger of the Covenant, Rashad Khalifa, was thus challenged, including the challenge to bring a new book, or bring down masses from the sky. Verse 3:81 defines the duties of God's Messenger of the Covenant. Overwhelming proof is detailed in Appendices 2 & 26.

---

104. And we said to the Children of Israel afterwards, "Go live in this land. When the final prophecy comes to pass, we will summon you all in one group."

The Quran Released Slowly
To Facilitate Memorization

105. Truthfully, we sent it down, and with the truth it came down. We did not send you except as a bearer of good news, as well as a warner.

106. A Quran that we have released slowly, in order for you to read it to the people over a long period, although we sent it down all at once.

107. Proclaim, "Believe in it, or do not believe in it." Those who possess knowledge from the previous scriptures, when it is recited to them, they fall down to their chins, prostrating.

108. They say, "Glory be to our Lord. This fulfills our Lord's prophecy."

109. They fall down on their chins, prostrating and weeping. For it augments their reverence.

110. Say, "Call Him **GOD**, or call Him Most Gracious; whichever name you use, to Him belongs the best names."

Tone of the Contact Prayers (Salat)
You shall not utter your Contact Prayers (*Salat*) too loudly, nor secretly; use a moderate tone.

111. And proclaim: "Praise be to **GOD**, who has never begotten a son, nor does He have a partner in His kingship, nor does He need any ally out

of weakness," and magnify Him constantly.

Sura 18: The Cave (Al-Kahf)

In the name of God,
Most Gracious, Most Merciful

1. Praise **GOD**, who revealed to His servant this scripture, and made it flawless.

2. A perfect (*scripture*) to warn of severe retribution from Him, and to deliver good news to the believers who lead a righteous life, that they have earned a generous recompense.

3. Wherein they abide forever.

4. And to warn those who said, "**GOD** has begotten a son!"

5. They possess no knowledge about this, nor did their parents. What a blasphemy coming out of their mouths! What they utter is a gross lie.

6. You may blame yourself on account of their response to this narration, and their disbelieving in it; you may be saddened.

The End of the World

7. We have adorned everything on earth, in order to test them, and thus distinguish those among them who work righteousness.

8. Inevitably, we will wipe out everything on it, leaving it completely barren.*

The Dwellers of the Cave

9. Why else do you think we are telling you about the people of the cave, and the numbers connected with them? They are among our wondrous signs.

10. When the youths took refuge in the cave, they said, "Our Lord, shower us with Your mercy, and bless our affairs with Your guidance."

11. We then sealed their ears in the cave for a predetermined number of years.

12. Then we resurrected them to see which of the two parties could count the duration of their stay therein.

13. We narrate to you their history, truthfully. They were youths who believed in their Lord, and we increased their guidance.

14. We strengthened their hearts when they stood up and proclaimed: "Our only Lord is the Lord of the heavens and the earth. We will never worship any other god beside Him. Otherwise, we would be far astray.

15. "Here are our people setting up gods beside Him. If only they could provide any proof to support their stand! Who is more evil than the one who fabricates lies and attributes them to **GOD**?

The Seven Sleepers
*of Ephesus**

16. "Since you wish to avoid them, and their worshiping of other than **GOD**,* let us take refuge in the cave. May your Lord shower you with His mercy and direct you to the right decision."

A Guiding Teacher
is a Prerequisite

17. You could see the sun when it rose coming from the right side of their cave, and when it set, it shone on them from the left, as they slept in the hollow thereof. This is one of **GOD**'s portents.* Whomever **GOD** guides is the truly guided one, and whomever He sends astray, you will not find for him a guiding teacher.

18. You would think that they were awake, when they were in fact asleep. We turned them to the right side and the left side, while their dog stretched his arms in their midst. Had you looked at them, you would have fled from them, stricken with terror.

18:8-9 As it turns out, the history of these Christian believers, the Seven Sleepers of Ephesus, is directly connected with the end of the world as stated in 18:9 & 21. The role of these believers in unveiling the end of the world is detailed in Appendix 25.

18:16-20 Ephesus is located about 200 miles south of ancient Nicene, and 30 miles south of today's Izmir in Turkey. The dwellers of the cave were young Christians who wanted to follow the teachings of Jesus, and worship God alone. They were fleeing the persecution of neo-Christians who proclaimed a corrupted Christianity three centuries after Jesus, following the Nicene Conferences, when the Trinity doctrine was announced. In 1928, Franz Miltner, an Austrian archeologist discovered the tomb of the seven sleepers of Ephesus. Their history is well documented in several encyclopedias.

18:17 This sign, or hint, tells us that the cave was facing north.

19. When we resurrected them, they asked each other, "How long have you been here?" "We have been here one day or part of the day," they answered. "Your Lord knows best how long we stayed here, so let us send one of us with this money to the city. Let him fetch the cleanest food, and buy some for us. Let him keep a low profile, and attract no attention.

20. "If they discover you, they will stone you, or force you to revert to their religion, then you can never succeed."

*Connection With
the End of the World**

21. We caused them to be discovered, to let everyone know that **GOD**'s promise is true, and to remove all doubt concerning the end of the world.* The people then disputed among themselves regarding them. Some said, "Let us build a building around them." Their Lord is the best knower about them. Those who prevailed said, "We will build a place of worship around them."

22. Some would say, "They were three; their dog being the fourth," while others would say, "Five; the sixth being their dog," as they guessed. Others said, "Seven," and the eighth was their dog. Say, "My Lord is the best knower of their number." Only a few knew the correct number. Therefore, do not argue with them; just go along with them. You need not consult anyone about this.

*Remembering God
Every Chance We Get*

23. You shall not say that you will do anything in the future,

24. without saying, "**GOD** willing."* If you forget to do this, you must immediately remember your Lord and say, "May my Lord guide me to do better next time."

*[300 + 9]**

25. They stayed in their cave three hundred years, increased by nine.*

26. Say, "**GOD** is the best knower of how long they stayed there." He knows all secrets in the heavens and the earth. By His grace you can see; by His grace you can hear. There is none beside Him as Lord and Master, and He never permits any partners to share in His kingship.

27. You shall recite what is revealed to you of your Lord's scripture. Nothing shall abrogate His words, and you shall not find any other source beside it.

Quranic Study Groups

28. You shall force yourself to be with those who worship their Lord day and night, seeking Him alone. Do not turn your eyes away from them, seeking the vanities of this world. Nor shall you obey one whose heart we rendered oblivious to our message; one who pursues his own desires, and whose priorities are confused.

18:21 As detailed in Appendix 25, this story helped pinpoint the end of the world.

18:24 This important commandment gives us daily opportunities to remember God.

18:25 The difference between 300 solar years and 300 lunar years is nine years. Thus, discovering the end of the world was predetermined by the Almighty to take place in 1980 AD (1400 AH), 300 years (309 lunar years) before the end of the world (see 72:27 & Appendix 25).

Absolute Freedom of Religion

29. Proclaim: "This is the truth from your Lord," then whoever wills let him believe, and whoever wills let him disbelieve. We have prepared for the transgressors a fire that will completely surround them. When they scream for help, they will be given a liquid like concentrated acid that scalds the faces. What a miserable drink! What a miserable destiny!

30. As for those who believe and lead a righteous life, we never fail to recompense those who work righteousness.

31. They have deserved gardens of Eden wherein rivers flow. They will be adorned therein with bracelets of gold, and will wear clothes of green silk and velvet, and will rest on comfortable furnishings. What a wonderful reward; what a wonderful abode!

Property as an Idol*

32. Cite for them the example of two men: we gave one of them two gardens of grapes, surrounded by date palms, and placed other crops between them.

33. Both gardens produced their crops on time, and generously, for we caused a river to run through them.

34. Once, after harvesting, he boastfully told his friend: "I am far more prosperous than you, and I command more respect from the people."

35. When he entered his garden, he wronged his soul by saying, "I do not think that this will ever end.

36. "Moreover, I think this is it; I do not think that the Hour (*the Hereafter*) will ever come to pass. Even if I am returned to my Lord, I will (*be clever enough to*) possess an even better one over there."

37. His friend said to him, as he debated with him, "Have you disbelieved in the One who created you from dust, then from a tiny drop, then perfected you into a man?

38. "As for me, **GOD** is my Lord, and I will never set up any other god besides my Lord.

Important Commandment

39. "When you entered your garden, you should have said, This is what **GOD** has given me (*Mã Shã Allãh*). No one possesses power except **GOD** (*Lã Quwwata Ellã Bellãh*).' You may see that I possess less money and less children than you.

40. "My Lord may grant me better than your garden. He may send a violent storm from the sky that wipes out your garden, leaving it completely barren.

41. "Or, its water may sink deeper, out of your reach."

42. Indeed, his crops were wiped out, and he ended up sorrowful, lamenting what he had spent on it in vain, as his property lay barren. He finally said, "I wish I never set up my property as a god beside my Lord."

---

*18:32-42 The Quran cites many examples of the different gods that people worship beside God; they include children (7:190), religious leaders and scholars (9:31), property (18:42), dead saints and prophets (16:20-21, 35:14, & 46:5-6), and the ego (25:43, 45:23).

---

43. No force on earth could have helped him against **GOD**, nor was it possible for him to receive any help.

44. That is because the only true Lord and master is **GOD**; He provides the best recompense, and with Him is the best destiny.

45. Cite for them the example of this life as water that we send down from the sky to produce plants of the earth, then they turn into hay that is blown away by the wind. **GOD** is able to do all things.

Rearranging Our Priorities

46. Money and children are the joys of this life, but the righteous works provide an eternal recompense from your Lord, and a far better hope.

47. The day will come when we wipe out the mountains, and you will see the earth barren. We will summon them all, not leaving out a single one of them.

48. They will be presented before your Lord in a row. You have come to us as individuals, just as we created you initially. Indeed, this is what you claimed will never happen.

49. The record will be shown, and you will see the guilty fearful of its contents. They will say, "Woe to us. How come this book leaves nothing, small or large, without counting it?" They will find everything they had done brought forth. Your Lord is never unjust towards anyone.

Classification of God's Creatures

50. We said to the angels, "Fall prostrate before Adam." They fell prostrate, except Satan. He became a jinn, for he disobeyed the order of His Lord.* Will you choose him and his descendants as lords instead of Me, even though they are your enemies? What a miserable substitute!

51. I never permitted them to witness the creation of the heavens and the earth, nor the creation of themselves. Nor do I permit the wicked to work in My kingdom.*

52. The day will come when He says, "Call upon My partners, whom you claimed to be gods beside Me;" they will call on them, but they will not respond to them. An insurmountable barrier will separate them from each other.

53. The guilty will see Hell, and will realize that they will fall into it. They will have no escape therefrom.

Disbelievers Refuse to Accept the Completeness of the Quran

54. We have cited in this Quran every kind of example, but the human being is the most argumentative creature.

55. Nothing prevented the people from believing, when the guidance came to them, and from seeking the forgiveness of their Lord, except that they demanded to see the same (*kind of miracles*) as the previous generations, or challenged to see the retribution beforehand.

---

*18:50 When the great feud in the heavenly society took place (38:69), all creatures became classified into angels, jinns, and humans (Appendix 7).

*18:51 God knew that Satan and his supporters (jinns and humans) were going to make the wrong decision. Hence their exclusion from witnessing the creation process.

---

56. We only send the messengers as simply deliverers of good news, as well as warners. Those who disbelieve argue with falsehood to defeat the truth, and they take My proofs and warnings in vain.

Divine Intervention

57. Who are more evil than those who are reminded of their Lord's proofs, then disregard them, without realizing what they are doing. Consequently, we place shields on their hearts to prevent them from understanding it (*the Quran*), and deafness in their ears. Thus, no matter what you do to guide them, they can never ever be guided.

58. Yet, your Lord is the Forgiver, full of mercy. If He called them to account for their deeds, He would annihilate them right there and then. Instead, He gives them a respite until a specific, predetermined time; then they can never escape.

59. Many a community we annihilated because of their transgressions, we designated a specific time for their annihilation.

Valuable Lessons from Moses and His Teacher

60. Moses said to his servant, "I will not rest until I reach the point where the two rivers meet, no matter how long it takes."

61. When they reached the point where they met, they forgot their fish, and it found its way back to the river, sneakily.

62. After they passed that point, he said to his servant, "Let us have lunch. All this traveling has thoroughly exhausted us."

63. He said, "Remember when we sat by the rock back there? I paid no attention to the fish. It was the devil who made me forget it, and it found its way back to the river, strangely."

64. (*Moses*) said, "That was the place we were looking for." They traced their steps back.

65. They found one of our servants, whom we blessed with mercy, and bestowed upon him from our own knowledge.

66. Moses said to him, "Can I follow you, that you may teach me some of the knowledge and the guidance bestowed upon you?"

67. He said, "You cannot stand to be with me.

68. "How can you stand that which you do not comprehend?"

69. He said, "You will find me, **GOD** willing, patient. I will not disobey any command you give me."

70. He said, "If you follow me, then you shall not ask me about anything, unless I choose to tell you about it."

71. So they went. When they boarded a ship, he bore a hole in it. He said, "Did you bore a hole in it to drown its people? You have committed something terrible."

72. He said, "Did I not say that you cannot stand to be with me?"

73. He said, "I am sorry. Do not punish me for my forgetfulness; do not be too harsh with me."

74. So they went. When they met a young boy, he killed him. He said, "Why did you kill such an innocent soul, who did not kill another soul? You have committed something horrendous."

75. He said, "Did I not tell you that you cannot stand to be with me?"

76. He said, "If I ask you about anything else, then do not keep me with you. You have seen enough apologies from me."

77. So they went. When they reached a certain community, they asked the people for food, but they refused to host them. Soon, they found a wall about to collapse, and he fixed it. He said, "You could have demanded a wage for that!"

There is a Good Reason
for Everything

78. He said, "Now we have to part company. But I will explain to you everything you could not stand.

79. "As for the ship, it belonged to poor fishermen, and I wanted to render it defective. There was a king coming after them, who was confiscating every ship, forcibly.

80. "As for the boy, his parents were good believers, and we saw that he was going to burden them with his transgression and disbelief.*

81. "We willed that your Lord substitute in his place another son; one who is better in righteousness and kindness.

82. "As for the wall, it belonged to two orphan boys in the city. Under it, there was a treasure that belonged to them. Because their father was a righteous man, your Lord wanted them to grow up and attain full strength, then extract their treasure. Such is mercy from your Lord. I did none of that of my own volition. This is the explanation of the things you could not stand."

Zul-Qarnain: The One With the
Two Horns or Two Generations

83. They ask you about Zul-Qarnain. Say, "I will narrate to you some of his history."

84. We granted him authority on earth, and provided him with all kinds of means.

85. Then, he pursued one way.

86. When he reached the far west, he found the sun setting in a vast ocean, and found people there. We said, "O Zul-Qarnain, you can rule as you wish; either punish, or be kind to them."

87. He said, "As for those who transgress, we will punish them, then, when they return to their Lord, He will commit them to more retribution.

88. "As for those who believe and lead a righteous life, they receive a good reward; we will treat them kindly."

89. Then he pursued another way.

90. When he reached the far east, he found the sun rising on people who had nothing to shelter them from it.

91. Naturally, we were fully aware of everything he found out.

92. He then pursued another way.

93. When he reached the valley between two palisades, he found people whose language was barely understandable.

18:80 Adolf Hitler was a cute and seemingly innocent child. Had he died as a child, many would have grieved, and many would have even questioned God's wisdom. We learn from these profound lessons that there is a good reason behind everything.

Gog and Magog*

94. They said, "O Zul-Qarnain, Gog and Magog are corruptors of the earth. Can we pay you to create a barrier between us and them?"

95. He said, "My Lord has given me great bounties. If you cooperate with me, I will build a dam between you and them.

96. "Bring to me masses of iron." Once he filled the gap between the two palisades, he said, "Blow." Once it was red hot, he said, "Help me pour tar on top of it."

97. Thus, they could not climb it, nor could they bore holes in it.

98. He said, "This is mercy from my Lord. When the prophecy of my Lord comes to pass, He will cause the dam to crumble. The prophecy of my Lord is truth."

99. At that time, we will let them invade with one another, then the horn will be blown, and we will summon them all together.

100. We will present Hell, on that day, to the disbelievers.

101. They are the ones whose eyes were too veiled to see My message. Nor could they hear.

102. Do those who disbelieve think that they can get away with setting up My servants as gods beside Me? We have prepared for the disbelievers Hell as an eternal abode.

Examine Yourself

103. Say, "Shall I tell you who the worst losers are?

104. "They are the ones whose works in this life are totally astray, but they think that they are doing good."

105. Such are the ones who disbelieved in the revelations of their Lord and in meeting Him. Therefore, their works are in vain; on the Day of Resurrection, they have no weight.

106. Their just requital is Hell, in return for their disbelief, and for mocking My revelations and My messengers.

107. As for those who believe and lead a righteous life they have deserved a blissful Paradise as their abode.

108. Forever they abide therein; they will never want any other substitute.

The Quran: Everything We Need

109. Say, "If the ocean were ink for the words of my Lord, the ocean would run out, before the words of my Lord run out, even if we double the ink supply."

110. Say, "I am no more than a human like you, being inspired that your god is one god. Those who hope to meet their Lord shall work right-eousness, and never worship any other god beside his Lord."

◆◆◆◆

Sura 19: Mary (Maryam)

In the name of God,
Most Gracious, Most Merciful

---

*18:94-98 One of my duties as God's Messenger of the Covenant is to state that Gog and Magog, the final sign before the end of the world, will reappear in 2270 AD (1700 AH), just 10 years before the end. Note that Gog and Magog occur in Suras 18 and 21, precisely 17 verses before the end of each sura, representing 17 lunar centuries (72:27). (See 72:27 and Appendix 25.)

1. K. H. Y. 'A. S.* (*Kãf Hã Yã 'Ayn Sãd*)

Zachariah

2. A narration about your Lord's mercy towards His servant Zachariah.

3. He called his Lord, a secret call.

4. He said, "My Lord, the bones have turned brittle in my body, and my hair is aflame with gray. As I implore You, my Lord, I never despair.

5. "I worry about my dependants after me, and my wife has been sterile. Grant me, from You, an heir.

6. "Let him be my heir and the heir of Jacob's clan, and make him, my Lord, acceptable."

John

7. "O Zachariah, we give you good news; a boy whose name shall be John (*Yahya*). We never created anyone like him before."

8. He said, "My Lord, will I have a son despite my wife's sterility, and despite my old age?"

9. He said, "Thus said your Lord: 'It is easy for Me to do. I created you before that, and you were nothing.' "

10. He said, "My Lord, give me a sign." He said, "Your sign is that you will not speak to the people for three consecutive nights."

11. He came out to his family, from the sanctuary, and signaled to them: "Meditate (*on God*) day and night."

12. "O John, you shall uphold the scripture, strongly." We endowed him with wisdom, even in his youth.

13. And (*we endowed him with*) kindness from us and purity, for he was righteous.

14. He honored his parents, and was never a disobedient tyrant.

15. Peace be upon him the day he was born, the day he dies, and the day he is resurrected back to life.

Mary

16. Mention in the scripture Mary. She isolated herself from her family, into an eastern location.

17. While a barrier separated her from them, we sent to her our Spirit. He went to her in the form of a human being.

18. She said, "I seek refuge in the Most Gracious, that you may be righteous."

19. He said, "I am the messenger of your Lord, to grant you a pure son."

20. She said, "How can I have a son, when no man has touched me; I have never been unchaste."

21. He said, "Thus said your Lord, 'It is easy for Me. We will render him a sign for the people, and mercy from us. This is a predestined matter.' "

---

*19:1 This is the maximum number of Quranic Initials, because this sura deals with such crucial matters as the miraculous birth of John and the virgin birth of Jesus, and strongly condemns the gross blasphemy that considers Jesus to be a son of God. The five initials provide a powerful physical evidence to support these issues (See Appendices 1 & 22).

The Birth of Jesus

22. When she bore him, she isolated herself to a faraway place.

23. The birth process came to her by the trunk of a palm tree. She said, "(*I am so ashamed;*) I wish I were dead before this happened, and completely forgotten."

24. (*The infant*) called her from beneath her, saying, "Do not grieve. Your Lord has provided you with a stream.

25. "If you shake the trunk of this palm tree, it will drop ripe dates for you.*

26. "Eat and drink, and be happy. When you see anyone, say, 'I have made a vow of silence; I am not talking today to anyone.' "

27. She came to her family, carrying him. They said, "O Mary, you have committed something that is totally unexpected.

28. "O descendant of Aaron, your father was not a bad man, nor was your mother unchaste."

The Infant Makes a Statement

29. She pointed to him. They said, "How can we talk with an infant in the crib?"

30. (*The infant spoke and*) said, "I am a servant of **GOD**. He has given me the scripture, and has appointed me a prophet.

31. "He made me blessed wherever I go, and enjoined me to observe the Contact Prayers (*Salat*) and the obligatory charity (*Zakat*) for as long as I live.

32. "I am to honor my mother; He did not make me a disobedient rebel.

33. "And peace be upon me the day I was born, the day I die, and the day I get resurrected."

The Proven Truth

34. That was Jesus, the son of Mary, and this is the truth of this matter, about which they continue to doubt.

35. It does not befit **GOD** that He begets a son, be He glorified. To have anything done, He simply says to it, "Be," and it is.

36. He also proclaimed, "**GOD** is my Lord and your Lord; you shall worship Him alone. This is the right path."*

37. The various parties disputed among themselves (*regarding the identity of Jesus*). Therefore, woe to those who disbelieve from the sight of a terrible day.

38. Wait till you hear them and see them when they come to face us. The transgressors on that day will be totally lost.

39. Warn them about the day of remorse, when judgment will be issued. They are totally oblivious; they do not believe.

40. We are the ones who inherit the earth and everyone on it; to us everyone will be returned.

Abraham

41. Mention in the scripture Abraham; he was a saint, a prophet.

---

*19:25 *Thus, Jesus was born in late September or early October. This is when dates ripen in the Middle East to the point of falling off the tree.*

*19:36 *This is similar to the statement attributed to Jesus in the Gospel of John 20:17.*

---

42. He said to his father, "O my father, why do you worship what can neither hear, nor see, nor help you in any way?

43. "O my father, I have received certain knowledge that you did not receive. Follow me, and I will guide you in a straight path.

44. "O my father, do not worship the devil. The devil has rebelled against the Most Gracious.

45. "O my father, I fear lest you incur retribution from the Most Gracious, then become an ally of the devil."

46. He said, "Have you forsaken my gods, O Abraham? Unless you stop, I will stone you. Leave me alone."

47. He said, "Peace be upon you. I will implore my Lord to forgive you; He has been Most Kind to me.

48. "I will abandon you and the gods you worship besides **GOD**. I will worship only my Lord. By imploring my Lord alone, I cannot go wrong."

49. Because he abandoned them and the gods they worshiped beside **GOD**, we granted him Isaac and Jacob, and we made each of them a prophet.

50. We showered them with our mercy, and we granted them an honorable position in history.

Moses

51. Mention in the scripture Moses. He was devoted, and he was a messenger prophet.

52. We called him from the right side of Mount Sinai. We brought him close, to confer with him.

53. And we granted him, out of our mercy, his brother Aaron as a prophet.

54. And mention in the scripture Ismail. He was truthful when he made a promise, and he was a messenger prophet.

55. He used to enjoin his family to observe the Contact Prayers (*Salat*) and the obligatory charity (*Zakat*); he was acceptable to his Lord.

56. And mention in the scripture Idrîs. He was a saint, a prophet.

57. We raised him to an honorable rank.

58. These are some of the prophets whom **GOD** blessed. They were chosen from among the descendants of Adam, and the descendants of those whom we carried with Noah, and the descendants of Abraham and Israel, and from among those whom we guided and selected. When the revelations of the Most Gracious are recited to them, they fall prostrate, weeping.

Losing the Contact Prayers (Salat)

59. After them, He substituted generations who lost the Contact Prayers (*Salat*), and pursued their lusts. They will suffer the consequences.

60. Only those who repent, believe, and lead a righteous life will enter Paradise, without the least injustice.

61. The gardens of Eden await them, as promised by the Most Gracious for those who worship Him, even in privacy. Certainly, His promise must come to pass.

62. They will not hear any nonsense therein; only peace. They receive their provisions therein, day and night.

63. Such is Paradise; we grant it to those among our servants who are righteous.

64. We do not come down except by the command of your Lord. To Him belongs our past, our future, and everything between them. Your Lord is never forgetful.

65. The Lord of the heavens and the earth, and everything between them; you shall worship Him and steadfastly persevere in worshiping Him. Do you know of anyone who equals Him?

66. The human being asks, "After I die, do I come back to life?"

67. Did the human being forget that we created him already, and he was nothing?

Special Warning to the Leaders

68. By your Lord, we will certainly summon them, together with the devils, and will gather them around Hell, humiliated.

69. Then we will pick out from each group the most ardent opponent of the Most Gracious.

70. We know full well those who are most deserving of burning therein.

Everyone Sees Hell*

71. Every single one of you must see it; this is an irrevocable decision of your Lord.

72. Then we rescue the righteous, and leave the transgressors in it, humiliated.

The Majority

73. When our revelations are recited to them, clearly, those who disbelieve say to those who believe, "Which of us is more prosperous? Which of us is in the majority?"

74. Many a generation have we annihilated before them; they were more powerful, and more prosperous.

75. Say, "Those who choose to go astray, the Most Gracious will lead them on, until they see what is promised for them—either the retribution or the Hour. That is when they find out who really is worse off, and weaker in power."

76. **GOD** augments the guidance of those who choose to be guided. For the good deeds are eternally rewarded by your Lord, and bring far better returns.

77. Have you noted the one who rejected our revelations then said, "I will be given wealth and children"?!

78. Has he seen the future? Has he taken such a pledge from the Most Gracious?

79. Indeed, we will record what he utters, then commit him to ever-increasing retribution.

80. Then we inherit everything he possessed, and he comes back to us all alone.

19:71 As detailed in Appendix 11, we will be resurrected prior to God's physical arrival to our universe. That will be a temporary taste of Hell, since the absence of God is Hell. When God comes (89:22), the righteous will be rescued. See 19:72.

---

81. They worship beside **GOD** other gods that may be of help to them.

The Idols Disown
Their Worshipers

82. On the contrary; they will reject their idolatry, and will be their enemies.

83. Do you not see how we unleash the devils upon the disbelievers to stir them up?

84. Do not be impatient; we are preparing for them some preparation.

85. The day will come when we summon the righteous before the Most Gracious in a group.

86. And we will herd the guilty to Hell, to be their eternal abode.

87. No one will possess the power to intercede, except those who conform to the laws of the Most Gracious.

Gross Blasphemy

88. They said, "The Most Gracious has begotten a son!"

89. You have uttered a gross blasphemy.

90. The heavens are about to shatter, the earth is about to tear asunder, and the mountains are about to crumble.

91. Because they claim that the Most Gracious has begotten a son.

92. It is not befitting the Most Gracious that He should beget a son.

93. Every single one in the heavens and the earth is a servant of the Most Gracious.

94. He has encompassed them, and has counted them one by one.

95. All of them will come before Him on the Day of Resurrection as individuals.

96. Surely, those who believe and lead a righteous life, the Most Gracious will shower them with love.

97. We thus made this (*Quran*) elucidated in your tongue, in order to deliver good news to the righteous, and to warn with it the opponents.

98. Many a generation before them we annihilated; can you perceive any of them, or hear from them any sound?

◆◆◆◆

Sura 20: T. H.
(Tã Hã)

In the name of God,
Most Gracious, Most Merciful

1. T.H.*

2. We did not reveal the Quran to you, to cause you any hardship.

3. Only to remind the reverent.

4. A revelation from the Creator of the earth and the high heavens.

5. The Most Gracious; He has assumed all authority.

6. To Him belongs everything in the heavens, and the earth, and everything between them, and everything beneath the ground.

7. Whether you declare your convictions (*or not*) He knows the secret, and what is even more hidden.

---

*20:1 The role of these Quranic initials as components of the Quran's awesome mathematical miracle is given in detail in Appendix 1.

---

8. **GOD**: there is no other god besides Him. To Him belong the most beautiful names.

9. Have you noted the history of Moses?

10. When he saw a fire, he said to his family, "Stay here. I have seen a fire. Maybe I can bring you some of it, or find some guidance at the fire."

11. When he came to it, he was called, "O, Moses.

12. "I am your Lord; remove your sandals. You are in the sacred valley, Tuwã.

13. "I have chosen you, so listen to what is being revealed.

14. "I am **GOD**; there is no other god beside Me. You shall worship Me alone, and observe the Contact Prayers (*Salat*) to remember Me.

*End of the World
is Not Hidden**

15. "The Hour (*end of the world*) is surely coming; I will keep it almost hidden. For each soul must be paid for its works.

16. "Do not be diverted therefrom by those who do not believe in it—those who pursue their own opinions—lest you fall.

17. "What is this in your right hand, Moses?"

18. He said, "This is my staff. I lean on it, herd my sheep with it, and I use it for other purposes."

19. He said, "Throw it down, Moses."

20. He threw it down, whereupon it turned into a moving serpent.

21. He said, "Pick it up; do not be afraid. We will return it to its original state.

22. "And hold your hand under your wing; it will come out white without a blemish; another proof.

23. "We thus show you some of our great portents.

24. "Go to Pharaoh, for he has transgressed."

25. He said, "My Lord, cool my temper.

26. "And make this matter easy for me.

27. "And untie a knot from my tongue.

28. "So they can understand my speech.

29. "And appoint an assistant for me from my family.

30. "My brother Aaron.

31. "Strengthen me with him.

32. "Let him be my partner in this matter.

33. "That we may glorify You frequently.

34. "And commemorate You frequently.

35. "You are Seer of us."

36. He said, "Your request is granted, O Moses.

37. "We have blessed you another time.

38. "When we revealed to your mother what we revealed.

39. "Saying: Throw him into the box, then throw him into the river. The river will throw him onto the shore, to be picked up by an enemy of Mine and an enemy of his.' I showered you with love from Me, and I had you made before My watchful eye.

---

*20:15 The end of the world is given in the Quran, God's final message (15:87).

---

40. "Your sister walked to them and said, 'I can tell you about a nursing mother who can take good care of him.' We thus returned you to your mother, that she may be happy and stop worrying. And when you killed a person, we saved you from the grievous consequences; indeed we tested you thoroughly. You stayed years with the people of Midyan, and now you have come back in accordance with a precise plan.

41. "I have made you just for Me.

42. "Go with your brother, supported by My signs, and do not waver in remembering Me.

43. "Go to Pharaoh, for he transgressed.

44. "Speak to him nicely; he may take heed, or become reverent."

45. They said, "Our Lord, we fear lest he may attack us, or transgress."

46. He said, "Do not be afraid, for I will be with you, listening and watching.

47. "Go to him and say, 'We are two messengers from your Lord. Let the Children of Israel go. You must refrain from persecuting them. We bring a sign from your Lord, and peace is the lot of those who heed the guidance.

48. " 'We have been inspired that the retribution will inevitably afflict those who disbelieve and turn away.' "

49. He said, "Who is your Lord, O Moses."

50. He said, "Our Lord is the One who granted everything its existence, and its guidance."

51. He said, "What about the past generations?"

52. He said, "The knowledge thereof is with my Lord in a record. My Lord never errs, nor does He forget."

53. He is the One who made the earth habitable for you, and paved in it roads for you. And He sends down from the sky water with which we produce many different kinds of plants.

54. Eat and raise your livestock. These are sufficient proofs for those who possess intelligence.*

55. From it we created you, into it we return you, and from it we bring you out once more.

56. We showed him all our proofs, but he disbelieved and refused.

57. He said, "Did you come here to take us out of our land with your magic, O Moses?

58. "We will surely show you similar magic. Therefore, set an appointment that neither we, nor you will violate; in a neutral place."

59. He said, "Your appointed time shall be the day of festivities. Let us all meet in the forenoon."

---

*20:54 Those who possess intelligence appreciate the fact that we are astronauts who were launched into space on this 'Spaceship Earth.' God provided us with renewable food, water, pets, wildlife, and livestock, as we embark on this temporary space odyssey. Compare God's provisions to 'Spaceship Earth' with the provisions we give to our astronauts (Appendix 7).

---

60. Pharaoh summoned his forces, then came.

61. Moses said to them, "Woe to you. Do you fabricate lies to fight **GOD** and thus incur His retribution? Such fabricators will surely fail."

62. They disputed among themselves, as they conferred privately.

63. They said, "These two are no more than magicians who wish to take you out of your land with their magic, and to destroy your ideal way of life.

64. "Let us agree upon one scheme and face them as a united front. The winner today will have the upper hand."

65. They said, "O Moses, either you throw, or we will be the first to throw."

66. He said, "You throw." Whereupon, their ropes and sticks appeared to him, because of their magic, as if they were moving.

67. Moses harbored some fear.

68. We said, "Have no fear. You will prevail.

69. "Throw what you hold in your right hand, and it will swallow what they fabricated. What they fabricated is no more than the scheming of a magician. The magician's work will not succeed."

The Experts Recognize The Truth

70. The magicians fell prostrate, saying, "We believe in the Lord of Aaron and Moses."

71. He said, "Did you believe in him without my permission? He must be your chief; the one who taught you magic. I will surely sever your hands and feet on alternate sides. I will crucify you on the palm trunks. You will find out which of us can inflict the worst retribution, and who outlasts whom."

72. They said, "We will not prefer you over the clear proofs that came to us, and over the One who created us. Therefore, issue whatever judgment you wish to issue. You can only rule in this lowly life.

73. "We have believed in our Lord, that He may forgive us our sins, and the magic that you forced us to perform. **GOD** is far better and Everlasting."

74. Anyone who comes to his Lord guilty will incur Hell, wherein he never dies, nor stays alive.

75. As for those who come to Him as believers who had led a righteous life, they attain the high ranks.

76. The gardens of Eden, beneath which rivers flow, will be their abode forever. Such is the reward for those who purify themselves.

77. We inspired Moses: "Lead My servants out, and strike for them a dry road across the sea. You shall not fear that you may get caught, nor shall you worry."

78. Pharaoh pursued them with his troops, but the sea overwhelmed them, as it was destined to overwhelm them.

79. Thus, Pharaoh misled his people; he did not guide them.

80. O Children of Israel, we delivered you from your enemy, summoned you to the right side of Mount Sinai, and we sent down to you manna and quails.

81. Eat from the good things we provided for you, and do not transgress, lest you incur My wrath. Whoever incurs My wrath has fallen.

82. I am surely Forgiving for those who repent, believe, lead a righteous life, and steadfastly remain guided.

The Children of Israel Rebel

83. "Why did you rush away from your people, O Moses?"

84. He said, "They are close behind me. I have rushed to You my Lord, that You may be pleased."

85. He said, "We have put your people to the test after you left, but the Samarian misled them."

86. Moses returned to his people, angry and disappointed, saying, "O my people, did your Lord not promise you a good promise? Could you not wait? Did you want to incur wrath from your Lord? Is this why you broke your agreement with me?"

87. They said, "We did not break our agreement with you on purpose. But we were loaded down with jewelry, and decided to throw our loads in. This is what the Samarian suggested."

88. He produced for them a sculpted calf, complete with a calf's sound.* They said, "This is your god, and the god of Moses." Thus, he forgot.

89. Could they not see that it neither responded to them, nor possessed any power to harm them, or benefit them?

90. And Aaron had told them, "O my people, this is a test for you. Your only Lord is the Most Gracious, so follow me, and obey my commands."

91. They said, "We will continue to worship it, until Moses comes back."

92. (*Moses*) said, "O Aaron, what is it that prevented you, when you saw them go astray,

93. "from following my orders? Have you rebelled against me?"

94. He said, "O son of my mother; do not pull me by my beard and my head. I was afraid that you might say, 'You have divided the Children of Israel, and disobeyed my orders.'"

95. He said, "What is the matter with you, O Samarian?"

96. He said, "I saw what they could not see. I grabbed a fistful (*of dust*) from the place where the messenger stood, and used it (*to mix into the golden calf*). This is what my mind inspired me to do."*

97. He said, "Then go, and, throughout your life, do not even come close. You have an appointed time (*for your final judgment*) that you can never evade. Look at your god that you used to worship; we will burn it and throw it into the sea, to stay down there forever."

You Have But One God

98. Your only god is **GOD**; the One beside whom there is no other god. His knowledge encompasses all things.

20:88 & 96 The Samarian went to the spot where God spoke to Moses, and grabbed a fistful of dust upon which God's voice had echoed. This dust, when mixed with the molten gold caused the golden statue to acquire the sound of a calf.

99. We thus narrate to you some news from the past generations. We have revealed to you a message from us.

100. Those who disregard it will bear a load (*of sins*) on the Day of Resurrection.

101. Eternally they abide therein; what a miserable load on the Day of Resurrection!

102. That is the day when the horn is blown, and we summon the guilty on that day blue.

103. Whispering among themselves, they will say, "You have stayed (*in the first life*) no more than ten days!"

104. We are fully aware of their utterances. The most accurate among them will say, "You stayed no more than a day."

On the Day of Resurrection

105. They ask you about the mountains. Say, "My Lord will wipe them out.

106. "He will leave them like a barren, flat land.

107. "Not even the slightest hill will you see therein, nor a dip."

108. On that day, everyone will follow the caller, without the slightest deviation. All sounds will be hushed before the Most Gracious; you will hear nothing but whispers.

109. On that day, intercession will be useless, except for those permitted by the Most Gracious, and whose utterances conform to His will.

110. He knows their past and their future, while none encompasses His knowledge.

111. All faces will submit to the Living, the Eternal, and those who are burdened by their transgressions will fail.

112. As for those who worked righteousness, while believing, they will have no fear of injustice or adversity.

113. We thus revealed it, an Arabic Quran, and we cited in it all kinds of prophecies, that they may be saved, or it may cause them to take heed.

114. Most Exalted is **GOD**, the only true King. Do not rush into uttering the Quran before it is revealed to you, and say, "My Lord, increase my knowledge."

Humans Fail to Make a Firm Stand*

115. We tested Adam in the past, but he forgot, and we found him indecisive.

116. Recall that we said to the angels, "Fall prostrate before Adam." They fell prostrate, except Satan; he refused.

117. We then said, "O Adam, this is an enemy of you and your wife. Do not let him evict you from Paradise, lest you become miserable.

118. "You are guaranteed never to hunger therein, nor go unsheltered.

119. "Nor will you thirst therein, nor suffer from any heat."

120. But the devil whispered to him, saying, "O Adam, let me show you the tree of eternity and unending kingship."

---

*20:115 When Satan challenged God's absolute authority (38:69), you and I did not make a firm stand against Satan. God is giving us a chance, on this earth, to redeem ourselves by denouncing Satan and upholding God's absolute authority (Appendix 7).

---

121. They ate from it, whereupon their bodies became visible to them, and they tried to cover themselves with the leaves of Paradise. Adam thus disobeyed his Lord, and fell.

122. Subsequently, his Lord chose him, redeemed him, and guided him.

123. He said, "Go down therefrom, all of you. You are enemies of one another. When guidance comes to you from Me, anyone who follows My guidance will not go astray, nor suffer any misery.

For the Disbelievers:
Miserable Life Unavoidable

124. "As for the one who disregards My message, he will have a miserable life, and we resurrect him, on the Day of Resurrection, blind."

125. He will say, "My Lord, why did you summon me blind, when I used to be a seer?"

126. He will say, "Because you forgot our revelations when they came to you, you are now forgotten."

127. We thus requite those who transgress and refuse to believe in the revelations of their Lord. The retribution in the Hereafter is far worse and everlasting.

128. Does it ever occur to them how many previous generations we have annihilated? They are now walking in the homes of those before them. These are signs for those who possess intelligence.

129. If it were not for your Lord's predetermined plan, they would have been judged immediately.

130. Therefore, be patient in the face of their utterances, and praise and glorify your Lord before sunrise and before sunset. And during the night glorify Him, as well as at both ends of the day, that you may be happy.

131. And do not covet what we bestowed upon any other people. Such are temporary ornaments of this life, whereby we put them to the test. What your Lord provides for you is far better, and everlasting.

The Parents' Responsibility

132. You shall enjoin your family to observe the contact prayers (*Salat*), and steadfastly persevere in doing so. We do not ask you for any provisions; we are the ones who provide for you. The ultimate triumph belongs to the righteous.

Why Messengers?

133. They said, "If he could only show us a miracle from his Lord!" Did they not receive sufficient miracles with the previous messages?

134. Had we annihilated them before this, they would have said, "Our Lord, had You sent a messenger to us, we would have followed Your revelations, and would have avoided this shame and humiliation."

135. Say, "All of us are waiting, so wait; you will surely find out who are on the correct path, and who are truly guided."

◆◆◆◆

Sura 21: The Prophets (Al-Anbyã')

In the name of God,
Most Gracious, Most Merciful

1. Fast approaching is the reckoning for the people, but they are oblivious, averse.

Opposition to the New Evidence

2. When a proof comes to them from their Lord, that is new, they listen to it heedlessly.

3. Their minds are heedless. And the transgressors confer secretly: "Is he not just a human being like you? Would you accept the magic that is presented to you?"*

4. He said, "My Lord knows every thought in the heaven and the earth. He is the Hearer, the Omniscient."

5. They even said, "Hallucinations," "He made it up," and, "He is a poet. Let him show us a miracle like those of the previous messengers."

6. We never annihilated a believing community in the past. Are these people believers?

7. We did not send before you except men whom we inspired. Ask those who know the scripture, if you do not know.

8. We did not give them bodies that did not eat, nor were they immortal.

9. We fulfilled our promise to them; we saved them together with whomever we willed, and annihilated the transgressors.

10. We have sent down to you a scripture containing your message. Do you not understand?

11. Many a community we terminated because of their transgression, and we substituted other people in their place.

12. When our requital came to pass, they started to run.

13. Do not run, and come back to your luxuries and your mansions, for you must be held accountable.

14. They said, "Woe to us. We were really wicked."

15. This continued to be their proclamation, until we completely wiped them out.

16. We did not create the heavens and the earth, and everything between them just for amusement.

17. If we needed amusement, we could have initiated it without any of this, if that is what we wanted to do.

18. Instead, it is our plan to support the truth against falsehood, in order to defeat it. Woe to you for the utterances you utter.

19. To Him belongs everyone in the heavens and the earth, and those at Him are never too arrogant to worship Him, nor do they ever waver.

20. They glorify night and day, without ever tiring.

21:3 Although the Bible (Malachi 3:1) and the Quran (3:81) prophesy the advent of God's Messenger of the Covenant, when he did appear, supported by 'one of the greatest miracles' (74:30-35), he was met with heedlessness and opposition. The divine assertion that every 'new' proof is opposed has been proven by the Arabs' opposition to the Quran's miracle (App. 1 & 2).

One God

21. Have they found gods on earth who can create?

22. If there were in them (*the heavens and the earth*) other gods beside **GOD**, there would have been chaos. Glory be to **GOD**; the Lord with absolute authority. He is high above their claims.

Never Question God's Wisdom

23. He is never to be asked about anything He does, while all others are questioned.

24. Have they found other gods beside Him? Say, "Show me your proof. This is the message to my generation, consummating all previous messages." Indeed, most of them do not recognize the truth; this is why they are so hostile.

One God/ One Message/ One Religion

25. We did not send any messenger before you except with the inspiration: "There is no god except Me; you shall worship Me alone."

26. Yet, they said, "The Most Gracious has begotten a son!" Glory be to Him. All (*messengers*) are (*His*) honored servants.

27. They never speak on their own, and they strictly follow His commands.

The Myth of Intercession

28. He knows their future and their past. They do not intercede, except for those already accepted by Him, and they are worried about their own necks.*

29. If any of them claims to be a god beside Him, we requite him with Hell; we thus requite the wicked.

The Big Bang Theory Confirmed*

30. Do the unbelievers not realize that the heaven and the earth used to be one solid mass that we exploded into existence? And from water we made all living things. Would they believe?

31. And we placed on earth stabilizers, lest it tumbles with them, and we placed straight roads therein, that they may be guided.

32. And we rendered the sky a guarded ceiling. Yet, they are totally oblivious to all the portents therein.

33. And He is the One who created the night and the day, and the sun and the moon; each floating in its own orbit.

34. We never decreed immortality for anyone before you; should you die, are they immortal?

35. Every soul will taste death, after we put you to the test through adversity and prosperity, then to us you ultimately return.

All Messengers Ridiculed

36. When those who disbelieve see you, they ridicule you: "Is this the one who challenges your gods?" Meanwhile, they remain totally heedless of the message from the Most Gracious.

---

*21:28 The myth of intercession is Satan's most effective bait (see Appendix 8).

*21:30 The Big Bang Theory is now supported by the Creator's infallible mathematical code (Appendix 1). Thus, it is no longer a theory; it is a law, a proven fact.

37. The human being is impatient by nature. I will inevitably show you My signs; do not be in such a hurry.

38. They challenge: "Where is that (*retribution*), if you are truthful?"

39. If only those who disbelieve could envision themselves when they try to ward off the fire; off their faces and their backs! No one will help them then.

40. Indeed, it will come to them suddenly, and they will be utterly stunned. They can neither avoid it, nor can they receive any respite.

41. Messengers before you have been ridiculed, and, consequently, those who ridiculed them incurred the retribution for their ridiculing.

Priorities Confused

42. Say, "Who can protect you from the Most Gracious during the night or during the day?" Indeed, they are totally oblivious to the message of their Lord.

43. Do they have gods who can protect them from us? They cannot even help themselves. Nor can they accompany one another when they are summoned to face us.

44. We have provided for these people and their ancestors, up until an old age. Do they not see that every day on earth brings them closer to the end? Can they reverse this process?

45. Say, "I am warning you in accordance with divine inspiration." However, the deaf cannot hear the call, when they are warned.

46. When a sample of your Lord's retribution afflicts them, they readily say, "We were indeed wicked."

47. We will establish the scales of justice on the Day of Resurrection. No soul will suffer the least injustice. Even the equivalent of a mustard seed will be accounted for. We are the most efficient reckoners.

Prophets Moses and Aaron

48. We gave Moses and Aaron the Statute Book, a beacon, and a reminder for the righteous.

49. The ones who reverence their Lord, even when alone in their privacy, and they worry about the Hour.

50. This too is a blessed reminder that we sent down. Are you denying it?

Abraham

51. Before that, we granted Abraham his guidance and understanding, for we were fully aware of him.*

52. He said to his father and his people, "What are these statues to which you are devoting yourselves?"

53. They said, "We found our parents worshiping them."

54. He said, "Indeed, you and your parents have gone totally astray."

21:51 Was Abraham so smart as to discover God, or, did God grant him the intelligence because He knew that he deserved to be saved? As it turns out, this whole world was created to redeem those among us who deserve redemption. When the angels suggested that all the rebels, humans and jinns, must be banished out of God's kingdom, 'I know what you do not know' (2:30). At the same time, this world proves Satan's incompetence as a god (App. 7).

55. They said, "Are you telling us the truth, or are you playing?"

56. He said, "Your only Lord is the Lord of the heavens and the earth, who created them. This is the testimony to which I bear witness.

57. "I swear by **GOD**, I have a plan to deal with your statues, as soon as you leave."

58. He broke them into pieces, except for a big one, that they may refer to it.

59. They said, "Whoever did this to our gods is really a transgressor."

60. They said, "We heard a youth threaten them; he is called Abraham."

61. They said, "Bring him before the eyes of all the people, that they may bear witness."

62. They said, "Did you do this to our gods, O Abraham?"

Abraham Proves His Point

63. He said, "It is that big one who did it. Go ask them, if they can speak."

64. They were taken aback, and said to themselves, "Indeed, you are the ones who have been transgressing."

65. Yet, they reverted to their old ideas: "You know full well that these can not speak."

66. He said, "Do you then worship beside **GOD** what possesses no power to benefit you or harm you?

67. "You have incurred shame by worshiping idols beside **GOD**. Do you not understand?"

Profound Miracle

68. They said, "Burn him and support your gods, if this is what you decide to do."

69. We said, "O fire, be cool and safe for Abraham."*

70. Thus, they schemed against him, but we made them the losers.

71. We saved him, and we saved Lot, to the land that we blessed for all the people.

72. And we granted him Isaac and Jacob as a gift, and we made them both righteous.

Abraham:
Delivered All
Religious Duties of Islam

73. We made them imams who guided in accordance with our commandments, and we taught them how to work righteousness, and how to observe the Contact Prayers (*Salat*) and the obligatory charity (*Zakat*).* To us, they were devoted worshipers.

Lot

74. As for Lot, we granted him wisdom and knowledge, and we saved him from the community that practiced abominations; they were wicked and evil people.

75. We admitted him into our mercy, for he was righteous.

Noah

76. And, before that, Noah called and we responded to him. We saved him and his family from the great disaster.

21:69 "Cool," without "and safe" would have caused Abraham to freeze.

21:73 When the Quran was revealed, all religious duties were already established through Abraham (2:128, 16:123, 22:78).

---

77. We supported him against the people who rejected our revelations. They were evil people, so we drowned them all.

David and Solomon

78. And David and Solomon, when they once ruled with regard to someone's crop that was destroyed by another's sheep, we witnessed their judgment.

79. We granted Solomon the correct understanding, though we endowed both of them with wisdom and knowledge. We committed the mountains to serve David in glorifying (*God*), as well as the birds. This is what we did.

80. And we taught him the skill of making shields to protect you in war. Are you then thankful?

81. For Solomon, we committed the wind gusting and blowing at his disposal. He could direct it as he wished, to whatever land he chose, and we blessed such land for him. We are fully aware of all things.

82. And of the devils there were those who would dive for him (*to harvest the sea*), or do whatever else he commanded them to do. We committed them in his service.

Job

83. And Job implored his Lord: "Adversity has befallen me, and, of all the merciful ones, You are the Most Merciful."

84. We responded to him, relieved his adversity, and restored his family for him, even twice as much. That was a mercy from us, and a reminder for the worshipers.

85. Also, Ismail, Idrîs, Zal-Kifl; all were steadfast, patient.

86. We admitted them into our mercy, for they were righteous.

Jonah

87. And Zan-Noon (*Jonah, "the one with an 'N' in his name"*), abandoned his mission in protest, thinking that we could not control him. He ended up imploring from the darkness (*of the big fish's belly*): "There is no god other than You. Be You glorified. I have committed a gross sin."

88. We responded to him, and saved him from the crisis; we thus save the believers.

Zachariah and John

89. And Zachariah implored his Lord: "My Lord, do not keep me without an heir, though You are the best inheritor."

90. We* responded to him and granted him John; we fixed his wife for him. That is because they used to hasten to work righteousness, and implored us in situations of joy, as well as fear. To us, they were reverent.

Mary and Jesus

91. As for the one who maintained her virginity, we blew into her from our spirit, and thus, we made her and her son a portent for the whole world.

One God / One Religion

92. Your congregation is but one congregation, and I alone am your Lord; you shall worship Me alone.

---

*21:90 The use of the plural tense throughout the Quran indicates participation of the angels. It is clear from 3:39 and from the Bible that the angels dealt with Zachariah extensively, as they gave him the good news about John. See Appendix 10.

93. However, they divided themselves into disputing religions. All of them will come back to us (*for judgment*).

94. As for those who work righteousness, while believing, their work will not go to waste; we are recording it.

95. It is forbidden for any community we had annihilated to return.

The End of the World*

96. Not until Gog and Magog reappear,* will they then return—they will come from every direction.

97. That is when the inevitable prophecy will come to pass, and the disbelievers will stare in horror: "Woe to us; we have been oblivious. Indeed, we have been wicked."

The Hereafter

98. You and the idols you worship besides **GOD** will be fuel for Hell; this is your inevitable destiny.

99. If those were gods, they would not have ended up in Hell. All its inhabitants abide in it forever.

100. They will sigh and groan therein, and they will have no access to any news.

101. As for those who deserved our magnificent rewards, they will be protected from it.

The Righteous

102. They will not hear its hissing. They will enjoy an abode where they can get everything they desire, forever.

103. The great horror will not worry them, and the angels will receive them joyfully: "This is your day, that has been promised to you."

The Day of Resurrection

104. On that day, we will fold the heaven, like the folding of a book. Just as we initiated the first creation, we will repeat it. This is our promise; we will certainly carry it out.

105. We have decreed in the Psalms, as well as in other scriptures, that the earth shall be inherited by My righteous worshipers.

106. This is a proclamation for people who are worshipers.

107. We have sent you out of mercy from us towards the whole world.

108. Proclaim, "I have been given divine inspiration that your god is one god. Will you then submit?"

109. If they turn away, then say, "I have warned you sufficiently, and I have no idea how soon or late (*the retribution*) will come to you.

110. "He is fully aware of your public utterances, and He is fully aware of everything you conceal.

111. "For all that I know, this world is a test for you, and a temporary enjoyment."

112. Say, "My Lord, Your judgment is the absolute justice. Our Lord is the Most Gracious; only His help is sought in the face of your claims."

❖❖❖❖

21:96 By the year 2270 AD, thanks to God's mathematical miracle in the Quran (Appendix 1), America will be the heart of Islam, and billions around the globe will have believed in the Quran (9:33, 41:53, 48:28, 61:9). Gog and Magog (allegorical names of villainous communities), will be the only bastions of heathenism, and they will attack the submitters. That is when the world will end (15:87, 18:94, Appendix 25). Gog and Magog are mentioned in 18:94 & 21:96, 17 verses before the end of each sura; this may indicate the time of their appearance.

Sura 22: Pilgrimage (Al-Hajj)

In the name of God,
Most Gracious, Most Merciful

1. O people, you shall reverence your Lord, for the quaking of the Hour is something horrendous.

2. The day you witness it, even a nursing mother will discard her infant, and a pregnant woman will abort her fetus. You will see the people staggering, as if they are intoxicated, even though they are not intoxicated. This is because, **GOD**'s retribution is so awesome.

3. Among the people, there are those who argue about **GOD** without knowledge, and follow every rebellious devil.

4. It is decreed that anyone who allies himself with him, he will mislead him and guide him to the agony of Hell.

Where Did We Come From?

5. O people, if you have any doubt about resurrection, (*remember that*) we created you from dust, and subsequently from a tiny drop, which turns into a hanging (*embryo*), then it becomes a fetus that is given life or deemed lifeless. We thus clarify things for you. We settle in the wombs whatever we will for a predetermined period.* We then bring you out as infants, then you reach maturity. While some of you die young, others live to the worst age, only to find out that no more knowledge can be attained beyond a certain limit. Also, you look at a land that is dead, then as soon as we shower it with water, it vibrates with life and grows all kinds of beautiful plants.

6. This proves that **GOD** is the Truth, and that He revives the dead, and that He is Omnipotent.

7. And that the Hour is coming, no doubt about it, and that **GOD** resurrects those who are in the graves.

A Common Occurrence

8. Among the people there is the one who argues about **GOD** without knowledge, and without guidance, and without an enlightening scripture.

9. Arrogantly he strives to divert the people from the path of **GOD**. He thus incurs humiliation in this life, and we commit him on the Day of Resurrection to the agony of burning.

10. This is what your hands have sent ahead for you. **GOD** is never unjust towards the people.

Fair Weather Friends

11. Among the people there is the one who worships **GOD** conditionally. If things go his way, he is content. But if some adversity befalls him, he makes an about-face. Thus, he loses both this life and the Hereafter. Such is the real loss.

12. He idolizes beside **GOD** what possesses no power to harm him or benefit him; such is the real straying.

22:5 The Quran's mathematical miracle is based on the number 19. As it turns out, this number represents the Creator's signature on His creations. Thus, you and I have 209 bones in our bodies (209=19x11). The length of pregnancy for a full term fetus is 266 days (19x14) (Langman's Medical Embryology, T. W. Sadler, Page 88, 1985).

13. He idolizes what is more apt to harm him than benefit him. What a miserable lord! What a miserable companion!

14. **GOD** admits those who believe and lead a righteous life into gardens with flowing streams. Everything is in accordance with **GOD**'s will.

Happiness Now, and Forever

15. If anyone thinks that **GOD** cannot support him in this life and in the Hereafter, let him turn completely to (*his Creator in*) heaven, and sever (*his dependence on anyone else*). He will then see that this plan eliminates anything that bothers him.

16. We have thus revealed clear revelations herein, then **GOD** guides whomever He wills.

God: The Only Judge

17. Those who believe, those who are Jewish, the converts, the Christians, the Zoroastrians, and the idol worshipers, **GOD** is the One who will judge among them on the Day of Resurrection. **GOD** witnesses all things.

18. Do you not realize that to **GOD** prostrates everyone in the heavens and the earth, and the sun, and the moon, and the stars, and the mountains, and the trees, and the animals, and many people? Many others among the people are committed to doom. Whomever **GOD** shames, none will honor him. Everything is in accordance with **GOD**'s will.

How Terrible is Hell!*

19. Here are two parties feuding with regard to their Lord. As for those who disbelieve, they will have clothes of fire tailored for them. Hellish liquid will be poured on top of their heads.

20. It will cause their insides to melt, as well as their skins.

21. They will be confined in iron pots.

22. Whenever they try to exit such misery, they will be forced back in: "Taste the agony of burning."

The Bliss of Heaven

23. **GOD** will admit those who believe and lead a righteous life into gardens with flowing streams. They will be adorned therein with bracelets of gold, and pearls, and their garments therein will be silk.

24. They have been guided to the good words; they have been guided in the path of the Most Praised.

25. Surely, those who disbelieve and repulse others from the path of **GOD**, and from the Sacred Masjid that we designated for all the people—be they natives or visitors—and seek to pollute it and corrupt it, we will afflict them with painful retribution.

22:19-22 People who have insisted upon going to Hell will inevitably complain: 'Had we known how bad this is, we would have behaved differently.' They will be told that the horrors of Hell have been pointed out to them in the most graphic, though symbolic, terms. It should be noted that Heaven and Hell are almost invariably mentioned together in the Quran.

Pilgrimage, Like All Duties in Islam, Decreed Through Abraham*

26. We appointed Abraham to establish the Shrine: "You shall not idolize any other god beside Me, and purify My shrine for those who visit it, those who live near it, and those who bow and prostrate.

27. "And proclaim that the people shall observe Hajj pilgrimage.* They will come to you walking or riding on various exhausted (*means of transportation*). They will come from the farthest locations."

28. They may seek commercial benefits, and they shall commemorate **GOD**'s name during the specified days for providing them with livestock. "Eat therefrom and feed the despondent and the poor."

29. They shall complete their obligations, fulfill their vows, and visit the ancient shrine.

30. Those who reverence the rites decreed by **GOD** have deserved a good reward at their Lord. All livestock is made lawful for your food, except for those specifically prohibited for you. You shall avoid the abomination of idol worship, and avoid bearing false witness.

31. You shall maintain your devotion absolutely to **GOD** alone. Anyone who sets up any idol beside **GOD** is like one who fell from the sky, then gets snatched up by vultures, or blown away by the wind into a deep ravine.

32. Indeed, those who reverence the rites decreed by **GOD** demonstrate the righteousness of their hearts.

Livestock Offerings During Pilgrimage *

33. The (*livestock*) provide you with many benefits for a period, before being donated to the ancient shrine.

34. For each congregation we have decreed rites whereby they commemorate the name of **GOD** for providing them with the livestock. Your god is one and the same god; you shall all submit to Him. Give good news to the obedient.

35. They are the ones whose hearts tremble upon mentioning **GOD**, they steadfastly persevere during adversity, they observe the Contact Prayers (*Salat*), and from our provisions to them, they give to charity.

36. The animal offerings are among the rites decreed by **GOD** for your own good.* You shall mention **GOD**'s name on them while they are standing in line. Once they are offered for sacrifice, you shall eat therefrom and feed the poor and the needy. This is why we subdued them for you, that you may show your appreciation.

37. Neither their meat, nor their blood reaches **GOD**. What reaches Him is your righteousness. He has subdued them for you, that you may show your appreciation by glorifying **GOD** for guiding you. Give good news to the charitable.

---

*22:26-27 Abraham was the original messenger of Submission (Islam). See 22:78 and Appendix 9.

*22:36 Animal offerings from the pilgrims conserve the resources at the pilgrimage site. Note that almost 2,000,000 pilgrims converge on Mecca during pilgrimage.

God Defends the Believers

38. **GOD** defends those who believe. **GOD** does not love any betrayer, unappreciative.

Synagogues, Churches, and Masjids

39. Permission is granted to those who are being persecuted, since injustice has befallen them, and **GOD** is certainly able to support them.

40. They were evicted from their homes unjustly, for no reason other than saying, "Our Lord is **GOD**." If it were not for **GOD**'s supporting of some people against others, monasteries, churches, synagogues, and masjids—where the name of **GOD** is commemorated frequently—would have been destroyed. Absolutely, **GOD** supports those who support Him. **GOD** is Powerful, Almighty.

41. They are those who, if we appointed them as rulers on earth, they would establish the Contact Prayers (*Salat*) and the obligatory charity (*Zakat*), and would advocate righteousness and forbid evil. **GOD** is the ultimate ruler.

42. If they reject you, the people of Noah, 'Ãd, and Thamoud have also disbelieved before them.

43. Also the people of Abraham, and the people of Lot.

44. And the dwellers of Midyan. Moses was also rejected. I led all those people on, then I called them to account; how (*devastating*) was My requital!

45. Many a community have we annihilated because of their wickedness. They ended up with ruins, stilled wells, and great empty mansions.

46. Did they not roam the earth, then use their minds to understand, and use their ears to hear? Indeed, the real blindness is not the blindness of the eyes, but the blindness of the hearts inside the chests.

47. They challenge you to bring retribution, and **GOD** never fails to fulfill His prophecy. A day of your Lord is like a thousand of your years.

48. Many a community in the past committed evil, and I led them on for awhile, then I punished them. To Me is the ultimate destiny.

*God's Messenger
of the Covenant*

49. Say, "O people, I have been sent to you as a profound warner."*

50. Those who believe and lead a righteous life have deserved forgiveness and a generous recompense.

51. As for those who strive to challenge our revelations, they incur Hell.

22:49 This command is directed specifically to God's Messenger of the Covenant. This fact, and the specific name of the messenger are mathematically coded into the Quran. See the details, together with the irrefutable proofs, in Appendices 2 and 26.

The System*

52. We did not send before you any messenger, nor a prophet, without having the devil interfere in his wishes. **GOD** then nullifies what the devil has done. **GOD** perfects His revelations. **GOD** is Omniscient, Most Wise.*

The Hypocrites Drop Out

53. He thus sets up the devil's scheme as a test for those who harbor doubts in their hearts, and those whose hearts are hardened. The wicked must remain with the opposition.

54. Those who are blessed with knowledge will recognize the truth from your Lord, then believe in it, and their hearts will readily accept it. Most assuredly, **GOD** guides the believers in the right path.

55. As for those who disbelieve, they will continue to harbor doubts until the Hour comes to them suddenly, or until the retribution of a terrible day comes to them.

Satan's Temporary Kingship

56. All sovereignty on that day belongs to **GOD**, and He will judge among them. As for those who believe and lead a righteous life, they have deserved the gardens of bliss.

57. While those who disbelieved and rejected our revelations have incurred a shameful retribution.

Striving in the Cause of God

58. Those who emigrate for the sake of **GOD**, then get killed, or die, **GOD** will surely shower them with good provisions. **GOD** is certainly the best Provider.

59. Most assuredly, He will admit them an admittance that will please them. **GOD** is Omniscient, Clement.

Divine Help for the Oppressed

60. It is decreed that if one avenges an injustice that was inflicted upon him, equitably, then is persecuted because of this, **GOD** will surely support him. **GOD** is Pardoner, Forgiving.

God's Omnipotence

61. It is a fact that **GOD** merges the night into the day, and merges the day into the night, and that **GOD** is Hearer, Seer.

62. It is a fact that **GOD** is the Truth, while the setting up of any idols beside Him constitutes a falsehood, and that **GOD** is the Most High, the Supreme.

63. Do you not see that **GOD** sends down from the sky water that turns the land green? **GOD** is Sublime, Cognizant.

64. To Him belongs everything in the heavens and everything on earth. Absolutely, **GOD** is the Most Rich, Most Praiseworthy.

22:52 Throughout this worldly test, Satan is allowed to present his point of view (we are born with a representative of Satan in our bodies). This allows the people to make a choice between God's evidence and Satan's evidence. Satan's evidence is invariably based on lies. This system explains the fact that the devil's agents continuously come up with the most absurd lies, insults and accusations against every messenger (see 6:33-34, 8:30, 17:76-77, 27:70).

65. Do you not see that **GOD** has committed in your service everything on earth? The ships run in the ocean by His command. He prevents the heavenly bodies from crashing onto the earth, except in accordance with His command. **GOD** is Most Kind towards the people, Most Merciful.

66. He is the One who granted you life, then He puts you to death, then He brings you back to life. Surely, the human being is unappreciative.

67. For each congregation, we have decreed a set of rites that they must uphold. Therefore, they should not dispute with you. You shall continue to invite everyone to your Lord. Most assuredly, you are on the right path.

68. If they argue with you, then say, "**GOD** is fully aware of everything you do."

69. **GOD** will judge among you on the Day of Resurrection regarding all your disputes.

70. Do you not realize that **GOD** knows everything in the heavens and everything on earth? All this is recorded in a record. This is easy for **GOD** to do.

71. Yet, they idolize beside **GOD** idols wherein He placed no power, and they know nothing about them. The transgressors have no helper.

*Violence & Belligerence:
Signs of Disbelief*

72. When our revelations are recited to them, clearly, you recognize wickedness on the faces of those who disbelieve. They almost attack those who recite our revelations to them. Say, "Shall I inform you of something much worse? Hell is promised by **GOD** for those who disbelieve; what a miserable destiny."

*Can They Create
A Fly?*

73. O people, here is a parable that you must ponder carefully: the idols you set up beside **GOD** can never create a fly, even if they banded together to do so. Furthermore, if the fly steals anything from them, they cannot recover it; weak is the pursuer and the pursued.

74. They do not value **GOD** as He should be valued. **GOD** is the Most Powerful, the Almighty.

75. **GOD** chooses from among the angels messengers, as well as from among the people. **GOD** is Hearer, Seer.

76. He knows their past and their future. To **GOD** belongs the ultimate control of all matters.

77. O you who believe, you shall bow, prostrate, worship your Lord, and work righteousness, that you may succeed.

*Abraham:Original
Messenger of Islam* *

78. You shall strive for the cause of **GOD** as you should strive for His cause. He has chosen you and has placed no hardship on you in practicing your religion—the religion of your father Abraham. He is the one who named you "Submitters" originally. Thus, the messenger shall serve as a witness among you, and you shall serve as witnesses among the people. Therefore, you shall observe the Contact Prayers (*Salat*) and give the obligatory charity (*Zakat*), and hold fast to **GOD**; He is your Lord, the best Lord and the best Supporter.

◆◆◆◆

Sura 23: The Believers (Al-Mu'minûn)

In the name of God,
Most Gracious, Most Merciful

1. Successful indeed are the believers;

2. who are reverent during their Contact Prayers (*Salat*).

3. And they avoid vain talk.

4. And they give their obligatory charity (*Zakat*).

5. And they maintain their chastity.

6. Only with their spouses, or those who are rightfully theirs, do they have sexual relations; they are not to be blamed.

7. Those who transgress these limits are the transgressors.

8. When it comes to deposits entrusted to them, as well as any agreements they make, they are trustworthy.

9. And they observe their Contact Prayers (*Salat*) regularly.

10. Such are the inheritors.

11. They will inherit Paradise, wherein they abide forever.

Accurate Embryology

12. We created the human being from a certain kind of mud.

13. Subsequently, we reproduced him from a tiny drop, that is placed into a well protected repository.

14. Then we developed the drop into a hanging (*embryo*), then developed the hanging (*embryo*) into a bite-size (*fetus*), then created the bite-size (*fetus*) into bones, then covered the bones with flesh. We thus produce a new creature. Most blessed is **GOD**, the best Creator.

15. Then, later on, you die.

16. Then, on the Day of Resurrection, you will be resurrected.

The Seven Universes

17. We created above you seven universes in layers, and we are never unaware of a single creature in them.

*Innumerable
Blessings From God*

18. We send down from the sky water, in exact measure, then we store it in the ground. Certainly, we can let it escape.

22:78 Although all messengers preached one and the same message, "Worship God alone," Abraham was the first messenger to coin the terms "Submission" (Islam) and "Submitter" (Muslim) (2:128). What did Abraham contribute to Submission? We learn from 16:123 that all religious duties in Submission were revealed through Abraham (see Appendices 9 & 26).

---

19. With it, we produce for you orchards of date palms, grapes, all kinds of fruits, and various foods.

20. Also, a tree native to Sinai produces oil, as well as relish for the eaters.

21. And the livestock should provide you with a lesson. We let you drink (*milk*) from their bellies, you derive other benefits from them, and some of them you use for food.

22. On them, and on the ships, you ride.

Noah

23. We sent Noah to his people, saying, "O my people, worship **GOD**. You have no other god beside Him. Would you not be righteous?"

24. The leaders who disbelieved among his people said, "This is no more than a human like you, who wants to gain prominence among you. Had **GOD** willed, He could have sent down angels. We never heard of anything like this from our ancestors.

25. "He is simply a man gone crazy. Just ignore him for awhile."

26. He said, "My Lord, grant me victory, for they have disbelieved me."

27. We then inspired him: "Make the watercraft* under our watchful eyes, and in accordance with our inspiration. When our command comes, and the atmosphere boils up, put on it a pair of every kind (*of your domesticated animals*), and your family, except those condemn-

ed to be doomed. Do not speak to Me on behalf of those who transgressed; they will be drowned.

28. "Once you are settled, together with those who are with you, on the watercraft, you shall say, Praise **GOD** for saving us from the evil people.'

29. "And say, 'My Lord, let me disembark onto a blessed location; You are the best deliverer.' "

30. These should provide sufficient proofs for you. We will certainly put you to the test.

31. Subsequently, we established another generation after them.

32. We sent to them a messenger from among them, saying, "You shall worship **GOD**. You have no other god beside Him. Would you not be righteous?"

33. The leaders among his people who disbelieved and rejected the idea of the Hereafter—although we provided for them generously in this life—said, "This is no more than a human being like you. He eats from what you eat, and drinks as you drink.

34. "If you obey a human being like you, then you are really losers.

35. "Does he promise you that, after you die and turn into dust and bones, you will come out again?

36. "Impossible, impossible indeed is what is promised to you.

23:27 The story tellers have created a mockery of Noah's history. Noah's ark was a flat watercraft made of logs, tied together with primitive ropes (54:13), the flood was local, around the Dead Sea area, and the animals were Noah's domesticated animals.

37. "We only live this life—we live and die—and we will never be resurrected.

38. "He is just a man who fabricated lies and attributed them to **GOD.** We will never believe him."

39. He said, "My Lord, grant me victory, for they have disbelieved me."

40. He said, "Soon they will be sorry."

41. The retribution struck them, equitably, and thus, we turned them into ruins. The wicked people perished.

42. Subsequently, we established other generations after them.

43. No community can advance its predetermined fate, nor delay it.

44. Then we sent our messengers in succession. Every time a messenger went to his community, they disbelieved him. Consequently, we annihilated them, one after the other, and made them history. The people who disbelieved have perished.

Moses and Aaron

45. Then we sent Moses and his brother Aaron with our revelations and a profound proof.

46. To Pharaoh and his elders, but they turned arrogant. They were oppressive people.

47. They said, "Shall we believe for two men whose people are our slaves?"

48. They rejected the two, and consequently, they were annihilated.

49. We gave Moses the scripture, that they may be guided.

50. We made the son of Mary and his mother a sign, and we gave them refuge on a mesa with food and drink.

One God/One Religion

51. O you messengers, eat from the good provisions, and work righteousness. I am fully aware of everything you do.

52. Such is your congregation—one congregation—and I am your Lord; you shall reverence Me.

53. But they tore themselves into disputing factions; each party happy with what they have.

54. Therefore, just leave them in their confusion, for awhile.

55. Do they think that, since we provided them with money and children,

56. we must be showering them with blessings? Indeed, they have no idea.

57. Surely, those who are reverently conscious of their Lord,

58. And who believe in the revelations of their Lord,

59. And who never set up any idols beside their Lord,

60. As they give their charities, their hearts are fully reverent. For they recognize that they will be summoned before their Lord,

61. They are eager to do righteous works; they compete in doing them.

The Disbelievers Unappreciative

62. We never burden any soul beyond its means, and we keep a record that utters the truth. No one will suffer injustice.

63. Because their minds are oblivious to this, they commit works that do not conform with this; their works are evil.

64. Then, when we requite their leaders with retribution, they complain.

65. Do not complain now; you have given up all help from us.

66. My proofs have been presented to you, but you turned back on your heels.

67. You were too arrogant to accept them, and you defiantly disregarded them.

68. Why do they not reflect upon this scripture? Do they not realize that they have received something never attained by their ancestors?

69. Have they failed to recognize their messenger? Is this why they are disregarding him?

70. Have they decided that he is crazy? Indeed, he has brought the truth to them, but most of them hate the truth.

71. Indeed, if the truth conformed to their wishes, there would be chaos in the heavens and the earth; everything in them would be corrupted. We have given them their proof, but they are disregarding their proof.

72. Are you asking them for a wage? Your Lord's wage is far better. He is the best Provider.

73. Most assuredly, you are inviting them to a straight path.

74. Those who disbelieve in the Hereafter will surely deviate from the right path.

75. Even when we showered them with mercy, and relieved their problems, they plunged deeper into transgression, and continued to blunder.

76. Even when we afflicted them with retribution, they never turned to their Lord imploring.

77. Subsequently, when we requited them with the severe retribution they had incurred, they were shocked.

78. He is the One who granted you the hearing, the eyesight, and the brains. Rarely are you appreciative.

79. He is the One who established you on earth, and before Him you will be summoned.

80. He is the One who controls life and death, and He is the One who alternates the night and day. Do you not understand?

81. They said what their ancestors said.

82. They said, "After we die and become dust and bones, we get resurrected?

83. "Such promises were given to us and to our parents in the past. These are no more than tales from the past."

*Most Believers are Destined for Hell**

84. Say, "To whom belongs the earth and everyone on it, if you know?"

85. They will say, "To **GOD**." Say, "Why then do you not take heed?"

86. Say, "Who is the Lord of the seven universes; the Lord of the great dominion?"

87. They will say, "**GOD**." Say, "Why then do you not turn righteous?"

---

*23:84-89 Belief in God is valid only if one recognizes God's qualities, such as the fact that God controls everything (8:17). Believers who do not know God are not really believers. Most believers nullify their belief by idolizing such powerless idols as the prophets and saints (6:106).

---

88. Say, "In whose hand is all sovereignty over all things, and He is the only one who can provide help, but needs no help, if you know?"

89. They will say, "**GOD**." Say, "Where did you go wrong?"

90. We have given them the truth, while they are liars.

91. **GOD** has never begotten a son. Nor was there ever any other god beside Him. Otherwise, each god would have declared independence with his creations, and they would have competed with each other for dominance. **GOD** be glorified; far above their claims.

92. The Knower of all secrets and declarations; be He exalted, far above having a partner.

93. Say, "My Lord, whether You show me (*the retribution*) they have incurred [*or not*],

94. "My Lord, let me not be one of the transgressing people."

95. To show you (*the retribution*) we have reserved for them is something we can easily do.

96. Therefore, counter their evil works with goodness; we are fully aware of their claims.

To Be Protected From Satan

97. Say, "My Lord, I seek refuge in You from the whispers of the devils.

98. "And I seek refuge in You, my Lord, lest they come near me."

The Dead Never Come Back
Until the Day of Resurrection

99. When death comes to one of them, he says, "My Lord, send me back.

100. "I will then work righteousness in everything I left." Not true. This is a false claim that he makes. A barrier will separate his soul from this world until resurrection.

101. When the horn is blown, no relations among them will exist on that day, nor will they care about one another.

102. As for those whose weights are heavy, they will be the winners.

103. Those whose weights are light are the ones who lost their souls; they abide in Hell forever.

104. Fire will overwhelm their faces, and they last miserably therein.

105. Were not My revelations recited to you, and you kept on rejecting them?

106. They will say, "Our Lord, our wickedness overwhelmed us, and we were people gone astray.

107. "Our Lord, take us out of this; if we return (*to our old behavior*), then we are really wicked."

108. He will say, "Abide therein, humiliated, and do not speak to Me.

They Ridiculed the Believers

109. "A group of My servants used to say, 'Our Lord, we have believed, so forgive us and shower us with mercy. Of all the merciful ones, You are the Most Merciful.'

110. "But you mocked and ridiculed them, to the extent that you forgot Me. You used to laugh at them.

111. "I have rewarded them today, in return for their steadfastness, by making them the winners."

112. He said, "How long have you lasted on earth? How many years?"

113. They said, "We lasted a day or part of a day. Ask those who counted."

114. He said, "In fact, you stayed but a brief interim, if you only knew.

115. "Did you think that we created you in vain; that you were not to be returned to us?"

116. Most exalted is **GOD**, the true Sovereign. There is no other god beside Him; the Most Honorable Lord, possessor of all authority.

117. Anyone who idolizes beside **GOD** any other god, and without any kind of proof, his reckoning rests with his Lord. The disbelievers never succeed.

118. Say, "My Lord, shower us with forgiveness and mercy. Of all the merciful ones, You are the Most Merciful."

◆◆◆◆

Sura 24: Light (Al-Noor)

In the name of God,
Most Gracious, Most Merciful

1. A sura that we have sent down, and we have decreed as law. We have revealed in it clear revelations, that you may take heed.

Adultery

2. The adulteress and the adulterer you shall whip each of them a hundred lashes. Do not be swayed by pity from carrying out **GOD**'s law, if you truly believe in **GOD** and the Last Day. And let a group of believers witness their penalty.*

3. The adulterer will end up marrying an adulteress or an idol worshiper, and the adulteress will end up marrying an adulterer or an idol worshiper. This is prohibited for the believers.

4. Those who accuse married women of adultery, then fail to produce four witnesses, you shall whip them eighty lashes, and do not accept any testimony from them; they are wicked.

5. If they repent afterwards and reform, then **GOD** is Forgiver, Merciful.

6. As for those who accuse their own spouses, without any other witnesses, then the testimony may be accepted if he swears by **GOD** four times that he is telling the truth.

7. The fifth oath shall be to incur **GOD**'s condemnation upon him, if he was lying.

8. She shall be considered innocent if she swears by **GOD** four times that he is a liar.

9. The fifth oath shall incur **GOD**'s wrath upon her if he was telling the truth.

10. This is **GOD**'s grace and mercy towards you. **GOD** is Redeemer, Most Wise.

24:2 Social pressure, i.e., public witnessing of the penalty, is the basic punishment (see also 5:38). The lashes shall be symbolic, not severe.

How to Deal With Rumors and Unproven Accusations

11. A gang among you produced a big lie.* Do not think that it was bad for you; instead, it was good for you. Meanwhile, each one of them has earned his share of the guilt. As for the one who initiated the whole incident, he has incurred a terrible retribution.

12. When you heard it, the believing men and the believing women should have had better thoughts about themselves, and should have said, "This is obviously a big lie."

13. Only if they produced four witnesses (*you may believe them*). If they fail to produce the witnesses, then they are, according to **GOD**, liars.

14. If it were not for **GOD**'s grace towards you, and His mercy in this world and in the Hereafter, you would have suffered a great retribution because of this incident.

15. You fabricated it with your own tongues, and the rest of you repeated it with your mouths without proof. You thought it was simple, when it was, according to **GOD**, gross.

What to Do

16. When you heard it, you should have said, "We will not repeat this. Glory be to You. This is a gross falsehood."

17. **GOD** admonishes you that you shall never do it again, if you are believers.

18. **GOD** thus explains the revelations for you. **GOD** is Omniscient, Wise.

19. Those who love to see immorality spread among the believers have incurred a painful retribution in this life and in the Hereafter. **GOD** knows, while you do not know.

20. **GOD** showers you with His grace and mercy. **GOD** is Most Kind towards the believers, Most Merciful.

The Devil Encourages Baseless Accusations

21. O you who believe, do not follow the steps of Satan. Anyone who follows the steps of Satan, should know that he advocates evil and vice. If it were not for **GOD**'s grace towards you, and His mercy, none of you would have been purified. But **GOD** purifies whomever He wills. **GOD** is Hearer, Knower.

22. Those among you who are blessed with resources and wealth shall be charitable towards their relatives, the poor, and those who have immigrated for the sake of **GOD**. They shall treat them with kindness and tolerance; do you not love to attain **GOD**'s forgiveness? **GOD** is Forgiver, Most Merciful.

Gross Sin

23. Surely, those who falsely accuse married women who are pious believers have incurred condemnation in this life and in the Hereafter; they have incurred a horrendous retribution.

---

*24:11 This refers to a historical incident where the Prophet's wife Aysha was left in the desert by mistake, and later found by a young man who helped her catch up with the Prophet's caravan. This triggered the famous 'Big Lie' against Aysha.

---

24. The day will come when their own tongues, hands, and feet will bear witness to everything they had done.

25. On that day, **GOD** will requite them fully for their works, and they will find out that **GOD** is the Truth.

26. The bad women for the bad men, and the bad men for the bad women, and the good women for the good men, and the good men for the good women. The latter are innocent of such accusations. They have attained forgiveness and a generous reward.

Divine Etiquette

27. O you who believe, do not enter homes other than yours without permission from their inhabitants, and without greeting them. This is better for you, that you may take heed.

28. If you find no one in them, do not enter them until you obtain permission. If you are told, "Go back," you must go back. This is purer for you. **GOD** is fully aware of everything you do.

29. You commit no error by entering uninhabited homes wherein there is something that belongs to you. **GOD** knows everything you reveal, and everything you conceal.

Dress Code for Believers*

30. Tell the believing men that they shall subdue their eyes (*and not stare at the women*), and to maintain their chastity. This is purer for them. **GOD** is fully Cognizant of everything they do.

31. And tell the believing women to subdue their eyes, and maintain their chastity. They shall not reveal any parts of their bodies, except that which is necessary. They shall cover their chests, and shall not relax this code in the presence of other than their husbands, their fathers, the fathers of their husbands, their sons, the sons of their husbands, their brothers, the sons of their brothers, the sons of their sisters, other women, the male servants or employees whose sexual drive has been nullified, or the children who have not reached puberty. They shall not strike their feet when they walk in order to shake and reveal certain details of their bodies. All of you shall repent to **GOD**, O you believers, that you may succeed.*

Encourage
Marriage to
Discourage Immorality

32. You shall encourage those of you who are single to get married. They may marry the righteous among your male and female servants, if they are poor. **GOD** will enrich them from His grace. **GOD** is Bounteous, Knower.

---

*24:30-31 Dressing modestly, therefore, is a trait of the believing men and women. The minimum requirements for a woman's dress is to lengthen her garment (33:59) and to cover her chest. Tyrannical Arab traditions have given a false impression that a woman must be covered from head to toe; such is not a Quranic or Islamic dress.

33. Those who cannot afford to get married shall maintain morality until **GOD** provides for them from His grace. Those among your servants who wish to be freed in order to marry, you shall grant them their wish, once you realize that they are honest. And give them from **GOD**'s money that He has bestowed upon you. You shall not force your girls to commit prostitution, seeking the materials of this world, if they wish to be chaste. If anyone forces them, then **GOD**, seeing that they are forced, is Forgiver, Merciful.

34. We have revealed to you clarifying revelations, and examples from the past generations, and an enlightenment for the righteous.

God

35. **GOD** is the light of the heavens and the earth. The allegory of His light is that of a concave mirror behind a lamp that is placed inside a glass container. The glass container is like a bright, pearl-like star. The fuel thereof is supplied from a blessed oil-producing tree, that is neither eastern, nor western. Its oil is almost self-radiating; needs no fire to ignite it. Light upon light. **GOD** guides to His light whoever wills (*to be guided*). **GOD** thus cites the parables for the people. **GOD** is fully aware of all things.

36. (*God's guidance is found*) in houses exalted by **GOD**, for His name is commemorated therein. Glorifying Him therein, day and night—

Those Who Frequent the Masjid

37. People who are not distracted by business or trade from commemorating **GOD**; they observe the Contact Prayers (*Salat*), and give the obligatory charity (*Zakat*), and they are conscious of the day when the minds and the eyes will be horrified.

38. **GOD** will certainly reward them for their good works, and will shower them with His grace. **GOD** provides for whomever He wills without limits.

Chasing A Mirage

39. As for those who disbelieve, their works are like a mirage in the desert. A thirsty person thinks that it is water. But when he reaches it, he finds that it is nothing, and he finds **GOD** there instead, to requite him fully for his works. **GOD** is the most efficient reckoner.

Exile From God: Total Darkness

40. Another allegory is that of being in total darkness in the midst of a violent ocean, with waves upon waves, in addition to thick fog. Darkness upon darkness—if he looked at his own hand, he could barely see it. Whomever **GOD** deprives of light, will have no light.

41. Do you not realize that everyone in the heavens and the earth glorifies **GOD**, even the birds as they fly in a column? Each knows its prayer and its glorification. **GOD** is fully aware of everything they do.

42. To **GOD** belongs the sovereignty of the heavens and the earth, and to **GOD** is the final destiny.

43. Do you not realize that **GOD** drives the clouds, then gathers them together, then piles them on each other, then you see the rain coming out of them? He sends down from the sky loads of snow to cover whomever he wills, while diverting it from whomever He wills. The brightness of the snow almost blinds the eyes.

44. **GOD** controls the night and day. This should be a lesson for those who possess eyes.

45. And **GOD** created every living creature from water. Some of them walk on their bellies, some walk on two legs, and some walk on four. **GOD** creates whatever He wills. **GOD** is Omnipotent.

46. We have sent down to you clarifying revelations, then **GOD** guides whoever wills in a straight path.

God Sends Instructions Through His Messenger

47. They say, "We believe in **GOD** and in the messenger, and we obey," but then some of them slide back afterwards. These are not believers.

48. When they are invited to **GOD** and His messenger to judge among them, some of them get upset.

49. However, if the judgment is in their favor, they readily accept it!

50. Is there a disease in their hearts? Are they doubtful? Are they afraid that **GOD** and His messenger may treat them unfairly? In fact, it is they who are unjust.

Believers Unhesitatingly Obey God and His Messenger

51. The only utterance of the believers, whenever invited to **GOD** and His messenger to judge in their affairs, is to say, "We hear and we obey." These are the winners.

52. Those who obey **GOD** and His messenger, and reverence **GOD** and ob-serve Him, these are the triumphant ones.

53. They swear by **GOD**, solemnly, that if you commanded them to mobilize, they would mobilize. Say, "Do not swear. Obedience is an obligation. **GOD** is fully Cognizant of everything you do."

54. Say, "Obey **GOD**, and obey the messenger." If they refuse, then he is responsible for his obligations, and you are responsible for your obligations. If you obey him, you will be guided. The sole duty of the messenger is to deliver (*the message*).

God's Promise Kings and Queens on Earth

55. **GOD** promises those among you who believe and lead a righteous life, that He will make them sovereigns on earth, as He did for those before them, and will establish for them the religion He has chosen for them, and will substitute peace and security for them in place of fear. All this because they worship Me alone; they never set up any idols beside Me. Those who disbelieve after this are the truly wicked.

Formula for Success

56. You shall observe the Contact Prayers (*Salat*) and give the obligatory charity (*Zakat*), and obey the messenger, that you may attain mercy.

57. Do not think that those who disbelieve will ever get away with it. Their final abode is Hell; what a miserable destiny.

Etiquette
Two Prayers Mentioned by Name

58. O you who believe, permission must be requested by your servants and the children who have not attained puberty (*before entering your rooms*). This is to be done in three instances—before the Dawn Prayer, at noon when you change your clothes to rest, and after the Night Prayer. These are three private times for you. At other times, it is not wrong for you or them to mingle with one another. **GOD** thus clarifies the revelations for you. **GOD** is Omniscient, Most Wise.

59. Once the children reach puberty, they must ask permission (*before entering*) like those who became adults before them have asked permission (*before entering*). **GOD** thus clarifies His revelations for you. **GOD** is Omniscient, Most Wise.

You Shall Dress Modestly

60. The elderly women who do not expect to get married commit nothing wrong by relaxing their dress code, provided they do not reveal too much of their bodies. To maintain modesty is better for them. **GOD** is Hearer, Knower.

Be Sure Your Meal is Lawful

61. The blind is not to be blamed, the crippled is not to be blamed, nor the handicapped is to be blamed, just as you are not to be blamed for eating at your homes, or the homes of your fathers, or the homes of your mothers, or the homes of your brothers, or the homes of your sisters, or the homes of your fathers' brothers, or the homes of your fathers' sisters, or the homes of your mothers' brothers, or the homes of your mothers' sisters, or the homes that belong to you and you possess their keys, or the homes of your friends. You commit nothing wrong by eating together or as individuals. When you enter any home, you shall greet each other a greeting from **GOD** that is blessed and good. **GOD** thus explains the revelations for you, that you may understand.

62. The true believers are those who believe in **GOD** and His messenger,* and when they are with him in a community meeting, they do not leave him without permission. Those who ask permission are the ones who do believe in **GOD** and His messenger. If they ask your permission, in order to tend to some of their affairs, you may grant permission to whomever you wish, and ask **GOD** to forgive them. **GOD** is Forgiver, Most Merciful.

63. Do not treat the messenger's requests as you treat each others' requests. **GOD** is fully aware of those among you who sneak away using flimsy excuses. Let them beware—those who disobey his orders—for a disaster may strike them, or a severe retribution.

64. Absolutely, to **GOD** belongs everything in the heavens and the earth. He fully knows every condition you may be in. The day you are returned to Him, He will inform them of everything they had done. **GOD** is fully aware of all things.

◆◆◆◆

24:62 This verse refers to God's Messenger of the Covenant; by adding the gematrical value of "Rashad" (505) plus the value of "Khalifa" (725), plus the verse number (62), we get 1292, a multiple of 19 (1292 = 19x68). See Appendix 2.

Sura 25:
The Statute Book
(Al-Furqãn)

In the name of God,
Most Gracious, Most Merciful

1. Most blessed is the One who revealed the Statute Book to His servant, so he can serve as a warner to the whole world.

2. The One to whom belongs all sovereignty of the heavens and the earth. He never had a son, nor does He have any partners in sovereignty. He created everything in exact measure; He precisely designed everything.*

3. Yet, they set up beside Him gods who do not create anything—they themselves are created—and who possess no power to even harm or benefit themselves, nor do they possess any power to control life, or death, or resurrection.

The Disbelievers Rebutted by the Quran's Mathematical Code

4. Those who disbelieved said, "This is a fabrication that he produced, with the help of some other people." They have uttered a blasphemy and a falsehood.

5. They also said, "Tales from the past that he wrote down; they were dictated to him day and night."*

6. Say, "This was revealed by the One who knows the Secret* in the heavens and the earth. He is Forgiving, Most Merciful."

Typical Utterances of Disbelievers

7. And they said, "How come this messenger eats the food and walks in the markets? If only an angel could come down with him, to serve with him as a preacher!"

8. Or, "If only a treasure could be given to him!" Or, "If only he could possess an orchard from which he eats!" The transgressors also said, "You are following a bewitched man."

9. Note how they called you all kinds of names, and how this led them astray, never to find their way back.

10. Most blessed is the One who can, if He wills, give you much better than their demands—gardens with flowing streams, and many mansions.

The Real Reason

11. In fact, they have disbelieved in the Hour (*Day of Resurrection*), and we have prepared for those who disbelieve in the Hour a flaming Hell.

25:2 When we launch astronauts into space, we measure precisely the amount of food, water, oxygen, and other needs throughout the journey. Similarly, God has launched us into space—on board spaceship Earth—and He has designed all kinds of renewable provisions for us and other creatures, a perfect design. Think, for example, of the symbiotic relationship between us and the plants; we use the oxygen they produce in photosynthesis, while they use the carbon dioxide we produce in respiration.

25:5 Muhammad's contemporaries knew that he was a literate man who could read and write; he wrote God's revelations with his own hand (see Appendix 28).

25:6 The Quran's miraculous mathematical code, the incontrovertible answer to the disbelievers' claims, remained a divinely guarded secret for 1400 years. God's Messenger of the Covenant was destined to unveil it by God's leave (Appendices 1, 2, & 26).

Retribution for the Disbelievers

12. When it sees them from afar, they will hear its rage and fuming.

13. And when they are thrown into it, through a narrow place, all shackled, they will declare their remorse.

14. You will not declare just a single remorse, on that day; you will suffer through a great number of remorses.

Reward for the Righteous

15. Say, "Is this better or the eternal Paradise that is promised for the righteous? It is their well deserved reward; a well deserved destiny."

16. They get anything they wish therein, forever. This is your Lord's irrevocable promise.

17. On the day when He summons them, together with the idols they had set up beside **GOD**, He will say, "Have you misled these servants of Mine, or did they go astray on their own?"

18. They will say, "Be You glorified, it was not right for us to set up any lords beside You. But You allowed them to enjoy, together with their parents. Consequently, they disregarded the message and thus became wicked people."

19. They have disbelieved in the message you have given them, and, consequently, you can neither protect them from the retribution they have incurred, nor can you help them in any way. Anyone among you who commits evil, we will commit him to severe retribution.

Messengers Are Just Human Beings

20. We did not send any messengers before you who did not eat food and walk in the markets. We thus test you by each other; will you steadfastly persevere? Your Lord is Seer.

21. Those who do not expect to meet us said, "If only the angels could come down to us, or we could see our Lord (*we would then believe*)!" Indeed, they have committed a gross arrogance, and have produced a gross blasphemy.

22. The day they see the angels, it will not be good news for the guilty; they will say, "Now, we are irreversibly confined."

23. We will look at all the works they have done, and render them null and void.

24. The dwellers of Paradise are far better on that day; they will hear better news.

25. The heaven will break apart, into masses of clouds, and the angels will descend in multitudes.

26. All sovereignty on that day belongs to the Most Gracious. For the disbelievers, it will be a difficult day.

*God's Messenger of the Covenant**

27. The day will come when the transgressor will bite his hands (*in anguish*) and say, "Alas, I wish I had followed the path with the messenger.

28. "Alas, woe to me, I wish I did not take that person as a friend.

29. "He has led me away from the message after it came to me. Indeed, the devil lets down his human victims."

30. The messenger* said, "My Lord, my people have deserted this Quran."

31. We also set up against every prophet enemies from among the guilty. Your Lord suffices as a guide, a master.

32. Those who disbelieved said, "Why did not the Quran come through him all at once?" We have released it to you gradually, in order to fix it in your memory. We have recited it in a specific sequence.

God's Evidence is Overwhelming

33. Whatever argument they come up with, we provide you with the truth, and a better understanding.

34. Those who are forcibly summoned to Hell are in the worst position; they are the farthest from the right path.

35. We have given Moses the scripture, and appointed his brother Aaron to be his assistant.

36. We said, "Go, both of you, to the people who rejected our revelations," and subsequently, we utterly annihilated the rejectors.

37. Similarly, when the people of Noah disbelieved the messengers, we drowned them, and we set them up as a sign for the people. We have prepared for the transgressors a painful retribution.

38. Also 'Ãd, Thamoud, the inhabitants of Al-Russ, and many generations between them.

39. To each of these groups, we delivered sufficient examples, before we annihilated them.

40. They have passed by the community that was showered with a miserable shower (*Sodom*). Did they not see it? The fact is, they never believed in resurrection.

Messengers Ridiculed

41. When they saw you, they always ridiculed you: "Is this the one chosen by **GOD** to be a messenger?

42. "He almost diverted us from our gods, if it were not that we steadfastly persevered with them." They will certainly find out, when they see the retribution, who are the real strayers from the path.

The Ego as a god

43. Have you seen the one whose god is his own ego? Will you be his advocate?

25:27-30 This verse refers also to God's Messenger of the Covenant whose name is mathematically coded in the Quran as "Rashad Khalifa." If you write down the gematrical value of "Rashad" (505), followed by the gematrical value of "Khalifa" (725), followed by this sura number (25), followed by verses 27, 28, 29, and 30, the final number (5057252527282930) is a multiple of 19 (see Appendices 2 & 26 for details). The prophet Muhammad will also make such a statement as in 25:30 on the Day of Judgment.

44. Do you think that most of them hear, or understand? They are just like animals; no, they are far worse.

Infinite Blessings From God

45. Have you not seen how your Lord designed the shadow? If He willed, He could have made it fixed, then we would have designed the sun accordingly.

46. But we designed it to move slowly.

47. He is the One who designed the night to be a cover, and for you to sleep and rest. And He made the day a resurrection.

48. He is the One who sends the winds with good omens of His mercy, and we send down from the sky pure water.

49. With it, we revive dead lands and provide drink for our creations—multitudes of animals and humans.

50. We have distributed it among them in exact measure, that they may take heed. But most people insist upon disbelieving.

51. If we willed, we could have sent to every community a warner.

52. Therefore, do not obey the disbelievers, and strive against them with this, a great striving.

53. He is the One who merges the two seas; one is fresh and palatable, while the other is salty and undrinkable. And He separated them with a formidable, inviolable barrier (*evaporation*).

54. He is the One who created from water a human being, then made him reproduce through marriage and mating. Your Lord is Omnipotent.

55. Yet, they still set up beside **GOD** idols that cannot benefit them, nor harm them. Indeed, the disbeliever is an enemy of his Lord.

56. We have sent you (*Rashad*) as a deliverer of good news, as well as a warner.

57. Say, "I do not ask you for any money. All I seek is to help you find the right path to your Lord, if this is what you choose."

The Prophets and the Saints Are Dead

58. You shall put your trust in the One who is Alive—the One who never dies—and praise Him and glorify Him. He is fully Cognizant of His creatures' sins.

59. He is the One who created the heavens and the earth, and everything between them, in six days, then assumed all authority. The Most Gracious; ask about Him those who are well founded in knowledge.

The Unappreciative Human

60. When they are told, "Fall prostrate before the Most Gracious," they say, "What is the Most Gracious? Shall we prostrate before what you advocate?" Thus, it only augments their aversion.

61. Most blessed is the One who placed constellations in the sky, and placed in it a lamp, and a shining moon.

62. He is the One who designed the night and the day to alternate: a sufficient proof for those who wish to take heed, or to be appreciative.

---

*25:56 The gematrical value of "Rashad Khalifa" (1230), plus the sura and verse number (25 + 56) give a total of 1230 + 25 + 56 = 1311 = 19x69.

Traits of the Righteous

63. The worshipers of the Most Gracious are those who tread the earth gently, and when the ignorant speak to them, they only utter peace.

64. In the privacy of the night, they meditate on their Lord, and fall prostrate.

65. And they say, "Our Lord, spare us the agony of Hell; its retribution is horrendous.

66. "It is the worst abode; the worst destiny."

67. When they give they are neither extravagant nor stingy; they give in moderation.

68. They never implore beside **GOD** any other god, nor do they kill anyone—for **GOD** has made life sacred—except in the course of justice. Nor do they commit adultery. Those who commit these offenses will have to pay.

69. Retribution is doubled for them on the Day of Resurrection, and they abide therein humiliated.

70. Exempted are those who repent, believe, and lead a righteous life. **GOD** transforms their sins into credits. **GOD** is Forgiver, Most Merciful.

71. Those who repent and lead a righteous life, **GOD** redeems them; a complete redemption.

Additional Traits of the Righteous

72. They do not bear false witness. When they encounter vain talk, they ignore it.

73. When reminded of their Lord's revelations, they never react to them as if they were deaf and blind.

74. And they say, "Our Lord, let our spouses and children be a source of joy for us, and keep us in the forefront of the righteous."

75. These are the ones who attain Paradise in return for their steadfastness; they are received therein with joyous greetings and peace.

76. Eternally they abide therein; what a beautiful destiny; what a beautiful abode.

77. Say, "You attain value at my Lord only through your worship. But if you disbelieve, you incur the inevitable consequences."

◆◆◆◆

Sura 26: The Poets (Al-Shu'arã')

In the name of God,
Most Gracious, Most Merciful

1. T.S.M.*

2. These (*letters*) constitute proofs of this clarifying scripture.

3. You may blame yourself that they are not believers.

---

*26:1 See Appendix 1 for the significance of these previously mysterious letters.

---

4. If we will, we can send from the sky a sign that forces their necks to bow.

The Quran's Mathematical Code

5. Whenever a reminder from the Most Gracious comes to them, that is new, they turn away in aversion.

6. Since they disbelieved, they have incurred the consequences of their heedlessness.

7. Have they not seen the earth, and how many kinds of beautiful plants we have grown thereon?

8. This should be a sufficient proof for them, but most of them are not believers.

9. Most assuredly, your Lord is the Almighty, Most Merciful.

Moses

10. Recall that your Lord called Moses: "Go to the transgressing people.

11. "Pharaoh's people; perhaps they reform."

12. He said, "My Lord, I fear lest they disbelieve me.

13. "I may lose my temper. My tongue gets tied; send for my brother Aaron.

14. "Also, they consider me a fugitive; I fear lest they kill me."

15. He said, "No, (*they will not*). Go with My proofs. We will be with you, listening.

16. "Go to Pharaoh and say, 'We are messengers from the Lord of the universe.

17. " 'Let the Children of Israel go.' "

18. He said, "Did we not raise you from infancy, and you spent many years with us?

19. "Then you committed the crime that you committed, and you were ungrateful."

20. He said, "Indeed, I did it when I was astray.

21. "Then I fled, when I feared you, and my Lord endowed me with wisdom and made me one of the messengers.

22. "You are boasting that you did me a favor, while enslaving the Children of Israel!"

23. Pharaoh said, "What is the Lord of the universe?"

24. He said, "The Lord of the heavens and the earth, and everything between them. You should be certain about this."

25. He said to those around him, "Did you hear this?"

26. He said, "Your Lord and the Lord of your ancestors."

27. He said, "Your messenger who is sent to you is crazy."

28. He said, "The Lord of the east and the west, and everything between them, if you understand."

29. He said, "If you accept any god, other than me, I will throw you in the prison."

30. He said, "What if I show you something profound?"

31. He said, "Then produce it, if you are truthful."

32. He then threw his staff, whereupon it became a profound snake.

33. And he took out his hand, and it was white to the beholders.

34. He said to the elders around him, "This is an experienced magician.

35. "He wants to take you out of your land, with his magic. What do you suggest?"

36. They said, "Respite him and his brother, and send summoners to every town.

37. "Let them summon every experienced magician."

38. The magicians were gathered at the appointed time, on the appointed day.

39. The people were told: "Come one and all; let us gather together here.

40. "Maybe we will follow the magicians, if they are the winners."

41. When the magicians came, they said to Pharaoh, "Do we get paid, if we are the winners?"

42. He said, "Yes indeed; you will even be close to me."

43. Moses said to them "Throw what you are going to throw."

44. They threw their ropes and sticks, and said, "By Pharaoh's majesty, we will be the victors."

45. Moses threw his staff, whereupon it swallowed what they fabricated.

The Experts See the Truth

46. The magicians fell prostrate.

47. They said, "We believe in the Lord of the universe.

48. "The Lord of Moses and Aaron."

49. He said, "Did you believe with him before I give you permission? He must be your teacher, who taught you magic. You will surely find out. I will cut your hands and feet on alternate sides. I will crucify you all."

50. They said, "This will not change our decision; to our Lord we will return.

51. "We hope that our Lord will forgive us our sins, especially that we are the first believers."

52. We inspired Moses: "Travel with My servants; you will be pursued."

53. Pharaoh sent to the cities callers.

54. (*Proclaiming,*) "This is a small gang.

55. "They are now opposing us.

56. "Let us all beware of them."

The Inevitable Retribution

57. Consequently, we deprived them of gardens and springs.

58. And treasures and an honorable position.

59. Then we made it an inheritance for the Children of Israel.

60. They pursued them towards the east.

61. When both parties saw each other, Moses' people said, "We will be caught."

62. He said, "No way. My Lord is with me; He will guide me."

63. We then inspired Moses: "Strike the sea with your staff," whereupon it parted. Each part was like a great hill.

64. We then delivered them all.

65. We thus saved Moses and all those who were with him.

66. And we drowned the others.

67. This should be a sufficient proof, but most people are not believers.

68. Most assuredly, your Lord is the Almighty, Most Merciful.

Abraham

69. Narrate to them Abraham's history.

70. He said to his father and his people, "What is this you are worshiping?"

71. They said, "We worship statues; we are totally devoted to them."

72. He said, "Can they hear you when you implore?

73. "Can they benefit you, or harm you?"

74. They said, "No; but we found our parents doing this."

75. He said, "Do you see these idols that you worship.

76. "You and your ancestors.

77. "I am against them, for I am devoted only to the Lord of the universe.

78. "The One who created me, and guided me.

79. "The One who feeds me and waters me.

80. "And when I get sick, He heals me.

81. "The One who puts me to death, then brings me back to life.

82. "The One who hopefully will forgive my sins on the Day of Judgment.

83. "My Lord, grant me wisdom, and include me with the righteous.

84. "Let the example I set for the future generations be a good one.

85. "Make me one of the inheritors of the blissful Paradise.

86. "And forgive my father, for he has gone astray.

87. "And do not forsake me on the Day of Resurrection."

88. That is the day when neither money, nor children, can help.

89. Only those who come to **GOD** with their whole heart (*will be saved*).

90. Paradise will be presented to the righteous.

91. Hell will be set up for the strayers.

They Will Disown Their Idols

92. They will be asked, "Where are the idols you had worshiped

93. "beside **GOD**? Can they help you now? Can they help themselves?"

94. They will be thrown therein, together with the strayers.

95. And all of Satan's soldiers.

96. They will say as they feud therein,

97. "By **GOD**, we were far astray.

98. "How could we set you up to rank with the Lord of the universe?

99. "Those who misled us were wicked.

100. "Now we have no intercessors.

101. "Nor a single close friend.

102. "If only we could get another chance, we would then believe."

103. This should be a good lesson. But most people are not believers.

104. Your Lord is the Almighty, Most Merciful.

Noah

105. The people of Noah disbelieved the messengers.

106. Their brother Noah said to them, "Would you not be righteous?

107. "I am an honest messenger to you.

108. "You shall reverence **GOD** and obey me.

109. "I do not ask you for any wage. My wage comes from the Lord of the universe.

110. "You shall reverence **GOD** and obey me."

111. They said, "How can we believe with you, when the worst among us have followed you?"

112. He said, "How do I know what they did?

113. "Their judgment rests only with my Lord, if you could perceive.

114. "I will never dismiss the believers.

115. "I am no more than a clarifying warner."

116. They said, "Unless you refrain, O Noah, you will be stoned."

117. He said, "My Lord, my people have disbelieved me.

118. "Grant me victory against them, and deliver me and my company of believers."

119. We delivered him and those who accompanied him in the loaded ark.

120. Then we drowned the others.

121. This should be a lesson, but most people are not believers.

122. Most assuredly, your Lord is the Almighty, Most Merciful.

Hûd

123. 'Ãd disbelieved the messengers.

124. Their brother Hûd said to them, "Would you not be righteous?

125. "I am an honest messenger to you.

126. "You shall reverence **GOD**, and obey me.

127. "I do not ask you for any wage; my wage comes from the Lord of the universe.

128. "You build on every hill a mansion for vanity's sake.

129. "You set up buildings as if you last forever.

130. "And when you strike, you strike mercilessly.

131. "You shall reverence **GOD** and obey me.

132. "Reverence the One who provided you with all the things you know.

133. "He provided you with livestock and children.

134. "And gardens and springs.

135. "I fear for you the retribution of an awesome day."

136. They said, "It is the same whether you preach, or not preach.

137. "That affliction was limited to our ancestors.

138. "No retribution will ever befall us."

139. They thus disbelieved and, consequently, we annihilated them. This should be a lesson, but most people are not believers.

140. Most assuredly, your Lord is the Almighty, Most Merciful.

Sãleh

141. Thamoud disbelieved the messengers.

142. Their brother Sãleh said to them, "Would you not be righteous?

143. "I am an honest messenger to you.

144. "You shall reverence **GOD**, and obey me.

145. "I do not ask you for any wage; my wage comes only from the Lord of the universe.

146. "Do you suppose you will be left forever, secure in this state?

147. "You enjoy gardens and springs.

148. "And crops and date palms with delicious fruits.

149. "You carve out of the mountains luxurious mansions.

150. "You shall reverence **GOD**, and obey me.

151. "Do not obey the transgressors.

152. "Who commit evil, not good works."

153. They said, "You are bewitched.

154. "You are no more than a human like us. Produce a miracle, if you are truthful."

155. He said, "Here is a camel that will drink only on a day that is assigned to her; a day that is different from your specified days of drinking.

156. "Do not touch her with any harm, lest you incur retribution on an awesome day."

157. They slaughtered her, and thus incurred sorrow.

158. The retribution overwhelmed them. This should be a lesson, but most people are not believers.

159. Most assuredly, your Lord is the Almighty, Most Merciful.

Lot

160. The people of Lot disbelieved the messengers.

161. Their brother Lot said to them, "Would you not be righteous?

162. "I am an honest messenger to you.

163. "You shall reverence **GOD**, and obey me.

164. "I do not ask you for any wage; my wage comes only from the Lord of the universe.

165. "Do you have sex with the males, of all the people?

166. "You forsake the wives that your Lord has created for you! Indeed, you are transgressing people."

167. They said, "Unless you refrain, O Lot, you will be banished."

168. He said, "I deplore your actions."

169. "My Lord, save me and my family from their works."

170. We saved him and all his family.

171. But not the old woman; she was doomed.

172. We then destroyed the others.

173. We showered them with a miserable shower; what a terrible shower for those who had been warned!

174. This should be a lesson, but most people are not believers.

175. Most assuredly, your Lord is the Almighty, Most Merciful.

Shu'aib

176. The People of the Woods disbelieved the messengers.

177. Shu'aib said to them, "Would you not be righteous?

178. "I am an honest messenger to you.

179. "You shall reverence **GOD**, and obey me.

180. "I do not ask you for any wage; my wage comes only from the Lord of the universe.

181. "You shall give full measure when you trade; do not cheat.

182. "You shall weigh with an equitable scale.

183. "Do not cheat the people out of their rights, and do not roam the earth corruptingly.

184. "Reverence the One who created you and the previous generations."

185. They said, "You are bewitched.

186. "You are no more than a human being like us. In fact, we think you are a liar.

187. "Let masses from the sky fall on us, if you are truthful."

188. He said, "My Lord is the One who knows everything you do."

189. They disbelieved him and, consequently, they incurred the retribution of the Day of the Canopy. It was the retribution of an awesome day.

190. This should be a lesson, but most people are not believers.

191. Most assuredly, your Lord is the Almighty, Most Merciful.

The Quran

192. This is a revelation from the Lord of the universe.

193. The Honest Spirit (*Gabriel*) came down with it.

194. To reveal it into your heart, that you may be one of the warners.

195. In a perfect Arabic tongue.

196. It has been prophesied in the books of previous generations.

197. Is it not a sufficient sign for them that it was known to the scholars among the Children of Israel?

The Quran Must Be Translated

198. If we revealed this to people who do not know Arabic.

199. And had him recite it (*in Arabic*), they could not possibly believe in it.

200. We thus render it (*like a foreign language*) in the hearts of the guilty.

201. Thus, they cannot believe in it; not until they see the painful retribution.

202. It will come to them suddenly, when they least expect it.

203. They will then say, "Can we have a respite?"

204. Did they not challenge our retribution?

205. As you see, we allowed them to enjoy for years.

206. Then the retribution came to them, just as promised.

207. Their vast resources did not help them in the least.

208. We never annihilate any community without sending warners.

209. Therefore, this is a reminder, for we are never unjust.

False Messengers
Incapable of Preaching
the Worship of God ALONE*

210. The devils can never reveal this.

211. They neither would, nor could.

212. For they are prevented from hearing.

213. Therefore, do not idolize beside **GOD** any other god, lest you incur the retribution.

God's Messenger of the Covenant*

214. You shall preach to the people who are closest to you.

215. And lower your wing for the believers who follow you.

216. If they disobey you, then say, "I disown what you do."

217. And put your trust in the Almighty, Most Merciful.

218. Who sees you when you meditate during the night.

219. And your frequent prostrations.

220. He is the Hearer, the Omniscient.

221. Shall I inform you upon whom the devils descend?

222. They descend upon every guilty fabricator.

223. They pretend to listen, but most of them are liars.

224. As for the poets, they are followed only by the strayers.

225. Do you not see that their loyalty shifts according to the situation?

226. And that they say what they do not do?

227. Exempted are those who believe, lead a righteous life, commemorate **GOD** frequently, and stand up for their rights. Surely, the transgressors will find out what their ultimate destiny is.

◆◆◆

Sura 27: The Ant (Al-Naml)

In the name of God,
Most Gracious, Most Merciful

1. T. S.* These (*letters*) constitute proofs of the Quran; a profound scripture.

2. A beacon, and good news, for the believers.

3. Who observe the Contact Prayers (*Salat*), give the obligatory charity (*Zakat*), and they are, with regard to the Hereafter, absolutely certain.

4. Those who do not believe in the Hereafter, we adorn their works in their eyes. Thus, they continue to blunder.

5. It is these who incur the worst retribution, and in the Hereafter, they will be the worst losers.

---

*26:210 A false messenger is a messenger of Satan, for he is the fabricator of the most horrendous lie. Such a messenger can never denounce idolatry, or preach the worship of God ALONE.

*26:214-223 These verses refer to God's Messenger of the Covenant: the sum of the gematrical value of "Rashad Khalifa" (1230), plus the verse number (214) is 1230 + 214 = 1444 = 19x76 = 19x19x4, and the sum of the verse numbers from 214 through 223 is 2185 = 19x115 (Appendix 1).

*27:1 See Appendix 1 for the meaning of these Quranic initials.

---

6. Surely, you are receiving the Quran from a Most Wise, Omniscient.

Moses

7. Recall that Moses said to his family, "I see a fire; let me bring you news therefrom, or a torch to warm you."

8. When he came to it, he was called: "Blessed is the One (*who is speaking from*) within the fire, and those around it." Glory be to **GOD**, Lord of the universe.

9. "O Moses, this is Me, **GOD**, the Almighty, Most Wise.

10. "Throw down your staff." When he saw it moving like a demon, he turned around and fled. "O Moses, do not be afraid. My messengers shall not fear.

11. "Except those who commit a transgression, then substitute righteousness after sinning; I am Forgiving, Most Merciful.

12. "Put your hand in your pocket; it will come out white, without a blemish. These are among nine miracles to Pharaoh and his people, for they are wicked people."

13. When our miracles were presented to them, clear and profound, they said, "This is obviously magic."

14. They rejected them and were utterly convinced of their wrong ways, due to their arrogance. Note the consequences for the evildoers.

David and Solomon

15. We endowed David and Solomon with knowledge, and they said,

"Praise **GOD** for blessing us more than many of His believing servants."

16. Solomon was David's heir. He said, "O people, we have been endowed with understanding the language of the birds, and all kinds of things have been bestowed upon us. This is indeed a real blessing."

17. Mobilized in the service of Solomon were his obedient soldiers of jinns and humans, as well as the birds; all at his disposal.

18. When they approached the valley of the ants, one ant said, "O you ants, go into your homes, lest you get crushed by Solomon and his soldiers, without perceiving."*

19. He smiled and laughed at her statement,* and said, "My Lord, direct me to be appreciative of the blessings You have bestowed upon me and my parents, and to do the righteous works that please You. Admit me by Your mercy into the company of Your righteous servants."

20. He inspected the birds, and noted: "Why do I not see the hoopoe? Why is he missing?

21. "I will punish him severely or sacrifice him, unless he gives me a good excuse."

22. He did not wait for long. (*The hoopoe*) said, "I have news that you do not have. I have brought to you from Sheba, some important information.

27:18-19 The more unusual the events in a given sura, the stronger the mathematical evidence supporting them. This helps assure us that such strange phenomena are indicative of God's power. This sura's initials, T.S., constitute a complex part of the mathematical miracles related to the Quranic initials. The unusual birth and miracles of Jesus are in Sura 19, which is prefixed with five Quranic Initials. See Appendix 1 for the details.

23. "I found a woman ruling them, who is blessed with everything, and possesses a tremendous palace.

24. "I found her and her people prostrating before the sun, instead of **GOD**. The devil has adorned their works in their eyes, and has repulsed them from the path; consequently, they are not guided."

25. They should have been prostrating before **GOD**, the One who manifests all the mysteries in the heavens and the earth, and the One who knows everything you conceal and everything you declare.

26. **GOD**: there is no other god beside Him; the Lord with the great dominion.

27. (*Solomon*) said, "We will see if you told the truth, or if you are a liar.

28. "Take this letter from me, give it to them, then watch for their response."

Back in Sheba

29. She said, "O my advisers, I have received an honorable letter.

30. "It is from Solomon, and it is, '**In the name of GOD, Most Gracious, Most Merciful.**'*

31. "Proclaiming: 'Do not be arrogant; come to me as submitters.' "

32. She said, "O my advisers, counsel me in this matter. I am not deciding anything until you advise me."

33. They said, "We possess the power, we possess the fighting skills, and the ultimate command is in your hand. You decide what to do."

34. She said, "The kings corrupt any land they invade, and subjugate its dignified people. This is what they usually do.

35. "I am sending a gift to them; let us see what the messengers come back with."

36. When the hoopoe returned to Solomon (*he told him the news*), and he responded (*to Sheba's people*): "Are you giving me money? What **GOD** has given me is far better than what He has given you. You are the ones to rejoice in such gifts."

37. (*To the hoopoe, he said,*) "Go back to them (*and let them know that*) we will come to them with forces they cannot imagine. We will evict them, humiliated and debased."

Faster Than the Speed of Light

38. He said, "O you elders, which of you can bring me her mansion, before they arrive here as submitters?"

39. One afrit from the jinns said, "I can bring it to you before you stand up. I am powerful enough to do this."

40. The one who possessed knowledge from the book said, "I can bring it to you in the blink of your eye." When he saw it settled in front of him, he said, "This is a blessing from my Lord, whereby He tests me, to show whether I am appreciative or unappreciative. Whoever is appreciative is appreciative for his own good, and if one turns unappreciative, then my Lord is in no need for him, Most Honorable."

27:30 The 'Basmalah' included in this verse compensates for the 'Basmalah' that is missing from Sura 9, 19 suras earlier. This restores the total occurrence of 'Basmalah' to 114, 19x6. See Appendix 29 for details of a vast and profound miracle attached to this 'Basmalah.'

---

41. He said, "Remodel her mansion for her. Let us see if she will be guided, or continue with the misguided."

42. When she arrived, she was asked, "Does your mansion look like this?" She said, "It seems that this is it." (*Solomon said,*) "We knew beforehand what she was going to do, and we were already submitters."

43. She had been diverted by worshiping idols instead of **GOD**; she belonged to disbelieving people.

44. She was told, "Go inside the palace." When she saw its interior, she thought it was a pool of water, and she (*pulled up her dress,*) exposing her legs. He said, "This interior is now paved with crystal." She said, "My Lord, I have wronged my soul. I now submit with Solomon to **GOD**, Lord of the universe."

Sãleh

45. We have sent to Thamoud their brother Sãleh, saying, "You shall worship **GOD**." But they turned into two feuding factions.

46. He said, "O my people, why do you hasten to commit evil instead of good works? If only you implore **GOD** for forgiveness, you may attain mercy."

47. They said, "We consider you a bad omen for us, you and those who joined you." He said, "Your omen is fully controlled by **GOD**. Indeed, you are deviant people."

48. There were nine gangsters in the city who were wicked, and never did anything good.

49. They said, "Let us swear by **GOD** that we kill him and his people, then tell his tribe, 'We know nothing about their death. We are truthful.' "

God Protects The Believers

50. They plotted and schemed, but we also plotted and schemed, while they did not perceive.

51. Note the consequences of their plotting; we annihilated them and all their people.

52. Here are their homes utterly ruined, because of their transgression. This should be a lesson for people who know.

53. We save those who believe and lead a righteous life.

Lot

54. Lot said to his people, "How could you commit such an abomination, publicly, while you see?

55. "You practice sex with the men, lustfully, instead of the women. Indeed, you are ignorant people."

56. The only response from his people was their saying, "Banish Lot's family from your town; they are people who wish to be pure."

57. Consequently, we saved him and his family, except his wife; we counted her among the doomed.

58. We showered them with a certain shower. It was a miserable shower upon people who had been warned.

Make No Distinction Among God's Messengers

59. Say, "Praise be to **GOD** and peace be upon His servants whom He chose. Is **GOD** better, or the idols some people set up?"

God ALONE Worthy of Worship

60. Who is the One who created the heavens and the earth? Who is the One who sends down to you from the sky water, whereby we produce gardens full of beauty—you could not possibly manufacture its trees? Is it another god with **GOD**? Indeed, they are people who have deviated.

Jesus, Mary, Muhammad, the Saints, etc. Never Participated

61. Who is the One who made the earth habitable, caused rivers to run through it, placed on it mountains, and created a barrier between the two waters? Is it another god with **GOD**? Indeed, most of them do not know.

62. Who is the One who rescues those who become desperate and call upon Him, relieves adversity, and makes you inheritors of the earth? Is it another god with **GOD**? Rarely do you take heed.

63. Who is the One who guides you in the darkness of land and sea? Who is the One who sends the winds with good news, signaling His mercy? Is it another god with **GOD**? Most exalted is **GOD**, above having any partner.

64. Who is the One who initiates the creation, then repeats it? Who is the One who provides for you from the heaven and the earth? Is it another god with **GOD**? Say, "Show me your proof, if you are truthful."

65. Say, "No one in the heavens and the earth knows the future except **GOD**. They do not even perceive how or when they will be resurrected."

Believing in the Hereafter: Great Obstacle for Most People

66. In fact, their knowledge concerning the Hereafter is confused. In fact, they harbor doubts about it. In fact, they are totally heedless thereof.

67. Those who disbelieved said, "After we turn into dust, and also our parents, do we get brought out?

68. "We have been given the same promise in the past. These are nothing but tales from the past."

69. Say, "Roam the earth and note the consequences for the guilty."

70. Do not grieve over them, and do not be annoyed by their scheming.

71. They say, "When will that promise come to pass, if you are truthful?"

72. Say, "You are already suffering some of the retribution you challenge."

73. Your Lord is full of grace towards the people, but most of them are unappreciative.

74. Your Lord fully knows what their chests hide, and what they declare.

75. There is nothing in the heavens and the earth that is hidden (*from God*); everything is in a profound record.

76. This Quran settles many issues for the Children of Israel; issues that they are still disputing.

77. And most assuredly, it is a guide and mercy for the believers.

78. Your Lord is the One who judges among them in accordance with His rules. He is the Almighty, the Omniscient.

79. Therefore, put your trust in **GOD**; you are following the manifest truth.

80. You cannot make the dead, nor the deaf, hear the call, if they turn away.

81. Nor can you guide the blind out of their straying. The only ones who will hear you are those who believe in our revelations, and decide to be submitters.

The Computer
Is The Creature*

82. At the right time, we will produce for them a creature, made of earthly materials, declaring that the people are not certain about our revelations.

83. The day will come when we summon from every community some of those who did not believe in our proofs, forcibly.

Study the
Quran's Mathematical Code

84. When they arrive, He will say, "You have rejected My revelations, before acquiring knowledge about them. Is this not what you did?"

85. They will incur the requital for their wickedness; they will say nothing.

86. Have they not seen that we made the night for their rest, and the day lighted? These should be sufficient proofs for people who believe.

87. On the day when the horn is blown, everyone in the heavens and the earth will be horrified, except those chosen by **GOD**. All will come before Him, forcibly.

Earth's Movement:
A Scientific Miracle

88. When you look at the mountains, you think that they are standing still. But they are moving, like the clouds. Such is the manufacture of **GOD**, who perfected everything. He is fully Cognizant of everything you do.

The Day of Judgment

89. Those who bring good works (*in their records*) will receive far better rewards, and they will be perfectly secure from the horrors of that day.

90. As for those who bring evil works, they will be forced into Hell. Do you not get requited for what you did?

91. I am simply commanded to worship the Lord of this town—He has made it a safe sanctuary—and He possesses all things. I am commanded to be a submitter.

92. And to recite the Quran. Whoever is guided is guided for his own good, and if they go astray, then say, "I am simply a warner."

93. And say, "Praise be to **GOD**; He will show you His proofs, until you recognize them. Your Lord is never unaware of anything you do."

◆ ◆ ◆ ◆

Sura 28: History (Al-Qasas)

In the name of God,
Most Gracious, Most Merciful

1. T.S.M.*

27:82 (2 + 7 + 8 + 2 = 19) The computer was required to unveil the Quran's mathematical miracle, and it proved that most people have discarded God's message (see Appendices 1 & 19).

28:1 See Appendix 1 for details of the Quran's miraculous mathematical code, and the meaning or significance of these Quranic Initials.

2. These (*letters*) constitute proofs of this profound book.

3. We recite to you herein some history of Moses and Pharaoh, truthfully, for the benefit of people who believe.

4. Pharaoh turned into a tyrant on earth, and discriminated against some people. He persecuted a helpless group of them, slaughtering their sons, while sparing their daughters. He was indeed wicked.

God Compensates the Oppressed

5. We willed to compensate those who were oppressed on earth, and to turn them into leaders, and make them the inheritors.

6. And to establish them on earth, and to give Pharaoh, Hamaan, and their troops a taste of their own medicine.

Confidence in God

7. We inspired Moses' mother: "Nurse him, and when you fear for his life, throw him into the river without fear or grief. We will return him to you, and will make him one of the messengers."

8. Pharaoh's family picked him up, only to have him lead the opposition and to be a source of grief for them. That is because Pharaoh, Hamaan, and their troops were transgressors.

Inside the Lion's Den

9. Pharaoh's wife said, "This can be a joyous find for me and you. Do not kill him, for he may be of some benefit for us, or we may adopt him to be our son." They had no idea.

10. The mind of Moses' mother was growing so anxious that she almost gave away his identity. But we strengthened her heart, to make her a believer.

11. She said to his sister, "Trace his path." She watched him from afar, while they did not perceive.

The Infant Returned to His Mother

12. We forbade him from accepting all the nursing mothers. (*His sister*) then said, "I can show you a family that can raise him for you, and take good care of him."

13. Thus, we restored him to his mother, in order to please her, remove her worries, and to let her know that **GOD**'s promise is the truth. However, most of them do not know.

14. When he reached maturity and strength, we endowed him with wisdom and knowledge. We thus reward the righteous.

Moses Commits Manslaughter

15. Once he entered the city unexpectedly, without being recognized by the people. He found two men fighting; one was (*a Hebrew*) from his people, and the other was (*an Egyptian*) from his enemies. The one from his people called on him for help against his enemy. Moses punched him, killing him. He said, "This is the work of the devil; he is a real enemy, and a profound misleader."

16. He said, "My Lord, I have wronged my soul. Please forgive me," and He forgave him. He is the Forgiver, Most Merciful.

17. He said, "My Lord, in return for Your blessings upon me, I will never be a supporter of the guilty ones."

18. In the morning, he was in the city, afraid and watchful. The one who sought his help yesterday, asked for his help again. Moses said to him, "You are really a troublemaker."

Moses' Crime Exposed

19. Before he attempted to strike their common enemy, he said, "O Moses, do you want to kill me, as you killed the other man yesterday? Obviously, you wish to be a tyrant on earth; you do not wish to be righteous."

20. A man came running from the other side of the city, saying, "O Moses, the people are plotting to kill you. You better leave immediately. I am giving you good advice."

21. He fled the city, afraid and watchful. He said, "My Lord, save me from the oppressive people."

In Midyan

22. As he traveled towards Midyan, he said, "May my Lord guide me in the right path."

23. When he reached Midyan's water, he found a crowd of people watering, and noticed two women waiting on the side. He said, "What is it that you need?" They said, "We are not able to water, until the crowd disperses, and our father is an old man."

24. He watered for them, then turned to the shade, saying, "My Lord, whatever provision you send to me, I am in dire need for it."

25. Soon, one of the two women approached him, shyly, and said, "My father invites you to pay you for watering for us." When he met him, and told him his story, he said, "Have no fear. You have been saved from the oppressive people."

Moses Marries

26. One of the two women said, "O my father, hire him. He is the best one to hire, for he is strong and honest."

27. He said, "I wish to offer one of my two daughters for you to marry, in return for working for me for eight pilgrimages; if you make them ten, it will be voluntary on your part. I do not wish to make this matter too difficult for you. You will find me, **GOD** willing, righteous."

28. He said, "It is an agreement between me and you. Whichever period I fulfill, you will not be averse to either one. **GOD** is the guarantor of what we said."

Back to Egypt

29. When he had fulfilled his obligation, he traveled with his family (*towards Egypt*), He saw from the slope of Mount Sinai a fire. He said to his family, "Stay here. I have seen a fire. Maybe I can bring to you news, or a portion of the fire to warm you."

Moses Appointed

30. When he reached it, he was called from the edge of the right side of the valley, in the blessed spot where the burning bush was located: "O Moses, this is Me. **GOD**; Lord of the universe."

31. "Throw down your staff." When he saw it moving like a demon, he turned around and fled. "O Moses, come back; do not be afraid. You are perfectly safe.

32. "Put your hand into your pocket; it will come out white without a blemish. Fold your wings and settle down from your fear. These are two proofs from your Lord, to be shown to Pharaoh and his elders; they have been wicked people."

33. He said, "My Lord, I killed one of them, and I fear lest they kill me.

34. "Also, my brother Aaron is more eloquent than I. Send him with me as a helper to confirm and strengthen me. I fear lest they disbelieve me."

35. He said, "We will strengthen you with your brother, and we will provide you both with manifest authority. Thus, they will not be able to touch either one of you. With our miracles, the two of you, together with those who follow you, will be the victors."

Pharaoh's Arrogance

36. When Moses went to them with our proofs, clear and profound, they said, "This is fabricated magic. We have never heard of this from our ancient ancestors."

37. Moses said, "My Lord knows best who brought the guidance from Him, and who will be the ultimate victors. Surely, the transgressors never succeed."

38. Pharaoh said, "O you elders, I have not known of any god for you other than me. Therefore, fire the adobe, O Hamaan, in order to build a tower, that I may take a look at the god of Moses. I am sure that he is a liar."

39. Thus, he and his troops continued to commit arrogance on earth, without any right, and thought that they would not be returned to us.

40. Consequently, we punished him and his troops, by throwing them into the sea. Note the consequences for the transgressors.

41. We made them imams who led their people to Hell. Furthermore, on the Day of Resurrection, they will have no help.

42. They incurred in this life condemnation, and on the Day of Resurrection they will be despised.

The Book of Moses*

43. We gave Moses the scripture—after having annihilated the previous generations, and after setting the examples through them—to provide enlightenment for the people, and guidance, and mercy, that they may take heed.

Addressing God's Messenger of the Covenant

44. You were not present on the slope of the western mount, when we issued the command to Moses; you were not a witness.*

45. But we established many generations, and, because of the length of time, (*they deviated*). Nor were you among the people of Midyan, reciting our revelations to them. But we did send messengers.

---

*28:43 *The Torah is the collection of all the scriptures revealed to all the prophets of Israel, including the book of Moses. The Quran consistently states that Moses was given a book, or "the Statute Book." Nowhere in the Quran do we see that Moses was given "the Torah." Today's Old Testament, therefore, is the Torah (see 3:50, 5:46).*

*28:44 *The name of this messenger is confirmed mathematically: by placing the gematrical value of "Rashad Khalifa" (1230) next to the verse number (44), we get 123044 = 19x6476.*

46. Nor were you on the slope of Mount Sinai when we called (*Moses*). But it is mercy from your Lord, (*towards the people,*) in order to warn people who received no warner before you, that they may take heed.

No Excuse

47. Thus, they cannot say, when a disaster strikes them as a consequence of their own deeds, "Our Lord, had You sent a messenger to us, we would have followed Your revelations, and would have been believers."

The Torah and The Quran

48. Now that the truth has come to them from us, they said, "If only we could be given what was given to Moses!" Did they not disbelieve in what was given to Moses in the past? They said, "Both (*scriptures*) are works of magic that copied one another." They also said, "We are disbelievers in both of them."

49. Say, "Then produce a scripture from **GOD** with better guidance than the two, so I can follow it, if you are truthful."

God Sends His Teachings to us Through His Messengers

50. If they fail to respond to you, then know that they follow only their own opinions. Who is farther astray than those who follow their own opinions, without guidance from **GOD**? **GOD** does not guide such wicked people.

All True Believers Accept the Quran

51. We have delivered the message to them, that they may take heed.

52. Those whom we blessed with the previous scriptures will believe in this.

53. When it is recited to them, they will say, "We believe in it. This is the truth from our Lord. Even before we heard of it, we were submitters."

Twice the Reward for Christians & Jews Who Recognize the Truth

54. To these we grant twice the reward, because they steadfastly persevere. They counter evil works with good works, and from our provisions to them, they give.

55. When they come across vain talk, they disregard it and say, "We are responsible for our deeds, and you are responsible for your deeds. Peace be upon you. We do not wish to behave like the ignorant ones."

Only God Guides

56. You cannot guide the ones you love. **GOD** is the only One who guides in accordance with His will, and in accordance with His knowledge of those who deserve the guidance.

57. They said, "If we follow your guidance, we will suffer persecution." Did we not establish for them a Sacred Sanctuary, to which all kinds of fruits are offered, as a provision from us? Indeed, most of them do not know.

58. Many a community we annihilated for turning unappreciative of their lives. Consequently, here are their homes, nothing but uninhabited ruins after them, except a few. We were the inheritors.

59. For your Lord never annihilates any community without sending a messenger in the midst thereof, to recite our revelations to them. We never annihilate any community, unless its people are wicked.

60. Everything that is given to you is only the material of this life, and its vanity. What is with **GOD** is far better, and everlasting. Do you not understand?

61. Is one whom we promised a good promise that will surely come to pass, equal to one whom we provide with the temporary materials of this life, then suffers eternal doom on the Day of Resurrection?

The Idols Disown Their Idolizers

62. The day will come when He calls upon them, saying, "Where are those idols you had set up beside Me?"

63. Those who incurred the judgment will say, "Our Lord, these are the ones we misled; we misled them only because we ourselves had gone astray. We now devote ourselves totally to You. They were not really worshiping us."

64. It will be said, "Call upon your idols (*to help you*)." They will call upon them, but they will not respond. They will suffer the retribution, and wish that they were guided!

Our Response to the Messengers

65. On that day, He will ask everyone, "How did you respond to the messengers?"

66. They will be so stunned by the facts on that day, they will be speechless.

67. As for those who repent, believe, and lead a righteous life, they will end up with the winners.

68. Your Lord is the One who creates whatever He wills, and chooses; no one else does any choosing. Glory be to **GOD**, the Most Exalted. He is far above needing partners.

69. Your Lord knows the innermost thoughts hidden in their chests, as well as everything they declare.

70. He is the one **GOD**; there is no other god beside Him. To Him belongs all praise in this first life, and in the Hereafter. All judgment belongs with Him, and to Him you will be returned.

God's Blessings

71. Say, "What if **GOD** made the night perpetual, until the Day of Resurrection? Which god, other than **GOD**, can provide you with light? Do you not hear?"

72. Say, "What if **GOD** made the daylight perpetual, until the Day of Resurrection? Which god, other than **GOD**, can provide you with a night for your rest? Do you not see?"

73. It is mercy from Him that He created for you the night and the day in order to rest (*during the night*), then seek His provisions (*during the day*), that you may be appreciative.

Idols Possess No Power

74. The day will come when He asks them, "Where are the idols you had fabricated to rank with Me?"

75. We will select from every community a witness, then say, "Present your proof." They will realize then that all truth belongs with **GOD**, while the idols they had fabricated will abandon them.

Qãroon

76. Qãroon (*the slave driver*) was one of Moses' people who betrayed them and oppressed them. We gave him so many treasures that the keys thereof were almost too heavy for the strongest band. His people said to him, "Do not be so arrogant; **GOD** does not love those who are arrogant.

77. "Use the provisions bestowed upon you by **GOD** to seek the abode of the Hereafter, without neglecting your share in this world. Be charitable, as **GOD** has been charitable towards you. Do not keep on corrupting the earth. **GOD** does not love the corruptors."

78. He said, "I attained all this because of my own cleverness." Did he not realize that **GOD** had annihilated before him generations that were much stronger than he, and greater in number? The (*annihilated*) transgressors were not asked about their crimes.

79. One day, he came out to his people in full splendor. Those who preferred this worldly life said, "Oh, we wish that we possess what Qãroon has attained. Indeed, he is very fortunate."

The Real Wealth

80. As for those who were blessed with knowledge, they said, "Woe to you, **GOD**'s recompense is far better for those who believe and lead a righteous life." None attains this except the steadfast.

The Tyrants' Inevitable Fate

81. We then caused the earth to swallow him and his mansion. No army could have helped him against **GOD**; he was not destined to be a winner.

82. Those who were envious of him the day before said, "Now we realize that **GOD** is the One who provides for whomever He chooses from among His servants, and withholds. If it were not for **GOD**'s grace towards us, He could have caused the earth to swallow us too. We now realize that the disbelievers never succeed."

The Ultimate Winners

83. We reserve the abode of the Hereafter for those who do not seek exaltation on earth, nor corruption. The ultimate victory belongs to the righteous.

84. Whoever works righteousness receives a far better reward. As for those who commit sins, the retribution for their sins is precisely equivalent to their works.

85. Surely, the One who decreed the Quran for you will summon you to a predetermined appointment. Say, "My Lord is fully aware of those who uphold the guidance, and those who have gone astray."

86. You never expected this scripture to come your way; but this is a mercy from your Lord. Therefore, you shall not side with the disbelievers.

87. Nor shall you be diverted from **GOD**'s revelations, after they have come to you, and invite the others to your Lord. And do not ever fall into idol worship.

88. You shall not worship beside **GOD** any other god. There is no other god beside Him. Everything perishes except His presence. To Him belongs all sovereignty, and to Him you will be returned.

◆◆◆◆

Sura 29: The Spider (Al-'Ankaboot)

In the name of God,
Most Gracious, Most Merciful

1. A.L.M.*

The Test is Mandatory

2. Do the people think that they will be left to say, "We believe," without being put to the test?

3. We have tested those before them, for **GOD** must distinguish those who are truthful, and He must expose the liars.

4. Do those who commit sins think that they can ever fool us? Wrong indeed is their judgment.

5. Anyone hoping to meet **GOD,** (*should know that*) such a meeting with **GOD** will most assuredly come to pass. He is the Hearer, the Omniscient.

6. Those who strive, strive for their own good. **GOD** is in no need of anyone.

7. Those who believe and lead a righteous life, we will certainly remit their sins, and will certainly reward them generously for their righteous works.

You Shall Honor Your Parents

8. We enjoined the human being to honor his parents. But if they try to force you to set up idols beside Me, do not obey them. To Me is your ultimate return, then I will inform you of everything you had done.

9. Those who believe and lead a righteous life, we will certainly admit them with the righteous.

Fair Weather Friends

10. Among the people there are those who say, "We believe in **GOD,**" but as soon as they suffer any hardship because of **GOD,** they equate the people's persecution with **GOD**'s retribution. But if blessings from your Lord come your way, they say, "We were with you." Is **GOD** not fully aware of the people's innermost thoughts?

11. **GOD** will most certainly distinguish those who believe, and He will most certainly expose the hypocrites.

12. Those who disbelieved said to those who believed, "If you follow our way, we will be responsible for your sins." Not true; they cannot bear any of their sins. They are liars.

13. In fact, they will carry their own sins, in addition to loads of other people's sins for which they were responsible. Most certainly, they will be asked on the Day of Resurrection about their false claims.

Noah

14. We sent Noah to his people, and he stayed with them one thousand years, less fifty.* Subsequently, they incurred the flood because of their transgressions.

29:1 See Appendix 1 for details of the Quran's mathematical composition, and the meaning of these previously mysterious Quranic Initials.

29:14 Since the Quran's miracle is mathematical, the numbers especially constitute an important part of the 19-based code. Thus, the numbers mentioned in the Quran add up to 162146, or 19x8534 (see Appendix 1 for the details).

15. We saved him and those who accompanied him in the ark, and we set it up as a lesson for all the people.

Abraham

16. Abraham said to his people, "You shall worship **GOD**, and reverence Him. This is better for you, if you only knew.

17. "What you worship instead of **GOD** are powerless idols; you have invented a lie."

God: The Only Source of Provisions
The idols you worship beside **GOD** do not possess any provisions for you. Therefore, you shall seek provisions only from **GOD**. You shall worship Him alone, and be appreciative of Him; to Him is your ultimate return.

18. If you disbelieve, generations before you have also disbelieved. The sole function of the messenger is to deliver *(the message)*.

Study the Origin of Life*

19. Have they not seen how **GOD** initiates the creation, then repeats it? This is easy for **GOD** to do.

20. Say, "Roam the earth and find out the origin of life."* For **GOD** will thus initiate the creation in the Hereafter. **GOD** is Omnipotent.

21. He condemns to retribution whomever He wills, and showers His mercy upon whomever He wills. Ultimately, to Him you will be turned over.

22. None of you can escape from these facts, on earth or in the heaven, and you have none beside **GOD** as a Lord and Master.

23. Those who disbelieve in **GOD**'s revelations, and in meeting Him, have despaired from My mercy. They have incurred a painful retribution.

Back to Abraham

24. The only response from his people was their saying, "Kill him, or burn him." But **GOD** saved him from the fire. This should provide lessons for people who believe.

Social Pressure: A Profound Disaster

25. He said, "You worship beside **GOD** powerless idols due to peer pressure, just to preserve some friendship among you in this worldly life. But then, on the Day of Resurrection, you will disown one another, and curse one another. Your destiny is Hell, wherein you cannot help one another."

26. Lot believed with him and said, "I am emigrating to my Lord. He is the Almighty, the Most Wise."

27. We granted him Isaac and Jacob, we assigned to his descendants prophethood and the scriptures, we endowed him with his due recompense in this life, and in the Hereafter he will surely be with the righteous.

Lot

28. Lot said to his people, "You commit such an abomination, no one in the world has ever done it before you.

29. "You practice sex with the men, you commit highway robbery, and you allow all kinds of vice in your society." The only response from his people was to say, "Bring to us **GOD**'s retribution, if you are truthful."

---

*29:19-20 We learn from the Quran that evolution is a divinely guided process. See Appendix 31 for the details.

30. He said, "My Lord, grant me victory over these wicked people."

Angels Visit Abraham and Lot

31. When our messengers went to Abraham with good news (*about Isaac's birth*), they also said, "We are on our way to annihilate the people of that town (*Sodom*). For its people have been wicked."

32. He said, "But Lot is living there." They said, "We are fully aware of everyone who lives in it. We will of course save him and his family, except his wife; she is doomed."

33. When our messengers arrived at Lot's place, they were mistreated, and he was embarrassed by their presence. But they said, "Have no fear, and do not worry. We will save you and your family, except your wife; she is doomed.

34. "We will pour upon the people of this town a disaster from the sky, as a consequence of their wickedness."

35. We left standing some of their ruins, to serve as a profound lesson for people who understand.

Shu'aib

36. To Midyan we sent their brother Shu'aib. He said, "O my people, you shall worship **GOD** and seek the Last Day, and do not roam the earth corruptingly."

37. They disbelieved him and, consequently, the earthquake annihilated them; they were left dead in their homes by morning.

38. Similarly, 'Ãd and Thamoud (*were annihilated*). This is made manifest to you through their ruins. The devil had adorned their works in their eyes, and had diverted them from the path, even though they had eyes.

God's Immutable System

39. Also Qãroon, Pharaoh, and Hã-mãn; Moses went to them with clear signs. But they continued to commit tyranny on earth. Consequently, they could not evade (*the retribution*).

40. All those disbelievers were doomed as a consequence of their sins. Some of them we annihilated by violent winds, some were annihilated by the quake, some we caused the earth to swallow, and some we drowned. **GOD** is not the One who wronged them; it is they who wronged their own souls.

The Spider

41. The allegory of those who accept other masters beside **GOD** is that of the spider and her home; the flimsiest of all homes is the home of the spider, if they only knew.*

42. **GOD** knows full well that whatever they worship beside Him are really nothing. He is the Almighty, the Most Wise.

43. We cite these examples for the people, and none appreciate them except the knowledgeable.*

44. **GOD** created the heavens and the earth, truthfully. This provides a sufficient proof for the believers.

29:41-43 It takes a knowledgeable person to know that the Black Widow spider kills her mate. The use of the feminine reference to the spider in 29:41 is thus significant. This is in addition to the fact that the spider web is physically very flimsy.

The Contact Prayers (Salat)

45. You shall recite what is revealed to you of the scripture, and observe the Contact Prayers (*Salat*), for the Contact Prayers prohibit evil and vice. But the remembrance of **GOD** (*through Salat*) is the most important objective.* **GOD** knows everything you do.

One God/One Religion

46. Do not argue with the people of the scripture (*Jews, Christians, & Muslims*) except in the nicest possible manner—unless they transgress—and say, "We believe in what was revealed to us and in what was revealed to you, and our god and your god is one and the same; to Him we are submitters."

47. We have revealed to you this scripture, and those whom we blessed with the previous scripture will believe in it. Also, some of your people will believe in it. Indeed, those who disregard our revelations are the real disbelievers.

*Quran: Muhammad's Miracle**

48. You did not read the previous scriptures, nor did you write them with your hand. In that case, the rejectors would have had reason to harbor doubts.

49. In fact, these revelations are clear in the chests of those who possess knowledge. Only the wicked will disregard our revelations.

50. They said, "If only miracles* could come down to him from his Lord!" Say, "All miracles come only from **GOD**; I am no more than a manifest warner."

51. Is it not enough of a miracle* that we sent down to you this book, being recited to them? This is indeed a mercy and a reminder for people who believe.

52. Say, "**GOD** suffices as a witness between me and you. He knows everything in the heavens and the earth. Surely, those who believe in falsehood and disbelieve in **GOD** are the real losers."

They Are in Hell

53. They challenge you to bring the retribution! If it were not for a predetermined appointment, the retribution would have come to them immediately.* Certainly, it will come to them suddenly, when they least expect it.

54. They challenge you to bring retribution! Hell already surrounds the disbelievers.

29:45 Your god is whatever occupies your mind most of the time (see 20:14 & Appendix 27).

29:48-51 It was the will of the Most Wise to separate the Quran from its awesome mathematical miracle by 1400 years. Seeing how the Muslims en masse have idolized Muhammad, it is obvious that if the Quran's mathematical miracle were also revealed through Muhammad, many people would have worshiped him as God incarnate. As it is, God willed that the great miracle of the Quran (74:30-35) shall await the computer age, and to have it revealed through His Messenger of the Covenant (see Appendices 1, 2, & 26).

29:53 Anyone who dies before the age of 40 goes to Heaven, and not everyone deserves this. People sometimes lament the slowness of justice when a vicious criminal is not executed promptly. God knows who deserves Heaven (see 46:15 and Appendix 32).

---

55. The day will come when the retribution overwhelms them, from above them and from beneath their feet; He will say, "Taste the consequences of your works."

Immigrate in the Cause of God

56. O My servants who believed, My earth is spacious, so worship Me.

57. Every soul will taste death, then to us you will be ultimately returned.

58. Those who believe and lead a righteous life, we will surely settle them in Paradise, with mansions and flowing streams. Eternally they abide therein. What a beautiful reward for the workers.

59. They are the ones who steadfastly persevere, and trust in their Lord.

60. Many a creature that does not carry its provision, **GOD** provides for it, as well as for you. He is the Hearer, the Omniscient.

Most Believers Destined for Hell

61. If you ask them, "Who created the heavens and the earth, and put the sun and the moon in your service," they will say, "**GOD**." Why then did they deviate?

62. **GOD** is the One who increases the provision for whomever He chooses from among His creatures, and withholds it. **GOD** is fully aware of all things.

63. If you ask them, "Who sends down from the sky water, to revive dead land," they will say, "**GOD**." Say, "Praise **GOD**." Most of them do not understand.

Re-arrange Your Priorities

64. This worldly life is no more than vanity and play, while the abode of the Hereafter is the real life, if they only knew.

65. When they ride on a ship, they implore **GOD**, devoting their prayers to Him. But as soon as He saves them to the shore, they revert to idolatry.

66. Let them disbelieve in what we have given them, and let them enjoy temporarily; they will surely find out.

67. Have they not seen that we have established a Sacred Sanctuary that we made secure, while all around them the people are in constant danger? Would they still believe in falsehood, and reject **GOD**'s blessings?

68. Who is more evil than one who fabricates lies and attributes them to **GOD**, or rejects the truth when it comes to him? Is Hell not a just retribution for the disbelievers?

69. As for those who strive in our cause, we will surely guide them in our paths. Most assuredly, **GOD** is with the pious.

◆◆◆◆

Sura 30: Romans (Al-Room)

In the name of God,
Most Gracious, Most Merciful

1. A.L.M.*

2. Certainly, the Romans will be defeated.

3. In the nearest land. After their defeat, they will rise again and win.

30:1 See Appendix 1 for the detailed explanation of these previously mysterious initials.

4. Within several years. Such is **GOD**'s decision, both in the first prophecy, and the second. On that day, the believers shall rejoice

5. in **GOD**'s victory. He grants victory to whomever He wills. He is the Almighty, Most Merciful.

Preoccupation With the Wrong Life

6. Such is **GOD**'s promise—and **GOD** never breaks His promise—but most people do not know.

7. They care only about things of this world that are visible to them, while being totally oblivious to the Hereafter.

8. Why do they not reflect on themselves? **GOD** did not create the heav-ens and the earth, and everything between them, except for a specific purpose, and for a specific life span. However, most people, with regard to meeting their Lord, are disbe-lievers.

9. Have they not roamed the earth and noted the consequences for those who preceded them? They used to be more powerful, more prosperous, and more productive on earth. Their messengers went to them with clear signs. Consequently, **GOD** was not the One who wronged them, they are the ones who wronged their own souls.

10. The consequences for those who committed evil had to be evil. That is because they rejected **GOD**'s revelations, and ridiculed them.

Idol Worshipers Disown Their Idols

11. **GOD** is the One who initiates the creation and repeats it. Ultimately, you will be returned to Him.

12. On the Day when the Hour comes to pass, the guilty will be shocked.

13. Their idols will have no power to intercede on their behalf; on the contrary, they will disown their idols.

14. On the day when the Hour comes to pass, they will part company.

15. As for those who believe and lead a righteous life, they will be in Paradise, rejoicing.

16. As for those who disbelieve, and reject our revelations and the meeting of the Hereafter, they will last in the retribution forever.

Remember God, Always

17. Therefore, you shall glorify **GOD** when you retire at night, and when you rise in the morning.

18. All praise is due to Him in the heavens and the earth, throughout the evening, as well as in the middle of your day.

19. He produces the live from the dead, and produces the dead from the live, and He revives the land after it had died; you are similarly resurrected.

Marriage: A Divine Institution

20. Among His proofs is that He created you from dust, then you became reproducing humans.

21. Among His proofs is that He created for you spouses from among yourselves, in order to have tranquility and contentment with each other, and He placed in your hearts love and care towards your spouses. In this, there are sufficient proofs for people who think.

More Proofs

22. Among His proofs are the creation of the heavens and the earth, and the variations in your languages and your colors. In these, there are signs for the knowledgeable.

23. Among His proofs is your sleeping during the night or the day, and your working in pursuit of His provisions. In this, there are sufficient proofs for people who can hear.

24. Among His proofs is that He shows you the lightning as a source of fear, as well as hope, then He sends down from the sky water to revive a land that has been dead. In these, there are sufficient proofs for people who understand.

25. Among His proofs is that the heaven and the earth are standing at His disposal. Finally, when He calls you out of the earth, one call, you will immediately come out.

26. To Him belongs everyone in the heavens and the earth; all are subservient to Him.

27. And He is the One who initiates the creation, then repeats it; this is even easier for Him. To Him belongs the most sublime similitude, in the heavens and the earth, and He is the Almighty, Most Wise.

Absurdity of Idol Worship

28. He cites for you herein an example from among yourselves: Do you ever elevate your servants or subordinates to the level where they rival you, and to the point that you pay them as much allegiance as is being paid to you? We thus explain the revelations for people who understand.

29. Indeed, the transgressors have followed their own opinions, without knowledge. Who then can guide those who have been sent astray by **GOD**? No one can ever help them.

Monotheism: Natural Instinct*

30. Therefore, you shall devote yourself to the religion of strict monotheism. Such is the natural instinct placed into the people by **GOD**. Such creation of **GOD** will never change. This is the perfect religion, but most people do not know.

31. You shall submit to Him, reverence Him, observe the Contact Prayers (*Salat*), and—whatever you do—do not ever fall into idol worship.

Sectarianism Condemned

32. (*Do not fall in idol worship,*) like those who divide their religion into sects; each party rejoicing with what they have.

Bad Weather Friends

33. When adversity afflicts the people, they turn to their Lord, totally devoting themselves to Him. But then, as soon as He showers them with mercy, some of them revert to idol worship.*

34. Let them be unappreciative of what we have given them. Enjoy temporarily; you will surely find out.

---

*30:30 Recognizing God ALONE as our Lord and Master is a natural instinct. We are born into this world with such an instinct. See 7:172-173 and Appendix 7.

*30:33 A common example is the classified advertisements we note in the newspapers, placed by people thanking St. Jude for healing them. Before undergoing surgery, they sincerely implore God to heal them. But as soon as the surgery succeeds, they thank St. Jude!!!

---

35. Have we given them authorization that justifies their idolatry?

36. When we bestow mercy upon the people, they rejoice therein. But when adversity befalls them, as a consequence of their own works, they become despondent.

37. Do they not realize that **GOD** increases the provision for whomever He wills, or reduces it? These should be lessons for people who believe.

38. Therefore, you shall give the relatives their rightful share (*of charity*), as well as the poor, and the traveling alien. This is better for those who sincerely seek **GOD**'s pleasure; they are the winners.

39. The usury that is practiced to increase some people's wealth, does not gain anything at **GOD**. But if you give to charity, seeking **GOD**'s pleasure, these are the ones who receive their reward manifold.

Who Is Worthy of Worship?

40. **GOD** is the One who created you. He is the One who provides for you. He is the One who puts you to death. He is the One who resurrects you. Can any of your idols do any of these things? Be He glorified. He is much too exalted to have any partners.

41. Disasters have spread throughout the land and sea, because of what the people have committed. He thus lets them taste the consequences of some of their works, that they may return (*to the right works*).

Learning From History

42. Say, "Roam the earth and note the consequences for those before you." Most of them were idol worshipers.

43. Therefore, you shall devote yourself completely to this perfect religion, before a day comes which is made inevitable by **GOD**. On that day, they will be shocked.

44. Whoever disbelieves, disbelieves to the detriment of his own soul, while those who lead a righteous life, do so to strengthen and develop their own souls.

45. For He will generously recompense those who believe and lead a righteous life from His bounties. He does not love the disbelievers.

46. Among His proofs is that He sends the winds with good omen, to shower you with His mercy, and to allow the ships to run in the sea in accordance with His rules, and for you to seek His bounties (*through commerce*), that you may be appreciative.

Guaranteed Victory for the Believers

47. We have sent messengers before you to their people, with profound signs. Subsequently, we punished those who transgressed. It is our duty that we grant victory to the believers.

48. **GOD** is the One who sends the winds, to stir up clouds, to be spread throughout the sky in accordance with His will. He then piles the clouds up, then you see the rain coming down therefrom. When it falls on whomever He chooses from among His servants, they rejoice.

49. Before it fell on them, they had resorted to despair.

50. You shall appreciate **GOD**'s continuous mercy, and how He revives the land that has been dead. He will just as certainly resurrect the dead. He is Omnipotent.

51. Had we sent upon them instead a yellow sandstorm, they would have continued to disbelieve.

52. You cannot make the dead, nor the deaf, hear the call, once they turn away.

53. Nor can you guide the blind out of their straying. You can only be heard by those who believe in our revelations, and decide to become submitters.

This Life is Very Short

54. **GOD** is the One who created you weak, then granted you after the weakness strength, then substituted after the strength weakness and gray hair. He creates whatever He wills. He is the Omniscient, the Omnipotent.

55. On the day when the Hour comes to pass, the guilty will swear that they lasted (*in this world*) only one hour. That is how wrong they were.

56. Those who are blessed with knowledge and faith will say, "You have lasted, according to **GOD**'s decree, until the Day of Resurrection. Now, this is the Day of Resurrection, but you failed to recognize it."

57. Therefore, no apology, on that day, will benefit the transgressors, nor will they be excused.

58. Thus, we have cited for the people in this Quran all kinds of examples. Yet, no matter what kind of proof you present to the disbelievers, they say, "You are falsifiers."

Divine Intervention

59. **GOD** thus seals the hearts of those who do not know.

60. Therefore, you shall steadfastly persevere—for **GOD**'s promise is the truth—and do not be intimidated by those who have not attained certainty.

◆◆◆

Sura 31: Luqmãn (Luqmãn)

In the name of God,
Most Gracious, Most Merciful

1. A.L.M.*

2. These (*letters*) constitute proofs of this book of wisdom.

3. A beacon and a mercy for the righteous.

4. Who observe the Contact Prayers (*Salat*), give the obligatory charity (*Zakat*), and as regards the Hereafter, they are absolutely certain.

5. They are following the guidance from their Lord, and they are the winners.

6. Among the people, there are those who uphold baseless *Hadith*, and thus divert others from the path of **GOD** without knowledge, and take it in vain. These have incurred a shameful retribution.

7. And when our revelations are recited to the one of them, he turns away in arrogance as if he never heard them, as if his ears are deaf. Promise him a painful retribution.

---

*31:1 See Appendix 1 for the important role of these initials.

---

8. Surely, those who believe and lead a righteous life have deserved the gardens of bliss.

9. Eternally they abide therein. This is the truthful promise of **GOD**. He is the Almighty, Most Wise.

10. He created the heavens without pillars that you can see. He established on earth stabilizers (*mountains*) lest it tumbles with you, and He spread on it all kinds of creatures. We send down from the sky water to grow all kinds of beautiful plants.

11. Such is the creation of **GOD**; show me what the idols you set up beside Him have created. Indeed, the transgressors are far astray.

Luqmãn's Wisdom

12. We have endowed Luqmãn with wisdom: "You shall be appreciative of **GOD**." Whoever is appreciative is appreciative for his own good. As for those who turn unappreciative, **GOD** is in no need, Praiseworthy.

13. Recall that Luqmãn said to his son, as he enlightened him, "O my son, do not set up any idols beside **GOD**; idolatry is a gross injustice."*

The Second Commandment

14. We enjoined the human being to honor his parents. His mother bore him, and the load got heavier and heavier. It takes two years (*of intensive care*) until weaning. You shall be appreciative of Me, and of your parents. To Me is the ultimate destiny.

15. If they try to force you to set up any idols beside Me, do not obey them.

But continue to treat them amicably in this world. You shall follow only the path of those who have submitted to Me. Ultimately, you all return to Me, then I will inform you of everything you have done.

Luqmãn's Advice

16. "O my son, know that even something as tiny as a mustard seed, deep inside a rock, be it in the heavens or the earth, **GOD** will bring it. **GOD** is Sublime, Cognizant.

17. "O my son, you shall observe the Contact Prayers (*Salat*). You shall advocate righteousness and forbid evil, and remain steadfast in the face of adversity. These are the most honorable traits.

18. "You shall not treat the people with arrogance, nor shall you roam the earth proudly. **GOD** does not like the arrogant showoffs.

19. "Walk humbly and lower your voice—the ugliest voice is the donkey's voice."

20. Do you not see that **GOD** has committed in your service everything in the heavens and the earth, and has showered you with His blessings—obvious and hidden? Yet, some people argue about **GOD** without knowledge, without guidance, and without the enlightening scripture.

Following the Parents Blindly: A Common Tragedy

21. When they are told, "Follow these revelations of **GOD**," they say, "No, we follow only what we found our parents doing." What if the devil is leading them to the agony of Hell?

31:13 How will you feel if you take care of a child, give him the best education, and prepare him for life, only to see him thank someone else? Thus is idolatry; injustice.

The Strongest Bond

22. Those who submit completely to **GOD**, while leading a righteous life, have gotten hold of the strongest bond. For **GOD** is in full control of all things.

23. As for those who disbelieve, do not be saddened by their disbelief. To us is their ultimate return, then we will inform them of everything they had done. **GOD** is fully aware of the innermost thoughts.

24. We let them enjoy temporarily, then commit them to severe retribution.

They Believe in God

25. If you ask them, "Who created the heavens and the earth," they will say, "**GOD**." Say, "Praise be to **GOD**." Yet, most of them do not know.

26. To **GOD** belongs everything in the heavens and the earth. **GOD** is the Most Rich, Most Praiseworthy.

These Are All the Words We Need

27. If all the trees on earth were made into pens, and the ocean supplied the ink, augmented by seven more oceans, the words of **GOD** would not run out. **GOD** is Almighty, Most Wise.

28. The creation and resurrection of all of you is the same as that of one person. **GOD** is Hearer, Seer.

God ALONE Worthy of Worship

29. Do you not realize that **GOD** merges the night into the day and merges the day into the night, and that He has committed the sun and the moon in your service, each running in its orbit for a specific life span, and that **GOD** is fully Cognizant of everything you do?

30. This proves that **GOD** is the truth, while any idol they set up beside Him is falsehood, and that **GOD** is the Most High, Most Great.

31. Do you not see that the ships roam the sea, carrying **GOD**'s provisions, to show you some of His proofs? Indeed, these should be sufficient proofs for everyone who is steadfast, appreciative.

32. When violent waves surround them, they implore **GOD**, sincerely devoting their prayers to Him alone. But as soon as He saves them to the shore, some of them revert. None discards our revelations except those who are betrayers, unappreciative.

33. O people, you shall reverence your Lord, and fear a day when a father cannot help his own child, nor a child can help his father. Certainly, **GOD**'s promise is truth. Therefore, do not be distracted by this life; do not be distracted from **GOD** by mere illusions.

Things We May and May Not Know*

34. With **GOD** is the knowledge regarding the Hour (*end of the world*).* He is the One who sends down the rain, and He knows the contents of the womb. No soul knows what will happen to it tomorrow, and no one knows in which land he or she will die. **GOD** is Omniscient, Cognizant.

---

*31:34 *God reveals His knowledge whenever He wills. We learn from this verse that we may be able to predict the rain, and the gender of the fetus. But we can never know the time or place of death. In accordance with 72:27, God has revealed the end of the world through His Messenger of the Covenant. See 15:87, 20:15, and Appendix 25 for the details.*

Sura 32: Prostration (Al-Sajdah)

In the name of God,
Most Gracious, Most Merciful

1. A.L.M.*

2. The book is, without a doubt, a revelation from the Lord of the universe.

3. They said, "He fabricated it." Indeed, this is the truth from your Lord, to warn people who never received a warner before you, that they may be guided.

*No Mediator
Between God and You*

4. **GOD** is the One who created the heavens and the earth, and everything between them in six days, then assumed all authority. You have none beside Him as Lord, nor do you have an intercessor. Would you not take heed?

5. All matters are controlled by Him from the heaven to the earth. To Him, the day is equivalent to one thousand of your years.

6. Knower of all secrets and declarations; the Almighty, Most Merciful.

The Origin of Man

7. He is the One who perfected everything He created, and started the creation of the human from clay.

8. Then He continued his reproduction through a certain lowly liquid.

9. He shaped him and blew into him from His spirit. And He gave you the hearing, the eyesight, and the brains; rarely are you thankful.

10. They wonder, "After we vanish into the earth, do we get created anew?" Thus, as regards meeting their Lord, they are disbelievers.

11. Say, "You will be put to death by the angel in whose charge you are placed, then to your Lord you will be returned."

Too Late

12. If only you could see the guilty when they bow down their heads before their Lord: "Our Lord, now we have seen and we have heard. Send us back and we will be righteous. Now we have attained certainty."*

13. Had we willed, we could have given every soul its guidance, but it is already predetermined that I will fill Hell with jinns and humans, all together.*

14. Taste the consequences of your forgetting this day; now we forget you. You have incurred eternal retribution in return for your own works.

---

*32:1 The meaning of these letters is given in the next verse: "This book is, without a doubt, a revelation from the Lord of the universe." See Appendix 1 for the details.

*32:12 If sent back, they would commit the same transgressions. See Footnote 6:28.

*32:13 The majority of humans "insist" upon going to Hell, by choosing to ignore God's invitations to redeem them. God will not put a single person in Hell. Those who fail to redeem themselves by denouncing idolatry and devoting themselves to God ALONE, and fail to develop their souls through the practices prescribed by our Creator, will have to run to Hell on their own volition. They will be too weak to stand the physical presence of God's energy.

15. The only people who truly believe in our revelations are those who fall prostrate upon hearing them. They glorify and praise their Lord, without any arrogance.

16. Their sides readily forsake their beds, in order to worship their Lord, out of reverence and hope, and from our provisions to them, they give.

Heaven: Indescribably Beautiful

17. You have no idea how much joy and happiness are waiting for you as a reward for your *(righteous)* works.

18. Is one who is a believer the same as one who is wicked? They are not equal.

19. As for those who believe and lead a righteous life, they have deserved the eternal Paradise. Such is their abode, in return for their works.

20. As for the wicked, their destiny is Hell. Every time they try to leave it, they will be forced back. They will be told, "Taste the agony of Hell which you used to disbelieve in."

Take A Hint

21. We let them taste the smaller retribution (*of this world*), before they incur the greater retribution (*of the Hereafter*), that they may (*take a hint and*) reform.

22. Who is more evil than one who is reminded of these revelations of his Lord, then insists upon disregarding them? We will certainly punish the guilty.

23. We have given Moses the scripture —do not harbor any doubt about meeting Him—and we made it a guide for the Children of Israel.

24. We appointed from among them imams who guided in accordance with our commandments, because

they steadfastly persevered and attained certainty about our revelations.

25. Your Lord is the One who will judge them on the Day of Resurrection, regarding everything they disputed.

26. Does it ever occur to them how many generations we have annihilated before them? They now live and walk in their ancestors' homes. This should provide sufficient proofs. Do they not hear?

27. Do they not realize that we drive the water to barren lands, and produce with it crops to feed their livestock, as well as themselves? Do they not see?

28. They challenge: "Where is that victory, if you are truthful?"

29. Say, "The day such a victory comes, believing will not benefit those who did not believe before that, nor will they be given another chance."

30. Therefore, disregard them and wait, they too are waiting.

Sura 33: The Parties (Al-Ahzāb)

In the name of God,
Most Gracious, Most Merciful

1. O you prophet, you shall reverence **GOD** and do not obey the disbelievers and the hypocrites. **GOD** is Omniscient, Most Wise.

2. Follow what is revealed to you from your Lord. **GOD** is fully Cognizant of everything you all do.

3. And put your trust in **GOD**. **GOD** suffices as an advocate.

Devotion to God Is Indivisible

4. **GOD** did not give any man two hearts in his chest. Nor did He turn your wives whom you estrange (*according to your custom*) into your mothers.* Nor did He turn your adopted children into genetic offspring. All these are mere utterances that you have invented. **GOD** speaks the truth, and He guides in the *(right)* path.

Do Not Change Your Names

5. You shall give your adopted children names that preserve their relationship to their genetic parents. This is more equitable in the sight of **GOD**. If you do not know their parents, then, as your brethren in religion, you shall treat them as members of your family. You do not commit a sin if you make a mistake in this respect; you are responsible for your purposeful intentions. **GOD** is Forgiver, Most Merciful.

6. The prophet is closer to the believers than they are to each other, and his wives are like mothers to them. The relatives ought to take care of one another in accordance with **GOD**'s scripture. Thus, the believers shall take care of their relatives who immigrate to them, provided they have taken care of their own families first. These are commandments of this scripture.

*Muhammad Pledges
to Support God's
Messenger of the Covenant**

7. Recall that we took from the prophets their covenant, including you (*O Muhammad*), Noah, Abraham, Moses, and Jesus the son of Mary. We took from them a solemn pledge.*

8. Subsequently, He will surely question the truthful about their truthfulness, and has prepared for the disbelievers (*in this Quranic fact*) a painful retribution.

The Battle of the Parties

9. O you who believe, remember **GOD**'s blessing upon you; when soldiers attacked you, we sent upon them violent wind and invisible soldiers. **GOD** is Seer of everything you do.

10. When they came from above you, and from beneath you, your eyes were terrified, your hearts ran out of patience, and you harbored unbefitting thoughts about **GOD**.

11. That is when the believers were truly tested; they were severely shaken up.

12. The hypocrites and those with doubts in their hearts said, "What **GOD** and His messenger promised us was no more than an illusion!"

---

*33:4 It was a custom in Arabia to estrange the wife by declaring that she was like the husband's mother. Such an unfair practice is abrogated herein.

*33:7 The covenant is detailed in 3:81. God took a covenant from the prophets that they shall support His Messenger of the Covenant who would come after Muhammad to purify and unify their messages. The Covenant was made before the earth's creation, and was fulfilled in Mecca Zul-Hijja 3, 1391 (Dec. 21, 1971). The sum of the Islamic month (12), plus the day (3), plus the year (1391) gives 1406, 19x74 Overwhelming proof identifying God's Messenger of the Covenant as Rashad Khalifa is provided throughout the Quran (Appendices 2 & 26).

---

13. A group of them said, "O people of Yathrib, you cannot attain victory; go back." Others made up excuses to the prophet: "Our homes are vulnerable," when they were not vulnerable. They just wanted to flee.

14. Had the enemy invaded and asked them to join, they would have joined the enemy without hesitation.

15. They had pledged to **GOD** in the past that they would not turn around and flee; making a pledge with **GOD** involves a great responsibility.

16. Say, "If you flee, you can never flee from death or from being killed. No matter what happens, you only live a short while longer."

17. Say, "Who would protect you from **GOD** if He willed any adversity, or willed any blessing for you?" They can never find, beside **GOD**, any other Lord and Master.

18. **GOD** is fully aware of the hinderers among you, and those who say to their comrades, "Let us all stay behind." Rarely do they mobilize for defense.

19. Also, they are too stingy when dealing with you. If anything threatens the community, you see their eyes rolling with fear, as if death had already come to them. Once the crisis is over, they whip you with sharp tongues. They are too stingy with their wealth. These are not believers, and, consequently, **GOD** has nullified their works. This is easy for **GOD** to do.

20. They thought that the parties might come back. In that case, they would wish that they were lost in the desert, asking about your news from afar. Had the parties attacked you while they were with you, they would rarely support you.

The Prophet's Courage*

21. The messenger of **GOD** has set up a good example for those among you who seek **GOD** and the Last Day, and constantly think about **GOD**.

22. When the true believers saw the parties *(ready to attack)*, they said, "This is what **GOD** and His messenger have promised us, and **GOD** and His messenger are truthful." This *(dangerous situation)* only strengthened their faith and augmented their submission.

23. Among the believers there are people who fulfill their pledges with **GOD**. Some of them died, while others stand ready, never wavering.

24. **GOD** will surely recompense the truthful for their truthfulness, and will punish the hypocrites, if He so wills, or redeem them. **GOD** is Forgiver, Most Merciful.

During Muhammad's Time

25. **GOD** repulsed those who disbelieved with their rage, and they left empty-handed. **GOD** thus spared the believers any fighting. **GOD** is Powerful, Almighty.

---

*33:21 Satan took this verse out of context, and relied on the people's idolization of the prophet Muhammad to innovate a whole set of unauthorized and unreasonable regulations called "Sunna of the Prophet." This created a totally different religion (see 42:21 and Appendix 18).

---

26. He also brought down their allies among the people of the scripture from their secure positions, and threw terror into their hearts. Some of them you killed, and some you took captive.

27. He made you inherit their land, their homes, their money, and lands you had never stepped on. **GOD** is in full control of all things.

Special Responsibility
For Being Close

28. O prophet, say to your wives, "If you are seeking this life and its vanities, then let me compensate you and allow you to go amicably.

29. "But if you are seeking **GOD** and His messenger, and the abode of the Hereafter, then **GOD** has prepared for the righteous among you a great recompense."

Special Responsibility

30. O wives of the prophet, if any of you commits a gross sin, the retribution will be doubled for her. This is easy for **GOD** to do.

31. Any one of you who obeys **GOD** and His messenger, and leads a righteous life, we will grant her double the recompense, and we have prepared for her a generous provision.

Setting the Example

32. O wives of the prophet, you are not the same as any other women, if you observe righteousness. *(You have a greater responsibility.)* Therefore, you shall not speak too softly, lest those with disease in their hearts may get the wrong ideas; you shall speak only righteousness.

33. You shall settle down in your homes, and do not mingle with the people excessively, like you used to do in the old days of ignorance. You shall observe the Contact Prayers (*Salat*), and give the obligatory charity (*Zakat*), and obey **GOD** and His messenger. **GOD** wishes to remove all unholiness from you, O you who live around the Sacred Shrine, and to purify you completely.

34. Remember what is being recited in your homes of **GOD**'s revelations and the wisdom inherent therein. **GOD** is Sublime, Cognizant.

Equality of Men and Women

35. The submitting men, the submitting women, the believing men, the believing women, the obedient men, the obedient women, the truthful men, the truthful women, the steadfast men, the steadfast women, the reverent men, the reverent women, the charitable men, the charitable women, the fasting men, the fasting women, the chaste men, the chaste women, and the men who commemorate **GOD** frequently, and the commemorating women; **GOD** has prepared for them forgiveness and a great recompense.

Major Error Committed
by Muhammad

Muhammad the Man Disobeys
Muhammad the Messenger

36. No believing man or believing woman, if **GOD** and His messenger issue any command, has any choice regarding that command. Anyone who disobeys **GOD** and His messenger has gone far astray.

37. Recall that you said to the one who was blessed by **GOD**, and blessed by you, "Keep your wife and reverence **GOD**," and you hid inside yourself what **GOD** wished to proclaim. Thus, you feared the people, when you were supposed to fear only **GOD**. When Zeid was completely through with his wife, we had you marry her, in order to establish the precedent that a man can marry the divorced wife of his adopted son. **GOD**'s commands shall be done.

38. The prophet is not committing an error by doing anything that is made lawful by **GOD**. Such is **GOD**'s system since the early generations. **GOD**'s command is a sacred duty.

39. Those who deliver **GOD**'s messages, and who reverence Him alone, shall never fear anyone but **GOD**. **GOD** is the most efficient reckoner.

*Not The Final Messenger***

40. Muhammad was not the father of any man among you. He was a messenger of **GOD** and the final prophet. **GOD** is fully aware of all things.

41. O you who believe, you shall remember **GOD** frequently.*

42. You shall glorify Him day and night.

43. He is the One who helps you, together with His angels, to lead you out of darkness into the light. He is Most Merciful towards the believers.

44. Their greeting the day they meet Him is, "Peace," and He has prepared for them a generous recompense.

45. O prophet, we have sent you as a witness, a bearer of good news, as well as a warner.

46. Inviting to **GOD**, in accordance with His will, and a guiding beacon.

47. Deliver good news to the believers, that they have deserved from **GOD** a great blessing.

48. Do not obey the disbelievers and the hypocrites, disregard their insults, and put your trust in **GOD**; **GOD** suffices as an advocate.

Marriage Laws

49. O you who believe, if you married believing women, then divorced them before having intercourse with them, they do not owe you any waiting interim *(before marrying another man)*. You shall compensate them equitably, and let them go amicably.

---

*33:40 Despite this clear definition of Muhammad, most Muslims insist that he was the last prophet and also the last messenger. This is a tragic human trait as we see in 40:34. Those who readily believe God realize that God sends His purifying and consolidating Messenger of the Covenant after the final prophet Muhammad (3:81, 33:7).
*33:41-42 Your god is whatever occupies your thoughts most of the time. Hence the commandment to commemorate God and glorify Him day and night. See Appendix 27.

---

50. O prophet, we made lawful for you your wives to whom you have paid their due dowry, or what you already have, as granted to you by **GOD**. Also lawful for you in marriage are the daughters of your father's brothers, the daughters of your father's sisters, the daughters of your mother's brothers, the daughters of your mother's sisters, who have emigrated with you. Also, if a believing woman gave herself to the prophet—by forfeiting the dowry—the prophet may marry her without a dowry, if he so wishes. However, her forfeiting of the dowry applies only to the prophet, and not to the other believers. We have already decreed their rights in regard to their spouses or what they already have. This is to spare you any embarrassment. **GOD** is Forgiver, Most Merciful.

51. You may gently shun any one of them, and you may bring closer to you any one of them. If you reconcile with any one you had estranged, you commit no error. In this way, they will be pleased, will have no grief, and will be content with what you equitably offer to all of them. **GOD** knows what is in your hearts. **GOD** is Omniscient, Clement.

52. Beyond the categories described to you, you are enjoined from marrying any other women, nor can you substitute a new wife (*from the prohibited categories*), no matter how much you admire their beauty. You must be content with those already made lawful to you. **GOD** is watchful over all things.

Etiquette

53. O you who believe, do not enter the prophet's homes unless you are given permission to eat, nor shall you force such an invitation in any manner. If you are invited, you may enter. When you finish eating, you shall leave; do not engage him in lengthy conversations. This used to hurt the prophet, and he was too shy to tell you. But **GOD** does not shy away from the truth. If you have to ask his wives for something, ask them from behind a barrier. This is purer for your hearts and their hearts. You are not to hurt the messenger of **GOD**. You shall not marry his wives after him, for this would be a gross offense in the sight of **GOD**.*

54. Whether you declare anything, or hide it, **GOD** is fully aware of all things.

55. The women may relax (*their dress code*) around their fathers, their sons, their brothers, the sons of their brothers, the sons of their sisters, the other women, and their (*female*) servants. They shall reverence **GOD**. **GOD** witnesses all things.

---

*33:53 We are enjoined in 4:22 from marrying women who were previously married to our fathers. Nor can the father marry the divorced wife of his son (4:23). This divine commandment preserves our respect for our fathers and their most private affairs. Similarly, the prophet was a father figure to the believers of his time. For the good of those believers, God enjoined them from marrying women who were previously married to the prophet. Marriage is a sacred and very private relationship, and the prophet's private life was better kept private.

During the Prophet's Life*

56. **GOD** and His angels help and support the prophet. O you who believe, you shall help and support him, and regard him as he should be regarded.*

57. Surely, those who oppose **GOD** and His messenger, **GOD** afflicts them with a curse in this life, and in the Hereafter; He has prepared for them a shameful retribution.

58. Those who persecute the believing men and the believing women, who did not do anything wrong, have committed not only a falsehood, but also a gross sin.

*Dress Code
for Women*

59. O prophet, tell your wives, your daughters, and the wives of the believers that they shall lengthen their garments. Thus, they will be recognized (*as righteous women*) and avoid being insulted. **GOD** is Forgiver, Most Merciful.

60. Unless the hypocrites, and those with disease in their hearts, and the vicious liars of the city refrain (*from persecuting you*), we will surely grant you the upper hand, then they will be forced to leave within a short while.

61. They have incurred condemnation wherever they go; *(unless they stop*

attacking you,) they may be taken and killed.

62. This is **GOD**'s eternal system, and you will find that **GOD**'s system is unchangeable.

End of the World Revealed*

63. The people ask you about the Hour (*end of the world*). Say, "The knowledge thereof is only with **GOD**. For all that you know, the Hour may be close."

*The Followers Turn
On Their Leaders*

64. **GOD** has condemned the disbelievers, and has prepared for them Hell.

65. Eternally they abide therein. They will find no lord, nor a supporter.

66. The day they are thrown into Hell, they will say, "Oh, we wish we obeyed **GOD**, and obeyed the messenger."

67. They will also say, "Our Lord, we have obeyed our masters and leaders, but they led us astray.

68. "Our Lord, give them double the retribution, and curse them a tremendous curse."

69. O you who believe, do not be like those who hurt Moses, then **GOD** absolved him of what they said. He was, in the sight of **GOD**, honorable.

70. O you who believe, reverence **GOD** and utter only the correct utterances.

---

*33:56 The word "prophet" (Nabi) consistently refers to Muhammad only when he was alive. Satan used this verse to entice the Muslims into commemorating Muhammad, constantly, instead of commemorating God as enjoined in 33:41-42.

*33:63 Less than a century ago, only God possessed knowledge about television and space satellites, for example. He revealed this knowledge at the predetermined time. Similarly, God has revealed the time appointed for the end of this world (Appendix 25).

---

71. He will then fix your works, and forgive your sins. Those who obey **GOD** and His messenger have triumphed a great triumph.

Freedom of Choice

72. We have offered the responsibility *(freedom of choice)* to the heavens and the earth, and the mountains, but they refused to bear it, and were afraid of it. But the human being accepted it; he was transgressing, ignorant.*

73. For **GOD** will inevitably punish the hypocrite men and the hypocrite women, and the idol worshiping men and the idol worshiping women. **GOD** redeems the believing men and the believing women. **GOD** is Forgiver, Most Merciful.

◆◆◆◆

Sura 34: Sheba (Saba')

In the name of God,
Most Gracious, Most Merciful

1. Praise be to **GOD**—to whom belongs everything in the heavens and the earth; all praise is also due to Him in the Hereafter. He is the Most Wise, the Cognizant.

2. He knows everything that goes into the earth, and everything that comes out of it, and everything that comes down from the sky, and everything that climbs into it. He is the Most Merciful, the Forgiving.

3. Those who disbelieve have said, "The Hour will never come to pass!" Say, "Absolutely—by my Lord—it will most certainly come to you. He is the Knower of the future. Not even the equivalent of an atom's weight is hidden from Him, be it in the heavens or the earth. Not even smaller than that, or larger *(is hidden)*. All are in a profound record."

4. Most certainly, He will reward those who believe and lead a righteous life. These have deserved forgiveness and a generous provision.

5. As for those who constantly challenge our revelations, they have incurred a retribution of painful humiliation.

6. It is evident to those who are blessed with knowledge that this revelation from your Lord to you is the truth, and that it guides to the path of the Almighty, the Most Praiseworthy.

7. Those who disbelieve have said, "Let us show you a man who tells you that after you are torn apart you will be created anew.

8. "Either he fabricated lies about **GOD**, or he is crazy." Indeed, those who disbelieve in the Hereafter have incurred the worst retribution; they have gone far astray.

9. Have they not seen all the things in front of them and behind them, in the heaven and the earth? If we willed, we could have caused the earth to swallow them, or caused masses to fall on them from the sky. This should be a sufficient proof for every obedient servant.

---

*33:72 The animals, trees, stars, etc. took advantage of this most gracious offer. See Appendix 7.

David and Solomon

10. We endowed David with blessings from us: "O mountains, submit with him, and you too, O birds." We softened the iron for him.

11. "You may make shields that fit perfectly, and work righteousness. Whatever you do, I am Seer thereof."

The First Oil Field

12. To Solomon we committed the wind at his disposal, traveling one month coming and one month going. And we caused a spring of oil to gush out for him. Also, the jinns worked for him, by his Lord's leave. Any one of them who disregarded our commands, we subjected him to a severe retribution.

13. They made for him anything he wanted—niches, statues, deep pools, and heavy cooking pots. O family of David, work *(righteousness)* to show your appreciation. Only a few of My servants are appreciative.

Jinns' Knowledge is Limited

14. When the appointed time for his death came, they had no clue that he had died. It was not until one of the animals tried to eat his staff, and he fell down, that the jinns realized that he was dead. They thus realized that if they really knew the unseen, they would have stopped working so hard as soon as he died.

15. Sheba's homeland used to be a marvel, with two gardens on the right and the left. Eat from your Lord's provisions, and be appreciative of Him—good land, and a forgiving Lord.

16. They turned away and, consequently, we poured upon them a disastrous flood, and we substituted their two gardens into two gardens of bad tasting fruits, thorny plants, and a skimpy harvest.

17. We thus requited them for their disbelief. Do we not requite only the disbelievers?

18. We placed between them and the communities that we blessed other oases, and we secured the journey between them: "Travel therein days and nights in complete security."

19. But they *(turned unappreciative and)* challenged: "Our Lord, we do not care if You increase the distance of our journeys *(without any stations)*." They thus wronged their own souls. Consequently, we made them history, and scattered them into small communities throughout the land. This should provide lessons for those who are steadfast, appreciative.

Satan Claims the Majority

20. Satan found them readily fulfilling his expectations. They followed him, except a few believers.

The Objective: Do We Believe in the Hereafter?*

21. He never had any power over them. But we thus distinguish those who believe in the Hereafter from those who are doubtful about it.* Your Lord is in full control of all things.

---

*34:21 The criteria that inform us whether we believe in the Hereafter or not are in 6:113, 17:45, & 39:45. These three criteria bring out our true convictions, regardless of our oral statements.

---

22. Say, "Implore the idols you have set up beside **GOD**. They do not possess as much as a single atom in the heavens, or the earth. They possess no partnership therein, nor does He permit them to be His assistants."

No Intercession

23. Intercession with Him will be in vain, unless it coincides with His will. When their minds are finally settled down, and they ask, "What did your Lord say," they will say, "The truth." He is the Most High, the Most Great.

24. Say, "Who provides for you, from the heavens and the earth?" Say, "**GOD**," and "Either we or you are guided, or have gone far astray."

25. Say, "You are not responsible for our crimes, nor are we responsible for what you do."

26. Say, "Our Lord will gather us all together before Him, then He will judge between us equitably. He is the Judge, the Omniscient."

27. Say, "Show me the idols you have set up as partners with Him!" Say, "No; He is the one **GOD**, the Almighty, Most Wise."

God's Messenger of the Covenant

28. We have sent you *(O Rashad)** to all the people, a bearer of good news, as well as a warner, but most people do not know.

29. They challenge, "When will this promise come to pass, if you are truthful?"

30. Say, "You have a specific time, on a specific day, that you cannot delay by one hour, nor advance."

31. Those who disbelieve have said, "We will not believe in this Quran, nor in the previous scriptures." If you could only envision these transgressors when they stand before their Lord! They will argue with one another back and forth. The followers will tell their leaders, "If it were not for you, we would have been believers."

On the Day of Resurrection

32. The leaders will say to those who followed them, "Are we the ones who diverted you from the guidance after it came to you? No; it is you who were wicked."

33. The followers will say to their leaders, "It was you who schemed night and day, then commanded us to be unappreciative of **GOD**, and to set up idols to rank with Him." They will be ridden with remorse, when they see the retribution, for we will place shackles around the necks of those who disbelieved. Are they not justly requited for what they did?

Every Time!

34. Every time we sent a warner to a community, the leaders of that community said, "We reject the message you are sent with."

34:28 As detailed in Appendix 2, the name of this messenger is mathematically coded into the Quran as "Rashad Khalifa." By adding the numerical value of the name "Rashad" (505), plus the numerical value of the name "Khalifa" (725), plus the number of the sura (34), plus the number of the verse (28), we obtain a total that conforms with the Quran's 19-based mathematical miracle, which was unveiled through Rashad Khalifa. (505 + 725 + 34 + 28= 1292 = 19x68). More information is given in 5:19 and its footnote.

35. They also said, "We are more powerful, with more money and children, and we will not be punished."

36. Say, "My Lord is the One who controls all provisions; He grants the provisions to whomever He wills, or reduces them, but most people do not know."

37. It is not your money or your children that bring you closer to us. Only those who believe and lead a righteous life will receive the reward for their works, multiplied manifold. In the abode of Paradise they will live in perfect peace.

38. As for those who consistently challenge our revelations, they will abide in retribution.

39. Say, "My Lord is the One who controls all provisions; He increases the provisions for whomever He chooses from among His servants, or reduces them. Anything you spend *(in the cause of God)*, He will reward you for it; He is the Best Provider."

40. On the day when He summons them all, He will say to the angels, "Did these people worship you?"

41. They will answer, "Be You glorified. You are our Lord and Master, not them. Instead, they were worshiping the jinns; most of them were believers therein."

42. On that day, you possess no power to help or harm one another, and we will say to the transgressors, "Taste the retribution of the Hell that you used to deny."

*Mathematical Miracle of the Quran**

43. When our proofs were recited to them, perfectly clear, they said, "This is simply a man who wants to divert you from the way your parents are worshiping." They also said, "These are fabricated lies." Those who disbelieved also said about the truth that came to them, "This is obviously magic."

44. We did not give them any other books to study, nor did we send to them before you another warner.

45. Those before them disbelieved, and even though they did not see one-tenth* of *(the miracle)* we have given to this generation, when they disbelieved My messengers, how severe was My retribution!

*God's Messenger of the Covenant**

46. Say, "I ask you to do one thing: Devote yourselves to **GOD**, in pairs or as individuals, then reflect. Your friend *(Rashad)* is not crazy. He is a manifest warner to you, just before the advent of a terrible retribution."

34:43 By adding the gematrical value of "Rashad" (505), plus the value of "Khalifa" (725), plus this verse number (43), we get 505 + 725 + 43= 1273 = 19x67. See Appendices 1&2.

34:45 The great miracles given to Moses and Jesus were limited in time and place; they were witnessed by a few people who happened to exist in that place at that time. But the mathematical miracle of the Quran is perpetual (see 74:30-35 & Appendix 1).

34:46 By placing the gematrical value of "Rashad" (505) next to the value of "Khalifa" (725), then the sura number (34), and the verse number (46), we get 5057253446= 19x266171234.

---

47. Say, "I do not ask you for any wage; you can keep it. My wage comes only from **GOD.** He witnesses all things."

48. Say, "My Lord causes the truth to prevail. He is the Knower of all secrets."

49. Say, "The truth has come; while falsehood can neither initiate anything, nor repeat it."

50. Say, "If I go astray, I go astray because of my own shortcomings. And if I am guided, it is because of my Lord's inspiration. He is Hearer, Near."

51. If you could only see them when the great terror strikes them; they cannot escape then, and they will be taken away forcibly.

52. They will then say, "We now believe in it," but it will be far too late.

53. They have rejected it in the past; they have decided instead to uphold conjecture and guesswork.*

54. Consequently, they were deprived of everything they longed for. This is the same fate as their counterparts in the previous generations. They harbored too many doubts.

◆◆◆◆

Sura 35: Initiator (Fāter)

In the name of God,
Most Gracious, Most Merciful

1. Praise be to **GOD,** Initiator of the heavens and the earth, and appointer of the angels to be messengers with wings—two, three, and four *(wings)*. He increases the creation as He wills. **GOD** is Omnipotent.

2. When **GOD** showers the people with mercy, no force can stop it. And if He withholds it, no force, other than He, can send it. He is the Almighty, Most Wise.

3. O people, remember **GOD**'s blessings upon you. Is there any creator other than **GOD** who provides for you from the heaven and the earth? There is no other god beside Him. How could you deviate?

4. If they disbelieve you, messengers before you have been disbelieved. **GOD** is in control of all things.

5. O people, **GOD**'s promise is the truth; therefore, do not be distracted by this lowly life. Do not be diverted from **GOD** by mere illusions.

6. The devil is your enemy, so treat him as an enemy. He only invites his party to be the dwellers of Hell.

7. Those who disbelieve have incurred a severe retribution, and those who believe and lead a righteous life have deserved forgiveness and a great recompense.

8. Note the one whose evil work is adorned in his eyes, until he thinks that it is righteous. **GOD** thus sends astray whoever wills *(to go astray)*, and He guides whoever wills *(to be guided)*. Therefore, do not grieve over them. **GOD** is fully aware of everything they do.

*34:53 People of all religions tend to forsake the word of God and uphold the words of men. The Jews and the Muslims uphold the Mishnah (Hadith) and Gemarrah (Sunna), while the Christians uphold a trinity invented by the Nicene Conference, 325 years after Jesus.

9. **GOD** is the One who sends the winds to stir up clouds, then we drive them towards barren lands, and revive such lands after they were dead. Thus is the resurrection.

All Dignity
Belongs With God

10. Anyone seeking dignity should know that to **GOD** belongs all dignity. To Him ascends the good words, and He exalts the righteous works. As for those who scheme evil works, they incur severe retribution; the scheming of such people is destined to fail.

God is in Full Control

11. **GOD** created you from dust, then from a tiny drop, then He causes you to reproduce through your spouses. No female becomes pregnant, nor gives birth, without His knowledge. No one survives for a long life, and no one's life is snapped short, except in accordance with a pre-existing record. This is easy for **GOD**.

*Appreciating God's Greatness**

12. The two seas are not the same; one is fresh and delicious, while the other is salty and undrinkable. From each of them you eat tender meat, and extract jewelry to wear. And you see the ships sailing through them, seeking His provisions, that you may be appreciative.

13. He merges the night into the day, and merges the day into the night. He has committed the sun and the moon to run for a predetermined period of time. Such is **GOD** your Lord; to Him belongs all kingship. Any idols you set up beside Him do not possess as much as a seed's shell.

The Idols
*Utterly Powerless **

14. If you call on them, they cannot hear you. Even if they hear you, they cannot respond to you. On the Day of Resurrection, they will disown you. None can inform you like the Most Cognizant.

15. O people, you are the ones who need **GOD**, while **GOD** is in no need of anyone, the Most Praiseworthy.

16. If He wills, He can get rid of you and substitute a new creation.

17. This is not too difficult for **GOD**.

18. No soul can carry the sins of another soul. If a soul that is loaded with sins implores another to bear part of its load, no other soul can carry any part of it, even if they were related. The only people to heed your warnings are those who reverence their Lord, even when alone in their privacy, and observe the Contact Prayers (*Salat*). Whoever purifies his soul, does so for his own good. To **GOD** is the final destiny.

---

*35:12-13 When we send our astronauts into space, we provide them with their minimum needs of food, water, and oxygen. When we sided with Satan's blasphemy billions of years ago (Appendix 7), God launched us into space aboard the spaceship Earth. But God has supplied our spaceship with awesome renewable systems that provide a great variety of fresh foods, water, oxygen, and even the reproduction of us astronauts.

*35:14 People idolize Jesus, Mary, Muhammad, Ali, and/or the saints; such idols are dead, unaware, and utterly powerless. Even when they were alive, they were powerless.

---

19. The blind and the seer are not equal.

20. Nor are the darkness and the light.

21. Nor are the coolness of the shade and the heat of the sun.

22. Nor are the living and the dead; **GOD** causes whomever He wills to hear. You cannot make hearers out of those in the graves.

23. You are no more than a warner.

*God's Messenger of the Covenant**

24. We have sent you* with the truth, a bearer of good news, as well as a warner. Every community must receive a warner.

25. If they disbelieve you, those before them have also disbelieved. Their messengers went to them with clear proofs, and the Psalms, and the enlightening scriptures.

26. Subsequently, I punished those who disbelieved; how terrible was My retribution!

God's Colorful Creations

27. Do you not realize that **GOD** sends down from the sky water, whereby we produce fruits of various colors? Even the mountains have different colors; the peaks are white, or red, or some other color. And the ravens are black.

28. Also, the people, the animals, and the livestock come in various colors. This is why the people who truly reverence **GOD** are those who are knowledgeable. **GOD** is Almighty, Forgiving.

29. Surely, those who recite the book of **GOD**, observe the Contact Prayers (*Salat*), and from our provisions to them they spend—secretly and publicly—are engaged in an investment that never loses.

30. He will recompense them generously, and will multiply His blessings upon them. He is Forgiving, Appreciative.

Quran: The Consummation of All the Scriptures

31. What we revealed to you in this scripture is the truth, consummating all previous scriptures. **GOD** is fully Cognizant of His servants, Seer.

32. We passed the scripture from generation to generation, and we allowed whomever we chose from among our servants to receive it. Subsequently, some of them wronged their souls, others upheld it only part of the time, while others were eager to work righteousness in accordance with **GOD**'s will; this is the greatest triumph.

The Believers

33. They will enter the gardens of Eden, where they will be adorned with bracelets of gold and pearls, and their garments in it will be made of silk.

34. They will say, "Praise **GOD** for removing all our worries. Our Lord is Forgiving, Appreciative.

35. "He has admitted us into the abode of eternal bliss, out of His grace. Never do we get bored herein, never do we get tired."

---

*35:24 The gematrical value of "Rashad Khalifa" (1230), plus the verse number (24) give us a total that is a multiple of 19 (1230 + 24 = 1254 = 19x66).

The Disbelievers

36. As for those who disbelieve, they have incurred the fire of Hell, where they are never finished by death, nor is the retribution ever commuted for them. We thus requite the unappreciative.

37. They will scream therein, "Our Lord, if you get us out of here, we will work righteousness, instead of the works we used to do." Did we not give you a life-long chance, with continuous reminders for those who would take heed? Did you not receive the warner? Therefore, taste *(the consequences)*. The transgressors will have no one to help them.

38. **GOD** is the Knower of the future of the heavens and the earth. He is the Knower of all innermost thoughts.

The Winners and the Losers

39. He is the One who made you inheritors of the earth. Subsequently, whoever chooses to disbelieve does so to his own detriment. The disbelief of the disbelievers only augments their Lord's abhorrence towards them. The disbelief of the disbelievers plunges them deeper into loss.

40. Say, "Consider the idols you have set up beside **GOD**; show me what on earth have they created." Do they own any partnership in the heavens? Have we given them a book wherein there is no doubt? Indeed, what the transgressors promise one another is no more than an illusion.

41. **GOD** is the One who holds the heavens and the earth, lest they vanish. If anyone else is to hold them, they will most certainly vanish. He is Clement, Forgiving.

Putting Them to the Test

42. They swore by **GOD** solemnly that if a warner went to them, they would be better guided than a certain congregation! However, now that the warner did come to them, this only plunged them deeper into aversion.

43. They resorted to arrogance on earth, and evil scheming, and the evil schemes only backfire on those who scheme them. Should they then expect anything but the fate of those who did the same things in the past? You will find that **GOD**'s system is never changeable; you will find that **GOD**'s system is immutable.

44. Have they not roamed the earth and noted the consequences for those who preceded them? They were even stronger than they. Nothing can be hidden from **GOD** in the heavens, nor on earth. He is Omniscient, Omnipotent.

45. If **GOD** punished the people for their sins, He would not leave a single creature on earth. But He respites them for a predetermined interim. Once their interim is fulfilled, then **GOD** is Seer of His servants.

◆◆◆◆

Sura 36: Y. S. (Yã Sîn)

In the name of God,
Most Gracious, Most Merciful

1. Y.S.*

2. And the Quran that is full of wisdom.

---

*36:1 See Appendix 1 for the detailed explanation of these initials.

---

3. Most assuredly, you *(Rashad)* are one of the messengers.*

4. On a straight path.

5. This revelation is from the Almighty, Most Merciful.

6. To warn people whose parents were never warned, and therefore, they are unaware.

7. It has been predetermined that most of them do not believe.

8. For we place around their necks shackles, up to their chins. Consequently, they become locked in their disbelief.

9. And we place a barrier in front of them, and a barrier behind them, and thus, we veil them; they cannot see.

10. It is the same whether you warn them or not, they cannot believe.*

11. You will be heeded only by those who uphold this message, and reverence the Most Gracious—even when alone in their privacy. Give them good news of forgiveness and a generous recompense.

12. We will certainly revive the dead, and we have recorded everything they have done in this life, as well as the consequences that continue after their death. Everything we have counted in a profound record.

*Rejecting The Messengers:
A Tragic Human Trait*

13. Cite for them the example of people in a community that received the messengers.

14. When we sent to them two *(messengers)*, they disbelieved them. We then supported them by a third. They said, "We are *(God's)* messengers to you."

15. They said, "You are no more than human beings like us. The Most Gracious did not send down anything. You are liars."

16. They said, "Our Lord knows that we have been sent to you.

17. "Our sole mission is to deliver the message."

18. They said, "We consider you bad omens. Unless you refrain, we will surely stone you, or afflict you with painful retribution."

19. They said, "Your omen depends on your response, now that you have been reminded. Indeed, you are transgressing people."

20. A man came from the other end of the city, saying, "O my people, follow the messengers.

21. "Follow those who do not ask you for any wage, and are guided.

22. "Why should I not worship the One who initiated me, and to Him is your ultimate return?

23. "Shall I set up beside Him gods? If the Most Gracious willed any harm for me, their intercession cannot help me one bit, nor can they rescue me.

24. "In that case, I would be totally astray.

---

*36:3 See Appendices 2 & 26 for the irrefutable physical evidence.

*36:10 Everyone is already stamped as a believer or a disbeliever. See Appendix 14.

*36:13-27 God's messengers have proof, advocate God alone, and do not ask for money.

25. "I have believed in your Lord; please listen to me."

The Righteous
Go Straight to Paradise*

26. *(At the time of his death)* he was told, "Enter Paradise." He said, "Oh, I wish my people knew.

27. "That my Lord has forgiven me, and made me honorable."

28. We did not send down upon his people, after him, soldiers from the sky; we did not need to send them down.

29. All it took was one blow, whereupon they were stilled.

Ridiculing The Messengers:
A Tragic Human Trait*

30. How sorry is the people's condition! Every time a messenger went to them, they always ridiculed him.

31. Did they not see how many generations we annihilated before them, and how they never return to them?

32. Every one of them will be summoned before us.

Signs of God

33. One sign for them is the dead land: we revive it and produce from it grains for their food.

34. We grow in it gardens of date palms, and grapes, and we cause springs to gush out therein.

35. This is to provide them with fruits, and to let them manufacture with their own hands whatever they need. Would they be thankful?

36. Glory be to the One who created all kinds of plants from the earth, as well as themselves, and other creations that they do not even know.

37. Another sign for them is the night: we remove the daylight therefrom, whereupon they are in darkness.

38. The sun sets into a specific location, according to the design of the Almighty, the Omniscient.

39. The moon we designed to appear in stages, until it becomes like an old curved sheath.

40. The sun is never to catch up with the moon—the night and the day never deviate—each of them is floating in its own orbit.

Invention of the First Ship

41. Another sign for them is that we carried their ancestors on the loaded ark.

42. Then created the same for them to ride in.

43. If we willed, we could have drowned them, so that their screaming would not be heard, nor could they be saved.

44. Instead, we shower them with mercy, and let them enjoy for awhile.

45. Yet, when they are told, "Learn from your past, to work righteousness for your future, that you may attain mercy,"

36:26 The righteous do not really die; they simply move on to the same Paradise where Adam & Eve lived. They join the prophets, saints and martyrs in an active and utopian life (see App. 17).

36:30 If the messenger presents solid proof of messengership, advocates the worship of God alone, and does not ask us for money, why should we not believe? (See Appendix 2.)

---

46. No matter what kind of proof is given to them from their Lord, they consistently disregard it.

47. When they are told, "Give from **GOD**'s provisions to you," those who disbelieve say to those who believe, "Why should we give to those whom **GOD** could feed, if He so willed? You are really far astray."

48. They also challenge, "When will that promise come to pass, if you are truthful?"

49. All they see will be one blow that overwhelms them, while they dispute.

50. They will not even have time to make a will, nor will they be able to return to their people.

51. The horn will be blown, whereupon they will rise from the grave and go to their Lord.

52. They will say, "Woe to us. Who resurrected us from our death? This is what the Most Gracious has promised. The messengers were right."

53. All it will take is one blow, whereupon they are summoned before us.

54. On that day, no soul will be wronged in the least. You will be paid precisely for whatever you did.

55. The dwellers of Paradise will be, on that day, happily busy.

56. They abide with their spouses in beautiful shade, enjoying comfortable furnishings.

57. They will have fruits therein; they will have anything they wish.

58. Greetings of peace from a Most Merciful Lord.

59. As for you, O guilty ones, you will be set aside.

The Devil is the Other Alternative

60. Did I not covenant with you, O Children of Adam, that you shall not worship the devil? That he is your most ardent enemy?

61. And that you shall worship Me alone? This is the right path.

62. He has misled multitudes of you. Did you not possess any understanding?

63. This is the Hell that was promised for you.

64. Today you will burn in it, as a consequence of your disbelief.

65. On that day we will seal their mouths; their hands and feet will bear witness to everything they had done.

66. If we will, we can veil their eyes and, consequently, when they seek the path, they will not see.

67. If we will, we can freeze them in place; thus, they can neither move forward, nor go back.

68. Whomever we permit to live for a long time, we revert him to weakness. Do they not understand?

69. What we taught him *(the messenger)* was not poetry, nor is he *(a poet)*. This is but a formidable proof,* and a profound Quran.

---

*36:69 The word "Zikr" refers frequently to the Quran's great mathematical code, which is certainly not literary, nor poetry. Please check out 38:1,8; 15:6,9; 16:44; 21:2,24; 26:5; & 36:11.

---

70. To preach to those who are alive, and to expose the disbelievers.

71. Have they not seen that we created for them, with our own hands, livestock that they own?

72. And we subdued them for them; some they ride, and some they eat.

73. They derive other benefits from them, as well as drinks. Would they not be appreciative?

Powerless Idols

74. They set up beside **GOD** other gods, perhaps they can be of help to them!

75. On the contrary, they cannot help them; they end up serving them as devoted soldiers.

76. Therefore, do not be saddened by their utterances. We are fully aware of everything they conceal and everything they declare.

77. Does the human being not see that we created him from a tiny drop, then he turns into an ardent enemy?

78. He raises a question to us—while forgetting his initial creation— "Who can resurrect the bones after they had rotted?"

79. Say, "The One who initiated them in the first place will resurrect them. He is fully aware of every creation."

80. He is the One who creates for you, from the green trees, fuel which you burn for light.

81. Is not the One who created the heavens and the earth able to re-create the same? Yes indeed; He is the Creator, the Omniscient.

82. All He needs to do to carry out any command is say to it, "Be," and it is.

83. Therefore, glory be to the One in whose hand is the sovereignty over all things, and to Him you will be returned.*

◆◆◆◆

Sura 37: The Arrangers (Al-Sãffãt)

In the name of God,
Most Gracious, Most Merciful

1. The arrangers in columns.

2. The blamers of those to be blamed.

3. The reciters of the messages.

4. Your god is only one.

5. The Lord of the heavens and the earth, and everything between them, and Lord of the easts.*

6. We have adorned the lowest heaven with adorning planets.*

7. We guarded it from every evil devil.

8. They cannot spy on the High Society; they get bombarded from every side.

---

*36:83 It is noteworthy that the gematrical value of "Rashad" (505), plus the gematrical value of "Khalifa" (725), plus the sura number (36), plus the number of verses (83), produces a total that is a multiple of 19 (505 + 725 + 36 + 83 = 1349=19x71). Also, Sura 36 is number 19 among the 29 initialed suras.

*37:5 Every heavenly body rises on the planet earth, and sets. Every rise is called "east."

*37:6 We live in the innermost and smallest universe. The jinns are confined to this universe.

9. They have been condemned; they have incurred an eternal retribution.

10. If any of them ventures to charge the outer limits, he gets struck with a fierce projectile.

11. Ask them, "Are they more difficult to create, or the other creations?" We created them from wet mud.

12. While you are awed, they mock.

13. When reminded, they take no heed.

14. When they see proof, they ridicule it.

15. They say, "This is obviously magic!

16. "After we die and become dust and bones, do we get resurrected?

17. "Even our ancient ancestors?"

18. Say, "Yes, you will be forcibly summoned."

19. All it takes is one nudge, whereupon they *(stand up)* looking.

20. They will say, "Woe to us; this is the Day of Judgment."

21. This is the day of decision that you used to disbelieve in.

22. Summon the transgressors, and their spouses, and the idols they worshiped

23. beside **GOD**, and guide them to the path of Hell.

24. Stop them, and ask them:

25. "Why do you not help one another?"

26. They will be, on that day, totally submitting.

Mutual Blaming

27. They will come to each other, questioning and blaming one another.

28. They will say *(to their leaders)*, "You used to come to us from the right side."

29. They will respond, "It is you who were not believers.

30. "We never had any power over you; it is you who were wicked.

31. "We justly incurred our Lord's judgment; now we have to suffer.

32. "We misled you, only because we were astray."

33. Thus, together they will all partake of the retribution on that day.

34. This is how we requite the guilty.

The First Commandment

35. When they were told, "*Lā Elāha Ella Allāh* [There is no other god beside **GOD**]," they turned arrogant.

36. They said, "Shall we leave our gods for the sake of a crazy poet?"

37. In fact, he has brought the truth, and has confirmed the messengers.

38. Most assuredly, you will taste the most painful retribution.

39. You are requited only for what you have done.

40. Only **GOD**'s servants who are absolutely devoted to Him alone *(will be saved)*.

41. They have deserved provisions that are reserved specifically for them.

42. All kinds of fruits. They will be honored.

43. In the gardens of bliss.

44. On furnishings close to one another.

45. Cups of pure drinks will be offered to them.

46. Clear and delicious for the drinkers.

47. Never polluted, and never exhausted.

48. With them will be wonderful companions.

49. Protected like fragile eggs.

The Dwellers of Heaven Visit the Dwellers of Hell

50. They will come to each other, and confer with one another.

51. One of them will say, "I used to have a friend.

52. "He used to mock: 'Do you believe all this?

53. " 'After we die and turn into dust and bones, do we get called to account?' "

54. He will say, "Just take a look!"

55. When he looks, he will see his friend in the heart of Hell.*

56. He *(will go to him and)* say, "By **GOD**, you almost ruined me.

57. "If it were not for my Lord's blessing, I would have been with you now.

58. *"(Do you still believe)* that we die,

59. "only the first death, and we never receive any requital?"

Redemption: The Greatest Triumph

60. Such is the greatest triumph.

61. This is what every worker should work for.

62. Is this a better destiny, or the tree of bitterness?

63. We have rendered it a punishment for the transgressors.

64. It is a tree that grows in the heart of Hell.

65. Its flowers look like the devils' heads.

66. They will eat from it until their bellies are filled up.

67. Then they will top it with a hellish drink.

68. Then they will return to Hell.

They Followed Their Parents Blindly

69. They found their parents astray.

70. And they blindly followed in their footsteps.

71. Most of the previous generations have strayed in the same manner.

72. We have sent to them warners.

73. Note the consequences for those who have been warned.

74. Only **GOD**'s servants who are absolutely devoted to Him alone *(are saved).*

Noah

75. Thus, Noah called upon us, and we were the best responders.

76. We saved him and his family from the great disaster.

77. We made his companions the survivors.

78. And we preserved his history for subsequent generations.

79. Peace be upon Noah among the peoples.

37:55 People who make it to Heaven will be able to visit their relatives and friends in Hell, without adverse consequences. In the Hereafter, anyone can move downward, but not upward beyond a certain limit. The limit is decided by one's degree of growth and development (App. 5).

---

80. We thus reward the righteous.

81. He is one of our believing servants.

82. We drowned all the others.

Abraham

83. Among his followers was Abraham.

84. He came to his Lord wholeheartedly.

85. He said to his father and his people, "What are you worshiping?

86. "Is it these fabricated gods, instead of **GOD**, that you want?

87. "What do you think of the Lord of the universe?"

88. He looked carefully at the stars.

89. Then he gave up and said, "I am tired of this!"

90. They turned away from him.

91. He then turned on their idols, saying, "Would you like to eat?

92. "Why do you not speak?"

93. He then destroyed them.

94. They went to him in a great rage.

95. He said, "How can you worship what you carve?

96. "When **GOD** has created you, and everything you make!"

97. They said, "Let us build a great fire, and throw him into it."

98. They schemed against him, but we made them the losers.

99. He said, "I am going to my Lord; He will guide me."

100. "My Lord, grant me righteous children."

101. We gave him good news of a good child.

Satanic Dream*

102. When he grew enough to work with him, he said, "My son, I see in a dream that I am sacrificing you. What do you think?" He said, "O my father, do what you are commanded to do. You will find me, **GOD** willing, patient."

103. They both submitted, and he put his forehead down (*to sacrifice him*).

*God Intervenes
to Save
Abraham and Ismail*

104. We called him: "O Abraham.

105. "You have believed the dream." We thus reward the righteous.

106. That was an exacting test indeed.

107. We ransomed (*Ismail*) by substituting an animal sacrifice.

108. And we preserved his history for subsequent generations.

109. Peace be upon Abraham.

110. We thus reward the righteous.

111. He is one of our believing servants.

Birth of Isaac

112. Then we gave him the good news about the birth of Isaac, to be one of the righteous prophets.

113. We blessed him and Isaac. Among their descendants, some are righteous, and some are wicked transgressors.

---

*37:102 The Most Merciful never advocates evil (7:28). As with Job, Satan claimed that Abraham loved his son too much, and was permitted to put Abraham to that severe test.

Moses and Aaron

114. We also blessed Moses and Aaron.

115. We delivered them and their people from the great disaster.

116. We supported them, until they became the winners.

117. We gave both of them the profound scripture.

118. We guided them in the right path.

119. We preserved their history for subsequent generations.

120. Peace be upon Moses and Aaron.

121. We thus reward the righteous.

122. Both of them were among our righteous servants.

Elias

123. Elias was one of the messengers.

124. He said to his people, "Would you not work righteousness?

125. "Do you worship a statue, instead of the Supreme Creator?

126. "**GOD**; your Lord, and the Lord of your forefathers!"

127. They disbelieved him. Consequently, they had to be called to account.

128. Only **GOD**'s servants who are absolutely devoted to Him alone (*are saved*).

129. We preserved his history for subsequent generations.

130. Peace be upon Elias, and all those like Elias.

131. We thus reward the righteous.

132. He was one of our believing servants.

Lot

133. Lot was one of the messengers.

134. We saved him and all his family.

135. Only the old woman was doomed.

136. We annihilated all the others.

137. You still pass by their ruins by day.

138. And by night. Would you understand?

Jonah

139. Jonah was one of the messengers.

140. He escaped to the loaded ship.

141. He rebelled and thus, he joined the losers.

142. Consequently, the fish swallowed him, and he was the one to blame.

143. If it were not that he resorted to meditation (*on God*),

144. he would have stayed in its belly until the Day of Resurrection.

145. We had him thrown up into the desert, exhausted.

146. We had a tree of edible fruit grown for him.

147. Then we sent him to a hundred thousand,* or more.

148. They did believe, and we let them enjoy this life.

149. Ask them if your Lord has daughters, while they have sons!

150. Did we create the angels to be females? Did they witness that?

---

*37:147 The Quran mentions 30 numbers: 1, 2, 3, 4, 5, 6, 7, 8, 9, 10, 11, 12, 19, 20, 30, 40, 50, 60, 70, 80, 99, 100, 200, 300, 1000, 2000, 3000, 5000, 50000, and 100000. The sum of these numbers is 162146, or 19x8534 (see Appendix 1).

151. Indeed, they grossly blaspheme when they say—

152. "**GOD** has begotten a son." Indeed, they are liars.

153. Did He choose the girls over the boys?

154. What is wrong with your logic?

Addressing the Disbelievers

155. Why do you not take heed?

156. Do you have any proof?

157. Show us your book, if you are truthful.

158. They even invented a special relationship between Him and the jinns. The jinns themselves know that they are subservient.

159. **GOD** be glorified; far above their claims.

160. Only **GOD**'s servants who are devoted to Him alone *(are saved)*.

161. Indeed, you and what you worship.

162. Cannot impose anything on Him.

163. Only you will burn in Hell.

The Angels

164. Each one of us has a specific job.

165. We are the arrangers.

166. We have duly glorified *(our Lord)*.

Following The Parents Blindly

167. They used to say,

168. "Had we received the correct instructions from our parents,

169. "we would have been worshipers; devoted to **GOD** alone."

170. But they disbelieved, and they will surely find out.

Victory for the Messengers Guaranteed

171. Our decision is already decreed for our servants the messengers.

172. They are surely the victors.

173. Our soldiers are the winners.

174. So disregard them for awhile.

175. Watch them; they too will watch.

176. Do they challenge our retribution?

177. When it hits them one day, it will be a miserable day; they have been sufficiently warned.

178. Disregard them for awhile.

179. Watch them; they too will watch.

180. Glory be to your Lord, the great Lord; far above their claims.

181. Peace be upon the messengers.

182. Praise be to **GOD,** Lord of the universe.

◆◆◆◆

Sura 38: S (Saad)

In the name of God,
Most Gracious, Most Merciful

1. S. (Saad),* and the Quran that contains the proof.**

2. Those who disbelieve have plunged into arrogance and defiance.

3. Many a generation before them we annihilated. They called for help; in vain.

38:1 This Initial (Saad) occurs in suras 7, 19, & 38 a total of 152 times, 19x8 (Appendix 1).

**38:1 The word "Zikr" is made distinct from the Quran and clearly points at the Quran's miraculous mathematical code. See 15:6, 9; 16:44; 21:2, 24; 26:5; & 36:11, 69.*

4. They wondered that a warner should come to them, from among them. The disbelievers said, "A magician; a liar.

5. "Did he make the gods into one god? This is really strange."

6. The leaders announced, "Go and steadfastly persevere in worshiping your gods. This is what is desired.

7. "We never heard of this from the religion of our fathers. This is a lie.

8. "Why did the proof come down to him, instead of us?" Indeed, they are doubtful of My proof. Indeed, they have not yet tasted My retribution.

9. Do they own the treasures of mercy of your Lord, the Almighty, the Grantor.

10. Do they possess the sovereignty of the heavens and the earth, and everything between them? Let them help themselves.

11. Instead, whatever forces they can muster—even if all their parties banded together—will be defeated.

12. Disbelieving before them were the people of Noah, 'Ãd, and the mighty Pharaoh.

13. Also, Thamoud, the people of Lot, the dwellers of the Woods (of Midyan); those were the opponents.

14. Each of them disbelieved the messengers and thus, My retribution was inevitable.

15. These people can expect a single blow, from which they never recover.

16. They challenged: "Our Lord, why do you not rush the retribution for us, before the Day of Reckoning."

17. Be patient in the face of their utterances, and remember our servant David, the resourceful; he was obedient.

18. We committed the mountains in his service, glorifying with him night and day.

19. Also the birds were committed to serve him; all were obedient to him.

20. We strengthened his kingship, and endowed him with wisdom and good logic.

21. Have you received news of the feuding men who sneaked into his sanctuary?

22. When they entered his room, he was startled. They said, "Have no fear. We are feuding with one another, and we are seeking your fair judgment. Do not wrong us, and guide us in the right path.

23. "This brother of mine owns ninety nine* sheep, while I own one sheep. He wants to mix my sheep with his, and continues to pressure me."

---

*38:23 This is the only place where the number 99 occurs. Thirty different numbers are mentioned in the Quran, and their total comes to 162146, 19x8534. See Appendix 1.

David's Exemplary Piety

24. He said, "He is being unfair to you by asking to combine your sheep with his. Most people who combine their properties treat each other unfairly, except those who believe and work righteousness, and these are so few." Afterwards, David wondered if he made the right judgment. He thought that we were testing him. He then implored his Lord for forgiveness, bowed down, and repented.*

25. We forgave him in this matter. We have granted him a position of honor with us, and a beautiful abode.

26. O David, we have made you a ruler on earth. Therefore, you shall judge among the people equitably, and do not follow your personal opinion, lest it diverts you from the way of **GOD**. Surely, those who stray off the way of **GOD** incur severe retribution for forgetting the Day of Reckoning.

27. We did not create the heaven and the earth, and everything between them, in vain. Such is the thinking of those who disbelieve. Therefore, woe to those who disbelieve; they will suffer in Hell.

28. Shall we treat those who believe and lead a righteous life as we treat those who commit evil on earth? Shall we treat the righteous as we treat the wicked?

29. This is a scripture that we sent down to you, that is sacred—perhaps they reflect on its verses. Those who possess intelligence will take heed.

Solomon's Exemplary Devotion

30. To David we granted Solomon; a good and obedient servant.

31. One day he became preoccupied with beautiful horses, until the night fell.

32. He then said, "I enjoyed the material things more than I enjoyed worshiping my Lord, until the sun was gone.*

33. "Bring them back." (*To bid farewell,*) he rubbed their legs and necks.

34. We thus put Solomon to the test; we blessed him with vast material wealth, but he steadfastly submitted.*

35. He said, "My Lord, forgive me, and grant me a kingship never attained by anyone else. You are the Grantor."

36. We (*answered his prayer and*) committed the wind at his disposal, pouring rain wherever he wanted.

37. And the devils, building and diving.

38. Others were placed at his disposal.

39. "This is our provision to you; you may give generously, or withhold, without limits."

38:24 In this clear example, 99 on one side vs. 1 on the other side, David's extreme care to render the correct judgment caused him to ask forgiveness. Are we this careful?

38:32 Solomon missed his afternoon prayer because of his horses. To nullify Satan's possible claim that Solomon loved his horses more than loving God, he got rid of his horses.

38:34 & 41 Solomon and Job represent both ends of the testing spectrum. We are put to the test through wealth, health, or lack of them, to see if we worship God alone under all circumstances.

40. He has deserved an honorable position with us, and a wonderful abode.

The Devil Afflicts Job *

41. Remember our servant Job: he called upon his Lord, "The devil has afflicted me with hardship and pain."

42. "Strike the ground with your foot. A spring will give you healing and a drink."

God Makes it up to the Believers

43. We restored his family for him; twice as many. Such is our mercy; a reminder for those who possess intelligence.

44. "Now, you shall travel the land and preach the message, to fulfill your pledge." We found him steadfast. What a good servant! He was a submitter.

45. Remember also our servants Abraham, Isaac, and Jacob. They were resourceful, and possessed vision.

46. We bestowed upon them a great blessing: awareness of the Hereafter.

47. They were chosen, for they were among the most righteous.

48. Remember Ismail, Elisha, and Zal-Kifl; among the most righteous.

The Righteous

49. This is a reminder: The righteous have deserved a wonderful destiny.

50. The gardens of Eden will open up their gates for them.

51. Relaxing therein, they will be given many kinds of fruits and drinks.

52. They will have wonderful spouses.

53. This is what you have deserved on the Day of Reckoning.

54. Our provisions are inexhaustible.

The Disbelievers:
Feuding With One Another

55. As for the transgressors, they have incurred a miserable destiny.

56. Hell is where they burn; what a miserable abode!

57. What they taste therein will be hellish drinks and bitter food.

58. And much more of the same kind.

59. "This is a group to be thrown into Hell with you." They will not be welcomed (*by the residents of Hell*). They have deserved to burn in the hellfire.

60. The newcomers will respond, "Nor are you welcomed. You are the ones who preceded us and misled us. Therefore, suffer this miserable end."

61. They will also say, "Our Lord, these are the ones who led us into this; double the retribution of hellfire for them."

Surprise!

62. They will say, "How come we do not see (*in Hell*) people we used to count among the wicked?

63. "We used to ridicule them; we used to turn our eyes away from them."

64. This is a predetermined fact: the people of Hell will feud with one another.

65. Say, "I warn you; there is no other god beside **GOD,** the One, the Supreme.

---

*38:41 See footnote for 38:38 & 41.

66. "The Lord of the heavens and the earth, and everything between them; the Almighty, the Forgiving."

The Great Feud

67. Say, "Here is awesome news.

68. "That you are totally oblivious to.

69. "I had no knowledge previously, about the feud in the High Society.*

70. "I am inspired that my sole mission is to deliver the warnings to you."

71. Your Lord said to the angels, "I am creating a human being from clay.

72. "Once I design him, and blow into him from My spirit, you shall fall prostrate before him."

73. The angels fell prostrate, all of them,

74. except Satan; he refused, and was too arrogant, unappreciative.

75. He said, "O Satan, what prevented you from prostrating before what I created with My hands? Are you too arrogant? Have you rebelled?"

76. He said, "I am better than he; You created me from fire, and created him from clay."

77. He said, "Therefore, you must be exiled, you will be banished.

78. "You have incurred My condemnation until the Day of Judgment."

79. He said, "My Lord, respite me till the Day of Resurrection."

80. He said, "You are respited.

81. "Until the appointed day."

82. He said, "I swear by Your majesty, that I will send them all astray.

83. "Except Your worshipers who are devoted absolutely to You alone."

84. He said, "This is the truth, and the truth is all that I utter.

85. "I will fill Hell with you and all those who follow you."

86. Say, "I do not ask you for any wage, and I am not an imposter.

87. "This is a reminder for the world.

88. "And you will certainly find out in awhile."

◆◆◆

Sura 39: The Throngs (Al-Zumar)

In the name of God,
Most Gracious, Most Merciful

1. This is a revelation of the scripture, from **GOD,** the Almighty, the Wise.

2. We sent down to you this scripture, truthfully; you shall worship **GOD,** devoting your religion to Him alone.

Idols as Mediators:
A Common Myth

3. Absolutely, the religion shall be devoted to **GOD** alone. Those who set up idols beside Him say, "We idolize them only to bring us closer to **GOD;** for they are in a better position!" **GOD** will judge them regarding their disputes. **GOD** does not guide such liars, disbelievers.

4. If **GOD** wanted to have a son, He could have chosen whomever He willed from among His creations. Be He glorified; He is **GOD,** the One, the Supreme.

38:69 The feud in the High Society was triggered by Satan's challenge to God's absolute authority. This is definitely the most important event in the history of the human race. We failed to make a firm stand regarding God's absolute authority. This life represents the third and final chance to redeem ourselves (See the Introduction and Appendix 7).

The Shape of the Earth*

5. He created the heavens and the earth truthfully. He rolls the night over the day, and rolls the day over the night.* He committed the sun and the moon, each running for a finite period. Absolutely, He is the Almighty, the Forgiving.

6. He created you from one person, then created from him his mate. He sent down to you eight kinds of livestock. He creates you in your mothers' bellies, creation after creation, in trimesters of darkness. Such is **GOD** your Lord. To Him belongs all sovereignty. There is no other god beside Him. How could you deviate?

Believe For Your Own Good

7. If you disbelieve, **GOD** does not need anyone. But He dislikes to see His servants make the wrong decision. If you decide to be appreciative, He is pleased for you. No soul bears the sins of any other soul. Ultimately, to your Lord is your return, then He will inform you of everything you had done. He is fully aware of the innermost thoughts.

8. When the human being is afflicted, he implores his Lord, sincerely devoted to Him. But as soon as He blesses him, he forgets his previous imploring, sets up idols to rank with **GOD** and to divert others from His path. Say, "Enjoy your disbelief temporarily; you have incurred the hellfire."

9. Is it not better to be one of those who meditate in the night, prostrating and staying up, being aware of the Hereafter, and seeking the mercy of their Lord? Say, "Are those who know equal to those who do not know?" Only those who possess intelligence will take heed.

10. Say, "O My servants who believed, you shall reverence your Lord." For those who worked righteousness in this world, a good reward. **GOD**'s earth is spacious, and those who steadfastly persevere will receive their recompense generously, without limits.

God ALONE

11. Say, "I have been commanded to worship **GOD**, devoting the religion absolutely to Him alone.

12. "And I was commanded to be the utmost submitter."

13. Say, "I fear, if I disobeyed my Lord, the retribution of a great day."

14. Say, "**GOD** is the only One I worship, devoting my religion absolutely to Him alone.

15. "Therefore, worship whatever you wish besides Him." Say, "The real losers are those who lose their souls, and their families, on the Day of Resurrection." Most certainly, this is the real loss.

16. They will have masses of fire on top of them, and under them. **GOD** thus alerts His servants: O My servants, you shall reverence Me.

---

*39:5 *This verse clearly informs us that the earth is round. The Arabic for "He rolls" (Yukawwir) is derived from the Arabic word for "ball" (Kurah). Since the Earth is not exactly round, a specific reference to its shape is given in 79:30. The Quran is replete with scientific information that became known to us centuries after the revelation of the Quran. See Appendix 20.*

17. As for those who discard the worship of all idols, and devote themselves totally to **GOD** alone, they have deserved happiness. Give good news to My servants.

Follow the Word of God

18. They are the ones who examine all words, then follow the best. These are the ones whom **GOD** has guided; these are the ones who possess intelligence.

19. With regard to those who have deserved the retribution, can you save those who are already in Hell?

The Righteous

20. As for those who reverence their Lord, they will have mansions upon mansions constructed for them, with flowing streams. This is **GOD**'s promise, and **GOD** never breaks His promise.

21. Do you not see that **GOD** sends down from the sky water, then places it into underground wells, then produces with it plants of various colors, then they grow until they turn yellow, then He turns them into hay? This should be a reminder for those who possess intelligence.

22. If **GOD** renders one's heart content with Submission, he will be following a light from his Lord. Therefore, woe to those whose hearts are hardened against **GOD**'s message; they have gone far astray.

The Best Hadith

23. **GOD** has revealed herein the best *Hadith*; a book that is consistent, and points out both ways (*to Heaven and Hell*). The skins of those who reverence their Lord cringe therefrom, then their skins and their hearts soften up for **GOD**'s message. Such is **GOD**'s guidance; He bestows it upon whomever He wills. As for those sent astray by **GOD**, nothing can guide them.

24. What is better than saving one's face from the terrible retribution on the Day of Resurrection? The transgressors will be told, "Taste the consequences of what you earned."

25. Others before them have disbelieved and, consequently, the retribution afflicted them whence they never expected.

26. **GOD** has condemned them to humiliation in this life, and the retribution in the Hereafter will be far worse, if they only knew.

Quran: No Ambiguity

27. We have cited for the people every kind of example in this Quran, that they may take heed.

28. An Arabic Quran, without any ambiguity, that they may be righteous.

29. **GOD** cites the example of a man who deals with disputing partners *(Hadith)*, compared to a man who deals with only one consistent source *(Quran)*. Are they the same? Praise be to **GOD**; most of them do not know.

Hadith: A Gross Blasphemy

30. You *(Muhammad)* will surely die, just like they will die.

31. On the Day of Resurrection, before your Lord, you people will feud with one another.

32. Who is more evil than one who attributes lies to **GOD**, while disbelieving in the truth that has come to him? Is Hell not a just requital for the disbelievers?

Quran: Absolute Truth

33. As for those who promote the truth, and believe therein, they are the righteous.

34. They will get everything they wish, at their Lord. Such is the reward for the righteous.

35. **GOD** remits their sinful works, and rewards them generously for their good works.

Profound Question

36. Is **GOD** not sufficient for His servant? They frighten you with the idols they set up beside Him. Whomever **GOD** sends astray, nothing can guide him.

37. And whomever **GOD** guides, nothing can send him astray. Is **GOD** not Almighty, Avenger?

They Believe in God Yet, They Are Going to Hell

38. If you ask them, "Who created the heavens and the earth?" they will say, "**GOD**." Say, "Why then do you set up idols beside **GOD**? If **GOD** willed any adversity for me, can they relieve such an adversity? And if He willed a blessing for me, can they prevent such a blessing?" Say, "**GOD** is sufficient for me." In Him the trusters shall trust.

39. Say, "O my people, do your best and I will do my best; you will surely find out.

40. "(*You will find out*) who has incurred shameful punishment, and has deserved an eternal retribution."

41. We have revealed the scripture through you for the people, truthfully. Then, whoever is guided is guided for his own good, and whoever goes astray goes astray to his own detriment. You are not their advocate.

42. **GOD** puts the souls to death when the end of their life comes, and also at the time of sleep. Thus, He takes some back during their sleep, while others are allowed to continue living until the end of their predetermined interim. This should provide lessons for people who reflect.

The Myth of Intercession

43. Have they invented intercessors to mediate between them and **GOD**? Say, "What if they do not possess any power, nor understanding?"

44. Say, "All intercession belongs to **GOD**." To Him belongs all sovereignty of the heavens and the earth, then to Him you will be returned.

The Greatest Criterion*

45. When **GOD** ALONE is mentioned, the hearts of those who do not believe in the Hereafter shrink with aversion. But when others are mentioned beside Him, they become satisfied.*

46. Proclaim: "Our god, Initiator of the heavens and the earth, Knower of all secrets and declarations, You are the only One who judges among Your servants regarding their disputes."

---

*39:45 Despite the clear commandment in 3:18 that the First Pillar of Islam is proclaiming: "Ash-hadu An Lã Elãha Ellã Allãh (there is no other god beside God)," the majority of "Muslims" insist upon adding the name of Muhammad. This Greatest Criterion alerts us that rejoicing in adding the name of Muhammad, or any other name, exposes disbelief in the Hereafter. See also Footnote 17:46.

47. If those who transgressed owned everything on earth, even twice as much, they would readily give it up to avoid the terrible retribution on the Day of Resurrection. They will be shown by **GOD** what they never expected.

48. The sinful works they had earned will be shown to them, and the very things they used to mock will come back to haunt them.

Human Fickleness

49. If the human is touched by adversity, he implores us, but as soon as we bestow a blessing upon him, he says, "I attained this because of my cleverness!" Indeed, this is only a test, but most of them do not know.

50. Those before them have uttered the same thing, and their earnings did not help them in the least.

51. They suffered the consequences of their evil works. Similarly, the transgressors among the present generation will suffer the consequences of their evil works; they cannot escape.

52. Do they not realize that **GOD** is the One who increases the provision for whomever He chooses, and withholds? These are lessons for people who believe.

God's Infinite Mercy

53. Proclaim: "O My servants who exceeded the limits, never despair of **GOD**'s mercy. For **GOD** forgives all sins. He is the Forgiver, Most Merciful."

54. You shall obey your Lord, and submit to Him totally, before the retribution overtakes you, then you cannot be helped.

55. And follow the best path that is pointed out for you by your Lord, before the retribution overtakes you suddenly when you least expect it.

56. Lest a soul may say, "How sorry I am for disregarding **GOD**'s commandments; I was certainly one of the mockers."

57. Or say, "Had **GOD** guided me, I would have been with the righteous."

58. Or say, when it sees the retribution, "If I get another chance, I will work righteousness."

59. Yes indeed *(you did get enough chances)*. My proofs came to you, but you rejected them, turned arrogant, and became a disbeliever.

60. On the Day of Resurrection you will see the faces of those who lied about **GOD** covered with misery. Is Hell not the right retribution for the arrogant ones?

61. And **GOD** will save those who have maintained righteousness; He will reward them. No harm will touch them, nor will they have any grief.

62. **GOD** is the Creator of all things, and He is in full control of all things.

63. To Him belongs all decisions in the heavens and the earth, and those who disbelieve in **GOD**'s revelations are the real losers.

64. Say, "Is it other than **GOD** you exhort me to worship, O you ignorant ones?"

Idol Worship Nullifies All Work

65. It has been revealed to you, and to those before you that if you ever commit idol worship, all your works will be nullified, and you will be with the losers.

66. Therefore, you shall worship **GOD** alone, and be appreciative.

Greatness of God*

67. They can never fathom the greatness of **GOD**. The whole earth is within His fist on the Day of Resurrection. In fact, the universes are folded within His right hand.* Be He glorified; He is much too high above needing any partners.

The Day of Judgment

68. The horn will be blown, whereupon everyone in the heavens and the earth will be struck unconscious, except those who will be spared by **GOD**. Then it will be blown another time, whereupon they will all rise up, looking.*

69. Then the earth will shine with the light of its Lord. The record will be proclaimed, and the prophets and the witnesses will be brought forth. Everyone will then be judged equitably, without the least injustice.

70. Every soul will be paid for whatever it did, for He is fully aware of everything they have done.

The Disbelievers

71. Those who disbelieved will be led to Hell in throngs. When they get to it, and its gates are opened, its guards will say, "Did you not receive messengers from among you, who recited to you the revelations of your Lord, and warned you about meeting this day?" They will answer, "Yes indeed. But the word 'retribution' was already stamped upon the disbelievers."

72. It will be said, "Enter the gates of Hell, wherein you abide forever." What a miserable destiny for the arrogant.

The Believers

73. Those who reverenced their Lord will be led to Paradise in throngs. When they get to it, and its gates are opened, its guards will say, "Peace be upon you; you have won. Therefore, you abide herein forever."

74. They will say, "Praise be to **GOD**, who fulfilled His promise to us, and made us inherit the earth, enjoying Paradise as we please." What a beautiful recompense for the workers!

75. You will see the angels floating around the throne, glorifying and praising their Lord. After the equitable judgment is issued to all, it will be proclaimed: "Praise be to **GOD**, Lord of the universe."

39:67 Our universe, with its billion galaxies, a billion trillion stars, uncountable decillions of heavenly bodies, spanning many billions of light-years, is the smallest and innermost of seven universes. This incomprehensible vastness of the seven universes is within God's hand. Such is the greatness of God. See Appendix 6.

39:68 The sequence of events on the Day of Resurrection begins with the symbolic blowing of the horn. The second blowing of the horn—by a creature who was spared from unconsciousness—marks the resurrection of all people; they will be resurrected on today's earth. This earth will then be destroyed by the physical coming of God, then a new earth and new heavens will be created (14:48). We will then be stratified according to our degree of development (Appendix 11).

Sura 40: Forgiver (Ghãfer)

In the name of God,
Most Gracious, Most Merciful

1. H.M.*

2. This revelation of the scripture is from **GOD**, the Almighty, the Omniscient.

3. Forgiver of sins, acceptor of repentance, strict in enforcing retribution, and possessor of all power. There is no other god beside Him. To Him is the ultimate destiny.

4. None argues against **GOD**'s revelations except those who disbelieve. Do not be impressed by their apparent success.

5. Disbelieving before them were the people of Noah, and many other opponents after them. Every community persecuted their messenger to neutralize him. And they argued with falsehood, to defeat the truth. Consequently, I punished them; how terrible was My retribution!

6. Thus, the judgment of your Lord is already stamped upon those who disbelieve, that they are the dwellers of Hell.

Angels Pray for the Believers

7. Those who serve the throne and all those around it glorify and praise their Lord, and believe in Him. And they ask forgiveness for those who believe: "Our Lord, Your mercy and Your knowledge encompass all things. Forgive those who repent and follow Your path, and spare them the retribution of Hell.

8. "Our Lord, and admit them into the gardens of Eden that You promised for them and for the righteous among their parents, spouses, and children. You are the Almighty, Most Wise.

9. "And protect them from falling in sin. Whomever You protect from falling in sin, on that day, has attained mercy from You. This is the greatest triumph."

God ALONE:
The Disbelievers Confess

10. Those who disbelieve will be told, "**GOD**'s abhorrence towards you is even worse than your own abhorrence towards yourselves. For you were invited to believe, but you chose to disbelieve."

God ALONE: The Disbelievers
*Suffer Two Deaths**

11. They will say, "Our Lord, you have put us to death twice, * and You gave us two lives; now we have confessed our sins. Is there any way out?"

God ALONE: Note the Reason

12. This is because when **GOD** A-LONE was advocated, you disbelieved, but when others were mentioned beside Him, you believed. Therefore, **GOD**'s judgment has been issued; He is the Most High, the Great.

40:1 The initials "Hã Mîm" occur in Suras 40-46, The total frequency of occurrence of the letters "Ha" and "Mîm" in the seven suras is 2147, or 19x113 (Appendix 1).

40:11-12 The disbelievers go through two deaths, while the righteous believers do not taste death, beyond the death we already experienced (44:56). Please see Appendix 17. The reason for going to Hell is obvious; even those who believe in God associate others with Him (see 39:45).

13. He is the One who continuously shows you His proofs, and sends down to you from the sky provisions. Only those who totally submit will be able to take heed.

14. Therefore, you shall devote your worship absolutely to **GOD** A-LONE, even if the disbelievers dislike it.

15. Possessor of the highest ranks, and Ruler of the whole dominion. He sends inspiration, bearing His commands, to whomever He chooses from among His servants, to warn about the Day of Summoning.

16. That is the day when everyone will be completely exposed; none of them will hide anything from **GOD**. To whom belongs all sovereignty on that day? To **GOD**, the One, the Supreme.

Prepare for the Big Day

17. On that day, every soul will be requited for whatever it had earned. There will be no injustice on that day. **GOD** is most efficient in reckoning.

No Intercession

18. Warn them about the imminent day, when the hearts will be terrified, and many will be remorseful. The transgressors will have no friend nor an intercessor to be obeyed.

19. He is fully aware of what the eyes cannot see, and everything that the minds conceal.

20. **GOD** judges equitably, while the idols they implore beside Him cannot judge anything. **GOD** is the One who is the Hearer, the Seer.

21. Did they not roam the earth and note the consequences for those before them? They used to be stronger than they, and more productive on earth. But **GOD** punished them for their sins, and nothing could protect them from **GOD**.

22. That is because their messengers went to them with clear proofs, but they disbelieved. Consequently, **GOD** punished them. He is Mighty, strict in enforcing retribution.

Moses

23. We sent Moses with our signs and a profound authority.

24. To Pharaoh, Hāmān, and Qāroon. But they said, "A magician; a liar."

25. And when he showed them the truth from us, they said, "Kill the sons of those who believed with him, and spare their daughters." Thus, the scheming of the disbelievers is always wicked.

Moses vs. Pharaoh

26. Pharaoh said, "Let me kill Moses, and let him implore his Lord. I worry lest he corrupts your religion, or spreads evil throughout the land."

27. Moses said, "I seek refuge in my Lord and your Lord, from every arrogant one who does not believe in the Day of Reckoning."

God Guides Not the Liars

28. A believing man among Pharaoh's people, who was concealing his belief, said, "How can you kill a man just for saying, 'My Lord is **GOD**,' and he has shown you clear proofs from your Lord? If he is a liar, that is his problem, and if he is truthful, you benefit from his promises. Surely, **GOD** does not guide any transgressor, liar.

29. "O my people, today you have kingship and the upperhand. But who will help us against **GOD**'s judgment, should it come to us?" Pharaoh said, "You are to follow only what I see fit; I will guide you only in the right path."

30. The one who believed said, "O my people, I fear for you the same fate as the previous opponents.

31. "The opponents of Noah, and 'Ãd, Thamoud, and others who came after them. **GOD** does not wish any injustice for the people.

32. "O my people, I fear for you the Day of Summoning.

33. "That is the day when you may wish to turn around and flee. But nothing will protect you then from **GOD**. Whomever **GOD** sends astray, nothing can guide him."

Who is the Last Messenger?*
A Tragic Human Trait

34. Joseph had come to you before that with clear revelations, but you continued to doubt his message. Then, when he died you said, "**GOD** will not send any other messenger after him. *(He was the last messenger)!"*** **GOD** thus sends astray those who are transgressors, doubtful.

35. They argue against **GOD**'s revelations, without any basis. This is a trait that is most abhorred by **GOD** and by those who believe. **GOD** thus seals the hearts of every arrogant tyrant.

36. Pharaoh said, "O Hãmãn, build for me a high tower, that I may reach out and discover.

37. "I want to reach the heaven, and take a look at the god of Moses. I believe he is a liar." Thus were the evil works of Pharaoh adorned in his eyes, and thus was he kept from following *(the right)* path. Pharaoh's scheming was truly evil.

38. The one who believed said, "O my people, follow me, and I will guide you in the right way.

39. "O my people, this first life is a temporary illusion, while the Hereafter is the eternal abode."

The Best Deal

40. Whoever commits a sin is requited for just that, and whoever works righteousness—male or female—while believing, these will enter Paradise wherein they receive provisions without any limits.

The Believing Egyptian Debates
With His People

41. "O my people, while I invite you to be saved, you invite me to the hellfire.

---

*40:34 *The Jews refused to believe in the Messiah when he came to them, the Christians refused to believe in Muhammad when he came to them, and a majority of today's Muslims believe that Muhammad was the last messenger. On that erroneous basis, they refused to accept God's Messenger of the Covenant. We learn from 3:81-90 and 33:7 that those who fail to accept the Quranic injunction to "believe in and support God's Messenger of the Covenant" are no longer believers. See Appendices 2 & 26.*

**40:34 *It is noteworthy that we find the name "Rashad" in the Arabic text precisely four verses ahead of the injunction against saying "the last messenger," and also four verses after it.*

42. "You invite me to be unappreciative of **GOD**, and to set up beside Him idols that I do not recognize. I am inviting you to the Almighty, the Forgiver.

43. "There is no doubt that what you invite me to do has no basis in this world, nor in the Hereafter, that our ultimate return is to **GOD**, and that the transgressors have incurred the hellfire.

44. "Some day you will remember what I am telling you now. I leave the judgment of this matter to **GOD**; **GOD** is the Seer of all the people."

45. **GOD** then protected him from their evil schemes, while the people of Pharaoh have incurred the worst retribution.

While in the Grave:
A Continuous Nightmare

46. The Hell will be shown to them day and night, and on the Day of Resurrection: "Admit Pharaoh's people into the worst retribution."

47. As they argue in Hell, the followers will say to their leaders, "We used to be your followers, can you spare us any part of this Hell?"

48. The leaders will say, "We are all in this together. **GOD** has judged among the people."

Too Late

49. Those in the hellfire will say to the guardians of Hell, "Call upon your Lord to reduce the retribution for us, for even one day."

50. They will say, "Did you not receive your messengers who delivered to you clear messages?" They will reply, "Yes we did." They will say, "Then implore *(as much as you wish)*; the imploring of the disbelievers is always in vain."

Guaranteed Victory;
Here and Forever

51. Most assuredly, we will give victory to our messengers and to those who believe, both in this world and on the day the witnesses are summoned.

52. On that day, the apologies of the disbelievers will not benefit them. They have incurred condemnation; they have incurred the worst destiny.

Learn From History

53. We have given Moses the guidance, and made the Children of Israel inherit the scripture.

54. *(Their history)* is a lesson and a reminder for those who possess intelligence.

55. Therefore, be patient, for **GOD**'s promise is true, and ask forgiveness for your sin, and glorify and praise your Lord night and day.

56. Surely, those who argue against **GOD**'s revelations without proof are exposing the arrogance that is hidden inside their chests, and they are not even aware of it. Therefore, seek refuge in **GOD**; He is the Hearer, the Seer.

Awesome Construction
of the Universe

57. The creation of the heavens and the earth is even more awesome than the creation of the human being, but most people do not know.

58. Not equal are the blind and the seer. Nor are those who believe and work righteousness equal to the sinners. Rarely do you take heed.

59. Most certainly, the Hour (*Day of Judgment*) is coming, no doubt about it, but most people do not believe.

*Supplication: A Form of Worship**

60. Your Lord says, "Implore Me, and I will respond to you. Surely, those who are too arrogant to worship Me will enter Gehenna, forcibly."

61. **GOD** is the One who designed the night so you can rest in it, and the day lighted. **GOD** bestows many blessings upon the people, but most people are not thankful.

62. Such is **GOD** your Lord, the Creator of all things. There is no god except He. How could you deviate?

63. Deviating are those who disregard **GOD**'s revelations.

64. **GOD** is the One who rendered the earth habitable for you, and the sky a formidable structure, and He designed you, and designed you well. He is the One who provides you with good provisions.* Such is **GOD** your Lord; Most Exalted is **GOD**, Lord of the universe.

65. He is the Living; there is no god except He. You shall worship Him alone, devoting your religion absolutely to Him alone. Praise be to **GOD**, Lord of the universe.

Before God's Blessings Upon Him, Muhammad Used to Worship Idols

66. Say, "I have been enjoined from worshiping the idols you worship beside **GOD**, when the clear revelations came to me from my Lord. I was commanded to submit to the Lord of the universe."*

67. He is the One who created you from dust, and subsequently from a tiny drop, then from a hanging embryo, then He brings you out as a child, then He lets you reach maturity, then you become old—some of you die earlier. You attain a predetermined age, that you may understand.

68. He is the only One who controls life and death. To have anything done, He simply says to it, "Be," and it is.

69. Have you noted those who argue against **GOD**'s proofs, and how they have deviated?

70. They are the ones who have disbelieved in the scripture, and in the messages we have sent with our messengers. Therefore, they will surely find out.

71. The shackles will be around their necks, and the chains will be used to drag them.

40:60 Supplication, imploring God for anything, even material luxuries, is a form of worship. Hence the commandment to implore God whenever we have any need. An atheist will never implore God for anything.

40:64 See Footnotes 15:20, 20:54, 25:2, and 35:12-13.

40:66 The Arabic word "Nahaa" used in this verse indicates the stopping of something that was going on. See for example the same word in 4:171. See also 93:7.

---

72. In the Inferno,* then in the Fire, they will burn.

73. They will be asked, "Where are the idols you used to worship,

They Worshiped Nothing

74. "beside **GOD**?" They will say, "They have abandoned us. In fact, when we worshiped them, we were worshiping nothing." Thus does **GOD** send the disbelievers astray.

75. This is because you used to rejoice in false doctrines, on earth, and you used to promote them.

76. Enter the gates of Gehenna, wherein you abide forever. What a miserable destiny for the arrogant ones.

77. You shall be patient, for **GOD**'s promise is truth. Whether we show you some of (*the retribution*) we have promised for them, or terminate your life before that, they will be returned to us.

God's Authorization for the Quran's Mathematical Miracle *

78. We have sent messengers before you—some of them we mentioned to you, and some we did not mention to you. No messenger can produce any miracle without **GOD**'s authorization.* Once **GOD**'s judgment is issued, the truth dominates, and the falsifiers are exposed and humiliated.

79. **GOD** is the One who created the livestock for you; some you ride, and some you eat.

80. They also provide you with additional benefits that satisfy many of your needs. On them, as well as on the ships, you are carried.

81. He thus shows you His proofs. Which of **GOD**'s proofs can you deny?

82. Have they not roamed the earth and noted the consequences for those who preceded them? They used to be greater in number, greater in power, and possessed a greater legacy on earth. Yet, all their achievements did not help them in the least.

83. When their messengers went to them with clear proofs, they rejoiced in the knowledge they had inherited, and the very things they ridiculed were the cause of their fall.

God ALONE

84. Subsequently, when they saw our retribution they said, "Now we believe in **GOD** ALONE, and we now disbelieve in the idol worship that we used to practice."

Too Late

85. Their belief then could not help them in the least, once they saw our retribution. Such is **GOD**'s system that has been established to deal with His creatures; the disbelievers are always doomed.

40:72 Those who did not prepare themselves will suffer tremendously in the presence of God, on the Day of Judgment. They cannot stand the closeness to God due to lack of sufficient growth and development of their souls. I am using "Inferno" to describe this particular situation (55:44). Preparation of the soul is accomplished by the rites decreed by God, such as the Contact Prayer.

40:78 We learn from 17:45-46, 18:57, and 56:79 that the unbelievers have no access to the Quran; only the believers and the sincere seekers are permitted by God to understand it. The Quran's mathematical code, "One of the great miracles" (74:30-35), was authorized by God, and revealed through His Messenger of the Covenant (Appendix 2).

Sura 41: Detailed (Fussilat)

In the name of God,
Most Gracious, Most Merciful

1. H.M.*

2. A revelation from the Most Gracious, Most Merciful.

3. A scripture whose verses provide the complete details, in an Arabic Quran, for people who know.

4. A bearer of good news, as well as a warner. However, most of them turn away; they do not hear.

5. They said, "Our minds are made up, our ears are deaf to your message, and a barrier separates us from you. Do what you want, and so will we."

6. Say, "I am no more than a human being like you, who has been inspired that your god is one god. You shall be devoted to Him, and ask His forgiveness. Woe to the idol worshipers.

7. "Who do not give the obligatory charity (*Zakat*), and with regard to the Hereafter, they are disbelievers."

8. As for those who believe and lead a righteous life, they receive a well deserved recompense.

9. Say, "You disbelieve in the One who created the earth in two days,* and you set up idols to rank with Him, though He is Lord of the universe."

10. He placed on it stabilizers (*mountains*), made it productive, and He calculated its provisions in four days, to satisfy the needs of all its inhabitants.

11. Then He turned to the sky, when it was still gas, and said to it, and to the earth, "Come into existence, willingly or unwillingly." They said, "We come willingly."

12. Thus, He* completed the seven universes in two days, and set up the laws for every universe. And we* adorned the lowest universe with lamps, and placed guards around it. Such is the design of the Almighty, the Omniscient.

Warning

13. If they turn away, then say, "I am warning you of a disaster like the disaster that annihilated 'Ād and Thamoud."

14. Their messengers went to them, as well as before them and after them, saying, "You shall not worship except **GOD**." They said, "Had our Lord willed, He could have sent angels. We are disbelievers in what you say."

41:1 For the significance of these Quranic Initials, see Footnote 40:1.

41:9-10 The "days" of creation represent a yardstick. Thus, the physical universe was created in two days, while the calculation of provisions for all the creatures on earth required four. This also teaches us that there is life only on this planet Earth.

41:12 God alone created the universe (18:51), but the angels participated in handling certain jobs in the lowest universe. Our universe cannot stand the physical presence of God (7:143). The plural tense acknowledges the angels' role in our universe (Appendix 10).

15. As for 'Ãd, they turned arrogant on earth, opposed the truth, and said, "Who is more powerful than we?" Did they not realize that **GOD**, who created them, is more powerful than they? They were unappreciative of our revelations.

16. Consequently, we sent upon them violent wind, for a few miserable days. We thus afflicted them with humiliating retribution in this life, and the retribution of the Hereafter is more humiliating; they can never win.

17. As for Thamoud, we provided them with guidance, but they preferred blindness over guidance. Consequently, the disastrous and shameful retribution annihilated them, because of what they earned.

18. We always save those who believe and lead a righteous life.

19. The day will come when the enemies of **GOD** will be summoned to the hellfire, forcibly.

20. Once they get there, their own hearing, eyes, and skins will bear witness to everything they had done.

The Video Record

21. They will say to their skins, "Why did you bear witness against us?" They will reply, "**GOD** made us speak up; He is the One who causes everything to speak. He is the One who created you the first time, and now you have been returned to Him."

22. There is no way you can hide from your own hearing, your eyes, or your skins. In fact, you thought that **GOD** was unaware of much of what you do.

23. This kind of thinking about your Lord will cause you to fall, and then you become losers.

24. If they continue the way they are, Hell will be their destiny, and if they make up excuses, they will not be excused.

The Jinn Companions

25. We assign to them companions who adorn everything they do in their eyes. Thus, they end up incurring the same fate as the previous communities of jinns and humans, who were also losers.

26. Those who disbelieved said, "Do not listen to this Quran and distort it, that you may win."

27. We will certainly afflict these disbelievers with a severe retribution. We will certainly requite them for their evil works.

28. Such is the requital that awaits **GOD**'s enemies. Hell will be their eternal abode; a just requital for discarding our revelations.

On the Day of Judgment

29. Those who disbelieved will say, "Our Lord, show us those among the two kinds—jinns and humans—who misled us, so we can trample them under our feet, and render them the lowliest."

Perfect Happiness: Now and Forever

30. Those who proclaim: "Our Lord is **GOD**," then lead a righteous life, the angels descend upon them: "You shall have no fear, nor shall you grieve. Rejoice in the good news that Paradise has been reserved for you.

31. "We are your allies in this life, and in the Hereafter. You will have in it anything you wish for; you will have anything you want.

32. "(*Such is your*) ultimate abode, from a Forgiver, Most Merciful."

Submitters

33. Who can utter better words than one who invites to **GOD**, works righteousness, and says, "I am one of the submitters?"

34. Not equal is the good response and the bad response. You shall resort to the nicest possible response. Thus, the one who used to be your enemy, may become your best friend.

35. None can attain this except those who steadfastly persevere. None can attain this except those who are extremely fortunate.

When the Devil Entices You

36. When the devil whispers an idea to you, you shall seek refuge in **GOD**. He is the Hearer, the Omniscient.

Proofs of God

37. Among His proofs are the night and the day, and the sun and the moon. Do not prostrate before the sun, nor the moon; you shall fall prostrate before the **GOD** who created them, if you truly worship Him alone.

38. If they are too arrogant to do this, then those at your Lord glorify Him night and day, without ever tiring.

39. Among His proofs is that you see the land still, then, as soon as we shower it with water, it vibrates with life. Surely, the One who revived it can revive the dead. He is Omnipotent.

40. Surely, those who distort our revelations are not hidden from us. Is one who gets thrown into Hell better, or one who comes secure on the Day of Resurrection? Do whatever you wish; He is Seer of everything you do.

Mathematical Miracle of the Quran*

41. Those who have rejected the Quran's proof* when it came to them, have also rejected an Honorable book.

42. No falsehood could enter it, in the past or in the future;* a revelation from a Most Wise, Praiseworthy.

God's Messenger of the Covenant*

43. What is said to you is precisely what was said to the previous messengers. Your Lord possesses forgiveness, and He also possesses painful retribution.

---

*41:41 The word "Zikr" refers to the Quran's mathematical code, as made clear in 38:1.

*41:42 One of the major functions of the Quran's mathematical miracle is to guard every letter and every aspect of the Quran. Thus, any tampering is immediately recognized (Apps. 1 & 24).

*41:43 Mathematical proof shows that this verse refers to God's Messenger of the Covenant. By adding the gematrical value of "Rashad"(505), plus the value of "Khalifa" (725), plus this verse number (43), we get 505 + 725 + 43 = 1273 = 19x67. See Appendix 2.

Language is Irrelevant

44. If we made it a non-Arabic Quran they would have said, "Why did it come down in that language?" Whether it is Arabic or non-Arabic, say, "For those who believe, it is a guide and healing. As for those who disbelieve, they will be deaf and blind to it, as if they are being addressed from faraway."

45. We have given Moses the scripture and it was also disputed. If it were not for your Lord's predetermined decision, they would have been judged immediately. Indeed, they harbor too many doubts.

46. Whoever works righteousness, does so for his own good, and whoever works evil does so to his own detriment. Your Lord is never unjust towards the people.

Idols Disown Their Followers

47. With Him is the knowledge about the Hour (*end of the world*).* No fruits emerge from their sheaths, nor does any female conceive or give birth, without His knowledge. The day will come when He asks them: "Where are those idols that you set up beside Me?" They will say, "We proclaim to You that none of us bears witness to that."

48. The idols they had idolized will disown them, and they will realize that there will be no escape.

Bad Weather Friends

49. The human being never tires of imploring for good things. And when adversity befalls him, he turns despondent, desperate.

50. And when we bless him after suffering some adversity, he says, "This belongs to me. I do not believe that the Hour will ever come to pass. Even if I am returned to my Lord, I will find at Him better things." Most certainly, we will inform the disbelievers of all their works, and will commit them to severe retribution.

51. When we bless the human being, he turns away, and drifts farther and farther away, and when he suffers any affliction, he implores loudly.

52. Proclaim: "What if this is truly from **GOD**, then you decide to reject it? Who are farther astray than those who decide to oppose this?"

A Great Prophecy

53. We will show them our proofs in the horizons, and within themselves, until they realize that this is the truth.* Is your Lord not sufficient, as a witness of all things?

54. Indeed, they are doubtful about meeting their Lord. He is fully aware of all things.

◆◆◆◆

Sura 42: Consultation (Al-Shoorã)

In the name of God,
Most Gracious, Most Merciful

41:47 God has revealed this knowledge through His Messenger of the Covenant (Appendix 25).

41:53 The letters that compose this verse are 19, and their gematrical values add up to 1387, 19x73. This great prophecy, together with 9:33, 48:28, 61:9 & 110:2 inform us that the whole world is destined to accept the Quran as God's unaltered message (See Appendix 38).

---

1. H.M.*

2. 'A.S.Q.*

3. Inspiring you, and those before you, is **GOD,** the Almighty, Most Wise.

4. To Him belongs everything in the heavens and everything on earth, and He is the Most High, the Great.

5. The heavens above them almost shatter, out of reverence for Him, and the angels praise and glorify their Lord, and they ask forgiveness for those on earth. Absolutely, **GOD** is the Forgiver, Most Merciful.

6. Those who set up other lords beside Him, **GOD** is the One in charge of them; you are not their advocate.

7. We thus reveal to you an Arabic Quran to warn the central community and all around it, and to warn about the Day of Summoning that is inevitable. Some will end up in Heaven, and some in Hell.

8. Had **GOD** willed, He could have made them one community. But He redeems into His mercy whomever He wills. As for the transgressors, they have no master, nor a helper.

9. Did they find other lords beside Him? **GOD** is the only Lord and Master. He is the One who resurrects the dead, and He is the Omnipotent One.

10. If you dispute any part of this message, the judgment for doing this rests with **GOD**. Such is **GOD** my Lord. In Him I trust, and to Him I submit.

None Equals God

11. Initiator of the heavens and the earth. He created for you from among yourselves spouses—and also for the animals. He thus provides you with the means to multiply. There is nothing that equals Him. He is the Hearer, the Seer.

12. To Him belongs absolute control of the heavens and the earth. He is the One who increases the provision for whomever He wills, or reduces it. He is fully aware of all things.

Only One Religion

13. He decreed for you the same religion decreed for Noah, and what we inspired to you, and what we decreed for Abraham, Moses, and Jesus: "You shall uphold this one religion, and do not divide it."

Monotheists vs. Idol Worshipers
The idol worshipers will greatly resent what you invite them to do. **GOD** redeems to Himself whomever He wills; He guides to Himself only those who totally submit.

14. Ironically, they broke up into sects only after the knowledge had come to them, due to jealousy and resentment among themselves. If it were not for a predetermined decision from your Lord to respite them for a definite interim, they would have been judged immediately. Indeed, the later generations who inherited the scripture are full of doubts.

---

*42:1 These initials constitute a significant part of the Quran's miracle (Footnote 40:1).

*42:2 This is the only sura where we see the initials 'A.S.Q. ('Ayn Seen Qaf), and the total occurrence of these three letters in this sura is 209, 19x11. Also, the letter "Q" occurs in this sura 57 times, 19x3. The only other sura where we see the initial "Q" is Sura 50, and this letter occurs in that sura also 57 times (See Appendix 1).

Message to the Christians
and the Jews

15. This is what you shall preach, and steadfastly maintain what you are commanded to do, and do not follow their wishes. And proclaim: "I believe in all the scriptures sent down by **GOD**. I was commanded to judge among you equitably. **GOD** is our Lord and your Lord. We have our deeds and you have your deeds. There is no argument between us and you. **GOD** will gather us all together; to Him is the ultimate destiny."

16. Those who argue about **GOD**, after receiving His message, their argument is nullified at their Lord. They have incurred condemnation, and have deserved a severe retribution.

17. **GOD** is the One who sent down the scripture, to deliver the truth and the law. For all that you know, the Hour (*Day of Judgment*) may be very close.

The Believers Mindful
of the Day of Judgment

18. Challenging it are those who do not believe in it. As for those who believe, they are concerned about it, and they know that it is the truth. Absolutely, those who deny the Hour have gone far astray.

19. **GOD** is fully aware of all His creatures; He provides for whomever He wills. He is the Powerful, the Almighty.

20. Whoever seeks the rewards of the Hereafter, we multiply the rewards for him. And whoever seeks the materials of this world, we give him therefrom, then he receives no share in the Hereafter.

The Idols:
Innovating New Religious Laws*

21. They follow idols who decree for them religious laws never authorized by **GOD**. If it were not for the predetermined decision, they would have been judged immediately. Indeed, the transgressors have incurred a painful retribution.*

22. You will see the transgressors worried about everything they had committed; everything will come back and haunt them. As for those who believed and led a righteous life, they will be in the gardens of Paradise. They will receive whatever they wish from their Lord. This is the great blessing.

23. This is the good news from **GOD** to His servants who believe and lead a righteous life. Say, "I do not ask you for any wage. I do ask each of you to take care of your own relatives." Anyone who does a righteous work, we multiply his reward for it. **GOD** is Forgiver, Appreciative.

42:21 The Islam of today's Muslim world has been so distorted, it has become a Satanic cult. The Ulama, or religious scholars, have added many extraneous laws, prohibitions, dress codes, dietary regulations, and religious practices never authorized by God. This is one of the main reasons for sending God's Messenger of the Covenant (9:31, 33:67, and Appendix 33).

---

*God Erases the Falsehood and
Affirms the Truth**

24. Are they saying, "He (*Rashad*)* has fabricated lies about **GOD**!"? If **GOD** willed, He could have sealed your mind, but **GOD** erases the falsehood and affirms the truth with His words. He is fully aware of the innermost thoughts.

25. He is the One who accepts the repentance from His servants, and remits the sins. He is fully aware of everything you do.

26. Responding to Him are those who believe and lead a righteous life. He will shower them with His blessings. As for the disbelievers, they have incurred a severe retribution.

27. If **GOD** increased the provision for His servants, they would transgress on earth. This is why He sends it precisely measured to whomever He wills. He is fully Cognizant and Seer of His servants.

28. He is the One who sends down the rain after they had despaired, and spreads His mercy. He is the only Master, Most Praiseworthy.

29. Among His proofs is the creation of the heavens and the earth, and the creatures He spreads in them. He is able to summon them, when He wills.

Only A Consequence

30. Anything bad that happens to you is a consequence of your own deeds, and He overlooks many *(of your sins)*.

31. You can never escape, and you have none beside **GOD** as a Lord and Master.

32. Among His proofs are the ships that sail the sea with sails like flags.

33. If He willed, He could have stilled the winds, leaving them motionless on top of the water. These are proofs for those who are steadfast, appreciative.

34. He can annihilate them, as a consequence of their own works. Instead, He overlooks many *(of their sins)*.

35. Those who argue against our proofs will find out that they have no basis.

36. Whatever you are given is no more than temporary material of this life. What **GOD** possesses is far better and everlasting, for those who believe and trust in their Lord.

Traits of the Believers

37. They avoid gross sins and vice, and when angered they forgive.

38. They respond to their Lord by observing the Contact Prayers (*Salat*). Their affairs are decided after due consultation among themselves, and from our provisions to them they give *(to charity)*.

39. When gross injustice befalls them, they stand up for their rights.

40. Although the just requital for an injustice is an equivalent retribution, those who pardon and maintain righteousness are rewarded by **GOD**. He does not love the unjust.

---

* *42:24 The disbelievers added 2 false statements at the end of Sura 9 to commemorate their idol, the prophet Muhammad. God has revealed overwhelming evidence to erase this blasphemy and establish the truth. By adding the gematrical value of "Rashad Khalifa" (1230), plus the verse number (24), we get 1254, 19x66 (please see Appendices 2 & 24 for the details).*

41. Certainly, those who stand up for their rights, when injustice befalls them, are not committing any error.

42. The wrong ones are those who treat the people unjustly, and resort to aggression without provocation. These have incurred a painful retribution.

43. Resorting to patience and forgiveness reflects a true strength of character.

44. Whomever **GOD** sends astray will never find any other lord, and you will see such transgressors, when they see the retribution, saying, "Can we get another chance?"

45. You will see them facing it, humiliated and debased, and looking, yet trying to avoid looking. Those who believed will proclaim: "The real losers are those who lost their souls and their families on the Day of Resurrection. The transgressors have deserved an everlasting retribution."

46. There will be no allies to help them against **GOD**. Whomever **GOD** sends astray can never be guided.

47. You shall respond to your Lord before a day comes which is decreed inevitable by **GOD**. There will be no refuge for you on that day, nor an advocate.

Sole Mission of the Messenger

48. If they turn away, we did not send you as their guardian. Your sole mission is delivering the message. When we shower the human beings with mercy, they become proud, and when adversity afflicts them, as a consequence of their own deeds, the human beings turn into disbelievers.

49. To **GOD** belongs the sovereignty of the heavens and the earth. He creates whatever He wills, granting daughters to whomever He wills, and granting sons to whomever He wills.

50. Or, He may have the males and the females marry each other, then render whomever He wills sterile. He is Omniscient, Omnipotent.

How God Communicates With Us

51. No human being can communicate with **GOD** except through inspiration, or from behind a barrier, or by sending a messenger through whom He reveals what He wills. He is the Most High, Most Wise.

52. Thus, we inspired to you a revelation proclaiming our commandments. You had no idea about the scripture, or faith. Yet, we made this a beacon to guide whomever we choose from among our servants. Surely, you guide in a straight path.

53. The path of **GOD**, to whom belongs everything in the heavens and everything on earth. Absolutely, all matters are controlled by **GOD**.

◆◆◆◆

Sura 43: Ornaments (Al-Zukhruf)

In the name of God,
Most Gracious, Most Merciful

1. H.M.*

2. And the enlightening scripture.

---

*43:1 See Footnote 40:1. The frequency of occurrence of the letters "H" (Hã) and "M" (Meem) in the seven H.M.-initialed suras is 292, and 1855, respectively. This adds up to 2147, or 19x113.

3. We have rendered it an Arabic Quran, that you may understand.*

4. It is preserved with us in the original master, honorable and full of wisdom.

5. Should we just ignore the fact that you have transgressed the limits?*

The Plan for Redemption

6. We have sent many a prophet to the previous generations.

7. Every time a prophet went to them, they ridiculed him.

8. Consequently, we annihilated people who were even more powerful than these. We thus set the examples from the previous communities.

9. If you asked them, "Who created the heavens and the earth," they would say, "The Almighty, the Omniscient has created them."

10. He is the One who made the earth habitable for you, and created for you roads therein, that you may follow the right way.

11. He is the One who sends down from the sky water, in exact measure, to revive dead lands therewith. Similarly, you will be resurrected.

12. He is the One who created all kinds, in pairs *(male and female)*, and He created for you ships and livestock to ride.

13. As you rest on top of them, you shall appreciate such a blessing from your Lord, and say, "Glory be to the One who subdued this for us. We could not have controlled them by ourselves.

14. "We ultimately return to our Lord."

Angels As Daughters: A Blasphemy

15. They even assigned for Him a share from His own creation! Surely, the human being is profoundly unappreciative.

16. Has He chosen from among His creations daughters for Himself, while blessing you with sons?

17. When one of them is given news *(of a daughter)* as they claimed for the Most Gracious, his face is darkened with misery and anger!

18. *(They say,)* "What is good about an offspring that is brought up to be beautiful, and cannot help in war?"

19. They claimed that the angels, who are servants of the Most Gracious, are females! Have they witnessed their creation? Their claims are recorded, and they will be asked.

20. They even said, "If the Most Gracious willed, we would not have worshiped them." They have no basis for such a claim; they only conjecture.*

21. Have we given them a book before this, and they are upholding it?

---

*43:3 Arabic is the most efficient language, especially in expressing commandments, statutes and exacting laws. Hence the revelation of the Quran in Arabic for the clear understanding of all peoples, regardless of their tongues. See Appendix 4 for the details.

*43:5 This refers to our original sin as detailed in the Introduction and Appendix 7.

*43:20 The idol worshipers cannot blame God for their idolatry, since we have absolute freedom of choice to worship God alone, or not.

Inherited Traditions Condemned

22. The fact is: they said, "We found our parents carrying on certain practices, and we are following in their footsteps."

23. Invariably, when we sent a warner to any community, the leaders of that community would say, "We found our parents following certain practices, and we will continue in their footsteps."

24. (*The messenger*) would say, "What if I brought to you better guidance than what you inherited from your parents?" They would say, "We are disbelievers in the message you brought."

25. Consequently, we requited them. Note the consequences for the rejectors.

Abraham's Example

26. Abraham said to his father and his people, "I disown what you worship.

27. "Only the One who initiated me can guide me."

28. This example (*of Abraham*) was rendered an everlasting lesson for subsequent generations; perhaps they redeem their souls.

29. Indeed, I have given these people and their ancestors sufficient chances, then the truth came to them, and a clarifying messenger.

30. When the truth came to them, they said, "This is magic, and we are disbelievers therein."

Muhammad Ridiculed

31. They said, "If only this Quran was sent down through another man from the two communities (*Mecca or Yathrib*) who is prominent!"

32. Are they the ones who assign your Lord's mercy? We have assigned their shares in this life, raising some of them above others in ranks, in order to let them serve one another. The mercy from your Lord is far better than any material they may hoard.

Materials of This World: All That The Disbelievers Get

33. If it were not that all the people might become one (*disbelieving*) congregation, we would have granted everyone who disbelieves in the Most Gracious mansions with silver roofs, and stairs upon which they could climb.

34. Their mansions would have impressive gates, and luxurious furnishings.

35. Also many ornaments. All these are the temporary materials of this lowly life. The Hereafter—at your Lord—is far better for the righteous.

Invisible, Devilish, Companions*

36. Anyone who disregards the message of the Most Gracious, we appoint a devil to be his constant companion.*

37. Such companions will divert them from the path, yet make them believe that they are guided.

---

*43:36-39 Each one of us has a representative of Satan as a constant companion (App. 7).

---

38. When he comes before us he will say, "Oh I wish you were as far from me as the two easts.* What a miserable companion!"

39. It will not console you on that day, as transgressors, that both of you will share in the retribution.

God's Messenger of
the Covenant

40. Can you make the deaf hear; can you make the blind see, or those who are far astray?

41. Whether we let you die before it or not, we will surely requite them.

42. Or, we may show you *(the retribution)* we promised for them. We are in full control over them.

43. You shall steadfastly preach what is revealed to you; you are in the right path.*

44. This is a message for you and your people; all of you will be questioned.

45. Check the messengers we sent before you: "Have we ever appointed any other gods—beside the Most Gracious—to be worshiped?"

46. For example, we sent Moses with our proofs to Pharaoh and his elders, proclaiming: "I am a messenger from the Lord of the universe."

47. When he showed them our proofs, they laughed at them.

Moses and Pharaoh

48. Every sign we showed them was bigger than the one before it. We afflicted them with the plagues, perhaps they repent.

49. They said, "O you magician, implore your Lord on our behalf, since you have an agreement with Him *(to relieve this plague);* we will then be guided."

50. But as soon as we relieved their affliction, they reverted.

51. Pharaoh announced to his people, "O my people, do I not possess the kingship over Egypt, and these flowing rivers belong to me? Do you not see?

52. "Which one is better; me or that one who is lowly and can hardly speak?

53. "How come he does not possess a treasure of gold; how come the angels do not accompany him?"

54. He thus fooled his people, and they obeyed him; they were wicked people.

55. When they persisted in opposing us, we punished them and drowned them all.

56. We rendered them a precedent and an example for the others.

Jesus: Another Example

57. When the son of Mary was cited as an example, your people disregarded it.

58. They said, "Is it better to worship our gods, or to worship him?" They said this only to argue with you. Indeed, they are people who have joined the opposition.

---

*43:38 The "easts" imply the locations of sunrise, moonrise, and the rising of heavenly bodies.

*43:43 The sum of the gematrical value of "Rashad Khalifa" (1230) plus 43 is 1273, 19x66.

59. He was no more than a servant whom we blessed, and we sent him as an example for the Children of Israel.

60. If we willed, we could have made you angels who colonize and reproduce on earth.

*Jesus and the End of the World**

61. He is to serve as a marker for knowing the end of the world, * so you can no longer harbor any doubt about it. You shall follow Me; this is the right path.

62. Let not the devil repel you; he is your most ardent enemy.

63. When Jesus went with the proofs, he said, "I bring to you wisdom, and to clarify some of the matters in which you dispute. You shall reverence **GOD** and obey me.

64. "**GOD** is my Lord and your Lord, you shall worship Him alone. This is the right path."

65. The opponents disputed among themselves. Woe to those who transgress from the retribution of a painful day.

66. Are they waiting for the Hour (*Day of Judgment*) to come to them suddenly when they least expect it?

67. The close friends on that day will become enemies of one another, except for the righteous.

The Righteous

68. O My servants, you will have no fear on that day, nor will you grieve.

69. They are the ones who believed in our revelations, and were submitters.

70. Enter Paradise, together with your spouses, and rejoice.

71. Offered to them will be golden trays and cups, and they will find everything the hearts desire and the eyes wish for. You live therein forever.

72. Such is the Paradise that you inherit, in return for your works.

73. You will have in it all kinds of fruits, from which you eat.

74. Surely, the guilty will abide in the retribution of Gehenna forever.

75. Never will the retribution be commuted for them; they will be confined therein.

76. It is not us who wronged them; it is they who wronged their own souls.

77. They will implore: "O Mālek, let your Lord finish us off." He will say, "You are staying forever.

They Hate The Truth

78. "We have given you the truth, but most of you hate the truth."

79. Have they schemed some scheme? We too are scheming.

80. Do they think that we do not hear their secrets and conspiracies? Yes indeed; our messengers are with them, recording.

81. Proclaim: "If the Most Gracious did have a son, I would still be the foremost worshiper."

43:61 As detailed in Appendix 25, the End of the World is given in the Quran, and the birthdate of Jesus provided one of the significant signs that the calculations are correct. We learn that the world will end in the year 2280 (19x120) after the birth of Jesus (see 47:18). Additionally, both the lunar year (1710) & the solar year (2280) are divisible by 570 (19x30), the number of years from the birth of Jesus to the birth of Muhammad Thus, the birth date of Jesus is a marker.

82. Be He glorified; He is the Lord of the heavens and the earth, the Lord with the great dominion, far above their claims.

83. Let them blunder and play until they meet their day that is awaiting them.

84. He is the only One who is a deity in the heaven and a deity on earth. He is the Most Wise, the Omniscient.

85. Most Exalted is the One who possesses all sovereignty of the heavens and the earth, and everything between them. With Him is the knowledge about the Hour (*end of the world*), and to Him you will be returned.

86. None of those whom they idolize beside Him possess any power to intercede, unless their intercession coincides with the truth, and they fully know.

87. If you asked them who created them, they would say, "**GOD.**" Why then did they deviate?

88. It will be proclaimed: "O my Lord, these people do not believe."

89. You shall disregard them and say, "Peace;" they will surely find out.

◆◆◆◆

Sura 44: Smoke (Al-Dukhãn)

In the name of God,
Most Gracious, Most Merciful

1. H.M.

2. And this enlightening scripture.

3. We have sent it down in a blessed night, for we are to warn.

4. In it (*the scripture*), every matter of wisdom is clarified.

5. It is a predetermined command from us that we send messengers.

6. This is a mercy from your Lord. He is the Hearer, the Omniscient.

7. Lord of the heavens and the earth, and everything between them. If only you could be certain!

8. There is no other god beside Him. He controls life and death; your Lord and the Lord of your ancestors.

9. Indeed, they are doubtful, heedless.

The Smoke: A Major Prophecy*

10. Therefore, watch for the day when the sky brings a profound smoke.*

11. It will envelope the people; this is a painful retribution.

12. "Our Lord, relieve this retribution for us; we are believers."

God's Messenger of the Covenant*

13. Now that it is too late, they remember! An enlightening messenger had come to them.*

14. But they turned away from him, saying, "Well educated, but crazy!"

15. We will relieve the retribution for awhile; you will soon revert.

16. The day we strike the big stroke, we will avenge.

17. We have tested before them the people of Pharaoh; an honorable messenger went to them.

44:10 Only two signs are yet to be fulfilled, this smoke and Gog and Magog (Appendix 25).

44:13 The sum of sura and verse numbers (44 + 13) is 57, 19x3, and this Quranic code was proclaimed by God's Messenger of the Covenant (Appendices 1, 2, & 26).

18. Proclaiming: "Listen to me, servants of **GOD**. I am an honest messenger to you."

19. And, "Do not transgress against **GOD**. I bring to you powerful proofs.

20. "I seek refuge in my Lord and your Lord, if you oppose me.

21. "If you do not wish to believe, then simply leave me alone."

22. Subsequently, he implored his Lord: "These are wicked people."

23. (*God said,*) "Travel with My servants during the night; you will be pursued.

24. "Cross the sea quickly; their troops will be drowned."

25. Thus, they left behind many gardens and springs.

26. Crops and a luxurious life.

27. Blessings that they enjoyed.

28. All these we caused to be inherited by other people.

29. Neither the heaven, nor the earth wept over them, and they were not respited.

30. Meanwhile, we saved the Children of Israel from the humiliating persecution.

31. From Pharaoh; he was a tyrant.

32. We have chosen them from among all the people, knowingly.

33. We showed them so many proofs, which constituted a great test.

Expect The Same Consequences

34. The present generations say,

35. "We only die the first death; we will never be resurrected!

36. "Bring back our forefathers, if you are truthful."

37. Are they better than the people of Tubba' and others before them? We annihilated them for their crimes.

38. We did not create the heavens and the earth, and everything between them, just to play.

39. We created them for a specific purpose, but most of them do not know.

40. The Day of Decision awaits them all.

41. That is the day when no friend can help his friend in any way; no one can be helped.

42. Only those who attain mercy from **GOD**. He is the Almighty, Most Merciful.

The Disbelievers

43. Surely, the tree of bitterness—

44. will provide the food for the sinful.

45. Like lye, it will boil in the stomachs.

46. Like the boiling of hellish drinks.

47. Take him and throw him into the center of Hell.

48. Then pour upon his head the retribution of the Inferno.

49. "Taste this; you were so powerful, so honorable."

50. This is what you used to doubt.

The Righteous

51. The righteous will be in a secure position.

52. Enjoying gardens and springs.

53. Wearing velvet and satin; close to each other.

54. We grant them wonderful spouses.

55. They enjoy in it all kinds of fruits, in perfect peace.

The Righteous Do Not Really Die*

56. They do not taste death therein— beyond the first death*—and He has spared them the retribution of Hell.

57. Such is the blessing from your Lord. Such is the great triumph.

58. We have thus clarified it in your language, that they may take heed.

59. Therefore, wait; they too will have to wait.

◆◆◆◆

Sura 45: Kneeling (Al-Jātheyah)

In the name of God,
Most Gracious, Most Merciful

1. H.M.

2. The revelation of this scripture is from **GOD**, the Almighty, Most Wise.

3. The heavens and the earth are full of proofs for the believers.

4. Also in your creation, and the creation of all the animals, there are proofs for people who are certain.

5. Also, the alternation of the night and the day, and the provisions that **GOD** sends down from the sky to revive dead lands, and the manipulation of the winds; all these are proofs for people who understand.

Which Hadith?*

6. These are **GOD**'s revelations that we recite to you truthfully. In which *Hadith* other than **GOD** and His revelations do they believe?

7. Woe to every fabricator, guilty.*

8. The one who hears **GOD**'s revelations recited to him, then insists arrogantly on his way, as if he never heard them. Promise him a painful retribution.

9. When he learns anything about our revelations, he mocks them. These have incurred a shameful retribution.

10. Awaiting them is Gehenna. Their earnings will not help them, nor the idols they had set up beside **GOD**. They have incurred a terrible retribution.

11. This is a beacon, and those who disbelieve in these revelations of their Lord have incurred condemnation and a painful retribution.

12. **GOD** is the One who committed the sea in your service, so that the ships can roam it in accordance with His laws. You thus seek His provisions, that you may be appreciative.

13. He committed in your service everything in the heavens and the earth; all from Him. These are proofs for people who reflect.

14. Tell those who believed to forgive those who do not expect the days of **GOD**. He will fully pay everyone for whatever they have earned.

---

*44:56 As detailed in Appendix 17, the righteous do not really die; they move on directly to the same Paradise where Adam and Eve once lived. Compare this statement with the disbelievers' statement in 40:11.

*45:6-7 God condemns "Hadith" by name, and informs us that it is a blasphemous fabrication.

---

15. Whoever works righteousness does so for his own good, and whoever works evil does so to his own detriment. To your Lord you will be returned.

16. We have given the Children of Israel the scripture, wisdom, and prophethood, and provided them with good provisions; we bestowed upon them more blessings than any other people.

17. We have given them herein clear commandments. Ironically, they did not dispute this until the knowledge had come to them. This is due to jealousy on their part. Surely, your Lord will judge them on the Day of Resurrection regarding everything they have disputed.

18. We then appointed you to establish the correct laws; you shall follow this, and do not follow the wishes of those who do not know.

19. They cannot help you at all against **GOD**. It is the transgressors who ally themselves with one another, while **GOD** is the Lord of the righteous.

20. This provides enlightenments for the people, and guidance, and mercy for those who are certain.

21. Do those who work evil expect that we will treat them in the same manner as those who believe and lead a righteous life? Can their life and their death be the same?* Wrong indeed is their judgment.

22. **GOD** created the heavens and the earth for a specific purpose, in order to pay each soul for whatever it earned, without the least injustice.*

*Common Form of Idolatry:
The Ego As A god*

23. Have you noted the one whose god is his ego? Consequently, **GOD** sends him astray, despite his knowledge, seals his hearing and his mind, and places a veil on his eyes. Who then can guide him, after such a decision by **GOD**? Would you not take heed?

24. They said, "We only live this life; we live and die and only time causes our death!" They have no sure knowledge about this; they only conjecture.

25. When our revelations are recited to them, clearly, their only argument is to say, "Bring back our forefathers, if you are truthful."

26. Say, "**GOD** has granted you life, then He puts you to death, then He will summon you to the Day of Resurrection, which is inevitable. But most people do not know."

27. To **GOD** belongs all sovereignty of the heavens and the earth. The day the Hour *(Judgment)* comes to pass, that is when the falsifiers lose.

Kneeling

28. You will see every community kneeling. Every community will be called to view their record. Today, you get paid for everything you have done.

---

*45:21 We now realize that the righteous do not really die—they go straight to Heaven (16:32)—while the unrighteous are beaten up by the angels of death (8:50 & 47:27).

*45:22 God granted us this life as a precious chance to redeem ourselves, denounce our ancient alliance with Satan, and rejoin God's kingdom. See Introduction & Appendix 7.

29. This is our record; it utters the truth about you. We have been recording everything you did.

30. As for those who believe and work righteousness, their Lord will admit them into His mercy. This is the great triumph.

31. As for those who disbelieve: "Were not My revelations recited to you, but you turned arrogant and were wicked people?"

32. When it is proclaimed that **GOD**'s promise is the truth and that the Hour *(of Judgment)* is inevitable, you said, "We do not know what the Hour is! We are full of conjecture about it; we are not certain."

33. The evils of their works will become evident to them, and the very things they mocked will come back and haunt them.

34. It will be proclaimed: "Today we forget you, just as you forgot the meeting of this day. Your abode is the hellfire, and you will have no helpers.

35. "This is because you took **GOD**'s revelations in vain, and were preoccupied with the first life." Consequently, they will never exit therefrom, nor will they be excused.

36. To **GOD** belongs all praise; Lord of the heavens, Lord of the earth, Lord of the universe.

37. To Him belongs all supremacy in the heavens and the earth. He is the Almighty, Most Wise.

◆◆◆◆

Sura 46: The Dunes (Al-Ahqãf)

In the name of God,
Most Gracious, Most Merciful

1. H.M.

2. The revelation of this scripture is from **GOD,** the Almighty, Most Wise.

3. We did not create the heavens and the earth, and everything between them except for a specific purpose, and for a finite interim. Those who disbelieve are totally oblivious to the warnings given to them.

4. Say, "Consider the idols you have set up beside **GOD.** Show me what on earth did they create. Do they own part of the heavens? Show me any other scripture before this one, or any piece of established knowledge that supports your idolatry, if you are truthful."

The Idols Totally Unaware

5. Who is farther astray than those who idolize beside **GOD** idols that can never respond to them until the Day of Resurrection, and are totally unaware of their worship?

The Idols Disown
Their Worshipers*

6. And when the people are summoned *(on the Day of Judgment),* their idols will become their enemies, and will denounce their idolatry.*

7. When our revelations were recited to them, perfectly clear, those who disbelieved said of the truth that came to them, "This is obviously magic!"

---

*46:6 See also Matthew 7:21-23: Jesus clearly disowns those who call him "Lord."

---

8. When they say, "He fabricated this," say, "If I fabricated this, then you cannot protect me from **GOD**. He is fully aware of everything you scheme. He suffices as a witness between me and you. He is the Forgiver, Most Merciful."

9. Say, "I am not different from other messengers. I have no idea what will happen to me or to you. I only follow what is revealed to me. I am no more than a profound warner."

Rabbi Judah the Pious*

10. Say, "What if it is from **GOD** and you disbelieved in it? A witness from the Children of Israel has borne witness to a similar phenomenon,* and he has believed, while you have turned arrogant. Surely, **GOD** does not guide the wicked people."

11. Those who disbelieved said about those who believed, "If it were anything good, they would not have accepted it before us." Because they were not guided to it, they said, "This is an old fabrication!"

12. Before this, the book of Moses provided guidance and mercy. This too is a scripture that confirms, in Arabic, to warn those who transgressed, and to give good news to the righteous.

Good News

13. Surely, those who say, "Our Lord is **GOD**," then lead a righteous life, will have no fear, nor will they grieve.

14. They have deserved Paradise, where they abide forever; a reward for their works.

40: The Age of Decision*

15. We enjoined the human being to honor his parents. His mother bore him arduously, gave birth to him arduously, and took intimate care of him for thirty months. When he reaches maturity, and reaches the age of forty,* he should say, "My Lord, direct me to appreciate the blessings You have bestowed upon me and upon my parents, and to do the righteous works that please You. Let my children be righteous as well. I have repented to You; I am a submitter."

16. It is from these that we accept the righteous works, and overlook their sins. They have deserved Paradise. This is the truthful promise that is promised to them.

17. Then there is the one who says to his parents, "Woe to you; are you telling me that (*after death*) I will come back to life? How come those who died before us never come back?" The parents would cry for **GOD**'s help and say, "Woe to you; please believe! **GOD**'s promise is the truth." He would say, "Tales from the past!"

18. Such are the ones stamped as disbelievers among every generation of jinns and humans; they are losers.

---

*46:10 *This witness is Rabbi Judah the Pious (11th Century A.D.), who discovered the same 19-based mathematical code in intact fragments of the scripture (see Appendix 1).*

*46:15 *God knows full well who deserves to go to Heaven and who deserves to go to Hell. It is His law that whomever He puts to death before the age of 40 shall go to Heaven. God's immense mercy is reflected in the fact that most people have difficulty accepting this divine mercy; they argue: "Put them in Hell!" See Appendix 32.*

19. They all attain the ranks they have deserved, in accordance with their works. He will pay them for their works, without the least injustice.

20. The day will come when those who disbelieved will be introduced to the hellfire: "You have wasted the good chances given to you during your worldly life, and you rejoiced in them. Consequently, today you incur a shameful retribution as a requital for the arrogance you committed on earth without any basis, and for your evil works."

Hûd

21. Recall that the brother of 'Ãd warned his people at the dunes— numerous warnings were also delivered before him and after him: "You shall not worship except **GOD**. I fear for you the retribution of a great day."

22. They said, "Did you come to divert us from our gods? We challenge you to bring (*the retribution*) you threaten, if you are truthful."

23. He said, "The knowledge about this is with **GOD**; I only deliver to you what I was sent to deliver. However, I see that you people are ignorant."

24. When they saw the storm heading their way, they said, "This storm will bring to us much needed rain." Instead, this is what you challenged (*Hûd*) to bring; violent wind wherein there is painful retribution.

25. It destroyed everything, as commanded by its Lord. By morning, nothing was standing except their homes. We thus requite the guilty people.

They Ridiculed the Messenger's Warnings

26. We had established them in the same way as we established you, and provided them with hearing, eyes, and minds. But their hearing, eyes, and minds did not help them at all. This is because they decided to disregard **GOD**'s revelations. Thus, the prophecies and warnings that they ridiculed have caused their doom.

27. We have annihilated many communities around you, after we had explained the proofs, that they might repent.

28. Why then did the idols they set up to bring them closer to **GOD** fail to help them? Instead, they abandoned them. Such were the false gods they idolized; such were the innovations they fabricated.

Believers Among the Jinns *

29. Recall that we directed a number of jinns to you, in order to let them hear the Quran. When they got there, they said, "Listen." As soon as it was over, they rushed to their people, warning.*

30. They said, "O our people, we have heard a book that was revealed after Moses, and confirms the previous scriptures. It guides to the truth; to the right path.

31. "O our people, respond to the call of **GOD**, and believe in Him. He will then forgive your sins, and spare you a painful retribution."

46:29 Jinns are the creatures who fully agreed with Satan when he initiated his famous blasphemy billions of years ago. They are brought into this world as descendants of Satan. One jinn is born every time a human being is born. The newly born jinn is assigned to the same body as the newly born human, and constantly pushes Satan's point of view (Appendix 7).

32. Those who fail to respond to **GOD**'s call cannot escape, and will have no Lord other than Him; they have gone far astray.

33. Do they not realize that **GOD**, who created the heavens and the earth without the least effort is able to revive the dead? Yes indeed; He is Omnipotent.

34. The day the disbelievers are introduced to the Hellfire, they will be asked, "Is this not the truth?" They will answer, "Yes indeed, by our Lord." He will say, "Then suffer the retribution for your disbelief."

God's Messenger of the Covenant*

35. Therefore, be patient like the messengers before you who possessed strength and resorted to patience. Do not be in a hurry to see the retribution that will inevitably come to them. The day they see it, it will seem as if they lasted one hour of the day. This is a proclamation: Is it not the wicked who are consistently annihilated?

❖❖❖❖

Sura 47: Muhammad

In the name of God,
Most Gracious, Most Merciful

1. Those who disbelieve and repel from the path of **GOD,** He nullifies their works.

2. Those who believe and work righteousness, and believe in what was sent down to Muhammad—which is the truth from their Lord—He re-mits their sins, and blesses them with contentment.

3. This is because those who disbelieve are following falsehood, while those who believe are following the truth from their Lord. **GOD** thus cites for the people, their examples.

4. If you encounter (*in war*) those who disbelieve, you may strike the necks. If you take them as captives you may set them free or ransom them, until the war ends. Had **GOD** willed, He could have granted you victory, without war. But He thus tests you by one another. As for those who get killed in the cause of **GOD**, He will never put their sacrifice to waste.

5. He will guide them, and bless them with contentment.

6. He will admit them into Paradise, that He described to them.

7. O you who believe, if you support **GOD**, He will support you, and strengthen your foothold.

8. Those who disbelieve incur misery; He causes their works to be utterly in vain.

9. That is because they hated what **GOD** revealed and consequently, He nullifies their works.

10. Did they not roam the earth and see the consequences for those before them? **GOD** destroyed their works; all disbelievers will suffer the same fate.

11. This is because **GOD** is the Lord of those who believe, while the disbelievers have no lord.

---

*46:35 Quranic and mathematical evidence proves that the messenger addressed here is Rashad Khalifa. By adding the gematrical value of "Rashad Khalifa" (1230), plus the sura number (46), plus the verse number (35), we get 1311, or 19x69. This conforms with the Quran's code (App. 2).

12. **GOD** admits those who believe and lead a righteous life into gardens with flowing streams. As for those who disbelieve, they live and eat like the animals eat, then end up in the hellfire.

13. Many a community was much stronger than the community that evicted you from your town; when we annihilated them, no one could help them.

14. Are those enlightened by their Lord the same as those whose evil works are adorned in their eyes, and they follow their own opinions?

15. The allegory of Paradise that is promised for the righteous is this: it has rivers of unpolluted water, and rivers of fresh milk, and rivers of wine—delicious for the drinkers—and rivers of strained honey. They have all kinds of fruits therein, and forgiveness from their Lord. *(Are they better)* or those who abide forever in the hellfire, and drink hellish water that tears up their intestines?

16. Some of them listen to you, then as soon as they leave they ask those who were enlightened, "What did he just say?" **GOD** thus seals their hearts and, consequently, they follow only their opinions.

17. As for those who are guided, He augments their guidance, and grants them their righteousness.

*End of the World**

18. Are they waiting until the Hour comes to them suddenly? All the signs thereof have already come.* Once the Hour comes to them, how will they benefit from their message?

Lã Elãha Ellã Allãh: First Commandment

19. You shall know that: **"There is no other god beside GOD,"*** and ask forgiveness of your sins and the sins of all believing men and women. **GOD** is fully aware of your decisions and your ultimate destiny.

Exposing the Hypocrites

20. Those who believed said: "When will a new sura be revealed?" But when a straightforward sura was revealed, wherein fighting was mentioned, you would see those who harbored doubts in their hearts looking at you, as if death had already come to them. They were thus exposed.

Proof of Faith During Muhammad's Era

21. Obedience and righteous utterances are expected of them. If only they showed confidence in **GOD**, when mobilization was called for, it would have been better for them.

22. Is it also your intention that as soon as you leave you will commit evil and mistreat your relatives?

23. It is those who incurred a curse from **GOD**, whereby He rendered them deaf and blind.

47:18 The Quran, being the Final Testament, provides all the signs needed to pinpoint the end of the world; AD 2280. See Appendix 25 for the details.

47:19 Significantly, the "First Pillar" of religion is stated in the sura entitled Muhammad, and is utterly devoted to God alone. Muhammad's name was added by his idolizers, against his will.

Study the Quran

24. Why do they not study the Quran carefully? Do they have locks on their minds?

25. Surely, those who slide back, after the guidance has been manifested to them, the devil has enticed them and led them on.

26. This is because they said to those who hated what **GOD** has sent down, "We will obey you in certain matters." **GOD** fully knows their secret conspiracies.

27. How will it be for them when the angels put them to death? They will beat them on their faces and their rear ends.

28. This is because they followed what angered **GOD** and hated the things that please Him. Consequently, He has nullified their works.

29. Did those who harbor doubts in their hearts think that **GOD** will not bring out their evil thoughts?

30. If we will, we can expose them for you, so that you can recognize them just by looking at them. However, you can recognize them by the way they talk. **GOD** is fully aware of all your works.

31. We will certainly put you to the test, in order to distinguish those among you who strive, and steadfastly persevere. We must expose your true qualities.

32. Those who disbelieve and repel from the path of **GOD**, and oppose the messenger after the guidance has been manifested for them, will never hurt **GOD** in the least. Instead, He nullifies their works.

33. O you who believe, you shall obey **GOD**, and obey the messenger. Otherwise, all your works will be in vain.

The Great Disaster

34. Those who disbelieve and repel from the path of **GOD**, then die as disbelievers, **GOD** will never forgive them.

35. Therefore, you shall not waver and surrender in pursuit of peace, for you are guaranteed victory, and **GOD** is with you. He will never waste your efforts.

36. This worldly life is no more than play and vanity. But if you believe and lead a righteous life, He will reward you, without asking you for any money.

37. If He asked you for money, to the extent of creating a hardship for you, you might have become stingy, and your hidden evil might be exposed.

38. You are invited to spend in the cause of **GOD,** but some of you turn stingy. The stingy are stingy towards their own souls. **GOD** is Rich, while you are poor.

Warning to the Arabs *

If you turn away, He will substitute other people in your place, and they will not be like you.

❖❖❖❖

Sura 48: Victory (Al-Fatt-h)

---

*47:38 The Quran was given to the Arabs, in their language, for 1400 years, but they clearly rejected it and refused to believe that it is complete; they fabricated Hadith & Sunna.

In the name of God,
Most Gracious, Most Merciful

1. We have bestowed upon you *(O Messenger)* a great victory.*

2. Whereby **GOD** forgives your past sins, as well as future sins, and perfects His blessings upon you, and guides you in a straight path.

3. Additionally, **GOD** will support you with an unwavering support.

4. He is the One who places contentment into the hearts of believers to augment more faith, in addition to their faith. To **GOD** belongs all forces of the heavens and the earth. **GOD** is Omniscient, Most Wise.

5. He will certainly admit the believing men and women into gardens with flowing streams, wherein they abide forever. He will remit their sins. This is, in the sight of **GOD**, a great triumph.

6. And He will requite the hypocrite men and women and the idol worshiping men and women, for they have harbored evil thoughts about **GOD**. Their evil will backfire against them. For **GOD** is angry with them, condemns them, and has prepared for them Gehenna. What a miserable destiny!

7. To **GOD** belongs all the forces in the heavens and the earth. **GOD** is Almighty, Most Wise.

8. We have sent you as a witness, a bearer of good news, and a warner.

9. That you people may believe in **GOD** and His messenger, and reverence Him, and observe Him, and glorify Him, day and night.

*You Shall Support
God's Messenger*

10. Surely, those who pledge allegiance to you, are pledging allegiance to **GOD**. **GOD** approves their pledge; He places His hand above their hands. Those who violate such a pledge, commit the violation to their own detriment. As for those who fulfill their pledge with **GOD**, He will grant them a great recompense.

11. The sedentary Arabs who stay behind will say, "We have been preoccupied with our money and our families, so ask forgiveness for us!" They utter with their tongues what is not in their hearts. Say, "Who can protect you from **GOD**, if He willed any adversity for you, or if He willed any blessing for you?" **GOD** is fully Cognizant of everything you do.

12. You secretly believed that the messenger and the believers will be defeated and never come back to their families, and this was firmly established in your hearts. You harbored evil thoughts and turned into wicked people.

13. Anyone who refuses to believe in **GOD** and His messenger, we have prepared for the disbelievers a hellfire.

48:1 This profound statement consists of 19 letters, indicating that our generation is the generation of victory for God's purified, unified, and consolidated religion— Submission (3:19, 85). It is our generation that witnessed the revelations of God's great miracle in the Quran (Appendix 1).

---

14. To **GOD** belongs the sovereignty of the heavens and the earth. He forgives whomever He wills, and punishes whomever He wills. **GOD** is Forgiver, Most Merciful.

15. The sedentary who stay behind will say, when you are expected to collect spoils of war, "Let us follow you to share in this!" They thus wish to alter **GOD**'s words. Say, "You will not follow us. This is **GOD**'s decision." They will then say, "You must be envious of us *(for staying behind)*." Indeed, they rarely understood anything.

The Test for Early Generations

16. Say to the sedentary Arabs who stay behind, "You will be invited to face powerful people and to fight them, unless they submit. If you obey, **GOD** will reward you with a generous recompense. But if you turn away again, as you did in the past, He will requite you with a painful retribution."

17. The blind is not to be blamed, the crippled is not to be blamed, and the sick is not to be blamed. Those who obey **GOD** and His messenger, He will admit them into gardens with flowing streams. As for those who turn away, He will requite them with a painful retribution.

18. **GOD** is pleased with the believers who pledged allegiance to you under the tree. He knew what was in their hearts and, consequently, He blessed them with contentment, and rewarded them with an immediate victory.

19. Additionally, they gained many spoils. **GOD** is Almighty, Most Wise.

20. **GOD** has promised you many spoils that you will gain. He thus advanced some benefits for you in this life, and He has withheld the people's hands of aggression against you, and has rendered this a sign for the believers. He thus guides you in a straight path.

21. As for the group that you could not possibly defeat, **GOD** took care of them; **GOD** is Omnipotent.

Victory
Guaranteed
for the Believers

22. If the disbelievers ever fought you, they would turn around and flee. They have no Lord and Master; they have no helper.

23. Such is **GOD**'s system throughout history, and you will find that **GOD**'s system is unchangeable.

24. He is the One who withheld their hands of aggression against you, and withheld your hands of aggression against them in the valley of Mecca, after He had granted you victory over them. **GOD** is Seer of everything you do.

25. It is they who disbelieved and barred you from the Sacred Masjid, and even prevented your offerings from reaching their destination. There were believing men and women *(within the enemy camp)* whom you did not know, and you were about to hurt them, unknowingly. **GOD** thus admits into His mercy whomever He wills. If they persist, He will requite those among them who disbelieve with a painful retribution.

26. While those who disbelieved were enraged, and their hearts were filled with the pride of the days of ignorance, **GOD** blessed His messenger and the believers with peaceful contentment, and directed them to uphold the word of righteousness. This is what they well deserved. **GOD** is fully aware of all things.

27. **GOD** has fulfilled His messenger's truthful vision: "You will enter the Sacred Masjid, **GOD** willing, perfectly secure, and you will cut your hair or shorten it *(as you fulfill the pilgrimage rituals)* there. You will not have any fear. Since He knew what you did not know, He has coupled this with an immediate victory."

The Great Prophecy*

28. He is the One who sent His messenger with the guidance and the religion of truth, to make it prevail over all other religions. **GOD** suffices as a witness.*

Qualities of the Believers

29. Muhammad—the messenger of **GOD**—and those with him are harsh and stern against the disbelievers, but kind and compassionate amongst themselves. You see them bowing and prostrating, as they seek **GOD** blessings and approval. Their

marks are on their faces, because of prostrating. This is the same example as in the Torah. Their example in the Gospel is like plants that grow taller and stronger, and please the farmers. He thus enrages the disbelievers. **GOD** promises those among them who believe and lead a righteous life forgiveness and a great recompense.

Sura 49: The Walls (Al-Hujurãt)

In the name of God,
Most Gracious, Most Merciful

1. O you who believe, do not place your opinion above that of **GOD** and His messenger. You shall reverence **GOD**. **GOD** is Hearer, Omniscient.

2. O you who believe, do not raise your voices above the voice of the prophet,* nor shall you shout at him as you shout at each other, lest your works become nullified while you do not perceive.

3. Surely, those who lower their voices at the messenger of **GOD** are the ones whose hearts are prepared by **GOD** to become righteous.* They have deserved forgiveness and a great recompense.

---

*48:28 This important prophecy informs us that Submission will inevitably dominate the whole world. This, together with Verses 9:33, 41:53, and 61:9 leave no doubt that God's mathematical miracle of the Quran will play a major role in this prophecy. Solid Quranic mathematical evidence points to God's Messenger of the Covenant as fulfilling this prophecy. See Appendices 2 & 26 for the evidence and specific details.

*49:2 Whenever the word "prophet" (Nabi) is used in reference to Muhammad, it invariably refers to him during his life, not after his death. Obviously, we cannot possibly raise our voices above Muhammad's voice, now that he is dead. See also 33:56.

*49:3 Respecting the messenger helps outsiders and visitors in coming to God's message.

4. As for those who call on you from outside the walls, most of them do not understand.

5. Had they been patient until you came out to them, it would have been better for them. **GOD** is Forgiver, Most Merciful.

Investigate Rumors Before Believing Them

6. O you who believe, if a wicked person brings any news to you, you shall first investigate, lest you commit injustice towards some people, out of ignorance, then become sorry and remorseful for what you have done.

7. And know that **GOD**'s messenger has come in your midst. Had he listened to you in many things, you would have made things difficult for yourselves. But **GOD** made you love faith and adorned it in your hearts, and He made you abhor disbelief, wickedness, and disobedience. These are the guided ones.

8. Such is grace from **GOD** and His blessings. **GOD** is Omniscient, Most Wise.

Reconcile The Believers

9. If two groups of believers fought with each other, you shall reconcile them. If one group aggresses against the other, you shall fight the aggressing group until they submit to **GOD**'s command. Once they submit, you shall reconcile the two groups equitably. You shall maintain justice; **GOD** loves those who are just.

The Real Family

10. The believers are members of one family; you shall keep the peace within your family and reverence **GOD**, that you may attain mercy.

Believers Set the Example

11. O you who believe, no people shall ridicule other people, for they may be better than they. Nor shall any women ridicule other women, for they may be better than they. Nor shall you mock one another, or make fun of your names. Evil indeed is the reversion to wickedness after attaining faith. Anyone who does not repent after this, these are the transgressors.

Suspicion Is Sinful

12. O you who believe, you shall avoid any suspicion, for even a little bit of suspicion is sinful. You shall not spy on one another, nor shall you backbite one another; this is as abominable as eating the flesh of your dead brother. You certainly abhor this. You shall observe **GOD**. **GOD** is Redeemer, Most Merciful.

The Only Criterion For Distinguishing Among The People

13. O people, we created you from the same male and female, and rendered you distinct peoples and tribes, that you may recognize one another. The best among you in the sight of **GOD** is the most righteous. **GOD** is Omniscient, Cognizant.

Muslim vs. Mu'men

14. The Arabs said, "We are *Mu'mens* (*believers*)." Say, "You have not believed; what you should say is, 'We are *Muslims* (*submitters*),' until belief is established in your hearts." If you obey **GOD** and His messenger, He will not put any of your works to waste. **GOD** is Forgiver, Most Merciful.

15. *Mu'mens (believers)* are those who believe in **GOD** and His messenger, then attain the status of having no doubt whatsoever, and strive with their money and their lives in the cause of **GOD.** These are the truthful ones.

16. Say, "Are you informing **GOD** about your religion? **GOD** knows everything in the heavens and the earth. **GOD** is Omniscient."

Who Is Doing
Whom A Favor?

17. They act as if they are doing you a favor by embracing Submission! Say, "You are not doing me any favors by embracing Submission. **GOD** is the One who is doing you a great favor by guiding you to the faith, if you are sincere."

18. **GOD** knows all the secrets in the heavens and the earth; **GOD** is Seer of everything you do.

Sura 50: Q (Qãf)

In the name of God,
Most Gracious, Most Merciful

1. Q., and the glorious Quran.*

2. They found it strange that a warner from among them came to them! The disbelievers said, "This is really strange.

3. "After we die and become dust; this is impossible."

4. We are fully aware of any one of them who gets consumed by the earth; we have an accurate record.

5. They rejected the truth when it came to them; they are utterly confused.

6. Have they not looked at the sky above them, and how we constructed it and adorned it, without a flaw?

7. And we created the earth, and scattered on it mountains, and grew in it all kinds of beautiful plants.

8. This is an enlightenment, and a reminder for every pious worshiper.

9. And we sent from the sky blessed water, to grow with it gardens and grains to be harvested.

10. Tall date palms, with clustered fruit.

11. Provisions for the people. And we revive with it dead lands; you are similarly resurrected.

12. Disbelieving before them were the people of Noah, the dwellers of Russ, and Thamoud.

13. And 'Aad, Pharaoh, and the brethren of Lot.

14. And the dwellers of the woods, and the people of Tubba'. All of them disbelieved the messengers and, consequently, My retribution befell them.

15. Were we too burdened by the first creation? Is this why they doubt resurrection?

16. We created the human, and we know what he whispers to himself. We are closer to him than his jugular vein.

17. Two recording *(angels)*, at right and at left, are constantly recording.

---

*50:1 See Appendix 1 for the awesome miracles connected with the Initial "Q."

18. Not an utterance does he utter without an alert witness.

19. Finally, the inevitable coma of death comes; this is what you tried to evade.

20. The horn is blown; this is the promised day.

21. Every soul comes with a herder and a witness.

22. You used to be oblivious to this. We now remove your veil; today, your vision is *(as strong as)* steel.

23. The companion said, "Here is my formidable testimony."*

24. Throw into Gehenna every stubborn disbeliever.

25. Forbidder of charity, aggressor, full of doubt.

26. He set up beside **GOD** another god. Throw him into severe retribution.

27. His companion said, "Our Lord, I did not mislead him; he was far astray."

28. He said, "Do not feud in front of Me; I have sufficiently warned you.

29. "Nothing can be changed now. I am never unjust towards the people."

30. That is the day when we ask Hell, "Have you had enough?" It will say, "Give me more."

31. Paradise will be offered to the righteous, readily.

32. This is what was promised to every repenter, steadfast.

33. They reverenced the Most Gracious, in their privacy, and came wholeheartedly.

34. Enter it in peace; this is the Day of Eternity.

35. They get anything they wish therein, and we have even more.

36. Many a generation before them, who were more powerful, we annihilated. They searched the land; did they find an escape?

37. This should be a lesson for everyone who possesses a mind, or is able to hear and witness.

38. We have created the heavens and the earth, and everything between them in six days, and no fatigue touched us.

39. Therefore, be patient in the face of their utterances, and praise and glorify your Lord before sunrise, and before sunset.

40. During the night you shall meditate on His name, and after prostrating.

41. Prepare for the day when the caller calls from a place that is near.

42. When they hear the inevitable cry; that is the day you come out.

43. We are the ones who control life and death; to us is the final destiny.

44. The day will come when the earth cracks in a hurry, giving rise to them. Such summoning is easy for us to do.

45. We are fully aware of everything they utter, while you have no power over them. Therefore, remind with this Quran, those who reverence My warnings.

---

*50:23-28 *Your life-time companion witnesses everything you do. See Appendix 7.*

Sura 51: Drivers of the Winds (Al-Dhãreyãt)

In the name of God,
Most Gracious, Most Merciful

1. The blowing winds.

2. Bearing rain.

3. Bringing provisions.

4. Distributing them as commanded.

5. What is promised to you will surely come to pass.

6. The Day of Judgment is inevitable.

7. Despite the perfectly created sky.

8. You continue to dispute the truth.

9. Deviating therefrom are the deviators.

10. Woe to the falsifiers.

11. In their blundering, they are totally heedless.

12. They question the Day of Judgment.

13. The day they are presented to the fire.

14. Taste the retribution; this is what you used to challenge.

15. The righteous have deserved gardens and springs.

16. They receive their Lord's rewards, for they used to be pious.

17. Rarely did they sleep the whole night.

18. At dawn, they prayed for forgiveness.

19. A portion of their money was set aside for the beggar and the needy.

20. The earth is full of signs for those who are certain.

21. And within yourselves; can you see?

22. In the heaven is your provision, and everything that is promised to you.

23. By the Lord of the heaven and the earth, this is as true as the fact that you speak.

24. Have you noted the history of Abraham's honorable guests?

25. They visited him, saying, "Peace." He said, "Peace to you, strangers!"

26. He asked his family to prepare a fat calf.

27. When he offered it to them, he remarked, "Do you not eat?"

28. He harbored fear of them. They said, "Have no fear," and they gave good news of a knowledgeable son.

29. His wife was astonished. Noting her wrinkled face: "I am a sterile old woman."

30. They said, "Thus said your Lord. He is the Most Wise, the Omniscient."

31. He said, "What are you up to, O messengers?"

32. They said, "We have been dispatched to criminal people.

33. "We will shower them with rocks of clay.

34. "Marked by your Lord for the transgressors."

35. We then delivered all the believers.

36. We did not find in it except one house of submitters.

37. We set it up as a lesson for those who fear the painful retribution.

38. In Moses *(there is a lesson)*. We sent him to Pharaoh with manifest proofs.

39. But he turned away, in arrogance, and said, "Magician, or crazy."

40. Consequently, we punished him and his troops. We threw them into the sea, and he is the one to blame.

41. In 'Aad *(there is a lesson)*. We sent upon them disastrous wind.

42. Anything that it came upon was utterly destroyed.

43. In Thamoud *(there is a lesson)*. They were told, "Enjoy temporarily."

44. They rebelled against the command of their Lord. Consequently, the lightning struck them as they looked.

45. They could never get up, nor were they helped.

46. And the people of Noah before that; they were wicked people.

"Expansion of the Universe Theory" Confirmed

47. We constructed the sky with our hands, and we will continue to expand it.

48. And we made the earth habitable; a perfect design.

49. We created a pair *(male and female)* of everything, that you may take heed.

50. You shall escape to **GOD**. I am sent by Him to you as a manifest warner.

51. Do not set up beside **GOD** any other god. I am sent by Him to you as a manifest warner.

52. Consistently, when a messenger went to the previous generations, they said, "Magician," or, "Crazy."

53. Did they make an agreement with each other? Indeed, they are transgressors.

54. You may disregard them; you cannot be blamed.

55. And remind, for the reminder benefits the believers.

The Purpose of Our Existence

56. I did not create the jinns and the humans except to worship Me alone.

57. I need no provisions from them, nor do I need them to feed Me.

58. **GOD** is the Provider, the Possessor of all power, the Supreme.

59. The transgressors have incurred the same fate as their previous counterparts; they should not challenge.

60. Woe to those who disbelieved from the day that is awaiting them.

Sura 52: Mt. Sinai (Al-Toor)

In the name of God,
Most Gracious, Most Merciful

1. Mt. Sinai.

2. The recorded scripture.

3. Published in books.

4. The frequented Shrine.

5. The exalted ceiling.

6. The sea that is set aflame.

7. Your Lord's requital is unavoidable.

8. No force in the universe can stop it.

9. The day will come when the sky will violently thunder.

10. The mountains will be wiped out.

11. Woe on that day to the disbelievers—

12. who are in their blundering, heedless.

13. They will be herded into Gehenna, forcibly.

14. This is the Fire in which you used to disbelieve.

15. Is this magic, or do you not see?

16. Suffer the burning. Whether you are patient or impatient, it will be the same for you. This is the just requital for what you did.

17. The righteous have deserved gardens and bliss.

18. They enjoy what their Lord has reserved for them; their Lord has spared them the retribution of Hell.

19. Eat and drink happily, in return for your works.

20. They relax on luxurious furnishings, and we match them with beautiful spouses.

21. For those who believed, and their children also followed them in belief, we will have their children join them. We never fail to reward them for any work. Every person is paid for what he did.

22. We will supply them with fruits and meats that they love.

23. They will enjoy drinks that are never polluted, and never sinful to drink.

24. Serving them will be servants like protected pearls.

25. They will meet each other and reminisce among themselves.

26. They will say, "We used to be kind and humble among our people.

27. "GOD has blessed us, and has spared us the agony of ill winds.

28. "We used to implore Him; He is the Most Kind, Most Merciful."

The Messenger

29. You shall remind the people. With your Lord's blessing's upon you, you are neither a soothsayer, nor crazy.

30. They may say, "He is a poet; let us just wait until he is dead."

31. Say, "Go on waiting; I will wait along with you."

32. Is it their dreams that dictate their behavior, or are they naturally wicked?

33. Do they say, "He made it all up?" Instead, they are simply disbelievers.

"Mohammedans" Challenge God and Produce Hadith

34. Let them produce a *Hadith* like this, if they are truthful.

35. Were they created from nothing? Are they the creators?

36. Did they create the heavens and the earth? Indeed, they have no certainty.

37. Do they possess the treasures of your Lord? Are they in control?

38. Do they climb a ladder that enables them to listen? Let their listeners show their proof.

39. Does He have daughters, while you have sons?

40. Are you asking them for any wage, and they are burdened thereby?

41. Do they know the future, and have it recorded?

42. Are they plotting and scheming? The disbelievers' schemes backfire against them.

43. Do they have another god besides **GOD**? **GOD** be glorified, far above having partners.

44. When they see masses falling from the sky, they will say, "Piled clouds!"

45. Disregard them until they meet the day in which they are struck.

46. On that day, their schemes will not protect them, nor will they be helped.

47. Those who transgress suffer retribution here, but most of them do not know.

48. You shall steadfastly persevere in carrying out your Lord's command—you are in our eyes—and glorify and praise your Lord when you get up.

49. Also during the night glorify Him, and at dawn as the stars fade away.

❖❖❖❖

Sura 53: The Stars (Al-Najm)

In the name of God,
Most Gracious, Most Merciful

1. As the stars fell away.*

2. Your friend *(Muhammad)* was not astray, nor was he deceived.

3. Nor was he speaking out of a personal desire.

4. It was divine inspiration.

5. Dictated by the Most Powerful.

6. Possessor of all authority. From His highest height.

7. At the highest horizon.

8. He drew nearer by moving down.

9. Until He became as close as possible.

10. He then revealed to His servant what was to be revealed.

11. The mind never made up what it saw.

12. Are you doubting what he saw?

13. He saw him in another descent.

14. At the ultimate point.

15. Where the eternal Paradise is located.

16. The whole place was overwhelmed.

17. The eyes did not waver, nor go blind.

18. He saw great signs of his Lord.

The Flimsy Idols

19. Compare this with the female idols Allaat and Al-'Uzzah.

20. And Manaat, the third one.

21. Do you have sons, while He has these as daughters?

22. What a disgraceful distribution!

23. These are but names that you made up, you and your fore-fathers. **GOD** never authorized such a blasphemy. They follow conjecture, and personal desire, when the true guidance has come to them herein from their Lord.

53:1-18 Muhammad was summoned to the highest universe to receive this Quran into his heart. The stars fell away as he traveled through them at millions of times the speed of light. Subsequently, the Quran was gradually released to his memory. Please see Appendix 28.

24. What is it that the human being desires?

25. To **GOD** belongs both the Hereafter, and this world.

26. Not even the angels in heaven possess authority to intercede. The only ones permitted by **GOD** are those who act in accordance with His will and His approval.

27. Those who disbelieve in the Hereafter have given the angels feminine names.

28. They had no knowledge about this; they only conjectured. Conjecture is no substitute for the truth.

Choose Your Friends Carefully

29. You shall disregard those who turn away from our message, and become preoccupied with this worldly life.

30. This is the extent of their knowledge. Your Lord is fully aware of those who strayed away from His path, and He is fully aware of those who are guided.

31. To **GOD** belongs everything in the heavens and everything on earth. He will requite those who commit evil for their works, and will reward the righteous for their righteousness.

32. They avoid gross sins and transgressions, except for minor offenses. Your Lord's forgiveness is immense. He has been fully aware of you since He initiated you from the earth, and while you were embryos in your mothers' bellies. Therefore, do not exalt yourselves; He is fully aware of the righteous.

33. Have you noted the one who turned away?

34. Rarely did he give to charity, and then very little.

35. Did he possess knowledge of the future? Could he see it?

36. Was he not informed of the teachings in the scripture of Moses?

37. And Abraham who fulfilled?

38. No soul bears the sins of another soul.

39. Every human being is responsible for his own works.

40. And everyone's works will be shown.

41. Then they will be paid fully for such works.

42. To your Lord is the final destiny.

43. He is the One who makes you laugh or cry.

44. He is the One who controls death and life.

The Husband Determines
The Baby's Gender

45. He is the One who created the two kinds, male and female—

46. from a tiny drop of semen.

47. He will effect the recreation.

48. He is the One who makes you rich or poor.

49. He is the Lord of the galaxies.

50. He is the One who annihilated ancient 'Aad.

51. And wiped out Thamoud.

52. Also the people of Noah before that; they were evil transgressors.

53. The evil communities *(of Sodom and Gomorrah)* were the lowliest.

54. Consequently, they utterly vanished.

55. Which of your Lord's marvels can you deny?

56. This is a warning like the older ones.

57. The inevitable is imminent.

58. None beside **GOD** can relieve it.

59. Are you questioning this matter?

60. Are you laughing, instead of crying?

61. Are you insisting on your ways?

62. You shall fall prostrate before **GOD**, and worship.

Sura 54: The Moon (Al-Qamar)

In the name of God,
Most Gracious, Most Merciful

1. The Hour has come closer, and the moon has split.*

2. Then they saw a miracle; but they turned away and said, "Old magic."

3. They disbelieved, followed their opinions, and adhered to their old traditions.

4. Sufficient warnings have been delivered to alert them.

5. Great wisdom; but all the warnings have been in vain.

6. Ignore them; the day will come when the caller will announce a terrible disaster.

7. With their eyes humiliated, they come out of the graves like scattered locusts.

8. As they respond to the caller, the disbelievers will say, "This is a difficult day."

9. The people of Noah disbelieved before them. They disbelieved our servant and said, "Crazy!" He was persecuted.

10. He implored his Lord, "I am oppressed; grant me victory."

11. We then opened the gates of the sky, pouring water.

12. And we caused springs to gush out of the earth. The waters met to effect a predetermined decision.

The Ark

13. We carried him on a watercraft made of logs and ropes.

14. It ran under our watchful eyes; a reward for one who was rejected.

15. We have set it up as a lesson. Does any of you wish to learn?

16. How terrible was My retribution after the warnings!

17. We made the Quran easy to learn. Does any of you wish to learn?

18. 'Aad disbelieved. Consequently, how terrible was My retribution after the warnings.

---

*54:1 This important sign of the approaching end of the world came to pass in 1969 when humans landed on the moon and brought pieces of the moon to earth. At the same time, God's mathematical Miracle of the Quran was being gradually unveiled. Traditional Muslims opposed it, since it exposed the fallacy of their practices (Appendix 25).

19. We sent upon them violent winds, on a day of continuous misery.

20. It tossed the people around as if they were decayed palm tree trunks.

21. How terrible was My retribution after the warnings!

22. We made the Quran easy to learn. Does any of you wish to learn?

23. Thamoud rejected the warnings.

24. They said, "Shall we follow one of us; a human being? We will then go astray, then end up in Hell.

25. "Did the message come down to him, instead of us? He is a flagrant liar."

26. They will find out tomorrow who the flagrant liar is.

27. We are sending the camel as a test for them. Watch them and be patient.

28. Inform them that the water shall be divided among them; *(the camel)* shall be allowed to drink on her designated day.

29. But they persuaded their friend to kill *(the camel)*, and he obliged.

30. Consequently, how terrible was My retribution! They have been warned.

31. We sent upon them one blow, whereupon they became like harvested hay.

32. We made the Quran easy to learn. Does any of you wish to learn?

33. The people of Lot rejected the warnings.

34. We showered them with rocks. Only Lot's family was saved at dawn.

35. We blessed him and his family; we thus reward the appreciative.

36. He warned them about our requital, but they ridiculed the warnings.

37. They negotiated with him about his guests; we blinded them. Suffer My retribution; you have been warned.

38. Early the next morning, a devastating retribution struck them.

39. Suffer My retribution; you have been warned.

40. We made the Quran easy to learn. Does any of you wish to learn?

41. Pharaoh's people were warned.

42. They rejected all our signs. Consequently, we requited them as an Almighty, Omnipotent should.

43. Are your disbelievers better than those disbelievers? Have you been absolved by the scripture?

44. Perhaps they think, "We will be the winners."

45. All of them will be defeated; they will turn around and flee.

46. The Hour is awaiting them, and the Hour is far worse and more painful.

47. Certainly, the guilty are astray, and will end up in Hell.

48. They will be dragged into the hellfire, forcibly. Suffer the agony of retribution.

49. Everything we created is precisely measured.

50. Our commands are done within the blink of an eye.

51. We annihilated your counterparts. Does any of you wish to learn?

52. Everything they did is recorded in the scriptures.

53. Everything, small or large, is written down.

54. Surely, the righteous have deserved gardens and rivers.

55. In a position of honor, at an Omnipotent King.

Sura 55: Most Gracious (Al-Rahmaan)

In the name of God,
Most Gracious, Most Merciful

1. The Most Gracious.

2. Teacher of the Quran.

3. Creator of the human beings.

4. He taught them how to distinguish.

5. The sun and the moon are perfectly calculated.

6. The stars and the trees prostrate.

7. He constructed the sky and established the law.

8. You shall not transgress the law.

9. You shall establish justice; do not violate the law.

10. He created the earth for all creatures.

11. In it there are fruits, and date palms with their hanging fruit.*

12. Also grains and the spices.

13. *(O humans and jinns,)* which of your Lord's marvels can you deny?

14. He created the human from aged clay, like the potter's clay.

15. And created the jinns from blazing fire.

16. *(O humans and jinns,)* which of your Lord's marvels can you deny?

17. Lord of the two easts and the two wests.

18. Which of your Lord's marvels can you deny?

19. He separates the two seas where they meet.

20. A barrier is placed between them, to prevent them from transgressing.

21. Which of your Lord's marvels can you deny?

22. Out of both of them you get pearls and coral.

23. Which of your Lord's marvels can you deny?

24. He gave you ships that roam the sea like flags.

25. Which of your Lord's marvels can you deny?

26. Everyone on earth perishes.

27. Only the presence of your Lord lasts. Possessor of Majesty and Honor.

28. Which of your Lord's marvels can you deny?

29. Imploring Him is everyone in the heavens and the earth. Every day He is in full control.

30. Which of your Lord's marvels can you deny?

---

*55:11 Compare the spaceship Earth's renewable systems and reproducing astronauts, with the most sophisticated spaceships that we launch into space. God be glorified.

31. We will call you to account, O humans and jinns.

32. Which of your Lord's marvels can you deny?

33. O you jinns and humans, if you can penetrate the outer limits of the heavens and the earth, go ahead and penetrate. You cannot penetrate without authorization.

34. Which of your Lord's marvels can you deny?

35. You get bombarded with projectiles of fire and metal, and you cannot win.

36. Which of your Lord's marvels can you deny?

37. When the sky disintegrates, and turns rose colored like paint.

38. Which of your Lord's marvels can you deny?

39. On that day, no human, nor a jinn, will be asked about his sins.

40. Which of your Lord's marvels can you deny?

41. *(This is because)* the guilty will be recognized by their looks; they will be taken by the forelocks and the feet.

42. Which of your Lord's marvels can you deny?

43. This is Gehenna that the guilty used to deny.

44. They will circulate between it and an intolerable inferno.*

45. Which of your Lord's marvels can you deny?

46. For those who reverence the majesty of their Lord, two gardens *(one for the jinns and one for the humans).*

47. Which of your Lord's marvels can you deny?

48. Full of provisions.

49. Which of your Lord's marvels can you deny?

50. Two springs are in them, flowing.

51. Which of your Lord's marvels can you deny?

52. Of every fruit in them, two kinds.

53. Which of your Lord's marvels can you deny?

54. While relaxing on furnishings lined with satin, the fruits are within reach.

55. Which of your Lord's marvels can you deny?

56. Their beautiful mates were never touched by any human or jinn.

57. Which of your Lord's marvels can you deny?

58. They look like gems and coral.

59. Which of your Lord's marvels can you deny?

60. Is the reward of goodness anything but goodness?

61. Which of your Lord's marvels can you deny?

62. Below them are two gardens *(one for the jinns and one for the humans).*

63. Which of your Lord's marvels can you deny?

64. Side by side.

55:44 Full details about the High Heaven, Low Heaven, the Purgatory, Hell, and the intolerable inferno are given in Appendices 5 and 11.

65. Which of your Lord's marvels can you deny?

66. In them, wells to be pumped.

67. Which of your Lord's marvels can you deny?

68. In them are fruits, date palms, and pomegranate.

69. Which of your Lord's marvels can you deny?

70. In them are beautiful mates.

71. Which of your Lord's marvels can you deny?

72. Confined in the tents.

73. Which of your Lord's marvels can you deny?

74. No human ever touched them, nor a jinn.

75. Which of your Lord's marvels can you deny?

76. They relax on green carpets, in beautiful surroundings.

77. Which of your Lord's marvels can you deny?

78. Most exalted is the name of your Lord, Possessor of Majesty and Honor.

❖❖❖❖

Sura 56: The Inevitable (Al-Waaqe'ah)

In the name of God,
Most Gracious, Most Merciful

1. When the inevitable comes to pass.

2. Nothing can stop it from happening.

3. It will lower some, and raise others.

4. The earth will be shaken up.

5. The mountains will be wiped out.

6. As if they never existed.

7. You will be stratified into three kinds.

8. Those who deserved bliss will be in bliss.

9. Those who deserved misery will be in misery.

10. Then there is the elite of the elite.

11. They are those who will be closest (*to God*).

12. In the gardens of bliss.

13. Many from the first generations.*

14. Few from the later generations.

15. On luxurious furnishings.

16. Enjoying everything, they will be neighbors.

17. Serving them will be immortal servants.

18. With cups, pitchers and pure drinks.

19. They never run out, nor do they get bored.

20. Fruits of their choice.

21. Meat of birds that they desire.

22. Beautiful mates.

23. Like protected pearls.

24. Rewards for their works.

56:13-40 People who believe and nourish their souls through worshiping God alone are destined for the High Heaven. The contemporary followers of each messenger invariably suffer persecution from the traditionalists and adherents of the corrupted religion. Thus, they have a special place reserved for them in the High Heaven. All people who die before the age of 40 go to the Lower Heaven, at least (46:15).

25. They never hear any nonsense therein, nor sinful utterances.

26. Only the utterance: "Peace, peace."

The Lower Heaven

27. Those of the right side, will be on the right side.

28. In lush orchards.

29. Fragrant fruits.

30. Extended shade.

31. Abundant water.

32. Many fruits.

33. Never ending; never forbidden.

34. Luxurious furnishings.

35. We create for them mates.

36. Never previously touched.

37. Perfectly matched.

38. For those on the right side.

39. Many from the early generations.

40. Many from the later generations.*

Hell

41. Those of the left, will be on the left.

42. In misery and inferno.

43. Even their shade is hot.

44. Never cool, never tolerable.

45. They used to be rich.

46. They insisted on the great blasphemy.

47. They said, "After we die and turn to dust and bones, we get resurrected?

48. "Does this include our forefathers?"

49. Say, "The early generations and the later generations.

50. "Will be summoned to a meeting on a predetermined day.

51. "Then you, O disbelieving strayers.

52. "Will eat from the trees of bitterness.

53. "Filling your bellies therefrom.

54. "Then drinking on top of it hellish drinks.

55. "Then adding drinks of sand."

56. Such is their share on the Day of Judgment.

Reflections

57. We have created you, if you could only believe!

58. Have you noted the semen that you produce?

59. Did you create it, or did we?

60. We have predetermined death for you. Nothing can stop us—

61. from substituting new generations in your place, and establishing what you do not know.

62. You know about the first creation. Do you not remember?

63. Have you noted the crops you reap?

64. Did you grow them, or did we?

65. If we will, we can turn it into hay. Then you will lament:

66. "We lost.

67. "We are deprived."

68. Have you noted the water you drink?

69. Did you send it down from the clouds, or did we?

70. If we will, we can make it salty. You should be thankful.

---

*56:40 See footnote for 56:13-40.

71. Have you noted the fire you ignite?

72. Did you initiate its tree, or did we?

73. We rendered it a reminder, and a useful tool for the users.

74. You shall glorify the name of your Lord, the Great.

Only the Sincere Can
Understand the Quran

75. I swear by the positions of the stars.

76. This is an oath, if you only knew, that is awesome.*

77. This is an honorable Quran.

78. In a protected book.

79. None can grasp it except the sincere.*

80. A revelation from the Lord of the universe.

81. Are you disregarding this narration?

82. Do you make it your business that you disbelieve?

83. When the time comes and it *(your soul)* reaches your throat—

84. you will then look around.

85. We are closer to it than you are, but you do not see.

86. If it is true that you do not owe any accounting—

87. why do you not restore *(your soul)*, if you are truthful?

88. If he is one of those close to Me—

89. then joy, flowers, and gardens of bliss.

90. And if he is one of the right—

91. peace is the lot of those on the right.

92. But if he is one of the disbelievers, the strayers—

93. then an abode of inferno—

94. and burning in Hell.

95. This is the absolute truth.

96. You shall glorify the name of your Lord, the Great.

Sura 57: Iron (Al-Hadeed)

In the name of God,
Most Gracious, Most Merciful

1. Glorifying **GOD** is everything in the heavens and the earth. He is the Almighty, Most Wise.

2. To Him belongs the kingship of the heavens and the earth. He controls life and death. He is Omnipotent.

3. He is the Alpha and the Omega. He is the Outermost and the Innermost. He is fully aware of all things.

56:75-76 Our universe, the smallest and innermost of seven universes, contains a billion galaxies, a billion trillion stars, spanning billions of light years. These uncountable decillions of heavenly bodies maintain their orbits in a divinely controlled precision. The more we learn, the more we realize how awesome this oath is. See Appendix 6.

56:79 The insincere who are not satisfied with the Quran alone are divinely prevented from understanding the Quran. This concept is repeated throughout the Quran (17:45, 18:57). Consequently, they cannot understand this verse. For example, compare this translation of 7:3, 17:46, 41:44, & 56:79 with other translations.

---

4. He is the One who created the heavens and the earth in six days,* then assumed all authority. He knows everything that enters into the earth, and everything that comes out of it, and everything that comes down from the sky, and everything that climbs into it. He is with you wherever you may be. **GOD** is Seer of everything you do.

5. To Him belongs the kingship of the heavens and the earth. All matters are controlled by **GOD**.

6. He merges the night into the day, and merges the day into the night. He is fully aware of the innermost thoughts.

7. Believe in **GOD** and His messenger, and give from what He has bestowed upon you. Those among you who believe and give *(to charity)* have deserved a great recompense.

8. Why should you not believe in **GOD** when the messenger is inviting you to believe in your Lord? He has taken a pledge from you, if you are believers.

9. He is the One who sends down to His servant clear revelations, in order to lead you out of the darkness into the light. **GOD** is Compassionate towards you, Most Merciful.

10. Why do you not spend in the cause of **GOD**, when **GOD** possesses all wealth in the heavens and the earth?

Special Honor

Distinguished from the rest are those among you who spend before the victory and strive. They attain a greater rank than those who spend after the victory and strive. For each, **GOD** promises salvation. **GOD** is Cognizant of everything you do.

11. Who would like to loan **GOD** a loan of righteousness, to have it multiplied for him manifold, and end up with a generous recompense?

The Great Triumph

12. The day will come when you see the believing men and women with their lights radiating ahead of them and to their right. Good news is yours that, on that day, you will have gardens with flowing streams. You will abide therein forever. This is the great triumph.

The Worst Losers

13. On that day, the hypocrite men and women will say to those who believed, "Please allow us to absorb some of your light." It will be said, "Go back behind you, and seek light." A barrier will be set up between them, whose gate separates mercy on the inner side, from retribution on the outer side.

14. They will call upon them, "Were we not with you?" They will answer, "Yes, but you cheated your souls, hesitated, doubted, and became misled by wishful thinking, until **GOD**'s judgment came. You were diverted from **GOD** by illusions.

15. "Therefore, today no ransom can be taken from you, nor from those who disbelieved. Your abode is the fire; it is your lord, and miserable abode."

57:4 The six days of creation are simply a yardstick to inform us of the relative importance of various components, to emphasize the significance of the planet Earth, and to let us know that the Earth is the only inhabited planet. See Footnote 41:9-10.

Deterioration of Religion

16. Is it not time for those who believed to open up their hearts for **GOD**'s message, and the truth that is revealed herein? They should not be like the followers of previous scriptures whose hearts became hardened with time and, consequently, many of them turned wicked.

17. Know that **GOD** revives the land after it had died. We thus explain the revelations for you, that you may understand.

18. Surely, the charitable men and women, have loaned **GOD** a loan of goodness. They will receive their reward multiplied manifold; they have deserved a generous recompense.

19. Those who believed in **GOD** and His messengers are the saints and martyrs. Reserved for them at their Lord are their rewards and their light. As for those who disbelieved and rejected our revelations, they have incurred Hell.

Preoccupation With This Life Condemned

20. Know that this worldly life is no more than play and games, and boasting among you, and hoarding of money and children. It is like abundant rain that produces plants and pleases the disbelievers. But then the plants turn into useless hay, and are blown away by the wind. In the Hereafter there is either severe retribution, or forgiveness from **GOD** and approval. This worldly life is no more than a temporary illusion.

The Intelligent Alternative

21. Therefore, you shall race towards forgiveness from your Lord, and a Paradise whose width encompasses the heaven and the earth. It awaits those who believed in **GOD** and His messengers. Such is **GOD**'s grace that He bestows upon whomever He wills. **GOD** is Possessor of Infinite Grace.

Profound Fact*

22. Anything that happens on earth, or to you, has already been recorded, even before the creation. This is easy for **GOD** to do.

23. Thus, you should not grieve over anything you miss, nor be proud of anything He has bestowed upon you. **GOD** does not love those who are boastful, proud.

24. They are stingy, and enjoin the people to be stingy. If one turns away, then **GOD** is the Rich, the Praiseworthy.

Iron: The Most Useful Metal

25. We sent our messengers supported by clear proofs, and we sent down to them the scripture and the law, that the people may uphold justice. And we sent down the iron, wherein there is strength, and many benefits for the people. All this in order for **GOD** to distinguish those who would support Him and His messengers, on faith. **GOD** is Powerful, Almighty.

57:22 We are absolutely free to side with God, or with Satan. God happens to know precisely what kind of decision each of us will make. The video tape of your life, from birth to death, is already recorded. See Appendix 14.

The Prophets

26. We sent Noah and Abraham, and we granted their descendants prophethood and the scripture. Some of them were guided, while many were wicked.

Deterioration of Religion

27. Subsequent to them, we sent our messengers. We sent Jesus the son of Mary, and we gave him the **Injeel** (*Gospel*), and we placed in the hearts of his followers kindness and mercy. But they invented hermitism which we never decreed for them. All we asked them to do was to uphold the commandments approved by **GOD**. But they did not uphold the message as they should have. Consequently, we gave those who believed among them their recompense, while many of them were wicked.

28. O you who believe, you shall reverence **GOD** and believe in His messenger. He will then grant you double the reward from His mercy, endow you with light to guide you, and forgive you. **GOD** is Forgiver, Most Merciful.

29. Thus, the followers of previous scripture should know that they have not monopolized **GOD**'s mercy and grace, and that all grace is in **GOD**'s hand. He bestows it upon whomever He wills. **GOD** is Possessor of Infinite Grace.

◆◆◆◆

Sura 58: The Debate (Al-Mujaadalah)

In the name of God,
Most Gracious, Most Merciful

1. **GOD** has heard the woman who debated with you about her husband, and complained to **GOD**. **GOD** heard everything the two of you discussed. **GOD** is Hearer, Seer.

2. Those among you who estrange their wives *(by declaring them as forbidden in sex)* as their mothers know full well that they are not their mothers.* Their mothers are the women who gave birth to them. Indeed, they are committing a blasphemy and a falsehood. **GOD** is Pardoner, Forgiver.

3. Those who estrange their wives in this manner, then reconcile thereafter, shall atone by freeing a slave before resuming their sexual relations. This is to enlighten you. **GOD** is Cognizant of everything you do.

4. If you cannot find a slave to free, you shall fast two consecutive months before resuming sexual relations. If you cannot fast, then you shall feed sixty poor people. You shall believe in **GOD** and His messenger. These are **GOD**'s laws. The disbelievers have incurred a painful retribution.

5. Surely, those who fight **GOD** and His messenger are committed to defeat, like their previous counterparts were committed to defeat. We have sent down clear proofs, and the rejectors have incurred a shameful retribution.

6. The day will come when **GOD** will resurrect them all, then inform them of everything they had done. **GOD** has recorded everything, while they have forgotten it. **GOD** witnesses all things.

58:2 Estranging a wife by declaring that she is like one's mother was an ancient tradition in Arabia. This is the only sura where the word "Allah" occurs in every verse.

God is With You Now

7. Do you not realize that **GOD** knows everything in the heavens and everything on earth? No three people can conspire secretly without Him being their fourth, nor five without Him being the sixth, nor less than that, nor more, without Him being there with them wherever they may be. Then, on the Day of Resurrection, He will inform them of everything they had done. **GOD** is fully aware of all things.

Do Not Conspire

8. Have you noted those who were enjoined from conspiring secretly, then insist on conspiring? They conspire to commit sin, transgression, and disobedience of the messenger. When they come to you, they greet you with a greeting other than that decreed by **GOD**. They say inside themselves, "**GOD** will not punish us for our utterances." Their only requital is Gehenna, wherein they burn; what a miserable destiny.

9. O you who believe, if you have to confer secretly, you shall not confer to commit sin, transgression, and to disobey the messenger. You shall confer to work righteousness and piety. You shall reverence **GOD**, before whom you will be summoned.

10. Secret conspiracy is the devil's idea, through which he seeks to hurt those who believed. However, he cannot hurt them against **GOD**'s will. In **GOD** the believers shall trust.

11. O you who believe, if you are told, "Please make room," you shall make room for each other to sit. **GOD** will then make room for you. If you are asked to get up and move,

get up and move. **GOD** raises those among you who believe, and those who acquire knowledge to higher ranks. **GOD** is fully Cognizant of everything you do.

12. O you who believe, when you wish to confer with the messenger, you shall offer a charity *(to the poor)* before you do so. This is better for you, and purer. If you cannot afford it, then **GOD** is Forgiver, Most Merciful.

13. If you failed to give to charity before conferring, then repented thereafter, **GOD** accepts your repentance. You shall observe the contact prayers *(Salat)*, give the obligatory charity *(Zakat)*, and obey **GOD** and His messenger. **GOD** is fully Cognizant of everything you do.

Choose Your Friends

14. Have you noted those who befriended people with whom **GOD** is angry? They neither belong with you, nor with them. They deliberately swear lies!

15. **GOD** has prepared for them a severe retribution. Miserable indeed is what they used to do.

16. They used their oaths as a means of repelling from the path of **GOD**. Consequently, they have incurred a shameful retribution.

17. Neither their money, nor their children will help them against **GOD**. They have incurred the hellfire, wherein they abide forever.

18. The Day will come when **GOD** resurrects them all. They will swear to Him then, just as they swear to you now, thinking that they really are right! Indeed, they are the real liars.

19. The devil has possessed them, and has caused them to disregard **GOD**'s message. These are the party of the devil. Absolutely, the party of the devil are the losers.

20. Surely, those who oppose **GOD** and His messenger will be with the lowliest.

21. **GOD** has decreed: "I and My messengers will most assuredly win." **GOD** is Powerful, Almighty.

Run For Your Life

22. You will not find people who believe in **GOD** and the Last Day befriending those who oppose **GOD** and His messenger, even if they were their parents, or their children, or their siblings, or their tribe. For these, He decrees faith into their hearts, and supports them with inspiration from Him, and admits them into gardens with flowing streams wherein they abide forever. **GOD** is pleased with them, and they are pleased with Him. These are the party of **GOD**. Most assuredly, **GOD**'s party are the winners.

◆◆◆◆

Sura 59: Exodus (Al-Hashr)

In the name of God,
Most Gracious, Most Merciful

1. Glorifying **GOD** is everything in the heavens and the earth, and He is the Almighty, Most Wise.

God Defends the Believers

2. He is the One who evicted those who disbelieved among the people of the scripture from their homes in a mass exodus. You never thought that they would leave, and they thought that their preparations would protect them from **GOD**. But then **GOD** came to them whence they never expected, and threw terror into their hearts. Thus, they abandoned their homes on their own volition, in addition to pressure from the believers. You should learn from this, O you who possess vision.

3. If **GOD** did not force them to leave, He would have requited them in this life *(even worse than forcing them to leave)*. In the Hereafter He will commit them to the retribution of Hell.

4. This is because they opposed **GOD** and His messenger. For those who oppose **GOD** and His messenger, **GOD** is most strict in enforcing retribution.

5. Whether you chop a tree, or leave it standing on its trunk, is in accordance with **GOD**'s will. He will surely humiliate the wicked.

6. Whatever **GOD** restored for His messenger was not the result of your war efforts, whether you fought on horses or on foot. **GOD** is the One who sends His messengers against whomever He wills. **GOD** is Omnipotent.

The Spoils of War

7. Whatever **GOD** restored to His messenger from the *(defeated)* communities shall go to **GOD** and His messenger *(in the form of a charity)*. You shall give it to the relatives, the orphans, the poor, and the traveling alien. Thus, it will not remain monopolized by the strong among you. You may keep the spoils given to you by the messenger, but do not take what he enjoins you from taking. You shall reverence **GOD**. **GOD** is strict in enforcing retribution.

8. *(You shall give)* to the needy who immigrated. They were evicted from their homes and deprived of their properties, because they sought **GOD**'s grace and pleasure, and because they supported **GOD** and His messenger. They are the truthful.

9. As for those who provided them with a home and a refuge, and were believers before them, they love those who immigrated to them, and find no hesitation in their hearts in helping them. In fact, they readily give them priority over themselves, even when they themselves need what they give away. Indeed, those who overcome their natural stinginess are the successful ones.

10. Those who became believers after them say, "Our Lord, forgive us and our brethren who preceded us to the faith, and keep our hearts from harboring any hatred towards those who believed. Our Lord, You are Compassionate, Most Merciful."

11. Have you noted those who are plagued with hypocrisy, and how they said to their companions in disbelief among the people of the scripture, "If you are evicted we will go out with you, and will never obey anyone who opposes you. If anyone fights you, we will fight on your side." **GOD** bears witness that they are liars.

12. In fact, if they were evicted, they would not have gone out with them, and if anyone fought them, they would not have supported them. Even if they supported them, they would have turned around and fled. They could never win.

13. Indeed, you strike more terror in their hearts than their fear of **GOD**. This is because they are people who do not comprehend.

14. They do not get together to fight you unless they are in well-shielded buildings, or behind walls. Their might appears formidable among themselves. You would think that they are united, when in fact their hearts are divided. This is because they are people who do not understand.

15. Their fate is the same as their counterparts who preceded them. They suffered the consequences of their decisions. They have incurred a painful retribution.

16. They are like the devil: he says to the human being, "Disbelieve," then as soon as he disbelieves, he says, "I disown you. I fear **GOD**, Lord of the universe."

17. The destiny for both of them is the Hellfire, wherein they abide forever. This is the requital for the transgressors.

18. O you who believe, you shall reverence **GOD**, and let every soul examine what it has sent ahead for tomorrow. You shall reverence **GOD**; **GOD** is fully Cognizant of everything you do.

19. Do not be like those who forgot **GOD**, so He made them forget themselves. These are the wicked.

20. Not equal are the dwellers of the Hellfire and the dwellers of Paradise; the dwellers of Paradise are the winners.

Greatness of the Quran

21. If we revealed this Quran to a mountain, you would see it trembling, crumbling, out of reverence for **GOD**. We cite these examples for the people, that they may reflect.

God

22. He is the One **GOD**; there is no other god besides Him. Knower of all secrets and declarations. He is the Most Gracious, Most Merciful.

23. He is the One **GOD**; there is no other god besides Him. The King, the Most Sacred, the Peace, the Most Faithful, the Supreme, the Almighty, the Most Powerful, the Most Dignified. **GOD** be glorified; far above having partners.

24. He is the One **GOD**; the Creator, the Initiator, the Designer. To Him belong the most beautiful names. Glorifying Him is everything in the heavens and the earth. He is the Almighty, Most Wise.

❖❖❖❖

Sura 60: The Test (Al-Mumtahanah)

In the name of God,
Most Gracious, Most Merciful

1. O you who believe, you shall not befriend My enemies and your enemies, extending love and friendship to them, even though they have dis-

believed in the truth that has come to you. They persecute the messenger, and you, just because you believe in **GOD**, your Lord. If you mobilize to struggle in My cause, seeking My blessings, how can you secretly love them? I am fully aware of everything you conceal, and everything you declare. Those among you who do this have indeed strayed off the right path.

2. Whenever they encounter you, they treat you as enemies, and hurt you with their hands and tongues. They want you to disbelieve.

3. Your relatives and your money can never help you. On the Day of Resurrection, He will judge among you. **GOD** is Seer of everything you do.

Abraham: An Example

4. A good example has been set for you by Abraham and those with him. They said to their people, "We disown you and the idols that you worship besides **GOD**. We denounce you, and you will see nothing from us except animosity and hatred until you believe in **GOD** ALONE."* However, a mistake was committed by Abraham when he said to his father, "I will pray for your forgiveness,** but I possess no power to protect you from **GOD**." "Our Lord, we trust in You, and submit to You; to You is the final destiny.

---

*60:4 The Arabic word for "ALONE" (WAHDAHU) occurs only six times in the Quran, one of them refers to upholding the Quran ALONE (17:46). The reference to God ALONE occurs in 7:70, 39:45, 40:12 & 84, and 60:4. The sum of these numbers (7+70+39+45+40+12+84+60+4) equals 361, or 19x19. This emphasizes that the main theme of the Quran is "Worship God ALONE." See Appendix 1.

**60:4 We can pray for guidance for the idolaters, not forgiveness, since God's law is that idolatry is the only unforgivable offense (4:48 & 116).

5. "Our Lord, let us not be oppressed by those who disbelieved, and forgive us. You are the Almighty, Most Wise."

6. A good example has been set by them for those who seek **GOD** and the Last Day. As for those who turn away, **GOD** is in no need (*of them*), Most Praiseworthy.

7. **GOD** may change the animosity between you and them into love. **GOD** is Omnipotent. **GOD** is Forgiver, Most Merciful.

Basic Law Regulating Relations With Unbelievers

8. **GOD** does not enjoin you from befriending those who do not fight you because of religion, and do not evict you from your homes. You may befriend them and be equitable towards them. **GOD** loves the equitable.

9. **GOD** enjoins you only from befriending those who fight you because of religion, evict you from your homes, and band together with others to banish you. You shall not befriend them. Those who befriend them are the transgressors.

In Case of War

10. O you who believe, when believing women (*abandon the enemy and*) ask for asylum with you, you shall test them. **GOD** is fully aware of their belief. Once you establish that they are believers, you shall not return them to the disbelievers. They are not lawful to remain married to them, nor shall the disbelievers be allowed to marry them. Give back the dowries that the disbelievers have paid. You commit no error by marrying them, so long as you pay them their due dowries. Do

not keep disbelieving wives (*if they wish to join the enemy*). You may ask them for the dowry you had paid, and they may ask for what they paid. This is **GOD**'s rule; He rules among you. **GOD** is Omniscient, Most Wise.

11. If any of your wives join the enemies' camp, and you are forced to fight, you shall force the enemy to compensate the men who lost their wives, by giving them what they spent on their wives. You shall reverence **GOD**, in whom you believe.

12. O you prophet, when the believing women (*who abandoned the disbelievers*) to seek asylum with you pledge to you that they will not set up any idols besides **GOD**, nor steal, nor commit adultery, nor kill their children, nor fabricate any falsehood, nor disobey your righteous orders, you shall accept their pledge, and pray to **GOD** to forgive them. **GOD** is Forgiver, Most Merciful.

13. O you who believe, do not befriend people with whom **GOD** is angry, and who are hopelessly stuck in disbelief; they are just as hopeless as the disbelievers who are already in the graves.

❖❖❖❖

Sura 61: The Column (Al-Saff)

In the name of God,
Most Gracious, Most Merciful

1. Glorifying **GOD** is everything in the heavens and everything on earth. He is the Almighty, Most Wise.

2. O you who believe, why do you say what you do not do?

3. Most abominable in the sight of **GOD** is that you say what you do not do.

4. **GOD** loves those who fight in His cause united in one column, like the bricks in one wall.

5. Recall that Moses said to his people, "O my people, why do you hurt me, even though you know that I am **GOD**'s messenger to you?" When they deviated, **GOD** diverted their hearts. For **GOD** does not guide the wicked people.

Messenger After Jesus

6. Recall that Jesus, son of Mary, said, "O Children of Israel, I am **GOD**'s messenger to you, confirming the Torah and bringing good news of a messenger to come after me whose name will be even more praised *(Ahmad)*." Then, when he showed them the clear proofs, they said, "This is profound magic."

7. Who is more evil than one who fabricates lies about **GOD**, and he is being invited to Submission? **GOD** does not guide the evil people.

8. They wish to put out **GOD**'s light with their mouths. But **GOD** insists upon perfecting His light, in spite of the disbelievers.

The Great Prophecy

9. He has sent His messenger* with the guidance and the true religion, and will make it dominate all religions, in spite of the idol worshipers.

The Best Deal

10. O you who believe, let Me inform you of a trade that will save you from painful retribution.

11. Believe in **GOD** and His messenger and strive in the cause of **GOD** with your money and your lives. This is the best deal for you, if you only knew.

12. In return, He forgives your sins, and admits you into gardens with flowing streams, with beautiful mansions in the gardens of Eden. This is the greatest triumph.

13. Additionally, you get something you truly love: support from **GOD** and guaranteed victory. Give good news to the believers.

14. O you who believe, be **GOD**'s supporters, like the disciples of Jesus, son of Mary. When he said to them, "Who are my supporters towards **GOD**," they said, "We are **GOD**'s supporters." Thus, a group from the Children of Israel believed, and another group disbelieved. We helped those who believed against their enemy, until they won.

◆◆◆◆

Sura 62: Friday (Al- Jumu'ah)

In the name of God,
Most Gracious, Most Merciful

1. Glorifying **GOD** is everything in the heavens and everything on earth; the King, the Most Sacred, the Almighty, the Most Wise.

---

*61:9 The specific name of this messenger is spelled out mathematically (Appendix 2).

2. He is the One who sent to the gentiles a messenger from among them, to recite to them His revelations, purify them, and teach them the scripture and wisdom. Before this, they had gone far astray.

3. And to many generations subsequent to them. He is the Almighty, Most Wise.

4. Such is **GOD**'s grace that He bestows upon whomever He wills. **GOD** is Possessor of Infinite Grace.

5. The example of those who were given the Torah, then failed to uphold it, is like the donkey carrying great works of literature. Miserable indeed is the example of people who rejected **GOD**'s revelations. **GOD** does not guide the wicked people.

6. Say, "O you who are Jewish, if you claim that you are **GOD**'s chosen, to the exclusion of all other people, then you should long for death if you are truthful!"

7. They will never long for it, because of what they have committed. **GOD** is fully aware of the wicked.

8. Say, "The death that you are trying to evade will catch up with you sooner or later. Then you will be returned to the Knower of all secrets and declarations, then He will inform you of everything you had done."

Important Commandments to All Believers

9. O you who believe, when the Congregational Prayer *(Salat Al-Jumu'ah)* is announced on Friday, you shall hasten to the commemoration of **GOD**, and drop all business. This is better for you, if you only knew.

10. Once the prayer is completed, you may spread through the land to seek **GOD**'s bounties, and continue to remember **GOD** frequently, that you may succeed.

11. When some of them come across a business deal, or some entertainment, they rush to it and leave you standing! Say, "What **GOD** possesses is far better than the entertainment or the business. **GOD** is the best Provider."

❖❖❖❖

Sura 63: The Hypocrites (Al-Munaafeqoon)

In the name of God,
Most Gracious, Most Merciful

1. When the hypocrites come to you they say, "We bear witness that you are the messenger of **GOD**."* **GOD** knows that you are His messenger, and **GOD** bears witness that the hypocrites are liars.

2. Under the guise of their apparent faith, they repel the people from the path of **GOD**. Miserable indeed is what they do.

---

*63:1 The "first pillar of Islam," as stated in 3:18 is to bear witness that God is the only god. But the corrupted "Muslim" scholars add "Muhammad is God's messenger," and this violates a number of commandments (see 2:285). Verse 63:1 is the only place in the Quran where such a statement is made. Only the hypocrites make such a statement.

---

3. This is because they believed, then disbelieved. Hence, their minds are blocked; they do not understand.

A Chip On Their Shoulders

4. When you see them, you may be impressed by their looks. And when they speak, you may listen to their eloquence. They are like standing logs. They think that every call is intended against them. These are the real enemies; beware of them. **GOD** condemns them; they have deviated.

5. When they are told, "Come let the messenger of **GOD** pray for your forgiveness," they mockingly turn their heads, and you see them repel others and act arrogantly.

The Myth of Intercession Shattered*

6. It is the same for them, whether you pray for their forgiveness, or not pray for their forgiveness; **GOD** will not forgive them. For **GOD** does not guide the wicked people.

7. They are the ones who say, "Do not give any money to those who followed the messenger of **GOD**, perhaps they abandon him!" However, **GOD** possesses the treasures of the heavens and the earth, but the hypocrites do not comprehend.

8. They say, "If we go back to the city, the powerful therein will evict the weak *(and we will be victimized).*" *(They should know that)* all dignity belongs to **GOD** and His messenger, and the believers. However, the hypocrites do not know.

9. O you who believe, do not be distracted by your money and your children from remembering **GOD**. Those who do this are the losers.

10. You shall give from our provisions to you before death comes to you, then you say, "My Lord, if only You could delay this for a short while! I would then be charitable and join the righteous!"

11. **GOD** never delays the appointed time of death for any soul. **GOD** is fully Cognizant of everything you do.

◆◆◆◆

Sura 64: Mutual Blaming (Al-Taghaabun)

In the name of God,
Most Gracious, Most Merciful

1. Glorifying **GOD** is everything in the heavens and everything on earth. To Him belongs all kingship, and to Him belongs all praise, and He is Omnipotent.

2. He is the One who created you, then among you there is the disbeliever, and the believer. **GOD** is fully Seer of everything you do.

3. He created the heavens and the earth for a specific purpose,* designed you and perfected your design, then to Him is the final destiny.

4. He knows everything in the heavens and the earth, and He knows everything you conceal and everything you declare. **GOD** is fully aware of the innermost thoughts.

63:6 Millions of people idolize their prophets because of this myth (Appendix 8).

64:3 We are in this world due to God's immense mercy. The Most Gracious has given us a chance to redeem ourselves. See the Introduction and Appendix 7.

5. Have you noted those who disbelieved in the past, then suffered the consequences of their decision? They incurred a painful retribution.

6. This is because their messengers went to them with clear proofs, but they said, "Shall we follow humans like us?" They disbelieved and turned away. **GOD** does not need them; **GOD** is in no need, Praiseworthy.

7. Those who disbelieved claim that they will not be resurrected! Yes indeed, by my Lord, you will be resurrected, and you will be held accountable for everything you have done. This is easy for **GOD** to do.

8. Therefore, you shall believe in **GOD** and His messenger, and the light that we have revealed herein. **GOD** is fully Cognizant of everything you do.

9. The day will come when He summons you to the Day of Summoning. That is the Day of Mutual Blaming. Anyone who believes in **GOD** and leads a righteous life, He will remit his sins, and will admit him into gardens with flowing streams. They abide therein forever. This is the greatest triumph.

10. As for those who disbelieve and reject our revelations, they are the dwellers of the Hell-fire; they abide therein forever. What a miserable destiny!

Divine Law

11. Nothing happens to you except in accordance with **GOD**'s will. Any-one who believes in **GOD**, He will guide his heart. **GOD** is fully aware of all things.

12. You shall obey **GOD** and you shall obey the messenger. If you turn away, then the sole mission of our messenger is to deliver the message.

13. **GOD**: there is no other god besides Him. In **GOD** the believers shall trust.

14. O you who believe, your spouses and your children can be your enemies; beware. If you pardon, forget, and forgive, then **GOD** is Forgiver, Most Merciful.

15. Your money and children are a test, and **GOD** possesses a great recompense.

16. Therefore, you shall reverence **GOD** as much as you can, and listen, and obey, and give *(to charity)* for your own good. Anyone who is protected from his own stinginess, these are the successful ones.

17. If you lend **GOD** a loan of righteousness, He will multiply the reward for you manifold, and forgive you. **GOD** is Appreciative, Clement.

18. The Knower of all secrets and declarations; the Almighty, Most Wise.

❖❖❖

Sura 65: Divorce (Al-Talaaq)

In the name of God,
Most Gracious, Most Merciful

1. O you prophet, when you people divorce the women, you shall ensure that a divorce interim is fulfilled. You shall measure such an interim precisely.* You shall reverence **GOD** your Lord. Do not evict them from their homes, nor shall you make life miserable for them, to force them to leave on their own, unless they commit a proven adultery. These are **GOD**'s laws. Anyone who transgresses **GOD**'s laws commits an injustice against himself. You never know; maybe **GOD** wills something good to come out of this.

2. Once the interim is fulfilled, you may reconcile with them equitably, or go through with the separation equitably. You shall have two equitable witnesses witness the divorce before **GOD**. This is to enlighten those who believe in **GOD** and the Last Day. Anyone who reverences **GOD**, He will create an exit for him.

3. And will provide for him whence he never expected. Anyone who trusts in **GOD**, He suffices him. **GOD**'s commands are done. **GOD** has decreed for everything its fate.

4. As for the women who have reached menopause, if you have any doubts, their interim shall be three months. As for those who do not menstruate, and discover that they are pregnant, their interim ends upon giving birth. Anyone who reverences **GOD**, He makes everything easy for him.

5. This is **GOD**'s command that He sends down to you. Anyone who reverences **GOD**, He remits his sins, and rewards him generously.

6. You shall allow them to live in the same home in which they lived with you, and do not make life so miserable for them that they leave on their own. If they are pregnant, you shall spend on them until they give birth. If they nurse the infant, you shall pay them for this service. You shall maintain the amicable relations among you. If you disagree, you may hire another woman to nurse the child.

7. The rich husband shall provide support in accordance with his means, and the poor shall provide according to the means that **GOD** bestowed upon him. **GOD** does not impose on any soul more than He has given it. **GOD** will provide ease after difficulty.

8. Many a community rebelled against the commands of its Lord and against His messengers. Consequently, we held them strictly accountable, and requited them a terrible requital.

9. They suffered the consequences of their decisions; a profound loss.

10. **GOD** has prepared for them severe retribution. Therefore, you shall reverence **GOD**, O you who possess intelligence and believed. **GOD** has sent down to you a message − *

65:1 The divorcee's interim, before becoming eligible for remarriage, is a waiting period of three menstruations. This ensures that the divorcee was not pregnant (2:228).

65:10-11 The "Messenger" here is clearly the Quran. Verse 10 talks about "sending down a message," and this points to the Quran as the messenger in 65:11 (App. 20).

11. a messenger* who recites to you **GOD**'s revelations, clearly, to lead those who believe and work righteousness out of the darkness into the light. Anyone who believes in **GOD** and leads a righteous life, He will admit him into gardens with flowing streams; they abide therein forever. **GOD** will generously reward him.

Seven Universes And Seven Earths

12. **GOD** created seven universes and the same number of earths. The commands flow among them. This is to let you know that **GOD** is Omnipotent, and that **GOD** is fully aware of all things.

❖❖❖❖

Sura 66: Prohibition (Al-Tahreem)

In the name of God,
Most Gracious, Most Merciful

1. O you prophet, why do you prohibit what **GOD** has made lawful for you, just to please your wives? **GOD** is Forgiver, Merciful.*

2. **GOD** has decreed for you the laws dealing with your oaths. **GOD** is your Lord, and He is the Omniscient, Most Wise.

3. The prophet had trusted some of his wives with a certain statement, then one of them spread it, and **GOD** let him know about it. He then informed his wife of part of the issue, and disregarded part. She asked him, "Who informed you of this?" He said, "I was informed by the Omniscient, Most Cognizant."

4. If the two of you repent to **GOD**, then your hearts have listened. But if you band together against him, then **GOD** is his ally, and so is Gabriel and the righteous believers. Also, the angels are his helpers.

5. If he divorces you, his Lord will substitute other wives in your place who are better than you; submitters (*Muslims*), believers (*Mu'mens*), obedient, repentant, worshipers, pious, either previously married, or virgins.

6. O you who believe, protect yourselves and your families from the Hellfire whose fuel is people and rocks. Guarding it are stern and powerful angels who never disobey **GOD**; they do whatever they are commanded to do.

7. O you who disbelieved, do not apologize today. You are being requited only for what you did.

The Believers Repent

8. O you who believe, you shall repent to **GOD** a firm repentance. Your Lord will then remit your sins and admit you into gardens with flowing streams. On that day, **GOD** will not disappoint the prophet and those who believed with him. Their light will radiate in front of them and to their right. They will say, "Our Lord, perfect our light for us, and forgive us; You are Omnipotent."

---

*65:11 See footnote for 65:10-11.

*65:12 Although God created six other planets that are identical to our Earth, there is life only on our planet. Thus, the evolutionists will be shown on the Day of Judgment that life did not just "evolve" on the planet because of its particular circumstances.

*66:1 Mohammedans around the world believe that Muhammad was infallible. This verse teaches us that he was indeed a fallible human being (18:110, 33:37, 40:66, 80:1).

9. O prophet, struggle against the disbelievers and the hypocrites and be stern with them. Their abode is Gehenna, and a miserable destiny.

The Myth of Intercession Shattered

10. **GOD** cites as examples of those who disbelieved the wife of Noah and the wife of Lot. They were married to two of our righteous servants, but they betrayed them and, consequently, they could not help them at all against **GOD**. The two of them were told, "Enter the Hellfire with those who deserved it."

Examples of the Believers: Pharaoh's Wife

11. And **GOD** cites as an example of those who believed the wife of Pharaoh. She said, "My Lord, build a home for me at You in Paradise, and save me from Pharaoh and his works; save me from the transgressing people."

Mary

12. Also Mary, the Amramite. She maintained her chastity, then we blew into her from our spirit. She believed in the words of her Lord and His scriptures; she was obedient.

◆◆◆◆

Sura 67: Kingship (Al-Mulk)

In the name of God, Most Gracious, Most Merciful

1. Most exalted is the One in whose hands is all kingship, and He is Omnipotent.

The Purpose of Our Life *

2. The One who created death and life for the purpose of distinguishing those among you who would do better.* He is the Almighty, the Forgiving.

3. He created seven universes in layers. You do not see any imperfection in the creation by the Most Gracious. Keep looking; do you see any flaw?

4. Look again and again; your eyes will come back stumped and conquered.

5. We adorned the lowest universe with lamps, and guarded its borders with projectiles against the devils; we prepared for them a retribution in Hell.

6. For those who disbelieved in their Lord, the retribution of Gehenna. What a miserable destiny.

7. When they get thrown therein, they hear its furor as it fumes.

8. It almost explodes from rage. Whenever a group is thrown therein, its guards would ask them, "Did you not receive a warner?"

9. They would answer, "Yes indeed; a warner did come to us, but we disbelieved and said, '**GOD** did not reveal anything. You are totally astray.' "

10. They also say, "If we heard or understood, we would not be among the dwellers of Hell!"

11. Thus, they confessed their sins. Woe to the dwellers of Hell.

12. As for those who reverence their Lord, when alone in their privacy, they have attained forgiveness and a great recompense.

67:2 See the Introduction and Appendix 7 for details of the purpose behind this world.

13. Whether you keep your utterances secret, or declare them, He is fully aware of the innermost thoughts.

14. Should He not know what He created? He is the Sublime, Most Cognizant.

15. He is the One who put the Earth at your service. Roam its corners, and eat from His provisions. To Him is the final summoning.

16. Have you guaranteed that the One in heaven will not strike the earth and cause it to tumble?

17. Have you guaranteed that the One in heaven will not send upon you a violent storm? Will you then appreciate the value of My warning?

18. Others before them have disbelieved; how terrible was My requital!

19. Have they not seen the birds above them lined up in columns and spreading their wings? The Most Gracious is the One who holds them in the air. He is Seer of all things.

20. Where are those soldiers who can help you against the Most Gracious? Indeed, the disbelievers are deceived.

21. Who is there to provide for you, if He withholds His provisions? Indeed, they have plunged deep into transgression and aversion.

22. Is one who walks while slumped over on his face better guided, or one who walks straight on the right path?

23. Say, "He is the One who initiated you, and granted you the hearing, the eyes, and the brains. Rarely are you appreciative."

24. Say, "He is the One who placed you on earth, and before Him you will be summoned."

25. They challenge: "When will that prophecy come to pass, if you are truthful?"

26. Say, "Such knowledge is with **GOD**; I am no more than a manifest warner."

27. When they see it happening, the faces of those who disbelieved will turn miserable, and it will be proclaimed: "This is what you used to mock."

28. Say, "Whether **GOD** decides to annihilate me and those with me, or to shower us with His mercy, who is there to protect the disbelievers from a painful retribution?"

29. Say, "He is the Most Gracious; we believe in Him, and we trust in Him. You will surely find out who is really far astray."

30. Say, "What if your water sinks away, who will provide you with pure water?"

❖❖❖

Sura 68: The Pen (Al-Qalam)

In the name of God,
Most Gracious, Most Merciful

1. NuN,* the pen, and what they (*the people*) write.

2. You have attained a great blessing from your Lord; you are not crazy.

68:1 "NuN" is unique among the Quran's miraculous initials. See Appendix 1.

3. You have attained a recompense that is well deserved.

4. You are blessed with a great moral character.

5. You will see, and they will see.

6. Which of you are condemned.

7. Your Lord is fully aware of those who strayed off His path, and He is fully aware of those who are guided.

8. Do not obey the rejectors.

9. They wish that you compromise, so they too can compromise.

10. Do not obey every lowly swearer.

11. A slanderer, a backbiter.

12. Forbidder of charity, a transgressor, a sinner.

13. Unappreciative, and greedy.

14. Even though he possessed enough money and children.

15. When our revelations are recited to him, he says, "Tales from the past!"

16. We will mark his face.

17. We have tested them like we tested the owners of the garden who swore that they will harvest it in the morning.

18. They were so absolutely sure.

19. A passing *(storm)* from your Lord passed by it while they were asleep.

20. By morning, it was barren.

21. They called on each other in the morning.

22. "Let us harvest the crop."

23. On their way, they confided to each other.

24. That from then on, none of them would be poor.

25. They were so absolutely sure of their harvest.

26. But when they saw it, they said, "We were so wrong!

27. "Now, we have nothing!"

They Should Have Said:
"God Willing."

28. The righteous among them said, "If only you had glorified *(God)*!"

29. They said, "Glory be to our Lord. We have transgressed."

30. They started to blame each other.

31. They said, "Woe to us. We sinned.

32. "May our Lord grant us a better one. We repent to our Lord."

33. Such was the requital. But the retribution of the Hereafter is far worse, if they only knew.

34. The righteous have deserved, at their Lord, gardens of bliss.

35. Shall we treat the Submitters like the criminals?

36. What is wrong with your logic?

37. Do you have another book to uphold?

38. In it, do you find anything you want?

39. Or, have you received solemn assurances from us that grant you whatever you wish on the Day of Resurrection?

40. Ask them, "Who guarantees this for you?"

41. Do they have idols? Let their idols help them, if they are truthful.

42. The day will come when they will be exposed, and they will be required to fall prostrate, but they will be unable to.

43. With their eyes subdued, humiliation will cover them. They were invited to fall prostrate when they were whole and able.

44. Therefore, let Me deal with those who reject this *Hadith*; we will lead them on whence they never perceive.

45. I will give them enough rope; My scheming is formidable.

46. Are you asking them for money, so they are burdened by the fine?

47. Do they know the future? Do they have it recorded?

48. You shall steadfastly persevere in carrying out the commands of your Lord. Do not be like *(Jonah)* who called from inside the fish.

49. If it were not for his Lord's grace, he would have been ejected into the desert as a sinner.

50. But his Lord blessed him, and made him righteous.

51. Those who disbelieved show their ridicule in their eyes when they hear the message and say, "He is crazy!"

52. It is in fact a message to the world.

❖❖❖❖

Sura 69: Incontestable (Al-Haaqqah)

In the name of God,
Most Gracious, Most Merciful

1. The incontestable *(event)*.

2. What an incontestable *(event)*!

3. It is truly incontestable.

4. Thamoud and 'Aad disbelieved in the Shocker.

5. As for Thamoud, they were annihilated by the devastating *(quake)*.

6. As for 'Aad, they were annihilated by a persistent, violent storm.

7. He unleashed it upon them for seven nights and eight days, violently. You could see the people tossed around like decayed palm trunks.

8. Can you find any trace of them?

9. Pharaoh, others before him, and the sinners *(of Sodom)* were wicked.

10. They disobeyed the messenger of their Lord. Consequently, He requited them a devastating requital.

11. The flood was devastating, so we carried you on the floating *(ark)*.

12. We rendered it a lesson for you, that any listening ear may understand.

13. When the horn is blown once.

14. The earth and the mountains will be carried off and crushed; utterly crushed.

15. That is the day when the inevitable event will come to pass.

16. The heaven will crack, and fall apart.

17. The angels will be all around, and Your Lord's dominion will then encompass eight *(universes)*. *

---

*69:17 This earth is full of misery because of its physical distance from God, since it is in the seventh universe (7:143). In the Hereafter, an eighth universe will be created that will be even farther than our seventh universe; it will be called "Hell" (89:23).

18. On that day, you will be exposed, nothing of you can be hidden.

The Believers

19. As for the one who receives his record with his right hand, he will say, "Come read my record.

20. "I did believe that I was going to be held accountable."

21. He has deserved a happy life.

22. In an exalted Paradise.

23. Its fruits are within reach.

24. Eat and drink happily in return for your works in days past.

The Disbelievers

25. As for him who is given his record in his left hand, he will say, "Oh, I wish I never received my record.

26. "I wish I never knew my account.

27. "I wish my death was eternal.

28. "My money cannot help me.

29. "All my power is gone."

30. Take him and shackle him.

31. Burn him in Hell.

32. In a chain that is seventy arms long, tie him up.

33. For he did not believe in **GOD**, Most Great.

34. Nor did he advocate the feeding of the poor.

35. Consequently, he has no friend here.

36. Nor any food, except the bitter variety.

37. Food for the sinners.

38. I swear by what you see.

39. And what you do not see.

40. This is the utterance of an honorable messenger.

41. Not the utterance of a poet; rarely do you believe.

42. Nor the utterance of a soothsayer; rarely do you take heed.

43. A revelation from the Lord of the universe.

Muhammad Forbidden from Issuing Any Religious Teachings

44. Had he uttered any other teachings.

45. We would have punished him.

46. We would have stopped the revelations to him.

47. None of you could have helped him.

48. This is a reminder for the righteous.

49. We know; some of you are rejectors.

50. It is but sorrow for the disbelievers.

51. It is the absolute truth.

52. Therefore, you shall glorify the name of your Lord, Most Great.

◆◆◆

Sura 70: The Heights (Al-Ma'aarej)

In the name of God,
Most Gracious, Most Merciful

1. A questioner may question the inevitable retribution.

2. For the disbelievers, none can stop it.

3. From **GOD**; Possessor of the highest Height.

4. The angels, with their reports, climb to Him in a day that equals fifty thousand years.

5. Therefore, you shall resort to a gracious patience.

6. For they see it far away.

7. While we see it very close.

8. The day will come when the sky will be like molten rocks.

9. The mountains will be like fluffy wool.

10. No friend will care about his close friend.

11. When they see them, the guilty will wish he could give his own children as ransom, to spare him the retribution of that day.

12. Also his spouse, and his brother.

13. Even his whole tribe that raised him.

14. Even all the people on earth, if it would save him.

15. No; it is aflame.

16. Eager to burn.

17. It calls on those who turned away.

18. Those who hoarded and counted.

19. Indeed, the human being is anxious.

20. If touched by adversity, despondent.

21. If blessed by wealth, stingy.

22. Except for the worshipers.

23. Who always observe their contact prayers (*Salat*).

24. Part of their money is set aside.

25. For the poor and the needy.

26. They believe in the Day of Judgment.

27. They reverence their Lord's requital.

28. Their Lord's requital is not taken for granted.

29. They keep their chastity.

30. *(They have relations)* only with their spouses, or what is legally theirs—

31. anyone who transgresses these limits is a sinner.

32. And the believers keep their word; they are trustworthy.

33. Their testimony is truthful.

34. They consistently observe their contact prayers (*Salat*) on time.

35. They have deserved a position of honor in Paradise.

36. What is keeping those who disbelieved from joining you?

37. To the right, and to the left, they flee.

38. How can any of them expect to enter the blissful Paradise?

39. Never; we created them, and they know from what.

40. I solemnly swear by the Lord of the easts and the wests; we are able—

41. to substitute better people in your place; we can never be defeated.

42. Therefore, let them blunder and play, until they meet the day that is awaiting them.

43. That is the day they come out of the graves in a hurry, as if herded to the *(sacrificial)* altars.

44. With their eyes subdued, shame will cover them. That is the day that is awaiting them.

❖❖❖❖

Sura 71: Noah

In the name of God,
Most Gracious, Most Merciful

1. We sent Noah to his people: "You shall warn your people before a painful retribution afflicts them."

2. He said, "O my people, I am a manifest warner to you.

3. "To alert you that you shall worship **GOD**, reverence Him, and obey me.

4. "He will then forgive you your sins and respite you for a predetermined period. Most assuredly, **GOD**'s appointment can never be delayed, once it is due, if you only knew."

5. He said, "My Lord, I have invited my people night and day.

6. "But my invitation only increased their aversion.

7. "Whenever I invited them to be forgiven by You, they placed their fingers in their ears, covered themselves with their clothes, insisted, and turned arrogant.

8. "Then I invited them publicly.

9. "Then I proclaimed to them loudly, and I spoke to them privately.

10. "I said, 'Implore your Lord for forgiveness; He is Forgiving.

11. " 'He will then shower you generously with rain.

12. " 'And provide you with money and children, and orchards, and streams.' "

13. Why should you not strive to reverence **GOD**?

14. He is the One who created you in stages.

15. Do you not realize that **GOD** created seven universes in layers?

16. He designed the moon therein to be a light, and placed the sun to be a lamp.

17. And **GOD** germinated you from the earth like plants.

18. Then He returns you into it, and He will surely bring you out.

19. **GOD** made the earth habitable for you.

20. That you may build roads therein.

21. Noah said, "My Lord, they disobeyed me, and followed those who were even more corrupted when blessed with money and children.

22. "They schemed terrible schemes.

23. "They said, 'Do not abandon your gods. Do not abandon Wadd, Suwaa', Yaghouth, Ya'ooq, and Nasr.'

24. "They misled many. Therefore, let the wicked plunge deeper into loss."

25. Because of their sins they were drowned and assigned to the hellfire. They found no helpers to protect them from **GOD**.

26. Noah also said, "My Lord, do not leave a single disbeliever on earth.

27. "For if you let them, they will only mislead your servants and give birth to nothing but wicked disbelievers.

28. "My Lord, forgive me and my parents, and anyone who enters my home as a believer, and all the believing men and women. But do not give the disbelievers anything but annihilation."

❖❖❖

Sura 72: Jinns (Al-Jinn)

In the name of God,
Most Gracious, Most Merciful

1. Say, "I was inspired that a group of jinns listened, then said, 'We have heard a wonderful Quran.*

2. " 'It guides to righteousness, and we have believed in it; we will never set up any idols beside our Lord.

3. " 'The Most High is our only Lord. He never had a mate, nor a son.

4. " 'It is the foolish among us who used to utter such nonsense about **GOD**.

5. " 'We thought that neither the humans, nor the jinns, could possibly utter lies about **GOD**.

6. " 'Human beings used to seek power through jinn beings, but they only afflicted them with a lot of adversity.

7. " 'They thought, just like you thought, that **GOD** would not send another *(messenger)*.

8. " 'We touched the heaven and found it filled with formidable guards and projectiles.

9. " 'We used to sit there in order to spy. Anyone who listens is pursued by a powerful projectile.

10. " 'We have no idea if something bad is intended for the inhabitants of Earth, or if their Lord wills to redeem them.

11. " 'Some of us are righteous, and some are less than righteous; we follow various paths.

12. " 'We knew full well that we can never run away from **GOD** on Earth; we can never run away and escape.

13. " 'When we heard the guidance, we believed therein. Anyone who believes in his Lord will never fear any injustice, nor any affliction.

14. " 'Among us are the submitters, and among us are the compromisers.' " As for those who submitted, they are on the right path.

15. As for the compromisers, they will be fuel for Gehenna.

16. If they remain on the right path, we will bless them with abundant water.

17. We will surely test them all. As for him who disregards the message of his Lord, He will direct him to ever increasing retribution.

18. The places of worship belong to **GOD**; do not call on anyone else beside **GOD**.

*God's Messenger of the Covenant**

19. When **GOD**'s servant* advocated Him alone, almost all of them banded together to oppose him.

20. Say, "I worship only my Lord; I never set up any idols beside Him."

21. Say, "I possess no power to harm you, nor to guide you."

72:1-28 The messenger here is named, mathematically, as "Rashad Khalifa," to whom God revealed the end of the world (Appendix 25). The number of verses from 1:1 to 72:27, where the messenger is mentioned, is 5472, 19x72x4. The word "Rashada" occurs 4 times in Sura 72. The value of "Rashada" is 504, and 504 + 28 (verses of Sura 72) is 532, 19x28. The value of "Rashad Khalifa" (1230) + 72 + 28 = 1330 = 19x70. The digits of Sura 72 and its number of verses (28) add up to 7 + 2 + 2 + 8 = 19. Also, the crucial expression, "only to a messenger that He chooses" has a value of 1919, 19x101.

22. Say, "No one can protect me from **GOD**, nor can I find any other refuge beside Him.

23. "I deliver **GOD**'s proclamations and messages." Those who disobey **GOD** and His messenger incur the fire of Hell, wherein they abide forever.

24. Once they see what is awaiting them, they will find out who is really weaker in power, and fewer in number.

25. Say, "I do not know if what is promised to you will happen soon, or if my Lord will delay it for awhile."

26. He is the Knower of the future; He does not reveal the future to anyone.

27. Only to a messenger that He chooses,* does He reveal from the past and the future, specific news.*

28. This is to ascertain that they have delivered their Lord's messages. He is fully aware of what they have. He has counted the numbers of all things.

◆◆◆◆

Sura 73: Cloaked (Al-Muzzammil)

In the name of God,
Most Gracious, Most Merciful

1. O you cloaked one.

2. Meditate during the night, except rarely.

3. Half of it, or a little less.

4. Or a little more. And read the Quran from cover to cover.

5. We will give you a heavy message.

6. The meditation at night is more effective, and more righteous.

7. You have a lot of time during the day for other matters.

8. You shall commemorate the name of your Lord, to come ever closer and closer to Him.

9. Lord of the east and the west; there is no other god besides Him. You should choose Him as your advocate.

10. And remain steadfast in the face of their utterances, and disregard them in a nice manner.

11. And let Me deal with the rejectors, who have been generously blessed; just give them a little time.

12. We have severe punishments, and Hell.

13. Food that can hardly be swallowed, and painful retribution.

14. The day will come when the earth and the mountains will quake, and the mountains will turn into a weightless pile.

15. We have sent to you a messenger, just as we sent to Pharaoh a messenger.

16. Pharaoh disobeyed the messenger and, consequently, we punished him severely.

17. If you disbelieve, how can you evade a day so terrible that it makes the infants gray-haired?

18. The heaven will shatter therefrom. His promise is true.

---

* 72:27 See footnote for 72:1-28.

---

19. This is a reminder; whoever wills, let him choose the path to his Lord.

20. Your Lord knows that you meditate during two-thirds of the night, or half of it, or one-third of it, and so do some of those who believed with you. **GOD** has designed the night and the day, and He knows that you cannot always do this. He has pardoned you. Instead, you shall read what you can of the Quran. He knows that some of you may be ill, others may be traveling in pursuit of **GOD**'s provisions, and others may be striving in the cause of **GOD**. You shall read what you can of it, and observe the contact prayers (*Salat*), give the obligatory charity (*Zakat*), and lend **GOD** a loan of righteousness. Whatever good you send ahead on behalf of your souls, you will find it at **GOD** far better and generously rewarded. And implore **GOD** for forgiveness. **GOD** is Forgiver, Most Merciful.

Sura 74: The Hidden Secret (Al-Muddath-thir)

In the name of God,
Most Gracious, Most Merciful

1. O you hidden secret.*

2. Come out and warn.

3. Extol your Lord.

4. Purify your garment.*

5. Forsake what is wrong.

6. Be content with your lot.

7. Steadfastly commemorate your Lord.

8. Then, when the horn is blown.

9. That will be a difficult day.

10. For the disbelievers, not easy.

11. Let Me deal with one I created as an individual.

12. I provided him with lots of money.

13. And children to behold.

14. I made everything easy for him.

15. Yet, he is greedy for more.

16. He stubbornly refused to accept these proofs.

17. I will increasingly punish him.

18. For he reflected, then decided.

19. Miserable is what he decided.

20. Miserable indeed is what he decided.

21. He looked.

22. He frowned and whined.

23. Then he turned away arrogantly.

24. He said, "This is but clever magic!

25. "This is human made."

26. I will commit him to retribution.

27. What retribution!

28. Thorough and comprehensive.

29. Obvious to all the people.

74:1 God's infinite wisdom willed to reveal the Quran through Muhammad, while the Quran's awesome 19-based mathematical miracle was revealed through God's Messenger of the Covenant 1406 lunar years after revelation of the Quran (1406 = 19x74 & 1974 AD was the Solar Year of discovery). In retrospect, we realize that the whole sura refers to the Quran's 19-based miracle (Appendices 1 & 2).

*74:4 Quran is the garment containing the secret code. This refers to removing 9:128-129.

The Quran's Common Denominator

30. Over it is nineteen.*

31. We appointed angels to be guardians of Hell, and we assigned their number *(19)*
(1) to disturb the disbelievers,
(2) to convince the Christians and Jews *(that this is a divine scripture),*
(3) to strengthen the faith of the faithful,
(4) to remove all traces of doubt from the hearts of Christians, Jews, as well as the believers, and
(5) to expose those who harbor doubt in their hearts, and the disbelievers; they will say, "What did **GOD** mean by this allegory?" **GOD** thus sends astray whomever He wills, and guides whomever He wills. None knows the soldiers of your Lord except He. This is a reminder for the people.

32. Absolutely, *(I swear)* by the moon.

33. And the night as it passes.

34. And the morning as it shines.

One of the Great Miracles

35. This is one of the great miracles.*

36. A warning to the human race.

37. For those among you who wish to advance, or regress.

38. Every soul is trapped by its sins.

39. Except for those on the right.

40. While in Paradise, they will ask.

41. About the guilty.

42. "What brought you to this retribution?"

43. They will say, "We did not observe the contact prayers (*Salat*).

44. "We did not feed the poor.

45. "We blundered with the blunderers.

46. "We disbelieved in the Day of Judgment.

47. "Until certainty came to us now."

48. The intercession of the intercessors will never help them.

49. Why are they so averse to this reminder?

50. Running like zebras.

51. Who are fleeing from the lion!

52. Does each one of them want to receive the scripture personally?

53. Indeed, they do not fear the Hereafter.

54. Indeed, this is a reminder.

55. For those who wish to take heed.

56. They cannot take heed against **GOD**'s will. He is the source of righteousness; He is the source of forgiveness.

◆◆◆◆

Sura 75: Resurrection (Al-Qeyaamah)

In the name of God,
Most Gracious, Most Merciful

1. I swear by the Day of Resurrection.

2. And I swear by the blaming soul.

3. Does the human being think that we will not reconstruct his bones?

4. Yes indeed; we are able to reconstruct his finger tip.

74:30-35 This "One of the great miracles" provides the first physical evidence that the Quran is God's message to the world. This 19-based miracle is detailed in Appendix 1.

5. But the human being tends to believe only what he sees in front of him.

6. He doubts the Day of Resurrection!

7. Once the vision is sharpened.

8. And the moon is eclipsed.

9. And the sun and the moon crash into one another.

10. The human being will say on that day, "Where is the escape?"

11. Absolutely, there is no escape.

12. To your Lord, on that day, is the final destiny.

13. The human being will be informed, on that day, of everything he did to advance himself, and everything he did to regress himself.

14. The human being will be his own judge.

15. No excuses will be accepted.

Muhammad Forbidden From
Explaining the Quran

16. Do not move your tongue to hasten it.

17. It is we who will collect it into Quran.

18. Once we recite it, you shall follow such a Quran.

19. Then it is we who will explain it.

20. Indeed, you love this fleeting life.

21. While disregarding the Hereafter.

22. Some faces, on that day, will be happy.

23. Looking at their Lord.

24. Other faces will be, on that day, miserable.

25. Expecting the worst.

26. Indeed, when *(the soul)* reaches the throat.

27. And it is ordered: "Let go!"

28. He knows it is the end.

29. Each leg will lay motionless next to the other leg.

30. To your Lord, on that day, is the summoning.

31. For he observed neither the charity, nor the contact prayers (*Salat*).

32. But he disbelieved and turned away.

33. With his family, he acted arrogantly.

34. You have deserved this.

35. Indeed, you have deserved this.

36. Does the human being think that he will go to nothing?

37. Was he not a drop of ejected semen?

38. Then He created an embryo out of it!

39. He made it into male or female!

40. Is He then unable to revive the dead?

Sura 76: The Human (Al-Insaan)

In the name of God,
Most Gracious, Most Merciful

1. Is it not a fact that there was a time when the human being was nothing to be mentioned?

2. We created the human from a liquid mixture, from two parents, in order to test him. Thus, we made him a hearer and a seer.

3. We showed him the two paths, then, he is either appreciative, or unappreciative.

4. We prepared for the disbelievers chains, shackles, and a blazing Hell.

5. As for the virtuous, they will drink from cups spiced with nectar.

6. A spring that is reserved for **GOD**'s servants; it will gush out as they will.

7. They fulfill their pledges, and reverence a day that is extremely difficult.

8. They donate their favorite food to the poor, the orphan, and the captive.

9. "We feed you for the sake of **GOD**; we expect no reward from you, nor thanks.

10. "We fear from our Lord a day that is full of misery and trouble."

11. Consequently, **GOD** protects them from the evils of that day, and rewards them with joy and contentment.

12. He rewards them for their steadfastness with Paradise, and silk.

13. They relax therein on luxurious furnishings. They suffer neither the heat of the sun, nor any cold.

14. The shade covers them therein, and the fruits are brought within reach.

15. They are served drinks in silver containers and cups that are translucent.

16. Translucent cups, though made of silver; they rightly deserved all this.

17. They enjoy drinks of delicious flavors.

18. From a spring therein known as "Salsabeel."

19. Serving them will be immortal servants. When you see them, they will look like scattered pearls.

20. Wherever you look, you will see bliss, and a wonderful dominion.

21. On them will be clothes of green velvet, satin, and silver ornaments. Their Lord will provide them with pure drinks.

22. This is the reward that awaits you, for your efforts have been appreciated.

23. We have revealed to you this Quran; a special revelation from us.

24. You shall steadfastly carry out your Lord's commandments, and do not obey any sinful disbeliever among them.

25. And commemorate the name of your Lord day and night.

26. During the night, fall prostrate before Him, and glorify Him many a long night.

27. These people are preoccupied with this fleeting life, while disregarding—just ahead of them—a heavy day.

28. We created them, and established them, and, whenever we will, we can substitute others in their place.

29. This is a reminder: whoever wills shall choose the path to his Lord.

30. Whatever you will is in accordance with **GOD**'s will. **GOD** is Omniscient, Wise.

31. He admits whomever He wills into His mercy. As for the transgressors, He has prepared for them a painful retribution.

❖❖❖

Sura 77: Dispatched (Al-Mursalaat)

In the name of God,
Most Gracious, Most Merciful

1. *(Angels)* dispatched in succession.

2. To drive the wind.

3. Stir up clouds.

4. Distribute the provisions.

5. Deliver messages.

6. Good news, as well as warnings.

7. What is promised will come to pass.

8. Thus, when the stars are put out.

9. The sky is opened up.

10. The mountains are blown up.

11. The messengers are summoned.

12. That is the appointed day.

13. The Day of Decision.

14. What a Day of Decision!

15. Woe on that day to the rejectors.

16. Did we not annihilate the earlier generations?

17. Then we made others follow them?

18. This is what we do to the criminals.

19. Woe on that day to the rejectors.

20. Did we not create you from a lowly liquid?*

21. Then we placed it in a well-protected repository.

22. For a specific period.

23. We measured it precisely.* We are the best designers.

24. Woe on that day to the rejectors.

25. Did we not make the earth an abode?

26. For the living and the dead?

27. We placed on it high mountains, and provided you with fresh water to drink.

28. Woe on that day to the rejectors.

29. Go to what you used to disbelieve in.

30. Go to a shade of three different densities.

31. Yet, it provides neither coolness, nor protection from the heat.

32. It throws sparks as big as mansions.

33. As yellow as the color of camels.

34. Woe on that day to the rejectors.

35. That is the day they do not speak.

36. Nor are they given permission to apologize.

37. Woe on that day to the rejectors.

38. This is the Day of Decision. We have summoned you and the previous generations.

77:20-23 According to Langman's Medical Embryology, *by T. W. Sadler (Fifth Edition, Page 88): "In general the length of pregnancy for a full term fetus is 266 days or 38 weeks after fertilization." Both 266 and 38 are multiples of 19 (Appendix 1).*

---

39. If you have any schemes, go ahead and scheme.

40. Woe on that day to the rejectors.

41. The righteous will enjoy shade and springs.

42. And fruits that they desire.

43. Eat and drink happily in return for your works.

44. We thus reward the virtuous.

45. Woe on that day to the rejectors.

46. Eat and enjoy temporarily; you are guilty.

47. Woe on that day to the rejectors.

48. When they are told, "Bow down," they do not bow down.

49. Woe on that day to the rejectors.

50. Which *Hadith,* other than this, do they uphold?

◆◆◆◆

Sura 78: The Event (Al-Naba')

In the name of God,
Most Gracious, Most Merciful

1. What are they questioning?

2. The great event.

3. That is disputed by them.

4. Indeed, they will find out.

5. Most assuredly, they will find out.

6. Did we not make the earth habitable?

7. And the mountains stabilizers?

8. We created you as mates *(for one another).*

9. We created sleeping so you can rest.

10. We made the night a cover.

11. And the day to seek provisions.

12. We built above you seven universes.

13. We created a bright lamp.

14. We send down from the clouds pouring water.

15. To produce with it grains and plants.

16. And various orchards.

17. The Day of Decision is appointed.

18. The day the horn is blown, and you come in throngs.

19. The heaven will be opened like gates.

20. The mountains will be removed, as if they were a mirage.

21. Gehenna is inevitable.

22. For the transgressors; it will be their abode.

23. They stay in it for ages.

24. They never taste in it coolness, nor a drink.

25. Only an inferno, and bitter food.

26. A just requital.

27. They never expected to be held accountable.

28. And utterly rejected our signs.

29. We counted everything in a record.

30. Suffer the consequences; we will only increase your retribution.

31. The righteous have deserved a reward.

32. Orchards and grapes.

33. Magnificent spouses.

34. Delicious drinks.

35. They will never hear in it any nonsense or lies.

36. A reward from your Lord; a generous recompense.

37. Lord of the heavens and the earth, and everything between them. The Most Gracious. No one can abrogate His decisions.

38. The day will come when the Spirit and the angels will stand in a row. None will speak except those permitted by the Most Gracious, and they will utter only what is right.

39. Such is the inevitable day. Whoever wills let him take refuge in his Lord.

40. We have sufficiently warned you about an imminent retribution. That is the day when everyone will examine what his hands have sent forth, and the disbeliever will say, "Oh, I wish I were dust."

❖❖❖❖

Sura 79: The Snatchers (Al-Naaze'aat)

In the name of God,
Most Gracious, Most Merciful

1. The *(angels who)* snatch *(the souls of the disbelievers)* forcibly.

2. And those who gently take *(the souls of the believers)* joyfully.

3. And those floating everywhere.

4. Eagerly racing with one another—

5. to carry out various commands.

6. The day the quake quakes.

7. Followed by the second blow.

8. Certain minds will be terrified.

9. Their eyes will be subdued.

10. They will say, "We have been recreated from the grave!

11. "How did this happen after we had turned into rotten bones?"

12. They had said, "This is an impossible recurrence."

13. All it takes is one nudge.

14. Whereupon they get up.

15. Have you known about the history of Moses?

16. His Lord called him at the holy valley of Tuwaa.

17. "Go to Pharaoh; he has transgressed."

18. Tell him, "Would you not reform?

19. "Let me guide you to your Lord, that you may turn reverent."

20. He then showed him the great miracle.

21. But he disbelieved and rebelled.

22. Then he turned away in a hurry.

23. He summoned and proclaimed.

24. He said, "I am your Lord; most high."

25. Consequently, **GOD** committed him to the retribution in the Hereafter, as well as in the first life.

26. This is a lesson for the reverent.

27. Are you more difficult to create than the heaven? He constructed it.

28. He raised its masses, and perfected it.

29. He made its night dark, and brightened its morn.

30. He made the earth egg-shaped.*

31. From it, He produced its own water and pasture.

32. He established the mountains.

33. All this to provide life support for you and your animals.

34. Then, when the great blow comes.

35. That is the day when the human will remember everything he did.

36. Hell will be brought into existence.

37. As for the one who transgressed.

38. Who was preoccupied with this life.

39. Hell will be the abode.

40. As for the one who reverenced the majesty of his Lord, and enjoined the self from sinful lusts.

41. Paradise will be the abode.

42. They ask you about the Hour, and when it will take place!

43. It is not you (*Muhammad*) who is destined to announce its time.

44. Your Lord decides its fate.

45. Your mission is to warn those who expect it.

46. The day they see it, they will feel as if they lasted one evening or half a day.

◆◆◆◆

Sura 80: He Frowned ('Abasa)

In the name of God,
Most Gracious, Most Merciful

1. He (*Muhammad*) frowned and turned away.

2. When the blind man came to him.

3. How do you know? He may purify himself.

4. Or he may take heed, and benefit from the message.

5. As for the rich man.

6. You gave him your attention.

7. Even though you could not guarantee his salvation.

8. The one who came to you eagerly.

9. And is really reverent.

10. You ignored him.

11. Indeed, this is a reminder.

12. Whoever wills shall take heed.

13. In honorable scriptures.

14. Exalted and pure.

15. (*Written*) by the hands of messengers.

16. Who are honorable and righteous.

17. Woe to the human being; he is so unappreciative!

18. What did He create him from?

19. From a tiny drop, He creates him and designs him.

20. Then He points out the path for him.

21. Then He puts him to death, and into the grave.

22. When He wills, He resurrects him.

23. He shall uphold His commandments.

24. Let the human consider his food!

79:30 The Arabic word "dahhaahaa" is derived from "Dahhyah" which means "egg."

25. We pour the water generously.

26. Then we split the soil open.

27. We grow in it grains.

28. Grapes and pasture.

29. Olives and palms.

30. A variety of orchards.

31. Fruits and vegetables.

32. To provide life support for you and your animals.

33. Then, when the blow comes to pass.

34. That is the day when one flees from his brother.

35. From his mother and father.

36. From his spouse and children.

37. Each one of them, on that day, worries about his own destiny.

38. Some faces on that day will be happy.

39. Laughing and joyful.

40. Other faces, on that day, will be covered with misery.

41. Overwhelmed by remorse.

42. These are the wicked disbelievers.

◆◆◆◆

Sura 81: The Rolling (Al-Takweer)

In the name of God,
Most Gracious, Most Merciful

1. When the sun is rolled.

2. The stars are crashed into each other.

3. The mountains are wiped out.

4. The reproduction is halted.

5. The beasts are summoned.

6. The oceans are set aflame.

7. The souls are restored to their bodies.

8. The girl who was buried alive is asked:

9. For what crime was she killed?

10. The records are made known.

11. The heaven is removed.

12. Hell is ignited.

13. Paradise is presented.

14. Every soul will know everything it brought.

God's Messenger of the Covenant

15. I solemnly swear by the galaxies.

16. Precisely running in their orbits.

17. By the night as it falls.

18. And the morn as it breathes.

19. This is the utterance of an honorable messenger.*

20. Authorized by the Possessor of the Throne, fully supported.

21. He shall be obeyed and trusted.

22. Your friend *(Rashad)* is not crazy.

23. He saw him at the high horizon.*

24. He is not holding back any news.

25. It is not the talk of a rejected devil.

26. Now then, where will you go?

27. This is a message to all the people.

---

*81:19 By adding the sura number, plus the verse number, plus the gematrical value of the name "Rashad" (505), plus the value of "Khalifa" (725), we get 1330, 19x70. This provides Quranic mathematical proof that this messenger is Rashad Khalifa.

*81:23 Rashad Khalifa was summoned to the high horizon as detailed in Appendix 2.

---

28. For those who wish to go straight.

29. Whatever you will is in accordance with the will of **GOD,** Lord of the universe.

❖❖❖❖

Sura 82: The Shattering (Al-Infitaar)

In the name of God,
Most Gracious, Most Merciful

1. When the heaven is shattered.

2. The planets are scattered.

3. The oceans are exploded.

4. The graves are opened.

5. Every soul will find out what caused it to advance, and what caused it to regress.

Reflect on God's Creations

6. O you human being, what diverted you from your Lord, Most Honorable?

7. The One who created you, designed you, and perfected you.

8. In whatever design He chose, He constructed it.

9. Indeed, you disbelieve in the religion.

10. Oblivious to the fact that there are *(invisible)* keepers around you.

11. They are honest recorders.

12. They record everything you do.

13. Surely, the pious have deserved bliss.

14. While the wicked have deserved Hell.

15. Will incur it on the Day of Judgment.

16. They never leave it.

17. Awesome is the Day of Judgment.

18. What a day; the Day of Judgment!

19. That is the day when no soul can help another soul, and all decisions, on that day, will belong to **GOD**.

❖❖❖❖

Sura 83: The Cheaters (Al-Mutaffifeen)

In the name of God,
Most Gracious, Most Merciful

1. Woe to the cheaters.

2. Who demand full measure when receiving from the people.

3. But when giving them the measures or weights, they cheat.

4. Do they not know that they will be resurrected?

5. On a tremendous day?

6. That is the day when all people will stand before the Lord of the universe.

Numerically Structured Books

7. Indeed, the book of the wicked is in *Sijjeen.*

8. Do you know what *Sijjeen* is?

9. A numerically structured book.

10. Woe on that day to the rejectors.

11. They do not believe in the Day of Judgment.

12. None disbelieves therein except the transgressor, the sinful.

13. When our revelations are recited to him, he says, "Tales from the past!"

14. Indeed, their hearts have become shielded by their sins.

15. Indeed, they will be isolated, on that day, from their Lord.

16. Then they will be thrown into Hell.

17. They will be told, "This is what you used to deny."

18. Indeed, the book of the righteous will be in *'Elleyyeen.*

19. Do you know what *'Elleyyeen* is?

20. A numerically structured book.

21. To be witnessed by those close to Me.

22. The righteous have deserved bliss.

23. On luxurious furnishings they watch.

24. You recognize in their faces the joy of bliss.

25. Their drinks will be spiced with nectar.

26. Its spice is like musk. This is what the competitors should compete for.

27. Mixed into it will be special flavors.

28. From a spring that is reserved for those close to Me.

29. The wicked used to laugh at those who believed.

30. When they passed by them, they used to poke fun.

31. When they got together with their people, they used to joke.

32. Whenever they saw them, they said, "These people are far astray!

33. "They have no such thing as *(invisible)* guards."

34. Today, those who believed are laughing at the disbelievers.

35. On luxurious furnishings they watch.

36. Most assuredly, the disbelievers are requited for what they did.

Sura 84: The Rupture (Al-Inshiqaaq)

In the name of God,
Most Gracious, Most Merciful

1. The time will come when the sky is ruptured.

2. It will submit to its Lord and expire.

3. The earth will be leveled.

4. It will eject its contents, as it erupts.

5. It will submit to its Lord and expire.

6. O humans, you are irreversibly heading for a meeting with your Lord.

7. As for the one who receives his record in his right hand,

8. His reckoning will be easy.

9. He will return to his people joyfully.

10. As for the one who receives his record behind his back,

11. He will be ridden with remorse.

12. And will burn in Hell.

13. He used to act arrogantly among his people.

14. He thought that he will never be called to account.

15. Yes indeed, his Lord was Seer of him.

16. I solemnly swear by the rosy dusk.

17. And the night as it spreads.

18. And the moon and its phases.

19. You will move from stage to stage.

20. Why do they not believe?

21. And when the Quran is recited to them, they do not fall prostrate.

22. This is because those who disbelieved are rejecting *(the Quran).*

23. **GOD** is fully aware of their innermost thoughts.

24. Promise them painful retribution.

25. As for those who believed and led a righteous life, they receive a recompense that is well deserved.

Sura 85: The Galaxies (Al-Burooj)

In the name of God,
Most Gracious, Most Merciful

1. The sky and its galaxies.

2. The promised day.

3. The witness and the witnessed.

4. Woe to the people of the canyon.

5. They ignited a blazing fire.

6. Then sat around it.

7. To watch the burning of the believers.

8. They hated them for no other reason than believing in **GOD**, the Almighty, the Praiseworthy.

9. To Him belongs the kingship of the heavens and the earth. And **GOD** witnesses all things.

10. Surely, those who persecute the believing men and women, then fail to repent, have incurred the retribution of Gehenna; they have incurred the retribution of burning.

11. Surely, those who believed and led a righteous life, have deserved gardens with flowing streams. This is the greatest triumph.

12. Indeed, your Lord's blow is severe.

13. He is the One who initiates and repeats.

14. And He is the Forgiving, Most Kind.

15. Possessor of the glorious throne.

16. Doer of whatever He wills.

17. Did you note the history of the troops?

18. Pharaoh and Thamoud?

19. Those who disbelieve are plagued with denial.

20. **GOD** is fully aware of them.

21. Indeed, it is a glorious Quran.

22. In a preserved master tablet.

Sura 86: The Bright Star (Al-Taareq)

In the name of God,
Most Gracious, Most Merciful

1. By the sky and Al-Taareq.

2. Do you know what Al-Taareq is?

3. The bright star.

4. Absolutely, everyone is well guarded.

5. Let the human reflect on his creation.

6. He was created from ejected liquid.

7. From between the spine and the viscera.

8. He is certainly able to resurrect him.

9. The day all secrets become known.

10. He will have no power, nor a helper.

11. By the sky that returns *(the water)*.

12. By the earth that cracks *(to grow plants)*.

13. This is a serious narration.

14. Not to be taken lightly.

15. They plot and scheme.

16. But so do I.

17. Just respite the disbelievers a short respite.

◆◆◆◆

Sura 87: The Most High (Al-A'alaa)

In the name of God,
Most Gracious, Most Merciful

1. Glorify the name of your Lord, the Most High.

2. He creates and shapes.

3. He designs and guides.

4. He produces the pasture.

5. Then turns it into light hay.

6. We will recite to you; do not forget.

7. Everything is in accordance with **GOD**'s will; He knows what is declared, and what is hidden.

8. We will direct you to the easiest path.

9. Therefore, you shall remind; perhaps the reminder will benefit.

10. The reverent will take heed.

11. The wicked will avoid it.

12. Consequently, he will suffer the great Hellfire.

13. Wherein he never dies, nor stays alive.

14. Successful indeed is the one who redeems his soul.

15. By remembering the name of his Lord and observing the contact prayers (*Salat*).

16. Indeed, you are preoccupied with this first life.

17. Even though the Hereafter is far better and everlasting.

18. This is recorded in the earlier teachings.

19. The teachings of Abraham and Moses.

Sura 88: Overwhelming (Al-Ghaasheyah)

In the name of God,
Most Gracious, Most Merciful

1. Are you aware of the Overwhelming?

2. Faces on that day will be shamed.

3. Laboring and exhausted.

4. Suffering in a blazing Hellfire.

5. Drinking from a flaming spring.

6. They will have no food except the useless variety.

7. It never nourishes, nor satisfies hunger.

8. Other faces on that day will be full of joy.

9. Satisfied with their work.

10. In an exalted Paradise.

11. In it, no nonsense is heard.

12. In it, a spring flows.

13. In it, there are luxurious furnishings.

14. And drinks made available.

15. And pitchers in rows.

16. And carpets throughout.

17. Why do they not reflect on the camels and how they are created?

18. And the sky and how it is raised.

19. And the mountains and how they are constructed.

20. And the earth and how it is built.

21. You shall remind, for your mission is to deliver this reminder.

22. You have no power over them.

23. As for those who turn away and disbelieve.

24. **GOD** will commit them to the great retribution.

25. To us is their ultimate destiny.

26. Then we will call them to account.

❖❖❖

Sura 89: Dawn (Al-Fajr)

In the name of God,
Most Gracious, Most Merciful

1. By the dawn.

2. And the ten nights.*

3. By the even and the odd.*

4. By the night as it passes.

5. A profound oath, for one who possesses intelligence.

6. Have you noted what your Lord did to 'Aad?

7. Erum; the town with tall buildings.

8. There was nothing like it anywhere.

9. Also Thamoud, who carved the rocks in their valley.

10. And Pharaoh who possessed might.

11. They all transgressed in the land.

12. They spread evil throughout.

13. Consequently, your Lord poured upon them a whipping retribution.

14. Your Lord is ever watchful.

15. When the human being is tested by his Lord, through blessings and joy, he says, "My Lord is generous towards me."

16. But if He tests him through reduction in provisions, he says, "My Lord is humiliating me!"

17. Wrong! It is you who brought it on yourselves by not regarding the orphan.

18. And not advocating charity towards the poor.

19. And consuming the inheritance of helpless orphans.

20. And loving the money too much.

21. Indeed, when the earth is crushed, utterly crushed.

---

*89:2 *The last ten nights of Ramadan, wherein many believers retreat to the masjids (2:187).*

*89:3 *See Appendix 1 for the role of the even numbers and the odd numbers.*

22. And your Lord comes, together with the angels in row after row.

23. On that day, Gehenna will be brought forth. On that day, the human being will remember—but what a remembrance—it will be too late.

24. He will say, "Oh, I wish I prepared for my *(eternal)* life."

25. On that day, no retribution could be worse than His retribution.

26. And no confinement is as effective as His confinement.

27. As for you, O content soul.

28. Return to your Lord, pleased and pleasing.

29. Welcome into My servants.

30. Welcome into My Paradise.

❖❖❖❖

Sura 90: The Town (Al-Balad)

In the name of God,
Most Gracious, Most Merciful

1. I solemnly swear by this town.

2. The town where you live.

3. The begetting and the begotten.

4. We created the human being to work hard *(to redeem himself).* *

5. Does he think that no one will ever call him to account?

6. He boasts, "I spent so much money!"

7. Does he think that no one sees him?

8. Did we not give him two eyes?

9. A tongue and two lips?

10. Did we not show him the two paths?

11. He should choose the difficult path.

12. Which one is the difficult path?

13. The freeing of slaves.

14. Feeding, during the time of hardship.

15. Orphans who are related.

16. Or the poor who is in need.

17. And being one of those who believe, and exhorting one another to be steadfast, and exhorting one another to be kind.

18. These have deserved happiness.

19. As for those who disbelieved in our revelations, they have incurred misery.

20. They will be confined in the Hellfire.

❖❖❖❖

Sura 91: The Sun (Al-Shams)

In the name of God,
Most Gracious, Most Merciful

1. By the sun and its brightness.

2. The moon that follows it.

3. The day that reveals.

4. The night that covers.

5. The sky and Him who built it.

6. The earth and Him who sustains it.

7. The soul and Him who created it.

8. Then showed it what is evil and what is good.

*90:4 See the Introduction and Appendix 7 for the purpose behind our creation.

9. Successful is one who redeems it.

10. Failing is one who neglects it.

11. Thamoud's disbelief caused them to transgress.

12. They followed the worst among them.

13. **GOD**'s messenger said to them, "This is **GOD**'s camel; let her drink."

14. They disbelieved him and slaughtered her. Their Lord then requited them for their sin and annihilated them.

15. Yet, those who came after them remain heedless.

◆◆◆◆

Sura 92: The Night (Al-Layl)

In the name of God,
Most Gracious, Most Merciful

1. By the night as it covers.

2. The day as it reveals.

3. And Him who created the male and the female.

4. Your works are of various kinds.

5. As for him who gives to charity and maintains righteousness.

6. And upholds the scripture.

7. We will direct him towards happiness.

8. But he who is stingy, though he is rich.

9. And disbelieves in the scripture.

10. We will direct him towards misery.

11. His money cannot help him when he falls.

12. We provide the guidance.

13. We control the Hereafter, as well as this life.

14. I have warned you about the blazing Hellfire.

15. None burns therein except the wicked.

16. Who disbelieves and turns away.

17. Avoiding it will be the righteous.

18. Who gives from his money to charity.

19. Seeking nothing in return.

20. Seeking only his Lord, the Most High.

21. He will certainly attain salvation.

◆◆◆◆

Sura 93: The Forenoon (Al-Duhaa)

In the name of God,
Most Gracious, Most Merciful

1. By the forenoon.

2. By the night as it falls.

3. Your Lord never abandoned you, nor did He forget.

4. The Hereafter is far better for you than this first *(life)*.

5. And your Lord will give you enough; you will be pleased.

6. Did He not find you orphaned and He gave you a home?

7. He found you astray, and guided you.

8. He found you poor, and made you rich.

9. Therefore, you shall not forsake the orphan.

10. Nor shall you reprimand the beggar.

11. You shall proclaim the blessing your Lord has bestowed upon you.

Sura 94: Cooling the Temper (Al-Sharrhh)

In the name of God,
Most Gracious, Most Merciful

1. Did we not cool your temper?

2. And we unloaded your load *(of sins).*

3. One that burdened your back.

4. We exalted you to an honorable position.

5. With pain there is gain.

6. Indeed, with pain there is gain.

7. Whenever possible you shall strive.

8. Seeking only your Lord.

Sura 95: The Fig (Al-Teen)

In the name of God,
Most Gracious, Most Merciful

1. By the fig and the olive.

2. Mount Sinai.

3. And this honored town *(Mecca).**

4. We created man in the best design.

5. Then turned him into the lowliest of the lowly.

6. Except those who believe and lead a righteous life; they receive a reward that is well deserved.

7. Why do you still reject the faith?

8. Is **GOD** not the Most Wise, of all the wise ones?

Sura 96: The Embryo (Al-'Alaq)

In the name of God,
Most Gracious, Most Merciful

1. Read, in the name of your Lord, who created.*

2. He created man from an embryo.

3. Read, and your Lord, Most Exalted.

4. Teaches by means of the pen.

5. He teaches man what he never knew.

6. Indeed, the human transgresses.

7. When he becomes rich.

8. To your Lord is the ultimate destiny.

9. Have you seen the one who enjoins.

10. Others from praying?

11. Is it not better for him to follow the guidance?

---

*95:1-3 The fig, olive, Sinai, and Mecca possibly symbolize Adam, Jesus, Moses, Abraham and Muhammad, respectively. Thus, all major religions are represented.

*96:1-19 From 96 to 114 is 19 suras. The first revelation (96:1-5) is 19 Arabic words, 76 letters (19x4). The sura consists of 19 verses and 304 Arabic letters (Appendices 1 & 23).

12. Or advocate righteousness?

13. If he disbelieves and turns away.

14. Does he not realize that **GOD** sees?

15. Indeed, unless he refrains, we will take him by the forelock.

16. A forelock that is disbelieving and sinful.

17. Let him then call on his helpers.

18. We will call the guardians of Hell.

19. You shall not obey him; you shall fall prostrate and draw nearer.

◆◆◆◆

Sura 97: Destiny (Al-Qadr)

In the name of God,
Most Gracious, Most Merciful

1. We revealed it in the Night of Destiny.*

2. How awesome is the Night of Destiny!

3. The Night of Destiny is better than a thousand months.

4. The angels and the Spirit descend therein, by their Lord's leave, to carry out every command.

5. Peaceful it is until the advent of the dawn.

◆◆◆◆

Sura 98: Proof (Al-Bayyinah)

In the name of God,
Most Gracious, Most Merciful

1. Those who disbelieved among the people of the scripture, as well as the idol worshipers, insist on their ways, despite the proof given to them.*

2. A messenger from **GOD** is reciting to them sacred instructions.*

3. In them there are valuable teachings.

4. In fact, those who received the scripture did not dispute until the proof was given to them.

5. All that was asked of them was to worship **GOD**, devoting the religion absolutely to Him alone, observe the contact prayers (*Salat*), and give the obligatory charity (*Zakat*). Such is the perfect religion.

6. Those who disbelieved among the people of the scripture, and the idol worshipers, have incurred the fire of Gehenna forever. They are the worst creatures.

7. Those who believed and led a righteous life are the best creatures.

8. Their reward at their Lord is the gardens of Eden with flowing streams, wherein they abide forever. **GOD** is pleased with them, and they are pleased with Him. Such is the reward for those who reverence their Lord.

97:1 The Quran was placed into Muhammad's soul on the 27th night of Ramadan, 13 B.H. (Before Hijrah). See also 17:1, 44:3, 53:1-18, and Appendix 28.

98:1-2 The proof is the Quran's mathematical code (Appendix 1) and the messenger is Rashad Khalifa. The number of the sura (98), plus the verse number (2), plus the numerical value of "Rashad Khalifa" (1230) add up to 1330 (19x70), the same total as in 81:19 (Appendix 2).

Sura 99: The Quake (Al-Zalzalah)

In the name of God,
Most Gracious, Most Merciful

1. When the earth is severely quaked.

2. And the earth ejects its loads.

3. The human will wonder: "What is happening?"

4. On that day, it will tell its news.

5. That your Lord has commanded it.

6. On that day, the people will issue from every direction, to be shown their works.

7. Whoever does an atom's weight of good will see it.

8. And whoever does an atom's weight of evil will see it.

Sura 100: The Gallopers (Al-'Aadeyaat)

In the name of God,
Most Gracious, Most Merciful

1. By the fast gallopers.

2. Igniting sparks.

3. Invading *(the enemy)* by morning.

4. Striking terror therein.

5. Penetrating to the heart of their territory.

6. The human being is unappreciative of his Lord.

7. He bears witness to this fact.

8. He loves material things excessively.

9. Does he not realize that the day will come when the graves are opened?

10. And all secrets are brought out.

11. They will find out, on that day, that their Lord has been fully Cognizant of them.

Sura 101: The Shocker (Al-Qaare'ah)

In the name of God,
Most Gracious, Most Merciful

1. The Shocker.

2. What a shocker!

3. Do you have any idea what the Shocker is?

4. That is the day when the people come out like swarms of butterflies.

5. The mountains will be like fluffy wool.

6. As for him whose weights are heavy.

7. He will lead a happy *(eternal)* life.

8. As for him whose weights are light.

9. His destiny is lowly.

10. Do you know what it is?

11. The blazing Hellfire.

Sura 102: Hoarding (Al-Takaathur)

In the name of God,
Most Gracious, Most Merciful

1. You remain preoccupied with hoarding.

2. Until you go to the graves.

3. Indeed, you will find out.

4. Most assuredly, you will find out.

5. If only you could find out for certain.

6. You would envision Hell.

7. Then you would see it with the eye of certainty.

8. Then you will be questioned, on that day, about the blessings you had enjoyed.

❖❖❖❖

Sura 103: The Afternoon (Al-'Asr)

In the name of God,
Most Gracious, Most Merciful

1. By the afternoon.

2. The human being is utterly lost.

3. Except those who believe and lead a righteous life, and exhort one another to uphold the truth, and exhort one another to be steadfast.

Sura 104: The Backbiter (Al-Humazah)

In the name of God,
Most Gracious, Most Merciful.

1. Woe to every backbiter, slanderer.

2. He hoards money and counts it.

3. As if his money will make him immortal.

4. Never; he will be thrown into the Devastator.

5. Do you know what the Devastator is?

6. **GOD**'s blazing Hellfire.

7. It burns them inside out.

8. They will be confined therein.

9. In extended columns.

Sura 105: The Elephant (Al-Feel)

In the name of God,
Most Gracious, Most Merciful

1. Have you noted what your Lord did to the people of the elephant?

2. Did He not cause their schemes to backfire?

3. He sent upon them swarms of birds.

4. That showered them with hard stones.

5. He made them like chewed up hay.

Sura 106: Quraish (The Quraish Tribe)

In the name of God,
Most Gracious, Most Merciful

1. This should be cherished by Quraish.

2. The way they cherish the caravans of the winter and the summer.

3. They shall worship the Lord of this shrine.

4. For He is the One who fed them after hunger, and provided them with security after fear.

❖❖❖❖

Sura 107: Charity (Al-Maa'oon)

In the name of God,
Most Gracious, Most Merciful

1. Do you know who really rejects the faith?

2. That is the one who mistreats the orphans.

3. And does not advocate the feeding of the poor.

4. And woe to those who observe the contact prayers (*Salat*)—

5. who are totally heedless of their prayers.

6. They only show off.

7. And they forbid charity.

Sura 108: Bounty (Al-Kawthar)

In the name of God,
Most Gracious, Most Merciful

1. We have blessed you with many a bounty.

2. Therefore, you shall pray to your Lord (*Salat*), and give to charity.

3. Your opponent will be the loser.

Sura 109: The Disbelievers (Al-Kaaferoon)

In the name of God,
Most Gracious, Most Merciful

1. Say, "O you disbelievers.

2. "I do not worship what you worship.

3. "Nor do you worship what I worship.

4. "Nor will I ever worship what you worship.

5. "Nor will you ever worship what I worship.

6. "To you is your religion, and to me is my religion."

Sura 110: Triumph (Al-Nassr) [Last Sura Revealed]*

In the name of God,
Most Gracious, Most Merciful

1. When triumph comes from **GOD**, and victory.

2. You will see the people embracing **GOD**'s religion in throngs.

3. You shall glorify and praise your Lord, and implore Him for forgiveness. He is the Redeemer.

Sura 111: Thorns (Al-Masad)

In the name of God,
Most Gracious, Most Merciful

1. Condemned are the works of Abee Lahab, and he is condemned.*

2. His money and whatever he has accomplished will never help him.

3. He has incurred the blazing Hell.

---

*110:1-3 *This last sura, chronologically, consists of 19 Arabic words (see 96:1), and the first verse consists of 19 letters. This indicates that this generation of believers shall attain the promised victory. Submission (true Islam) will prevail throughout the world (48:28).*

*111:1 *Abee Lahab was Muhammad's uncle and the leader of the opposition. His wife carried out a campaign of persecution against Muhammad and the believers. Like all descriptions of Heaven and Hell, the rope of thorns is an allegory.*

4. Also his wife, who led the persecution.

5. She will be *(resurrected)* with a rope of thorns around her neck.

Sura 112: Absoluteness (Al-Ikhlaas)

In the name of God,
Most Gracious, Most Merciful

1. Proclaim, "He is the One and only **GOD.**

2. "The Absolute **GOD.**

3. "Never did He beget. Nor was He begotten.

4. "None equals Him."

Sura 113: Daybreak (Al-Falaq)

In the name of God,
Most Gracious, Most Merciful

1. Say, "I seek refuge in the Lord of daybreak.

2. "From the evils among His creations.

3. "From the evils of darkness as it falls.

4. "From the evils of the troublemakers.

5. "From the evils of the envious when they envy."

Sura 114: People (Al-Naas)

In the name of God,
Most Gracious, Most Merciful

1. Say, "I seek refuge in the Lord of the people.

2. "The King of the people.

3. "The god of the people.

4. "From the evils of sneaky whisperers.

5. "Who whisper into the chests of the people.

6. "Be they of the jinns, or the people."

2698*   118123*

*Thus, the total occurrence of the crucial word "God" (Allah) throughout the Quran is 2698,19x142. The reader can ascertain the accuracy of this total by randomly checking the numbers of the word "God" at the bottom of any page in this book. Additionally, if one adds the verse numbers wherever the word "God" occurs, the total comes to 118123, also a multiple of 19 (118123 = 19x6217). Details of the Quran's unique mathematical composition are given in Appendices 1, 2, 24, 25, 26, and 29.

APPENDICES

Appendices

Appendix   1

One of the Great Miracles   [74:35]

The Quran is characterized by a unique phenomenon never found in any human authored book. Every element of the Quran is mathematically composed—the suras, the verses, the words, the number of certain letters, the number of words from the same root, the number and variety of divine names, the unique spelling of certain words, the absence or deliberate alteration of certain letters within certain words, and many other elements of the Quran besides its content. There are two major facets of the Quran's mathematical system: (1) The mathematical literary composition, and (2) The mathematical structure involving the numbers of suras and verses. Because of this comprehensive mathematical coding, the slightest distortion of the Quran's text or physical arrangement is immediately exposed.

Simple to Understand
Impossible to Imitate

For the first time in history we have a scripture with built-in proof of divine authorship—a superhuman mathematical composition.

Any reader of this book can easily verify the Quran's mathematical miracle. The word "God" *(Allah)* is written in bold capital letters throughout the text. The cumulative frequency of occurrence of the word "God" is noted at the bottom of each page in the left hand corner. The number in the right hand corner is the cumulative total of the numbers for verses containing the word "God." The last page of the text, Page 372, shows that the total occurrence of the word "God" is 2698, or 19x142. The total sum of verse numbers for all verses containing the word "God" is 118123, also a multiple of 19 (118123 = 19x6217).

Nineteen is the common denominator throughout the Quran's mathematical system.

This phenomenon alone suffices as incontrovertible proof that the Quran is God's message to the world. No human being(s) could have kept track of 2698 occurrences of the word "God," and the numbers of verses where they occur. This is especially impossible in view of (1) the age of ignorance during which the Quran was revealed, and (2) the fact that the suras and verses were widely separated in time and place of revelation. The chronological order of revelation was vastly different from the final format (Appendix 23). However, the Quran's mathematical system is not limited to the word "God;" it is extremely vast, extremely intricate, and totally comprehensive.

The Simple Facts

Like the Quran itself, the Quran's mathematical coding ranges from the very simple, to the very complex. The Simple Facts are those observations that can be ascertained without using any tools. The complex facts require the assistance of a calculator or a computer. The following facts do not require any tools to be verified, but please remember they all refer to the original Arabic text:

1. The first verse (1:1), known as "*Basmalah*" consists of........... 19 letters.
2. The Quran consists of 114 suras, which is .... 19 x 6.
3. The total number of verses in the Quran is 6346, or .... 19 x 334. [6234 numbered verses & 112 un-numbered verses *(Basmalahs)* 6234 + 112 = 6346] Note that 6 + 3 + 4 + 6 = ... 19.
4. The *Basmalah* occurs 114 times, despite its conspicuous absence from Sura 9 (it occurs twice in Sura 27) & 114 =....... 19 x 6.
5. From the missing *Basmalah* of Sura 9 to the extra *Basmalah* of Sura 27, there are precisely .... 19 suras.
6. It follows that the total of the sura numbers from 9 to 27 (9 +10 +11 +12 +... + 26 + 27) is 342, or............. 19 x 18.
7. This total (342) also equals the number of words between the two *Basmalahs* of Sura 27, and 342 =.................. 19 x 18.
8. The famous first revelation (96:1-5) consists of........................ 19 words.
9. This 19-worded first revelation consists of 76 letters............... 19 x 4.
10. Sura 96, first in the chronological sequence, consists of .... 19 verses.
11. This first chronological sura is placed atop the last .... 19 suras.
12. Sura 96 consists of 304 Arabic letters, and 304 equals .... 19 x 16.
13. The last revelation (Sura 110) consists of................................ 19 words.
14. The first verse of the last revelation (110:1) consists of.......... 19 letters.
15. 14 different Arabic letters, form 14 different sets of "Quranic Initials" (such as A.L.M. of 2:1), and prefix 29 suras. These numbers add up to 14 + 14 + 29 = 57 = ... 19 x 3.
16. The total of the 29 sura numbers where the Quranic Initials occur is 2 + 3 + 7 +... + 50 + 68 = 822, and 822 + 14 (14 sets of initials) equals 836, or .... 19 x 44.
17. Between the first initialed sura (Sura 2) and the last initialed sura (Sura 68) there are 38 un-initialed suras............. 19 x 2.
18. Between the first and last initialed sura there are.................... 19 sets of alternating "initialed" and "uninitialed" suras.
19. The Quran mentions 30 different numbers: 1, 2, 3, 4, 5, 6, 7, 8, 9, 10, 11, 12, 19, 20, 30, 40, 50, 60, 70, 80, 99, 100, 200, 300, 1000, 2000, 3000, 5000, 50,000, & 100,000. The sum of these numbers is 162146, which equals .... 19x8534.

This is a condensed summary of the Simple Facts.

The Literary Mathematical Composition

The Quran is characterized by a unique phenomenon never found in any other book; 29 suras are prefixed with 14 different sets of "Quranic Initials," consisting of one to five letters per set. Fourteen letters, half the Arabic alphabet, participate in these initials. The significance of the Quranic initials remained a divinely guarded secret for 14 centuries.

The Quran states in 10:20 and 25:4-6 that its miracle, i.e., proof of divine authorship, was destined to remain secret for a specific predetermined interim:

They said, "Why hasn't a miracle come down to him from his Lord?" Say, "Only God knows the future. Therefore, wait, and I will wait along with you." [10:20]

******

Those who disbelieved said, "This is no more than a fabrication by him, with the help of other people." Indeed, they uttered a blasphemy; a falsehood. Others said, "Tales from the past that he wrote down; they were dictated to him day and night." Say, "This was sent down from the One who knows 'the secret' in the heavens and the earth." Surely, He is Forgiving, Most Merciful. [25:4-6]

The Quranic Initials constitute a major portion of the Quran's 19-based mathematical miracle.

Table 1: List of the Quranic Initials and Their Suras

No.	Sura No.	Sura Title	Quranic Initials
1.	2	The Heifer	A.L.M.
2.	3	The Amramites	A.L.M.
3.	7	The Purgatory	A.L.M.S
4.	10	Jonah	A.L.R.
5.	11	Hûd	A.L.R.
6.	12	Joseph	A.L.R.
7.	13	Thunder	A.L.M.R.
8.	14	Abraham	A.L.R.
9.	15	Al-Hijr Valley	A.L.R.
10.	19	Mary	K.H.Y.'A.S.
11.	20	T.H.	T.H.
12.	26	The Poets	T.S.M.
13.	27	The Ant	T.S.
14.	28	History	T.S.M.
15.	29	The Spider	A.L.M.
16.	30	The Romans	A.L.M.
17.	31	Luqmaan	A.L.M.
18.	32	Prostration	A.L.M.
19.	36	Y.S.	Y.S.
20.	38	S.	S.
21.	40	Forgiver	H.M.
22.	41	Elucidated	H.M.
23.	42	Consultation	H.M. 'A.S.Q.
24.	43	Ornaments	H.M.
25.	44	Smoke	H.M.
26.	45	Kneeling	H.M.
27.	46	The Dunes	H.M.
28.	50	Q.	Q.
29.	68	The Pen	NuN

Historical Background

In 1968, I realized that the existing English translations of the Quran did not present the truthful message of God's Final Testament. For example, the two most popular translators, Yusuf Ali and Marmaduke Pickthall, could not overcome their corrupted religious traditions when it came to the Quran's great criterion in 39:45.

> **When God ALONE is mentioned, the hearts of those who do not believe in the Hereafter shrink with aversion. But when others are mentioned beside Him, they rejoice.   [39:45]**

Yusuf Ali omitted the crucial word "ALONE" from his translation, and altered the rest of the verse by inserting the word "(gods)." Thus, he utterly destroyed this most important Quranic criterion. He translated 39:45 as follows:

> **When God, the One and Only, is mentioned, the hearts of those who believe not in the Hereafter are filled with disgust and horror; but when (gods) other than He are mentioned, behold, they are filled with joy.   [39:45]**
> **(according to A. Yusuf Ali)**

The expression "When God, the One and Only, is mentioned," is not the same as saying, "When God <u>alone</u> is mentioned." One can mention "God, the One and Only," and also mention Muhammad or Jesus, and no one will be upset. But if "God ALONE is mentioned," you cannot mention anyone else, and a lot of people—those who idolize Muhammad or Jesus—will be upset. Thus, Yusuf Ali could not bring himself to present the truth of the Quran, if it exposed his corrupted belief.

Marmaduke Pickthall translated "ALONE" correctly, but destroyed the criterion by inserting his personal belief in parentheses; he translated 39:45 as follows:

> **And when Allah alone is mentioned, the hearts of those who believe not in the Hereafter are repelled, and when those (whom they worship) beside Him are mentioned, behold! they are glad.   [39:45]**
> **(according to Marmaduke Pickthal)**

When I saw the truth of God's word thus distorted, I decided to translate the Quran, at least for the benefit of my own children. Since I was a chemist by profession, and despite my extensive religious background—my father was a renowned Sufi leader in Egypt—I vowed to God that I would not move from one verse to the next unless I fully understood it.

I purchased all the available books of Quranic translations and exegeses *(Tafseer)* I could find, placed them on a large table, and began my translation. The first sura, The Key, was completed in a few days. The first verse in Sura 2 is "A.L.M." The translation of this verse took four years, and coincided with the divine unveiling of "the secret," the great mathematical Miracle of the Quran.

The books of Quranic exegeses unanimously agreed that "no one knows the meaning or significance of the Quranic Initials A.L.M., or any other initials." I decided to write the Quran into the computer, analyze the whole text, and see if there were any mathematical correlations among these Quranic initials.

I used a time-share terminal, connected by telephone to a giant computer. To test my hypothesis, I decided to look at the single-lettered Quranic Initials—"Q" (Qaaf) of Suras 42 and 50, "S" (Saad) of Suras 7, 19, and 38, and "N" (Noon) of Sura 68. As detailed in my first book *MIRACLE OF THE QURAN: SIGNIFICANCE OF THE MYSTERIOUS ALPHABETS* (Islamic Productions, 1973), many previous attempts to unravel the mystery had failed.

The Quranic Initial "Q" (Qaaf)

The computer data showed that the text of the only Q-initialed suras, 42 and 50, contained the same number of Q's, 57 and 57. That was the first hint that a deliberate mathematical system might exist in the Quran.

Sura 50 is entitled "Q," prefixed with "Q," and the first verse reads, "Q, and the glorious Quran." This indicated that "Q" stands for "Quran," and the total number of Q's in the two Q-initialed suras represents the Quran's 114 suras (57 + 57 = 114 = 19x6). This idea was strengthened by the fact that "the Quran" occurs in the Quran 57 times.

The Quran is described in Sura "Q" as "Majid" (glorious), and the Arabic word "Majid" has a gematrical value of 57: M (40) + J (3) + I (10) +D (4) = 57.

Sura 42 consists of 53 verses, and 42 + 53 = 95 = 19x5.

Sura 50 consists of 45 verses, and 50 + 45 = 95, same total as in Sura 42.

By counting the letter "Q" in every "Verse 19" throughout the Quran, the total count comes to 76, 19x4. Here is a summary of the Q-related data:

---

1. The frequency of occurrence of "Q" in Sura "Q" (No. 50) is 57, 19x3.
2. The letter "Q" occurs in the other Q-initialed sura (No. 42) exactly the same number of times, 57.
3. The total occurrence of the letter "Q" in the two Q-initialed suras is 114, which equals the number of suras in the Quran.
4. "The Quran" is mentioned in the Quran 57 times.
5. The description of the Quran as "Majid" (Glorious) is correlated with the frequency of occurrence of the letter "Q" in each of the Q-initialed suras. The word "Majid" has a gematrical value of 57.
7. Sura 42 consists of 53 verses, and 42 + 53 is 95, or 19x5.
8. Sura 50 consists of 45 verses, and 50 + 45 is also 95, 19x5.
9. The number of Q's in all verses numbered "19" throughout the Quran is 76, 19x4.

Glimpses of the Quran's mathematical composition began to emerge. For example, it was observed that the people who disbelieved in Lot are mentioned in 50:13 and occur in the Quran 13 times—7:80; 11:70, 74, 89; 21:74; 22:43; 26:160; 27:54, 56; 29:28; 38:13; 50:13; and 54:33. Consistently, they are referred to as "*Qawm*," with the single exception of the Q-initialed Sura 50 where they are referred to as *"Ikhwaan."* Obviously, if the regular, Q-containing word *"Qawm"* were used, the count of the letter "Q" in Sura 50 would have become 58, and this whole phenomenon would have disappeared. With the recognized absolute accuracy of mathematics, the alteration of a single letter destroys the system.

Another relevant example is the reference to Mecca in 3:96 as *"Becca"*! This strange spelling of the renowned city has puzzled Islamic scholars for many centuries. Although Mecca is mentioned in the Quran properly spelled in 48:24, the letter "M" is substituted with a "B" in 3:96. It turns out that Sura 3 is an M-initialed sura, and the count of the letter "M" would have deviated from the Quran's code if "Mecca" was spelled correctly in 3:96.

NuN (Noon)

This initial is unique; it occurs in one sura, 68, and the name of the letter is spelled out as three letters—*Noon Wow Noon*—in the original text, and is therefore counted as two N's. The total count of this letter in the N-initialed sura is 133, 19x7.

The fact that "N" is the last Quranic Initial (see Table 1) brings out a number of special observations. For example, the number of verses from the first Quranic Initial (A.L.M. of 2:1) to the last initial (N. of 68:1) is 5263, or 19x277.

The word "God" (Allah) occurs 2641 (19x139) times between the first initial and the last initial. Since the total occurrence of the word "God" is 2698, it follows that its occurrence outside the initials "A.L.M." of 2:1 on one side, and the initial "N" of 68:1 on the other side, is 57, 19x3. Tables 9 to 20 prove that the initial "NuN" must be spelled out to show two N's.

Table 2: The Frequency of Occurrence of the Letter "S" in the Saad-initialed Suras

S (Saad)

This initial prefixes three suras, 7, 19, and 38, and the total occurrence of the letter "S" (Saad) in these three suras is 152, 19x8 (Table 2). It is noteworthy that in 7:69, the word "Bastatan" is written in some printings with a "Saad," instead of "Seen." This is an erroneous distortion that violates the Quran's code. By looking at the

Sura	Frequency of "S"
7	97
19	26
38	29
	152
	(19x8)

oldest available copy of the Quran, the Tashkent Copy, it was found that the word "Bastatan" is correctly written with a "Seen" (see photocopy below).

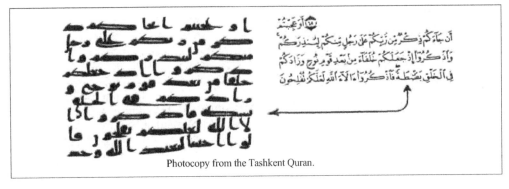

Photocopy from the Tashkent Quran.

Historical Note

The momentous discovery that "19" is the Quran's common denominator became a reality in January 1974, coinciding with Zul-Hijjah 1393 A.H. The Quran was revealed in 13 B.H. (Before Hijrah). This makes the number of years from the revelation of the Quran to the revelation of its miracle 1393 + 13 = 1406 = 19x74. As noted above, the unveiling of the Miracle took place in January 1974. The correlation between 19x74 lunar years and 1974 solar years could not escape notice. This is especially uncanny in view of the fact that "19" is mentioned in Sura 74.

Y.S. (Ya Seen)

These two letters prefix Sura 36. The letter "Y" occurs in this sura 237 times, while the letter "S" (Seen) occurs 48 times. The total of both letters is 285, 19x15.

It is noteworthy that the letter "Y" is written in the Quran in two forms; one is obvious and the other is subtle. The subtle form of the letter may be confusing to those who are not thoroughly familiar with the Arabic language. A good example is the word "*Araany* أراني ," which is mentioned twice in 12:36. The letter "Y" is used twice in this word, the first "Y" is subtle and the second is obvious. Sura 36 does not contain a single "Y" of the subtle type. This is a remarkable phenomenon, and one that does not normally occur in a long sura like Sura 36. In my book *QURAN: VISUAL PRESENTATION OF THE MIRACLE* (Islamic Productions, 1982) every "Y" and "S" in Sura 36 is marked with a star.

H.M. (Ha Mim)

Seven suras are prefixed with the letters "H ح " and "M م ;" Suras 40 through 46. The total occurrence of these two letters in the seven H.M.-initialed suras is 2147, or 19x113. The detailed data are shown in Table 3.

Naturally, the alteration of a single letter "H" or "M" in any of the seven H.M.-initialed suras would have destroyed this intricate phenomenon.

'A.S.Q. ('Ayn Seen Qaf)

These initials constitute Verse 2 of Sura 42, and the total occurrence of these letters in this sura is 209, or 19x11. The letter " 'A" ('Ayn) occurs 98 times, the letter "S" (Seen) occurs 54 times, and the letter "Q" (Qaf) occurs 57 times.

Table 3: Occurrence of the Letters "H" and "M" in the Seven H.M.-initialed Suras

Sura No.	Frequency of Occurrence "H"	"M"	"H + M"
40	64	380	444
41	48	276	324
42	53	300	353
43	44	324	368
44	16	150	166
45	31	200	231
46	36	225	261
	292	1855	2147
			(19x113)

A.L.M. (Alef Laam Mim)

The letters "A," "L," and "M" are the most frequently used letters in the Arabic language, and in the same order as we see in the Quranic Initials—"A," then "L," then "M." These letters prefix six suras—2, 3, 29, 30, 31, and 32—and the total occurrence of the three letters in each of the six suras is a multiple of 19 [9899 (19x521), 5662 (19x 298), 1672 (19x88), 1254 (19x66), 817 (19x43), and 570 (19x30), respectively]. Thus, the total occurrence of the three letters in the six suras is 19874 (19x 1046), and the alteration of one of these letters de-stroys this phenomenon.

Table 4: Occurrence of the Letters "A," "L," and "M" in the A.L.M.-Initialed Suras

Sura No.	Frequency of Occurrence			
	"A"	"L"	"M"	Total
2	4502	3202	2195	9899 (19x521)
3	2521	1892	1249	5662 (19x298)
29	774	554	344	1672 (19x88)
30	544	393	317	1254 (19x66)
31	347	297	173	817 (19x43)
32	257	155	158	570 (19x30)
	8945	6493	4436	19874 (19x1046)

A.L.R.
(Alef Laam Ra)

These initials are found in Suras 10, 11, 12, 14, and 15. The total occurrences of these letters in these suras are 2489 (19x131), 2489 (19x131), 2375 (19x 125), 1197 (19x63), and 912 (19x48), respectively (Table 5).

Table 5: Occurrence of the Letters "A," "L," and "R" in the A.L.R.-initialed Suras

Sura No.	Frequency of Occurrence			
	"A"	"L"	"R"	Total
10	1319	913	257	2489 (19x131)
11	1370	794	325	2489 (19x131)
12	1306	812	257	2375 (19x125)
14	585	452	160	1197 (19x63)
15	493	323	96	912 (19x48)
	5073	3294	1095	9462 (19x498)

A.L.M.R. (Alef Laam Mim Ra)

These initials prefix one sura, No. 13, and the total frequency of occurrence of the four letters is 1482, or 19x78. The letter "A" occurs 605 times, "L" occurs 480 times, "M" occurs 260 times, and "R" occurs 137 times.

A.L.M.S. (Alef Laam Mim Saad)

Only one sura is prefixed with these initials, Sura 7, and the letter "A" occurs in this sura 2529 times, "L" occurs 1530 times, "M" occurs 1164 times, and "S" (Saad) occurs 97 times. Thus, the total occurrence of the four letters in this sura is 2529 + 1530 + 1164 + 97 = 5320 = 19x280.

An important observation here is the interlocking relationship involving the letter "S" (Saad). This initial occurs also in Suras 19 and 38. While complement-ing its sister letters in Sura 7 to give a total that is divisible by 19, the frequency of this letter also complements its sister letters in Suras 19 and 38 to give a multiple of 19 (see Page 380).

Additionally, the Quranic Initial "S" (Saad) interacts with the Quranic Initials "K.H.Y. 'A." (Kaaf Haa Ya 'Ayn) in Sura 19 to give another total that is also a multiple of 19 (see Page 383). This interlocking relationship—which is not uni-que to the initial "S" (Saad)—contributes to the intricacy of the Quran's numeri-cal code.

K.H.Y.'A.S. (Kaaf Ha Ya 'Ayn Saad)

This is the longest set of initials, consisting of five letters, and it occurs in one sura, Sura 19. The letter "K" in Sura 19 occurs 137 times, "H" occurs 175 times, "Y" occurs 343 times, " 'A" occurs 117 times, and "S" (Saad) occurs 26 times. Thus, the total occurrence of the five letters is 137 + 175 + 343 + 117 + 26 = 798 = 19x42.

H., T.H. (Ta Ha), T.S. (Ta Seen),
& T.S.M. (Ta Seen Mim)

An intricate interlocking relationship links these overlapping Quranic Initials to produce a total that is also a multiple of 19. The initial "H." is found in Suras 19 and 20. The initials "T.H." prefix Sura 20. The initials "T.S." are found in Sura 27, while the initials "T.S.M." prefix its surrounding Suras 26 & 28.

It should be noted at this time that the longer, more complex, interlocking and overlapping initials are found in the suras where uncommonly powerful miracles are narrated. For example, the virgin birth of Jesus is given in Sura 19, which is prefixed with the longest set of initials, K.H.Y.'A.S.

The interlocking initials "H.," "T.H.," "T.S.," and "T.S.M." prefix suras describing the miracles of Moses, Jesus, and the uncommon occurrences surrounding Solomon and his jinns. God thus provides stronger evidence to support stronger miracles. The frequencies of occurrence of these initials are presented in Table 6.

Table 6: Occurrence of the Quranic Initials "H.," "T.H.," "T.S.," and "T.S.M." in Their Suras

Sura	Frequency of			
	"H"	"T"	"S"	"M"
19	175	—-	—- -	—-
20	251	28	—- -	—-
26	—-	33	94	484
27	—-	27	94	—-
28	—-	19	102	460
	426	107	290	944

426 + 107 + 290 + 944=1767=(19x93)

What Is A "Gematrical Value"?

When the Quran was revealed, 14 centuries ago, the numbers known today did not exist. A universal system was used where the letters of the Arabic, Hebrew, Aramaic, and Greek alphabets were used as numerals. The number assigned to each letter is its "Gematrical Value." The numerical values of the Arabic alphabet are shown in Table 7.

Table 7: Gematrical Values of the Arabic Alphabet

								ا 1
ي 10	ط 9	ح 8	ز 7	و 6	ه 5	د 4	ج 3	ب 2
ق 100	ص 90	ف 80	ع 70	س 60	ن 50	م 40	ل 30	ك 20
غ 1000	ظ 900	ض 800	ذ 700	خ 600	ث 500	ت 400	ش 300	ر 200

Other Mathematical Properties of the Initialed Suras

Fourteen Arabic letters, half the Arabic alphabet, participate in the formation of 14 different sets of Quranic Initials. By adding the gematrical value of each one of these letters, plus the number of suras which are prefixed with Quranic Initials (29), we obtain a total of 722, or 19x19x2.

Additionally, if we add the total gematrical value of all 14 initials, plus the number of the first sura where the initial occurs, we get a grand total of 988, 19x52. Table 8 presents these data.

If we add the number of occurren-ces of each of the 14 letters listed in Table 8 as an initial, plus the numbers of the suras where it occurs as an initial, the Grand Total comes to 2033, 19x107. See Table 9.

Table 8: The 14 Letters Used in Forming Quranic Initials

Letter	Value	First Sura
A (Alef)	1	2
L (Laam)	30	2
M (Mim)	40	2
S (Saad)	90	7
R (Ra)	200	10
K (Kaf)	20	19
H (Ha)	5	19
Y (Ya)	10	19
'A ('Ayn)	70	19
T (Ta)	9	20
S (Seen)	60	26
H (Ha)	8	40
Q (Qaf)	100	42
N (Noon)	50	68
	693	295

693 + 295 = 988 = 19x52

also 693 + 29 (suras) = 722 = 19x19x2

Table 9: Mathematically Structured Distribution of the Quranic Initials

Initial	Number of Occurences	Sura Where It Occurs	Total
A (Alef)	13	[+ 2 + 3 + 7 + 10 + 11 + 12 + 13 + 14 + 15 + 29 + 30 + 31 + 32]	222
L (Laam)	13	[+ 2 + 3 + 7 + 10 + 11 + 12 + 13 + 14 + 15 + 29 + 30 + 31 + 32]	222
M (Mim)	17	[+ 2 + 3 + 7 + 13 + 26 + 28 + 29 + 30 + 31 + 32 + 40 + 41 + 42 + 43 + 44 + 45 + 46]	519
S (Saad)	3	+ 7 + 19 + 38	67
R (Ra)	6	+ 10 + 11 + 12 + 13 + 14 + 15	81
K (Kaf)	1	+ 19	20
H (Ha)	2	+ 19 + 20	41
Y (Ya)	2	+ 19 + 36	57
'A ('Ayn)	2	+ 19 + 42	63
T (Ta)	4	+ 20 + 26 + 27 + 28	105
S (Seen)	5	+ 26 + 27 + 28 + 36 + 42	164
H (HHa)	7	+ 40 + 41 + 42 + 43 + 44 + 45 + 46	308
Q (Qaf)	2	+ 42 + 50	94
N (Noon)	2	+ 68	70
	79	1954	2033 (19x107)

Table 10 presents the total frequency of Quranic Initials, plus the total gematrical value of these letters in the whole sura. The Grand Total for all initialed suras is 1089479. This number, in excess of one million, is a multiple of 19 (1089479 = 19 x 57341). The slightest alteration or distortion destroys the system.

Note: The total gematrical value of the Quranic Initials in a given sura equals the gematrical value of each initial multiplied by the frequency of occurrence of that initial in the sura.

Major Parameters of the Quranic, Initials (Suras, Verses, Frequency, First Sura, & Last Sura)

Table 11 shows that the sum of numbers of suras and verses where the Quranic Initials are found, plus the initial's frequency of occurrence in that sura,

Table 10: Total Gematrical Values of All Quranic Initials In Their Suras

Sura	Initials	Frequency Of Initials	Tot. G. Val. in Sura
2	A.L.M.	9899	188362
3	A.L.M.	5662	109241
7	A.L.M.S.	5320	103719
10	A.L.R.	2489	80109
11	A.L.R.	2489	90190
12	A.L.R.	2375	77066
13	A.L.M.R.	1482	52805
14	A.L.R.	1197	46145
15	A.L.R.	912	29383
19	K.H.Y.'A.S.	798	17575
20	T.H.	279	1507
26	T.S.M.	611	25297
27	T.S.	121	5883
28	T.S.M.	581	24691
29	A.L.M.	1672	31154
30	A.L.M.	1254	25014
31	A.L.M.	817	16177
32	A.L.M.	570	11227
36	Y.S.	285	5250
38	S.	29	2610
40	H.M.	444	15712
41	H.M.	324	11424
42	H.M.-'A.S.Q.	562	28224
43	H.M.	368	13312
44	H.M.	166	6128
45	H.M.	231	8248
46	H.M.	261	9288
50	Q	57	5700
68	N,N	133	6650
		41388	1048091

41388 + 1048091 = 1089479 (19X57341)

plus the number of the first sura where the initials occur, plus the number of the last sura where the initials occur, produces a total that equals 44232, or 19x2348. Thus, the distribution of the Quranic Initials in the initialed suras is so intricate that their counts and their placement within suras are intertwined to give a grand total that is a multiple of 19.

It is noteworthy that the initial "N" must be counted as two N's. This reflects the fact that the original Quranic text spells out this initial with 2 N's.

Table 11: Parameters of the 14 Individual Quranic Initials

Initial	Sura, Verse, & (Frequency) of Initial in Each Sura	First Sura	Last Sura
A (Alef)	2:1 (4502), 3:1 (2521), 7:1 (2529), 10:1 (1319) 11:1 (1370), 12:1 (1306), 13:1 (605), 14:1 (585), 15:1 (493), 29:1 (774), 30:1 (544), 31:1 (347), 32:1 (257)	2	32
L (Laam)	2:1 (3202), 3:1 (1892), 7:1 (1530), 10:1 (913), 11:1 (794), 12:1 (812), 13:1 (480), 14:1 (452), 15:1 (323), 29:1 (554), 30:1 (393), 31:1 (297), 32:1 (155)	2	32
M (Mim)	2:1 (2195), 3:1 (1249), 7:1 (1164), 13:1 (260) 26:1 (484), 28:1 (460), 29:1 (344), 30:1 (317), 31:1 (173), 32:1 (158), 40:1 (380), 41:1 (276), 42:1 (300), 43:1 (324), 44:1 (150), 45:1 (200), 46:1 (225)	2	46
S (Saad)	7:1 (97), 19:1 (26), 38:1 (29)	7	38
R (Ra)	10:1 (257), 11:1 (325), 12:1 (257), 13:1 (137), 14:1 (160), 15:1 (96)	10	15
K (Kaf)	19:1 (137)	19	19
H (Ha)	19:1 (175), 20:1 (251)	19	20
Y (Ya)	19:1 (343), 36:1 (237)	19	36
'A ('Ayn)	19:1 (117), 42:2 (98)	19	42
T (Ta)	20:1 (28), 26:1 (33), 27:1 (27), 28:1 (19)	20	28
S (Seen)	26:1 (94), 27:1 (94), 28:1 (102), 36:1 (48), 42:2 (54)	26	42
H (HHa)	40:1 (64), 41:1 (48), 42:1 (53), 43:1 (44) 44:1 (16), 45:1 (31), 46:1 (36)	40	46
Q (Qaf)	42:2 (57), 50:1 (57)	42	50
N (Nun)	68:1 (133)	68	68
	43423	295	514
Grand Total =	43423 + 295 + 514 = 44232 = 19x2328.		

A special mathematical coding authenticates the number of verses where the Quranic Initials themselves are found. As detailed in Table 11, all Quranic Initials occur in Verse 1, except in Sura 42 (initials in Verses 1 and 2). This fact is supported by the remarkable mathematical phenomenon detailed in Table 12. If we multiply the first two columns of Table 12, instead of adding, we still end up with a Total that is divisible by 19 (see Table 13).

| Table 12: Mathematical Coding of the Number of Verses With Initials |

Sura No.	No. of Initials	Initialed Verses
2	3	1
3	3	1
7	4	1
10	3	1
11	3	1
12	3	1
13	4	1
14	3	1
15	3	1
19	5	1
20	2	1
26	3	1
27	2	1
28	3	1
29	3	1
30	3	1
31	3	1
32	3	1
36	2	1
38	1	1
40	2	1
41	2	1
42	5	2
43	2	1
44	2	1
45	2	1
46	2	1
50	1	1
68	2	1
822	79	30

822 + 79 + 30 = 931 (19x49)

| Table 13: Multiplying the First Two Columns of Table 12, Instead of Adding |

Sura No.		No. of Initials	No. of Init'ld Verses
2	x	3	1
3	x	3	1
7	x	4	1
-		-	-
42	x	5	2
-		-	-
50	x	1	1
68	x	2	1
....		2022	30

2022 + 30 = 2052 (19x108)

Obviously, it is crucial to have two different initialed verses in Sura 42 in order to conform with the Quran's mathematical code. The fact that Verse 1 of Sura 42 consists of the two Quranic Initials "H.M." and the second verse consists of the three Initials " 'A.S.Q." has perplexed Muslim scholars and orientalists for 14 centuries.

By the end of this Appendix, the reader will see that every element of the Quran is mathematically authenticated. The elements we are dealing with now are "the number of Quranic Initials in each initialed sura" and "the number of verses that contain Quranic Initials." Tables 11 through 13 have dealt with these two elements.

Additional mathematical authentication is shown in Tables 14 and 15. In Table 14, we have the numbers of all initialed suras added to the number of verses in each sura, plus the number of verses containing initials, plus the gematrical values of those initials. The Grand Total is 7030, or 19x370.

Table 14: Mathematical Properties of the Initialed Suras

Sura Number	Number of Verses	Number of Initialed Verses	Gematrical Value of the Initials	TOTAL
2	286	1	71	360
3	200	1	71	275
7	206	1	161	375
10	109	1	231	351
11	123	1	231	366
12	111	1	231	355
13	43	1	271	328
14	52	1	231	298
15	99	1	231	346
19	98	1	195	313
20	135	1	14	170
26	227	1	109	363
27	93	1	69	190
28	88	1	109	226
29	69	1	71	170
30	60	1	71	162
31	34	1	71	137
32	30	1	71	134
36	83	1	70	190
38	88	1	90	217
40	85	1	48	174
41	54	1	48	144
42	53	2	278	375
43	89	1	48	181
44	59	1	48	152
45	37	1	48	131
46	35	1	48	130
50	45	1	100	196
68	52	1	50 + 50	221
— — —	— — —	— — —	— — — —	— — — —
822 +	2743 +	30	+ 3435	= 7030 (19x370)

Remarkably, if we multiply the first two columns of Table 14, instead of adding them, **we still get a Grand Total that is divisible by 19** (Table 15).

The number of verses per sura, and the numbers assigned to each verse are among the basic elements of the Quran. Not only are these elements authenticated mathematically, but both initialed and un-initialed suras are independently coded. Since we are now dealing with the initialed suras, Table 16 presents the numbers assigned to these suras, added to the numbers of verses in each sura, plus the sum of verse numbers (1 + 2 + 3+ ... + n). The Grand total is 190133, or 19x10007.

Table 15: Multiplying the First 2 Columns of Table 14, Instead of Adding Them

Sura Number		Number of Verse		Number of Initialed Verses		Gematrical Value of the Initials		TOTAL
2	x	286	+	1	+	71	=	644
3	x	200	+	1	+	71	=	672
7	x	206	+	1	+	161	=	1604
-		-		-		-		-
50	x	45	+	1	+	100	=	2351
68	x	52	+	1	+	(50 + 50)	=	3637
	60071		+	30	+	3435	=	63536
								(19x3344)

By adding the number of every sura to the number of the next sura, and accumulating the sums of sura numbers as we continue this process to the end of the Quran, we will have a value that corresponds to each sura. Thus, Sura 1 will have a corresponding value of 1, Sura 2 will have a value of $1 + 2 = 3$, Sura 3 will have a value of $3 + 3 = 6$, Sura 4 will have a value of $6 + 4 = 10$, and so on to

Table 16: Mathematical Structuring of the Verses of Initialed Suras

Sura No.	No. of Verses	Sum of Verses #s	Total
2	286	41041	41329
3	200	20100	20303
7	206	21321	21534
-	-	-	-
50	45	1035	1130
68	52	1378	1498
822	2743	186568	190133
			(19x10007)

Table 17: Values Obtained by Successive Addition of Sura Numbers

Sura Number	Calculated Value
2	3
3	6
7	28
10	55
11	66
12	78
13	91
14	105
15	120
19	190
20	210
-	-
44	990
45	1035
46	1081
50	1275
68	2346
	15675
	(19x825)

the end of the Quran. The total values for the initialed and the un-initialed suras are independently divisible by 19. The values for the initialed suras are shown in Table 17.

The values calculated for the un-initialed suras add up to a total of 237785, which is also a multiple of 19 ($237785 = 19\text{x}12515$).

Mathematical Coding of Special Words
The Word "God" (Allah)

[1] As shown earlier the word "God" occurs in the Quran 2698 times, 19x142.

[2] The numbers of verses where the word "God" occurs add up to 118123, also a multiple of 19 (118123 = 19x6217).

These simple phenomena gave us many difficulties while simply counting the word "God." We were a group of workers, equipped with computers, and all of us college graduates. Yet, we made several errors in counting, calculating, or simply writing the counts of the word "God." Those who still claim that Muhammad was the author of the Quran are totally illogical; he never went to college, and he did not have a computer.

Table 18: Occurrence of the Word "God" Outside the Initialed Section

Number of Sura	Numbers of Verses	Times Occurs
1	1, 2	2
69	33	1
70	3	1
71	3,4,13,15,17,19,25	7
72	4,5,7,12,18,19,22,23	10
73	20	7
74	31, 56	3
76	6, 9, 11, 30	5
79	25	1
81	29	1
82	19	1
84	23	1
85	8, 9, 20	3
87	7	1
88	24	1
91	13	2
95	8	1
96	14	1
98	2, 5, 8	3
104	6	1
110	1, 2	2
112	1, 2	2
1798	634	57 (19x3)

Sum of numbers of the suras & Verses = 1798 + 634 = 2432 = 19x128
Total occurrence of the word "God" outside the initialed section = 57 (19x3).

[3] From the first Quranic Initials (A.L.M. 2:1) to the last initial (N. 68:1), there are 2641, 19 x 139, occurrences of the word "God."

[4] The word "God" occurs 57 times in the section outside the Initials (Table 18).

[5] By adding the numbers of the suras and verses where these 57 occurrences of the word "God" are found, we get a total of 2432, or 19x128. See Table 18.

[6] The word "God" occurs in 85 suras. If we add the number of each sura to the number of verses between the first and last occurrences of the word "God," both verses inclusive, the Grand Total comes to 8170 or 19 x 430. An abbreviated representation of the data is shown in Table 19.

Table 19: All Suras in Which the Word "God" (Allah) Is Mentioned

	Sura No.	First Verse	Last Verse	Verses 1st to Last
1.	1	1	2	2
2.	2	7	286	280
3.	3	2	200	199
-	-	-	-	-
84.	110	1	2	2
85.	112	1	2	2
	3910			4260

3910 + 4260 = 8170 = 19x430
These mathematical properties cover all Occurrences of the word "God."

[7] The Quran's dominant message is that there is only "One God." The word "One," in Arabic *"Wahed"* occurs in the Quran 25 times. Six of these occurrences refer to other than God (one kind of food, one door, etc.). The other 19 occurrences refer to God. These data are found in the classic reference *INDEX TO THE WORDS OF QURAN*.

The crucial importance of the word "ONE" as the Quran's basic message is manifested in the fact that the Quran's common denominator, 19, happens to be the gematrical value of the word "ONE."

WHY 19!

As pointed out later in this Appendix, all God's scriptures, not only the Quran, were mathematically coded with the number "19." Even the universe at large bears this divine mark. The number 19 can be looked upon as the Almighty Creator's signature on everything He created (see Appendix 38). The number "19" possesses unique mathematical properties beyond the scope of this Appendix. For example:

[1] It is a prime number.

[2] It encompasses the first numeral (1) and the last numeral (9), as if to proclaim God's attribute in 57:3 as the "Alpha and the Omega."

[3] It looks the same in all languages of the world. Both components, 1 and 9, are the *only* numerals that look the same in all languages.

[4] It possesses many peculiar mathematical properties. For example, 19 is the sum of the first powers of 9 and 10, and the difference between the second powers of 9 and 10.

We now understand that the universal coding of God's creations with the number 19 rests in the fact that it is the gematrical value of the word "ONE" in all the scriptural languages—Aramaic, Hebrew, and Arabic.

The number 19, therefore, proclaims the First Commandment in all the scriptures: that there is only ONE God.

The Lord our God is ONE!
Therefore, you shall worship
the Lord your God
with all your heart,
with all your soul,
with all your mind,
and with all your strength.

[Deuteronomy 6:4-5]
[Mark 12:29]
[Quran 2:163,17:22-23]

Table 20: Why "19!"

	Letter		
Hebrew		Arabic	Value
V		W	6
A		A	1
H		H	8
D		D	4
			.....
			19

As shown in Table 7, the Aramaic, Hebrew, and Arabic alphabets used to double as numerals in accordance with a universally established system. The Hebrew word for "ONE" is "VAHD" (pronounced V-AHAD). In Arabic, the word for "ONE" is "WAHD" (pronounced WAAHED). See Table 20.

The Word "Quran"

The word "Quran" occurs in the Quran 58 times, with one of them, in 10:15, referring to "another Quran." This particular occurrence, therefore, must be excluded. Thus, the frequency of occurrence of "this Quran" in the Quran is 57, or 19x3.

Two other grammatical forms of the word "Quran" occur in 12 verses. These include the word "Quranun" and the word "Quranahu." One of these occurrences, in 13:31 refers to "another Quran" that cause the mountains to crumble. Another occurrence, in 41:44, refers to "a non-Arabic Quran." These two occurrences, therefore, are excluded. Table 21 shows a list of the suras and verses where the word "Quran," in all its grammatical forms, occurs.

Table 21: Suras and Verses Where "Quran" Occurs

Sura	Verse	Sura	Verse
2	185	30	58
4	82	34	31
5	101	36	2
6	19	-	69
7	204	38	1
9	111	39	27
10	37	-	28
-	61	41	3
12	2	-	26
-	3	42	7
15	1	43	3
-	87	-	31
-	91	46	29
16	98	47	24
17	9	50	1
-	41	-	45
-	45	54	17
-	46	-	22
-	60	-	32
-	78	-	40
-	82	55	2
-	88	56	77
-	89	59	21
-	106	72	1
18	54	73	4
20	2	-	20
-	113	75	17
-	114	-	18
25	30	76	23
-	32	84	21
27	1	85	21
-	6	......	......
-	76	1356	3052
-	92		
28	85	1356 + 3052 = 4408	
		(19x232)	

A STRONG FOUNDATION

The Quran's first verse, "In the Name of God, Most Gracious, Most Merciful," known as *Basmalah*, consists of 19 Arabic letters. Its constituent words occur in the Quran consistently in multiples of 19.

The first word............ "Ism" (Name)........... occurs .... 19 times.
The second word .... "Allah" (God) .... occurs .... 2698 times (19x142).
The third word............ "Al-Rahman" (Most Gracious)........... 57 times, 19x3.
The fourth word.......... "Al-Raheem" (Most Merciful)........... 114 times, 19x6.

Professor Cesar Majul looked at the gematrical value of more than 400 attributes of God, and found only four names whose gematrical vaues are multiples of 19:

Divine Name	Gematrical Value
1. "Waahed" (One)	19
2. "Zul Fadl Al-'Azim" (Possessor of Infinite Grace)	2698
3. "Majid" (Glorious)	57
4. "Jaami'" (Summoner)	114

As noted above, the only Divine Names whose gematrical values are divisible by 19 correspond exactly to the frequencies of occurrence of the **Basmalah**'s four words. The figure below illustrates this remarkable phenomenon:

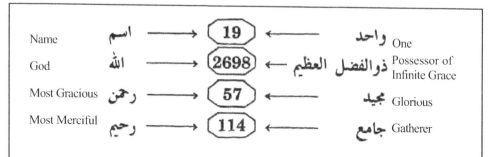

The four words of Basmalah are shown on the left side, and the only four divine names whose gematrical values are divisible by 19 are on the right side. The numbers in the middle are the frequencies of occurrence of the words of Basmalah, and, at the same time, the gematrical values of the four divine names.

The Five Pillars of Islam

Although the Quran provides numerous important commandments governing all aspects of our lives (see for example 17:22-38), five basic "pillars" have been traditionally emphasized. They are:

1. *Shahaadah:* Bearing witness that there is no other god besides God.

2. *Salat:* Observing five daily Contact Prayers.

3. *Seyaam:* Fasting during the ninth month of the Islamic calendar (Ramadan).

4. *Zakat:* Giving away 2.5% of one's net income as a charity to specified people.

5. *Hajj:* Pilgrimage to Mecca once in a lifetime for those who can afford it.

Like everything else in the Quran, these are mathematically structured.

1. **One God (Shahaadah):**

As mentioned earlier, the word "ONE" that refers to God occurs in the Quran 19 times. The reference to God "ALONE" occurs 5 times, and the sum of the sura and verse numbers where we find these five occurrences is 361, 19x19.

The "First Pillar of Islam" is stated in 3:18 as **"LAA ELAAHA ELLA HOO"** (There is no other god besides Him). This most important expression occurs in 19 suras. The first occurrence is in 2:163, and the last occurrence is in 73:9. Table 22 shows that the total of sura numbers, plus the number of verses between the first and last occurrences, plus the sum of these verse numbers is 316502, or 19x 16658.

Also, by adding the numbers of the 19 suras where **LAA ELAAHA ELLA HOO** occurs, plus the verse numbers where this crucial expression is found, plus the total number of occurrences (29), the Grand

Table 22: All Suras and Verses from the First Occurrence of LAA ELAAHA ELLA HOO to the Last Occurrence.

Sura No.	No. of Verses	Sum of Verse #s	Total
2	123	27675	27800
3	200	20100	20303
-	-	-	-
9	127	8128	8264
-	-	-	-
72	28	406	506
73	9	45	127
....	....	....	....
2700	5312	308490	316502
			(19x16658)

Table 23: List of All Occurrences of the Crucial Phrase: "LAA ELAAHA ELLA HOO" (There is no other god besides Him).

No.	Sura No.	Verses with Shahadah	Frequency of Shahadah
1.	2	163, 255	2
2.	3	2, 6, 18 (twice)	4
3.	4	87	1
4.	6	102, 106	2
5.	7	158	1
6.	9	31	1
7.	11	14	1
8.	13	30	1
9.	20	8, 98	2
10.	23	116	1
11.	27	26	1
12.	28	70, 88	2
13.	35	3	1
14.	39	6	1
15.	40	3, 62, 65	3
16.	44	8	1
17.	59	22, 23	2
18.	64	13	1
19.	73	9	1
	....	....	....
	507	1592	29

$507 + 1592 + 29 + 2128 = 19 \times 112$

Total comes to 2128, or 19x112. The details are shown in Table 23.

2. The Contact Prayers "Salat":

The word "Salat" occurs in the Quran 67 times, and when we add the numbers of suras and verses of these 67 occurrences, the total comes to 4674, or 19x246 (see *INDEX OF THE QURAN*).

3. Fasting (Seyaam):

The commandment to fast is mentioned in 2:183, 184, 185, 187, 196; 4:92; 5:89, 95; 33:35, 35; & 58:4. The total of these numbers is 1387, or 19x73. It is noteworthy that 33:35 mentions fasting twice, one for the believing men, and the other for the believing women.

4. The Obligatory Charity (Zakat):&
5. Hajj Pilgrimage to Mecca:

While the first three "Pillars of Islam" are obligatory upon all Muslim men and women, the *Zakat* and Hajj are decreed only for those who can afford them. This explains the interesting mathematical phenomenon associated with *Zakat* and Hajj.

The *Zakat* charity is mentioned in 2:43, 83, 110, 177, 277; 4:77, 162; 5:12, 55, 7:156; 9:5, 11, 18, 71; 18:81; 19:13, 31, 55; 21:73; 22:41, 78; 23:4; 24:37, 56; 27:3; 30:39; 31:4; 33:33; 41:7; 58:13; 73:20; and 98:5. These numbers add up to 2395. This total does not quite make it as a multiple of 19; it is up by 1.

The Hajj Pilgrimage occurs in 2:189, 196, 197; 9:3; and 22:27. These numbers add up to 645, and this total does not quite make it as a multiple of 19; it is down by 1.

Thus, *Zakat* and Hajj, together, give a total of 2395 + 645 = 3040 = 19x160.

THE QURAN'S
MATHEMATICAL STRUCTURE

The Quran's suras, verses, words, and letters are not only mathematically composed, but also arranged into a superhuman structure that is purely mathematical, i.e., the literary content has nothing to do with such an arrangement.

Since the physical construction of the Quran is purely mathematical, it would be expected that the numbers mentioned in the Quran must conform with the Quran's 19-based code.

A total of 30 unique numbers are mentioned throughout the Quran, and the sum of all these numbers is 162146, a multiple of 19 (162146 = 19x8534). Table 24 lists all the numbers mentioned in the Quran, without the repetitions.

The numbers which are mentioned only once in the Quran are: 11, 19, 20, 50, 60, 80, 99, 300, 2000, 3000, 5000, 50000, and 100000.

All the numbers mentioned in the Quran, with repetitions, occur 285 times, and this number is a multiple of 19; 285 = 19x15.

The Numbers of Suras and Verses

The numbering system of the Quran's suras and verses has been perfectly preserved. Only a few unauthorized and easily detectable printings deviate from the standard system that is divinely guarded.

When we add the numbers of all suras, plus the number of verses in every sura, plus the sum of verse numbers, the Grand total for the whole Quran comes to 346199, 19x19x959. Table 25 is an abbreviated presentation of these data. Thus, the slightest alteration of a single sura or verse would have destroyed this system. As shown in Table 16, if we consider only the 29 initialed suras, these same data produce a Grand Total which is also a multiple of 19. It follows that the data for the un-initialed suras are also divisible by 19.

Table 25: Mathematical Coding of the Sura and Verse Numbers.

Sura No.	No. of Verses	Sum of Verse #s	TOTAL
1	7	28	36
2	286	41041	41329
-	-	-	-
9	127	8128	8264
-	-	-	-
113	5	15	133
114	6	21	141
— —	— —	— —	— — —
6555	6234	333410	346199 (19x19x959)

Table 24: All the Quranic Numbers.

Number	Location Example
1	2:163
2	4:11
3	4:171
4	9:2
5	18:22
6	25:59
7	41:12
8	69:17
9	27:48
10	2:196
11	12:4
12	9:36
19	74:30
20	8:65
30	7:142
40	7:142
50	29:14
60	58:4
70	9:80
80	24:4
99	38:23
100	2:259
200	8:65
300	18:25
1000	2:96
2000	8:66
3000	3:124
5000	3:125
50000	70:4
100000	37:147
162146 (19x8534)	

Table 26 is an abbreviated presentation of the same data related to the 85 un-initialed suras.

Now let us look at another set of miracles involving the sura and verse numbers.

Write down the sura number, followed by the number of verses in that sura, then the number of every verse, and finally, the sum of verse numbers. So, for Sura 1 you would write 1 for the sura, then 7 for the number of verses, 1234567 for each verse number, and finally 28 for the sum of verse numbers, i.e. 1 7 1234567 28. The number for Sura 2 will look like this: 2 286 123456.... 286 41041. Do the same for all the 114 suras, and than add these numbers. The total consists of 759 digits, and is a multiple of 19.

Table 26: Mathematical Coding of the 85 Un-initialed Suras

Sura No.	No. of Verses	Sum of Verse #s	TOTAL
1	7	28	36
4	176	15576	15756
-	-	-	-
9	127	8128	8264
-	-	-	-
113	5	15	133
114	6	21	141
5733	3491	146842	156066
			(19x8214)

Table 27: Sura, Total Number of Verses, Verse numbers & Sum of Verse numbers for every sura.

Sura	Sura,# of Verses, Verse #'s & Sum of Verse #'s
1	17123456728
2	228612345........28641041
-	-
114	114123456621
Total is 759 digits and a multiple of 19	

Now write down the total number of verses in a sura, followed by the sum of verse numbers, and keep all numbers justified to the left. For example, the number of verses in Sura 1 is 7, and the sum of verse numbers is 28. Thus, the combined number for Sura 1 will be 7 28, for Sura 2 it will be 286 41041, for Sura 3 it will be 200 20100; and so on to Sura 114 for which the combined number is 6 21. Remember that these numbers are written all the way to the left, as shown in Table 28. Then add them in the usual manner, from right to left. The total of all these left justified numbers is 4,859,309,774, or 19 x 255753146.

Finally, do the same thing as above (continuing to keep all numbers left justified), except write down the number of every verse, instead of the total number of verses. For example, the number for Sura 1 consists of its seven verse numbers (1234567) combined with the sum of those numbers

Table 28: Number of verses for every sura & sum of verse numbers, justified to the left.

Sura	Total Verses & Sum of Verses
1	728
2	28641041
3	20020100
-	-
114	621
	4859309774=
	19x255753146

(28). Thus, the combined number for Sura 1 will be 1234567 28. The combined number for Sura 114 will be 123456 21. Table 29 demonstrates this process. The total of all these left justified numbers consists of 757 digits, and is still a multiple of 19.

Table 29: Verse numbers and Sum of Verse numbers, justified to the left.

Sura	Verse #'s & Sum of Verses
1	123456728
2	1234...28641041
-	-
114	12345621
Total is 757 digits & a multiple of 19	

Superhuman Numerical Combinations

Let us write down the number of each verse in the Quran, preceded for each sura by the number of verses in that sura. Thus, Sura 1, which consists of seven verses, will be represented by the number 7 1234567. What we are doing here is forming long numbers by writing the numbers of verses next to each other. To find the number representing Sura 2, you write down the number of verses in this sura, 286, followed by the number of every verse, written next to each other. Thus, the number representing Sura 2 will look like this: 286 12345.....284285286. The two numbers representing the first two suras are:

7 1 2 3 4 5 6 7   &   286 1 2 3 4 5.....284 285 286.

Putting these two numbers together to form one number representing the first two suras, we get this number:

7 1 2 3 4 5 6 7 2 8 6 1 2 3 4 5.....284 285 286.

This process is continued until every verse in the Quran is written down, thus forming one very long number encompassing the number of every verse in the Quran. The number representing the whole Quran is **a multiple of 19 & consists of 12692 digits, which is also a multiple of 19.**

---

7 1234567 286 12345...286 ...5 12345 6 123456

FIRST No: This very long number consists of 12692 digits (19x668) and and includes every verse in the Quran. The number of verses in each sura precedes its verses. A special computer program that divides very long numbers has shown that this long number is a multiple of 19.

Instead of putting the total number of verses in every sura ahead of the sura, let us put it at the end of every sura. Thus, the number representing Sura 1 will look like this: 1234567 7, instead of 7 1234567. The number representing Sura 2 will look like this: 12345.....284 285 286 286 instead of 286 12345......284285286. The numbers representing the first two suras will look like this:

1 2 3 4 5 6 7 7   &   1 2 3 4 5.....284 285 286 286.

Putting these two numbers together to form a longer number representing the first two suras, we get a number that looks like this:

1 2 3 4 5 6 7 7   1 2 3 4 5.....284 285 286 286.

Since we are putting the total number of verses per sura at the end of each sura, we must put the total number of numbered verses (6234) at the end of the Quran. The last numbers, therefore, represent the last sura (123456 6), followed by the total number of numbered verses in the Quran (6234):

1 2 3 4 5 6 6 & 6234 > > > 1 2 3 4 5 6 6 6234.

Putting together all the verses of all the suras, produces a long number that consists of 12696 digits, and **is a multiple of 19.**

> **1234567 7 12345...286 286 12345 5...123456 6 6234**

> **SECOND No:** The number of every verse in every sura is followed by the number of verses per sura. The last 11 digits shown here are the 6 verses of the last sura, followed by its number of verses (6), followed by the total number of numbered verses in the Quran (6234). The complete, very long number, is a multiple of 19.

Now let us include the number of every sura.

Write down the number of every verse in every sura, followed by the number of the sura, followed by the number of verses in the sura. Thus, the number representing Sura 1 looks like this: 1234567 1 7. The number representing Sura 2 looks like this: 1 2 3 4 5......284 285 286 2 286. The number representing the last sura (No. 114) looks like this: 1 2 3 4 5 6   114 6. Again, the total number of numbered verses (6234) is added at the end. This number, representing the whole Quran, **is a multiple of 19;** it looks like this:

> **1234567 1 7 12345...286 2 286 ...123456 114 6 6234**

> **THIRD No:** The number of every verse, followed by the sura number, then the number of verses in the sura. The total number of numbered verses is added at the end. The long number (12930 digits) is a multiple of 19.

Instead of putting the total number of verses in every sura after the sura, let us now put it ahead of the sura. Thus, the number representing Sura 1 looks like this: 7 1234567 1, instead of 1234567 1 7, and the number representing Sura 2 looks like this: 286 12345.... 284 285 286 2, instead of 12345.....284 285 286 2 286. This very long number representing the whole Quran **is a multiple of 19.**

> **7 1234567 1 286 12345...286   2...6 123456 114 6234**

> **FOURTH No:** The total number of verses in each sura is followed by the number of every verse, then the sura number. The last 14 digits shown above are the number of verses in the last sura (6), followed by the numbers of the six verses (123456), followed by the number of the sura (114), then the total number of numbered verses in the Quran.
> The very long number (consisting of 12930 digits) is a multiple of 19.

Now, let us write down the number of every verse in every sura, followed by the sum of verse numbers for every sura. Sura 1 consists of 7 verses, and the sum of verse numbers is $1 + 2 + 3 + 4 + 5 + 6 + 7 = 28$. Thus, the number representing Sura 1 looks like this: 1234567 28.

The sum of verse numbers for Sura 2 is 41041 ($1 + 2 + 3 + ... + 286$). Thus, the number representing Sura 2 looks like this: 12345...284 285 286 41041.

The number representing the last sura, which consists of 6 verses, looks like this: 123456 21, since $1 + 2 + 3 + 4 + 5 + 6 = 21$.

The complete number, representing the whole Quran, consists of 12836 digits and **is a multiple of 19.** It looks like this:

1234567 28 12345...284285286 41041...123456 21

FIFTH No: The number of every verse in every sura is followed by the sum of verse numbers. The long number consists of 12836 digits, and is a multiple of 19.

Remarkably, if we take the "Fifth No." shown above and reverse the order of verse numbers and sum of verse numbers, i.e., move the sum of verse numbers, and put it ahead of the sura, the resulting long number **is still a multiple of 19.**

28 1234567 41041 12345...285286....21 123456

SIXTH No: Placing the sum of verse numbers ahead of each sura, instead of after it, produces a long number (12836 digits) that is also a multiple of 19.

Even writing the suras backward, i.e., reversing the order of suras by starting with the last sura and ending with the first sura, and placing the sum of verse numbers after the verses of each sura, the product **is still a multiple of 19**

123456 21 12345 15..12345..286 41041 1234567 28

SEVENTH No: Reversing the order of suras—starting from the last sura and ending with the first sura—and writing down the number of every verse, with the sum of verse numbers for every sura after its verses, the product is a long number consisting of 12836 digits. This long number is a multiple of 19.

Write the sum of verse numbers for the whole Quran (333410), followed by the total number of numbered verses in the Quran (6234), then the number of suras (114). Every sura is then represented by its number followed by its number of verses. The numbers representing Suras 1 and 2 are 1 7 and 2 286. The complete number, covering all suras of the Quran, consists of 474 digits, and **is a multiple of 19**—it looks like this:

333410 6234 114 1 7 2 286 3 200..113 5 114 6

EIGHTH No: The Grand Sum of verse numbers (333410) is followed by the total number of numbered verses (6234), the number of suras (114), then the sura numbers and numbers of verses of every sura.

Now let us reverse the order of sura number and its number of verses as presented in the "Eighth No." Thus, the numbers representing the first two suras look like this: 7 1 & 286 2, instead of 1 7 & 2 286. The complete number also consists of 474 digits and **is still a multiple of 19.** It looks like this:

333410 6234 114 7 1 286 2 200 3...5 113 6 114

NINTH No: Reversing the sequence of sura number and number of verses still gives us a long number that is a multiple of 19

If we write down the sum of verse numbers for Sura 1 (28), followed by the sum of verse numbers for Sura 2 (41041), and so on to the end of the Quran, and placing the Grand Sum of verse numbers (333410) at the end, the resulting long number (Tenth No.) consists of 377 digits, and **is a multiple of 19.**

28 41041 20100 .... 15 21 333410

TENTH No: The sums of verse numbers for every sura in the Quran, are written next to each other, followed at the end by the Grand Sum of verse numbers (333410).
This long number (377 digits) is a multiple of 19.

If we write down the number of suras in the Quran (114), followed by the total number of numbered verses (6234), followed by the number of every sura and its sum of verse numbers, the final long number (612 digits) **is a multiple of 19.**

114 6234 1 28 2 41041 3 20100...113 15 114 21

ELEVENTH No: The number of suras, followed by the total number of numbered verses, then the number of every sura and its sum of verse numbers, produce this long number (612 digits) that is a multiple of 19.

Lest anyone may think that any Quranic parameter is left un-guarded with this awesome mathematical code, let us look at more parameters.

If we write down the number of suras (114), followed by the total number of numbered verses, followed by the Grand Sum of verse numbers in the whole Quran (333410), followed by the numbers of every sura and its verses, we end up with a very long number (12712 digits) that is a multiple of 19.

114 6234 333410 1 1 2 3 4 5 6 7...114 1 2 3 4 5 6

TWELFTH NUMBER

If we write down the numbers of verses in every sura next to each other, we end up with a 235-digit number that **is a multiple of 19.** To do this, write down the total number of numbered verses in the Quran (6234), followed by the number of verses in every sura, then close with the total number of numbered verses in the Quran. The final long number looks like this:

6234   7 286 200 176 .... 127 ...   5 4 5 6   6234

(total verses)   (First 4 suras)   (Sura 9)   (Last 4 suras)   (total verses)

THIRTEENTH NUMBER

If we write down the number of numbered verses in the Quran (6234), followed by the number of suras (114), followed by the number of every verse in every sura, then close with the number of numbered verses in the Quran (6234) and the number of suras (114), the final number consists of 12479 digits, **and is a multiple of 19.**

6234 114 1234567 12345...286...123456 6234 114

FOURTEENTH NUMBER

Another long number that consists of 12774 digits is formed by writing down the number of every verse in every sura, followed by the number of every sura added to its number of verses. Sura 1 consists of 7 verses, and the total 1 + 7 is 8. Therefore, the number representing Sura 1 looks like this: 1234567 8. Since Sura 2 consists of 286 verses, the number representing Sura 2 looks like this:

12345...286 288. This is done for every sura in the Quran. The final combined number consists of 12774 digits, and **is a multiple of 19.**

1234567 8 12345.....286 288 ....123456 120
(1 + 7)   (2 + 286)   (114 + 6)
FIFTEENTH NUMBER

More specialized features are in Appendices 2, 9, 19, 24, 25, 26, 29, and 37.

A Witness From the Children of Israel [46:10]

Proclaim: "What if it is from God, and you disbelieved in it? A witness from the Children of Israel has borne witness to a similar phenomenon, and he has believed, while you have turned too arrogant to believe. God does not guide the wicked" [46:10]

The following quotation is taken from *STUDIES IN JEWISH MYSTICISM,* (Association for Jewish Studies, Cambridge, Mass., Joseph Dan & Frank Talmage, eds., Page 88, 1982). The quotation refers to the work of Rabbi Judah the Pious (12th Century AD):

The people [Jews] in France made it a custom to add [in the morning prayer] the words: " 'Ashrei temimei derekh [blessed are those who walk the righteous way]," and our Rabbi, the Pious, of blessed memory, wrote that they were completely and utterly wrong. It is all gross falsehood, because there are only nineteen times that the Holy Name is mentioned [in that portion of the morning prayer]... and similarly you find the word 'Elohim nineteen times in the pericope of Ve-'elleh shemot. . . . Similarly, you find that Israel were called "sons" nineteen times, and there are many other examples. All these sets of nineteen are intricately intertwined, and they contain many secrets and esoteric meanings, which are contained in more than eight large volumes... Furthermore, in this section there are 152 (19x8) words.

Acknowledgments

All praise and thanks are due to God who has willed that His miracle of the Quran shall be revealed at this time. He has distinguished the following individuals and blessed them by revealing through them many portions of this momentous discovery: Abdullah Arik, Mohamoud Ali Abib, Lisa Spray, Edip Yuksel, Ihsan Ramadan, Feroz Karmally, Ismail Barakat, Gatut Adisoma, Ahmed Yusuf, Cesar A. Majul, Muhtesem Erisen, and Emily Kay Sterrett.

Appendix 2

God's Messenger of the Covenant

God's Messenger of the Covenant is a consolidating messenger. His mission is to purify and unify all existing religions into one: Islam (Submission).

Islam is NOT a name; it is a description of one's total submission and devotion to God ALONE, without idolizing Jesus, Mary, Muhammad, or the saints. Anyone who meets this criterion is a "Muslim" (Submitter). Therefore, one may be a Muslim Jew, a Muslim Christian, a Muslim Hindu, a Muslim Buddhist, or Muslim Muslim.

God's Messenger of the Covenant delivers God's proclamation that "The only religion approved by God is Submission" (3:19) and that "Anyone who seeks other than Submission as a religion, it will not be accepted from him/her" (3:85).

A messenger of God must present proof that he is God's messenger. Every messenger of God is supported by incontrovertible divine signs proving that he is authorized by the Almighty to deliver His messages. Moses threw down his staff and it turned into a serpent, Jesus healed the leprous and revived the dead by God's leave, Saaleh's sign was the famous camel, Abraham walked out of the fire, and Muhammad's miracle was the Quran (29:50-51).

The Quran (3:81, 33:7, 33:40) and the Bible (Malachi 3:1-3) have prophesied the advent of the consolidating messenger, God's Messenger of the Covenant. It is only befitting that a messenger with such a crucial mission must be supported by the most powerful miracle (74:30-35). While the miracles of previous messengers were limited in time and place, God's miracle supporting His Messenger of the Covenant is perpetual; it can be witnessed by anyone, at anytime, in any place.

This Appendix presents physical, examinable, verifiable, and irrefutable evidence that Rashad Khalifa is God's Messenger of the Covenant.

A Quranic Truth

One of the major prophecies in the Quran is that God's Messenger of the Covenant will be sent after all the prophets have come to this world, and after all of God's scriptures have been delivered.

> **God took a covenant from the prophets, saying, "I will give you the scripture and wisdom. Afterwards, a messenger will come to confirm all existing scriptures. You shall believe in him and support him." He said, "Do you agree with this, and pledge to fulfill this covenant?" They said, "We agree." He said, "You have thus borne witness, and I bear witness along with you."**
>
> **(3:81)**

Muhammad Marmaduke Pickthall translated 3:81 as follows:

> **When Allah made (His) covenant with the Prophets, (He said): Behold that which I have given you of the Scripture and knowledge. And afterward there will come unto you a messenger, confirming that which ye possess. Ye shall believe in him and ye shall help him. He said: Do ye agree, and will ye take up My burden (which I lay upon you) in this (matter)? They answered: We agree. He said: Then bear witness. I will be a witness with you.**

We learn from Sura 33 that Muhammad was one of the prophets who made that solemn covenant with God.

> **And when we exacted a covenant from the Prophets, and from thee (O Muhammad) and from Noah and Abraham and Moses and Jesus son of Mary, We took from them a solemn covenant.** **(33:7)**
> **(according to Muhammad Marmaduke Pickthall)**

Verse 3:81, among many other verses, provides the definitions of *"Nabi"* (Prophet) and *"Rasoul"* (Messenger). Thus, *"Nabi"* is a messenger of God who delivers a new scripture, while *"Rasoul"* is a messenger commissioned by God to confirm existing scripture; he does not bring a new scripture. According to the Quran, every *"Nabi"* is a *"Rasoul"* but not every *"Rasoul"* is a *"Nabi"*

Not every messenger was given a new scripture. It is not logical that God will give a scripture to a prophet, then ask him to keep it exclusively for himself, as stated by some Muslim "scholars" (2:42, 146, 159). Those who are not sufficiently familiar with the Quran tend to think that Aaron was a *"Nabi"* as stated in 19:53, who did not receive a scripture. However, the Quran clearly states that the statute book was given specifically "to both Moses and Aaron" (21:48, 37:117).

We learn from the Quran, 33:40, that Muhammad was the last prophet *(Nabi),* but not the last messenger *(Rasoul):*

> **Muhammad was not the father of any of your men; he was a messenger (Rasoul) of God and the last prophet (Nabi).** **[33:40]**

This crucial definition is confirmed by the Quran's mathematical code. The expression used in 33:40, *"Muhammad Khaatum Al-Nabiyyeen"* (the last prophet) has a gematrical value of 1349, 19x71, while the value of the erroneous expression *"Muhammad Khaatum Al-Mursaleen"* (the last messenger) is not a multiple of 19.

From time immemorial, it has been a human trait to reject a contemporary, living messenger. Joseph was declared "the last messenger" (40:34). Yet, many messengers came after him, including Moses, David, Solomon, Jesus, and Muhammad.

The Covenant Fulfilled

Although the prophets are dead, as far as this world is concerned, we know that their souls, the real persons, are now in the Garden of Eden where Adam and Eve lived. Several verses enjoin us from thinking that the believers who shed their bodies and departed this world are dead (2:154, 3:169, 4:69). Although they cannot come back to our world (23:100), they are "alive" in Paradise. Please see Appendix 17.

During my Hajj pilgrimage to Mecca, and before sunrise on Tuesday, Zul-Hijjah 3, 1391, December 21, 1971, I, Rashad Khalifa, the soul, the real person, not the body, was taken to some place in the universe where I was introduced to all the prophets as God's Messenger of the Covenant. I was not informed of the details and true significance of this event until Ramadan 1408.

What I witnessed, in sharp consciousness, was that I was sitting still, while the prophets, one by one, came towards me, looked at my face, then nodded their heads. God showed them to me as they had looked in this world, attired in their respective mode of dress. There was an atmosphere of great awe, joy, and respect.

Except for Abraham, none of the prophets were identified to me. I knew that all the prophets were there, including Moses, Jesus, Muhammad, Aaron, David, Noah, and the rest. I believe that the reason for revealing Abraham's identity was that I asked about him. I was taken aback by the strong resemblance he had with my own family—myself, my father, my uncles. It was the only time that I wondered, "Who is this prophet who looks like my relatives?" The answer came: "Abraham." No language was spoken. All communication was done mentally.

It is noteworthy that the date of this fulfillment of the prophets' covenant was **Zul-Hijjah 3, 1391**. If we add the month (12), plus the day (3), plus the year (1391), we get a total of 1406, 19x74. Sura 74 is where the Quran's common denominator, the number 19, is mentioned. Note that the number 1406 is also the number of years from the revelation of the Quran to the revelation of its miracle (Appendix 1).

The mission of God's Messenger of the Covenant is to confirm existing scriptures, purify them, and consolidate them into one divine message. The Quran states that such a messenger is charged with restoring God's message to its pristine purity, to lead the righteous believers—Jews, Christians, Muslims, Buddhists, Sikhs, Hindus, and others—out of darkness into the light (5:19 & 65:11). He is to proclaim that *Islam (total submission to God) is the only religion acceptable by God (3:19)*.

> Lo, I am sending my messenger to prepare the way before me;
> and suddenly there will come to the temple
> the Lord whom you seek and the messenger of the covenant whom you
> desire.
> Yes, he is coming, says the Lord of hosts.
> But who will endure the day of his coming?
> And who can stand when he appears?
> For he is like the refiner's fire, or like the fuller's lye.   [Malachi 3:1-2]

The Proof

The name of God's Messenger of the Covenant is mathematically coded into the Quran as "Rashad Khalifa." This is certainly the most appropriate method of introducing God's messenger to the world in the computer-age.

(1) As shown in Appendix 1, God's great miracle in the Quran is based on the prime number 19, and it remained hidden for 1406 years (19x74). This awesome miracle was predestined by Almighty God to be unveiled through Rashad Khalifa. Hundreds of Muslim and Orientalist scholars during the last 14 centuries have tried in vain, but none of them was permitted to decipher the significance of the Quranic Initials.

(2) The Quran is made easy for **the sincere believers and seekers** (54:17, 22, 32, 40 & 39:28). It is an irrevocable divine law that no one is permitted access to the Quran, let alone its great miracle, unless he or she is a sincere believer who is given specific divine authorization (17:45-46, 18:57, 41:44, 56:79). The unveiling of the Quran's miracle through Rashad Khalifa is a major sign of his messengership.

(3) The root word of the name "Rashad رَشَاد " is "Rashada رَشَدَ " (to uphold the right guidance). This root word is mentioned in the Quran 19 times. Nineteen is the Quran's common denominator (see *INDEX TO THE WORDS OF*

Table 1: Suras and Verses of "Rashada" and "Khalifa"

No.	"Rashada" Sura	"Rashada" Verse	"Khalifa" Sura	"Khalifa" Verse
1.	2	186	(2)	30
2.	-	256	38	26
3.	4	6		
4.	7	146		
5.	11	78		
6.	-	87		
7.	-	97		
8.	18	10		
9.	-	17		
10.	-	24		
11.	-	66		
12.	21	51		
13.	40	29		
14.	-	38		
15.	49	7		
16.	72	2		
17.	-	10		
18.	-	14	(Sura 2	
19.	-	21	is a Repeat)	
	224	1145	38	56

224 + 1145 + 38 + 56 = 1463 = 19x77

QURAN, First Printing, Page 320).

(4) The word "Rashad" occurs in 40:29 & 38. The word "Khalifa" occurs in 2:30 and 38:26. The first "Khalifa" refers to a non-human "Khalifa," namely, Satan, while the second occurrence (Sura 38), refers to a human "Khalifa." If we add the numbers of suras and verses of "Rashad" (40:29, 38) and "Khalifa" (38:26) we get $40 + 29 + 38 + 38 + 26 = 171 = 19 \times 9$.

(5) The sum of all sura and verse numbers where all "Rashada" and all "Khalifa" occur, without discrimination, add up to 1463, 19×77 (Table 1).

(6) The total of all suras and verses where the root word "Rashada" occurs is 1369, or $(19 \times 72) + 1$, while the total for all occurrences of "Khalifa" is 94, $(19 \times 5)-1$. The fact that "Rashada" is up by one and "Khalifa" is down by one pins down the name as "Rashad Khalifa," and not any "Rashad" or any "Khalifa."

(7) The gematrical value of "Rashad" is 505 and the value of "Khalifa" is 725 (Table 7, Appendix 1). If we add the value of "Rashad Khalifa" (1230) to the sura numbers, and the number of verses, from the beginning of the Quran to the first occurrence of "Rashada," the total is 1425, 19×75. The details are given in Table 2.

Table : The Suras and Verses from the Beginning of the Quran to the First Occurrence of the Root Word "Rashada"

Sura No.	No. of Verses	Sum of Verse #s
1	7	28
2	185	17205
3	192	17233 (19×907)

Also, "Rashad" (505) + "Khalifa" (725) + Sura Total (3) + Total of Verses (192) = 1425 (19×75)
$505 + 725 + 3 + 192 = 1425 = 19 \times 75$

(8) If we add the numbers of all the verses in every sura, i.e., the sum of verse numbers $(1 + 2 + 3 + ... + n)$ from the beginning of the Quran to the first occurrence of the root word "Rashada," the total comes to 17233, 19×907 (Table 2).

(9) The Quranic Initials constitute the basic foundation of the Quran's miracle. These initials occur in suras 2, 3, 7, 10, 11, 12, 13, 14, 15, 19, 20, 26, 27, 28, 29, 30, 31, 32, 36, 38, 40, 41, 42, 43, 44, 45, 46, 50, and 68. If we add the sum of these numbers (822) to the value of "Rashad Khalifa" (1230), the total is 2052, 19×108.

(10) As shown in Table 3, if we add the numbers of all suras where the root word "Rashada" occurs, plus the number of verses, we get 1368, or 19×72.

(11) If we write down the sura number, followed by the number of verses per sura, followed by the individual

Table 3: The Suras Where the Root Word "Rashada" Occurs.

Sura No.	No. of Verses	Total
2	286	288
4	176	180
7	206	213
11	123	134
18	110	128
21	112	133
40	85	125
49	18	67
72	28	100
224	1144	1368 (19×72)

verse numbers, from the first occurrence of the root word "Rashada" (2:186) to the last occurrence of "Rashada" (72:21), and place these numbers next to each other, we get a very long number that consists of 11087 digits, and is a multiple of 19. This very long number begins with the number of Sura 2, followed by the number of verses in Sura 2 from the first occurrence of "Rashada" at verse 186 to the end of the sura (100 verses). Thus, the beginning of the number looks like this: 2 100. The numbers of these 100 individual verses (187 to 286) are placed next to this number. Thus, the number representing Sura 2 looks like this: 2 100 187 188 189 .... 285 286. The same process is carried out all the way to 72:21, the last occurrence of the root "Rashada." The complete number looks like this:

> **2 100 187 188 189 ..... 72 21 1 2 3 ..... 19 20 21**
> **The Sura number is followed by the number of verses, then the numbers of individual verses, from the first to the last occurrence of "Rashada" (2:187 through 72:21).**
> **The complete number consists of 11087 digits, and is divisible by 19.**

(12) If we examine the suras and verses from the first occurrence of the root word "Rashada" to the word "Khalifa" in 38:26, we find that the sum of sura numbers and their numbers of verses is 4541, or 19x239. The details are in Table 4.

(13) When we write down the value of "Rashad" (505), followed by the value of "Khalifa" (725), followed by every sura number where the root word "Rashada" occurs, followed by the numbers of its verses, from the first "Rashada" (2:186) to the word "Khalifa" (38:26), we get a long number that is divisible by 19.

The first occurrence of "Rashada" is in 2:186. So, we write down 2 186. The second occurrence is in 2:256, so we write down 256. The next occurrence is in 4:6, so we write down 4 6, and so on, until we write down 38 26 ("Khalifa" occurs in 38:26). The complete number looks like this:

Table 4: The Suras and Verses from the First "Rashada" to "Khalifa."

Sura No.	No. of Verses	Total
2	100 (187-286)	102
3	200	203
4	176	180
5	120	125
-	-	-
36	83	119
37	182	219
38	26	64
740	3801	4541 (19x239)

> **505   725   2   186   256   4   6 38   26**

> **The gematrical value of "Rashad" is followed by the value of "Khalifa," followed by the sura number and verse numbers of every occurrence of the root word "Rashada" from the first occurrence of "Rashada" to the occurrence of "Khalifa" in 38:26.**

The Only Religion Approved by God is Islam
[3:19]

(14) The Quran specifies three messengers of Islam (Submission):

Abraham delivered all the practices of Islam. The value of his name	= 258
Muhammad delivered the Quran. The value of his name	= 92
Rashad delivered Islam's proof of authenticity. The value of his name	= 505
Total gematrical value of the 3 names = 258 + 92 + 505	= 855.
	(19x45)

The true Judaism, Christianity, and Islam will be consolidated into one religion—complete submission and absolute devotion to God ALONE.

The existing religions, including Judaism, Christianity, and Islam are severely corrupted and will simply die out (9:33, 48:28, 61:9).

(15) Since the Quran sometimes refers to "Abraham, Ismail, and Isaac," it was suggested that Ismail and Isaac should be included. Remarkably, the addition of Ismail and Isaac gave a total that is still a multiple of 19. As shown in Table 5, the new total is 1235, or 19x65. This divisibility by 19 is not possible if any of the 3 names Abraham, Muhammad, or Rashad is omitted.

Why 81:   Verse 81 & Sura 81

(16) God's Messenger of the Covenant is prophesied in Verse 81 of Sura 3.

The addition of the gematrical value of "Rashad" (505), plus the gematrical value of "Khalifa" (725), plus the Verse number (81), produces 505 + 725 + 81 = 1311 = 19x69.

(17) If we look at **Sura 81**, we read about a messenger of God who is powerfully supported and authorized by the Almighty (Verse 19). Thus, Verse 81 of Sura 3, and Sura 81, Verse 19 are strongly connected with the name "Rashad Khalifa" 505 + 725 + 81 = 1311 = 19x69.

(18) If we add the sura numbers plus the number of verses from the beginning of the Quran to Verse 3:81, where the Messenger of the Covenant is prophesied, the total comes to 380, 19x20. These data are in Table 6.

Table 5: Gematrical Value of the 5 Messengers

Name	Value of Individual Letters	Total
Abraham	1 + 2 + 200 + 5 + 10 + 40	258
Ismail	1 + 60 + 40 + 70 + 10 + 30	211
Isaac	1 + 60 + 8 + 100	169
Muhammad	40 + 8 + 40 + 4	92
Rashad	200 + 300 + 1 + 4	505
	1235	1235 (19x65)

Table 6: The Suras and Verses from 1:1 to 3:81

Sura No.	No. of Verses	Total
1	7	8
2	286	288
3	81	84
6	374	380 (19x20)

(19) The gematrical value of Verse 3:81 is 13148, 19x692. This value is obtained by adding the gematrical values of every letter in the verse.

(20) If we look at that portion of Verse 3:81 which refers specifically to the messenger of the Covenant: "A messenger will come to you, confirming what you have," in Arabic:

"JAA'AKUM RASOOLUN MUSADDIQUN LEMAA MA'AKUM"

جَآءَكُمْ رَسُولٌ مُّصَدِّقٌ لِّمَا مَعَكُمْ

we find that the gematrical value of this key phrase is 836, 19x44.

"Surely, You Are One of the Messengers" (36:3)

(21) I was told most assertively, through the angel Gabriel, that Verse 3 of Sura 36 refers specifically to me. If we arrange the initialed suras only, starting with Sura 2, then Sura 3, then Sura 7, and so on, we find that Sura 36, Ya Seen, occupies position number 19.

(22) Verse 3 of Sura 36 says, "Surely, you are one of the messengers." The gematrical value of this phrase is 612. By adding this value (612), plus the sura number (36), plus the verse number (3), plus the gematrical value of "Rashad Khalifa" (505+ 725), we get 36 + 3 + 612 + 505 + 725 = 1881 = 19x99.

(23) Sura 36 consists of 83 verses. If we add the sura number (36), plus its number of verses (83), plus the gematrical value of "Rashad Khalifa" (505 + 725), we get 36 + 83 + 505 + 725 = 1349 = 19x71.

(24) From 3:81, where the Messenger of the Covenant is prophesied, to Sura 36, there are 3330 verses. By adding the value of "Rashad Khalifa" (1230), to this number of verses (3330), we get 505 + 725 + 3330 = 4560, 19x240.

(25) From 3:81 to 36:3 there are 3333 verses. By adding this number to the gematrical value of "Rashad" (505), we get 3333 + 505 = 3838 = 19x202.

(26) The number of verses from 1:1 to 36:3 is 3705, 19x195 (Table 7).

Table 7: Suras and Verses From Sura 1 to Verse 3 of Sura 36.

Sura No.	No. of Verses	Sum of Verse #s
1	7	28
2	286	41041
3	200	20100
-	-	-
9	127	8128
-	-	-
34	54	1485
35	45	1035
36	2	3
666	3705 (19x195)	257925 (19x137575)

(27) The sum of verse numbers of every sura from 1:1 to 36:3 is 257925, 19x13575 (Table 7).

(28) The sum of sura numbers from Sura 1 to Sura 36 is 666 (Table 7). If we add this sum to the gematrical value of "Rashad Khalifa" (505 + 725), plus the gematrical value of verse 36:3 "Surely, you are one of the messengers," (612), the total is: 666 + 505 + 725 + 612 = 2508= 19x132.

(29) If we add the sum of verse numbers (1 + 2 + 3 + ... + n) from the first occurrence of the root word "Rashada" (2:186) to 36:3 (You are one of the messengers) to the total of suras (35), plus the sura numbers themselves, the total is 241395, or 19x12705 (Table 8).

(30) The sum of sura numbers from the first occurrence of the root word "Rashada" to 36:3 is 665, 19x35. Note that these are 35 suras (Table 8).

Table 8: The Suras and Verses from the First "Rashada" to 36:3.

No.	Sura No.	Sum of Verse #s
1.	2 (186-286)	23836
2.	3	20100
3.	4	15576
4.	5	7260
-	-	-
10.	9	8128
-	-	-
33.	34	1485
34.	35	1035
35.	36 (1-3)	6
------	——	——
35	665	240695

35 + 665 + 240695 = 241395 (19x12705)

"A Messenger to the People of the Scripture"
(Jews, Christians, and Muslims)

O people of the scripture, our messenger has come to you, to clarify things for you, after a long period without messengers. Lest you say, "No preacher or warner has come to us." A preacher and warner has come to you. God is Omnipotent.   [5:19]

(31) Obviously, the number of this verse is 19, the Quran's common denominator discovered by Rashad, and the number of occurrences of "Rashada" in the Quran.

(32) If we add the value of "Rashad Khalifa" (1230), plus the sura number (5), plus the verse number (19), we get 1230 + 5 + 19 = 1254 = 19x66.

(33) The sum of the sura numbers and the number of verses from the beginning of the Quran to this verse (5:19) is 703,19x37. See Table 9.

(34) Sura 98, "The Proof," Verse 2, proclaims the advent of God's Messenger of the Covenant for the benefit of "The People of the Scripture (Jews, Christians, and Muslims)." By adding the gematrical value of "Rashad Khalifa"

Table 9: The Suras and Verses from the Beginning to 5:19.

Sura No.	No. of Verses	Total
1	7	8
2	286	288
3	200	203
4	176	180
5	19	24
——	——	——
15	688	703
		(19x73)

(505 + 725) to the sura number (98), plus the verse number (2), we get:
505 + 725 + 98 + 2 = 1330 = 19x70.

> **Those who disbelieved among the people of the scripture (Jews, Christians, Muslims), and the idolators, will not believe, despite the profound sign given to them. [98:1]**
> **A messenger from God, reciting Sacred Scriptures.**
> **[98:2]**

(35) It is noteworthy that the word "Bayyinah," which means "Profound Sign," and is the title of Sura 98, occurs in the Quran 19 times. This is another mathematical confirmation that the Quran's proof of divine authorship is based on the prime number 19, and that "Rashad Khalifa" is the messenger in 98:2.

A Profound Messenger Has Come [44:13]

(36) By adding the sura numbers, plus the number of verses in each sura, from the 1:1 to 44:13, the total comes to 5415, 19x19x15 (Table 10).

(37) The sum of the sura number (44) plus the number of the verse where the messenger is predicted (13) equals 57, 19x3. See Table 10.

END OF THE WORLD

(38) God is the only Knower of the future; He knows exactly when this world will end (7:187, 31:34, 33:63, 41:47, 43:85). We learn from the Quran that God reveals certain aspects of the future to His chosen messengers. In Appendix 25, evidence is presented that Rashad Khalifa was blessed with unveiling the End of the World, in accordance with 72:27.

(39) The number of verses from the beginning of the Quran to Verse 72:27 is 5472, or 19x72x4. Note that the messenger who is given information about the future in 72:27, and that this sura contains 4 "Rashada" words (72:2, 10, 14, & 21). By adding the value of "Rashad Khalifa" (1230), plus the sura number (72), plus the numbers of the 4 verses where "Rashada" is mentioned, we get 1230 + 72 + 2 + 10 +14 + 21 = 1349 = 19x71.

(40) Verse 72:27 begins with the statement.

" الا من ارتضى من رسول "

(Only the Messenger that He chooses). This reference to the messenger who is chosen by God to receive news about the future has a gematrical value of 1919. Table 11 presents the data.

Table 10: The Suras and Verses from 1:1 to 44:13.

Sura No.	No. of Verses	Total
1	7	8
2	286	288
3	200	203
4	176	180
5	120	125
-	-	-
9	127	136
-	-	-
41	54	95
42	53	95
43	89	132
44	13	57
990	4425	5415
		(19 x19 x15)

Table 11: Gematrical Value of
the Chosen Messenger in 72:27.

إِلَّا مَنِ ٱرْتَضَىٰ مِن رَّسُولٍ

Letter	Gematrical Value
A	1
L	30
A	1
M	40
N	50
A	1
R	200
T	400
D	800
Y	10
M	40
N	50
R	200
S	60
W	6
L	30
	....
	1919

HOW TO DISTINGUISH GOD'S MESSENGER FROM A FAKE MESSENGER

The Quran provides straightforward criteria to distinguish the true messengers of God from the false messengers:

[1] God's messenger advocates the worship of God ALONE, and the abolition of all forms of idol worship.

[2] God's messenger never asks for a wage for himself.

[3] God's messenger is given divine, incontrovertible proof of his messengership.

Anyone who claims to be God's messenger, and does not meet the three minimum criteria listed above is a false claimant.

The most important difference between God's messenger and a fake messenger is that God's messenger is supported by God, while the fake messenger is not:

* God's messenger is supported by God's invisible soldiers (3:124-126, 9:26&40, 33:9, 37:171-173, 48:4&7, 74:31).

* God's messenger is supported by God's treasury (63:7-8).

* God's messenger, as well as the believers, are guaranteed victory and dignity, in this world and forever (40:51 & 58:21).

Thus, the truthfulness of God's messenger invariably prevails, while the falsehood of a fake messenger invariably, sooner or later, is exposed.

PRINCIPAL DUTIES OF GOD'S MESSENGER OF THE COVENANT

As stated in the Quran, 3:81, God's Messenger of the Covenant shall confirm all the scriptures, which were delivered by all the prophets, and restore them to their original purity.

MERCY FROM GOD [21:107]

When the believers are faced with a problem, they develop a number of possible solutions, and this invariably leads to considerable bickering, disunity, and disarray. We learn from 2:151, 3:164, and 21:107 that it is but mercy from God that He sends to us messengers to provide the final solutions to our problems. We learn from 42:51 that God sends His messengers to communicate with us, and to disseminate new information. Hence the strong injunction in 4:65, 80 to accept, without the slightest hesitation, the teachings delivered to us through God's messengers.

The following is a list of the principal duties of God's Messenger of the Covenant:

---

1. Unveil and proclaim the Quran's mathematical miracle (Appendix 1).
2. Expose and remove the two false verses 9:128-129 from the Quran (App. 24).
3. Explain the purpose of our lives; why we are here (Appendix 7).
4. Proclaim one religion for all the people, and point out and purge away all the corruptions afflicting Judaism, Christianity, and Islam (Appendices 13, 15,19).
5. Proclaim that Zakat (obligatory charity) is a prerequisite for redemption (7:156), and explain the correct method of observing Zakat (Appendix 15).
6. Unveil the end of the world (Appendix 25).
7. Proclaim that those who die before the age of 40 go to Heaven (Appendix 32).
8. Explain Jesus' death (Appendix 22).
9. Explain the Quran's delivery to, then through Muhammad (Appendix 28).
10. Announce that Muhammad wrote God's revelations (the Quran) with his own hand (Appendix 28).
11. Explain why most believers in God do not make it to Heaven (Appendix 27).
12. Proclaim that God never ordered Abraham to kill his son (Appendix 9).
13. Proclaim the secret of perfect happiness (Introduction, xx).
14. Establish a criminal justice system (Appendix 37).

Appendix 3

We Made the Quran Easy [54:17]

Verse 11:1 informs us that the Quran's Miracle involves [1] the superhuman mathematical design of its physical structure and [2] the simultaneous composition of a literary work of extraordinary excellence.

One may be able to meet the numerical distribution requirements of a simple mathematical pattern. However, this is invariably accomplished at the expense of the literary quality. The simultaneous control of the literary style and the intricate mathematical distribution of individual letters throughout the Quran (Appendix 1) is evident in the fact that the Quran is made easy to memorize, understand, and enjoy. Unlike a human-made book, the Quran is enjoyable to read over and over, infinitely.

The title of this Appendix is repeated in Sura 54, verses 17, 22, 32, and 40. As it turns out, the Quran's Arabic text is composed in such a way as to remind the reader or the memorizer of the next correct expression, or the next verse. God created us and He knows the most efficient way for fixing literary materials into our memory. Memorization of the Quran has played a vital role in preserving the original text generation after generation at a time when written books were a rarity.

Without even realizing it, the person who memorizes the Quran is divinely helped by an intricate literary system as he utters the sounds of the Quranic words. Almost every verse in the Quran contains what I call "Memory Bells." Their function is to remind the reader of what comes next. This system is so vast, I will give only two illustrative examples:

1. In Sura 2, Verses 127, 128, and 129 end with two different names of God each. These pairs of names are *"Al-Samee' Al-'Aleem* (The Hearer, the Omniscient)," *"Al-Tawwaab Al-Raheem* (The Redeemer, Most Merciful)", and *"Al-'Azeez Al-Hakeem* (The Almighty, Most Wise)," respectively. If this were a regular book, one would easily mis-match these six names. Not so in the Quran. Each one of these pairs is preceded in the same verse by a "Memory Bell" that reminds us of the correct pair of names. Thus, Verse 127 talks about Abraham and Ismail raising the foundations of the Ka'abah. The verse ends with the names *"Al-Samee' Al-'Aleem."* The prominent sounds here are the "S," "M," and " 'Ayn." These three letters are prominent in the word "Ismail." We find that this word is conspicuously delayed in the sentence, while improving its literary quality. Thus, we find that the verse goes like this: "When Abraham raised the foundations of the *Ka'abah,* together with Ismail ..." Normally, a human writer would say, "When Abraham and Ismail raised the foundations of the *Ka'abah...*" But delaying the sounds in "Ismail" brings them closer to the end of the verse, and thus reminds us that the correct names of God in this verse are *"Al-Samee' Al-'Aleem."*

Verse 128 has the prominent word *"Tubb"* just before the names *"Al-Tawwaab Al-Raheem."* The word *"Tubb"* thus serves as the memory bell. The names of God at the end of 2:129 are *"Azeez, Hakeem."* The prominent sounds here are

"Z" and "K." Obviously, the memory bell in this verse is the word *"Yuzak-keehim"*

2. Another good example is found in 3:176, 177, & 178, where the retribution for disbelievers is described as " *'Azeem* (Terrible)," *Aleem* (Painful)," and *"Muheen* (Humiliating)," respectively. In a human-made book, the memorizer could easily mix up these three descriptions. But we find that each of these adjectives is preceded by powerful memory bells that prevent such a mix-up. The word " *'Azeem"* of Verse 176 is preceded by the word *"Huzzun"* which is characterized by a stressed letter "Z." This serves to remind us of the particular adjective at the end of this verse. The word *"Aleem"* of Verse 177 is preceded by the sound of the word *"Iman"* to serve as a memory bell, and the word *"Muheen"* of 3:178 is preceded by an abundance of "M" and "H" throughout this verse.

Other examples of memory bells include the ending of 3:173 and the beginning of 3:174, the ending of 4:52 and the beginning of 4:53, the ending of 4:61 and the beginning of 4:62, the ending of 18:53 and the beginning of 18:54, and many more.

****

Appendix 4
Why Was the Quran Revealed in Arabic?

We learn from 41:44 that the sincere believers have access to the Quran, regardless of their mother tongue. The disbelievers, on the other hand, are not permitted access to the Quran, even if they are professors of the Arabic language (17:45, 18:57, 41:44, & 56:79).

Arabic is the most efficient language in the world, especially when it comes to the precise statement of laws. Since the Quran is a Statute Book, it was crucial that such laws must be clearly stated. God chose Arabic for His Final Testament because of the obvious reason that it is the most suitable language for that purpose. Arabic is unique in its efficiency and accuracy. For example, the word "they" in English does not tell you if "they" are males or females. In Arabic there is a "they" for the males, *"HUM,"* and a "they" for the females, *"HUNNA."* There is even a "they" for two males, *"HUMAA,"* and a "they" for two females, *"HAATAAN."* This feature does not exist in any other language in the world. I came to appreciate this efficiency of the Arabic language when I translated, for example, 2:228. This verse enjoins the divorcee to give up her own wishes to divorce her husband, if she discovers that she is pregnant, and the husband wishes to reconcile—the welfare of the child takes a priority. The efficiency of the Arabic language was extremely helpful in stating this law. Any other language would have made it almost impossible to point out whose wishes are to be superseded, at least not in such a few words as we see in 2:228.

The word *"Qaalataa"* of 28:23, for example, translates into four English words: "the two women said." Such is the efficiency of the Arabic language.

Another possible reason for choosing Arabic is the fact that "He" and "She" do not necessarily imply natural gender. Thus, when God is referred to as "He," this does not imply gender at all. God be glorified; He is neither male, nor female. The usage of "He" to refer to God in the English language, for example, has contributed to a false image of God. This was not helped by such distorted expressions as "Father" when referring to God. You never find such a reference to God in the Quran.

****

Appendix 5

Heaven and Hell

The descriptions of Heaven and Hell throughout the Quran are allegorical. And the Quran tells us so whenever such descriptions occur as independent statements, not within a general subject. See 2:24-26, 13:35, and 47:15. The word *"Mathal"* (allegory) is used in these verses. Linguistically, the word "Mathal" in these verses can be removed, and we still have perfect sentences. But it is there because the descriptions of Heaven and Hell are allegorical.

What Heaven and Hell are really like is far beyond our comprehension. Hence the need for allegory.

How can one describe, for example, the taste of chocolate to a person who never tasted chocolate? Allegory will have to be used. The person has to wait to actually taste chocolate in order to know what chocolate tastes like. Whatever allegory we use to describe the taste of chocolate can never approximate the real thing.

Heaven already exists, since Adam and Eve were placed in it during their days of innocence (2:35). We learn from Sura 55 that there are two "High Heavens"—one for the humans and one for the jinns—and two "Lower Heavens"—one for the humans and one for the jinns (see Appendix 11 for more details).

Hell is not created yet. It will be created on the Day of Judgment (69:17 & 89:23). More details are given in Appendix 11.

The High Heaven vs. The Lower Heaven

There are profound differences between the High Heaven and the Lower Heaven. Allegorically, water in the High Heaven flows freely (55:50), while the water of the Lower Heaven needs to be pumped out (55:66).

Allegorically, the High Heaven has all kinds of fruit (55:52), while the Lower Heaven has a limited variety of fruits (55:68).

Allegorically, the pure spouses readily join their spouses in the High Heaven (55:56), while the dwellers of the Lower Heaven must go fetch their spouses (55:72).

Yet, even the Lower Heaven is an incredibly fantastic prize for those who are fortunate enough to escape Hell and end up in the Lower Heaven (3:185)— going to the Lower Heaven is a great triumph. People who depart this life before reaching their 40th birthday, and did not sufficiently develop their souls, will go to the Lower Heaven (46:15, Appendices 11 & 32). The High Heaven is reserved for those who believed, led a righteous life, and developed their souls sufficiently.

> **Whoever succeeds in barely missing Hell, and is admitted into Heaven, has attained a great triumph.** [3:185]

****

Appendix 6

Greatness of God

We learn from Verse 39:67 that God's greatness is far beyond human comprehension—the verse states that all seven universes are "folded within God's hand."

Supported by the Quran's formidable mathematical code, we are taught that our universe is the smallest and innermost of seven universes (41:12, 55:33, 67:5, & 72:8-12). Meanwhile, our scientific advances have shown us that our galaxy, the Milky Way, is 100,000 light years across, and that our universe contains a billion such galaxies and a billion trillion stars, plus countless decillions of heavenly bodies. Our universe is estimated to span distances in excess of 20,000,000,000 light years.

Count the Stars!

If we take only a quintillion [1,000,000,000,000,000,000] of the stars and simply count them [from 0 to quintillion] one count per second, day and night, this will take 32 billion years (more than the age of the universe). That is how long it will take to just "count" them; but God "created" them. Such is the greatness of God.

We can appreciate the vastness of our universe if we imagine going on a space odyssey. When we leave the planet Earth towards the sun, at the speed of light, we reach the sun after 93,000,000 miles and 8 minutes. It will take us more than 50,000 years at the speed of light to exit our galaxy. From the outer limit of the Milky Way, our planet Earth is invisible. Not even the most powerful telescope can detect our tiny "Earth."

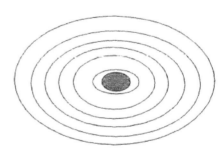

We have to spend more than 2,000,000 years at the speed of light to reach our next-door galaxy. At least 10,000,000,000 years, at the speed of light, must be spent to reach the outer limit of our universe. From the outer limit of our universe, even the Milky Way is like a speck of dust in a large room.

The second universe surrounds our universe. The third universe is larger than the second, and so on. More accurately, our universe should be considered the seventh universe, surrounded by the sixth universe, which is surrounded by the fifth universe, and so on. Can you imagine the vastness of the first, outermost universe? No number exists to describe the circumference of the first universe. This incomprehensible vastness is "within the fist of God's hand." From the outer limit of the outermost universe, where is the planet Earth? How significant is it? On the infinitesimal mote called Earth, such minuscule creatures as Mary, Jesus, and Muhammad lived. Yet, some people set up these powerless humans as gods!

God's greatness is represented not only by the fact that He holds the seven universes in His hand, but also by the fact that He fully controls every atom, even subatomic components, everywhere in the greater universe (6:59, 10:61, & 34:3).

****

Appendix 7
Why Were We Created ?

We are in this world because we committed a horrendous crime, and this life is our chance to redeem ourselves, denounce our crime, and rejoin God's kingdom.

It all began a few billion years ago when "a feud arose in the Heavenly Society" (38:69). One of the high-ranking creatures, Satan, entertained supercilious thoughts that his God-given powers qualified him to be a god besides God. He thus challenged God's absolute authority. Not only was Satan's idea blasphemous, it was wrong—only God, and no one else, possesses the qualifications and ability to be a god. Consequent to Satan's blasphemy, a division occurred in the Heavenly Society, and all constituents of God's kingdom became classified into four categories:

1. Angels: Creatures who upheld God's absolute authority.
2. Animals: Creatures who rebelled but then accepted God's invitation to repent.
3. Jinns: Creatures who agreed with Satan; that he is capable of being a "god."
4. Humans: Creatures who did not make up their minds; they failed to make a firm stand with God's absolute authority.

The Most Merciful

The angels expected God to banish the creatures who did not uphold His absolute authority (2:30). But God is Most Merciful; He decided to give us a chance to denounce our mistake, and informed the angels that He knew what they did not know (2:30). God knew that some creatures deserved a chance to be redeemed.

If you claim the ability to fly a plane, the best way to test your claim is to give you a plane and ask you to fly it. This is precisely what God decided to do in response to Satan's claim. God created seven vast universes, then informed the angels that He was appointing Satan as a god on the tiny mote called "Earth" (2:30). The Quranic accounts related to appointing Satan as a temporary "god" (36:60) confirm the previous scripture.

God's plan called for creating death (67:1-2), then bringing the humans and jinns into this world. Thus, they start over without any biases, and exercise full freedom to uphold God's absolute authority or Satan's polytheistic theory. To make this crucial decision, every human being receives a message from God advocating His absolute authority, as well as a message from Satan pushing his polytheistic principles.

To give us a headstart, the Most Merciful gathered all the human beings before Him, prior to sending us to this world, and we bore witness that He alone is our Lord and Master (7:172). Thus, upholding God's absolute authority is a natural instinct that is an integral part of every human being.

After putting the rebels to death, the souls of humans and jinns were placed in a special depository. God then created the appropriate bodies to house the souls of jinns and humans during the test period. The first jinn body was made from fire,

> You, Lucifer, said in your heart:
> "I will scale the heavens.
> Above the stars of God.
> I will set up my throne.
> I will take my seat
> on the Mount of Congregation,
> in the recesses of the North.
> I will ascend above the tops of the clouds;
> I will be like the Most High!"
>   [Isaiah 14:13-15]
>
> The devil then took Jesus up a very high mountain and displayed before him all the kingdoms of the world in their magnificence, promising: "All these will I bestow on you if you prostrate yourself in homage before me." At this, Jesus said to him, "Away with you, Satan! Scripture has it:
> 'You shall worship the Lord your God; Him ALONE shall you adore.' "
>   [Matthew 4:8-10] & [Luke 4:5-8]

and Satan was assigned to that body (15:27). The first human body was created from earthly material, clay (15:26), and God assigned the first human soul to that body. The divine plan called for the angels to serve the humans on earth—guard them, drive the wind and rain for them, distribute provisions, etc. This fact is stated in the Quran allegorically: "Your Lord said to the angels, 'Fall prostrate before Adam.' " Satan of course refused to have anything to do with serving the human race (2:34, 7:11, 17:61, 18:50, 20:116).

While Adam's body remained on earth, the real person, the soul, was admitted into Heaven in the outermost universe. God gave Adam certain commandments, represented by the forbidden tree, and Satan was appointed as Adam's companion to deliver to Adam his satanic message. The rest is history.

Every time a human being is born, a human person is assigned to the new baby from the depository of souls. God assigns the souls in accordance with His knowledge (28:68). Every soul deserves to be assigned to a certain body, and live under certain circumstances. God alone knows which souls are good and which souls are evil. Our children are assigned to our homes in accordance with God's plan.

An independent jinn soul is also assigned to the new human being to represent Satan's point of view. While the physical body of any jinn is reproduced from the parent jinns, the jinn soul is that of an independent individual. Jinns are descendants of Satan (7:27, 18:50). The assigned jinn remains with the human being from birth to death, and serves as the main witness on the Day of Judgment (50:23). A continuous debate takes place in our heads between the human soul and the jinn soul until both of them are convinced of one point of view.

The Original Sin

Contrary to common belief, the "Original Sin" was not Adam's violation of God's law when he ate from the forbidden tree. The original sin was our failure to uphold God's absolute authority during the Great Feud. If the human person convinces his or her jinn companion to denounce that original sin, and uphold God's absolute authority, both creatures are redeemed to God's eternal kingdom on the Day of Judgment. But if the jinn companion convinces the human being to uphold Satan's idolatrous views, then both creatures are exiled forever from God's kingdom.

To promote his point of view, Satan and his representatives advocate the idolization of such powerless creatures as Muhammad, Jesus, Mary, and the saints. Since we are here due to our polytheistic tendencies, most of us are easy prey for Satan.

Satan's incompetence as a "god" has already been proven by the prevalence of chaos, disease, accidents, misery, and war throughout his dominion (36:66). On the other hand, the human beings who denounce Satan, uphold God's absolute authority, and refrain from idolizing powerless and dead creatures like Jesus and Muhammad, are restored to God's protection—they enjoy a perfect life here in this world and forever.

Because our life in this world is a series of tests designed to expose our polytheistic ideas, idol worship is the only unforgivable offense (4:48, 116). The world is divinely designed to manifest our decision to uphold either God's absolute authority, or Satan's idolatrous views (67:1-2). The day and the night change constantly to test our willingness to uphold God's laws by observing the Dawn Prayer and fasting during the hottest and longest days. Only those who are totally certain about God's absolute authority are redeemed (26:89).

$$\ast\ast\ast\ast\ast\ast\ast\ast\ast\ast\ast\ast\ast\ast\ast\ast\ast\ast\ast\ast\ast\ast$$

Appendix 8

The Myth of Intercession

To believe that anyone, other than God, can intercede on our behalf to have our sins forgiven or our wishes fulfilled, is to set up partners with God. This is idolatry. The Quran proclaims that "All intercession belongs to God" (39:44), and that there will be "no intercession on the Day of Judgment" (2:254).

The myth of intercession is one of Satan's most effective tricks to dupe millions of people into idol worship. Millions of Christians believe that Jesus will intercede for them at God, and millions of Muslims believe that Muhammad will intercede on their behalf. Consequently, these people idolize Jesus and Muhammad.

The concept of intercession is utterly illogical. Those who believe in Muhammad's intercession, for example, claim that he will ask God to forgive them and admit them into Paradise. They imagine Muhammad on the Day of Judgment choosing the candidates for his intercession. If you ask those who believe in intercession: "How will Muhammad recognize those who deserve his intercession?" they tell you, "God will tell him!" According to this concept, a person will go to Muhammad and request his intercession. Muhammad will then ask God whether this person deserves his intercession or not. God will inform Muhammad that the person deserves to go to Paradise. Muhammad will then turn around and tell God that the person deserves to go to Paradise! The blasphemy is obvious; those who believe in intercession make God a secretary of their idol Muhammad. God be glorified.

Since the Quran is the most accurate book, it acknowledges that everyone in Paradise will intercede on behalf of his or her loved ones: "Please God, admit my mother into Paradise." This intercession will work if the person's mother deserves to go to Paradise (2:255, 20:109, 21:28). Thus, intercession, though it will take place in this manner, is utterly useless.

We learn from the Quran that Abraham, God's beloved servant, could not intercede on behalf of his father (9:114). Noah could not intercede on behalf of his son (11:46). Muhammad could not intercede on behalf of his uncle (111:1-3) or relatives (9:80). What makes anyone think that a prophet or a saint will intercede on behalf of a perfect stranger?! See 2:48, 123; 6:51, 70, 94; 7:53; 10:3; 19:87; 26:100; 30:13; 32:4; 36:23; 39:44; 40:18; 43:86; 53:26 & 74:48. Muhammad's intercession is in 25:30.

****

Appendix 9
Abraham: Original Messenger of Islam

One of the prevalent myths is that Muhammad was the founder of Islam. Although Islam, total submission to God alone, is the only religion recognized by God since the time of Adam (3:19, 85), Abraham is reported in the Quran as the first user of the word "Islam" (Submission) and the one who called us "Muslims", i.e., Submitters (22:78). Abraham's exemplary submission to God is demonstrated by his famous willingness to sacrifice his only son, Ismail, when he thought that that was God's command. As it turns out, such a command was in fact from Satan.

God Never Ordered Abraham to Sacrifice His Son

God is the Most Merciful. He never violates His own law (7:28). Any person who believes that the Most Merciful ordered Abraham to kill his son cannot possibly make it to God's Heaven. Such evil thought about God is grossly blasphemous. Nowhere in the Quran do we see that God ordered Abraham to kill his son. On the contrary, God intervened to save Abraham and Ismail from Satan's plot (37:107), and He told Abraham: "You believed the dream" (37:105). Undoubtedly, it was a dream inspired by Satan. God's irrevocable law is: "God never advocates sin" (7:28).

Millat Ibrahim

Islam is called *"Millat Ibrahim"* (The Religion of Abraham) throughout the

Quran (2:130, 135; 3:95; 4:125; 6:161; 12:37-38; 16:123; 21:73; 22:78). Moreover, the Quran informs us that Muhammad was a follower of Abraham (16:123).

Due to a general unawareness of the fact that Abraham was the original messenger of Islam, many so-called Muslims challenge God: "If the Quran is complete and fully detailed (as claimed by God), where can we find the number of *Rak'ahs* (units) in each contact prayer (*Salat*)?" We learn from the Quran that all religious practices of Islam (Submission) were already established before the Quran's revelation (8:35, 9:54, 16:123, 21:73, 22:27, 28:27). Verse 16:123 is direct proof that all religious practices in Islam were intact when Muhammad was born. Muhammad was enjoined to "follow the religion of Abraham." If I ask you to buy a color TV, it is assumed that you know what a color TV is. Similarly, when God enjoined Muhammad to follow the practices of Abraham (16:123), such practices must have been well known.

Another proof of divine preservation of the Islamic practices given to Abraham is the "Universal Acceptance" of such practices. There is no dispute concerning the number of *Rak'ahs* in all five daily prayers. This proves the divine preservation of *Salat*. The Quran's mathematical code confirms the number of *Rak'ahs* in the five prayers 2, 4, 4, 3, and 4, respectively. The number 24434 is a multiple of 19.

The Quran deals only with practices that were distorted. For example, the distorted ablution is restored in 5:6 to its original four steps. The tone of voice during the contact prayers (*Salat*) was distorted—many Muslims pray silently. This was corrected in the Quran, 17:110. The fasting during Ramadan was modified in the Quran to allow intercourse during the night (2:187). *Zakat* is restored in 6:141, and *Hajj* is restored to the four correct months (see Appendix 15).

✱✱✱✱✱✱✱✱✱✱✱✱✱✱✱✱✱✱✱✱

Appendix 10
God's Usage of the Plural Tense

In the English speaking world, where the trinity doctrine is prevalent, some people are intrigued by God's usage of the plural tense in the Quran. The overwhelming message of the Quran, where there is absolutely no compromise is that "GOD IS ONE" (2:133, 163; 4:171; 5:73; 6:19; 9:31; 12:39; 13:16; 14:48, 52; 16:22, 51; 18:110; 21:108; 22:34; 37:4; 38:65; 39:4; 40:16; 41:6; 112:1).

Whenever the first person plural form is used by the Almighty, it invariably indicates participation of other entities, such as the angels. For example, the revelation of this Quran involved participation of the angel Gabriel and the prophet Muhammad. Hence the use of the plural form in 15:9: "*We* revealed this scripture, and *we* will preserve it." The plural form here simply reflects the fact that the angel Gabriel and the prophet Muhammad participated in the process of delivering the Quran.

Another example has to do with blowing the breath of life into Adam and Jesus. The creation of Adam took place in heaven and God directly blew into him the breath of life. Thus, the first person singular form is consistently used: "I blew into Adam from My spirit" (15:29, 38:72). The creation of Jesus, on the other hand, took place on earth, and Gabriel carried God's "word" to Mary. The plural form is consistently used when referring to the creation of Jesus (21:91, 66:12).

When God spoke to Moses directly, without the mediation of angels, we see that God is speaking exclusively in the singular tense: *"I am* God. There is no other god besides *Me.* You shall worship *Me* alone, and observe the regular contact prayers (*Salat*) to commemorate *Me."* (20:12-14).

Whenever the worship of God is mentioned, the singular tense is used (51:56).

****

Appendix 11

The Day of Resurrection

> The horn is blown, whereupon everyone in the heavens and the earth is struck unconscious, except those spared by God. Then it is blown a second time, whereupon they rise up. [39:68]

All generations of humans and jinns will be resurrected on this earth; about 150 billion of them. But we will not be earthbound. God teaches us through the example of the caterpillar; it turns into a pupa in the cocoon (grave), then exits the cocoon as an airborne butterfly. Similarly, we live here on earth, and when we exit the grave on the Day of Resurrection we will not be earthbound; like the butterfly (101:4).

The earth will shine with the light of God (39:69) as He comes to our universe, together with the angels (89:22). Since our universe is a temporary dominion for Satan, it cannot stand the physical presence of God (7:143). As the Almighty approaches, the stars will crash into one another (77:8, 81:2), and the earth will shatter under our feet (69:14, 89:21). These horrors will not worry the believers (21:103).

The High Heaven

Upon arrival of Almighty God, all the humans and jinns will be automatically stratified according to their degree of growth and development. Those who nourished their souls through worshiping God alone, believing in the Hereafter, and leading a righteous life will be strong enough to stay close to God; they will occupy the highest ranks (see Appendix 5).

The Lower Heaven

Those who developed their souls to a lesser degree, as well as those who die before the age of forty, will move downward to the Lower Heaven. They will go to the location where they can be as close to God as their degree of growth and development permits them to be.

The Purgatory

There will be people who nourished their souls just enough to spare them Hell, but not enough to enter the Lower Heaven. They are neither in Hell, nor in Heaven. They will implore God to admit them into the Lower Heaven (7:46-50). God will have mercy on them, and will merge the Purgatory into the Lower Heaven.

Hell

A new, eighth universe will be created to house those who run away from God due to their weakness; they failed to nourish and develop their souls (69:17). God does not put a single being in Hell; they go to it of their own volition (Appendix 5).

****

Appendix 12
Role of the Prophet Muhammad

The Prophet's sole mission was to deliver Quran, the whole Quran, and nothing but Quran (3:20; 5:48-50, 92, 99; 6:19; 13:40; 16:35, 82; 24:54; 29:18; 42:48; 64:12).

Delivering the Quran was such a momentous and noble mission that the Prophet did not have any time to do anything else. Moreover, the Prophet was enjoined in the strongest words from issuing any religious teachings besides the Quran (69:38-47). He was even enjoined from explaining the Quran (75:15-19)—God is the only teacher of the Quran (55:1-2) and the Quran is the best *Hadith* (39:23 & 45:6).

These Quranic facts are manifested in the historical reality that the words and actions *(Hadith & Sunna)* attributed to the Prophet did not appear until the second century after his death. The Quran has prophesied the fabrication of *Hadith* and *Sunna* by the Prophet's enemies (6:112-115). The Quran teaches us that it was God's will to permit the invention of *Hadith* and *Sunna* to serve as criteria for exposing those who believe only with their lips, not in their hearts. Those who are attracted to *Hadith* and *Sunna* are proven to be false believers (6:113). Ironically, the books of *Hadith* report the Prophet's orders to write down nothing from him except the Quran! Shown below are two such *Hadiths* taken from the Hadithists' most reliable sources, Sahih Muslim and Is-haah Ahmad Ibn Hanbal:

عَنْ أَبِى سَعِيدٍ الْخُدْرِىِّ رَضِىَ اللهُ عَنْهُ قَالَ : قَالَ رسُولُ اللهِ صَلَّى اللهُ

عَلَيْهِ وَسَلَّمَ : «لَاتَكْتُبُوا عَنِّى شَيْئاً سِوَى الْقُرْآنِ . مَنْ كَتَبَ شَيْئاً

سِوَى الْقُرْآنِ فَلْيَمْحُهُ »(١) .

The Prophet said, "Do not write down anything from me except the Quran."
[Ahmed, Vol. 1, Page 171, and Sahih Muslim]

عَنْ عَبْدِ الْمُطَّلِبِ بْنِ عَبْدِ اللهِ قَالَ : [دَخَلَ زَيْدُ بْنُ ثَابِتٍ رَضِيَ اللهُ

عَنْهُ عَلَى مُعَاوِيَةَ رَضِيَ اللهُ عَنْهُ ، فَحَدَّثَهُ حَدِيثاً ، فَأَمَرَ إِنْسَاناً أَنْ يَكْتُبَ ،

فَقَالَ زَيْدٌ : إِنَّ رَسُولَ اللهِ صَلَّى اللهُ عَلَيْهِ وَسَلَّمَ نَهَى أَنْ نَكْتُبَ شَيْئاً

مِنْ حَدِيثِهِ ، فَمَحَاهُ] .

This Hadith states that the Prophet maintained his anti-Hadith stand until death.   [Ahmed, Vol. 1, Page 192]

****

Appendix 13
The First Pillar of Islam (Submission): "Laa Elaaha Ellaa Allah" (No god except God)

Verse 3:18 states the First Pillar of Islam (Submission): "God bears witness that there is no other god besides Him, and so do the angels and those who possess knowledge."

This most crucial pillar has been distorted. Millions of Muslims have adopted Satan's polytheistic version, and insist upon mentioning the name of Muhammad besides the name of God. However, the Quran's great criterion in 39:45 stamps such Muslims as disbelievers: "When God ALONE is mentioned, the hearts of those who do disbelieve in the Hereafter shrink with aversion, but when others are mentioned with Him, they become satisfied."

I have conducted extensive research into this criterion, and I have reached a startling conclusion: the idol worshipers who do not uphold the First Pillar of Islam as dictated in 3:18 are forbidden by God from uttering the correct *Shahadah.* They simply cannot say: *"Ash-hadu Allaa Elaaha Ellaa Allah"* by it-self, without mentioning the name of Muhammad. Try it with any idol worshiper who claims to be a Muslim. Challenge them to say: *"Ash-hadu Allaa Elaaha Ellaa Allah."* They can never say it. Since this is the religion of Abraham (2:130, 135; 3:95; 4:125; 6:161; 12:37-38; 16:123; 22:78; Appendix 9), the ONLY creed must be *"LAA ELAAHA ELLAA ALLAH* (there is no god except the One God)". Muhammad did not exist on earth before Abraham.

A Gross Blasphemy

There is no greater blasphemy than distorting the Quran to idolize the prophet Muhammad against his will. Verse 19 of Sura "Muhammad" (47:19) states: "You shall know that there is no god except the one God." Shown below is a photocopy of the regular logo of a Muslim publication *THE REVIEW OF RELIGIONS* (The London Mosque, 16 Gressenhall Road, London SW18 5QL, England). Using the Quran's calligraphic style, the publishers of *THE REVIEW*

OF RELIGIONS added the phrase *"Muhammad Rasool Allah"* in such a way that gives a false impression that such is the Quranic statement of 47:19. What a blasphemy!

You shall know that there is no god besides the One God, Allah. Muhammad is a messenger of God.
[The blasphemy]

Typical Example of the Distorted Islam

****

Appendix 14

Predestination

We are absolutely free to believe or disbelieve in God. It is God's will that we will freely (18:29, 25:57, 73:19, 74:37, 76:29, 78:39, 80:12).

After committing our original sin (Appendix 7), God gave us a chance to denounce our crime and accept His absolute authority (33:72). But we decided that we wanted to see a demonstration of Satan's competence as a god. Many people protest the fact that God has created them, to put them through this gruesome test. Obviously, such people are not aware that [1] they have committed a horrendous crime (Introduction & Appendix 7), and [2] that they were given a chance to denounce their crime and redeem themslves, but they chose to go through the test.

We learn from 57:22 that our lives, along with everything else around us, are pre-recorded on something like a videotape. God fully knows what kind of decision each of us is destined to make; He knows which of us are going to Heaven and which are going to Hell. Even before we were born into this world, God knew which souls are good and which souls are evil. As far as God's omniscience is concerned, we can imagine a stamp on everyone's forehead that says "Heaven" or "Hell." Yet, as far as we are concerned, we are totally free to side with God's absolute authority, or Satan's polytheistic views. Predestination, therefore, is a fact as far as God is concerned, not as far as we are concerned.

This understanding explains the numerous verses stating that "God guides whomever He wills, and misleads whomever He wills." Based on His knowledge, God assigns our souls to the circumstances that we deserve. When God said to the angels, "I know what you do not know" (2:30), this meant that some of us deserved a chance to redeem ourselves. One example of God's guidance for those who deserve guidance is found in 21:51: "We granted Abraham his guidance, for we were fully aware of him." In other words, God knew that Abraham was a good soul who deserved to be guided, and God granted him his guidance and understanding. Another good example is stated in 12:24. Joseph fell for the Egyptian nobleman's wife, and almost committed adultery "if it were not that he saw a sign from his Lord." God teaches us in 12:24 that He "diverted evil and sin from Joseph, for he was one of My devoted worshipers." Was it Joseph who controlled his lust? Or, was it God's protection from sin that rendered him chaste? Such is predestination.

****

Appendix 15

Religious Duties: A Gift From God

When Abraham implored God in 14:40, he did not ask for wealth or health; the gift he implored for was: "Please God, make me one who observes the contact prayers (*Salat*)." The religious duties instituted by God are in fact a great gift from Him. They constitute the nourishment required for the growth and development of our souls. Without such nourishment, we cannot survive the immense energy associated with God's physical presence on the Day of Judgment. Belief in God does not by itself guarantee our redemption; we must also nourish our souls (6:158, 10:90-92). Additionally, 15:99 states that observing the religious duties instituted by God is our means of attaining certainty: "Worship your Lord in order to attain certainty."

The Contact Prayers (Salat)

The five daily contact prayers are the main meals for the soul. While a soul may attain some growth and development by leading a righteous life, and without observing the contact prayers, this would be like surviving on snacks without regular meals.

We learn from 2:37 that we can establish contact with God by uttering the specific Arabic words given to us by God. Sura 1, The Key, is a mathematically composed combination of sounds that unlocks the door between us and God:

1. The Dawn Prayer must be observed during two hours before sunrise (11:114, 24:58).
2. The Noon Prayer is due when the sun declines from its highest point at noon (17:78).
3. The Afternoon Prayer can be observed during the 3-4 hours preceding sunset (2:238).
4. The Sunset Prayer becomes due after sunset (11:114).
5. The Night Prayer can be observed after the twilight disappears from the sky (24:58).
* The Friday noon congregational prayer is an obligatory duty upon every Submitting man and woman (62:9). Failure to observe the Friday Prayer is a gross offense.

Each contact prayer is valid if observed anytime during the period it becomes due until the next prayer becomes due. Once missed, a given contact prayer is a missed opportunity that cannot be made up; one can only repent and ask forgiveness. The five prayers consist of 2, 4, 4, 3, and 4 units *(Rak'ahs),* respectively.

The proof that *Salat* was already established through Abraham is found in

8:35, 9:54, 16:123, & 21:73. This most important duty in Islam (Submission) has been so severely distorted that the contact prayers (*Salat*) have become a practice in idolatry for the vast majority of Muslims. Although the Quran commands that our contact prayers must be devoted to God alone (20:14; 39:3, 45), today's Muslims insist on commemorating "Muhammad and his family" and "Abraham and his family" during their prayers. This renders the prayers null and void (39:65).

The following text, pertaining to the miracles confirming the contact prayers, is excerpted from the January 1990 issues of the Submitter's Perspective (the regular and special bonus issues), as written by Dr. Rashad Khalifa:

AWESOME MATHEMATICAL MIRACLE CONFIRMS ALL THE 5 CONTACT PRAYERS

[1] Sura 1 is God's gift to us, to establish contact with Him (Salat). Write the sura number and the number of verses next to each other and you get 17, the total number of units in the 5 daily prayers.

[2] Let us write down the sura number, followed by the number of every verse in the sura. This is what we get:

1 1 2 3 4 5 6 7   This number is a multiple of 19.

[3] Now, let us replace each verse number by the number of letters in that verse. This is what we get:

Properties of Sura 1, The Key

Verse No	No of Letters	Gematrical Value
1	19	786
2	17	581
3	12	618
4	11	241
5	19	836
6	18	1072
7	43	6009

1 19 17 12 11 19 18 43 also a multiple of 19. Theoretically, one can alter the letters of Sura 1, and still keep the same number of letters, However, the following mathematical phenomena rule out that possibility. For the gematrical value of every single letter is taken into consideration. Here it is:

[4] Let us include the gematrical value of every verse, and write it down following the number of letters in each verse:

1 19 786 17 581 12 618 11 241 19 836 18 1072 43 6009 also a multiple of 19.

[5] Now, let us add the number of each verse, to be followed by the number of letters in that verse, then the gematrical value of that verse. This is what we get:

1 1 19 786 2 17 581 3 12 618 4 11 241 5 19 836 6 18 1072 7 43 6009 a multiple of 19.

[6] Instead of the gematrical values of every verse, let us write down the gematrical values of every individual letter in Sura 1. This truly awesome miracle, shows that the resulting long number, consisting of 274 digits, is also a multiple of 19. ALLAHU AKBAR.

1 7 1 19 2 60 40 1 30 30 5 1 30 200 8 40 50 1 30 200 8 10 40 2 17 ... 50

This number starts with the sura number, followed by the number of verses in the sura, followed by the verse number, followed by the number of letters in this verse, followed by the gematrical values of every letter in this verse, followed by the number of the next verse, followed by the number of letters in this verse, followed by the gematrical values of every letter in this verse, and so on to the end of the sura. Thus, the last component is 50, the value of "N" (last letter).

[7] Since I cannot write very long numbers here, let us substitute [*] for the long number consisting of the number of every verse, followed by the number of letters in the verse, followed by the gematrical value of every individual letter in the verse. If we write down the number of the sura, followed by its number of verses, we get 17, the number of units (Rak'aas) in the 5 daily prayers. Next to the 17, write down the number of the first prayer (1), followed by its number of Rak'aas, which is 2, then two [*]'s, followed by the number of the second prayer (2), followed by the number of Rak'aas in this second prayer (4), followed by four [*]'s, and so on. Not only is the resulting long number a multiple of 19, but also the number of its component digits is 4636 (19x244).... Please note that any representation of Sura 1 can replace the [*] without affecting the outcome; all of them give multiples of 19. For example, a short representation of "The Key" consists of the Sura number (1), followed by the number of verses (7), followed by the total number of letters in Sura 1 (139) followed by the total gematrical value of the whole sura (10143). The resulting number (1713910143) can also represent [*].

1712[*][*]24[*][*][*][*]34[*][*][*][*]43[*][*][*]54[*][*][*][*]

CONFIRMATION OF FRIDAY PRAYERS

[8] Since the Friday prayer consists of two sermons and two Rak'aas (total is still 4 units), we read only 15 "Keys" on Friday, compared with 17 on the other days. Abdullah Arik discovered that if we replace the 17 by 15 in the long number in [7] and remove two "Keys" from the noon prayer, we still get a multiple of 19. This confirms the Friday Prayer, at noon, with 2 "Keys." The long number shown below represents Friday's five payers; it is a multiple of 19.

1512[*][*]24[*][*]34[*][*][*][*]43[*][*][*][*]54[*][*][*][*]

"THE KEY" (Al-Fateha) MUST BE RECITED IN ARABIC

[9] The first sura in the Quran is mathematically composed in a manner that challenges and stumps the greatest mathematicians on earth. Now we appreciate the fact that when we recite Sura 1, "The Key," during our Contact Prayers, something happens in the universe, and we establish contact with our Creator. The result is perfect happiness, now and forever. By contacting our Almighty Creator 5 times a day, we nourish and develop our souls in preparation for the Big Day when we meet God. Only those who nourish their souls will be able to withstand and enjoy the physical presence of Almighty God.

All submitters, of all nationalities, recite the words of "The Key" which were

	Word	Letter	Value
	written by God Himself, and given to us to establish contact with Him (2:37).		
1.	Bism	B	2
2.	Bism	M	40
3.	Rahman	M	40
4.	Rahim	M	40
5.	Al-Hamdu	M	40
6.	Rub	B	2
7.	'Alamin	M	40
8.	Rahman	M	40
9.	Rahim	M	40
10.	Malik	M	40
11.	Yawm	M	40
12.	Na'budu	B	2
13.	Mustaqim	M	40
14.	Mustaqim	M	40
15.	An'amta	M	40
16.	'Alayhim	M	40
17.	Maghdub	M	40
18.	Maghdub	B	2
19.	'Alayhim	M	40
			608 (19x32)

written by God Himself, and given to us to establish contact with Him (2:37).

Edip Yuksel's discovery adds to the awesomeness of "The Key" and proclaims clearly that it must be recited in Arabic.

When you recite "The Key" in Arabic, your lips touch each other precisely 19 times.

Your lips touch each other where the letters "B" and "M" occur. There are 4 "B's" and 15 "M's" and this adds up to 19. The gematrical value of the 4 "B's" is 4x2 = 8, and the gematrical value of the 15 "M's" is 15x40 = 600. The total gematrical value of the 4 "B's" and 15 "M's" is 608, that is 19x32.

CONFIRMATION OF THE 5 DAILY PRAYERS, NUMBER OF BOWINGS (Ruku'), PROSTRATIONS (Sujood), and TASHAHHUD

[10] One of the common challenges...is: "If the Quran is complete and detailed (as claimed in 6:19, 38 & 114), where are the details of the Contact Prayers (Salat)?" These people ask this question because they are not aware that the Quran informs us that the Contact Prayers came from Abraham (21:73 & 22:78). If we write down the numbers of the prayers with their bowings, prostrations and Tashahhuds, we get:

1 1 2 2 4 1 2 4 4 8 2 3 4 4 8 2 4 3 3 6 2 5 4 4 8 2

This long number consists of the sura that we recite in the 5 prayers (1) followed by the number of the first prayer (1), then the number of "Keys" that we recite in this prayer (2), then the number of bowings (Ruku') (2), then the number of prostrations (4), then the number of Tashahhuds (in the sitting position) (1), then the number of the second prayer (2), then the number of "Keys" that we recite in the second prayer (4), then the number of bowings (Ruku') in this prayer (4), then the number of prostrations (8), then the number of Tashahhuds (2), then the number of the third prayer (3), and so on to the last prayer. This long number is a multiple of 19, and this confirms the minutest details of the prayers, even the numbers of Ruku', Sujud, and Tashahhud.

The Obligatory Charity (Zakat)

Zakat must be given away "on the day of harvest" (6:141). Whenever we receive "net income," we must set aside 2.5% and give it to the specified recipients—the parents, relatives, orphans, the poor, and the traveling alien, in this order (2:215). The vital importance of *Zakat* is reflected in God's law: "My mercy encompasses all things, but I will specify it for the righteous who give *Zakat*" (7:156).

Zakat must be carefully calculated and given away on a regular basis whenever we receive any income. Government taxes should be deducted, but not other expenses such as debts, mortgages, and living expenses. If one does not know needy persons, he or she may give the Zakat to a mosque or charitable organization with the distinct purpose of helping poor people. Charities given to mosques or hospitals or organizations cannot be considered *Zakat.*

Fasting

The full details of fasting are given in 2:183-187.

Pilgrimage: Hajj & 'Umrah

Once in a lifetime, Hajj and *'Umrah* are decreed for those who can afford it. Pilgrimage commemorates Abraham's exemplary submission to God (Appendix 9), and must be observed during the four Sacred Months—Zul-Hijjah, Muharram, Safar, & Rabi' I (12th, 1st, 2nd, 3rd months) (2:197; 9:2, 36). *'Umrah* can be observed any time. Like all other duties in Islam, Hajj has been distorted. Most Muslims observe Hajj only during a few days in Zul-Hijjah, and they consider Rajab, Zul-Qi'dah, Zul-Hijjah, and Muharram (7th, 11th, 12th, 1st months) to be the Sacred Months. This is a distortion that is strongly condemned (9:37).

The pilgrimage begins with a bath or shower, followed by a state of sanctity called *"Ihraam,"* where the male pilgrim wears seamless sheets of material, and the woman wears a modest dress (2:196). Throughout Hajj, the pilgrim abstains from sexual intercourse, vanities such as shaving and cutting the hair, arguments, misconduct, and bad language (2:197). Cleanliness, bathing, and regular hygiene practices are encouraged. Upon arrival at the Sacred Mosque in Mecca, the pilgrim walks around the Ka'bah seven times, while glorifying and praising God (2:125, 22:26-29). The common formula is: *"Labbayka Allaahumma Labbayk"* (My God, I have responded to You). *"Labbayka Laa Shareeka Laka Labbayk"* (I have responded to You, and I proclaim that there is no other god besides You; I have responded to You). The next step is to walk the half-mile distance between the knolls of Safa and Marwah seven times, with occasional trotting (2:158). This completes the *'Umrah* portion of the pilgrimage.

The pilgrim then goes to 'Arafat to spend a day of worship, meditation, and glorification of God, from dawn to sunset (2:198). After sunset, the pilgrim goes to Muzdalifah where the Night Prayer is observed, and 21 pebbles are picked up for the symbolic stoning of Satan at Mina. From Muzdalifah, the pilgrim goes to Mina to spend two or three days (2:203). On the first morning at Mina, the pilgrim offers an animal sacrifice to feed the poor and to commemorate God's intervention to save Ismail and Abraham from Satan's trick (37:107, Appendix

9). The stoning ceremonies symbolize rejection of Satan's polytheism and are done by throwing seven pebbles at each of three stations, while glorifying God (15:34). The pilgrim then returns to Mecca and observes a farewell circumvolution of the Ka'bah seven times.

Unfortunately, most of today's Muslim pilgrims make it a custom to visit the prophet Muhammad's tomb where they commit the most flagrant acts of idolatry and thus nullify their Hajj. The Quran consistently talks about "The Sacred Mosque," while today's Muslims talk about "The Two Sacred Mosques"! In a glaring act of idolatry, the Muslims have set up Muhammad's tomb as another "Sacred Mosque"! This is a blasphemous violation of the Quran, and, ironically, even violates *Hadith.* The *Hadith* shown below illustrates this strange irony:

لَعْنَةُ اللهِ عَلَى الْيَهُودِ وَالنَّصَارَى اتَّخَذُوا قُبُورَ أَنْبِيَائِهِمْ مَسَاجِدَ

Translation of this false statement: "God has cursed the Jews and Christians for turning the tombs of their prophets into mosques."
[Bukhari, Nawawi Edition, Vol. 6, Page 14]

Physical Benefits

In addition to their invaluable spiritual benefits, there is a plethora of physical, economic, and health benefits from observing the contact prayers (*Salat*), obligatory charity (*Zakat*), fasting during the month of Ramadan, and Hajj.

Observing the Dawn prayer interrupts long periods of stillness during sleep; this is now proven to help prevent arthritis. Also, getting up early in the morning helps combat depression and other psychological problems. The prostration position which is repeated during the contact prayers expands the blood vessels in our brains to accommodate more blood, and this prevents headaches. The repeated bending of the back and the joints is a healthful exercise. All these are scientifically established facts.

The ablutions required prior to the contact prayers encourage us to use the toilet more frequently. This habit protects us from a common and devastating cancer, colon cancer. Harmful chemicals are excreted in the urine and fecal matter. If these excretions are kept in the colon for prolonged periods of time, the harmful materials are re-absorbed into the body, and cause cancer.

Fasting during the month of Ramadan restores our expanded stomachs to their normal sizes, lowers our blood pressure through temporary dehydration, rids the body of harmful toxins, gives our kidneys a much needed rest, and reduces our weight by removing excessive and harmful fat.

Zakat charity and Hajj pilgrimage have far reaching economic and social benefits.

Appendix 16

Dietary Prohibitions

The Quran teaches that God is extremely displeased with those who prohibit anything that was not specifically prohibited in the Quran (16:112-116). The upholding of any prohibitions not specifically mentioned in the Quran is tantamount to idolatry (6:142-152). Such prohibitions represent some other god(s) besides God. If you worship God ALONE, you will uphold His teachings ALONE and honor the commandments and prohibitions instituted only by Him.

The absolute specificity of dietary prohibitions in the Quran is best illustrated in 6:145-146. We learn from these two verses that when God prohibits "meat," He prohibits "meat" and nothing else, and when He prohibits "fat," that is what He specifically prohibits. These two verses inform us that "the meat" of pigs is prohibited, not "the fat." Obviously, God knew that in many countries, lard would be used in baked goods and other food products, and that such usage does not render the foods *Haraam* (prohibited). The Quran specifically prohibits four meats (2:173, 5:3, 6:142-145, and 16:112):

Say, "I do not find in what was revealed to me
anything prohibited for any eater
unless it is (1) carrion, (2) running blood,
(3) the meat of pigs, for it is unclean, and
(4) meat blasphemously dedicated to other than God."
If one is forced to eat these
without being malicious or deliberate,
then your Lord is Forgiver, Most Merciful.   [6:145]

****

Appendix 17

Death

Death is a great mystery to most people. Not so for the students of the Quran. We learn that death is exactly like sleeping; complete with dreams (6:60, 40:46). The period between death and resurrection passes like one night of sleep (2:259; 6:60; 10:45; 16:21; 18:11, 19, 25; 30:55).

At the moment of death, everyone knows his or her destiny; Heaven or Hell. For the disbelievers, death is a horrible event; the angels beat them on the faces and rear ends as they snatch away their souls (8:50, 47:27, 79:1).

Consistently, the Quran talks about two deaths, the first death took place when we failed to make a stand with God's absolute authority (Appendix 7). That first death lasted until we were born into this world. The second death terminates our life in this world (2:28, 22:66, 40:11).

Note: The following is a reproduction of the lead article from the February, 1990 issue of the <u>Submitters Perspective,</u> the montly bulletin of United Submitters Inter-

completed and mailed ahead of time, in December, 1989. Dr. Khalifa was martyred on January 31, 1990 and his soul was taken directly to Paradise.

The Righteous Do Not Really Die
They Go Straight to Heaven

رَبَشِّرِ ٱلَّذِينَ ءَامَنُوا وَعَمِلُوا ٱلصَّـٰلِحَـٰتِ أَنَّ لَهُمْ جَنَّـٰتٍ تَجْرِى مِن تَحْتِهَا ٱلْأَنْهَـٰرُ كُلَّمَا رُزِقُوا مِنْهَا مِن ثَمَرَةٍ رِّزْقًا قَالُوا هَـٰذَا ٱلَّذِى رُزِقْنَا مِن قَبْلُ وَأُتُوا بِهِۦ مُتَشَـٰبِهًا وَلَهُمْ فِيهَآ أَزْوَٰجٌ مُّطَهَّرَةٌ وَهُمْ فِيهَا خَـٰلِدُونَ ﴿٢٥﴾

Give good news to those who believe and work righteousness that they will have gardens with flowing streams. When provided with provisions of fruits therein, they will say, "This is what was given to us in the past." They will be given similar provisions, and they will have pure spouses therein. They abide therein forever. (2:25)

وَلَا تَحْسَبَنَّ ٱلَّذِينَ قُتِلُوا فِى سَبِيلِ ٱللَّهِ أَمْوَٰتًۢا بَلْ أَحْيَآءٌ عِندَ رَبِّهِمْ يُرْزَقُونَ ﴿١٦٩﴾

Do not think that those who are killed in the cause of God are dead; they are alive at their Lord, being provided for. (3:169)

وَلَا تَقُولُوا لِمَن يُقْتَلُ فِى سَبِيلِ ٱللَّهِ أَمْوَٰتٌۢ بَلْ أَحْيَآءٌ وَلَـٰكِن لَّا تَشْعُرُونَ ﴿١٥٤﴾

Do NOT say about those who are killed in the cause of God, "They ar dead." For they are alive, but you do not perceive. (2:154)

يَـٰٓأَيُّهَا ٱلَّذِينَ ءَامَنُوا ٱسْتَجِيبُوا لِلَّهِ وَلِلرَّسُولِ إِذَا دَعَاكُمْ لِمَا يُحْيِيكُمْ

O you who believe, you shall respond to God and the messenger when he invites to what keeps you alive. (8:24)

وَٱلَّذِينَ هَاجَرُوا فِى سَبِيلِ ٱللَّهِ ثُمَّ قُتِلُوا أَوْ مَاتُوا لَيَرْزُقَنَّهُمُ ٱللَّهُ رِزْقًا حَسَنًا

Those who emigrate in the cause of God, then get killed or die, God will surely provide for them a good provision. (22:58)

لَا يَذُوقُونَ فِيهَا ٱلْمَوْتَ

They do not taste death, beyond the first death, and God spares them the retribution of Hell. (44:56)

إِلَّا ٱلْمَوْتَةَ ٱلْأُولَىٰ وَوَقَىٰهُمْ عَذَابَ ٱلْجَحِيمِ ﴿٥٦﴾

He was told, "Enter Paradise." He said, "I wish my people (on earth) know; that my Lord has forgiven me and honored me." (36:26-27)

قِيلَ ٱدْخُلِ ٱلْجَنَّةَ قَالَ يَـٰلَيْتَ قَوْمِى يَعْلَمُونَ ﴿٢٦﴾ بِمَا غَفَرَ لِى رَبِّى وَجَعَلَنِى مِنَ ٱلْمُكْرَمِينَ ﴿٢٧﴾

> The wages of sin is death [Romans 6:23]

As stated in 3:81 and 46:9, God's Messenger of the Covenant does not bring anything new; everything I receive and pass on to you is already in the Quran. However, the Quran is full of information that is kept by Almighty God for revelation at a specific time. Now is the time to look at the verses shown above and learn the great news: THE RIGHTEOUS DO NOT DIE; when their lives on this earth come to the predetermined end, the angel of death simply invites them to leave their earthly bodies and move on to Heaven, the same Paradise where Adam and Eve once lived. Heaven has been in existence since Adam and Eve. We learn from 89:27-30 that God invites the believers' souls: "Enter My Paradise."

MY OWN EXPERIENCE

When God's covenant with the prophets was fulfilled in accordance with 3:81, I was taken to Heaven where the righteous live NOW (4:69). While my body was down here on earth, I was in the same Paradise of Adam & Eve.

THE DISBELIEVERS

As for the disbelievers, they know at the moment of death that they are destined for Hell. The angels beat them up on the faces and rear ends (8:50 & 47:27), order them to evict their souls (6:93), then "snatch their souls" (79:1). The Quran teaches that the disbelievers go through 2 deaths (2:28 & 40:11). They will be put to death — a state of nothingness during which they see Hell day and

night in a continuous nightmare that lasts until the Day of Judgment (40:46). Hell is not yet in existence (40:46, 89:23).

Of Course, the Righteous Depart

As far as people on earth are concerned, the righteous "die." People do not realize that the righteous simply leave their bodies, and move on to Paradise. The verses shown above are self explanatory. They tell us that the righteous die only once — the one death we have already experienced as a consequence of the great feud (38:69). In 36:26-27, we see the best evidence that the righteous go to Paradise, while their friends and relatives are still living on earth. Like going to Hawaii and waiting for us there.

See also 16:32 & 6:60-62.

Appendix 18

Quran: All You Need For Salvation

The words of the Quran speak in 19:64, saying, "We come down in accordance with the commandments of your Lord. To Him belongs the past, present, and the future. Your Lord never forgets." God did not forget, for example, to tell us how to sleep (18:109, 31:27). Yet, the fabricators of such false doctrine as *Hadith & Sunna* have come up with religious teachings dictating to their followers how to sleep, and even how to cut your nails. The Sacred Mosque in Mecca and the illegal "Sacred Mosque" of Medina, hire some individuals to seek out the exhausted visitors and beat them with a stick if they fall asleep on the wrong side!

The Quran proclaims that the Quran is complete, perfect, and fully detailed (6:19, 38, 114, 115; 50:45), and that religious regulations not specifically instituted in the Quran constitute a religion other than Islam, i.e., Submission (42:21, 17:46). The true believers uphold the Quran, the whole Quran, and nothing but the Quran. This principle is confirmed by the Quran's mathematical code. Verse 46 of Sura 17 proclaims that we shall uphold the Quran ALONE. The word "ALONE" occurs in the Quran 6 times: 7:70, 17:46, 39:45, 40: 12 & 84, and 60:4. All these occurrences refer to God, except 17:46. When we add the numbers of suras and verses which refer to "GOD ALONE," we get 361, 19x19. This proves that 17:46 refers to "the Quran ALONE."

****

Appendix 19

Hadith & Sunna: Satanic Innovations

> **Which** *Hadith*, **other than God and His revelations, do they uphold?**
> **[45:6]**
> **The Quran is not a fabricated** *Hadith*; **...it details everything.**
> **[12:111]**
> **Some people uphold vain** *Hadith* **to divert others from the path of God.**
> **[31:6]**
> **The only** *Sunna* **to follow shall be God's** *Sunna.*
> **[17:77, 33:62, 48:23, 6:114]**

The Quran informs us that some enemies of the Prophet, described as "human and jinn devils," will fabricate lies and attribute them to the Prophet (6:112, 25:31). This is precisely what happened after the prophet Muhammad's death; *Hadith* (oral) and *Sunna* (actions) were invented and attributed to the Prophet. *Hadith* and *Sunna* are satanic innovations because they: [1] defy the divine assertions that the Quran is complete, perfect, fully detailed, and shall be the only source of religious guidance (6:19, 38, 114 & 45:6-7), [2] blaspheme against the Prophet and depict him as a vicious tyrant who did not uphold the Quran, and [3] create false doctrines based on superstition, ignorance, and indefensible nonsensical traditions. The prophet Muhammad was enjoined, in very strong words, from issuing any religious teachings besides the Quran (69:38-48).

Some Muslims compromise: "If a *Hadith* agrees with the Quran we will accept it, and if it contradicts the Quran, we will reject it!" Such premise proves that these people do not believe God's assertions that the Quran is "complete, perfect and fully detailed." The moment they seek guidance from anything besides the Quran, no matter how "right" it seems, they fall into Satan's trap (see 63:1). For they have rejected God's word and set up another god besides God (18:57). See Appendix 33.

The Quran's mathematical miracle provides mathematical evidence that the Quran shall be our only source of religious teachings. Here are just 2 examples:

1. " ما فرطنا فى الكتب من شئ = We did not leave anything out of this book," is in Verse 38 (19x2) and consists of 19 Arabic letters (6:38).

2. " انزل اليكم الكتب مفصلا = He sent down this book fully detailed," is in Verse 114 (19x6) and consists of 19 Arabic letters (6:114).

****

Appendix 20

Quran: Unlike Any Other Book

The Quran is God's Final Testament to the world, and He has pledged to protect it from the slightest distortion (15:9). Thus, the Quran is surrounded by invisible forces that guard it and serve it (13:39, 41:42, 42:24).

Unlike any other book, the Quran is taught by God (55:1-2); He teaches us what we need at the time we need it. This is why we read the Quran hundreds of times without getting bored. We can read a novel, for example, only once. But the Quran can be read an infinite number of times, and we derive new and valuable information from it every time. On the other hand, the insincere readers—those who read the Quran to find fault with it—are diverted from the Quran (7:146, 17:45, 18:57, 41:44). In fact, God's invisible forces help them find the faults they seek. Since the Quran is perfect, such "faults" serve only to reveal the stupidity of God's enemies.

God uses His own attributes to describe the Quran; He calls the Quran " *'Azeem* = Great" (15:87), *"Hakeem* = Full of wisdom" (36:2), *"Majid* = Glorious"* (50:1), and *"Karim* = Honorable" (56:77). What can we say?

Since the Quran is God's message to all the people, regardless of their language, the Quran is accessible to the believers, regardless of their language (41:44). This explains a profound phenomenon: the believers who do not know Arabic know the Quran better than the Arabic speaking unbelievers. Because of the invisible forces serving the Quran, it is readily and enjoyably accessible to the sincere believers, and utterly inaccessible to the unbelievers (17:45, 18:57, 56:79).

Appendix 21

Satan: Fallen Angel

In God's kingdom, certain creatures are necessarily given the powers needed to perform their duties. Satan believed that his God-given powers qualified him to function as an independent god. As evidenced by the prevalence of misery, disease, accidents, and war in his dominion, we now know that Satan is incompetent.

The Quran clearly states that Satan was an angel, by virtue of the immense powers and rank bestowed upon him. This is why he is addressed as an angel (2:34, 7:11, 15:29, 17:61,18:50, 20:116, 38:71) prior to his fall. By definition, a jinn is a fallen angel (18:50). Satan's rebellion teaches us that the angels were created with minds of their own, and absolute freedom of choice (2:34).

****

Appendix 22

Jesus

The Quran, informs us that Jesus was a human messenger of God whose sole mission was to deliver God's message; he never possessed any power, and is now dead (4:171, 5:75, 117). Those who consider Jesus to be God, or Son of God, or part of a trinity are "pagans" (5:17, 72, 73). Outstanding Christian scholars have reached these same conclusions *(THE MYTH OF GOD INCARNATE,* John Hick, ed., The Westminster Press, Philadelphia, 1977 & *THE MYTH MAKER,* Hyam Maccoby, Harper & Row 1986). Christianity is the product of Nicene (AD 325).

The Bible's Jesus

Jesus proclaimed aloud: "Whoever puts faith in me believes not so much in me as in him who sent me; .... For I have not spoken on my own; no, the Father who sent me has commanded me what to say and how to speak. Since I know that his commandment means eternal life, whatever I say is spoken just as he instructed me."   *[John 12:44-50]*

"I cannot do anything of myself. I judge as I hear, and my judgment is honest because I am not seeking my own will but the will of him who sent me."
                    [John 5:30]

Jesus said: "My doctrine is not my own; it comes from him who sent me."
                    [John 7:16]

"Men of Israel, listen to me! Jesus the Nazorean was a man whom God sent to you with miracles, wonders, and signs as his credentials. These God worked through him in your midst, as you well know."
                    [Acts 2:22]

"...The man who hears my word and has faith in him who sent me possesses eternal life."   *[John 5:24]*

"Whoever welcomes me welcomes, not me, but him who sent me."
[Matthew 10:40, Mark 9:37, Luke 9:48, & John 13:20]

"...I have not come of myself. I was sent by One who has the right to send, and him you do not know. I know him because it is from him I come; he sent me."
[John 7:28-29]

Jesus looked up to heaven and said, "...Eternal life is this: to know you, the only true God, and him whom you have sent, Jesus Christ." *[John 17:1-3]*

All who are led by the Spirit of God are sons of God.   *[Romans 8:14]*

Jesus looked upward and said, "Father, I thank you for having heard me. I know that you always hear me but I have said this for the sake of the crowd, that they may believe that you sent me."   *[John 11:41-42]*

As he was setting out on a journey a man came running up, knelt down before him and asked, "Good Teacher, what must I do to share in everlasting life?" Jesus answered, "Why do you call me good? No one is good but God alone."
[Mark 10:17-18]

"None of those who call me 'Lord' will enter the kingdom of God, but only the one who does the will of my Father in heaven."   *[Matthew 7:21]*

"...Go to my brothers and tell them, I am ascending to my Father and your Father, to my God and your God.' "   *[John 20:17]*

"God is my Lord and your Lord; you shall worship Him alone. This is the right path."   *[Quran 3:51, 19:36, & 43:64]*

Trinity, the doctrine of God taught by Christians asserts that God is one in essence but three in "person," Father, Son, and Holy Spirit. Neither the word Trinity, nor the explicit doctrine as such, appears in the New Testament, nor did Jesus and his followers intend to contradict the Shema in the Old Testament: "Hear O Israel: The Lord our God is one" *(Deut. 6:4).*
[Encyclopaedia Britannica, 1975]

Jesus' Death

This has been the single most controversial subject in the world. The Quran's miraculous mathematical code has now provided the final answer to this topic:

> Jesus' soul was raised, i.e., he was put to death prior to the arrest and crucifixion of his body. Thus, his persecutors arrested, tortured, and crucified an empty body—Jesus was already gone to the world of souls (3:55, 4:157).

They plotted and schemed,
but so did God,
and God is the best schemer.
Thus, God said, "O Jesus,
I am putting you to death,
and raising you to Me;
I will save you from the disbelievers."

[Quran 3:54-55]

They claimed that they killed the Messiah,
Jesus, the son of Mary, the messenger of God!
In fact, they never killed him;
they never crucified him;
they were led to believe that they did.

[Quran 4:157]

Mercifully, God has given our generation a living example of a person whose soul departed this world, but his body continued to live for 19 months. On November 25, 1984, doctors at the Humana Hospital of Louisville, Kentucky removed the diseased heart of Mr. William Schroeder and replaced it with a plastic and metal pump (*THE NEW YORK TIMES,* Monday, November 26, 1984).

On the 19th day after this historic operation—Thursday, December 13, 1984—Mr. Schroeder, the soul, the real person, departed this world. Mr. Schroeder died. But his body continued to function with the artificial heart implanted in his body. The world was told that he "probably suffered a stroke" (*THE NEW YORK TIMES,* December 14, 1984). Significantly, only one day before Mr. Schroeder's departure, he talked with President Ronald Reagan on national TV, and demanded that the Social Security Administration send his overdue check. He was perfectly alert. From the moment "he suffered a stroke," he did not recognize the day or time, nor his family members. In fact, Mr. Schroeder was no longer in this world.

The Gospels state clearly that the arrested body of Jesus was oblivious to the events surrounding it:

The chief priests, meanwhile,
brought many accusations against Jesus.
Pilate interrogated him again:
"Surely you have some answer?
See how many accusations
they are leveling against you."
But greatly to Pilate's surprise,
<u>*Jesus made no further response.*</u>   *[Mark 15:3-5]*

Herod was extremely pleased to see Jesus. From the reports about him he had wanted for a long time to see him, and he was hoping to see him work some miracles. He questioned Jesus at considerable length, but <u>Jesus made no response.</u> *The chief priests and scribes were at hand to accuse him vehemently. Herod and his guards then treated him with contempt and insult.*

[*Luke 23:8-11*]

The Savior said to me, "He whom you saw on the tree, glad and laughing, this is the living Jesus. But this one into whose hands and feet they drive the nails is the fleshy part. [Apocalypse of Peter, VII, 3, 81] from THE NAG HAMMADI LIBRARY (Harper & Row, 1977, James M. Robinson, ed, Page 339).

The facts that (1) Mr. Schroeder's soul departed on the 19th day after the operation, and (2) his body survived for 19 months, are uncanny reminders that God wanted the world to know the parallel between Schroeder's situation, and the proven account of Jesus' departure prior to the arrest, torture, and crucifixion of his soulless body.

****

Appendix 23

Chronological Sequence of Revelation

Order	Sura	Order	Sura	Order	Sura	Order	Sura	Order	Sura	Order	Sura	Order	Sura
		17	107	34	50	51	10	68	88	85	29	102	24
1	96	18	109	35	90	52	11	69	18	86	83	103	22
2	68	19	105	36	86	53	12	70	16	87	2	104	63
3	73	20	113	37	54	54	15	71	71	88	8	105	58
4	74	21	114	38	38	55	6	72	14	89	3	106	49
5	1	22	112	39	7	56	37	73	21	90	33	107	66
6	111	23	53	40	72	57	31	74	23	91	60	108	64
7	81	24	80	41	36	58	34	75	32	92	4	109	61
8	87	25	97	42	25	59	39	76	52	93	99	110	62
9	92	26	91	43	35	60	40	77	67	94	57	111	48
10	89	27	85	44	19	61	41	78	69	95	47	112	5
11	93	28	95	45	20	62	42	79	70	96	13	113	9
12	94	29	106	46	56	63	43	80	78	97	55	114	110
13	103	30	101	47	26	64	44	81	79	98	76		
14	100	31	75	48	27	65	45	82	82	99	65		
15	108	32	104	49	28	66	46	83	84	100	98		
16	102	33	77	50	17	67	51	84	30	101	59		

APPENDIX 24

Tampering With the Word of God

> *A superhuman mathematical system pervades the Quran and serves to guard and authenticate every element in it.*
> *Nineteen years after the Prophet's death, some scribes injected two false verses at the end of Sura 9, the last sura revealed in Medina. The evidence presented in this Appendix incontrovertibly removes these human injections, restores the Quran to its pristine purity, and illustrates a major function of the Quran's mathematical code, namely, to protect the Quran from the slightest tampering. Thus, the code rejects ONLY the false injections 9:128-129.*

> **Surely, we have revealed this scripture, and surely, we will preserve it.**
>
> **[15:9]**

The Quran is God's Final Testament. Hence the divine pledge to keep it perfectly preserved. To assure us of both the divine authorship, and the perfect preservation of the Quran, the Almighty author has rendered the Quran mathematically composed. As proven by the physical evidence in Appendix 1, such mathematical composition is far beyond human capabilities. The slightest violation of God's Final Testament is destined to stand out in glaring disharmony. A deviation by only 1—one sura, one verse, one word, even one letter—is immediately exposed.

Nineteen years after the Prophet Muhammad's death, during the reign of Khalifa 'Uthman, a committee of scribes was appointed to make several copies of the Quran to be dispatched to the new Muslim lands. The copies were to be made from the original Quran which was written by Muhammad's hand (Appendix 28).

This committee was supervised by 'Uthman Ibn 'Affaan, 'Ali Ibn Abi Taaleb, Zeid Ibn Thaabet, Ubayy Ibn Ka'ab, 'Abdullah Ibn Al-Zubair, Sa'eed Ibn Al-'Aas, and 'Abdul Rahman Ibn Al-Haareth Ibn Heshaam. The Prophet, of course, had written the Quran in its chronological order of revelation (Appendix 23), together with the necessary instructions to place every piece in its proper position. The last sura revealed in Medina was Sura 9. Only Sura 110, a very short sura, was revealed after Sura 9, in Mina.

The committee of scribes finally came to Sura 9, and put it in its proper place. One of the scribes suggested adding a couple of verses to honor the Prophet. The majority of scribes agreed. 'Ali was outraged. He vehemently maintained that the word of God, written down by the hand of His final prophet, must never be altered.

Ali's protest is documented in many references, but I cite and reproduce here the classic reference *AL ITQAAN FEE 'ULUM AL QURAN* by Jalaluddin Al-Suyuty, Al-Azhareyyah Press, Cairo, Egypt, 1318 AH, Page 59 [see Insert 1].

قعد على بن أبي طالب في بيته فقيل ما أقعدك؟ قال رأيت كتاب الله يزاد فيه
فذرت نفسي أن لا ألبس ردائي الا الصلاة حتى اجمعه

Translation: 'Ali was asked: "Why are you staying home?" He said, "Something has been added to the Quran, and I have pledged never to put on my street clothes, except for the prayer, until the Quran is restored."
[Insert 1]

The horrendous dimensions of this crime can be realized once we look at the consequences:

(1) 'Uthman was assassinated, and 'Ali was installed as the fourth Khalifa.

(2) A 50-year war erupted between the new Khalifa and his supporters on one side, and the Mohammedan distorters of the Quran on the other side.

(3) 'Ali was martyred, and eventually his family, the prophet Muhammad's family, except for some women and children, were killed.

(4) The disaster culminated in the infamous Battle of Karbala, where 'Ali's son, Hussein, and his family were massacred.

(5) The Muslims were deprived of the pure, unaltered, Quran for 1400 years.

The distorters of the Quran finally won the war, and the "official" history that came to us represented the victors' point of view. This apparent victory for God's enemies was, of course, in accordance with God's will. In just two decades after the Prophet's death, the idol worshipers who were defeated by the Prophet in the conquest of Mecca (632 AD) reverted to idolatry. Ironically, this time around their idol was the Prophet himself. Such idol worshipers obviously did not deserve to possess the pure Quran. Hence the blessed martyrdom of the true believers who tried to restore the Quran, and the apparent victory for the distorters of God's word.

The first peace time ruler after this lengthy and disastrous war was Marwan Ibn Al Hakam (died 65 AH/684 AD). One of the first duties he performed was to destroy the original Quran, the one that was so scrupulously written by the Prophet's own hand, "fearing it might become the cause of <u>NEW</u> disputes" [see *'ULUM AL-QURAN,* by Ahmad von Denffer, Islamic Foundation, Leicester, United Kingdom, 1983, Page 56]. The question an intelligent person must ask is: "If the original Quran were identical to the Quran in circulation at that time, why did Marwan Ibn Al-Hakam have to destroy it?!"

Upon examining the oldest Islamic references, we realize that the false injections, 9:128-129, were always suspect. For example, we read in Bukhary's famous *Hadith,* and Al-Suyuty's famous *Itqaan,* that every single verse in the Quran was verified by a multiplicity of witnesses "except Verses 128 and 129 of Sura 9; they were found only with Khuzeimah Ibn Thaabet Al-Ansaary." When some people questioned this improper exception, someone came up with a *Hadith* stating that "the testimony of Khuzeimah equals the testimony of two men!!!"

Strangely, the false injections 9:128-129 are labeled in the traditional Quran printings as "Meccan" [see Insert 2].

The Title Figure of Sura 9 from a standard Quran, showing that this sura is Medinan, "except for the last two verses; they are Meccan"!!!

[Insert 2]

How could these 'Meccan' verses be found with Khuzeimah, a late 'Medinan' Muslim?! How could a Medinan sura contain Meccan verses, when the universal convention has been to label as 'Medinan' all revelations after the Prophet's *Hijerah* from Mecca??!! Despite these discrepancies, plus many more glaring contradictions associated with Verses 9:128-129, no one dared to question their authenticity. The discovery of the Quran's mathematical code in 1974, however, ushered in a new era where the authenticity of every element in the Quran is proven (Appendix 1).

As it turns out, the injection of the two false Verses 9:128-129 resulted in:
(1) demonstrating the major function of the Quran's mathematical system, and
(2) producing an awesome miracle in its own right, and
(3) distinguishing the true believers from the hypocrites (they uphold traditions).

The translation of the two false verses is shown in Insert 3:

"A messenger has come to you from among you who wants no hardship to afflict you, and cares about you, and is compassionate towards the believers, merciful. If they turn away, then say, 'Sufficient for me is God, there is no god except He. I put my trust in Him. He is the Lord with the great throne.' "

[Insert 3]

THE PHYSICAL EVIDENCE

[1] The first violation of the Quran's code by Verses 9:128-129 appeared when the count of the word "God" (Allah) in the Quran was found to be 2699, which is not a multiple of 19, unless we remove one. The count of the word "God" is shown at the bottom of each page in this translation. The total shown at the end of the Quran is 2698, 19x142, because the false injections 9:128-129 have been removed.

[2] The sum of all the verse numbers where the word "God" occurs is 118123, or 19x6217. This total is obtained by adding the numbers of verses wherever the word "God" is found. If the false Verse 9:129 is included, this phenomenon disappears.

[3] As shown at the end of Sura 9 in this translation, the total occurrence of the word "God" to the end of Sura 9 is 1273, 19x67. If the false injections 9:128-129 were included, the total would have become 1274, not a multiple of 19.

[4] The occurrence of the word "God" from the first Quranic initial ("A.L.M." of 2:1) to the last initial ("N." of 68:1) totals 2641, or 19x139. Since it is easier to list the suras outside the initialed section of the Quran, Table 1 shows the 57 occurrences of the word "God" in that section. Subtracting 57 from the total occurrence of the word "God" gives us 2698-57 = 2641 = 19x139, from the first initial to the last initial. If the human injections 9:128 and 129 were included, the count of the word "God" in the initialed section would have become 2642, not a multiple of 19.

[5] Sura 9 is an un-initialed sura, and if we look at the 85 un-initialed suras, we find that the word "God" occurs in 57 of these suras, 19x3. The total number of verses in the suras where the word "God" is found is 1045, 19x55. If 9:128-129 were included, the verses containing the word "God" would increase by 1.

[6] The word "God" from the missing *Basmalah* (Sura 9) to the extra *Basmalah* (Sura 27) occurs in 513 verses, 19x27, within 19 suras (Table 2). If the false Verses 9:128-129 were included, the number of verses containing the word "God" would have become 514, and this phenomenon would have disappeared.

[7] The word *"Elaah"* which means "god" occurs in Verses 9:129. The total

Table 1: Occurrence of the word "God" outside the initialed section.

Sura No.	No. of "God"	Sura No.	No. of "God"
1	2	84	1
69	1	85	3
70	1	87	1
71	7	88	1
72	10	91	2
73	7	95	1
74	3	96	1
76	5	98	3
79	1	104	1
81	1	110	2
82	1	112	2
			57
			19x3

Table 2: The word "God" from the missing Basmalah to the extra Basmalah.

No.	Sura No.	No. of Verses with "God"
1.	9	100
2.	10	49
3.	11	33
4.	12	34
5.	13	23
6.	14	28
7.	15	2
8.	16	64
9.	17	10
10.	18	14
11.	19	8
12.	20	6
13.	21	5
14.	22	50
15.	23	12
16.	24	50
17.	25	6
18.	26	13
19.	27	6
......	......	......
19	342	513

No. of suras = 19,
Total of sura numbers = 342 = 19x18
Total of verses = 513 = 19x27.

occurrence of this word in the Quran is 95, 19x5. The inclusion of 9:128-129 causes this word to increase by 1, to 96.

[8] The *INDEX TO THE WORDS OF THE QURAN,* lists 116 *"Rasool"* (Messenger) words. One of these words is in 9:128. By removing this false verse, 115 *"Rasool"* words remain. Another *"Rasool"* word which must be excluded from counting is in 12:50, since it refers to the "messenger of Pharaoh," not the messenger of God. Thus, the total occurrence of *"Rasool"* of God is 114, 19x6.

[9] Another important word that occurs in the false Verses 9:128-129 is the word *"Raheem"* (Merciful). This word is used in the Quran exclusively as a name of God, and its total count is 114,19x6, after removing the word *"Raheem"* of 9:128, which refers to the prophet. According to 7:188, 10:49, and 72:21 the Prophet did not possess any power of mercy.

[10] The *INDEX* lists 22 occurrences of the word " *'Arsh"* (Throne). After removing the false injection 9:129, and the " *'Arsh"* of Joseph which occurs in 12:100, and the " *'Arsh"* of the Queen of Sheba (27:23), we end up with 19 " *'Arsh"* words. This proves that the word " *'Arsh"* of 9:129 does not belong in the Quran.

[11] The Quranic command *"Qul"* (Say) occurs in the Quran 332 times. Also, the word *"Qaaloo"* (They said) occurs the same number of times, 332. Since the false Verse 9:129 contains the word *"Qul"* (Say), its inclusion would have destroyed this typical Quranic phenomenon.

[12] The Quran contains 6234 numbered verses and 112 un-numbered verses (*Basmalahs*). Thus, the total number of verses in the Quran is 6346, 19x334. The false Verses 9:128-129 violate this important criterion of the Quran's code.

[13] In addition to violating the numbers of words as listed above, 9:128-129 violate the Quran's mathematical structure. When we add the number of verses in each sura, plus the sum of verse numbers (1 + 2 + 3 +... + n, where n = number of verses), plus the number of each sura, the cumulative total for the whole Quran comes to 346199, or 19x19x959. This phenomenon confirms the authenticity of every verse in the Quran, while excluding 9:128-129. Table 3 is an abbreviated illustration of the calculations of Item 13. This phenomenon is impossible if the false Verses 9:128-129 are included.

[14] When we carry out the same calculations as in Item 13 above, but for the 85 un-initialed suras only, which include Sura 9, the cumulative total is also a multiple of 19. The cumulative total for all

Table 3: Mathematical coding of the Quran's suras & verses, based on "19".

Sura No.	No. of Verses	Sum of Verse #'s	Total
1	7	28	36
2	286	41041	41329
.	.	.	.
9	127	8128	8264
.	.	.	.
114	6	21	141
6555	6234	333410	346199
			(19 x 19 x 959)

un-initialed suras is 156066, or 19x8214. This result depends on the fact that Sura 9 consists of 127 verses, not 129. The data are shown in Table 4. The false verses would have destroyed this criterion.

Table 4: Mathematical coding of the Quran's 85 un-initialed suras.

Sura No.	No. of Verses	Sum of Verse #'s	Total
1	7	28	36
4	176	15576	15756
.	.	.	.
9	127	8128	8264
.	.	.	.
114	6	21	141
			156066
156066 = (19x8214)			

[15] By adding the sura numbers of all un-initialed suras (85 suras), plus their number of verses, from the beginning of the Quran to the end of Sura 9 we get 703, 19x37. The detailed data are shown in Table 5.

This phenomenon depends on the fact that Sura 9 consists of 127 verses.

Table 5: Un-initialed suras and their verses from the beginning to Sura 9.

Sura	# Verses	Total
1	7	8
4	176	180
5	120	125
6	165	171
8	75	83
9	127	136
		703
		(19x37)

[16] By adding the sura number of the un-initialed suras, plus the number of verses, plus the sum of verse numbers from the missing *Basmalah* (9:1) to the end of the Quran, the grand total comes to 116090, or 19x6110. These data are in Table 6. If Verses 9:128-129 are included, the number of verses for Sura 9 becomes 129, and the grand total becomes 116349, not a multiple of 19.

Table 6: The un-initialed suras & their verses from missing Basmalah (Sura 9) to the end of the Quran.

Sura No.	No. of Verses	Sum of Verse #s	Total
9	127	8128	8264
16	128	8256	8400
.	.	.	.
113	5	15	133
114	6	21	141
			116090
			(19x6110)

[17] When the same calculations of Item 16 are done for all the verses from the missing *Basmalah* of Sura 9 to the extra *Basmalah* of Sura 27, the grand total comes to 119966, or 19x6314. This phenomenon would be destroyed, and the total would no longer be divisible by 19, if the number of verses in Sura 9 were 129. Since this phenomenon is also related to the absence of *Basmalah* from Sura 9, it is explained and the detailed data are given in table form in Appendix 29.

[18] When the same calculations of Items 16 and 17 are carried out from the missing *Basmalah* (9:1) to the verse where the number 19 is mentioned (74:30), we find that the grand total comes to 207670, or 19x10930 (Table 7). Sura 9 must consist of 127 verses.

[19] Sura 9 consists of 127 verses. The digits of 127 add up to 1 + 2 + 7 = 10. Let us look at all the verses whose digits add up to 10, from the missing *Basmalah* of Sura 9, to the extra *Basmalah* of Sura 27. If Sura 9 consisted of 129 verses, the grand total would be 2472, instead of 2470

Table 7: The suras and verses from the missing Basmalah to 74:30.

Sura No.	No. of Verses	Sum of Verse #s	Total
9	127	8128	8264
10	109	5995	6114
.	.	.	.
73	20	210	303
74	30	465	569
2739	4288	200643	207670
			(19x10930)

(19x130); 2472 is not a multiple of 19, and this phenomenon would have disappeared. The data are in Table 8.

[20] The falsifiers wanted us to believe that Sura 9 consists of 129 verses. The number 129 ends with the digit "9." Let us look at the first sura and the last sura whose number of verses ends with the digit "9." These are Sura 10 and Sura 104. By adding the sura number, plus the number of verses, plus the sum of verse numbers, from Sura 10 to Sura 104, we get a grand total that equals 23655, or 19x1245. The details are shown in Table 9.

The inclusion of Sura 9 with the wrong number of verses, 129, would have altered both the sum of verse numbers and the cumulative total—the sum of verse numbers would have become 627 + 129 = 756, and the cumulative total would not be 23655—and the Quran's code would have been violated (Table 9).

[21] The false injection consisted of Verses 128 and 129 at the end of Sura 9. If we look at the numbers 128 and 129, we see two 1's, two 2's, one 8, and one 9. Now let us look at all the verses in the Quran, and count all the 1's we see. This means the 1's we see in verses 1, 10, 11, 12, 13... 21, 31, and so on. The total count of the 1's is 2546 (19x134), provided the correct number of verses in Sura 9, 127, is used. If 128 and 129 are included, the grand total becomes 2548, which is not a multiple of 19 (Table 11).

Table 10: Counting all the 1's in the 85 un-initialed suras.

[22] Since Sura 9 is an un-initialed sura, let us look at all the verse numbers in the 85 un-initialed suras and count all the 1's we see.

Table 8: The verses whose digits add up to 10 from 9:1 to 27:29.

Sura No.	No. of Verses	How many add up to 10	No. of Total
9	127	12	148
10	109	10	129
11	123	11	145
12	111	10	133
13	43	3	59
14	52	4	70
15	99	9	123
16	128	12	156
17	111	10	138
18	110	10	138
19	98	9	126
20	135	12	167
21	112	10	143
22	78	7	107
23	118	11	152
24	64	6	94
25	77	7	109
26	227	22	275
27	29	2	58
342	1951	177	2470

342 = 19x18 & 2470 = 19x130

Table 9: All the suras whose number of verses ends with "9."

Sura No.	No. of Verses	Sum of Verse #s	Total
10	109	5995	6114
15	99	4950	5064
29	69	2415	2513
43	89	4005	4137
44	59	1770	1873
48	29	435	512
52	49	1225	1326
57	29	435	521
81	29	435	545
82	19	190	291
87	19	190	296
96	19	190	305
104	9	45	158
748	627	22280	23655

(19x1245)

Sura	# of Verse	# of 1's
1	7	1
4	176	115
.	.	.
9	127	61
.	.	.
113	5	1
114	6	1
....		
1406		
(19x74)		

As shown in Table 10, the total count of the digit "1" in the un-initialed suras is 1406, or 19x74. Obviously, if Sura 9 consisted of 129 verses, we would see two additional 1's, from 128 and 129, and the code would be violated.

[23] Following the same process explained in Items 22 and 23 for the digit "1," let us count all the 2's, 8's and 9's in all the verse numbers of the whole Quran. As shown in Table 11, the total count of all the 2's, 8's, and 9's is 3382, or 19x178. This makes the grand total of all the 1's, 2's, 8's, and 9's 2546 + 3382 = 5928, 19x312.

Table 11: Counting the digits that make up 128 and 129 in the whole Quran.

Sura	# of 1's	# of 2's	# of 8's	# of 9's	Total
1	1	1	0	0	2
2	159	146	55	48	408
.	.	.	.	.	.
9	61	31	22	22	136
10	31	21	21	21	94
.	.	.	.	.	.
114	1	1	0	0	2
....	....	....	....	....	....
	2546	1641	908	833	5928
	(19 x 134)				(19x 312)

In this remarkable phenomenon, we considered every single verse in the Quran, and examined the individual digits that make up Verses 128 and 129. Since 128 and 129 contain 6 digits, the inclusion of these human injections causes the total count of these digits in the whole Quran to be 5928 + 6 = 5934, not a multiple of 19.

[24] The total count of all the digits (1 through 9) in all the verse numbers of the 85 un-initialed suras, including Sura 9 with 127 verses, is 27075, or 19x19x75.

[25] Adding up the digits of the Quran's suras and verses produces a multiple of 19, provided the correct number of verses for Sura 9, 127, is taken. To do this, you make a list of the Quran's 114 suras and the number of verses in each sura. Add the digits of every sura number. The sum of digits of 10 = 1, 11 = 2, 12 = 3, 99 = 18, and so on. The total for all the suras is 975. The same thing is done for the numbers of verses in every sura. For example, Sura 2 consists of 286 verses. The digits of 286 add up to 2 + 8 + 6 = 16. For Sura 9, the digits of its number of verses add up to 1 + 2 + 7 = 10. The total for all 114 suras is 906. Thus, the grand total for the sum of digits of all the suras and verses is 975 + 906 = 1881 = 19x99. Naturally, this observation would not be possible if

Table 12: Sum of digits of all suras & verse numbers in the whole Quran.

Sura No.	No. of Verses	Sum of Digits of Suras	Sum of Digits of Verses
1	7	1	7
2	286	2	16
3	200	3	2
.	.	.	.
9	127	9	10
.	.	.	.
114	6	6	6
		....	....
		975	906

975 + 906 = 1881 = 19x99

Sura 9 consisted of 129 verses. Table 12 is abbreviated to illustrate the calculations.

[26] Miraculously, if we calculate the sum of digits for every sura in the Quran, and *multiply* the sum for each sura by the sum of digits of its number of verses, *instead of adding*, we still end up with a grand total that is a multiple of 19. For example, Sura 2 has 286 verses. The sum of digits of $2 + 8 + 6 = 16$. So you multiply 2 by 16, and you get 32, instead of adding $2 + 16$ as we did in Item 26. This is done for every sura in the Quran. The grand total for all the suras is 7771, or 19x409. Once again, every single verse in the Quran is confirmed, while the false verses are utterly rejected. See Table 13.

Table 13: Multiplication of the sum of digits of the Quran's suras and verses.

Sura No.	No. of Verses	Sum of Digits of Suras		Verses		Multiplication Product
1	7	1	x	7	=	7
2	286	2	x	16	=	32
3	200	3	x	2	=	6
.	.	.		.		.
9	127	9	x	10	=	90
.	.	.		.		
114	6	6	x	6	=	36
		....		....		....
		975		906		7771 (19x409)

$$975 + 906 = 1881 = 19\text{x}99$$

[27] Another truly awesome phenomenon: Sura 9 is an odd-numbered sura, and if we carry out the calculations described above for the odd-numbered suras only, we find that the total for the suras is 513 (19x27), the total for the verses is 437 (19x23), and the grand total for both is $513 + 437 = 950$ (19x50). Table 14 illustrates this remarkable phenomenon.

[28] Let us take all the suras that consist of 127 verses or less. There are 105 such suras. The sum of the sura numbers of these 105 suras, plus the sum of their verse numbers is 10963, or 19x577. Sura 9 is the only sura that has 127 verses. See Table 15. If Sura 9 did consist of 129 verses, it would not be included in this list of suras, the total would be 10827 (10963-136), this phenomenon would have disappeared, and the Quran's code would have been violated.

[29] Since Sura 9 is odd-numbered, and its number of

Table 14: Same data as in Table 12, but only for the odd-numbered suras.

Sura No.	No. of Verses	Sum of Digits of Suras	Verses	Total
1	7	1	7	8
3	200	3	2	5
.	.	.	.	
9	127	9	10	19
.	.	.	.	
113	5	5	5	10
		....	....	....
		513 (19x27)	437 (19x23)	950 (19x50)

verses is also odd, let us look at all the odd-numbered suras whose number of verses is also odd. This gives us 27 suras: 1, 9, 11, 13, 15, 17, 25, 27, 29, 33, 35, 39, 43, 45, 57, 63, 81, 87, 91, 93, 97, 101, 103, 105,107, 111, and 113. They consist of 7, 127, 123, 43, 99, 111, 77, 93, 69, 73, 45, 75, 89, 37, 29, 11, 29, 19, 15, 11, 5, 11, 3, 5, 7, 5, and 5 verses, respectively. The sum of these sura numbers, plus their sum of verse numbers is 2774, 19x146. If we take the wrong number of verses for Sura 9 , i.e., 129, this miracle disappears.

[30] The correct number of verses in Sura 9 is 127, and this is a prime number—it is not divisible by any number except 1, and itself. Let us look at all the suras whose number of verses is a prime number. These are Suras 1, 9, 13, 33, 43, 45, 57, 63, 81, 87, 93, 97, 101, 103, 105, 107, 111, and 113. The numbers of verses in these suras are 7, 127, 43, 73, 89, 37, 29, 11, 29, 19,11, 5, 11, 3, 5, 7, 5, and 5, respectively. If you add the digits of these suras, you get 137, while the digits of the verses add up to 129. This makes the grand total of all the digits 137 + 129 = 266 = 19x14.

[31] The distorters added two false verses to Sura 9, and this caused the sura to have 129 verses. Since 129 consists of 3 digits, and is divisible by 3, let us look at the suras whose number of verses is divisible by 3, and consists of 3 digits. The total of these sura numbers is 71, and the total number of verses is 765. This produces a grand total of 71 + 765 = 836, or 19x44. The data are shown in Table 16.

If Sura 9 had 129 verses, it would have been included in this table, and would have destroyed this phenomenon.

Table 15: Mathematical coding of all suras consisting of 127 verses or less.

Sura Number	No. of Verses	Total
1	7	8
5	120	125
8	75	83
9	127	136
.	.	.
113	5	118
114	6	120
6434	4529	10963
		(19x577)

Table 16: All suras whose number of verses is 3 digits, and is divisible by 3.

Sura	# of Verses	Total
5	120	125
6	165	171
11	123	134
12	111	123
17	111	128
20	135	155
71	765	836
		(19 x 44)

Table 17: All the suras that consist of 129 verses or more.

Sura No.	No. of Verses
2	286
3	200
4	176
6	165
7	206
20	135
26	227
37	182
	1577
	(19x83)

[32] If Sura 9 consisted of 129 verses, as the falsifiers would like us to believe, then let us look at all the suras which consist of 129 verses or more. There are 8 such suras. Their data are shown Table 17.

If Sura 9 consisted of 129 verses, the total number of verses would have been 1577 +129 = 1706, not a multiple of 19.

[33] The numbers 127, 128 and 129 have two digits in common, "1" and "2." Let us consider all the suras whose number of verses contains the digits 1 and 2. By adding the sura numbers plus

the numbers of verses, we get 1159, 19x61. See Table 18.

If Sura 9 consisted of 129 verses, the total would have become 1159 + 2 = 1161, not a multiple of 19.

[34] Sura 9 is a single-digit sura whose number of verses contains the digits 1 and 2. There is only one other sura that possesses these traits: Sura 5 is a single-digit sura, and it consists of 120 verses. As shown in Table 19, the number of verses in these two suras is 120 +127 = 247 = 19x13.

Table 18: Suras whose final verse have the numerals "1" and "2" in common with the verses in question (127, 128, and 129).

Sura No.	No. of Verses	Total
5	120	125
9	127	136
11	123	134
16	128	144
21	112	133
37	182	219
65	12	77
66	12	78
92	21	113
....	....	....
322	837	1159 (19x61)

Table 19: The only suras whose number is a single digit, and the number of verses contains the numerals "1" and "2."

Sura Number	No. of Verses
5	120
9	127
....	
	247 (19x13)

If Sura 9 consisted of 129 verses, the total would have been 247 + 2 = 249, not a multiple of 19.

[35] We looked at all the suras whose number of verses contains "1" and "2." Let us now look at all the suras whose number of verses begins with the digit "1." There are 30 suras that possess this quality: Suras 4, 5, 6, 9, 10, 11, 12, 16, 17, 18, 20, 21, 23, 37, 49, 60, 61, 62, 63, 64, 65, 66, 82, 86, 87, 91, 93, 96, 100, and 101.

Their numbers of verses are 176, 120, 165, 127, 109, 123, 111, 128, 111, 110, 135, 112, 118, 182, 18, 13, 14, 11, 11, 18, 12, 12, 19, 17, 19, 15, 11, 19, 11, and 11. The sum of verse numbers (1 + 2 + 3 + ... + n) for these 30 suras is 126122, or 19x6638.

If Sura 9 consisted of 129 verses, the sum of their verse numbers would have been 126122 + 128 + 129 = 126379, and this total is not a multiple of 19.

Table 20: All the suras where the digits of sura number and number of verses add up to 19.

Sura No.	No. of Verses	Total
9	127	136
22	78	100
26	227	253
45	37	82
54	55	109
64	18	82
72	28	109
77	50	82
78	40	118
84	25	109
....	....	....
531	685	1216 (19x64)

[36] Sura 9 consists of 127 verses, and 9 + 1 + 2 + 7 equals 19. Let us look at all the suras whose digits of sura and verses add up to 19. There are 10 suras that meet this specification, and the total of their sura numbers and numbers of verses is 1216, or 19x64. The data are shown in Table 20.

Mr, Gatut Adisoma of Masjid Tucson made the following two discoveries.

[37] Sura 9 consists of 127 verses, and (9) plus (1 + 2 + 7) add up to 19. There are three other suras in the whole Quran whose sura digits add up to 9 and the digits of their number of verses add up to 10. These are suras 9, 45, 54, and 72. They consist of 127, 37, 55, and 28 verses, respectively. The total number of verses in these three suras is 247, 19x13.

If Sura 9 consisted of 129 verses, it would not be included in this table to begin with. See Table 21.

[38] If Sura 9 consisted of 129 verses as the distorters claimed, then there is only one other sura in the whole Quran whose sura digits add up to 9, and its number of verses' digits add up to 12, namely Sura 27.

As shown in Table 22, this combination, with 129 verses for Sura 9, does not conform with the Quran's code.

[39] Let us assume for awhile that Sura 9 consists of 129 verses. Since the number 129 ends with the digit "9," let us look at all the suras where the number of verses ends with the digit "9."

Table 21: All the suras where the digits of sura number add up to 9 and the digits of number of verses add up to 10.

Sura No.	No. of Verses
9	127
45	37
54	55
72	28
	247
	(19x13)

Table 22: The suras where the digits of sura number add up to 9, and the digits of the number of verses add up to 12, assuming that Sura 9 is 129 verses.

Sura No.	No. of Verses
9	129
27	93
	222
(not a multiple of 19)	

Table 23: All suras whose number of verses end with the digit "9."

Sura No.	No. of Verses	Sum of Verse #'s	Total
10	109	5995	6114
15	99	4950	5064
29	69	2415	2513
43	89	4005	4137
44	59	1770	1873
48	29	435	512
52	49	1225	1326
57	29	435	521
81	29	435	545
82	19	190	291
87	19	190	296
96	19	190	305
104	9	45	158
748	627	22280	23655
	(19x33)		(19x1245)

We find 13 suras in the Quran whose number of verses ends with the digit "9." They are Suras 10, 15, 29, 43, 44, 48, 52, 57, 81, 82, 87, 96, and 104. Their numbers of verses are 109, 99, 69, 89, 59, 29, 49, 29, 29, 19,19,19, and 9, respectively.

As illustrated by Table 23, many results conform with the Quran's code only if Sura 9 is excluded; it does not not consist of 129 verses. Without Sura 9, the total number of verses in these 13 suras is 627, 19x33. Additionally, the sura number, plus the number of verses, plus the sum of verse numbers, add up to 23655, or 19x1245. These phenomena would have disappeared if Sura 9 consisted of 129 verses.

[40] Sura 9 is an odd-numbered sura whose number of verses ends with the digit "9." Let us now look at all the odd-num-

bered suras whose number of verses ends with "9." As shown in Table 24, the total of sura number and number of verses in these suras is 646, or 19x34. If Sura 9 had 129 verses, it would have been included in this group, and the total would have been 646 + 129 + 9 = 784, which is not a multiple of 19.

[41] By now, it is incontrovertibly proven that Sura 9 consists of 127 verses. Let us now look at the suras whose number of verses ends with "7." There are 7 such suras; they are Suras 1, 9, 25, 26, 45, 86, and 107. Their numbers of verses are 7, 127, 77, 227, 37, 17, and 7 verses, respectively. The grand total of sura numbers plus number of verses for these seven suras is 798, 19x42. The details are shown in Table 25. Thus, every sura whose number of verses ends with the digit "7," including Sura 9, conforms with the code.

[42] The last two verses of Sura 9 are 126 and 127. Since the falsifiers added two verses, let us look at the last two verses of every sura in the Quran, and count the digit "7," all of them, among these last two verses.

As shown in Table 26, the total number of the digit "7" among the last two verses of every sura in the Quran is 38, 19x2.

If the last verse in Sura 9 was 129 instead of 127, the number of occurrences of the digit "7" would have been 37, not 38, and this criterion would have been destroyed.

[43] Assuming that Sura 9 consists of 129 verses, let us look at all the suras that contain a verse No. 129. This means that we look at all the suras that consist of 129 or more verses. For example, Sura 2 consists of 286 verses. Therefore, it contains a verse that is assigned the number "129." We then take this verse and add it to all the other verses assigned the number 129 throughout the Quran. Under this assumption, there are 9 suras that contain a verse No. 129. Interestingly, we find that the total of sura numbers of these 9 suras is a multiple of 19 (114), while the total for the nine 129's can be a multiple of 19 if 2 is deducted from their

Table 24: Odd numbered suras whose number of verses ends with "9."

Sura No.	No. of Verses	Total
15	99	114
29	69	98
43	89	132
57	29	86
81	29	110
87	19	106
312	334	646
		(19x34)

Table 25: The suras whose number of verses ends with the digit "7."

Sura No.	No. of Verses	Total
1	7	8
9	127	136
25	77	102
26	227	253
45	37	82
86	17	103
107	7	114
299	499	798
		(19x42)

Table 26: The total number of the digit "7" among the last two verses of every sura in the Quran.

Sura No	Last 2 Verses	7's in Last 2 Verses
1	6,7	1
2	285, 286	0
3	199, 200	0
4	175, 176	2
.	.	.
9	126, 127	1
.	.	.
25	76, 77	3
.	.	.
114	5,6	0
		38

total. In other words, we are told that one of these 9 suras contains 2 extra verses. The details are in Table 27.

When we add 114, plus 1161, and remove 2, we get 1273, or 19x67. Compare this total (1273) with the total reported in the Item 44 below. Of the 9 suras listed in Table 27, which one has the extra 2 verses? The answer is provided in Item 44.

[44] To pinpoint the location of these two false verses, let us look at all the suras that contain a verse No. 128, while continuing to assume that Sura 9 consists of 129 verses. This will give us the same list of suras as in Table 27, and also bring in Sura 16 which has precisely 128 verses.

As shown in Table 28, Sura 9 stands out in glaring disharmony; it is singled out as the sura that contains the false verses. The total of suras and verses becomes divisible by 19 **only** if Sura 9 is removed. Note that the divisible total, after removing Sura 9, is 1273, 19x67, which is the same total obtained in Item 43 above after removing 2 verses. This remarkable phenomenon proves that Sura 9 could not contain a verse No. 128.

[45] Sura 9 is an un-initialed sura whose last two verses are 126 and 127. Let us take the 85 un-initialed suras, and add up the numbers of the last two verses in each sura. For example, the last two verses in Sura 1 are 6 and 7. Add 6 + 7 and you get 13. The next un-initialed sura is Sura 4; its last two verses are 175 and 176. Add 175 +176 and you get 351. Do this for all un-initialed suras. The data are in Table 29. Thus, the last two verses of Sura 9 are confirmed to be 126 and 127.

[46] Let us now take the last two verses in every sura in the Quran, initialed and un-initialed, and add the digits of the last two verses in each sura (Table 30).

It is readily obvious that the last two verses of every sura in the Quran are divinely fixed, and divinely guarded through this intricate mathematical code. The last two verses of Sura 9 are confirmed to be 126 & 127, not 128 & 129.

Table 27: All suras which contain a verse number "129."

Sura No.	Verse No.
2	129
3	129
4	129
6	129
7	129
9 ?	129
20	129
26	129
37	129
114	1161

$(114 + 1161 - 2 = \mathbf{1273} = 19\text{x}67)$

Table 28: All suras containing a verse number "128."

Sura No.	Verse No.
2	128
3	128
4	128
6	128
7	128
9?	128
16	128
20	128
26	128
37	128
130	1280

$(130 + 1280 = 1410,$ not a multiple of 19) If we remove sura 9, with its 128 verses, we get 1410 - 9 - 128 = **1273** = 19x67.

Table 29: Abbreviated table of the last two verses in the un-initialed suras.

Sura No.	Last 2 Verses	Total
1	6 + 7	13
4	175 + 176	351
5	119 + 120	239
.	.	.
9	126 + 127	253
.	.	.
114	5 + 6	13
		6897
		(19x363)

[47] Sura 9 consists of 127 verses, and 127 consists of 3 digits. Let us look at all the suras whose number of verses consists of 3 digits; these are suras 2, 3, 4, 5, 6, 7, 9, 10, 11, 12, 16, 17, 18, 20, 21, 23, 26, and 37. Their verse numbers are 286, 200, 176, 120, 165, 206, 127, 109, 123, 111, 128, 111, 110, 135, 112, 118, 227, and 182, respectively. By taking the last digit in each number of verses, and adding up these digits, we get 6 + 0 + 6 + 0 + 5 + 6 + 7 + 9 + 3 + 1 + 8 + 1 + 0 + 5 + 2 + 8 + 7 + 2 = 76 = 19x4.

If Sura 9 consisted of 129 verses, the last digit in its number of verses would be 9 instead of 7, and the total of last digits would be 78 instead of 76, and this phenomenon would disappear.

Table 30: Sum of digits of the last two verses of every sura in the Quran.

Sura No.	Last 2 Verses	Sum the Digits
1	6, 7	6 + 7
2	285, 286	2+8+5+2+8+6
3	199, 200	1+9+9+2+0+0
.	.	.
9	126, 127	1+2+6+1+2+7
.	.	.
113	4, 5	4 + 5
114	5, 6	5 + 6
	....	
		1824 = 19x96

[48] Let us look at the list of suras shown in Item 47 above. Since the number of verses in Sura 9 is an odd number, let us now consider the odd-numbered verse numbers. There are 8 suras with a 3-digit, odd number of verses: Suras 6, 9, 10, 11, 12, 17, 20, and 26. Their numbers of verses are 165, 127, 109, 123, 111, 111, 135, & 227.

Table 31: All suras whose number of verses is odd, and consists of 3 digits.

Sura No.	No. of Verses	Last Digit
6	165	5
9	127	7
10	109	9
11	123	3
12	111	1
17	111	1
20	135	5
26	227	7
		....
		38
		(19x2)

The last digits in these numbers of verses are 5, 7, 9, 3, 1, 1, 5, and 7, respectively, and the sum of these digits is 38, or 19x2. Obviously, if Sura 9 consisted of 129 verses, its last digit would be 9, not 7, and the sum of the last digits would be 40, not a multiple of 19. The detailed data are shown in Table 31. Thus, we are getting more and more specific, as we zoom in on the last digit in the number of verses.

[49] Let us continue to work with the same group of suras of Items 47 and 48. Since Sura 9 is an odd-numbered sura, let us now remove all the even-numbered suras from the list of suras shown in Item 47. Now we have odd-numbered suras, with odd-numbered verses. There are only three such suras in the whole Quran: 9, 11, and 17. Their numbers of verses are 127, 123, and 111 (Table 32). If Sura 9 consisted of 129 verses, this remarkable phenomenon would have been destroyed.

[50] Let us continue to work with the three suras listed in Item 49. These are all the suras in the Quran whose number is odd (like Sura 9), their number of

verses consists of 3 digits (like Sura 9), and their number of verses is also odd (like Sura 9).

As shown in Table 32, the verse numbers of these 3 suras are 127, 123, and 111. Just add the individual digits, and you get $1 + 2 + 7 + 1 + 2 + 3 + 1 + 1 + 1 = 19$.

Obviously, this phenomenon depends on the now proven truth that Sura 9 consists of 127 verses. If Sura 9 consisted of 129 verses, the only suras in the Quran that possess the above stated qualities would have added up to $1 + 2 + 9 + 1 + 2 + 3 + 1 + 1 + 1 = 21$. In other words, this important component of the Quran's mathematical code would have disappeared.

Table 32: Odd numbered suras whose number of verses is odd and consists of 3 digits.

Sura No.	No. of Verses
9	127
11	123
17	111
	361
	(19x19)

[51] There are three suras (1) whose numbers are odd, (2) their numbers of verses are odd, and (3) the number of verses consists of 3 digits. They are Suras: 9, 11, and 17 (see Items 48 through 50 for the flow of this point). Just add the individual digits that make up the three sura numbers, and you get $9 + 1 + 1 + 1 + 7 = 19$.

[52] The number 129 is divisible by 3. If Sura 9 consisted of 129 verses as the distorters claimed, then it would be (1) an odd-numbered sura that (2) consists of a 3-digit number of verses, (3) the number of verses is odd, and (4) the number of verses is divisible by 3. There are only two suras in the whole Quran that possess these qualities: Sura 11 with 123 verses, and Sura 17 with 111 verses. The sum of digits of both sura numbers and the numbers of verses comes to $1 + 1 + 1 + 2 + 3 + 1 + 7 + 1 + 1 + 1 = 19$. This can be observed only if Sura 9 consists of 127 verses.

[53] Sura 9 is (1) odd-numbered, (2) its number of verses is odd, (3) its number of verses ends with the digit "7," (4) its number of verses is a prime number, and (5) the sura number is divisible by 3 & 9. The only two suras that possess these qualities are: Sura 9 (127 verses), and Sura 45 (37 verses). Just add the digits you see:

$9 + 1 + 2 + 7 = 19$ & $4 + 5 + 3 + 7 = 19$; **Total for both suras = $19 + 19 = 38$.**

[54] Let us assume that Sura 9 does have 129 verses. In that case we will have only two suras in the whole Quran whose number begins with 9, and their number of verses ends with 9: Sura 9 (129 verses) and Sura 96 (19 verses). As detailed in Table 33, the grand total of sura number, plus the number of verses, plus the sum of verse numbers is 8828, not a multiple of 19.

Now let us remove the false verses (128 & 129) from Sura 9, and repeat the same calculations. The result of this correction

Table 33: Suras whose number begins with "9" and their number of verses ends with "9."

Sura No.	No. of Verses	Sum of Verse #s	Total
9	129?	8385	8523
96	19	190	305
105	148	8575	8828
		(Not multiple of 19)	

is shown in Table 34. The grand total becomes 8569, 19x451.

[55] Let us assume that Sura 9 consists of 129 verses. The total of these digits is 9 + 1 + 2 + 9 = 21. Let us look at all the suras where the digits of their number of verses add up to 21. There are 7 such suras: 9, 25, 27, 37, 68, 94, and 97.

By adding the sura numbers, plus the number of verses in each sura, plus the sum of verse numbers, the grand total comes to 34744, not a multiple of 19 (Table 35).

Now, let us use the correct number of verses for Sura 9, 127, and repeat the same calculations as in Table 35. This causes the grand total to become 34485, or 19x1815. See Table 36.

[56] For the last time, let us assume that Sura 9 consists of 129 verses. We have here a sura that (1) is an odd numbered sura, (2) its number is divisible by 3, (3) the number of verses, 129, is also divisible by 3, and (4) the number of verses ends with the digit "9." There is only one sura that possesses these qualities: Sura 15 is divisible by 3, its number of verses is 99, which is divisible by 3 and ends with the digit "9." If Sura 9 consisted of 129, and we added the sura and verse numbers for these two suras, we would end up with the following results: 9 + 129 + 15 + 99 = 252—not a multiple of 19.

If we throw away the false number 129, we have one sura in the Quran whose number is odd, and its number of verses is divisible by 3 and ends with the digit 9—Sura 15. Now we have the following result:

Table 34: Same data as in Table 33, after correcting the number of verses in Sura 9.

Sura No.	No. of Verses	Sum of Verse #s	Total
9	127	8128	8264
96	19	190	305
105	146	8318	8569
			(19 x 451)

Table 35: Suras whose digits of sura numbers and verse numbers add up to 21, assuming that Sura 9 consists of 129 verses.

Sura No.	No. of Verses	Sum of Verse #s	Total
9	129?	8385	8523
25	77	3003	3105
27	93	4371	4491
37	182	16653	16872
68	52	1378	1498
94	8	36	138
97	5	15	117
......	......	....	....
357	546	33841	34744
		(not divisible by 19)	

Table 36: Calculations of Table 35, after correcting the verses in Sura 9.

Sura No.	No. of Verses	Sum of Verse #'s	Total
9	127	8128	8264
25	77	3003	3105
27	93	4371	4491
37	182	16653	16872
68	52	1378	1498
94	8	36	138
97	5	15	117
......	....	....	....
357	544	33584	34485
			(19x1815)

15 + 99 = 114 = 19x6.

[57] For some time now, we have been dealing with numbers. Let us now look at specific words and letters that occur in the false injections 9:128-129.

The last statement in 9:127 describes the disbelievers as *"LAA YAF-QAHOON"* (they do not comprehend). Thus, the last letter in Sura 9 is "N" (Noon).

According to the falsifiers, the last verse is 129, and the last letter is "M" (Meem), since the last false word is *"AZEEM."*

Now let us look at the first letter and the last letter of every sura from the beginning of the Quran to Sura 9, and calculate their gematrical (numerical) values. Table 37 shows that the last true letter in Sura 9 must be "N," not "M."

Table 37: Gematrical value of the first and last letters of every sura from the beginning of the Quran to Sura 9.

Sura No.	First Letter	Last Letter	Total
1	B = 2	N = 50	52
2	A = 1	N = 50	51
3	A = 1	N = 50	51
4	Y = 10	M = 40	50
5	Y = 10	R = 200	210
6	A = 1	M = 40	41
7	A = 1	N = 50	51
8	Y = 10	M = 40	50
9	B = 2	N = 50	52
....	....	......	
	38 (19x2)	570 (19x30)	608 (19x32)

[58] Sister Ihsan Ramadan of Masjid Tucson counted all the suras in the Quran which end with the letter "N" (Noon), the last letter in Sura 9.

She found that 43 suras end with the same letter as Sura 9 (N)—suras 1, 2, 3, 7, 9, 10, 11, 12, 15, 16, 21, 23, 26, 27, 28, 29, 30, 32, 36, 37, 38, 39, 40, 43, 44, 46, 49, 51, 58, 61, 62, 63, 66, 67, 68, 70, 77, 81, 83, 84, 95, 107, and 109. Just add the sura numbers + number of suras that end with "N", and you get:

1919.

Thus, the last letter in Sura 9 is once again confirmed to be "N," not "M."

[59] Now let us look at the crucial expression **"LA ELAAHA ELLA HOO"** (There is no god except He). This phrase occurs in the false injection 9:129.

This very special expression occurs 29 times in 19 suras (Table 38). By adding the sura numbers of the 19 suras, plus the verse numbers where the phrase **"LAA ELAAHA ELLA HOO"** occurs, plus the number of occurrences of this crucial phrase, the grand total comes to 2128, or 19x112. This awesome result is dependent on the fact that 9:128-129 do not belong in the Quran.

Obviously, if 9:129 were included, the crucial expression **"LA ELAAHA ELLA HOO,"** the First Pillar of Islam, would not conform with the mathematical code.

[60] The first occurrence of **"LA ELAAHA ELLA HOO"** is in 2:163, and the last occurrence is in 73:9. If we add the sura number, plus the number of verses, plus the sum of verse numbers from the first occurrence to the last occurrence, the grand total comes to 316502, or 19x16658.

Table 38: List of all occurrences of the crucial phrase : "LAA ELAAHA ELLA HOO" (There is no other god besides Him), after removing 9:129.

No.	Sura No.	Verses with the key phrase	Frequency of the phrase
1.	2	163, 225	2
2.	3	2, 6, 18 (2x)	4
3.	4	87	1
4.	6	102, 106	2
5.	7	158	1
6.	9	31	1
7.	11	14	1
8.	13	30	1
9.	20	8, 98	2
10.	23	116	1
11.	27	26	1
12.	28	70, 88	2
13.	35	3	1
14.	39	6	1
15.	40	3, 62, 65	3
16.	44	8	1
17.	59	22, 23	2
18.	64	13	1
19.	73	9	1
	....	....	....
	507	1592	29

507 + 1592 + 29 = 2128 = 19x112

Table 39: All suras and verses from the first occurrence to the last occurrence of "LAA ELAAHA ELLA HOO."

Sura No.	No. of Verses	Verses #s	Total
2	123 (286-163)	27675	27800
3	200	20100	20303
.	.	.	.
9	127	8128	8264
.	.	.	.
72	28	406	506
73	9	45	127
....	....	....	....
2700	5312	308490	316502
			(19x16658)

Table 39 presents the detailed data. Naturally, if "**LAA ELAAHA ELLA HOO**" of the false verse 129 were included, this phenomenon would have disappeared.

[61] The phrase "**LAA ELAAHA ELLA HOO**" occurs 7 times between the missing Basmalah of Sura 9 and the extra Basmalah of Sura 27, in 9:31, 11:14, 13:30, 20:8, 20:98, 23:116, and 27:26. By adding the numbers of the 7 verses, we get 323, or 19x17. The detailed data are shown in Table 40.

Table 40: Occurrences of the phrase "LAA ELAAHA ELLA HOO" from the missing Basmalah to the extra Basmalah.

Sura No.	Verse Numbers With Phrase
9	31
11	14
13	30
20	8
20	98
23	116
27	26
	323
	(19x17)

If 9:129 were part of the Quran, the total in Table 40 would have been: 323+129 = 452, not a multiple of 19. God rejects what the hypocrites utter, even if it is the truth (63:1).

The Ultimate Quranic Miracle

[62] Brother Abdullah Arik has discovered what I consider to be the ultimate Quranic miracle. This miraculous phenomenon incontrovertibly authenticates every single verse in the Quran—the number of verses in every sura, and the numbers assigned to every single verse in the Quran—while exposing and rejecting the false injections, 9:128-129. To witness this great phenomenon, see Page 398. Putting the number of every verse in the Quran in sequence from the beginning to the end, with the number of verses in each sura ahead of the verse numbers of each sura, the final number consists of 12692 digits (19x668), and the number itself is also a multiple of 19. If the wrong number of verses for Sura 9 was used—129 instead of 127—neither the number of digits, nor the number itself would be divisible by 19.

[63] Since the subject of this Appendix is Sura 9 and its number of true verses, it is noteworthy that if we write down the number of the sura, 9, followed by the correct number of verses, 127, followed by the numbers of all the verses from 1 to 127, the resulting long number is a multiple of 19. Needless to say, if the wrong number of verses is used, i.e., 129 instead of 127, this remarkable miracle would have disappeared:

---

9 127 1 2 3 4 5 122   123   124   125   126   127.

The total number of verses in Sura 9 is followed by the numbers of every verse in the sura from 1 to 127. The resulting long number is a multiple of 19.

---

[64] The number of verses in Sura 9, 127, is an odd number. The falsifiers added two fake verses, and this made the number of verses 129, which is also an odd number. Mr. Arik used the same computer program he devised for Item 62 above to check all odd-numbered verses in the Quran. Thus, the number of verses in every sura was written down, followed only by the last digit of each of the odd-numbered verses in that sura. Sura 1 was represented by the number 71357. Sura 2 was represented by the number 28613579....5, and so on through the last sura. The result is a long number, with 3371 digits, that is divisble by 19. Obviously, Sura 9 was represented by the number 12713579...... 7:

---

7 1 3 5 7 286 1 3 5 ... 3 5 ...... 5 1 3 5 6 1 3 5.

The number of verses in every sura is followed by the last digit of each odd-numbered verse. The resulting long number, 3371 digits, is a multiple of 19.

---

[65] Since Sura 9 is an un-initialed sura, Mr. Arik applied the same computer program to all 85 un-initialed suras. The number of every verse in each of the 85 suras was written down, without the number of verses in the sura. Thus, Sura 1 was represented by the number 1234567, not 71234567. This was done with all un-initialed suras. The final result is a number that consists of 6635 digits, and is a multiple of 19. These awesome phenomena would be destroyed if we used the wrong number of verses for Sura 9, i.e., 129 instead of 127.

God's Messenger of the Covenant
Destined to Purify the Quran

[66] Finally, in a profound demonstration of the foreknowledge of the Almighty Author of the Quran, it is mathematically coded that "The person destined to prove that Sura 9 consists of 127 verses is Rashad Khalifa, God's Messenger of the Covenant" (see Appendix 2). The item presented here is another one of those numerous proofs; it is chosen for its relevance to this Appendix.

The gematrical value of the word "Rashad," as written in the Quran (40:29, 38) is 505 (R = 200, Sh = 300, A = 1, and D = 4). The gematrical value of the word "Khalifa," as written in the Quran (38:26) is 725 (Kh = 600, L = 30, I = 10, F = 80, and H = 5). By writing down the value of "Rashad," followed by the value of "Khalifa," followed by the number of Sura 9, followed by the correct number of verses in this sura, the product is 5057259127. This number is a multiple of 19; it equals 19 x 266171533.

[67] The number of verses from 3:81, where God's Messenger of the Covenant is prophesied, to 9:127, the end of Sura 9, is 988 (19x52). Table 41.

[68] The sum of verse numbers from 3:81 to 9:127 is also a multiple of 19 (Table 41).

[69] In Verse 3:78, just 3 verses before proclaiming God's Messenger of the Covenant, the word "God" number 361 (19x19) occurs. This verse (3:78) informs us that some falsifiers will "add falsehood to the Quran, then claim that it is part of the Quran; they attribute lies to God, knowingly."

[70] The word "God" occurs 912 times (19x48) from Verse 3:78, which exposes the falsifiers, to 9:127.

[71] The number of letters, plus the number of words in 3:78 and in the false verses 9:128-129, give the same total, 143. Verse 3:78 consists of 27 words and 116 letters, & 9:128-129 consist of 115 letters and 28 words.

Table 41: The number of verses from 3:81 to the end of Sura 9.

Sura No.	No. of Verses	Sum of Verse #s
3	119	16860
4	176	15576
5	120	7260
6	165	13695
7	206	21321
8	75	2850
9	127	8128
———	———	———
	988 (19x52)	85690 (19x4510)

Table 42: Occurrence of the word "God" from 3:78 to the end of Sura 9

Sura Number	Frequency of "God"
3	132
4	229
5	147
6	87
7	61
8	88
9	168
———	———
	912 (19x48)

What Can We Say?

The overwhelming physical evidence provided by the Almighty to protect and authenticate His message leaves no doubt that: (1) no distortion of any kind can enter the Quran, (2) Verses 9:128-129 do not belong in the Quran, and (3) every element in the Quran is mathematically structured far beyond human capabilities—the number of suras, the number of verses, the numbers assigned to the suras and verses, the frequency of occurrence of key expressions, the number of words, the number of letters, and the unique and often uncommon spelling of certain words.

This Appendix documents a profound miracle in its own right. Vast and utterly overwhelming as it is, it does not surpass or even match the overall mathematical miracle of the Quran which is detailed in Appendix One. This merely confirms the fact that the Almighty Author of the Quran has deliberately permitted the blasphemous addition of two verses to Sura 9 in order to:

---

(1) Demonstrate an essential function of the Quran's mathematical composition.

(2) Prove the impossibility of tampering with the Quran.

(3) Fulfill God's promise to distinguish the believers and expose the hypocrites.

Why Did God Permit It For 1400 Years??

Due to the mass corruption of Islam shortly after the prophet Muhammad's death, God obviously has fulfilled His pledge in 47:38. A divine decree issued in Sura 47, which is entitled "Muhammad," Verse 38 (19x2), stipulates that "if the Arabs failed to uphold the Quran, God will dismiss them from His grace, and substitute other people in their place."

When the Arabs distorted the Quran a few years after the Prophet's death, and exterminated the Prophet's family in the process, they incurred God's pledge of 47:38, and no longer deserved to possess the Quran; the true Quran. The evidence is irrefutable that the Arabs have abandoned the Quran en masse.

For example, there is not a single mosque in the so-called Muslim world today (1989) that upholds the crucial commandment: "The mosques belong to God; you shall not invoke anyone else besides God" (72:18).

The call to prayer (*Azan*) and the prayer itself are no longer devoted to God alone; Muhammad's name is invariably invoked along with the name of God.

The "First Pillar of Islam" is clearly stated in the Quran, 3:18 & 47:19, and its words are decreed to be: **LAA ELAAHA ELLA ALLAH** (There is no other god besides God). But the Muslims, as early as the first century AH, do not want God if Muhammad is not invoked along with Him. This is easily demonstrable today by going into any mosque and declaring: "**LAA ELAAHA ELLA ALLAH**;" this will actually enrage today's Muslims. This behavior is documented in the Quran, 39:45. Moreover, my own research has now convinced me that the traditional Muslims are **forbidden by God** from uttering the Quranic, divinely dictated *Shahaadah*: *"Ash-hadu Allaa Elaaha Ellaa Allah."* They can never say this *Shahaadah* (without invoking Muhammad's name). Test them yourself. The First Pillar of the distorted Islam, **LAA ELAAHA ELLA ALLAH, MUHAMMAD RASOOL ALLAH,** does not conform with God's commandments that came to us through Muhammad (see Appendix 13).

A number of other commandments are violated as well by this Mohammedan *Shahaadah*. For example, the Quran enjoins us repeatedly from making any distinction among God's messengers (2:136, 285; 3:84). The distorted *Shahaadah* gives more distinction to Muhammad, against his will. Despite the Quran's repeated assertions that it is "complete, perfect, and fully detailed" (6:19, 38, & 114), the "Muslims" have refused to believe their Creator; they uphold such ridiculous and nonsensical sources as *Hadith* and *Sunna*. This unanimous rebellion against God and His messenger, and the mass reversion to glaring idolatry—idolizing the Prophet and the saints—called for fulfillment of God's pledge in 47:38.

In view of the incontrovertible divine evidence presented here, and in Appendices 1, 2, and 26, one can truly appreciate the following verses:

> **Surely, we have revealed this message,**
> **and surely, we will preserve it.**   **[15:9]**
>
> **Say, "If all the humans, and all the jinns,**
> **banded together, in order to produce a Quran like this,**
> **they will surely fail, no matter how much assistance**
> **they lend one another."**   **[17:88]**
>
> **The disbelievers rejected this message**
> **when it came to them, though it is a profound scripture.**
> **No falsehood can enter it,**
> **through addition or deletion.**
> **For it is a revelation from**
> **the Most Wise, Most Praiseworthy.**   **[41:41-42]**
>
> **If we revealed this Quran to a mountain,**
> **you would see it trembling,**
> **crumbling,**
> **out of reverence for God.**   **[59:21]**

I acknowledge with thanks the valuable contributions of Mahmoud Ali Abib, Gatut Adisoma, Abdullah Arik, Ihsan Ramadan, Lisa Spray, and Edip Yuksel. Some of the astounding mathematical facts presented in this Appendix were discovered by these hard working researchers at Masjid Tucson.

Appendix 25
End Of The World

> **(God is) the Knower of the future;**
> **He does not permit anyone to unveil such knowledge.**
> **Only through the messengers that He chooses**
> **does He reveal future and past events.**   **[72:27]**

Among the duties charged to me as God's Messenger of the Covenant is unveiling the end of the world (Page 415). We learn from 18:7-8 and 69:13-15 that this world will come to an end. A new earth and new heavens will replace the present heavens and earth (14:48).

Signs of the Approaching End of the World

The Quran provides many signs, and states that the means for unveiling the end of the world have been given (47:18). The signs given in the Quran include:

1. **The splitting of the moon:** This already happened in June 1969 when we landed on the moon and brought back moon rocks. People on earth can go now to many museums, colleges and observatories to look at pieces of the moon.

2. **Discovering the Quran's 19-based mathematical code** (74:30-37): Fulfilled in 1969-1974.

3. **The creature** (27:82): "Made from the earth, it alerts the people that they have been oblivious to their Creator." The Creature, made from the earth, did appear and was instrumental in unveiling the Quran's numerical code, and proclaiming that the world has neglected God's message; the creature is the computer. Note that the digits that make up 27:82 add up to 19.

4. **Appearance of God's Messenger of the Covenant** (3:81): As detailed in Appendix 2, a consolidating messenger, prophesied in the Quran, comes after all the prophets have delivered the scriptures, to purify and unify. This prophecy was fulfilled in Ramadan 1408.

5. **The Smoke** (44:10): occurs after God's Messenger of the Covenant has delivered the unified message and proclaimed Islam (Submission) as the only religion acceptable by God.

6. **Gog and Magog**: they re-appear, in accordance with God's plan, in the year 1700 AH (2271 AD). Gog and Magog are mentioned in 18:94 and 21:96. If you count the verses from 18:94 to the end of Sura 18, you find them 17. If you count the verses from 21:96 to the end of Sura 21, you find them also 17. This is the Quran's sign that Gog and Magog will re-appear in 1700 AH.

It Will Not Remain Hidden [20:15]

Verse 15 of Sura 20 informs us that the end of the world will be revealed by God before the end of the world, and Sura 15, Verse 87, gives the time for that event:

> **We have given you the seven pairs, and the great Quran.   [15:87]**

The seven pairs are the 14 Quranic Initials. The total gematrical value of these profound pillars of the Quran's miracle pinpoints the year of the end of the world. It is noteworthy that Verse 85 of Sura 15 states: "The end of the world will surely come to pass." The next verse, 15:86, tells us that God is the Creator of this world, and, of course, He knows when it will end. The following verse, 15:87, tells us when the world will end. As shown in Table 1, the gematrical values of "The Seven Pairs" of Quranic Initials total 1709 (see also Table 1 of Appendix 1). According to 15:87, the world will survive for 1709 lunar years from the time this prophecy is stated in the Quran. This means that the world will end in the year 1710 AH. This number is a multiple of 19; 1710 = 19x90.

The unveiling of this information took place in the year 1400 AH, 309 years before the prophesied end of the world (1709-1400 = 309). The number 309 is a Quranic number (18:25), and is connected with the end of the world (18:21). The peculiar way of writing 309 in 18:25, "Three hundred years, increased by nine," indicates that the 309 are lunar years. The difference between 300 solar years and 300 lunar years is 9 years.

The year of this discovery, 1400 AH, coincided with 1980 AD, and 1980 plus 300 solar years is 2280, also a multiple of 19, 19x120. Thus the world ends in 1710 AH, 19x90, which coincides with 2280 AD, 19x120. For the disbelievers who do not accept these powerful Quranic proofs, the end of the world will come suddenly (6:31, 44, 47; 7:95, 187; 12:107; 21:40, 22:55; 26:202; 29:53; 39:55; 43:66; and 47:18).

Table 1: Total Gematrical Value of "The Seven Pairs" of Quranic Initials.

Quranic Initial	Gematrical Value
1. Q	100
2. N	50
3. S (Saad)	90
4. H.M.	48
5. Y.S.	70
6. T.H.	14
7. T.S.	69
8. A.L.M.	71
9. A.L.R.	231
10. T.S.M	109
11. 'A.S.Q.	230
12. A.L.M.S.	161
13. A.L.M.R.	271
14. K.H.Y.'A.S.	195
	1709

While *Hadith* is forbidden as a source of religious teachings (Appendix 19), it can be a useful source of history. We can derive a lot of information about historical events and local customs and traditions during the early centuries of Islam. The books of Hadith indicate that the Quranic Initials were believed to determine the life span of the Muslim *Ummah*. The classic exegesis by Al-Baydaawy cites the following historical event as a possible explanation of the Quranic Initials. The same event is detailed in Al-Suyooty's *ITQAAN,* First Printing, 1318 AH, Vol 2, Page 10:

The Jews of Medina went to the Prophet and said, "Your Quran is initialed with A.L.M., and these Initials determine the life span of your religion. Since 'A' is 1, 'L' is 30, and 'M' is 40, this means that your religion will survive only 71 years." Muhammad said, "We also have A.L.M.S." They said, "The 'A' is 1, the '*L*' is 30, the 'M' is 40, and the 'S' is 90. This adds up to 161. Do you have anything else?" The Prophet said, "Yes, A.L.M.R." They said, "This is longer and heavier; the 'A' is 1, 'L' is 30, 'M' is 40, and 'R' is 200, making the total 271." They finally gave up, saying, "We do not know how many of these Initials he was given!"

[Al-Suyuty's Famous Reference *ITQAAN*]

Although this narration is well known, many scholars have been reluctant to accept the unmistakable connection between the Quranic Initials and the end of the world. They could not bring themselves to deal with this subject for the simple reason that the calculation makes the end of the world, and judgment, a reality.

****

Appendix 26

The Three Messengers of Islam

This Appendix provides the Quranic mathematical evidence that [1] Abraham was the original messenger of Islam, i.e., Submission (22:78), [2] Muhammad was the scripture delivering messenger (47:2), and [3] Rashad is the purifying and consolidating messenger who delivered the religion's authenticating proof (3:81, & Appendix 2).

Perpetual and Verifiable Evidence

[1] As pointed out in Appendix 2, the gematrical value of "Abraham" is 258, the gematrical value of "Muhammad" is 92, the gematrical value of "Rashad" is 505, and 258 + 92 + 505 =855 = 19x45.

[2] If we include "Ismail," whose gematrical value is 211 and "Isaac," whose gematrical value is 169, we still end up with a total gematrical value of 855 + 211 + 169 = 1235 = 19x65. The total gematrical value of the three messengers, or the five, cannot conform with the Quran's 19-based mathematical code if either Abraham, Muhammad, or Rashad is not included.

Table 1: The Suras & Verses from the First to the Last Occurrence of Abraham.

Sura No.	No. of Verses	Sum of Verse #'s	Total
2	163	33415	33580
3	200	20100	20303
4	176	15576	15756
5	120	7260	7385
-	-	-	-
9	127	8128	8264
-	-	-	-
84	25	325	434
85	22	253	360
86	17	153	256
87	19	190	296
3827	5835	323598	333260 (19x17540)

Table 2: The Suras and Occurrences of Abraham, Muhammad, and Rashada.

Sura No.	Number of Occurrences		
	Abraham	Muhammad	Rashada
2	15	-	2
3	7	1	-
4	4	-	1
6	4	-	-
7	-	-	1
9	3	-	-
11	4	-	3
12	2	-	-
14	1	-	-
15	1	-	-
16	2	-	-
18	-	-	4
19	3	-	-
21	4	-	1
22	3	-	-
26	1	-	-
29	2	-	-
33	1	1	-
37	3	-	-
38	1	-	-
40	-	-	2
42	1	-	-
43	1	-	-
47	-	1	-
48	-	1	-
49	-	-	1
51	1	-	-
53	1	-	-
57	1	-	-
60	2	-	-
72	-	-	4
87	1	-	-
....	....	......	.....
991	69	4	19

$991 + 69 + 4 + 19 = 1083 = 19 \times 19 \times 3$

* "Rashada" occurs 19 times
*Total is 19x19x3, the 3 messengers

[3] The first and last occurrences of "Abraham" are in 2:124 and 87:19. By adding the sura numbers plus the number of verses, plus the sum of verse numbers from the first occurrence to the last occurrence, the grand total is 333260, 19x17540 (Table 1).

[4] As pointed out in Appendix 2, the name of God's Messenger of the Covenant is introduced to the computer age through mathematical coding. If the name was specified in the Quran, as is the case with past messengers, millions of people would have named their children "Rashad Khalifa." Thus, the root word "Rashada" is mentioned in the Quran 19 times (Appendix 2).

[5] "Abraham" is mentioned in 25 suras, "Muhammad" is mentioned in 4 suras, and "Rashada" occurs in 9 suras. The total of these suras is 25 + 4 + 9 = 38 = 19x2 *(INDEX TO THE WORDS OF QURAN,* Abdul Baqi).

[6] If we add the numbers of the suras where Abraham, Muhammad, and Rashada occur, plus the number of occurrences per sura, the total comes to 1083, 19x19x3 (Table 2).

[7] If we take all the suras where Abraham, Muhammad, and the root word "Rashada" are mentioned, and add the sura numbers, plus the number of the first verse in each sura where each of the three words is mentioned, the total comes to 2793, 19x147 (Table 3).

[8] The sum of all sura numbers where the three words occur, without repetition, plus the sum of all the verse numbers, without repetition, add up to 6479,

19x341. The suras are 2, 3, 4, 6, 7, 9, 11, 12, 14, 15, 16, 18, 19, 21, 22, 26, 29, 33, 37, 38, 40, 42, 43, 47, 48, 49, 51, 53, 57, 60, 72, and 87. The sum of these numbers is 991 (see Table 3). The verses where the three words are mentioned, without repetition, are 2, 4, 6, 7, 10, 13, 14, 16, 17, 19, 21, 24, 26, 29, 31, 33, 35, 37, 38, 40, 41, 43, 45, 46, 51, 54, 58, 60, 62, 65, 66, 67, 68, 69, 70, 74, 75, 76, 78, 83, 84, 87, 95, 97, 104, 109, 114, 120, 123, 124, 125, 126, 127, 130, 132, 133, 135, 136, 140, 144, 146, 161, 163, 186, 256, 258, and 260. The sum of these numbers is 5488, and:

5488 + 991 = 6479 = 19x341.

[9] If we add the sura number, plus the verse number, plus the number of verses where Abraham, Muhammad, and Rashada occur, we get a grand total that equals 7505, 19x395 (Table 4).

Table 3: The Suras & First Verse Where Abraham, Muhammad, & Rashada Occur.

Sura No.	Number of Occurrences		
	Abraham	Muhammad	Rashada
2	124	-	186
3	33	144	-
4	54	-	6
6	74	-	-
7	-	-	146
9	70	-	-
11	69	-	78
12	6	-	-
14	35	-	-
15	51	-	-
16	120	-	-
18	-	-	10
19	41	-	-
21	(51)	-	(51)
22	26	-	-
26	69	-	-
29	16	-	-
33	7	40	-
37	83	-	-
38	45	-	-
40	-	-	29
42	13	-	-
43	26	-	-
47	-	2	-
48	-	29	-
49	-	-	7
51	24	-	-
53	37	-	-
57	26	-	-
60	4	-	-
72	-	-	2
87	19	-	-
.....	.....	......	.....
991	1123	215	464

991 + 1123 + 215 + 464 = 2793 = 19x147

* Verse 21:51 cannot be added twice

*Table 4: The Suras, Verses, and Occurrences of
'Abraham," "Muhammad," and "Rashada."*

Sura No.	Verse Where the 3 Words are Mentioned			No. of Verses
	Abraham	Muhammad	Rashada	
2	124,125,126,127, 130,132,133,135 136,140,258,260	-	186, 256	14
3	33,65,67,68 84,95,97	144	-	8
4	54,125,163	-	6	4
6	74,75,83,161	-	-	4
7	-	-	146	1
9	70,114	-	-	2
11	69,74,75,76	-	78,87,97	7
12	6,38	-	-	2
14	35	-	-	1
15	51	-	-	1
16	120,123	-	-	2
18	-		10,17,24,66	4
19	41,46,58	-	-	3
21	51,60,62,69	-	51	5
22	26,43,78	-	-	3
26	69	-	-	1
29	16,31	-	-	2
33	7	40	-	2
37	83,104,109	-	-	3
38	45	-	-	1
40	-	-	29,38	2
42	13	-	-	1
43	26	-	-	1
47	-	2	-	1
48	-	29	-	1
49	-	-	7	1
51	24	-	-	1
53	37	-	-	1
57	26	-	-	1
60	4	-	-	1
72	-	-	2,10,14,21	4
87	19	-	-	1
......	......	......	......	......
991	5068	215	1145	86

$$991 + 5068 + 215 + 1145 + 86 = 7505 = 19 \times 395$$

Thus, it is mathematically coded into the Quran that Abraham, Muhammad, and Rashad are the three messengers of Islam (Submission).

[10] As shown in Table 4, the 19 occurrences of the root word "Rashada" are in verses 186, 256, 6, 146, 78, 87, 97, 10, 17, 24, 66, 51, 29, 38, 7, 2, 10, 14, and 21. These are 38 digits, 19x2.

[11] Table 4 shows that the sum of the verse numbers where we see the 19 occurrences of the root word "Rashada" is 1145. By adding this total of verse numbers (1145), to the gematrical value of the name "Rashad" (505), plus the gematrical value of the name "Khalifa" (725), we get 1145 + 505 + 725 = 2375, 19x125.

[12] If we write down these numbers next to each other, i.e., the total of verse numbers (1145), followed by the gematrical value of the name "Rashad" (505), followed by the gematrical value of the name "Khalifa" (725), we also get a number that is a multiple of 19: 1145505725 = 19x60289775.

Sum of Verse Numbers Where the 19 "Rashada" Occur..........................	= 1145
Gematrical Value of the Name "Rashad"	= 505
Gematrical Value of the Name "Khalifa"	= 725

1145 + 505 + 725 = 2375 = 19x125

1145 505 725 = 1145505725 = 19x60289775

****

Appendix 27

Who Is Your God?

Most people are outraged upon hearing this question. "What do you mean, 'Who is your god?' " they ask. "My god is the Creator of the heavens and the earth." And most of these people will be shocked to find out that their proclamation that their god is the Creator of the heavens and the earth is no more than lip service, and that they are in fact destined for Hell (12:106).

> **Your god is whoever or whatever occupies your mind most of the time.**

Your god can be your children (7:190), your spouse (9:24), your business (18:35), or your ego (25:43). This is why we note that one of the most important and most repeated commandments in the Quran is:

> **O you who believe, you shall remember God frequently; glorify Him day and night. [33:41]**

To put this commandment into practice, we must establish certain habits whereby we guarantee that God occupies our minds more than anything else. The Quran helps us establish such soul saving habits:

1. The Contact Prayers (*Salat*): those who observe the 5 daily prayers come a

long way towards commemorating God a significant proportion of their waking hours. *Salat* helps us remember God not only during the few minutes of prayer, but also throughout the times of anticipation. At 11:00 AM, one may look at his or her watch to see if the noon prayer is due yet. This act causes one to think about God, and one is credited accordingly (20:14).

2. Commemorate God before eating: Verse 6:121 enjoins us to mention God's name before we eat: "You shall not eat from that upon which God's name has not been mentioned."

3. God Willing (*IN SHAA ALLAH*): "You shall not say, 'I will do this or that tomorrow,' without saying, 'God willing' *(IN SHAA ALLAH)*. If you forget to do this, then apologize and say, 'May my Lord guide me to do better next time.' " [18:24]. This is a direct commandment that we must carry out, no matter who we are talking with.

4. God's Gift (*MAA SHAA ALLAH*): To invoke God's protection for our beloved objects—our children, our cars, our homes, etc.—we are enjoined in 18:39 to say "MAA SHAA ALLAH" (This is God's gift).

5. Glorify God day and night: When we eat anything, we shouldn't be like animals; we must reflect on God's creation of the food we are eating—the flavor, our enjoyment due to the senses God has given us, the perfect packaging of the banana or the orange, the varieties of sea foods created by God, etc.—and glorify Him as we enjoy His provisions. When we see a beautiful flower, or animal, or sunsets, we must glorify God. We must seize every possible opportunity to remember and glorify God, so that God may be our God.

6. First Utterance: Make it a habit to say: "In the name of God, Most Gracious, Most Merciful. There is no other god besides God," the moment you wake up every morning. If you establish this good habit, this is what you will utter when you are resurrected.

****

Appendix 28

Muhammad Wrote God's Revelations With His Own Hand

The first revelation was "Read," and included the statement "God teaches by means of the pen" (96:1-4), and the second revelation was "The Pen" (68:1). The only function of the pen is to write.

Ignorant Muslim scholars of the first two centuries after the Quran could not understand the Quran's challenge to produce anything like it. They had no idea about the Quran's mathematical composition, and they knew that many literary giants could have composed works comparable to the Quran. In fact, many such literary giants did claim the ability to produce a literary work as excellent as the Quran. The latest claim came from Taha Hussein, the renowned Egyptian writer.

The ignorant Muslim scholars then decided to proclaim Muhammad an illiterate man! They figured that this would make the Quran's extraordinary literary excellence truly miraculous. The word they relied on to bestow illiteracy upon the Prophet was *"UMMY."* Unfortunately for those "scholars," this word clearly means "Gentile," or one who does not follow any scripture (Torah, Injeel, or Quran) [see 2:78, 3:20 & 75, 62:2]; it does NOT mean "illiterate."

The Prophet was a successful merchant. The "Muslim scholars" who fabricated the illiteracy lie forgot that there were no numbers during the Prophet's time; the letters of the alphabet were used as numbers. As a merchant dealing with numbers every day, the Prophet had to know the alphabet, from one to one-thousand.

The Quran tells us that Muhammad wrote down the Quran—Muhammad's contemporaries are quoted as saying, "These are tales from the past that he wrote down. They are being dictated to him day and night" (25:5). You cannot "dictate" to an illiterate person. The Prophet's enemies who accuse him of illiteracy abuse Verse 29:48, which relates specifically to previous scriptures.

On the 27th night of Ramadan 13 B.H. (Before Hijerah), Muhammad the soul, the real person, not the body, was summoned to the highest universe and the Quran was given to him (2:97, 17:1, 44:3, 53:1-18, 97:1-5). Subsequently, the angel Gabriel helped Muhammad release a few verses of the Quran at a time, from the soul to Muhammad's memory. The Prophet wrote down and memorized the verses just released into his mind. When the Prophet died, he left the complete Quran written down with his own hand in the chronological order of revelation, along with specific instructions as to where to place every verse. The divine instructions recorded by the Prophet were designed to put the Quran together into the final format intended for God's Final Testament to the world (75:17). The early Muslims did not get around to putting the Quran together until the time of Khalifa Rashed 'Uthmaan. A committee was appointed to carry out this task. Read Appendix 24 for the details.

✶✶✶✶✶✶✶✶✶✶✶✶✶✶✶✶✶✶✶✶

Appendix 29
The Missing Basmalah

Every sura in the Quran opens with the statement "In the name of God, Most Gracious, Most Merciful," known as the *Basmalah,* with the exception of Sura 9. This conspicuous absence of the *Basmalah* from Sura 9 has been an intriguing feature of the Quran for 14 centuries. Many theories have been advanced to explain this phenomenon.

Now we learn that the missing Basmalah plays a significant role as [1] a significant constituent of the Quran's mathematical miracle, and [2] a glaring sign from the Most Gracious, Most Merciful, that Sura 9 has been tampered with and must be purified (Appendix 24). Both roles of the missing *Basmalah* were

Table 1: The Verses Containing the Word "Allah" from the Missing Basmalah to the Extra Basmalah.

Sura Number	Verses w/ "Allah"
9	100
10	49
11	33
12	34
13	23
14	28
15	2
16	64
17	10
18	14
19	8
20	6
21	5
22	50
23	12
24	50
25	6
26	13
27	6
342	513
(19x18)	(19x27)

revealed with the discovery of the Quran's mathematical code. The following list of factual observations illustrate the miraculous features of the missing *Basmalah*:

[1] Since the *Basmalah* consists of 19 Arabic letters, and prefixes all the suras except one, it can be considered the foundation upon which the Quran's 19-based code is built. But the absence of the *Basmalah* from Sura 9 causes the number of this crucial opening statement to be 113, a number that does not conform with the Quran's code. However, we find that this deficiency is compensated for in Sura 27. Two *Basmalahs* occur in Sura 27, one as an opener and one in Verse 30. This restores the total number of *Basmalahs* in the Quran to 114, 19x6.

[2] From the missing *Basmalah* of Sura 9 to the extra *Basmalah* of Sura 27, there are 19 suras.

[3] The sum of sura numbers from the missing *Basmalah* (Sura 9) to the extra *Basmalah* (Sura 27) is 9 + 10 + 11 + 12 + ... + 25 + 26 + 27 = 342, 19x18. This is a mathematical property, any consecutive 19 numbers will add up to a multiple of 19. But the miraculous phenomenon is that this number, 342, equals the number of words from the first *Basmalah* of Sura 27 to the second *Basmalah* in 27:30.

[4] The occurrence of the extra *Basmalah* in 27:30 conforms with the Quran's code in that the sura number, plus the verse number is a multiple of 19 (27 + 30 = 57 = 19x3).

[5] The occurrence of the extra *Basmalah* in Verse 30 compares with the occurrence of the number 19 itself in Verse 30 (Sura 74).

[6] The Quran contains 6234 numbered verses. The absence of the *Basmalah* from Sura 9, and compensating for it in Verse 30 of Sura 27 gives us two numbered *Basmalahs*, 1:1 & 27:30, and 112 un-numbered *Basmalahs*. This causes the

Table 2: Suras & Verses From the Missing Basmalah to the Extra Basmalah.

Sura	Verses	Sum of Verse #
9	127	8128
10	109	5995
11	123	7626
12	111	6216
13	43	946
14	52	1378
15	99	4950
16	128	8256
17	111	6216
18	110	6105
19	98	4851
20	135	9180
21	112	6328
22	78	3081
23	118	7021
24	64	2080
25	77	3003
26	227	25878
27	29	435
342	1951	117673
1951 + 117673 = 119624 = 19x6296		

total number of verses in the Quran to be 6234 + 112 = 6346, 19x334.

[7] From the missing *Basmalah* to the extra *Basmalah,* the number of verses containing the word "Allah" is 513, 19x27. Note that 27 is the sura number where the extra *Basmalah* occurs. The data are in Table 1.

[8] The sum of verse numbers (1 + 2 + 3 + ... + n), plus the number of verses, from the missing *Basmalah* to the extra *Basmalah* is 119624, 19x6296. See Table 2.

[9] This item also proves that Sura 9 consists of 127 verses, not 129 (see Appendix 24). The sum of digits of 127 is 1 + 2 + 7 = 10. By finding all the verses whose digits add up to 10, from the missing Basmalah of Sura 9 to the extra Basmalah of Sura 27, then adding the number of these verses to the total number of verses from the missing Basmalah to the extra Basmalah, we get 2128, or 19x112 (Table 3).

[10] Sura 9 is an odd-numbered sura whose number of verses (127) is also odd. From the missing Basmalah to the extra Basmalah, there are 7 suras that possess this property; they are odd-numbered suras whose numbers of verses are also odd. As detailed in Table 4, these are Suras 9, 11, 13, 15, 17, 25, and 27. By adding the digits that make up the sura numbers and the numbers of verses, the grand total is 114, 19x6.

Table 3: The Verses Whose Digits Add Up to 10, from the Missing Basmalah to the Extra Basmalah.

Sura No.	No. of Verses	No. of Occurrences
9	127	12
10	109	10
11	123	11
12	111	10
13	43	3
14	52	4
15	99	9
16	128	12
17	111	10
18	110	10
19	98	9
20	135	12
21	112	10
22	78	7
23	118	11
24	64	6
25	77	7
26	227	22
27	29	2
342	1951	177

(19x18) & 1951 + 177 = 2128 = 19x112.

Table 4: The Odd-numbered Suras Whose Number of Verses are Also Odd.

Sura No.	Sum of Digits	No. of Verses	Sum of Digits
9	9	127	10
11	2	123	6
13	4	43	7
15	6	99	18
17	8	111	3
25	7	77	14
27	9	29	11
	45		69

45 + 69 = 114 = 19x6

[11] The next two features authenticate both the missing *Basmalah* and the number of verses in Sura 9 (where two false verses had been injected). If we take the same suras listed in Table 4, odd-numbered suras whose numbers of verses are also odd, and write down the number of every sura, followed by its number of verses, the resulting long number (30 digits) is a multiple of 19 (Figure 1).

[12] Let us take the last digit of all the verses from the missing Basmalah to the extra Basmalah. If we write down the number of every sura, followed by the last digit in every verse in that sura, we end up with a long number, of 1988 digits, which is divisible by 19 (Figure 2).

---

9 127 11 123 13 43 15 99 17 111 25 77 27 29
Every sura number is followed by the number of verses in that sura.
This long number equals 19 x 4803742753338505219532409091.
[Figure 1]

---

9 1234567890123... ...27 1234567890 ... 789
The sura number is followed by the last digit in every verse number from
Sura 9 to Sura 27, Verse 29.   **[Figure 2]**

****

Appendix 30

Polygamy

Polygamy was a way of life until the Quran was revealed 1400 years ago. When the earth was young and under-populated, polygamy was one way of populating it and bringing in the human beings needed to carry out God's plan. By the time the Quran was revealed, the world had been sufficiently populated, and the Quran put down the first limitations against polygamy.

Polygamy is permitted in the Quran, but under strictly observed circumstances. Any abuse of this divine permission incurs severe retribution. Thus, although polygamy is permitted by God, it behooves us to examine our circumstances carefully before saying that a particular polygamous relationship is permissible.

Our perfect example here is the prophet Muhammad. He was married to one wife, Khadijah, until she died. He had all his children, except one, from Khadijah. Thus, she and her children enjoyed the Prophet's full attention for as long as she was married to him; twenty-five years. For all practical purposes, Muhammad had one wife—from the age of 25 to 50. During the remaining 13 years of his life, he married the aged widows of his friends who left many children. The children needed a complete home, with a fatherly figure, and the Prophet provided that. Providing a fatherly figure for orphans is the only specific circumstance in support of polygamy mentioned in the Quran (4:3).

Other than marrying widowed mothers of orphans, there were three political marriages in the Prophet's life. His close friends Abu Bakr and Omar insisted that he marry their daughters, Aisha and Hafsah, to establish traditional family ties among them. The third marriage was to Maria the Egyptian; she was given to him as a political gesture of friendship from the ruler of Egypt.

This perfect example tells us that a man must give his full attention and loyalty in marriage to his wife and children in order to raise a happy and wholesome family.

The Quran emphasizes the limitations against polygamy in very strong words: "If you fear lest you may not be perfectly equitable in treating more than one wife, then you shall be content with one." (4:3) "You cannot be equitable in a polygamous relationship, no matter how hard you try." (4:129)

The Quranic limitations against polygamy point out the possibility of abusing God's law. Therefore, unless we are absolutely sure that God's law will not be abused, we had better resist our lust and stay away from polygamy. If the circumstances do not dictate polygamy, we had better give our full attention to one wife and one set of children. The children's psychological and social well-being, especially in countries where polygamy is prohibited, almost invariably dictate monogamy. A few basic criteria must be observed in contemplating polygamy:

1. It must alleviate pain and suffering and not cause any pain or suffering.

2. If you have a young family, it is almost certain that polygamy is an abuse.

3. Polygamy to substitute a younger wife is an abuse of God's law (4:19).

****

Appendix 31

Evolution: Divinely Controlled

We learn from the Quran that evolution is a divinely designed fact:

Life began in water:	**"From water we initiated all living things."** **(21:30, 24:45)**

Humans not descendants of monkeys:	**"He started the creation of man from mud." (32:7)**
Man created from "aged" mud:	**"I am creating the human being from 'aged' clay." (15:28)**

Evolution is possible only within a given species. For example, the navel orange evolved from seeded oranges, not from apples. The laws of probablity preclude the possibility of haphazard evolution between species. A fish cannot evolve into a bird; a monkey can never evolve into a human.

Probability Laws Preclude Darwin's Evolution

In this computer age, we have mathematical laws that tell us whether a certain event is probable or not. If we throw five numbered cubes up in the air and let them fall into a guided straight line, the probability laws tell us the number of possible combinations we can get: $1 \times 2 \times 3 \times 4 \times 5 = 120$ combinations. Thus, the probability of obtaining any combination is 1 in 120, or 1/120, or 0.0086. This probability diminishes fast when we increase the number of cubes. If we increase them by one, the number of combinations becomes $1 \times 2 \times 3 \times 4 \times 5 \times 6 = 720$, and the probability of getting any combination diminishes to 1/720, 0.0014. Mathematicians, who are very exacting scientists, have agreed that the probability diminishes to "Zero" when we increase the number of cubes to 84. If we work with 84 cubes, the probability diminishes to 209×10^{-50}, or 0.000000000000000000 00000000000000000000000000000000000000209

Darwin's famous statement that "life began as a 'simple' cell" is laughable. As recently as 50 years ago, Wells, Huxley, and Wells wrote in their classic textbook that "nothing can be seen inside the nucleus but clear fluid." We know now that the cell, is an extremely complex unit, with billions of nucleotides in the gene material inside the nucleus, and millions of biochemical reactions. The probability laws tell us that the probability of the haphazard creation of the exacting sequences of nucleotides into DNA is Zero, many times over. We are not talking about 84 nucleotides; we are talking about billions of nucleotides that must be arranged in a specific sequence.

Some evolutionists have stated that the human gene and the monkey's gene are 90% similar. However, even if the similarity was 99%, we are still talking about 300,000,000 nucleotides that must be haphazardly re-arranged to change the monkey into a human. The probability laws preclude this as an utter impossibility. The human gene contains 30,000,000,000 nucleotides; 1% of that is 300,000,000.

A fitting quote here is that of Professor Edwin Conklin; he stated:

> **The probability of life originating from accident is comparable to the probability of the Unabridged Dictionary resulting from an explosion in a printing factory.**

****

Appendix 32

The Crucial Age of 40

What is the age of responsibility? If a child dies at the age of 12, without even hearing about God, does this child go to Heaven or Hell? What if the child is 15 years old, or 21, or 25? At what age will the human being be held responsible for his or her beliefs? This question has puzzled researchers of all religions for a long time.

The Quran sets the age of responsibility at 40; anyone who dies before this age goes to Heaven (46:15). If the person believed in God and benefitted from belief by nourishing and developing the soul (see Appendix 15), he or she goes to the High Heaven. Otherwise, the person goes to the Lower Heaven.

Your first reaction to this piece of information is objection: "What if the person was really bad, evil, and an atheist, will he go to Heaven if he died before the age of 40?" This is because you are mean, while God is the Most Merciful. Our tendency is to "put them all in Hell."

People who object strongly to this Divine mercy cannot come up with a cut-off age of responsibility. They ask questions like, "What if the person was really wicked?" The answer is, "Does God know that this person was wicked?" "Yes." "Does God know that this person does not deserve to go to Heaven?" "Yes." "Therefore, this person will not die before the age of 40." As simple as that. God is the only one who terminates our lives on this earth. He knows exactly who deserves to go Heaven and who deserves to go to Hell.

Early in 1989 a man by the name of Theodore Robert Bundy was executed for killing a number of women. The whole nation agreed that he was one of the most vicious criminals in history. So much so that his execution was one of the rare occasions where the opponents of capital punishment did not protest. On the contrary, many people actually celebrated his execution. Numerous journalists, editorials, and politicians lamented the fact that justice took eleven years to execute Ted Bundy. They stated that Bundy should have been executed within a maximum of six years after his conviction. According to the Quran, this would have been the greatest favor anyone could have done to Bundy. He was 42 years old when executed. Had he been executed five years earlier, at the age of 37, he would have gone straight to Heaven, and he did not deserve that.

As it turns out, Bundy was one of the signs God has given us to confirm that anyone who dies before 40 goes to Heaven. Bundy's name, Theodore Robert Bundy, consists of 19 letters, and he confessed to killing 19 women just one day before his execution. There were many other signs from God.

Delivering this important piece of information is one of the responsibilities given to me as God's Messenger of the Covenant. It is not *my* personal opinion.

It is noteworthy that both Martin Luther King and Malcolm X were assassinated just a couple of months before their 40th birthdays.

****

Appendix 33

Why Did God Send A Messenger Now?

As stated in 3:81, and in Appendix 2, God has sent a messenger to consolidate the messages delivered by all the prophets, purify them, and unify them into one religion: Submission. The timing is certainly ripe for fulfillment of this important prophecy, for the following reasons:

1. Judaism, Christianity, and Islam have been corrupted beyond recognition.

2. All God's messages have been delivered; the Quran is the Final Testament.

3. More than 93% of the human beings destined to live in this world are yet to come. As illustrated in the Introduction, Page xiv, the people who have lived on this earth since Adam are only one-fifteenth of the total projected human population.

Judaism

The best illustration of today's corrupted Judaism can be found in the books of a famous Rabbi; Harold S. Kushner. In his best seller *WHEN BAD THINGS HAPPEN TO GOOD PEOPLE,* Avon Books, 1981, Rabbi Kushner states the following:

..., we would be advised to take this world as seriously as we can, in case it turns out to be the only one we will ever have, and to look for meaning and justice here. (P. 29)

Bad things do happen to good people in this world, but it is not God who wills it. God would like people to get what they deserve, but He cannot always arrange it. (P. 42)

God does not reach down to interrupt the workings of laws of nature to protect the righteous from harm. This is a second area of our world which causes bad things to happen to good people, and God does not cause it and cannot stop it. (P. 58)

God can't do everything, but He can do some important things. (P. 113)

We can't ask Him to make us immune to disease, because He can't do that. (P. 125)

I recognize His limitations. He is limited in what He can do by law of nature, and by the evolution of human nature and human moral freedom. (P. 134)

Christianity

If Jesus came back to life today, the Christians would crucify him. Outstanding Christian scholars have reached solid conclusions that today's Christianity has nothing to do with Jesus, and that its doctrine was mortally distorted at the infamous Nicene Conferences (325 A.D.). See *THE MYTH OF GOD INCARNATE,* Westminster Press, Philadelphia, 1977.

Islam

If Muhammad came back to this world, the "Muslims" would stone him to death. The religion they follow today has nothing to do with the Islam, i.e. Submission, preached by Abraham and Muhammad. Everything the "Muslims" do is wrong: the First Pillar (*Shahaadah*), the call to *Salat* prayer (*Azan*), the ablution (*Wudu*), the daily *Salat* prayers, the *Zakat* charity, Hajj, and all other practices of Islam (see Appendices 2, 13, & 15).

"A Religion Never Authorized by God" (42:21)

The extent to which Islam (Submission) has been corrupted is illustrated in the following table:

Innovation	*Violated Quranic Principles*
Hadith & Sunna	*6:19, 38, 114; 7:1-3; 12:111; 17:46; 31:6; 45:6; 69:38-47; plus more.*
Killing whomever they consider an apostate	*2:256; 4:90; 10:99; 18:29; 88:21-22.*
Vicious criminal justice system:	
Cutting off the hand of the thief	*5:38, 12:31.*
Stoning the adulterers to death	*4:25, 24:2.*
Killing anyone who does not observe Salat	*2:256, 18:29.*
Killing one who drinks alcohol for the 4th time	*2:256, 18:29.*
Forbidding menstruating women from worshiping	*2:222.*
Forbidding women from the Friday Prayer	*62:9.*
Idolizing Muhammad against his will:	
calling him "the most honorable messenger"	*2:285.*
claiming that he was infallible	*4:79; 9:117; 17:73-74; 33:37; 40:66, 66:1; 80:1-10; 93:7.*
setting up his tomb as a "Sacred Mosque"	*2:149-150.*
claiming that he possesses power of intercession	*2:48,123,254; 6:70,94; 7:53; 10:3; 39:44; 43:86; 74:48.*
inventing an indefensible story about his ascension to the heavens on a horse, at the speed of light, and talking God out of 50 Salat prayers. At the speed of light, he would still be traveling within the Milky Way Galaxy.	*17:1; 53:1-18.*
Adding his name in the Salat prayers & Azan	*20:14; 72:18.*
Adding his name to the First Pillar of Islam	*3:18; 37:35; 39:45.*
Insulting Muhammad by depicting him as a vicious man:	
they claim he gouged out people's eyes	*3:159, 68:4.*
claiming he possessed sexual power of 30 men	*18:110; 25:20.*
Nullifying the fact that Muhammad was the last prophet by teaching that Jesus will come back to this world. This makes Jesus the last prophet.	*33:40.*
Claiming that Muhammad was illiterate, un-intelligent.	*see Appendix 28.*
A bizarre dietary system with multitudes of prohibitions	*6:145-150; 16:115-116.*
Altering the Sacred Months	*9:37.*
Neglecting the Zakat charity through distortion	*6:141, Appendix 15.*
Oppressing women and forcing them to wear head-covers and unreasonable clothes; and depriving them of all rights in marriage, divorce, inheritance, etc.	*2:228; 3:195; 4:19, 32; 9:71.*
Insulting women by instituting that "if a monkey, dog or a woman passes in front of a praying person, his prayer is nullified" (Hadith)	
Inventing numerous rules from ablution, to prayer, to sleeping to cutting one's nails	*2:67-71; 5:101;42:21.*
Prohibiting gold and silk for men	*5:48-49; 7:31-32.*
Prohibiting music and the arts	*7:32; 34:13; 42:21.*
Ridiculing Islam by stating that the earth is built on top of a giant whale!! (79:30; Ibn Kathir, 1200 AD & Ben Baz, 1975 AD)	

This is only a minute sample of the violations committed by the "Muslims" on a daily basis. This is why God has sent His Messenger of the Covenant now.

****

Appendix 34
Virginity

> *Sons and daughters of the true believers must be taught that their happiness throughout their lives depends on following God's law and preserving their chastity. This means that they must keep themselves for their spouses only, and never allow anyone else to touch them in a sexual manner (23:5-6, 24:30, 33:35, 70:29-30).*

Today's society is replete with powerful temptations. In America's society of the eighties, even parents start talking about boyfriends for their daughters and girlfriends for their sons. When they reach their teens, many parents even supply birth control means to their children. An alarming percentage of teen-agers are sexually active, even though they are not physiologically mature, and without any moral limitations. Millions of illicit pregnancies and the tragedies associated with them, plus millions of tragic abortions, happen every month in the USA.

Among the results of this moral breakdown: unwanted and unsupported children, delinquent and irresponsible fathers, criminals who have no regard for people's lives or properties, millions of social misfits, incurable genital herpes, incurable genital warts, devastating syphilis and gonorrhea, dysplasia, the killer AIDS, and new diseases never known before.

What most people do not know is that this moral breakdown costs them dearly throughout their lives. For the only law that rules the world is God's law, and these flagrant violations of God's law cost them a lot of misery and problems (20:124).

The true believers who care about their children will advise them and remind them repeatedly and persistently (20:132) to keep their chastity. This means staying a virgin until their wedding night, then staying loyal to one's spouse—never committing adultery—for their own happiness. God's advice to keep our chastity, before and after marriage, is for our own good. God is the one who controls our health, wealth, and happiness or misery (53:43, 48).

****

Appendix 35
Drugs & Alcohol

There is no compromise whatsoever regarding illicit drugs and alcoholic beverages; they are called "abominations and the work of Satan" (5:90). In 2:219 and 5:90, we see that "intoxicants, gambling, the idols' altars, and games of chance" are strictly prohibited. The word used for intoxicants is *"Khamr"* from the root word *"Khamara"* which means "to cover." Thus, anything that covers or hinders the mind is prohibited. This includes anything that alters the mind, such as marijuana, heroin, cocaine, alcohol, hashish, and anything else that affects the mind.

Appendix 36

What Price A Great Nation

If the people of the scripture (Jews, Christians, and Muslims) believe and maintain a righteous life, we will remit their sins and admit them into the blissful Heaven. Had they observed the Torah, the Gospel, and what is revealed herein from their Lord, they would have enjoyed provisions from above them, and from beneath their feet. Some of them are righteous, but most of them are evil doers. **[5:65-66]**

If only the people of the various communities believed and maintained a righteous life, we would have showered them with blessings from the heaven and the earth. **[7:96]**

God is the One who controls your happiness, or misery.
.... God is the One who makes you rich or poor. **[53:43, 48]**

A nation that upholds God's laws is guaranteed prominence among the nations of the world, victory, prosperity, and happiness (10:62-64, 16:97, 24:55, 41:30-31). On the other hand, a nation that violates God's laws incurs a miserable life (20:124). A nation that upholds God's laws is guaranteed to be a great nation. This is not a mere idealistic dream; since God is in full control (10:61), His guarantees and promises are done. A nation that upholds God's laws is characterized by:

1. Maximum freedom for the people—freedom of religion, freedom of expression, freedom to travel, and freedom of economy (2:256, 10:99, 88:21-22).

2. Guaranteed human rights for all the people, regardless of their race, color, creed, social status, financial situation, or political affiliation (5:8, 49:13).

3. Prosperity for all the people. God's economic system is based on constant circulation of wealth, no usury, and productive investment. Non-productive economy such as gambling, lottery, and high interest loans are not permitted (2:275-7, 59:7).

4. Social justice for all. Because of the obligatory charity (*Zakat*), no one will go hungry or un-sheltered (2:215, 70:24-25, 107:1-7).

5. A political system that is based on unanimous consensus. Through mutual consultation and freedom of expression, one side of any given issue convinces all participants in the discussion. The end result is a unanimous agreement, not the opinion of a 51% majority rammed down the throat of the 49% minority (42:38).

6. A society that upholds and maintains the highest standards of moral behavior. There will be a strong family, no alcoholism, no illicit drugs, no illegitimate pregnancies, no abortions, and practically no divorce.

7. Maximum regard for people's lives and properties. Therefore, there will be no crime against the people's lives or properties.

8. Prevalence of love, courtesy, peace, and mutual respect among the people, and between this nation and other world communities (3:110, 60:8-9).

9. Environmental protection is guaranteed through conservation and prohibition of wasteful practices (30:41).

****

Appendix 37
Criminal Justice

If a thief steals a thousand dollars from you, and they put him in prison, what do you get? If the thief has a wife and children, what is their crime? Why should they be deprived of their father?

The Quran solves this problem, as well as the problems associated with the criminal justice systems prevalent in today's world.

Equivalence is the Law [2:178-179]

According to the Quranic criminal justice, the thief who is convicted of stealing a thousand dollars from you must work for you until you are fully paid for the thousand dollars you lost, plus any other damage and inconvenience the theft may have caused you. At the same time, the thief's innocent wife and children are not deprived of their man, and the expensive prison system is eliminated. Imprisonment is a cruel and inhumane punishment that has proven useless to all concerned.

Contrary to common belief, the thief's hand shall not be cut off. Thank God for His mercy and His mathematical miracle in the Quran, we know now that the thief's hand is to be marked. Marking the hand of the thief is stated in 5:38. The sura and verse numbers add up to 5 + 38 = 43. The other place in the Quran where "the hand is cut" is found in 12:31. This is where we see the women who admired Joseph so much, they "cut" their hands. Obviously, they did not sever their hands; no one can do that. The sura and verse numbers add up to 12 + 31 = 43, the same total as in 5:38. This gives mathematical confirmation that the Quranic law calls for marking the hand of the thief, not severing it. Additional mathematical confirmation is provided: 19 verses after 12:31, we see the "cutting of the hand" again. Punishment in Islam (Submission) is based on equivalence and social pressure (2:178, 5:38, 24:2).

The blasphemy called "*Hadith & Sunna*" has instituted stoning to death as the punishment for married adulterers. This is not God's law. As stated in 24:2, the punishment for adultery is whipping in public; a hundred symbolic lashes. As pointed out above, the basic punishment is social pressure and scandalizing the criminal. Whipping in public achieves this goal.

In dealing with murder, the Quran definitely discourages capital punishment (2:179). "The free for the free, the slave for the slave, and the female for the female" (2:178). Due to human meanness and injustice, many people cannot even imagine what this Quranic law says. They refuse to accept the clear injunctions that strict equivalence must be observed—if a woman kills a man, or a man kills a woman, or a slave kills a free person, or a free person kills a slave, capital punishment cannot be applied. The Quran prefers that the murderer compensate the victim's family. Killing the murderer does not bring the victim back, nor does the family of the victim benefit from executing the murderer. The compensation, however, must be sufficient to be a deterrent for others. In Islam (Submission), the victim and/or the victim's family are the judges for all crimes; they decide what the punishment shall be under the supervision of a person who knows the Quran.

✱✱✱✱✱✱✱✱✱✱✱✱✱✱✱✱✱✱✱✱✱✱✱✱✱

Appendix 38

19: The Creator's Signature

The scriptures are not the only mathematically composed creations of God where the number 19 is the common denominator. It is profound indeed that Galileo made his famous statement: "Mathematics is the language with which God created the universe." A plethora of scientific findings have now shown that the number 19 represents God's signature upon certain creations. This divine stamp appears throughout the universe in much the same manner as the signature of Michelangelo and Picasso identify their works. For example:

1. The sun, the moon, and the earth become aligned in the same relative positions once every 19 years (see *ENCYCLOPEDIA JUDAICA* under "Calendar").

2. Halley's comet, a profound heavenly phenomenon, visits our solar system every 76 years, 19x4.

3. God's stamp on you and me is manifested in the fact that the human body contains 209 bones, 19x11.

4. *LANGMAN'S MEDICAL EMBRYOLOGY,* by T. W. Sadler, is used as a textbook in most of the Medical Schools in the U.S.A. On Page 88 of the Fifth edition, we read the following statement: "In general the length of pregnancy for a full term fetus is considered to be 280 days or 40 weeks after onset of the last menstruation, or more accurately, 266 days or 38 weeks after fertilization." The numbers 266 and 38 are both multiples of 19.

✱✱✱✱✱✱✱✱✱✱✱✱✱✱✱✱✱✱✱✱✱✱✱✱✱

GOD BE GLORIFIED.

INDEX

)

Made in the USA
Middletown, DE
24 January 2025

69941327R00309